LINOTTE

The Early Diary of Anaïs Nin

1914 – 1920

WORKS BY ANAÏS NIN

[*Published by The Swallow Press*]
D. H. Lawrence: An Unprofessional Study
House of Incest (a prose poem)
Winter of Artifice
Under a Glass Bell (stories)
Ladders to Fire
Children of the Albatross
The Four-Chambered Heart
A Spy in the House of Love
Solar Barque
Seduction of the Minotaur
Collages
Cities of the Interior
A Woman Speaks

[*Published by Harcourt Brace Jovanovich*]
The Diary of Anaïs Nin, 1931–1934
The Diary of Anaïs Nin, 1934–1939
The Diary of Anaïs Nin, 1939–1944
The Diary of Anaïs Nin, 1944–1947
The Diary of Anaïs Nin, 1947–1955
The Diary of Anaïs Nin, 1955–1966
A Photographic Supplement to the Diary of Anaïs Nin
In Favor of the Sensitive Man and Other Essays
Delta of Venus: Erotica by Anaïs Nin
Linotte: The Early Diary of Anaïs Nin, 1914–1920

[*Published by Macmillan*]
The Novel of the Future

Translated from the French

by Jean L. Sherman

With a Preface by Joaquin Nin-Culmell

———

Harcourt Brace Jovanovich

New York • London

❧ *LINOTTE* ❧

THE EARLY DIARY
OF ANAÏS NIN
1914 - 1920

Printed in the United States of America

Library of Congress Cataloging in Publication Data
Nin, Anaïs, 1903–1977.
Linotte: the early diary of Anaïs Nin, 1914–1920.
1. Nin, Anaïs, 1903–1977—Diaries.
2. Authors, American—20th century—Biography.   I. Title.
PS3527.I865Z522   1978   818'.5'203   77-20314
ISBN 0-15-152488-2

First edition

B C D E

❧ *Preface* ❧

When Anaïs left Barcelona for New York in 1914, she began writing in French what she later called her Childhood Diary. "By beginning a diary," Anaïs said in a commencement address in June 1973, "I was already conceding that life would be more bearable if I looked at it as an adventure and a tale. I was telling myself the story of a life, and this transmutes into an adventure the things which can shatter you." She also thought of this early diary as a means of communication with her absent father, but above all it stemmed from her overwhelming vocation to observe, comment and set down. Her laughter, her tears, her sadness, her enthusiasm, come to the surface like bubbles of oxygen from the deep waters of her introspection. She was a deep-sea diver from the start, and the diary was her indispensable lifeline.

Anaïs inherited many physical traits from our Cuban-born parents, both musicians, both handsome, both spirited although in quite different ways. Intellectual and inventive activities were not uncommon on both sides of the family, but Anaïs was no echo of past personalities, however close, however strong, however meaningful they may have been. She was an extraordinary individual who refused to be subdivided, taken apart or fragmented. As mysterious as Anaïs will always be, when you read the early diary you will know as much about her as anybody ever has.

This volume of the diary begins with our departure from Barcelona, continues with our early years in New York and ends in Richmond Hill when Anaïs began to write in English. It depicts our uprooted family, very close, very unified and very loving.

Mother's efforts, our interest and pride in one another's achievements and our common religious and cultural background are all flawlessly described, albeit through the eyes of a child. It is precisely the child in Anaïs, the clarity of her vision and the purity of her heart that enabled her to remain indestructible and delicate at the same time. I used to call her my steel hummingbird. And so she was.

Later she reinterpreted many events, many situations, many impressions. *Linotte* may seem to contradict these later interpretations, but I do not feel that this is so. After all, reality is many layered. We peel off one layer only to discover that the process must be repeated. It is evident from the very beginning that Anaïs's heart went out to the intuitive, to the poetic, to the magic of subjectivity. This was her world, her refuge, her shatterproof glass bell.

As a child Anaïs narrated stories that would make us laugh and cry and above all held us enthralled. Later, I participated in these narrations by improvising appropriate sounds at the piano as background music. May these words serve the same purpose.

Joaquin Nin-Culmell

Berkeley, California
June 1977

🌿 *Editor's Note* 🌿

This is the first volume of Anaïs Nin's diary to be published essentially in the form in which it was written. It is thus unlike the six volumes already in print, which the author consciously shaped, using "a craft like that of the fiction writer," and moving through a loosely connected time sequence to some peak moment of her life. Except for an unexplained gap of three months from August 31 to December 1, 1917, and another from January 1918 to March 1919 (here, an entire journal was lost), the chronology is continuous. Deletions have been made solely for the sake of producing a book of publishable length and sustained interest. It was Anaïs's custom to greet and take leave of her diary; most of these passages have been cut, but enough remain to serve as examples. Several poems have been omitted, and so have occasional routine entries and a few outbursts of religious or patriotic fervor, common in the earlier section of the diary, which tended to be repetitive. Those who wish to read the uncut version in the original French can look forward to an edition to be published in France by Editions Stock.

Anaïs's editing of the other volumes of her diary has been the model here: she chose to preserve the spontaneity of her writing in preference to a polished, rule-book approach. Therefore editorial intrusions have been kept to a minimum. Deletions are not indicated unless they occur within quoted text, such as letters; and likewise, changes in paragraphing, punctuation and spelling are unrecorded. Anaïs, by her own admission, wrote ungrammatical French, and English was a new language for her. Her errors in both languages, while charming in the original, would have been a distraction to the reader if carried over to the published book. Phrases that were written in English usually appear in quotation marks, and longer passages in English are also noted. The principal people in Anaïs's life and many of the minor ones have been identified in footnotes where necessary; a Glossary of Family Names can be found in the Appendix. Some names eluded all research and must be left in obscurity.

The manuscripts used for this translation are in seven volumes. Each of the first four contain several notebooks that Anaïs's mother bound together by hand in leather and marbleized paper. (The fifth volume was lost, possibly during one of the Nin family's frequent moves.) The remaining three volumes are standard commercial diaries, one bearing the imprint of Lord & Taylor. All contain line drawings and photographs, most of which have been reproduced here, with the addition of related illustrations from the same period.

A word must be said about the title. Anaïs always referred to this portion of her journal as "The Childhood Diary." While there was good reason to feel loyal to the author's own title, it failed to suggest the true character of the book. Anaïs was an adolescent, not a child, when she started the diary, and in 1920 she was seventeen, a young woman. "Linotte," or little bird (linnet), Anaïs's self-mocking nickname, seemed more appropriate as a title, evoking the fragile dreamer that she was throughout this period of her life.

At the time of her death in January 1977, the translation was for the most part complete and had Anaïs's unreserved approval. Had she recovered from her illness, she would doubtlessly have undertaken further work on it herself. As it was, preparation of the manuscript required the efforts of several people. Rupert Pole, executor of the Anaïs Nin Trust, made available photographs and manuscripts and was called upon continually to consult the original journals; Joaquin Nin-Culmell dated photographs, contributed to the Glossary of Family Names and the footnotes, and plumbed his memory to resolve many questions; Jean Sherman was drawn into problems that often went beyond the duties of a translator. A number of other people were helpful with translations from French, Spanish and Latin and with research on Metropolitan Opera performances. To Anaïs Nin we all owe our deep gratitude for the pleasure she gave us during the editing of *Linotte*.

John Ferrone

Harcourt Brace Jovanovich, Inc.
April 1978

LINOTTE

The Early Diary of Anaïs Nin

1914 – 1920

25 Juillet 14

Dernier regard dans
Barcelone et
dernières pensées.

Les montagnes s'élèvent avec une
festueuse beauté. Le soleil couchant laisse
voir ses dernières et pâles lueurs. Le ciel
bleu, taché de ci de là de petits nuages
blancs.

Parmis ces paysages des pensées diverses viennent
en foule.

Nous allions quité Barcelone, ce pays se
joli ? Nous ne verions plus ce ciel bleu, troub-
et de mon charme. Je ne poserai plus m-
lèvres sur la douce figure de grand' mère
chéri. Je ne pourai plus contemplé avec tou-
ces magnifique paysages. je ne pourai plume livrai a mes pense, sans noms, qui me
venai toujours, les soirs que, acuclé sur le
balcon, avec le silence de la nuit, je m'y
livré.

Et enfin je m'atriste en pensant que
nous allons quiter une pays qui a été
pour nous une mère, et un porte bonheur
A Dieu

❧ *1914* ❧

July 25. Last look at Barcelona and last thoughts. The mountains rise up in majestic beauty. The setting sun shows its last pale rays. Here and there, the blue sky holds little white clouds. As I look at this landscape, my mind is crowded with thoughts. We are going to leave Barcelona, leave this beautiful country. No more shall we see this blue sky which delights me so. No more shall I be able to touch my lips to the sweet face of dearest Grandmother.[1] No more shall I be able to surrender to nameless thoughts that always come to me in the evening when I lean on the railing of our balcony, in the silence of the night. And last of all, I am sad to think that we are leaving a country that has been like a mother and a lucky charm for us.

July 26. The ship sailed at 4. We were laden down with flowers and candy, also with kisses. Everyone wept because dearest Maman was leaving. I understand why everyone loves her. She is so sweet, so lovable and above all so good, oh, so good. She never says no to us if she can help it. We spent a very bad night, the heat did not let us rest. At 5, we arrived at Valencia. I have written a lot to finish my story, but luckily I have also managed to devote a moment to my diary. The sea is lovely, and I think we will have a very nice trip. The ship is not crowded; we can do whatever we like because Joaquina Sánchez gave Maman a letter of recommendation for the purser, a very pleasant man who seems very

1 *Angela Castellanos de Nin.*

nice. I shall stop for now, with a promise to write more tomorrow. The ship is called the "Montserrat."

July 27. I am keeping my promise to come back to this page. This time, the title of the page will be "Poetry Page."

Toward the Horizon

Far far away toward the horizon
I still seem to see
Someone dear to me,
My Grandmother.
Far far away toward the horizon,
I can still see that sweet face,
My Grandmother's face.
Far far away toward the horizon,
I feel a warm hand caressing me,
My Grandmother's hand.
Far far away toward the horizon,
I can still feel someone
Leaning down to kiss me.
It is Grandmother.
During the good-byes,
I saw a tear fall.
Grandmother wept!

July 28. Yesterday I had to stop quickly, so on this page there will still be a little of the Past. Yesterday, then, we reached Málaga. After eating, we left the ship, but we couldn't do anything because Madam the Mad Englishwoman interfered. Therefore we went back immediately. Today we got up very early in the morning and after drinking our daily cup of café au lait, we got off the ship, and this time we were all alone, that is, without anyone to interfere with what we wanted to do. We took a carriage and went shopping, and after that we went for a walk along a drive lined with palms and other trees. In the background we could see magnificent rocky mountains decorated with a few little houses that disappeared among the leaves and flowers. The houses in this country look a lot like Cuba. The women cannot go out except to go to church or to the bullfight, and even that is unusual. I consider it a very ugly custom, and if I couldn't go out as I wished, I would leave this country, if only because of that one custom of the inhabitants. One thing I find very strange is that the hawkers and other people who go about the town, can you imagine, ride on a burro or a little white donkey or even on mares. The countryside is very picturesque. Everything is mountainous, nothing flat. The town is small. I noticed that there are very beautiful grapes, olives, and wine. I read the part about the wine in my geography book, but the other things are my own observations. We sail at two o'clock.

July 29. Today we arrived at Cadiz at 5 in the morning. This is the city that everyone says is so wonderful. At 7 we were all washed and dressed and got up to the bridge just in time to watch the departure of the Golondrina (a small steamboat), for we were far from the harbor and had to take the Golondrina to get there. We went down to breakfast, after which each of us went about his own work until noon. Exactly at noon we got on the boat, and there we were, on our way. After a trip that took half an hour, we finally reached Cadiz, a city where there is nothing to see except beggars on every corner. The few inhabitants, or the few who go out, all look ready for the undertaker; they are all old, infirm, blind, lame, etc. The town seems dead to me and the only pretty thing is a drive overlooking the sea, lined with trees, where one sees an occasional bouquet of flowers amid the leaves. But even that is sad because half the plants are dry and uncared for and look so mournful. The only thing that interested me and that had dignity was the cathedral. I am going to describe it for you:

The cathedral

The first thing I saw was a large door supporting two life-size angels on two columns. A priest guided us through the church. The gilded silver altar was very large indeed. In front of it, on an antique table built entirely of oak was a huge book, a very old Bible.[1] Great beams everywhere in every nook and cranny of the altar. At one moment, when I had lagged a little behind, it became very dark. It was impressive and I felt as though I were in an ancient castle, but all those ideas flew away when Maman called me. After crossing several galleries supported by beams and columns carved with Latin scripture, the priest led us down a dark little staircase. We went down, not without risk of breaking our necks, and found ourselves in something like a walled dungeon. A shudder chilled my blood. The priest explained that this room was dug twelve feet below the sea, his voice resounding loudly amid

[1] *Very likely a missal.*

those gigantic walls. Next he led us into a kind of cave dug into the wall; at the back a 200-year-old crucifix dominated the cave. The priest showed us three graves of priests and a bishop. Then he led us farther on to where the wall was entirely made up of holes that were used as tombs. He showed us a Virgin sculptured out of a single block of stone, very beautiful. The priest guided us toward a little staircase which we climbed, opened a large door to a kind of sacristy, but very big. He spoke a word to another priest, who opened a wardrobe and took out a huge bunch of keys. He opened another big wardrobe where we could see a magnificent miniature altar, 18 inches high, all in gold. The cross was made of pearl mixed with gold thread, a marvel. The priest locked the wardrobe carefully and opened another, in which we could admire a magnificent gold chalice set with pearls and with a big emerald in the center. What wealth! After closing that wardrobe, he opened another where we admired the hilt of a sword that had belonged to a king of Spain. Maman then remarked, "Here you are able to preserve these things because the churches have never been pillaged, but in France all the relics were burned and looted." It's true, my poor country expelled her priests, her nuns, threw out everything, everything. I blush to think of it. For the first time France committed an act of which I shall always be ashamed. No, I don't mean France, but her people, who really were not the French people but proud, envious, evil-minded, selfish people who joined together under the name of the French people. A Frenchman could never have had a dishonorable idea like that of driving out priests and nuns who only did good. No, no, I repeat, they were not French.

July 30. I had already written these last pages when the purser came to ask Maman's permission to take us for a boat ride on the Golondrina. Maman couldn't make up her mind, but the purser insisted, saying: just over and back. Maman agreed and we left. It was 9:30. The moon had just risen, the stars were shining, the boat got under way. It was a lovely trip, and after a half-hour ride, we disembarked. The purser sent a boy for meringue glacé. We waited for about a quarter of an hour, and during that time Thorvald[1] and I amused ourselves by asking riddles of the purser, the captain and a priest who came with us. I still don't understand why a priest who is a passenger should wear a captain's uniform,

---

[1] *The older of A.N.'s two brothers.*

as ours did.[1] Finally the boy came back and the purser came triumphantly, singing Au Clair de la Lune and carrying the package of meringue glacé. We got back on board the Golondrina and left. I had difficulty eating my meringue; there was a big piece that I couldn't bite into and that dripped on my dress, so I took advantage of the darkness to take it out with my fingers and throw it away. After that delicious treat, we began to talk, then sing, and since I remembered Marlborough s'en Va-t-en Guerre,[2] I began to sing it. Everyone happened to know it, so there we all were in the moonlight, singing Marlborough s'en Va-t-en-guerre at the top of our lungs. Then we began to talk about stars, and the trip, I described Brussels, etc. When we got back to the ship, it was 11:30. I told all this to Maman, then went to bed. Now here I am awake again, bathed and breakfasted. Today at 2 we leave Cadiz to travel 13 days to New York.

[1] A "castrense" (military chaplain) generally wore an officer's uniform.
[2] "Marlborough's Off to War."

July 31. Here I am again, and this time I have nothing to say. The sea is not bad but the ship rolls a lot, so that not one passenger has escaped being seasick. I was seasick too but not too much. I leave you quickly but only because I have nothing to tell you. Till tomorrow.

August 1. This is a new month, and there will be happy days because we are going to see our aunts again. We are still on the ship and since I have nothing to tell, I will have a little chat with my dear diary.

I am eleven years old, I know, and I am not serious enough. Last night I said to myself: tomorrow I will be good. Good? I wasn't any better than I was the day before. Now here is a new month, and I haven't yet thought out how to be more sensible, how to master my impulses and my temper. I am ashamed to be so undisciplined. I hereby resolve that with God's help I will be more reasonable. Today the day is nearly over and it isn't much, but for the rest of the day I will observe silence. Not talk, but answer politely. Not seek out conversation, but work on my shawl, which must be finished at least by day after tomorrow.

August 2. It is evening, I have been lost in contemplation and here is all my achievement:

The moon, my visions

The moon shines, the stars come out, a soft breeze caresses my meditation. On the right, one still sees the setting sun showing itself humbly behind the moon, which now rules the heavens.

Finally the sun disappears altogether and then the moon, shining still more brightly, proudly ascends the throne of the sun. I greet you, Madam, the stars seem to say. Then as in a dream I catch sight of:

> Grandmother who kisses me
> Papa who is working
> Mama who weeps
> Thorvald who plays his violin
> Someone saying to me, "I love you"
> And I see myself in truth
> In contemplation.

August 3. I had the idea that in my diary I would do a portrait of each member of the family. Today I have a portrait of Papa that I am going to exhibit:

This is my Papa, my dear Papa. This is the face of the greatest pianist in the world. Sometimes he plays softly, sometimes powerfully. The way he plays tells me whether he is sad or gay. It is majestic to see his hands make the keys obey, everyone is spellbound. Every concert crowns him with success, thousands of laurel wreaths rest upon his brow, wreaths of glory that he has won and well deserves. His name is on every tongue, he is invoked as the god of music. No one can compare to my Papa, no one plays like him, no one can imitate him.

There, it's finished! Now I shall talk about Maman. I am carried away: Dearest Maman, oh! I love you, I love you, I will do anything for you. Just ask! ask! and I will do it.

Maman delightful singer, Maman, tender loving mother, Maman, a mother devoted to her children.

Maman deserves better than heaven. God should have a special heaven for a mother like my Maman, and that heaven would be only for her and for Grandmother, as no one else deserves it.

Mme. Rosa C. Nin, Singer and tender loving Mother.

You are looking at a great singer, my Maman. She has met with great success everywhere and, like Papa, she wears many laurel wreaths to reward her efforts. Besides being a great singer, she is devoted to us, more than any other mother in the world. Maman has a heart of gold, the kindness of her glance says so. I love her so much and she loves us deeply too, I know. My dear Maman does everything to give us pleasure, all her sacrifices are for us, she works only to assure the future for all of us. When I was sick, she was at my bedside day and night. Anything she could do to please me, she did, with never a second to herself. My dear Maman showed such kindness that I could never repay her by myself, but God will help me. She kisses me goodnight with so much sweetness, and without a kiss from my angel I couldn't even close my eyes. No mother on earth does more than Maman. Love, love to Maman, my dearest beloved angel.

August 3. Today I almost finished my scarf and while I was working on it, I thought, is it for Maman? for Grandmother? for my godmother? I haven't decided yet, but I think it will be for Grandmother. Thorvald was sick and spent the day in bed. From time to time I went by to see if he needed anything, which earned me the title of little "Sister of Charity." The sea continues to be very calm and I am not bored a minute.

August 4. The second mate invited us to his cabin. He has a typewriter and I would have liked to type my diary on it because no one in the family will be able to decipher my horrible hand-writing, but Maman gave me to understand that it would be better if I left it handwritten the way it is. I haven't too much to say. I have my shawl almost finished, I just have to do the edge which I will decorate with wool of the same color. Maman tells me not to write too much because she doesn't like me to be indoors, so I will finish, but not without saying one last thing: every day I try to practice one virtue. I believe in that way I will get to be a better person.

August 5. Still nothing to tell, but anyhow, let's try. My shawl is almost finished. Maman has started the trimming. I have started a story. I haven't found the title but I think I will call it:

Touching Memory of
the Shipwrecked Charles Ledoure
and of Captain
Lucien Couragon

August 7. Excuse me for writing in pencil, but I am on the bridge. I will give you a description of the weather: There is no sun, the sky is gray, the wind blows, the sea is covered with foam, the waves throw a fine spray over the bridge, the water is gray. The ship ducks its head so deep that water got into several of the cabins.

Marguerite in first class
a lady in second
a lady in second
two other ladies in second
a man in first
Maman in first
two other ladies in first
are seasick.

I thought I would copy here something that happened to me before my trip. I wrote it in my notebook but am afraid of losing it. I begin:

July 16, 1913, Barcelona. We were at Carmen Karr's[1] place where Maman was to sing one last time, a farewell performance because we were leaving for New York. Many friends were there and among them three nuns wearing the same habit as in the clinic where I stayed when I was sick. All evening I could think of nothing but the clinic and the nuns. Two of the nuns who were there looked a lot like Sister Norberta and Sister Regina. Finally I couldn't contain myself and feeling sure it was they, I went to Maman and whispered in her ear: "Maman, ask the name of those nuns. They look like Sister Norberta and Sister Regina." Maman paid no attention and after a few minutes I asked her again. Then Maman took me over to the nuns, saying, "This is my daughter, who thinks she has a vocation." One of the nuns then leaned down and kissed me. That gentle kiss seemed to say

Come with us.

This impressed me so that I felt like crying, but Maman went on, "My daughter was nursed by two nuns who wore a habit like yours and she would like to know your order, because she thinks you look like them." The nun answered, "We are Dominican nuns." Maman then turned to me and said, "You see, these aren't the nuns you thought they were." Then Maman put me in a chair next to the nuns and went away. The nun asked me, "Would you like to become a nun?" I was embarrassed and answered, "Yes, but not if I have to leave Maman." The sister smiled. I am still intrigued by that adventure.

August 9. I have started to make a neat copy of the story I wrote. I must announce to my diary that we are going to arrive in New York. I shall be happy to see my aunts. But I am also sadder and sadder to leave Grandmother. It's true, I miss her kisses, I miss her sweet expression as much as her kisses, but perhaps we shall go back to Barcelona, I hope so. My shawl is nearly finished, just one row still to be added. I have decided it will be for Maman because Grandmother can't wear a light color like blue.

August 12. Yesterday we reached New York.[2] It was hot and humid, the thunder rumbled, and on account of the fog we had to wait between the entrance to the port and the dock. A heavy rain began to fall, there was thunder and finally lightning. All the Spaniards fell on their knees and prayed. All that finished and

[1] *Carmen Karr (1865–1943), Catalan writer and feminist of French origin.*
[2] *A.N.'s revised version of her arrival can be found in the Appendix.*

about eight o'clock we started up again and 20 minutes later we were in New York. We expected to see our aunts but no one was there. We were beginning to despair when a lady came up to us and said that a lady was there with 3 boys. Oh, happiness. There was my godmother[1] with Coquito,[2] Carlos[3] and Felo.[4] After saying good-bye to everyone, we got off, and we all kissed each other. They decided that Thorvald and I would spend the night at my Aunt Antolina's,[5] and Maman and Joaquin[6] at Aunt Edelmira's.[7]

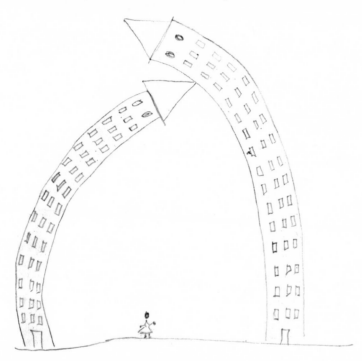

New York is big, with buildings of 20, 19 or 17 stories on each side of the street. These are office buildings. Godmother explained that since land is very expensive, they build the buildings very tall to make the most of it. We kept walking until we reached the underground electric train station. We took the train, then transferred to another, and at last we were there, but instead of being underground we were on a very high bridge. We went down a few steps

[1] *A.N.'s aunt, Juana Culmell.*
[2] *Gilbert Chase, a cousin.*
[3] *Carlos de Cárdenas, a cousin.*
[4] *Rafael de Cárdenas, a cousin.*
[5] *Antolina Culmell de Cárdenas.*
[6] *The younger of A.N.'s brothers.*
[7] *Edelmira Culmell de Chase.*

and afterward went on a staircase that goes down all by itself, what fun. Finally we reached home [Riverside Drive]. It is a very beautiful house, I slept with my aunt. In the morning I got up, had a lovely bath, and at 9:30 we had a delicious breakfast of melon, hot rolls with a cup of hot chocolate, cornbread. Then I dressed and we took the train to Kew.[1] It is beautiful! In the country, pretty houses with little gardens, flowers, small neat white streets. Among the houses was my aunt's house. My little cousin Nuna[2] was at the door and in a few minutes we were friends. I made a little garden, I played, I swung in a swing and tried to ride a bicycle. I rediscovered my little house in Cuba, my dream, a villa surrounded by fields, flowers, a little garden, all white furniture, order, and something in all this that one cannot explain. I am writing this in my aunt's study. I think of my Grandmother, Barcelona, the trip, Brussels, Paris where my Papa is, the war. And I say to myself that I want France to win. Maman sings, I admire everything, I think to myself that I am in a foreign land, I watch my cousins and brothers playing, and finally I think I will leave my diary to go and play too.

August 13. Description of heaven on earth. Green lawns strewn with flowers, tiny houses, little white roads neatly designed, a few trees, bright sunshine, small gardens full of flowers. My Aunt Edelmira's house is arranged in exquisite taste, white furniture, everything is small, nice, very clean and orderly. A swing, bicycles, a nice little girl cousin, a friendly boy cousin, a good kind aunt whom no one could help loving. I have to say hurrah for Kew Gardens, hurrah for the house, hurrah for my aunt, hurrah for the flowers and the fields, hurrah for God who has sent us to this earthly Paradise.

After thinking it over, how imperfect I am. Oh, how could I think for one moment of a heaven on earth. I do believe the fields of flowers intoxicated me and I wrote as though I were insane. I know only too well that there is no heaven on earth, much less in a country that is not my fatherland, with Papa so far away and having to bear the pain of leaving Barcelona.

August 14. After I finished my diary yesterday, Uncle Gilbert[3] took us for a walk. I picked flowers in the country, I caught but-

[1] *A.N. spelled this "Kiou."*
[2] *Maria Teresa Chase, a cousin.*
[3] *Gilbert P. Chase.*

terflies, we came to a very pretty wood that reminded me of my
dear wood in Cambria,[1] only wilder and uglier for there was no
lawn, no little path. A sandy road runs straight through this wood.
I am writing now at a very early hour. I got up early to write. The
sun is up, I am waiting to have breakfast with my uncle, and then
we will accompany him to the train. In the meantime I will try to
write a letter to Grandmother. I forgot to say that last night my
aunt gave a party for the grownups and Maman sang a tonadilla. I
don't know why but I began to cry and cry, no doubt I thought I
was back in Barcelona. I don't know myself why I cried while
Maman was singing and everyone laughing.

August 15. Today my Uncle Gilbert and I got up at 6:30. We
straightened up, raked, planted and watered my uncle's little garden. What fun! Then we went to breakfast with a good appetite,

[1] *La Cambre, a park near Brussels.*

La casa de Edelmira

Mrs. E. S. Karr and G. P. Chase Residence Kew Gardens, L. I.

we played a little while, then we got dressed and left for Aunt Antolina's. I forgot to say that my aunt has been sick, she had a kind of fainting spell and she cried, and has been fasting. Our little cousins were waiting for us and we were received with cries of joy. When we were about to eat, a lady named Emilia Quintero[1] came in, greeted everyone, and came to me, saying: "Esta es la niña que escribe tan bien."[2] I stared at Maman in astonishment at these words, which are hardly true. Anyhow, we ate and my godmother suggested that we go to the cinema with the governess. From the first day this woman displeased me and there are no words to describe how much I dislike her. But it was done and willy-nilly I had to go. Since I can't read English, I asked my older cousin Felo, who is 12, to sit next to me and translate, but out of meanness the governess put me at the end of the row with Thorvald and my little cousin Carlos. I held back my tears, I had to put up with being bored, not understanding, hold my tongue and mind that woman against my will. No one knows this except Maman, and now my diary.

August 16. I have played a lot with my doll and am beginning to ride the bicycle, but without pedaling.

[1] *Pianist, accompanist to Metropolitan Opera singers, and Joaquin Nin-Culmell's first piano teacher.*
[2] *"This is the little girl who writes so well."*

August 17. I know how to ride the bicycle. Yesterday I forgot to say in my diary that we went to Mass, not in a church but in a house. I don't understand the way they said the Mass, serving it quite brusquely, no elevation of the Host, no silent prayer, everything aloud. It seemed as though the priest was angry and was scolding. I found I miss my little French chapel in Barcelona, so I have resolved to read the Mass for myself, as if it were being said.

August 23. We went to New York to my Aunt Antolina's. I am going to write down my observations. In the train or bus, not one man gives his seat to a woman because they say the men work and often come back tired, whereas the women go out for amusement. There are more Protestants here than Catholics. The churches are hung with mourning because the Pope[1] died. All I do is dream about the chief purser on the ship. I don't know why. Last night in the train going home, even as I watched the bridges, fields and villages going by, I saw as in a daydream the purser taking me onto a boat, leaving New York, then I saw myself reaching Barcelona, kissing Grandmother, marrying the imaginary son of the purser. Mother, Grandmother and the purser talked about the past while I was kissing my children.

August 25. Today we went to see an American ship. Nothing interesting, everything made of iron with some cannons bigger than the boat and an American flag at the end. I understand a lot of English and I read all the ads. It appears that when my aunt leaves, she will let us have her house in New York. Maman has to become known and I understand that she has to live in New York, but I am sad just the same to leave the country.

August 30. Today is the last full day that we shall spend at Kew, the last day, and I have been neglecting my diary. Today I think I shall write a little more. Coquito's birthday is drawing near. Now I am thinking of doing something that I should have done since the beginning, and that is describing the arrangement of the house at Kew. From the street, one sees a nicely kept garden, a nice entrance. A little hall with two armchairs, a rocking chair, two or three benches decorated with flowers, a tall door that separates the hall from a nice little living room. In the living room, a little table

[1] *Pius X (1835–1914).*

with flowers, three armchairs, two chairs, a piano, all of very pretty brown wood. Through a big door on the right is the dining room, with a table and chairs, a buffet and a cabinet full of dishes painted by my godmother. Across from the dining room is a small room with a little desk, a chair, two armchairs, a table with a phonograph and books. I must stop, Maman is telling me to go to bed.

August 31. Here I am in New York at my aunt's apartment. I can't go on with the plan of the house for I am afraid to get it mixed up. Here I have a nice little room with Thorvald.

September 1. We have moved in. We go for walks, it's lots of fun. What do you think of the war? It's dreadful. I only hope that France will win. I would give my most precious possession to save France. It all makes a great impression on me, but I hope and trust that France will win. Now I think that I should make a vow to help France win, but it should be something big. I shall think about it, but it's difficult.

September 3. We went downtown. What magnificent stores! We saw the Public Library. It is magnificent, all made of marble, and contains everything from the first books [printed] to modern books. I would have liked to take out a book, but to do that one must have a permanent address in New York, and since we aren't yet sure, it was impossible. Maman bought me another notebook.

September 5. The weather is very cool. Another birthday, this time Joaquinito's. I think that we are all going to get together here again. It is early, so I have nothing to say, see you later. This afternoon we went to the Five and Ten cent store,[1] it's marvelous. Everything costs 5 or 10 cents. Uncle Thorvald[2] bought Thorvald and me a paint box and bought Joaquinito a sand bucket. Maman gave me permission to spend 10 cents and I bought 4 very pretty handkerchiefs.

September 6. It is Sunday. Godmother couldn't take us to the French chapel because she was tired, so we went to an American church. We had never seen anything like it. To make music, they had an organ, a piano, a violin, the entire Mass with theatre

---

[1] *A.N. wrote this in English as the "Fay and Ten Cent."*
[2] *Thorvald Culmell.*

music, and even at the moment of the elevation, they played a serenade. Godmother said she would complain to her confessor.

September 7. Time hangs heavy for me. Maman went out to find us a little apartment. Uncle Thorvald is still here. It is very hot. When Maman came back (she didn't find anything), she took us to the park, we played, then came back. Here in this apartment, if we make the slightest noise or run around, the old lady who lives upstairs comes down and begins, blah blah, police, blah blah, police, etc. Which means, "If this continues, I am going to call the police." What a nuisance. I wrote Grandmother and we have already mailed the letter.

September 8. What cold weather! It is early in the morning. I got up because I thought that I would be better off warmly dressed. Now I don't know because my hands are freezing, I can hardly hold the pen. Godmother says this is nothing and I believe her, but for me it's terrible because I haven't been in a cold climate for three years.

September 10. I am delighted! Godmother just made me a present of a pretty red flannel kimono. It's so warm, so soft! The cold weather continues, dry and freezing. Maman went out again and found a tiny apartment in a house. She took it, that's done, and at the end of the month we shall move again.

September 12. We went to Kew, I was very happy, but my aunt told us that the Montserrat, our ship, had been captured. All afternoon I could think of nothing but the poor purser. I liked that man very much and am sad to think that he is a prisoner too. I decided to pray for him so that he may be set free, along with the others. Well, let's change the subject. Every day I become more fond of Uncle Gilbert, my American uncle. I am going to tell my diary a secret, something very silly, but for which I have my reasons. I have made a resolution not to have any friends and not to be attached to anyone outside my family. One can't be sure of staying anywhere and if one leaves, there is too much sadness. I prefer to care only for my family, you see?

September 13. Our apartment was rented to someone else because they didn't allow children. Maman looked again and today she found another one [on 80th Street]. We went to see it. It's a very small apartment with a big living room, a small bedroom, a beautiful bathroom and a tiny kitchen. It is all painted white, very nice. I don't forget to say my prayers and this morning at Mass I prayed for everyone.

The war is going well, the Germans are thrown back everywhere, and everyone says the same thing, that the Germans work like demons. They throw themselves into the war blindly, like wild beasts, with the single aim of taking Paris, whereas France works more with her head, preparing herself, and her only aim is to defend Paris, nothing more.

September 27. I haven't had anything to write these last days, but now I have. Yes, I received a letter from Papa that goes like this:

My dear little girl, how many things have happened in this last month. I have just received your first letter from Long Island with a postcard from Thorvald written by order of Kiki [Joaquin]. I can see it wouldn't be Thorvald who would reinvent writing if it ever became a lost art! I came back to Paris yesterday morning at 4 in the morning. I wanted to pick up some books and music and things for the winter in Spain. I rode 70 hours on the train, almost half of them in a cattle car, sitting on straw and having as provisions only two bottles of beer and a few chocolate bars. In the same wagon there were a lot of rich people who hardly had any more to eat than I and also had to sit on the straw. And in spite of all that I could take neither the music nor the books and was just able to take my winter underwear, a suit and an overcoat, nothing more. At the railway stations they don't accept checked baggage, one must carry everything, and even then one isn't allowed to take too much. While I waited for my train in a crowd of 10,000 on the Quai d'Austerlitz, a second German plane flew over and dropped a bomb near the Opéra, then another near the Salle Erard. The day before, another German plane had dropped three bombs. All the women and children, all the old people and almost all foreigners are fleeing Paris, leaving behind their homes, furniture, silver, bric-à-brac, books and all, carrying with them only a package or two of the most necessary things. It is thought in spite of the heroism and bravery of the French that the Germans with their superior numbers will force their way into Paris, sacking and burning as they did in Belgium. They don't fight like men but like beasts, killing women, children, and the aged. They drop bombs on the cities without the advance warning required by the rules of war. They demolish old churches and works of art, burning statues and relics. At Malines, near Brussels, after having left the city once, they came back to break the stained glass windows in the cathedral, although they left the church itself standing because they know there is none other like it. But I think they are going to lose. I don't believe they will do the same thing with Paris. I think that sooner or later I shall again see Paris, the city where you were born, where you learned to talk. I couldn't take your pictures with me because of the heavy frames, nor a single one of my books, not even any music. I am just glad to be in Spain safe and sound. A few of my students have found refuge here in Spain, in Madrid, and in a day or two I shall join them, so don't write me until you have my new address, or if you write send the letters in care of Grandmother, who will forward them to me. I write to her often because she is sad that you left and also is worried.

Today I answered Papa's letter with another one just as long.

The things Papa wrote have made a deep impression on me. I am sad to think Papa had to leave everything behind. This morning I prayed with all my soul and all my fervor to the Virgin Mary and if she heard me, my dearest Papa will be here with me for Christmas. That is my prayer, my dream, my dearest wish.

October 4. On September 30, I spent the day helping Maman pack the trunks, then on the 1st we moved and I couldn't find the inkwell. Uncle Gilbert took us to the Hippodrome, the biggest theatre in the world. It was magnificent. Then we went to Kew to sleep because the beds had not yet come. We spent a very nice day, then went to bed and didn't come back until three o'clock. My dear godmother left for Cuba with Uncle Thorvald and my aunt. I am still sad because he has gone. We left my aunt and came back to the apartment. Each of us found a handkerchief box, a present from Godmother, and I also had 4 pairs of long black stockings and one yellow pair. I think Godmother is an angel just like Grandmother. I shall always be grateful to her and shall always love her. Yesterday we spent a very busy day straightening up and I was too tired to write. Godmother made me a present of a table croquet game. Tomorrow . . . we . . . start . . . school . . . in English. I am scared. Br-r-r-r-r.

October 5. We started going to English school. A little Spanish girl made friends with me. Today we didn't do anything. I already know several words in English.

October 7. I am in bed because I'm very tired, but just the same I want to tell my diary what has happened at school. Yesterday I didn't do anything, but when we came home at three o'clock, Maman took us to the park. I played with two little Spanish girls. Today I did a page of multiplication and got a *C*, which means "correct." In the afternoon I wrote a composition in French entitled "My Class Room" and I got a "very very good." Maman bought me a red pencil and a black one, a magnificent eraser and a thing to sharpen my pencils. All the little girls would like to have my ruler, my pencil, etc. because they say mine are the best. One of them had me kiss my crucifix and then said "good girl." They have fun getting me to say all kinds of things in English like "pencil," "pen," "teacher," etc., and when I pronounce them incorrectly they laugh uproariously.

October 16.

A Dream by Anaïs

One day at my window, where I had so often wept and where so many bitter tears had fallen, I saw the one I love, the one I adore, suddenly appear. Full of love, I rushed into the arms that were stretched out toward me. Oh, what joy! Oh, what happiness! The sweetness of a father's kiss! Oh, happiness! I can't believe it! That day I knew the happiness of my father's kiss.

October 17. Saturday, so no school. Maman was hanging curtains when Madame Adele [Van Name][1] called her on the phone to invite us for a ride in the car. We dressed and she came to pick us up. We had a lovely ride, after which the lady left us at the French Chapel, at Maman's request. We went to confession to a venerable old priest, then we came home. I am going to bed after making a long prayer for tomorrow's Communion.

October 18. How happy I am! I took Communion this morning and I have Jesus in my heart, so I feel very calm. I had lunch, prayed again, and here I am. I shall stop for now. . . . It is late, everything is quiet, and in this silence I come to entrust my thoughts to my faithful confidant. I have thought deeply about the happiness that some children must feel having their father and mother near them. This morning at Communion I saw a father and mother with a little girl of about six, all three taking Communion. Why can I not have my father with me as well? Why

[1] *An old friend of A.N.'s mother since the Spanish-American War, when the entire Culmell family took refuge in New York.*

can I not have the joy of Communion together with Papa and Maman? Alas, how long it has been since I had a papa to kiss! That idea makes me weep many times. Today I thought about it even more deeply and my Communion was just for Papa. For a long time I repeated Papa, Maman. What sweet words! But afterward the truth came to me and my heart wept, wept. No one but God knows my bitter sorrow. My dreams are always about Papa. He comes back, I kiss him, he presses me to his heart. That moment is sweet, but afterward sadness comes again with the truth and my heart weeps and weeps again. Tonight I am sadder than ever and my sorrow is greater still. I am too sad to continue.

October 21. I am beginning to like school, my teacher and my schoolmates. I am working hard at my studies. Today we were given a child's book to teach us English.

October 22. Things are going better and better. I get up at 7:30, I get bathed and dressed by 8 and I am ready. I have breakfast and am finished by 8:30. Then I rest 15 minutes and leave at quarter to 9. I come back at 12, have lunch, and leave again at quarter to 1. I come back at 3, practice the piano for half an hour, then I play, I read, and at 7 o'clock I set the table. I help Maman and we eat at 7:30. Afterward Maman does the dishes while I turn down the beds. Sometimes when Maman is tired, I do the dishes. I like to do them. I am very fond of our little house, as I call it.

October 27. Already the third notebook of my diary since we left Barcelona. In my new diary I have promised to watch my hand-writing and now I promise also to stop writing "nothing" the way I did in the last volume. Nothing? Never. There was never a day when I did nothing, so it's out of laziness that I wrote that. I shall have to correct myself very often and during the 4 remaining days of October I am going to prepare myself to do better in November. I shall correct myself and try to be better and to behave. I shall do this in thinking always of Papa and I shall say, if I do that, will Papa be pleased? No? Well then, I won't do it, and so on. Today I didn't do anything that would be interesting to tell. I go to school as usual. I am getting used to it and that's all.

October 28. I ask my diary to pardon me for writing in pencil but I am in bed. Maman has visitors so we three children are in bed together. Joaquinito just pushed my arm. I finished the letter to

Papa. I am cold and I have a headache. I shall stop so that I can hide under the covers.

October 29. Today I have to write with a pencil again. I have a bad cold. It is very cold and last night there was frost. My hands are frozen. I had a piano lesson with Mrs. Quintero. Today she told me, "If you want to, you can play as well as your Papa." If it were true, how glad I would be, but play like Papa? Impossible.

November 2. Yesterday was Sunday and a great holiday, All Saints' Day. We went to my aunt's house [Kew Gardens], put on costumes, danced and ate ice cream. We came home very late and laden down with packages, things from a trunk that Maman had left over there. Today Mrs. Quintero came to give me my lesson, and later she showed us a muffler like those she is making for the French soldiers. The idea intrigued me and I asked her to explain. She told me a French lady has organized a group of ladies to knit mufflers for the soldiers. Maman has promised to take me next Monday. Mrs. Quintero gives her work to someone else to do because she hasn't enough time. Maman asked her to leave it with us. She was willing and here I am knitting a muffler for a French soldier.

November 11. I have already finished the muffler, with help from Maman, of course. Today Mrs. Quintero came over and picked it up. She also invited Maman and me to visit her on Thursday from 3 to 7. I shall certainly not stay that long because it is a party for ladies and I am only a child. Yesterday evening I wrote a poem. Here it is:

The Beggar
People and birds of every kind are going to bed,
only the poor beggar stays shivering behind the door.
He has no bed, nothing to eat either,
the snow is falling, he is cold.
Finally he can stand it no longer, he weeps!
A little girl warmly dressed in a heavy coat
goes out and sees the poor man,
she is good-hearted and is moved.
She goes up to him and says: Come,
I shall make room for you in my bed.
He goes, follows the child, and her mother

who is as kind as her daughter, makes a bed for him.
That night the poor man tasted long-lost happiness:
A roof, a meal, a bed and more than that . . .
a child . . . for she was his daughter.

Would you like another one?

The Orphan's Friend
The whole village is celebrating, it is Christmas.
Only one little orphan laughs not
for it is the day his mother died
and the memory is too sad for him to smile.
He weeps, the poor little one,
he weeps for his lost mother, and alas,
his father too has gone that day to rejoin
the mother, and the child thinks of that.
Instead of going to the celebration
he turns toward the cemetery,
he walks toward a humble grave.
There he kneels and begs his mother with all his heart
to send him a little brother, a companion.
He thinks of his mother's soft caress,
his father's kiss, and he weeps! he weeps!
Then suddenly he sees another little orphan
who weeps for his mother and father, too.
The two children share their sorrow
and from that day on they loved each other
like brothers and gave each other tender care.
The child is ever grateful to his mother
for having sent him a little brother.

November 12. I am so happy. Today after I got dressed I went with Maman and Mrs. Quintero to the party that I have awaited impatiently for 3 days. We saw many ladies who were knitting. Mrs. Quintero introduced us. One lady was Mrs. Carlo Polifeme, a great French writer. Maman bought me wool and knitting needles and I sat down with a group of girls. I was the youngest, then another girl 13 years old and some ladies 19, 20 and 21 years old. I worked and during that time someone read a piece called The Knitters, about wounded soldiers who wanted to be useful, so the nuns taught them to knit. Then someone said, Oh, how many good things come from kindness! I deeply admired that lady, first because she is French, then also because she has all the French feelings of charity, sweetness, goodness, etc. Afterward she gave a prize to the one who did the best work. She introduced my dear Maman as heaven-sent because the person she was expecting hadn't been able to come, she said. She made a speech in which she said that Monsieur Poincaré absolutely had to save France and that he would do it. When we left, she kissed me and said, Au revoir, mignonne. I shall always remember the moment when Mrs. Quintero played La Marche Lorraine. I had not heard it for a long, long time and I was terribly moved. I dreamed of being back in France, I could see the soldiers marching triumphantly back from this great war.

November 14. It is 9. I left a little candle lighted in front of Thorvald's crucifix. I offered it for Maman and Papa, so that God may bless them. Maman asked me which of the two I loved more and I answered, "I love you first of all for being my Maman, then I love you out of gratitude because you took care of me, whereas I love Papa because he is my Papa." Maman is singing, Joaquinito is sleeping, Thorvald is getting undressed, I am writing. Today Maman was given the news of the purser's arrival, but she didn't want to go see him. I am so very very sorry. I practice the piano with all my heart because that pleases Maman and I am progressing rather well. I work hard at my muffler. I have been thinking deeply that I am eleven years old and I don't know anything yet. I have resolved to apply myself to everything I do to make up for lost time.

November 15. Each time I take Communion the thought of Papa becomes sadder and I don't know why. Last night I dreamed that I received a letter from Papa in which he said: I am coming. Oh, if it were true! What happiness, I would be the happiest girl in the world. I write to Papa and always ask him to come. I keep hoping and perhaps he will come. At the moment of Communion, it seems more as though I am kissing and hugging Papa, rather than receiving the body of Christ. That moment is sweet. I am tired of saying to Papa, I send you a big hug. I would like to hug him for real. I am jealous of the other little girls with their papas. I think that I might also be with my Papa, but I console myself by saying: Soon I shall be with him again. Well, no more about that.

I think that here I shall never have occasion to write poetry because everywhere all one sees are busy people, red stores and houses that are so tall one can hardly see the sky, which is always gray. Since this morning there hasn't been one minute without rain. The sky is darker still and the day is sad. Well, to amuse myself I shall do the portrait of Thorvald. What is Thorvald like? Here he is. Thorvald is nine and a half years old, of medium height. He has blue eyes, his hair is cut up over his ears. One lock, light brown in color, falls over his eyes. A little round nose, a little mouth, pretty teeth, small feet and hands. He plays the violin beautifully, it's wonderful to hear him. His disposition usually is calm and he works hard, but when he plays, he plays like a madman. Not very often grumpy, so he has only one fault but that a big one. He cries a long time about everything. But one can forgive that. He doesn't like to write and makes very hard work of writing a note to Papa once or twice a month in my letters to him. He is never sick; he is very strong and very healthy. Today Thorvald and I invented a new kind of ink that I shall try out tomorrow.

November 18. Today we went to Lord and Taylor to hear a concert.[1] Nothing pretty, just tired voices and bellowing. Then they played Hansel and Gretel, which would have been pretty except for the voices, and the Secret of Suzanne, which I liked the best.

November 19. Today I have nothing to say, so I am going to have a chat with my diary, or rather, my confidant, for I write many things that I never tell anyone and that no one knows. Let's begin:

Today I opened a book at random and read, Life is only sad reality. Is that true? Perhaps! I have never discussed that. Today I want to know and although my diary is mute, I am going to ask it anyhow. Is it true? Oh, if anyone asked me that on the sad, somber days when I think about Papa, oh, I would answer immediately, Yes, but that's all. It's true that I haven't suffered yet, I am only eleven, and I can't say, I must wait awhile before answering that question. Although my curiosity isn't satisfied, I shall resign myself and talk about something else.

When I see a poor person, I would like to be rich if only to help. I wonder, when there are so many rich people, why there are poor people. But it's true that there are many rich people who don't give anything and if I could I would give, give. With that in mind, I collected some little toys that I want to give to the church.

[1] *Apparently an event to celebrate the opening of the Fifth Avenue store.*

November 21. After lunch Maman went out and we played together. Maman made up a prize for the one who wouldn't quarrel, and in the evening we had *O* or *X*, meaning quarreled or not. That way we kept quiet and when Maman came home we had dinner. Now the daughter of one of Maman's best friends is here. I am bored and shall do the portrait of my little brother Joaquinito. He is 6 years old, he has long light-brown hair, a little round nose, a little mouth, pretty white teeth. He is terribly intelligent, he has a stormy disposition but isn't mean; when he hurts us or when I cry, he hugs me and asks to be forgiven. I always forgive him, he is so nice. He is a little anemic like me, but he is very strong. I forgot to say that he is destructive and you will see that he never has a toy in one piece.

What is Maman like? Maman has light-brown hair, a long nose, small gray-green eyes, a rather large mouth, very pretty teeth. She is a little short but not too much so. She is very strong, in good health, and her disposition is admirable. She is an angel as sweet as can be. Maman is never tired, she does everything for us. I have to confess that there are days when I don't help her at all. She is good, very good. Her patience is inexhaustible. Do what I may, I shall never be able to give a good description of the angelic nature of my darling Maman. Yesterday I couldn't restrain myself, I asked Maman if life was a sad reality. Here is what she answered. Life is a sad reality for old people who have tasted all of life's bitter pain, but not for young people who haven't suffered at all. A good answer. So I cannot say that life is a sad reality for I am still young, and so I am satisfied.

December 3. Here I am alone at home for I didn't feel well enough to go to Maman's concert.[1] My favorite amusement is to talk to my diary and that is what I am going to do. These last days I haven't been able to find my diary. Finally today I found it hidden behind the folding screen. Thorvald hid it there to play a trick on me. All three of us have had a bad cold and I have been in bed five days with a terrible earache. Last night Thorvald began playing the pieces that Maman is going to sing on Sunday, and he played them so well and so beautifully that Maman said perhaps he will play on Sunday, too. He is a real artist and plays the violin wonderfully. Later he will support Maman. As for me, I can't do that well. My only pleasure is reading and writing. Maman doesn't like that very much, she says I will never earn any money, but my idea isn't to make money like the Americans, who drink it and eat it and jingle it in their hands. I don't want that, I don't aspire to anything, I just want to be allowed to think and contemplate the landscape and to be left to read in peace, that's the truth. I prefer not to think unless I am alone. When I am alone I read, I think and I write. These last days I have written many stories. Then when I am tired I sit at the window which looks out on the ugly courtyard, but as a consolation I imagine that it's a countryside. I pretend the ugly dry plants are beautiful flowers, the ugly red wall a beautiful golden gate that is the entrance to the grounds of a pretty chateau. Then once I am inside I think endlessly, I imagine that the Negro servants are handsome little princes who walk about in their chateau. Perhaps those are foolish ideas, but they are true and perhaps I am mad. So much the worse for me. I like being like that and I shall always be that way, for I have no intention of changing until someone more sensible than I tells me to, and even then it will be with regret.

December 6. Yesterday Maman took us to Gimbels to see the Christmas toys. How beautiful it was! The greatest variety of toys was spread out to tempt all the children. Dolls that cry or laugh,

---

[1] *At Chickering Hall. Under the name Rosa Joachim, she sang English, French and Italian songs of the seventeenth and eighteenth centuries, accompanied by Emilia Quintero.*

cradles trimmed in blue, little white furniture, etc. I looked at them, I loved them, but those are not the things I want most. Maman bought each of us a pad, crayons and writing paper. I am now writing a story called The Savior, or Clovis the Savior. Maman also bought me a notebook for the story of my life.

Let's talk about today. Maman was supposed to sing at the house of Mrs. Guerin, a lady who gives benefit lectures for the children of Brittany. We went and the lady had us sell programs. I sold them saying, "for the children of Brittany, 25 cents for a program with 5 pictures." I sold a lot. Afterward Mrs. Guerin gave a lecture on Marie Antoinette. First she came out in a green crinoline dress with yellow flowers, with a long yellow train printed with gold flowers, a long green necklace falling onto her bosom, and a big black hat trimmed on one side with a big black feather. Then she wore the costume of the queen when she came to France, a long white silk dress trimmed with lace, short sleeves, a long string of pearls, and over all, a long sky-blue coat with white fur trimming fastened across the bosom by a wide band of diamonds. Her hair was held up with a pretty comb trimmed in small white pearls and the white hair hung down in curls. Then she came dressed as a shepherdess when the queen lived at the Trianon, a very bouffant red and white dress and a large light-gray straw hat decorated with roses, and she held in her hand a stick trimmed with red and white ribbons. Next she wore a shroud, and how sad she was when she told how they had taken away the Dauphin. Then she spoke these mournful words to the judge. "As the queen, you have taken away my throne; as a woman, you have killed my husband; as a mother, you have taken away my children. What more can you ask of me? I have only my life, do you want that?" Poor Marie Antoinette! What a sad life! What a heroic woman!

December 8. Today we had a holiday for the Immaculate Conception. Now, when Maman goes out, I give lectures to amuse Thorvald and Joaquinito. Nothing like real lectures, of course. What amuses them the most is when I dress up as Marat and shout at the top of my lungs, One hundred thousand French heads. The whole house shakes. Sometimes I put on one of Maman's long black dresses and my little Marie Antoinette hat, then I climb on a box and stand like Marie Antoinette in the wagon. I love to do that. Sometimes Thorvald and I act out plays that are so sad Joaquinito really cries.

December 9. In school, as usual. I have grown used to it, although I don't like it. I already know a lot of words. Today I reread several sections of my diary. I would like to do the trip from Spain here over again. What fun I had there; here I am bored, everything is sad. There are moments when I feel like crying, crying and never stopping. The weather, school, the streets, everything seems dark, dark. Only at home with Maman and my brothers I find a little more gaiety. Well, the true word: I detest New York and everything modern. I am not the only one. For example, day before yesterday Mrs. Guerin asked me, "Do you like New York?" I didn't dare answer, but when she exclaimed, "Oh, I don't like it, myself," then I said to her, "Neither do I." Another example: Aunt Lolita[1] said in front of her entire family, "Yo no puedo ver a Nueva York,"[2] and even Maman says that living in New York is hell.

[1] *First wife of Thorvald Culmell.*
[2] *I can't stand New York.*

December 15. Maman sang yesterday at Aeolian Hall, the largest concert hall in New York. I pasted in the program to remind me, when I am grown up, of Maman's concert in New York. Maman wore a Spanish costume and sang the tonadillas of Granados. She was a great success, as I keep saying about each of her concerts. Now Maman's picture is going to be published in the Musical Courier, the editor of which has become one of her greatest admirers.

In ten days it will be Christmas. It will be a sad day for it is the anniversary of my illness and New Year's Day the anniversary of my operation. I can't help crying when I think of Brussels and the people that I know there. I would like to be able to share their sorrow and suffering, those dear friends who were so good to me. Their kind care will always be engraved in my memory and I shall always try to prove my gratitude to them, as soon and as much as I can. Miss Zoe, Mrs. Rhode's daughter, is now teaching me to draw. Today I copied two things. Most of it I do from memory. I wanted to draw the way it looked when we arrived from Spain, with the moon reflected on the water.

December 16. I have some very bad news to announce to my diary. My dear little cousin Tina[1] died of typhoid fever. Grandmother wrote to Maman and she let me read the letter. Grandmother says she died like an angel. She was given the last rites and the whole family was moved by the gentle way she bore her pain. She will be another angel in heaven. I shall do her portrait as I remember her. Constantina (Tina for short) was 10 years old when she died. She was very pretty, with large black eyes, a rather round nose, a small mouth that went in a little bit, small and very pretty teeth, rather short but very pretty hair that fell to her shoulders. She was very tall for her age, not very heavy. Her eyes were sad. When I saw her, I often came back touched by her expression. Her disposition was calm, silent. She was very intelligent, very nice. I remember that she used to love to play with dolls and to dress up in old hats and mantillas. I used to play with her and we had a lot of fun. Today I wrote Grandmother. I tried to console her, but since I was sad myself, I don't even know what I told her.

It is terribly cold. We went out and came back with our eyes running. I covered up with every blanket in the house. Maman fixed a hot water bottle for me. Now I am better, but I am wearing two shawls, my bathrobe, and a blanket over my knees. I feel the cold! There's no cure for that. I shiver in advance for all the chilly weather I have to go through.

December 24. I haven't been able to write because Maman left me here [at Kew] on Sunday and my diary was in New York. I love to be here! Today is Christmas Eve. Everyone is excited, the shops are full, people are running around, the gifts are ready. Father and Mother are anxious for the children to go to bed so that with their tender hands they can trim the tree, the pretty Christmas tree. How the children's eyes will shine, and ours too. My uncle, aunt and Maman hurried the children off to bed. Since I am the oldest, I was allowed to stay up a little while, but only a little. Maman watched me out of the corner of her eye and said, hurry up, and I answered, In a minute. Alas, darling Papa is still missing from the family. Oh, if God granted my wish, tomorrow I would hug Papa, but I have no hope of that for today I received a card from him. Papa says he is at Arcachon. It's a long trip for one night to come from Arcachon. That is where Papa left us and he didn't come

---

[1] *Constantina Xuclà.*

LA COTE D'ARGENT

HENRY GUILLIER, r. F........

(6976) ARCACHON. — Les Ruines.

rne. — HENRY Guillier, rue Fonneuve   LA COTE D'ARGENT

) ARCACHON. — Les Ruines, le Grand Salon.

back. We were living in a villa called The Ruins, and they actually were ruins. Since that time I haven't kissed Papa, since then the family is ruined and Maman has to sing in order to earn a living. I am giving in to sadness. No, if I go on I shall cry and I mustn't do that.

December 25. "Merry Christmas!" That was the shout when we woke up. What a surprise, hanging near the bed . . . a stocking for each of the three of us. What a lovely Christmas. There was a top for Thorvald, caramels for Joaquinito, oranges, holly, snow (imitation), how beautiful! And that's not all. Coquito led the way downstairs. New joy, new shouts. A beautiful Christmas tree, all lighted, and toys, it was wonderful. I was in the group of children too. Finally Uncle Gilbert calmed us down and it was with happy hearts and smiling faces that we sang "Adeste Fideles" all together. Then the blond heads and dark heads bent down to read the names and see a beautiful gun, skates, a box of chocolates for Coquito, a little car, a doll for Nuna, shiny proud soldiers for Thorvald, a little boat for Joaquinito, for Anaïs, a beautiful white bed from Aunt Edelmira, a book and a box of writing paper from Maman. Oh, I really don't deserve it. The cries of joy ended and we had breakfast. The house is full of holly. Holly wreaths hang at the windows. The dining room lamp is ornamented with a beautiful white bell tied round with red ribbon, a charming effect. Afterward Uncle Gilbert, Thorvald and I went to take Communion. How sweet it is to be able to say, I belong to Jesus. The rest of the day was calm and happy. In spite of that, in spite of my happiness, I did not forget Papa. If he had been there, I could have shouted, I am in paradise. I have thought a lot about God's goodness. I am here with my family, warm, needing nothing. How many children over there are dying of cold and hunger. Here I have Maman, I am happy and can feel her tender kiss. How many children over there weep for their mothers or weep for the father who will never return. I can console myself knowing that I have Papa, who is far away, it's true, but he is there and I have the hope of receiving his kiss that I long for so much.

It's not right to be sad on such a happy day, and to avoid that I am going to bed and dream about Papa's homecoming. One word more. Today I couldn't help thinking of Christmas 1912, which I spent in Brussels in a sickbed, with an operation in prospect. I couldn't help telling God, O Jesus, your kindness is infinite. Thanks to your mercy, I have been allowed to have a merry Christmas here in New York with my family. I shall stop. I feel like crying when I remember my dear Brussels.

December 29. On the 28th I wrote Papa and sent him a little calendar that Mrs. Rhode gave me on Sunday. Papa sent me some beautiful magazines for Christmas. I read them from cover to cover. I spent a long time studying some sad pictures of a tearful mother holding out her arms toward the child that has just been torn away from her, a father looking at his burned house, the body of his child in the ashes, then some patriotic pictures showing a smiling young soldier, his arm bandaged with a handkerchief, who is shouting, Forward, it's nothing! It's all so beautiful that I get tears in my eyes. After dinner I felt dizzy and couldn't do anything, so at last today I can get back to my diary. It rained all day and we had to stay in the house. I read the "Letters of Madame de Sévigné" that Mrs. Rhode lent me, but since it wasn't interesting I put it aside. At Kew the snow was very pretty, but what a difference here. They pile it up in the corners and what is left turns into black mud. What a pity that snow, which is so beautiful, is pushed aside here. It's so beautiful, so soft, so white! To describe it better, I am going to copy here a poem that I wrote in Barcelona one day when it snowed:

> ### Snow   January 1914
> How beautiful the snow is!
> Pure and white as an angel.
> The children play in it,
> And even babies stretch their arms
> As a sign of welcome.
> She should be happy in her white gown
> Which is real fur, although very cold.
> It is pure and spotless
> Except where people walk on it.

December 31. I am at Kew, here is why. This morning Coquito called us on the phone to say that Aunt Edelmira is sick and would like Maman to come. In a wink of an eye we had packed the suitcase and left. My aunt had a terrible headache and was so faint that she moaned all day long. Now she is better, so I could leave Thorvald, Joaquinito, Nuna and Coquito to play alone while I write. I played with a clay set that belongs to Coquito and my aunt made me a present of it, saying that Coquito never plays with it. I like it very much and modeled a cannon, a little house and a face, not to mention little things like candlesticks, holly, a cross, and some tables and chairs, which I can make easily. Tonight they decided we should stay in case my aunt is still not quite well and can't get along without Maman's care. I am going to help Maman put Joaquinito to bed because I hear him crying and yelling.

❦ *1 9 1 5* ❧

January 1. New Year! We didn't celebrate because Aunt Edelmira is still not quite well. We just went out for a walk and played. Everyone here keeps shouting all the time, Happy New Year! I have not forgotten Papa's absence, Brussels, the clinic, the little house, the friends, all so far away, and perhaps I shall never again see the nuns who were so kind, our house with its beautiful rooms, small, sweet and calm, the friends, Mr. and Mrs. Hostelé to whom along with God I owe my life, Clairette, the nice little girl, and so many others who must now be suffering! All of that makes me terribly sad. Papa's name alone makes me dream for hours on end. Only my heart can explain how I feel, my pen cannot do it. Perhaps my feelings are absurd, I think so and I shall stop. All that makes me feel like crying and I contain myself only with great difficulty. I can't explain this state of mind. Luckily I manage to conceal it and no one sees or guesses. If I suffer, I mustn't make the others suffer too. Besides, what good would it do? Would their sorrow help console me for mine? No, so only my diary has the right to suffer like me, to think like me, since its destiny is to hold my heart's most secret thoughts. To return to what we were saying, why does the thought of Papa make me so sad? Perhaps I want so much to have him near me, I want so much to give him a long, tender hug as I see the other children do. I cry because I think, who is it who keeps Papa from being here with me? Is there someone dearer over there who holds him back? How many times I have asked myself that question. I think that might be it, for I am just a silly girl, full of fancies, of crazy ideas, so I can understand that Papa might love an intelligent girl more, someone with the right kind of ideas who may have taken my place. Although I try to think it out and make myself understand that, I cannot accept it, I cry and get into the state of sadness that I have already explained to my diary.

January 2. Still at Kew. That is what my aunt wanted. Tomorrow is Sunday, so we must go back to New York to get ready for school, which begins on Monday. I have made a resolution to keep my diary all year long. Nothing comforts me like being able to tell all my sorrows, my joys and my thoughts to a silent friend. No one will ever know the things I have written in these mute pages which will keep my secrets. Now let's talk seriously. In February I will have a birthday, 12 years old. I am so old! It's high time for me to become a little woman. I have tried so often to do that, and then for the least thing I get angry, and I must start over again. I get back on my feet, but the road is slippery, be careful. Yes, I am a big girl and I must become perfect. Afterward it will be too late. Maman is calling me. I shall go, I don't want to slip down the path of disobedience.

January 3. The day is not yet over but I feel so blue that I want to chat a bit. This afternoon we are going to leave. My aunt is out of bed and has eaten a little, a sign that she is better. Thorvald went to skate and Coquito is drawing. I am alone here in my uncle's office. There is total silence. My thoughts can unroll and expand among these confidential pages. I am not discouraged because God didn't grant my wish. I am only more determined. I have renewed my vow, and if God is willing, Papa will be here on February 21, which is my twelfth birthday. I am full of hope. Why should God refuse to let me be with my Papa? Why should He refuse me this happiness that I have waited for all year? Since I realized that Papa wasn't coming, why did I begin to wish for his return? Alas, New York is far away, I am afraid that Papa won't be here the 21st of February either, that date that I have set my heart on.

January 4. Last night I couldn't write. As soon as Maman came home, Mr. Diaz,[1] a friend of Aunt Antolina's, took us out for tea, and later he and Maman went out together. We had to go to bed immediately. Today the daily round began, school. I hate it. The blackboard looks a hundred times blacker, the yellow desks are dirty and smell bad. The teacher is severe with us, the yellow tablet they give us to write on tires my eyes. School has become a nightmare for me and I hate it to the utmost.

January 7. Today was a day that I liked. We went to the meeting [at Mrs. Polifeme's], which was just as pleasant as usual. Maman bought me another skein of wool with some money that Papa sent. This was the anniversary of Joan of Arc's birth. First we sang, then various ladies volunteered to make speeches on the subject of upbringing at home. It was very good. Really, the French lan-

[1] *Rafael Diaz, an American tenor from Texas who collaborated with Rosa Nin in her concert at Aeolian Hall.*

guage is admirable. Then a gentleman named Emile Villemin spoke very well on the same subject. He ended by reciting Le Pot de Confiture[1] by Victor Hugo and was very well received. The gentleman asked me if I would like to eat the jam, which made everyone laugh. Then he said something I still remember, that if one knows two languages, one is two people. If one knows three, one is three people. So then, what am I? He promised to send me the poem about the jam. I have to work hard on my muffler so that I finish it. Ah, one more thing: Day before yesterday my aunt came to have dinner in New York and while she was away all her jewelry was stolen. The detectives are looking for it. Everyone thinks it was the governess, for she had the keys and was alone there. All right, now I am a gossip.

January 9. Today we went walking in the wood with a little friend of Thorvald's. We went to see the cave of the bandits who were captured 20 years ago. The little boy told us that they robbed everyone in New York and hid what they stole in the cave. While I walk, I knit. Afterward we went to visit the Museum of Natural History. It is very pretty, first the mummies from Egypt, then animals from elephants to butterflies and ants. Then there were fish, from a very large whale down to little fish. We saw everything, then saw things made by the Indians, weapons, necklaces, costumes in brilliant colors, and the chief's garments, some of them covered with delicate bird feathers, some with ivory beads with gold thread. Baskets, combs, necklaces, then vases painted by the Chinese and Japanese. Finally we saw the Eskimos, but if I tell about everything I shall never finish, and all the time I knitted. Finally on the way home Thorvald and I went to confession in the French chapel. When we reached home, Maman had a letter with the poem Jeanne au Pain Sec[2] by Victor Hugo. Mr. Emile Villemin sent it to me. I hurried to write and thank him. I promised my diary to write each day what has been happening about my aunt's stolen jewels. Julia, a very good faithful servant, has been put in jail over my aunt's protests, although she knew very well she was the one who did it. My aunt is very upset, my uncle too. Tomorrow we are going to spend Sunday with them.

January 10. This morning we got up at 8 to take Communion. I love that moment when I can close my eyes and imagine that Papa is beside me. Oh, it is impossible to describe the sweetness of the

[1] *"Jam Pot."*
[2] *"Bread-and-water Jane."*

kisses that he gives me in my imagination. But it was very brief, since we came back right away to get dressed, for my aunt had invited us to spend Sunday. We took the tram. It was a superb afternoon. Seeing that, I left the games and, taking Coquito's bicycle, I went to wander in the fields. Oh, how I love that. The setting sun painted the sky a delicate pink against the blue, then white. The fields were yellow and pale green since it is winter. The trees, trembling in a light breeze, swayed sadly as they await the end of winter to put on their pretty leaves. Far away a few chilly little birds pecked at the sparse crumbs. But I left all that behind and went to a small hill that overlooks the countryside. I know that spot because I often go there to give free rein to my thoughts. The place is a hill surrounded by trees, and the trees are not so thick that they prevent one from seeing the beautiful pale-pink sky. A large rock serves as my chair. Once there, I put the bicycle aside and give in to my thoughts, thoughts without end. First Papa. I started again to explain this to myself logically, as I have already told my diary, but since I finish by weeping real tears, I put that subject aside. I thought of my dear grandmother whom I left so far behind. I thought of the brave and heroic soldiers who fight for the glory of their French fatherland. I thought of my dear Brussels and wept again. I would have continued to cry except that I saw a painter coming in my direction. Regretfully I got on my bicycle and went home, still thinking, but I stopped all that as soon as I reached the house because that ended my melancholy reverie.

January 11. Today went by in the usual way. We went to school, I work as hard as I can but that doesn't interfere with my doing the things I like best. I am now writing a story, "Poor Little Boy." I only like things that are sad or funny.

I now hate school and everything American. Why, Maman asked me and my aunt too. Why? Here is the answer. Because I love only silence and here there is noise all the time. Everything here is dark, enclosed, severe, and I love sunny landscapes, I love to see the sky. I love to admire the beauties of nature in silence and here the buildings are so high, so high that one sees nothing, or if one sees a little something out of the window, it isn't a beautiful sky that is pale blue, pale pink or a calm white. No, that isn't what one sees here. One sees a dark sky, heavy, mournful, soiled and darkened by the vanity and pride of modern men and women. I say that because I don't like anything modern. I would like to live in the first century in ancient Rome, I would like to live in the time of the grand castles and gracious ladies. I would like to live in the time of Charlotte Corday when every woman could become a heroine, and so on. The truth is I would like to save France from its afflictions, but we are no longer living in the era of Joan of Arc or Jeanne Hachette,[1] and the best thing I can do is keep quiet and out of sight. Where was I when I asked why I don't like America and got into the period when I would like to live? I shall go on and I'm sure my diary has guessed the answer and I can give my imagination free rein. Oh, if I could rise up and annihilate all those ambitious countries that are the cause of Belgium's misfortune and France's tears. But once again I must bow my head and give way to older people who will come along later, perhaps, as I hope. I have to recognize that I am crazy, but since my diary is the diary of a madwoman, I can't write only reasonable things, and if I did they wouldn't be my own thoughts. So while I await the great woman who will save France, I shall go to bed.

January 18. Yesterday, Sunday, we went to Kew, but I didn't enjoy it at all because it was raining and I couldn't go for my lonely walk in the woods. Now that is the only thing I like. The house doesn't seem so charming, I see only sad faces, but let's admit that I am sad too. The news from France is very bad. The Germans have taken several French cities and there is much to fear for the glory of France. Alas, the heroine may come too late and then there will be no more France! Oh, no, that cannot be. If the heroine doesn't come, all of us together will replace her. I who am so small, in thinking that, I feel myself strong, so strong, but it isn't enough. Ah, if I could save France, if only I could put a smile back on the faces of the poor mothers by driving back the barbarians who destroy whole cities, who kill children, old people and women. But I know very well the rôle isn't meant for me, and yet if no one comes I must help to take her place. That is my illusion, but I know my thoughts are impossible and I shall keep them to myself. For now I shall quiet my thoughts and let my pen work.

Day before yesterday Mrs. Polifeme sent me a book that she wrote, Jeanne d'Arc à Domrémy.[2] I read it. That is, I devoured it, I was hungry for that book. What an admirable book! I wrote her to say thank you. Today Maman went to see her. I was very sad,

---

[1] *French heroine who defended her native Beauvais in 1472 by chopping off the head of the Burgundian standard-bearer.*
[2] Joan of Arc in Domrémy.

my muffler was finished but Maman couldn't buy me the material for another one. Mrs. Polifeme seemed to guess that and said that beginning today, she would make me a present of the wool. Isn't that a French heart?

January 19. I am in bed. Thorvald is reading, Maman has gone out, Joaquinito is asleep, the wind shakes the windowpanes mournfully, the rain is falling, it is cold. In spite of my deep sadness, I have my pen in hand and have opened my diary. The news is very bad. The misfortunes of my dear France make me weep all day long. It doesn't show, of course. It is my heart that weeps, since I must wear a smile in order not to make others unhappy. In a word, mine is a secret sorrow and only in the evening by lamplight can I give in to my sad thoughts, until Maman's tender voice advises me to go to bed. Once in bed, with the lights out, I can cry again and think, although I find that moment all too short. This time it will be long and I am going to take advantage of it. Above all I must say one thing. The other day I received a picture postcard of Mouleau from Maria Luisa.[1] I asked Papa to thank her for me, but I confess to my diary that I don't like her. Isn't it she who has stolen my Papa from me? Yes, it is she, for she keeps him from coming to hold me in his arms and I shall never forgive her. If I go on, I will cry and I must not. I still have time to write but my hand refuses. There now, I can't hold back the tears at the thought of my darling Papa so far, so far away!

January 22. Yesterday Jack [Cosgrove][2] invited us to the cinema. Thorvald went but I didn't want to go. Would it be right for me to have fun while Frenchmen are dying, while mothers weep and France suffers? No, I shouldn't, should I? That thought kept me from going and afterward I was much happier. Joaquinito stayed home too and we went to the park with a bag of crumbs. The little birds are so nice! I like them very much. They take the place of the flowers scattered by the wind, the snow and the winter rain. Speaking of snow, we wrote a composition at school. I had to write in English. Here is what I wrote about, although I had to change some of it because I couldn't find all the words in English. The Snow in Belgium. Here, the snow is welcomed with joy, children love it and smile, but there the shivering little ones weep at the

---

[1] *Maria Luisa Rodríguez ("Maruca"), who was to become the second wife of A.N.'s father. The marriage ended in divorce.*
[2] *A friend of Thorvald's.*

sight. Here it makes the children happy because they go out on
sleds or on ice skates, but alas, the children over there have no
shoes and they are cold. Thus the pure white snow that gives happiness here causes tears to flow over there. As I think of the poor
soldiers and children who cry, I leave my diary, but not without
sending a last thought to Papa.

January 23. I take up my diary in this new notebook that Maman
bought for me today. We didn't go out because it was raining, so
we played alone all afternoon and I was very bored. I want to
wear black now. I would like to wear mourning for France's sorrows. I am still very sad. I pray to St. Joan of Arc and St.
Geneviève and I always add, Oh, dear God, oh, beloved savior, I
beg you in your mother's name, in the name of the French people
to save France. Oh Jesus, give back her glory and her sons who are
also yours. Divine Master, grant our prayer. In my prayers I
always remember Papa and all my fervor is for him. If God hears
me, my darling Papa will be here for the 21st of February, so I am
waiting and wishing for that date because it may mark the greatest celebration, the happiest day of my life, next to my first Communion, which shall never be forgotten. If God still doesn't hear
my prayer, I feel myself very strong and able to try again, and I
shall try again and again until I leave this place, God willing. I
must stop. I have to put my little devil of a brother to bed.

January 24. It is very cold. This morning we went to Mass, then
we came home. We didn't go to Kew because Uncle Gilbert is sick.
We had a very boring day. In the afternoon I pretended to have a
little party and I fixed a little tea. We drank sugared water and ate
jam, then I read stories. Thorvald played a piece on the violin
which was very pretty, but we didn't have an audience to applaud
and that rather spoiled it. We were beginning to feel downhearted
when I made up a raffle of some little thing and that put Thorvald
and Joaquinito in a good humor again. Then each of us read his
book and thanks to all that we were not too bored. Afterward we
went to the park. What dreadfully cold weather! I fed the little
birds, then we came home and had supper. There are the things
that we do on Sundays. I am tired so I shall stop, but before I do I
am going to copy something that I just wrote.

The Nuns
Look at those gentle creatures of the Lord taking care of the
wounded, encouraging the dying, distributing charity to the poor.

How good they are! How holy! How many acts of devotion are hidden under their veils, how many kind deeds their humble downcast eyes must conceal. Their tender hands serve only to take care of everything. On the battlefield they do not fear death, but rush in, and in poor villages they dedicate themselves to teaching the children, consoling the mothers, caring for the sick. Therefore in appreciation of their goodness, let us love them, respect them, and above all try to be like them, let us try to be devoted, good, as tender as they. If we can't do that on the battlefield, let us do it in our homes. If we have no family, let us serve the poor. Let us not merely admire those heroic women, but let us imitate them.

January 25. Here I am once more, still in my humdrum life. My efforts are crowned by small successes that make me very happy. Ah, what wouldn't I do to please Maman and Papa. I don't like the piano, but if it's Maman who gives me my lesson, then I go at it with a great deal of pleasure. Maman sings, which makes me very sad because I remember when Papa accompanied her, and then I think of Brussels and the war. Today I fought against it but I am seized by a desire to become a nurse or something that would take me to France. I would like to become a man so that I could bear arms. Oh, how many things I would like to be, for I envy the sisters, too, who care for the soldiers, but alas, I am too little and I should give up those ideas. It's music that makes me sad. I am going to try to amuse myself. Last night I dreamed about piano music slow as a lullaby, about languorous and sad songs, about the harp with its sweet harmonious sounds, then about the faint voice of the guitar. I woke up crying, but I fell back asleep and dreamed that I was saving France, that I was Joan of Arc and that she sang, Rise up, Anaïs, save France since that is your wish. I rushed forward and a quarter of an hour later the whole city shouted, Victory! Vive la France, vive Joan of Arc who gave Anaïs her strength. How happy I was. If it were only true. Vain illusions, I a girl, I who am so small, saving France.

January 27. I didn't write yesterday because Maman had to go out and I had to take her place, and I might add that I was very tired. Today I didn't go to school because I had a pain in my back, but that didn't keep me from writing. I wrote a story, Duty and the Sacrifice of Louis and Jeanne. I love to write stories, only I don't know how to make them gay, they are always sad. That's because I am very sad. Oh, yes, France deserves a martyr's crown. How much she has suffered, yet she is always beautiful, always admirable, always glorious. I am very proud to be French. I have written so much that my eyes are tired, so I must stop, but I shall say one more thing. My diary wonders why I now write only my thoughts. It's because things here are always the same.

January 28. Once again I thought that I wouldn't be able to write because when we came back from a walk, I had dreadful back pains again. Now it is better. Maman just went out, Thorvald is reading, the wind blows and shakes the panes, the rain falls without stopping. I am in bed, there isn't a sound, and the silence makes me sadder than ever. I feel like crying but I promised myself to write everything in my diary and I will do it. During the day I make myself smile and act happy, but in the evening I cry all the tears that I wanted to cry all day long. When it is dark, after my prayer, I give in to sad thoughts and often I cry, I cry so much that when the clock chimes 11 I am only at the beginning. In spite of that, those hours are sweet, for I talk to Papa, I hug him as in a waking dream, but I do all that with tears. I realize it's very foolish to cry like that, since I don't want Maman to know, but the tears I shed almost always free me from the dark sadness that surrounds me. Besides the evening, I have another time, although only rarely. When Maman takes Thorvald and Joaquinito out during the day and I stay home on one pretext or another, I sit at the window and then I also think. But alas, my thoughts don't travel very far. Doubtless frightened by the tall buildings and the dark sky, the birds don't fly close enough to carry them away. So all I do is wish that my thoughts might go far away, but it's very sad always to wish for something that one knows is impossible. . . . No, I am not telling the truth, because I wish for Papa to come and that is not impossible. I wish France to win and that is also very possible. Don't they say that to God all things are possible? And these lines carry my wishes to Him, so it is quite possible that my thoughts travel far . . . very far, to get to Papa and to my beloved country, who are the reasons for my sadness, my wishes, and my thoughts. . . .

January 30. Today being a holiday, I have something to tell. This morning I went out with Joaquinito. I took bread and gave it to the birds, then I fed the squirrels. What pretty animals. When they catch sight of you, they come forward, then stop, then come forward again and again. If you move, they run away at top speed, but I don't move, so they come close and take what I give them from my hand. Then they run on the grass, coming and going, eating in the shadow of a tree, and we do it all over again. It's delightful. In the afternoon I went out with Maman, I ran errands, then I came back and started to write Papa. I wanted to send him my diary, but Maman explained that it might be lost, so I copied a few paragraphs. I forgot to say that we went to the French chapel to confess. Tomorrow we are going to take Communion. I am impatient and I want that moment, for it is then that I am together with Papa and with France, more than ever.

January 31. What a nice day. This morning at Communion I wept, my heart was full of happiness, a nameless joy, an unexplainable happiness came over me, and as I said, I cried tears of joy. That moment when I close my eyes and speak to Papa and kiss him makes an impression on me that lasts all day long, for it seems to me I hear Papa's voice, I see him, and when I open my eyes that vision that I love disappears and I weep. Today that moment lasted longer than usual for I thought of France and prayed. The moment lasted also because I added the thought of Maman to it. She was not there and I had to imagine her. I love her with all my heart and admire her with my mind. And so the Communion is turned into visions. This is how it is right now. First I kiss Maman, I hear her voice, I speak to Papa and he answers me, I see the sufferings of France and I feel myself grow strong, stronger than ever, and even so strong that I think of saving France. But then I wake up, I understand the foolishness of those thoughts, those visions. I say vision because neither Maman nor Papa is there and yet I hear them, I see them and seem to feel them near me. I have let myself go, but that's the truth, and when I reread this I say to myself, all foolishness, all madness, so am I crazy? Yes, I recognize it, so I am going to keep my madness in my head and not write anymore for my diary.

February 3. It's beautiful these days. Every day it snows, but so much and so deep that the streets, the houses, everything stays white in spite of the rage of human beings who work to get rid of it. So the streets are white, as I said, and it's beautiful to see. Even the sky has joined this celebration of pure color and now I love it, but that won't last because when the snow disappears, driven away by everyone, the sky will put on mourning again and I won't love it anymore. I say driven away by everyone, but not the children. In class we open the window and when the teacher turns her back, we all rush to the window and try to catch the pretty flakes. When one of the children catches some, you can see his face break into a beautiful smile. I took part also and had several flakes when the teacher, jealous of our joy, rolled her eyes, closed the windows, and the children all went back to their desks, but more determined than ever to try again. I am now going to dream about the snow and the birds that I like so much.

February 7. Without knowing it, my diary went for a trip. Here is how and why. Aunt Edelmira came to dinner at our house on Friday and invited us to spend Saturday and Sunday at Kew, so we packed a suitcase and left, including my inseparable companion, my diary. Only in spite of wanting to write, I couldn't manage to do it, and that is how my diary took a trip without knowing about it. But I know that it is indulgent and will forgive me. I am going to talk a little and we will make peace. I have so many things to say! Friday Maman went out with me by myself and bought me some beautiful black shoes with rubber soles to keep me from the damp. I was very pleased and kept looking at them, but Maman hadn't finished. She also bought me a pretty dress in navy-blue serge with light-blue trimming at the neck and a smart white collar. I was so happy. After that we came home. At Kew the snow has melted because it has been so warm these last few days. The sun shines brightly, everything is singing, everything smiling. How I love to walk among the trees stirred by a light February wind and in the fields where one can see the clear horizon. Ah, how I love that! How sweet it is to me! In those dreamy moments I feel as though I have left this sad earth, I feel as though I catch a glimpse, a tiny glimpse, of the air and fragrance of heaven, it seems as though I fly away toward the infinite. If my Maman's sweet voice didn't call me back, I would spend hours, long hours, contemplating nature . . . it's so beautiful! . . . it's the only thing that is pure and beautiful in this world. I don't know about the world to come.

February 22. Yesterday, February 21, was my birthday, but I went to bed with swollen feet and was terribly sleepy and I couldn't write. I am going to tell everything that happened on that day, at what is called here a "party." At 4 o'clock my aunt, uncle and cousins came over. They gave me a box of chocolates. Then Jack, a little friend of Thorvald's, who gave me a pretty pencil box. Then Pauline, a little friend of mine who is in my class and is the best student, then Mrs. Rhode, followed by William. We played, then had cake, chocolates, ice cream, etc., then they all went home very happy.

February 25. I brought my diary to school so that I could write a few words. We are reciting geography but I can't follow it. I am going to describe the classroom, that place that I detest. The classroom is a large square room with gray woodwork, a glass door, and on the right a big cloak closet with red curtains. After hanging up my coat and hat, I go to the 4th yellow desk in the 3rd row. Before that, when I come in, I say, Good Morning, Miss Bring. I get out a pencil, a pen, an eraser and a ruler. I take a book and study. The teacher goes bing on her bell, we stand up and say a prayer made up of an Our Father, Glory to God, Hail Mary, and the blessing for the day. After that we recite the catechism, then geography, then we do arithmetic until noon. At 1 school starts again. We do dictation, composition, reading and grammar. At 3 it's finished. There are 24 boys, 12 girls in our class. The teacher is stern but not mean, but there are many unfair things because she has a favorite who is the meanest girl in class and accuses everyone else very unfairly. The teacher is watching me, so I have to close my notebook.

February 27. I wanted to write the evening of the 25th but I had a horrible pain in my legs; however, that isn't interesting. I want to tell about a strange dream that I had that night. First I was in a large room with gray wallpaper, very dark. I can still remember exactly how it was, but that isn't interesting. I was sitting on a small wooden chair that smelled of pine. Then a great lady dressed in black velvet and wearing a belt of diamonds or some shiny material came into the room. First she went to the grand piano in the corner and played, a long melody that was so sad it seems to me I cried, or at least I felt sad. When she had finished, she went to a large easel, took a brush and began to paint on very dark wood. In the distance the sky was pale blue. She painted gently and in a moment had finished. Then she went to a big desk, took a pen and a big book with white pages, and first looking at me with her big blue eyes, then at the sky, she slowly began to write and she wrote pages and pages. I could see that they were long beautiful poems full of charm, tenderness and sweetness. Oh, I couldn't read them, but they seemed to me to be very beautiful. Finally she shut the book gently, laid down her pen, and came silently toward me. Then I heard her say, Choose. Oh, how I hesitated. First I remembered the beautiful melody she played on the piano, then suddenly I turned toward the easel, with the beautiful painting where I could describe all the lovely and charming landscapes, all the beauty of nature. But quickly I turned toward the big desk covered with books, an invisible force pulled me toward it, without even trying my hand took up the pen. Then the great lady smiled, came closer and gave me the big book, saying, Write, I shall guide you. Without any trouble I wrote some things that I think were very beautiful, for the lady pointed to a place where venerable bearded old men and also queens and beautiful ladies were seated in great armchairs, writing endlessly. If they raised their eyes, it was to question nature, the horizon, infinity. Your place is there, she said to me. As soon as she left, I gently let go of my book and my pen and went to the piano. I wanted to try it and at first my fingers moved very well, I liked what I was playing, but suddenly I stopped, I couldn't remember any more. So looking sadly at the piano, I said to myself, I can't play. I tried to paint and was doing a beautiful landscape, but I stopped and instead of paint, there was a lot of heavy daubing on my canvas, so I said, Adieu, I don't want you. Then I picked up my pen and began to write without stopping.

March 17. Lots of new things! If I haven't written, I have had good reasons. First I caught a pleurisy that lasted four days (it seemed like a year), four long days, as I said, and in bed. But that was nothing. The very day I got up, Maman fell sick and had to go to bed. Maman in bed and no one to take her place. I had to shake myself a little and so I have become a cook. I do everything. I get dinner, straighten up, clean the house, and do the laundry, because Messieurs, my brothers, do me the honor of dirtying a pair of socks and a handkerchief every day. Then I have to mend the stockings and sew on buttons that are forever coming off. It certainly is hard work to take Maman's place and I couldn't have managed it without her counsels. She is teaching me the order that it takes to keep a house. I have been excused from school for these occupations, but I must say also that the doctor ordered me to stay home from school for a week to rest. I haven't rested much, but I like this kind of work and do it with pleasure, and the American school bores and tires me. Today Maman got up, but since she still doesn't feel quite well, my dear Maman had to stretch out on the

sofa. I have been interrupted after every line because I found time to bake a cake and I have to watch it. Maman calls me, too, from time to time. Having so many duties to take care of, I shall stop this diary of my life.

March 19. Just a few words in pencil because my time isn't my own, it belongs to the house, to Maman, to my brothers, and to my housekeeping. I don't belong to myself but to others. I have never been so happy because the work prevents me from having the painful thoughts that I used to have. I feel happy, my conscience is clear, and I am sure of doing my duty as I should, whereas I used to feel remorse watching Maman do all the work. Finally, I feel happy because I have been good for something, oh, very little, but something just the same. I feel a soft beam of light in my soul and I have found the secret and the source of happiness in working, not always for myself, but for Maman, for my brothers. If I am a little tired when I go to bed, it doesn't matter. Only now Maman is better and next week I have to go back to school. However, I understand now that even if I don't do the housekeeping, I can give my dear Maman another kind of pleasure in working well in school and applying myself to the little bit of work that I do outside of the schoolroom. I am full of good resolutions and full of good intentions about keeping them, and each time I would like to break them, my faithful diary and friend will remind me.

March 20. At Kew! We are at Kew. The doctor recommended it for a complete cure.

March 21. Three beautiful logs are burning gaily in the pretty red brick fireplace. Sitting on the green sofa, I think of many things, so many, many things hurry under my pen. I want to resolve the question of gratitude toward New York. New York has certainly accepted us, but that's all. Maman has had to work, oh, so hard. No one has enough admiration for her constant courage and her energy. No one has admired the ardor with which she works. All is vanity in this world, vanity underlined, because no one realizes that Maman does not take part in any of those frivolous pleasures that are against the rules of the wise man, who says, What must be done? Oh, certainly there are some people who like work, who recognize its sweetness, but there are not many of them. Besides his work, the laborer must have courage and the patience of perseverance to defend himself against the thousands of lazy ones who would carry him away, patience to withstand the isolation, disdain and mockery that frivolous people impose on him. Oh, how different from France, my dear beautiful motherland. I am speaking of la belle France, full of heroism, of courage, and so industrious. I am not talking about certain parts of France (which are French in name only). I don't mean those places where, under the name of Frenchmen, certain people have taken refuge who are selfish, mean, lazy, and inhuman, let's say the scum of the pestilential earth. On the way to Mass, I contemplated the blue sky (which is rare here) and it seemed as though I glimpsed more than ever the beauties of France. I saw as in a dream the glory, the beautiful and true glory that she deserves, and I thought (not without pride) what good fortune it is to be French, to be a child of that country under such a pure sky. As one French poet wrote, may a little bit of that pure sky cling to me and give me a little purity, and above all courage and strength to fight for my country. As I reread these lines, I notice the disorder of my thought, which began with New York and finished with France. But oh, it's that her sweet name offers so much to admire, to respect, and above all to love.

March 22. Now I am back again in our house in New York. We found a lot to do and have been working almost all morning. Since we got back too late, we couldn't go to school in the morning, but in the afternoon, what a cold welcome from the teacher. It wasn't a very encouraging way to begin the week. Just the same, I weathered the storm, although a hundred times I felt like throwing my books in the teacher's face. Oh, I am not afraid of her, I am not afraid of anyone, I fear God, Papa and Maman, but that's all. I don't say that I don't obey, I do obey, but my thoughts are in revolt against the unjust severity of Miss Bring.

March 24. The dear name of France inspired me to write a poem which I shall copy here:

Salute to France

I salute you, O beautiful France,
I salute you, lovely fatherland.
Only you have won my heart,
You, amidst your trials and misfortunes.
I salute your beautiful courage,
France whose goodness encourages
Our sacrifices for you.
I salute your voice
That calls us to our duty
and to the joy of seeing you again.
I salute your fields, your flowers,
You who dance amidst your trials,
Send us a ray of happiness.
Last, I salute you for your supreme energy.
We are your children, sweet France.
Let us care for you always
And give us your courage
To fulfill our wish
So that glory may be yours.

Life goes on as usual. Only school seems different to me, as the teacher is nicer. I am beginning to enjoy studying, but that isn't much. I am disgusted with my classmates. I can't understand the way they think and talk. I have never heard such dumb subjects of conversation. Are you going out in the car this afternoon, where are you going, with whom? Or else they say bad things about people behind their backs and make up thousands of lies. I keep quiet, and go away from them and think of other things. If I take an interest in my studies, it is only to learn another language. Mr. Villemin's words haunt me. He who knows one language is one man, he who knows two is two men. I would like to be ten strong men, I would like to know how to fight and help France. Unfortunately, I realize with sadness that I am only two children, and a female at that. When shall I be the equal of at least one man?

March 29. Peace until day after tomorrow. Yesterday was Palm Sunday, which was in no way different from any other day, and I had to remind myself sadly that we are in New York, where no Christian holidays are observed. At Mass they gave me a tiny bit of palm branch that had been blessed, but such a tiny thing. To keep the memory forever, I am going to describe one Palm Sunday in Spain.

It is a beautiful spring day. Brilliant sunshine bathes the mountains in its light. Having put on their best clothes, people begin to put their heads out of the windows to wish one another a joyful, friendly good morning. The children await the time to go to church very impatiently. Ding, ding, bing, bang, the bells, let's go, and with happy shouts the children run toward the church, proudly waving their beautiful palm branches. The palm branches, bought the night before, are made of a very long yellowish branch braided and decorated with candied fruit, shiny balls, and a large bright-colored bow, red, black, white, blue, green, etc. It's very pretty. The grownups wear a little branch of laurel. All the people stop in front of the church (The Conception). The bells ring. Everyone taps on the ground to show their impatience. At times the palms rustle in the breeze. The sun makes them shine in such a way that they look like an enormous field of wheat stalks. The bows look like scattered flowers. O God, who reigneth in heaven, look down on the fields that belong to you and bless them! The bells begin to ring again, the palms are waved, and the pious crowd makes way to let the procession through. Then all voices are lifted in a Gloria, the crowd is still, the palms are blessed solemnly and the procession returns to the church, followed by the part of the crowd that wants to hear Mass. The rest of the people scatter happily in all directions, to meet again around the family table for dinner. That is how Palm Sunday is celebrated in Spain.

March 30. The days seem short to me now, only now that I have nothing to do, I am sad once again. I think about France. Not for a moment do I despair of her glory, but I am sad because of her suffering. I am becoming famous as a storyteller, which isn't much fun, because each time I start to write, Coquito, Nuna and my brothers take me by the arm, make me sit down and I have to tell all the stories that I can think of. I'm lucky that I can remember so many. I'm afraid I will run out because I tell at least two long ones every day. It's tiring but I am rewarded by their thanks and their joy. I wrote to Papa and sent a postcard to Emilia, who wrote me to ask how I am. I don't deserve so much attention. Maman went to New York to give a singing lesson, and she came back with a package that she took pains to hide. I know what it is, it's for Easter. For my dear Maman I shall always be a little girl who likes surprises. I like that, it's so nice to be able to lean on her, close my eyes, and let her steer our bark amid life's tempests. Often I open my eyes to take lessons from her, so that later on I will have nothing to worry about. God grant that I may still have Maman when I am grown, for it's in those serious moments that I shall need her the most.

April 1. This morning Maman went to visit my cousin Billin[1] who has been at boarding school. Tonight she phoned to say she was bringing Billin home for a few days of vacation. I am very happy. Aunt Edelmira gave me permission to wait up for them; she will come at 2:30, so I haven't long to wait, fortunately, or I would die of impatience. When I was going through things, I found a French book, Marie Clair. Maman read it first, then gave me permission to read it. I do nothing except read, I like it so much, but that's just an excuse. But really, I couldn't give up reading, since I learn everything from books. Today is April 1, but it isn't celebrated here. I remember what fun we had in Brussels, exchanging gifts of chocolate fish or even real fish. Poor Brussels, how changed things must be now!

April 3. I shall need a whole page to describe my cousin Billin. He is 12 years old and has very pretty dark-brown eyes, light-blond

1 *Thorvald Sánchez.*

hair, a small mouth with rather thick lips, and a very pretty straight nose. He is very polite, very nice, he never disobeys and is very pious, so he is constantly held up to us as an example. We love him already. Joaquinito follows him everywhere and I try to be like him. Every evening he sings and plays the piano, and the whole family listens. He plays without rushing and without pounding. All in all, I find him very nice and very likable. I have written a story, "Mabel," and I think it's interesting, at least it seems so to me. I am thinking of rewriting my arrival in New York because the account that is in my diary is badly done and not my real thoughts. My aunt was reading over my shoulder and I didn't want to say anything against New York because she likes it so much.[1] Tomorrow is Easter. We shall have bad weather, according to the prediction. A dreadful wind is blowing which makes all the windowpanes shake and the doors slam. The terrible wind raises great whirlwinds of hail and snow that are blinding. Mountains of snow two meters high pile up in all the corners, the trees bend under the weight of the snow, the little houses seem swallowed up, for the snow sticks to the windows, the doors, the walls and everywhere, and the sky is heavy. It will be a sad Easter. Papa never leaves me, I carry him in my heart, but many times I feel like crying when I see Uncle Gilbert put his arms around Nuna and kiss her gently. How sweet that must be, how good. When will I have such kisses? It's hard to hold back my tears. Afterward I scold myself and tell myself it's jealousy. That's why, when Uncle Gilbert kisses his lucky little girl so tenderly, that wish that I have felt for so long becomes sharper and more ardent, and I wonder how long I shall have to wait for that kiss which is so far away and perhaps may never come, and the repressed tears fall in my soul, burning and bitter.

April 13. I am in New York and have become reacquainted with school. Papa has written me several letters and sent packages of newspapers and a grammar. I am going to study it by correspondence, and my diary is supposed to notice the difference. I write, I write, and I think a lot. I spend my time dreaming, but with a purpose; I have written another poem, a sad one as usual. I am always sad about a lot of things. Papa is going back to Paris and I fear the dangers he will be exposed to. Why did he leave Arcachon, which is such a calm place? Papa knows what he should do, so I shall keep quiet. Mrs. Rhode is leaving New York to go to Havana and Maman will go with them to the ship. I just heard

[1] *See Appendix.*

that the ship is called the Antonio López and that the purser from the Montserrat is in charge of it. Maman will see him. I would have liked to go along, only Maman received two invitations to the French theatre and I must go or risk offending Mrs. Polifeme. So tomorrow, against my will, I am going to the theatre. I have had no news from Grandmother. She doesn't write, could she be sick? Please God that she isn't. Poor Grandmother, that would be too much sorrow. Maman went out this evening. Thorvald is in bed. It is too quiet.

April 14. The French theatre this afternoon was very well received. It was beautiful. First I saw Il était une bergère,[1] a funny play, then Jeanne d'Arc à Domrémy, which is both beautiful and admirable, and what fine language. I held my breath so as not to miss a word, only I couldn't stop the pounding of my heart. Oh, Joan, how I love you, how I admire you, oh, why did you have to leave this world! Look down upon the dangers to the glory of France, save her, protect her, oh, beautiful sweet heroine, and from heaven on high send us another heroine like yourself. I tried to read the expression of Joan of Arc on stage, I tried to guess her thoughts, to absorb her strength. I was so impressed by her words that involuntarily my eyes were wet. Oh, how I would love to be like her. Finally a singer wearing a white dress and carrying a long red and blue banner over her arm came out and sang the Marseillaise. Her voice was vibrant and I was really moved. My brain swam with overwhelming thoughts, my heart burned with love, admiration and respect, my fingers twisted nervously as though they wanted to fight for France. I had to close my eyes to hold back the tears and I could hardly stand up. It was wonderful, so glorious! I managed to applaud just the same, and I noticed a lot of people weeping and feeling just as I did, so I think that theatre is very patriotic and very French. Maman and Joaquinito went to the ship and saw the purser, who laughed when Maman told him that I don't like New York.

April 18. My heart is full of a slow sadness and I feel like crying. Mrs. Quintero is playing the piano, Maman talks about the war and the news, and I pour a heavy heart into my diary. This morning I took Communion, and during Communion I just murmured, *God, France, Papa!* God knows what that means and like my diary, He will understand. When Maman takes me to the park

[1] There Was a Shepherdess.

I don't play, I think sweet sad thoughts. My heart is weary of living far away from my father. Maman does everything she can to make us happy and I am grateful. She takes us for walks in different woods and I love those walks, which are very picturesque, calm, far from all the noise. That does me good. Now I am sad but sensible.

April 19. School is again keeping me busy all day long, but I shall not neglect my diary. On the contrary, I shall talk to it as much as I can, to take my mind off other things. Today right after school, Maman came for me and we went to the dentist, who filled my teeth. They hurt a lot and I can't chew at all on the left side. I am going to copy a poem that I wrote.

Maman Sings

Maman sings, her voice is so pure.
When Maman sings, heaven opens,
God and the angels want to hear.
Maman sings, brilliant in her jewels,
Her sweet voice stills my heart.
Her voice tries to erase her sorrow
As with tender lips she says the words.
Where do songs go in their flight?
When I cry, her voice dries my tears
And I smile at her voice that can do so much.
The echo repeats the sound of that heavenly voice,
Maman's voice resounds from the mountain tops,
It rises from the highest peaks to heaven.
Ah, how beautiful it is, how beautiful!
When Maman sings I am in heaven.
Those are my dreams
When Maman sings.

April 20. I brought my diary to school with me, only I can't chat because the teacher is making her rounds and if she saw me writing she would take my diary away. Until this evening.

I said I would return, and here I am, ready to confide my thoughts to my diary. After school Maman took us to Riverside Drive, a beautiful drive overlooking the Hudson River. Maman and I sat in the shade while Thorvald and Joaquinito played. Maman was mending and I embroidered a little table mat that I am making for Aunt Edelmira. I don't play much. I can't help feeling serious and sad when I think of this horrible war that is costing so many lives, so much suffering. It seems that the terrain retaken by the French is already being sown with crops in order to prevent famine. The seeds must be bathed in blood! But the news is good, rather comforting, although until the war is over I shall always be sad and my heart will weep. Fortunately winter is over, so the soldiers won't suffer with the cold; now they will have to bear the heat of the sun. We must hope and be patient. May God protect France and her children.

April 21. It is unbearably hot, and such a warm spring makes us think that summer will be three times as hot. It's really too much. Such changes are to be feared. I received a pretty white jacket from Godmother and a hat for school. Maman is going to buy me another one for dressing up. Also I must report that Maman has had a little good luck, she has three pupils who will attract others. I go out every day with Joaquinito and Thorvald because Maman is very busy. I haven't had a letter from Papa. I shall write to him tomorrow. I continue to do good work in school, only I am not good in arithmetic. This evening Mrs. Quintero came to supper. I feel sorry for the poor woman, and Maman says she is afraid she is losing her mind. I would be very sorry. If she had more energy and didn't worry so much, I think she could avoid that sickness. She is very downhearted. Perhaps Maman's example will lift her tired spirits. Maman made me a present of a geranium that I am caring for the best I can, as it represents the fields and flowers that I love.

April 22. I wrote to Papa, and always I tell him of my ardent wish, "that he may come here, not as a concert musician but as a father who is awaited and longed for."

April 26. Yesterday, Sunday, we went to Kew, only I didn't enjoy the trip because I have a bad toothache. I came back so tired I could not write. I have finished the little table mat. I put it in a box tied with ribbon, and if my aunt comes over I shall give it to her. Maman says that her health is very bad, poor Aunt Edelmira. School is as usual. I would like to help Maman, but how? I can only write and not very well as yet. I must keep looking, just the same. Papa sent me a packet of newspapers. Ah, how I enjoy them; when I read them, I am back in the atmosphere of France. At school I am teaching my classmates French. Bit by bit I communicate my love for France, and I have won over a few hearts. Maman is going out, and I must hurry to my tasks as substitute mother.

April 27. Maman has the only inkwell, it is late and I can't wait, so I am writing in pencil. I am sitting on the floor, and next to me is Bouby, who has become my favorite doll. Why? Because he reminds me of Mr. and Mrs. Hostelé, to whom I am so grateful. He reminds me too of the calm and happy days that I spent in dear Brussels. My Bouby has always traveled with me. He was there at the painful separation from Grandmother, he has seen me laugh and cry, but I hold it against him that he doesn't remember anything, and I don't love him as much as I do my diary. Bouby is the only child I shall ever have, for I want to be free, always free, I don't want anyone except Papa and Maman to judge what I do. I want to give myself completely to poetry, to writing, to stories, but man proposes, God disposes. I shall let God determine my future.

April 30. I have just finished reading "Les Grandes Tristesses d'Alice."[1] It was beautiful. A proud rebellious girl, an orphan for two years, is sheltered by an uncle. Things look dark, she is always serious, always in a bad frame of mind. Her uncle is very unhappy, and so is his brother, his sister-in-law, his friends. One day Alice runs away and hides behind a bush to weep over what she terms the world's wickedness toward her. She overhears a conversation between her cousin Henri and her brother Robert. Poor girl, growing up without her mother, and without anyone to tell her she has the wrong idea. . . . The name "Mother" had never been mentioned, but now Alice promises herself to do better and to change her thoughts. That sweet word brought her to herself and she becomes cheerful and obliging. Her uncle is very happy and everyone is pleased when Henri asks for Alice's hand in marriage. She accepts, for it was he who invoked her mother, it is he who made her happy and will continue to do so. This story is full of sadness, painful separations and death, so I was moved in spite of myself, and Alice makes me think that more than ever I should listen to darling Maman's counsels. While I have her I should love her always and in return God will keep her for me always.

May 4. Maman received a trunk full of clothing from Cuba. I received a beautiful pair of shoes and a jar of "guava cream," a

[1] Alice's Great Sorrows.

specialty of Havana. Sunday we went to Kew. I took the mat to my aunt and I think she was very pleased. Apropos of my aunt, she is in very bad health and is very thin and nervous. Everything makes her cross and upsets her, and she worries terribly about every little thing. She makes the children and Uncle Gilbert unhappy, herself too. Poor Aunt! Aunt Anaïs[1] has asked Maman if I might go to Havana. For the time being Maman is not willing, and I would not like either to go anywhere unless Maman goes with me. I am too unhappy without her. I am going now to a very good dentist recommended to Maman by Uncle Gilbert. I am not allowed to eat many sweets. Lucky that I don't like them too much. I still write very often to Papa. I know that pleases him, so I write long letters. His letters bring me a touch of the atmosphere in France. Papa has undertaken to give me French lessons by correspondence. He hasn't given me any for a long time, though, because he was moving out of Paris. From his letters I learn that he arrived safely. God keep him safe from danger! Papa also is sending me gifts by one of his pupils. I hope that they will get here. The torpedoes are so dangerous.

I am working hard in school, not to please my teacher (I don't care at all about that), but only to learn another language and to become "more than one man." I have used the same words here as in the letter to Papa because that is what I think.

We laughed a lot in school this afternoon because after the teacher dictated some numbers, a boy asked, Do we have to add, Miss Breen? And the teacher answered, You don't have to add Miss Breen, just the numbers. That is the first time she has let us laugh. She is terribly severe. She can pound but we shall not change. My teacher should learn this proverb: "One cannot catch flies with vinegar." I am very chatty tonight, but sleep is stronger than my urge to write.

May 5. I am very tired but it was because I wanted to do something to please Maman. Coming home from the dentist, I walked instead of taking the streetcar, from 116th Street to 72nd. With the five-cent streetcar fare, I bought Maman a bouquet of lilacs that now decorates the living room. Maman deserves much more than that and I regret that I can't give her a thousand times more.

May 7. Yesterday Maman gave an afternoon tea for some of her friends. I was so tired at bedtime that I couldn't write. I confess

[1] *Anaïs Culmell de Sánchez.*

with some remorse that I went to the French theatre, but instead of being happy I am sorry that I didn't refuse. It moves me so that I lose all my usual peace of mind. I know there is one thing that attracts me to that theatre. Each time I go I hear the Marseillaise, and that is so wonderful! I can't help feeling deeply moved. I can't explain what I feel. My heart pounds and I tremble. At the words "Aux armes, citoyens" I feel as though I have wings, as though a divine force has hold of me. Could it be Joan of Arc who hovers over us in that happy moment? She comes to beautify that song which symbolizes France.

May 11. I wonder, when I let so many days go by without writing, if my diary thinks I have abandoned it! Oh, no, never. Fortunately I am not an ungrateful person, and I promise my diary never to give it up, oh, no, never. I already feel very remorseful because I didn't begin my diary sooner. But I must admit that it was only when I began to keep a diary that my ideas began to take shape and pour forth. To whom could I have confided all the thoughts that fill my mind if not to a diary? Confidant that I love, do you promise always to keep the heart that I have given you, the thoughts that I have expressed only to you?

May 12. I wish that no one knew me, I would like to live alone and apart. Ah, how I envy the life of those souls who find so much peace, so much sweetness in solitude. In one of my stories I described the sweetness of that kind of life, which so many people fear, and why? Because they are sick, they have a disease called blindness. Alas, why did God veil the horrible things in the world from their gaze? Perhaps it was for their good. I say nothing and feel pity for them. What do I know, perhaps I am as blind as those I pity. God put us in this world to make us hate sin. All of us humans are weak and we are dazzled by a brilliant light full of reflections that weigh on us too late. We are dazzled, I say, and instead of realizing that the world is laden with sin and vices, we admire it and have chosen it as our mother. Horror and remorse which forever seize us too late, poor blind ones that we are! God has granted me infinite grace, He has allowed me to see a tiny light which revealed the vice, the horror that encumbers the world. He has explained to me the sweetness that His heart holds and I have understood; thus I have given myself completely to that divine heart. I am full of pity for the blind ones. I am full of gratitude toward God.

May 16. Two years, two years since Papa left me at Arcachon. A terrible betrayal seized me that day, I have never felt the pain of separation so deeply. Ah, poor Papa, when will you come, when shall I be able to kiss you and carry out my filial duties toward you? The other day I had a visit from a gentleman who is an uncle of one of Papa's pupils; he brought two packages from Papa. What a nice surprise! As soon as he left I opened the first package, a box camera with films for Thorvald, a gold stickpin for Joaquinito and a pretty leather purse with my initials on it for me. I was mad with joy. Dear little Papa, how nice you are! Yesterday Maman bought me a beautiful blue ribbon for my hair and a pair of white shoes. I am so spoiled. I keep trying to think of something that will give pleasure to Maman. Every time I go to the dentist, I walk and with the streetcar fare I buy lilacs. It's not much, not enough to show Maman a tiny little ember of the burning love she has kindled in my heart.

Yesterday I had a terrible toothache. My cheek was all swollen with neuralgia. That was what I call a black day, oh, so black and heavy, so heavy that by evening I felt broken with pain, boredom, and fatigue. Today things are better. I am writing to console myself, to lift the burden that is weighing me down and which happens each time that I don't have a little chat with my diary. Ah, I would like to know what will become of me when I am grown. Perhaps I shall seek happiness in a cloister, perhaps I shall sacrifice my life for the sick, the wounded, the poor, perhaps I shall share my life with a man and give myself completely to my children. I prefer to give myself to my pen, I prefer to write, not for glory or to become known, no, only to write, to let those who want to understand my heart know it, in order to reform it.

It is to choose one's future that one has a guardian angel and Providence. As for me, silence. I shall not try to explore the mystery of my future or to become Providence, although that would be a "terrific" thing. That word really isn't too elegant, but that means it's the right word. I hope I won't use too many of those right words because then I wouldn't be French anymore but a "boche." I don't know what's the matter with me tonight, but I can't find any nice words, so before I wound my dear diary, I shall close it quickly, quickly.

May 19. I am still the same Anaïs and for my diary I shall always be. I now have to work twice as hard because I have to learn catechism in English. I have gone many days without writing but it's because I have been having terrible pain in my teeth. I am cutting my twelve-year molars. I am over that now, but I go every other day to the dentist. It certainly is not much fun, but these miserable cavities will be taken care of. The first thing my class-mates asked me was: When will I be able to eat candy. I quickly answered: Oh, even if I am cured I shall never eat any. I am exactly the opposite of other children. Is that foolish? Perhaps. So much the worse for me. Each person has his own disposition and that is mine. Last night I wrote to Papa and tried to express the pleasure that his gifts gave me. I described my life to him, I let him see how ardently I long for him to come. Thorvald seems to be developing a taste, a tiny taste, for writing, he who likes only numbers. I described how nicely Joaquin behaves. All my letters are full of thoughts, memories, wishes. I write often since Papa told me my letters give him pleasure. I have had to stop walk-ing to bring flowers to Maman because of the pain in my legs. I am a bundle of illnesses that should be thrown out for fear they may be catching. But I close up my bundle and no one catches anything.

May 20. I forgot (I blame it on my occupations) I forgot to buy a notebook in which I could reunite with my diary, so I am writing on this sheet of paper and shall insert it in my notebook.

I have never taken the trouble to make a portrait of myself for my diary. It's fun to talk to someone without saying who one is. Now I think I shall perform that little duty.

I am Angela Anaïs Juana Antolina Rosa Edelmira Nin et Culmell. I am twelve years old at present. I am rather tall for my age, everyone says. I am thin. I have large feet and large hands with fingers that often are clenched from nervousness. My face is very pale and I have big brown eyes[1] that are vague and that I am afraid reveal my crazy thoughts. My mouth is big. I have a funny laugh, a passably nice smile. When I am angry, my mouth be-comes an ugly pout. Usually I am serious and somewhat dis-tracted. My nose is a bit the Culmell nose, by which I mean it is a little long, like Grandmother's. I have chestnut hair, not very light in color, which falls a little below the shoulder. Maman calls them locks of hair. I have always hidden them, either in a braid or tied back with a hair ribbon.

My disposition: I get angry easily. I can't stand to be teased

[1] *They were changeable in color. In her later years, they could be described as green.*

but I like a little to tease others. I like to work. I adore my mother and father and above all my aunts and all the rest of the family, not counting Maman, Papa, Thorvald and Joaquinito. I love Grandmother. I am crazy about reading, and writing is a passion with me. I believe fervently in God and in everything that God tells me through His holy Church. Prayer is something to which I have always had recourse. I don't love easily and become attached only to people whom I respect in my own way. I am a French girl who loves, admires, and respects her country, a real French girl. I admire Spain, although less, of course, and I especially admire Belgium.

My diary knows my thoughts as well as I know them myself. I have finished my portrait now, because a very sweet magnet has just attracted a kiss from Maman for me, and with the dream of Papa's arrival I am going to sleep after this day of work.

May 23. Here I am at last, with my diary again. I am sitting on an old bench in the park and while Thorvald and Joaquinito play, I shall try to write. The weather is beautiful. The grass has grown tall and stands in pretty fields that one can roll in as though it were cotton. The majestic trees have on their green adornment. Summer is a fairy who, in three or four days, turns nature green again. The sun, it's true, is not like the hot sun of Spain. Here it is paler, but warm just the same. This morning I took Communion and my soul is wrapped in the sweetness of that wonderful moment. I let myself go hazily with my thoughts, my illusions. I would try to describe them here, but I am distracted and preoccupied by a thousand projects for a new story that I am going to write.

May 27. The other day I wanted to arrive at the dentist's on time, so I took the subway. It was the first time I have taken it without Maman, and an employee, probably to make fun of me, told me to go downtown but pointed to the uptown train. I took it and rode for a quarter of an hour in the wrong direction. I was scared, alone in the subway! But a kind lady, who happened to be French, put me back on the right track. I have made myself a promise not to do that again, not even to get to the dentist's on time.

My friend Pauline Ryan, or rather my classmate, is a real American character. She likes me a lot, but she can't stand it if another girl talks to me or if I talk to another girl. She is very proud, she never will admit that she thinks another girl is pretty.

JOACHIM NIN.

PAIOR EDIT

She has a nerve. For instance, without asking Maman or a word of warning, she telephones and comes to dinner. In class, she sits at my desk, takes my notebook and scribbles silly things in it, which means I have to tear out almost all the pages to hide her drawings. She puts her nose into everything that concerns me and soon she will want to know, line for line, the story of my life. Naturally, I won't tell her. Although I want to be pleasant to her, I almost never answer her indiscreet questions. She is my friend because she is the best-mannered girl in my class, and I don't want to have anything to do with the badly brought-up girls who would teach me their ordinary language. And yet, that's the kind of girl that everyone likes in this country. Certainly no one here will like me for my personality. It's better to obey than give orders. That suits me and I have adopted it. My ideas certainly aren't reasonable, I know. They are free, they fly away in all directions, they are full of illusions.

May 29. Today I went by myself to visit Mrs. Quintero, who is sick. I read to her, I took her flowers, and all day long all I did was say over to myself Mrs. Quintero's words of thanks. In the evening I felt remorseful and asked myself, Am I becoming vain and frivolous? Am I full of the wish to be admired? If that happens, I shall be like those vain and frivolous people that I dislike, and I should dislike myself. Heaven help me not to let that happen! My dear diary will scold me and judge me severely so that I don't let myself be full of pride and the wish to be admired. I am a little bird[1] as in these preceding pages. I am a little bird, I say, who has neither strength nor energy, no nest, no place where I can lean and learn to be reasonable. My diary will be my anchor and a harbor for my thoughts. Reason must be my conscience guided by God. And it's up to me to develop strength.

May 30. At Kew! When I come to Kew, I forget that I am in New York. The fields, the flowers make me happy and remind me of my Country, France, Queen of the most exquisite, most charming, sweetest flowers. Above all else, I love to dream. I love to leave this harsh world and soar toward the infinite where there is only sweetness. I am not saying I am unhappy, oh, no! Maman is so good to me. But just the same, who can keep me from weeping over my country's misfortunes? Who can keep me from waiting

[1] "Linotte" (*linnet*) *in the original. One of A.N.'s nicknames for herself. Later her favorite was "Mandra," Catalan for "lazy bones."*

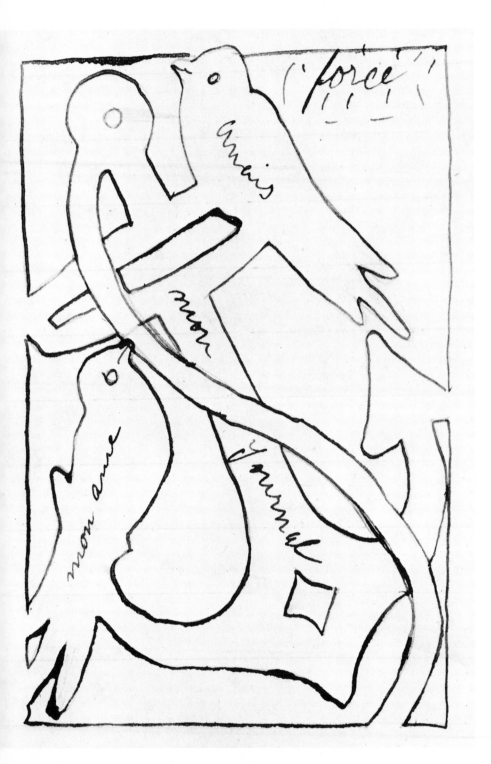

impatiently for Papa's arrival? Who can keep me from suffering because of my faults?

Uncle Gilbert is leaving on a warship where duty calls him. I am very sad that he is going away. I shall not see him for two years, this uncle whom I love more than all the others. He is so silent! A strong man who knows how to command. Where did he find the patience to care for my aunt, who is so capricious, when she was sick? My uncle never refuses her anything.

Those Eyes

Those gentle gray eyes
When one is good.
Those eyes, so terrible
When one deserves it.
Those eyes that pierce the night,
Following me when I run away,
Those dark eyes that pierce
My heart.

Those tempting eyes that I sometimes run from
Because they are too sweet,
Alas, where can I hide?
If I do wrong, they are so angry!
If I do right, so good, so sweet
That my heart melts.

Those eyes, an illusion, perhaps,
They are the eyes of the conscience
Of my soul.

Copies of My First Poems

Arcachon (at the age of 9)
The Painting
Under the shady leaves
Sat a painter
Painting on his beautiful canvas
A lovely landscape.

Badalona (at the age of 10)
The beautiful sea,
The enchanting blue sky
That lend gaiety and enthusiasm

Even if one is sad.
To think that it is God who gave us this beauty
And this delightful enchantment!

Badalona (at the age of 10)

I approach the altar,
My heart full of love for God.   .
My Savior!
My happiness is so great,
And my long white veil,
Which reveals my joy to others,
Hides me like a Virgin.

Thoughts on the Day of My First Communion
When I see the miseries of this World, I think that if
I were rich, there would not be one poor person on Earth.

Barcelona, July 2 (at the age of 11)
The Shy Violet

One day, the queen of flowers
Saw blooming in her field
A graceful violet
Endowed with every charm.
But one day the queen of flowers
Said to the violet:
Child of my kingdom,
What other gift can I give you?
And the shy flower answered:
A blade of grass to hide me.

Barcelona, July 2 (at the age of 11)

Here below, everything takes flight.
Thus the birds fly to their nests,
The Saints fly toward God,
The sailboats swiftly fly
Toward unknown shores,
And my heart flies to my mother.

Barcelona, July 6 (at the age of 11)

If the weather is good,
Said a shining butterfly,
If the weather is good,

I shall go roving
Through my favorite meadow.
If the weather is good,
The busy bee answered,
If the weather is good,
I shall push forward with my task
Of searching out the nectar
That will go to make my honey.

Collection of My Last Thoughts

To you, dear parents, I open my heart with the same intention as did Saint Theresa of the Child Jesus and the Holy Face. That intention was to show her heart exactly as it was. But she opened her heart to the Superior in her convent, whereas I open mine to the Mother and Father Superior of the family. When you read this collection of my last thoughts, I shall be far away, far from this world. I don't know exactly what the word Testament means. I think it means to reveal the last thoughts of the heart, those that will never change. I would like to make mine. It's silly, but just the same, even though I am only twelve, death can come suddenly, so I shall proceed.

I would like us to remember always that we owe everything to our Wonderful Creator. And that we must always love Him and pray to Him. Oh! yes, we should love Him, sweet Jesus and the God who made us and who forgives us always whenever we ask it.

I would like you not to be sad about my death. Rather you should consider it a grace that has been granted, for in heaven I shall pray to God for you. I would like all my toys to be divided among the poor. I would like all my papers to be burned except my diary and such of my stories and my poems as you think deserve to be read. I would like everyone to forget the bad things I have done and for which I am very sorry. Especially you, dear parents, pardon your daughter. I would like the whole family to love the Hostelé family and help them if they are in need. They should be considered part of the family, and those who love me should do what I am not able to do. They must try to repay what was done for me.

Forgive me, forget me, care nothing for this world where you will find only bitterness except in the service of God. Be modest, charitable and pious. Prayer heals our sick hearts. Dearest Thorvald, beloved Joaquinito, you who have such a place in my heart, I thought of you with my last breath. In return, forgive me, I love you, I forgive you. Maman, Papa, dear ones that I have loved all my life, you who alone detained me on this earth, farewell, farewell, farewell. Be kind, you will see me again.

My diary, I leave you at the same time I leave this world. Thank you, thank you, companion of my thoughts. . . .

I imagined that I might die and wrote down here what would be my last thoughts and eternal wishes. They will never change. I shall always have the same love for God, the same tenderness toward my parents, the same love for my brothers. If my thoughts ever change, I shall not be the same Anaïs Nin.

June 2. Maman has gone out with Oscar and Amanda Rhode. She is going to Aunt Edelmira's, where there is a get-together. I am alone with Thorvald, who is reading, and Joaquinito, who is asleep. The wind is blowing hard. Is it possible that a day in June can be exactly like winter?

I closed my eyes a little while ago and imagined that I was in a castle, a prison. A wicked lord tore me from the arms of Maman and Papa. I suffered indescribable torments. It was a waking nightmare. I don't know why I always dream of suffering. In the morning when I wake up and realize it was a dream I am angry with myself.

June 7. Yesterday Maman held a musical evening and I helped her serve tea. They made me read my poems and I was ashamed, because I know they are bad. I write them only for myself. Maman is very busy because my aunts have her buy things for them. We are often alone and I practice giving little lectures, with Thorvald and Joaquin as my audience. I give little parties where I read, or we drink tea in doll cups.

I am going to copy a short poem:

New York, June 2, 1915
My Bewildered Heart
In the shadow of the night
As the bells rang the hour of midnight,
I walked, I sought to catch a shadow,
But the shadow grew darker and darker.
It was my shadow that fled.
I wanted to get it back,
I wasn't ready to die,

The thought made me sad.
But as I ran
I heard a noise in the thicket.
I looked and what did I see?
It was myself!
Only a game
Of my bewildered heart.

June 12. I have been to confession and I feel a great peace take possession of my heart. It is this virtue, Patience, that I find terribly hard to practice. The lack of it causes me a lot of suffering and I am very unhappy for having been impatient.

As I write, I look at my watch. I have only a quarter of an hour. The hands seem to turn quickly for I forget the time when I talk to my companion. Maman sang night before last. She was rehearsing with Mrs. Quintero. I let go of my book and slipped into the bedroom. There I threw myself on the bed and painful sobs escaped from my heart. I saw all the horrors of the war, the saddest things passed before my eyes. And Maman continued singing. I grew dizzy, and her songs, happy or sad, seemed like a murmur that made my tears flow twice as fast. It seemed to me that I was fighting, and on the battlefield I saw Papa as he lay dying. Maman was taken prisoner. I saw blood everywhere, then cottages, houses, castles and monuments, all on fire, and I felt my heart break. The murmur continued and I still wept. My tears burned my cheeks. I closed my eyes and my breast trembled with the sobs that shook me. It was an unexplainable sorrow. Maman heard and came to comfort me. This happens every time Maman sings, and I don't know why I feel so unhappy in those moments. They say I have been doing this since I was little. Music makes such an impression on me, all of it sounding like the cry of a human heart or the description of a heart that is never really happy on this earth. I was quiet all the rest of the evening, and after my "crisis of sadness" I wasn't even strong enough to hold the pen.

The quarter of an hour went by in a minute, because my heart overflowed.

June 21. I left school feeling a little sad, because the teacher was nice to me. We will see each other again in a few months, after vacation. Now we are free. I want to write more than ever during this vacation. Thorvald is at Far Rockaway for ten days.

Now I have many things to say. Tonight I started to think, perhaps my grandchildren will read my diary, so they will have the story of Mlle. Anaïs Nin. That seems funny. But I imagine they will find my thoughts old-fashioned. They will condescendingly notice how little progress has been made and will say, as I say now, You see, everything is invented, we have surpassed all the past centuries.

I just have time to copy my two latest poems:

Hope

Here is the coming on of Spring,
Turning the fields green and flowery.
The bells that ring in unison
Used to sound the hour
Of running through the fields.
Alas! How can we hear them now
Except with tears
And longing for that peaceful time?
Never more shall we await Spring,
Never more shall we smile for an hour,
Never more shall we expect joy.
We still have a time to wait,
A time full of faith,
Which is our only Hope.

Reverie

When the sun sets,
When the wind caresses me,
I think of him who fights off
Those who come endlessly to trouble our peace.
And then my tears fall
When I think of his death.
It is only a painful reverie.
Perhaps happiness will return
And the home be rebuilt
Perhaps I shall smile again
Before I die,
But that is only a happy reverie.
I would like to possess riches
To give all, all of it away.
I would like to be a friend of good folk
And plan a campaign of charity.

I would like to have the strength
And a thick skin
To follow life's road,
But that is only an ambitious reverie.

Dream of my soul,
Dream that gives life,
Dream that helps us believe in distant things,
Dream, fly away, leave me.
Begone! I don't want to dream, but live.

June 24. Aunt Antolina wrote Maman that she is coming back. I am glad. But a great sadness comes over me. I realize that I am going to spend another vacation without Papa. Am I condemned to live far away from my beloved father? Since God refuses to reunite me with Papa, He cannot refuse to go on watching over him . . . and later? later? . . . We shall see. In his last letter Papa spoke of a tour, a trip which perhaps will bring him to New York. But that is only a tiny hope and I can't believe it, because each time the disillusionment is more painful than the time before. To forget my sorrow, I read more than ever, but never, never, no never shall I forget to miss Papa.

I forgot to say that yesterday Maman took us to Coney Island.[1] We had dinner at the beach and afterward went to see the

[1] *Shown in the photograph at Coney Island are: top, Isabel Duarte (an old friend of Mrs. Nin's), Mrs. Nin and Isabel's daughter, Belica Tallet; below, Joaquin (Joaquinito) and A.N.*

amusements. Joaquinito rode on the merry-go-round and I played at bowls. I won two ugly little brooches. We went to the cinema. Then after eating ice cream, we came back home.

July 1. During an hour of reading, my mind was transported to a battlefield. My heart trembled with impatience, together with the soldiers. I felt with them the desire to win new glory for France. I wept and my heart broke when they had to lower the flag in front of the enemy. Like the Red Cross nurses, it seemed to me that I gave life to many poor soldiers and it seemed that, like them, I deserved the glances of the poor sons of Mother Country. Above all, I felt and I understood the depth of their love for their country and that it made them give their lives as though they were little seeds. But the little seeds, once planted, grow tall and become the wealth of the field or the greater glory of France.

At night I often weep and think, Alas! If I were a man, ah! I would avenge the insults of our enemies. How happy I would be if I could die on the battlefield, after having done my duty! And I shiver, I tremble, I clench my fists when I realize I am not even half a seed. I am so little. If I could put on a man's skin, my soul could go ahead and accomplish this thing I want so much. Perhaps I could content myself with being a woman and I would be a nurse: "Since I can't give my life, I shall dedicate it to others." How long will it take? 4 years, 4 endless years to become a half-woman, to be 16 years old.

But then, if I could cut my hair . . . an idle ornament! and put on a soldier's helmet, then making my eyes shine and holding a weapon by sheer strength of will, my soul in readiness and my ardent love for my Country summoning all my strength . . . perhaps . . . perhaps I could be a soldier. I dare not think of it. It would be the realization of my dearest dream as a Frenchwoman. After that, I would be content and I could say, not just in dreams: I fought for France! These visions dazzle me, and how I envy, yes I envy those who right now are shedding their blood in France. Unhappy creature that I am, why dream about things that are *impossible?* That word really upsets me. I am ashamed to be a girl. I am so sad when I think about my crazy wish and how impossible it is that my tears flow, my heart breaks, my whole being trembles, I close my eyes and when I awake, I fall into an abyss.

Ah ! If I were only strong! If I were a man! If I were grown up! Alas! When I look at my thin little hands, still clenched into fists, I understand, and the abyss seems afire, and I repeat what I said in one of my poems:

> Dream that gives life,
> Dream that helps us believe in distant things,
> Dream, fly away, leave me.
> I don't want to dream but live.

But the dream doesn't go away. I don't want to live, the pain is too great now. I would rather dream of my happiness at being a soldier and fighting for France.

The last rays of bright sunshine disappear in the distance, and the air and I are wrapped in a light mist. I am sitting in an armchair. I breathe the cool evening air and I feel more sensible now. I am in a frame of mind to talk seriously with my diary. Of the thoughts that I described this afternoon, only great sadness and bleak desolation remain. Now, I live. By talk seriously, I mean explain to my diary what I am doing and where we are. Where are we? At Kew, where we are going to spend a month. My aunt [Edelmira] is leaving tomorrow morning for Newport to see Uncle Gilbert one last time. It is dark and I can't see too well what I am writing, but my hand finds its own way. I wouldn't give up this little place where, all alone, I feel a great peace, for anything in the world.

In my prayers, I have stopped asking for Papa to come here. This is the reason. The ships are in great danger because of mines and enemy submarines. I would rather Papa stayed in Paris where there is no danger for the moment and where I firmly hope that Papa will always be safe. But I pray even more fervently that God will bless him.

July 11. I am leaning on the windowsill of my room, breathing the cool evening air. There is not a sound except for the occasional meowing of a little cat or a cricket that, in jumping, gives off the strange little noise with which the Creator endowed him. My gaze is fixed on the starry sky and I try to forget the great sadness, the regrets, the desires that preoccupy my mind endlessly. Suddenly, instead of stars, I seem to see flaming bombs, and the sky looks on fire. I feel as though the gentle breeze carries moaning and lamentation. Everything trembles, I shiver. It seems as if I am in the midst of a battle. My heart beats very fast. Before my troubled eyes stands a poor woman surrounded by skeletal children who are dying of hunger. That disappears and I see before me bloody corpses. I hear an agonized voice crying: Help. Thousands of imploring eyes look at me. I am powerless to console these miseries, I feel myself falling into an abyss. Always, always a vision of the war. Another shiver brings me to myself and Reality surrounds me. I see that I am far from the battle, sitting calmly in Kew Gardens, in the country. Then I fall to my knees and my heart thanks God and asks His pardon for not realizing the favor He has done me. That is all. I go down, sit on the porch, breathe.

Now . . . another idea, a question. What can I do to help France, help her children? I have no money to give. I haven't the time to knit. So what to do . . . I found it . . . Pray. Yes, pray that the hungry children may be fed. Pray that the lonely mothers may be consoled. Pray that the soldiers may be given strength and courage, and pray for France. May God hear my prayer!

July 13. Copy of a biography of Maman that I wrote today:

I had the pleasure of hearing the harmonious voice of Mrs. Nin. It was very sweet, very smooth and very clear. The entire audience was transported toward the ideal, the perfection and beauty that are felt when someone really knows how to sing. This celebrated singer has appeared in France, Belgium, Germany, Havana, Spain and New York. Everywhere she has always been received with the warm appreciation that she inspires.

Mrs. Nin has always refused to sing popular music. She has always sung good music, true art. She is one of those women who knows what is beautiful and sublime in music and her rôle is to acquaint others with it.

Mrs. Nin, who lives in New York at present, came to this city to form a group of pupils who in a very short time will do her honor.

She communicates all of her musical skill to her students as a missionary imparts knowledge. If all singers were like Mrs. Nin, the science of music would not be profaned nowadays as it is by certain people. Because she is modest, Mrs. Nin remained too long in the shadow of her famous husband. The few times that she sang for friends remain engraved in the memory of those fortunate enough to have heard her.

The few artists who have been privileged to hear her admired her at her true worth. Now that she has come out into the light and been recognized, Mrs. Nin is receiving the praise that she deserves.

I hope the reader may have the pleasure of hearing this sweet voice and will dream, as I did, and soar into the space which separates us from the ideal in music.

Maman thinks this is quite good and may have it edited in the leaflets she is going to have printed for her publicity. If she does, my name will be printed for the first time underneath a biography. However, it isn't sure as yet and perhaps someone else won't like it . . . so . . . it will be written just for me or for some indulgent reader in the family.

August 8. We were still at Kew Gardens when a letter came announcing the happy arrival of Aunt Antolina, Godmother, my two cousins Rafael and Charlie and my cousin Antolinita,[1] who is 9 years old. We were supposed to wait 3 more days for them. Maman left me in the care of Mercedes (an elderly lady who came to help Maman during the week), along with Thorvald and Joaquinito, and she left for New York. With the help of a cleaning woman, our little apartment was cleaned, scrubbed, swept and put in order. After having closed the apartment, Maman came back to Kew where we spent 3 days counting the minutes. The happy day arrived. Dressed in our best, we went to meet the boat. It was noon, the time the boat was scheduled to arrive. After waiting an hour, we learned that the boat would not arrive until 3. Maman bought a few sandwiches and with that and a glass of milk we had a delicious little lunch. We waited a long time and suddenly the boat came slowly into sight. My head began to spin and I thought, When will it be Papa's turn to arrive? I couldn't smile any more. I felt very sad for a quarter of an hour, during which I waved my handkerchief sadly to welcome my aunts, whom I could already see. Two minutes later, we were hugging each other joyfully and I

[1] *Antolina de Cárdenas.*

was totally taken up with the pleasure of seeing Godmother and Aunt Antolina again. When we reached the apartment, Maman made plans with my aunt and it was decided that she would stay over at the apartment and that Godmother, Rafael and one of the two maids would go to Kew with us. It was late and with each one helping as best he could, we made a rather good supper to satisfy our Nin, Cardenas and Culmell appetites. That same evening my aunt went to look at a small apartment in our house. It has 2 bedrooms, a large living room, bath and kitchen. My aunt found it attractive. That evening at 9, the apartment was hers. It's true that money can do everything. . . .

From that day on, life was nothing but pleasant rides. My aunt had brought her automobile with her. Separated as we were by the distance between Kew and New York, we couldn't see each other often, so Maman packed her trunk and there we were, back in New York. Between trips, cinema and theatre. I haven't had a minute to myself. But this evening, after going to see the park in Brooklyn, I said to myself, I must write in my diary and I have done it.

But always and everywhere, I think of my absent Papa who is the only one I need to be happy. And when we are riding along at top speed in the automobile, I look bitterly at the beautiful country, those beautiful fields and beaches that Papa doesn't see.

August 13. In front of me stretches a green lawn shining in the sun. On the left, a clump of trees. In the distance, in front of me and behind me, the main avenue through the park. I am sitting all alone on a bench in the shade of a big tree. I was looking for solitude. I would have liked to be even more alone, but Joaquinito didn't want to walk any farther, so without paying attention to the passersby, without listening to the murmur of the branches that are shaken by a very cool wind, I shall begin. Now, that is to say exactly today, if I am not mistaken, we have been here just a year. At this hour (noon) we were having dinner for the last time on the Montserrat, which now has been replaced by a new boat whose name I can't remember. It is one year, one year I have been in New York, a year full of work, of walks, and of endless dreams. I am too fond of dreaming. Is it because reality seems to me too sad? I am afraid so. Papa's absence turns into wishes, into dreams that are full of melancholy. But let's stay on the track. I said it was a year, a year that we are here, that I breathe the air full of ambition that fills New York, and heaven help me not to fall victim to it because ambition counts many victims. If I am not mistaken, it is two and a half years that I have been away from Papa. . . .

So I always come back to Papa and I shall stop because I don't want my diary to become as melancholy as I am.

August 17. I am not in the park now, but in the little living room. Thorvald is studying catechism, Maman is starching my ribbons. I have just finished the arithmetic lesson that Maman gives me every evening.

Every evening we have supper upstairs, then we discuss. Carlos is German, or rather on the side of the Germans. We spend hours arguing. France inspires me with good arguments that send him packing.

I am going to copy a short poem that I wrote this afternoon in the park.

Vengeance

Heartless man, do you believe
That your crimes will go unpunished?
Do you believe that the tears and misery
You have caused and that you commit in the night,
Do you think there is no one to bring your misdeeds
To the light of the truth?
Do you think that under the ruins your dreadful deeds
Will be forever hidden?
No. And under those ruins that your cruel breath made
There is still someone breathing
Who one day will rise from the grave
To summon all your victims
And this new king of the overthrown,
Who shall march in rhythm to the sound of bells,
Shall be Vengeance.

August 20. Papa sent me, or rather sent us, $5.50 each. At the same time he sent me one of his latest portraits, taken in profile. When I sit next to the portrait, Maman tells me I look exactly like Papa.

I answer all of his letters with long letters describing my life in New York and all that I do. I tell him, using words from prayers, how much I wish he would come and I say, When will I be able to do my duty as a loving daughter? I think of Papa always and I often say, Dear Papa . . .

My cousins call me The Serious One, and today they told me that my face looked more cheerful because I played tennis for a little while with another little girl of my age. I try to do better, but it seems I always look like an old maid. My face expresses too clearly the sad thoughts that preoccupy me.

September 22. On September 13, school opened its doors and drew us into the arms of: Learning. We all went to chapel and in the middle of a great silence, the priest gave a sermon on the good intentions we should have for the new school year. After that, the Superior, Sister Angelita, began to read the names of those whose work and good conduct have deserved advancement to a higher class. My heart pounded and I thought how happy the mothers of my classmates will be when they announce: I am "promoted." Suddenly, my name was read, and I slowly followed the others. Then I thought how happy Maman will be and that is what gives me the greatest pleasure.

The new classroom is smaller, better lighted, with many pictures on the walls. Three American flags look down on their children, except for Thorvald and me. We were born of another mother who has the same heart and the same name of Mother Country. I hardly had time to look around the room when our new teacher came in. At that moment I was missing Miss Breen and feeling sad, but when I raised my eyes I saw a pair of small brown eyes looking at me mildly, and immediately I found the new teacher likable. She is small and rather thin. Her features are regular but not pretty. Her lips wear a perpetual mischievous smile. Beginning today, our days will be fuller than before and the lessons longer. For arithmetic, which we have from eleven o'clock until noon, I go to another smaller class to learn my division tables. From 3 to 5:30 every day, we go for a walk. When I come home from the park, I just have time to do a little homework. At 6 we have supper and after that I practice the piano, do the rest of my lessons, and go to bed, sometimes tired and other times regretfully. This evening I was excused from piano practice and immediately I thought of my diary. Papa sent me an issue of "La Science et la Vie" that I received this morning. I plan to write to him tonight if I have time.

Mrs. Quintero came over the other night and Maman, who considers her one of the family, had me read Vengeance to her, knowing that she is very French. She gave me so many compliments on the beauty of my poetry and went on and on in such a way that if I weren't, I must confess, a little pleased about it, I would make fun of her to my diary. I understand she even spoke about it to the Countess, who would like to print it in the Annals or the Gazette du Salon, because it seems she has music parties at her home. It isn't certain, and when she sees my pitiful little poem, she won't know what to say. Maman told me this when I came home at noon and I said to myself: Give the credit to Inspiration, as it certainly isn't due to me or my pen. That way, too, if the poem is bad, it will be Inspiration's fault and not mine.

I am sitting on the grass with my eyes half-closed, thinking of Papa, of the war. I have been reliving my life from the earliest days I can remember. Then, as in a dream, I saw myself grown up. Writing stories, with Papa and Maman nearby, it seemed as though I saw the sea in front of me. The waves rocked me gently as I described my impressions to Papa and Maman. Suddenly I arose and it seemed to me I said, How I love you, Papa and Maman. And I heard a murmured answer, Together. But the wind rose, the trees bent, and among the whirlwinds of dead leaves, I saw the sky suddenly darken. Then a sharp pain went through me. The leaves were my dream, a gust of wind. Reality swept them up and carried them far, far away so that I shall never see them and the blue sky of my dreams became the dark sky of the truth, yes, the truth. Papa wasn't with me. Why? It seemed as though I wept inside and I held my head in my hand. My mind could hardly resist the tempest that assailed it. Yes, and among the angry waves an everlasting Why? kept repeating. Why? Why? I tell myself there is a simple reason. Papa's work keeps him in Paris. He doesn't come here because he has nothing to do here. He is waiting for us in Paris. My heart leaped and said, No, no, but didn't say why. One day I shall know why. But my heart, which is never wrong, said no to that natural response.

October [?]. I am in Central Park. It is a beautiful day, but since I started school the sun is less bright. With little cries of distress, the birds huddle before the first winter wind. The trees lose their leaves and the yellow leaves soar into space and whirl in every direction before fleeing on a last gust of wind. People who go for a walk hurry back home immediately with their hands in their pockets, saying, It is cold today, I have to put on my big coat, the winter comes too early. Yes, especially for me, winter has come too early. The wind has carried away all my dreams, those that I believed were real. A veil has been torn away from my heart and again I must say, Papa won't come. Why not? Today I think I have the answer, and this mournful phrase constantly runs through my head and wounds me: Papa is angry with Maman. Suddenly, various pictures come to my unhappy mind. Papa was severe, and often Maman tried to intervene. They have two different personalities, they weren't meant for each other and that has separated them. That and a thousand things that I didn't understand now are clear to me. And I forgive Maman for having led us along so as not to spoil our childhood. But now, little by little, with God's help, I have come to understand; the truth is more painful, more terrible, and more so since I was not prepared for it. The trip to Spain to visit Grandmother was a partial separation. That rekindles a hope in me of seeing Papa and Maman together again before I leave this unjust world.

Could the parting be my fault? Must I go on living as a witness to the separation of the two people that I love most in the world? Oh, my confidant, what it costs me to admit that! To tell the truth, if I haven't opened your pages for a long time, it was because I knew I had to make this painful confession. My mind was asleep, I didn't want to see it, and today, yes, in spite of myself . . . It's too much, too much! God has struck me in my weakest spot. He has struck those I love. I bless Him, may His will be done, but I still have my diary and I can pour out my sorrow. A mother's caress cannot console my broken heart. I need the union of the two.

Right now, I envy the poor man with no coat, no food, but let our family and our home be as solid as a rock, made by God's hand, that nothing can dissolve or break apart! Such families are fortunate, but unfortunate are those that the world can separate.

People want to renounce God's commandments, they want to improve on them, and what is the result? What has become of the sacred union of man and woman? A violent union seen as a game of dolls, a doll marriage that can be broken whenever they please, as in a game. The name of this disgrace is divorce. How can the tree be cut off from its roots? The tree, the leaves will die. One cannot live without the other. How then can one separate two lives that are interwoven, two who have shared the same breath? The two will perish miserably without happiness, like the tree without its root. Modern marriage has become like everything else these days, madness, frivolity, ostentation and the intoxication of eternal youth, and the result is, old, young, and middle-aged are all children, thoughtless people, guided only by their natural impulses, the passion God has given us, not so that we may give in to it, but that we may earn the promised reward by subduing it and going counter to it.

But it isn't just the parents who are made unhappy by divorce. What happens to the children? Shall I finally be one of those children? What a terrible uncertainty. Oh, no, it is bad enough that Papa and Maman should be angry, but who says it must come to divorce? I can't think of it without trembling. I imagine my hurt, and if it should happen, I know I would no longer have the strength to smile, and I could say, of all the bad things in the world, divorce is the worst.

One day I will know whether what I have written today is true. But please God may that day never come and may our family never die, that is, never be shattered!

Now I am calmer. I have reread these last pages and I think that if, one day when I am gone, someone reads them (with an indiscretion that I forgive in advance), he will say, The child must have read that somewhere, to write about divorce as she does. No. In spite of my age, I know life and I can judge people at first glance. I have one example as my measuring stick and that is my ideas, my impressions, if you prefer. Try to find a book these days that speaks ill of divorce.

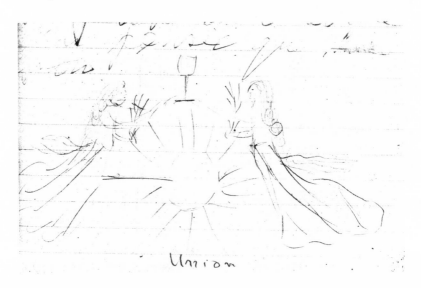

Union

October 23. In school, I won first prize for a composition in English about Columbus. I immediately wrote Papa about this little success. I included some poems. I write him long letters and I love him more than ever, because he is my Papa and I haven't seen him for a long time. Ah! how sorry I am that he is so far away.

I wanted to tell my confidant about one of my aunt's nephews who came here to go to college, but now he doesn't want to stay in New York and is going back to Cuba. He seemed very nice and very well educated. The first of those qualities, especially, is hard to find. I have noticed that there are very few really nice people. Perhaps I am hard to please. So much the worse for me. He is only 15 but is big, tall and strong. His name is Miguel Antonio Riva. He knows all about literature and it's a pleasure to hear him talk. Maman showed him my poems and I was ashamed, as I wrote them for myself. I think he was being polite when he said they were very pretty.

October 25. Everything is quiet. I am in bed and I am writing in ink as I have a board on my knees that serves as a table.

Maman was invited to go to the Opera. There again, she will meet people who will help her in business.

Yesterday Mrs. Quintero came over. My aunts Antolina and Juanita [Godmother], three gentlemen and Miguel Antonio were also here. Mrs. Quintero began to play. A strange thing, an immense sadness overcame me and I cried and cried. I pushed my head into the pillow to stifle my sobs. I don't know what makes me cry when the sound grows loud. The war comes to my mind then and my heart cries out, Vengeance. When the music and the sounds become softer, I think of the bells and put myself in their place, and so on. All the bitterness, all the pain that is distilled in my soul then overflows. Does music hold the key to my heart? I understand its language. It is the only one that doesn't wound my heart. It is the only sweetness remaining on this earth. Yes, everything is profaned. All that is most sacred has been adapted to the pleasure of human passion. Only one thing is missing, the desecration of that sublime art, which has been tried and tried without success. God took pity on the innocent. What do I mean by desecration? I mean, to profane music by using it for mad dances, for accompanying people who can't sing, by deserting Chopin, Beethoven, Schubert, Grieg for tuneless songs. Alas, real music is becoming like a lamp without a wick that slowly goes out. What a shame! Even that will be lost, will be engulfed. Courage, true artists. The priests of your sublime profession are preparing an altar where your glory will be celebrated with sounds as sweet as those you used to beautify the world for a time.

I could say more, but I fear I am the only one who thinks like that. I don't say this to anyone except my faithful diary who alone understands Anaïs's foolish ideas. For better or for worse, she doesn't want to change the way she thinks.

October 26. It is raining, I can hear thunder. The sky is dark, the stars have disappeared. It is late, but I have a few minutes to write. The gloomy weather corresponds to my state of mind. Now, the only star that shines is my diary. I don't want to communicate my dark melancholy, for my diary must be joyful in order to give me hope. Assuredly, I think there is no one who understands the sadness in my soul. I smile and laugh like everyone else, but each smile is another tear distilled in my soul until those pearls of bitterness overflow onto these pages, where they remain. There are several reasons for all this sadness: I must remember that Papa won't come here until there is a chance meeting in which each one sees how foolish he has been, foolish to separate because of some misunderstanding. It's a delicate situation; I can't arrange it and I lament not being able to reunite the two people I love.

October 27. So that they can't make fun of me any more, I am learning the entire Marseillaise by heart. That way my cousins will see that when a Frenchwoman wants to do something . . . At the words, Tremble, tyrants . . . I feel as though I am singing to the worthless Kaiser. Ah! if he were Marat and I were Charlotte Corday. What a big if. Yes, I have come to envy Charlotte and her kind. If she were alive, how she would punish Marat's descendant, that dreadful Emperor who dishonors his father and his country. But alas, she is in heaven and the only thing she can do is guide the avenging hand, but since that avenging hand hasn't come along, Charlotte must think, Must I come myself? Yes, O thou who killed the tyrant, the ancient tyrant, yes, no one here can imitate thee. In spite of the fact that we are French, we cannot do it.

My heart is ready for any sacrifice. I cry Vengeance and do not tremble, except with impatience, I am ready to rush forward, I have wings, but nothing to tie them to, nothing to guide them. Yes, and I must say something else. My heart wants to imitate Charlotte Corday but my strength and size belong to someone who was made to be spoiled and pampered. What a perpetual struggle in prospect, since the two are not well matched. Why did God create me, then, since I am good for nothing? I can only regret being born since I cannot accomplish what should have been my mission on this earth. Regrets? Yes, but since I cannot change, I am going to try not to think about it any more. I am going to try to accomplish the mission, the only mission that I can carry out in view of my size and strength, and that is to be my Maman's little girl who works hard and who, later on, will care for her own little ones. No, no, when all is said: no. I feel that with my disposition I couldn't be a good mother and I prefer not to be one. I want to be free, free to cry over my unfortunate smallness by myself, since my size is coupled with a heart that has no limits to its dreams of glory, of distant action, of the ambition of a Frenchwoman.

November 15. What a great change has taken place. Now we have moved away from 166 West 72nd Street and have gone to 219 West 80 Street. A pretty little apartment on the third floor. It is cheerful, painted all in white. The view isn't very poetic, since that is impossible to find in New York, but the park is next door

and Riverside not far away. We go to the same school. I was very pleased when I saw the apartment. It seemed to me that we were starting a new, more orderly life, and I was lighthearted, full of good resolutions, as I helped Maman unpack the trunks. As if by chance, Papa's picture stands in the bedroom. When I went through there, it seemed to me that his eyes were fastened on me, and I felt sad, thinking this would be another place where Papa wouldn't be with me. Everything became cloudy, my spirits fell, and a terrible sadness took hold of me. Why did that thought have to come to mind just when I wanted to be joyful? Am I condemned always to feel sad after I feel happy? Happiness is every child's right, happiness to be alive, living all together with the family.

Last night I wrote to Grandmother and I told her, speaking of my poems: The bells in my poem are the bells for the mobilization, but in my heart they also ring, slow, sad and lonely, the bells for the sadness of life. Yes, life is sad! Instead of dreaming of the natural ambitions of youth, instead of dreaming of the future, I must feel regret and envy of other children. And yes, I confess, I keep looking for a way to reunite the two people I love most in the world. That would make them happy, and I, oh, I would want nothing else, nothing, because I would think about the future later on. I shall certainly be alone and I feel that I must avoid people, for no one will love me. I feel that, because my disposition will surely make me unhappy and no one will ever want to live with me or be my companion. Then my diary will be doubly dear because it will not desert me.

Today Godmother took us to the cinema. We saw the life of Edgar Poe. Oh! I cried sincerely over his sad life. I understood the sorrow he felt in losing Virginia, his wife, and it seems to me that the life he led, full of dreams and illusions, will also be mine. Yes, I shall live on dreams because reality is too cruel for me. I think I shall be the kind of person that nobody understands, like Edgar Poe, although later he was understood while I shall never be. I think differently from everyone else. I admire the classic author who wrote, honor above all. I hate the modern laws which allow divorce and allow homes to be destroyed. And it seems to me that if I had a man as master, I would be submissive and, even if he deceived me, I think that I would never love another, never. And it seems to me that if I had to divorce, I would rather die, because I think it is dishonorable. Oh! How can one love a person one time and another time come to hate him? Myself, I have only one heart, only one promise, only one answer, and once a deed is done, I would never go against it. It seems to me it is impossible to change one's mind like that, and if that can be, then I say all minds are false, their decisions do not come from the heart, which has only one thought and can't change like that.

November 17. In my sadness, my diary is the only one at whom I smile.

Today my aunts went away, went away. Once again we are alone. I am happy, though, that Godmother will still be here for a while, but just the same I was sad to see Aunt Antolina leave. They all went on the train and I couldn't see them this morning before eight o'clock. We went to tell them good-bye, and Felo went ahead. I shook hands with everyone. When Miguel Antonio took my hand, I thought, I won't shake the hand of many men like this one: honest, sincere, well educated and respectful, for those are now rare virtues. Everything today is the offspring of that unworthy mother, "Modern Times," a term that embraces all the vices, all dishonor, the desecration of morals, persons, and the laws.

When I saw Miguel for the last time, I realized that my liking for him is true and sincere. But isn't it always like that? It's natural, for aren't all friends sincere? No, not for me. I am hard to please and in spite of all the people I have known, all that I have had dealings with, of all those many characters, only a very few stand out.

November 18. After an ordinary day, after having studied my lessons, knitted, and read, I am here for a little chat. I have been thinking about something: I feel that I am different from everyone else. I have noticed that none of the other children in my class, of my age, think as I do. They are all alike, they agree about everything. I know how people think, I know about modern life and about the ambitions that lie in every heart. And I compare. I am completely different. Instead of feeling that they are my brothers, they seem like strangers to me. My hopes, my dreams, my ambitions, my opinions are quite different. Why am I not like everyone else? In glancing at random over the lines written in this notebook, I said to myself: Yes, those are my thoughts, but they are the opposite of other people's. Am I odd? Do people look at me as someone strange? When I analyze my impressions in these pages, I know I didn't mean to contradict what people think nowadays, and yet when I reread them and put myself in the place of a divorced woman, a frivolous or spendthrift woman, a pleasure-seeker or in fact any woman today, I think that my ideas go against what people call happiness. I speak ill of the divorce laws, I criticize the silly flirts, I look down on the modern. It will be better if I live poor and ignorant, because with those ideas, I shall be spurned, as is natural. But just the same, I won't be sorry. When I read and reread these pages, I am glad to be able to say: this is a special story. What does it matter if nobody understands it. Am I writing for other people? No. I write for me, for myself. My voice is unknown. What joy if I am looked down on. My treasure will then belong only to me. When the end comes, I shall burn these pages, and my thoughts, scribbled on them, will live on through eternity with the person who wrote them.

Surely, if someone understands, if someone hears the contradictory words, the fresh impressions, these thoughts, these vagabond dreams that climb the slow mountain of life, I shall be glad of that too. But since that won't happen, I look on these impressions as belonging just to me. If, advertently, they outlive me, after lingering yet a while on earth, after being read and perhaps disdained, these dreams will die. They won't be able to fly without wings, and when I am gone, after having once more cursed the world, those wings will soar toward the infinite where they will be united to the only soul that understood and felt and dreamed them.

November 23. Maman has a visitor. I have turned out the light in the bedroom and, now that Maman can't notice my sadness, I have opened the window, put on a heavy shawl because it is cold, and having pulled up a bench, I am taking deep breaths of the cold night air. The view isn't pretty, a dirty garage, two tall buildings, across the street another house, everything dark and sad. Added to my own deep pain, it is so sad that I lift my eyes in prayer. The deep-blue sky seems deaf to my prayer, although it is a fervent one. I am, I feel so unhappy. To lighten the load, I cry, but ashamed, I dry my tears, close my eyes, and as though bent under a burden, I lower my head. I remain, pouring out into the mysterious night all the bitterness, the deep, unending sorrow, with no help for it, that wounds my heart, that makes my life nothing but a cry of pain. Suddenly the young face of Miguel Antonio Riva comes to my mind and it seems as though he looks at me with an expression of pity. Why should his face surprise me in these moments of sorrowful dreams? And yet, I am not so sad any more. I begin to think of him. I remember the first time Aunt Antolina introduced him to me. He leaned down and smiled as he gave me his hand. I like to remember what he said in reply to my aunt, who said, Here is the French girl. He said, She is pretty. He seemed sincere. It was the first time anyone has told me that. I remember with regret the last moment, when with a voice that I tried to keep steady I told him good-bye.

Oh, my diary, what is happening to me! How and why should I talk all the time about Miguel Antonio? Why does the thought of him interrupt the pouring out of my heart's bitterness? Why is it that his image calms my pain? What is this passion that moves me? I remember the words of a song that said, Young girls, flee from love.

Oh, what a big word. Now I've gone too far. Oh, I am embarrassed. Just writing it disturbs me and makes me exclaim oh. Go away, I don't want you for a friend. I rule out all that foolishness, all that madness and I repeat the only thing that is true, real, and unaffected: I simply liked Miguel Antonio better than anyone else I have known, although naturally I have not known many.

What is my rôle in this world? My eyes shine, I long to pierce the dark night from which the secrets of the future are hidden and I push from me a mad, happy dream of youth, telling myself my rôle is that of someone who is despised, repulsed, whom no one loves, alas! That is harsh, but then my soul, freed from the earth, can soar toward the infinite, toward the blue sky and the land of dreams. "Life," a word that means pain, the devouring passion that seizes us and lets go only with death. Life, a mournful word that weighs down my heart, but that draws near. Life begins when one is grown and without parents to shape it. My Life is coming closer. In a little while I shall have to support Maman and Papa. I must live. If I am looked down on, Life for me will be like something despised. Life will no longer be my friend. Dreams are my Life, the dream that sustains the solitary person that I shall be, for I say again, no man will want to be my master. A disposition such as mine is made to live in union only with solitude.

The other evening, our warm, well-lighted living room suddenly became quiet. Maman was reading, Thorvald also, Joaquinito was working on the alphabet, and I was knitting. I almost broke down and let them see my tears. This thought came to disturb the moment: Only Papa is missing. Oh! Papa, Papa, how many times that cry has escaped my lips like a call. Papa, Papa, come, come, let me be happy, let me live in reality!

November 24.

Cruel Flag

Cruel German flag,
Emblem of tyranny,
All Europe mocks
Your cruel gloomy colors.
The eagle your symbol,
Blind Germany without honor,
Peopled by heartless folk,
Led by a new Marat
Who strikes without pity

All that is beauty and art,
If you come to yourself it will be too late.
Children stretch their innocent hands to you,
The indignant sky fills in the distance with clouds,
The weeping mothers will never forgive you
For the home destroyed and your frightful guns
That broke their hearts forever
And caused their misfortune.
The sword of God will strike
And all your ambitious dreams
Will turn into an abyss
Where your miserable eagle
Will fling himself,
Confused, shamed and dying.
Then Europe in song will say,
Thanks, thanks,
Now that the tyrant is gone,
Dear liberty, return, return.

After copying my poetry, I saw that it wasn't late and decided to add a few lines. This begins a new notebook and I wonder if one of these pages will receive the news of my happiness, the news that Papa is coming.

Last night I had the following dream. I was seated at a table covered with papers. Moved by an invisible force, I got up and opened a very heavy door. I saw a picture that represented family life. But that disappeared and I thought I saw written in large letters, That is not your place, and I was seized with a great pain. Slowly, my heart breaking, I opened the other door. It was a world full of light, full of bitter pleasures, and I read, Against whom will you fight? I shall fight against the world. It's my destiny. I shall live only to curse it. No happiness will be permitted me on earth. Oh, that is so hard. Then a dark shadow, richly dressed but looking very unhappy, appeared to me and a pale light shone on the gloomy word Life. The shadow looked at me hatefully, sank its claws into my shoulders, and with sad moans, it held me in a frightful embrace. I woke up in a sweat, but that word Life remains engraved in my heart to show me the hard road with no respite that I must follow. Don't dream of happiness any more, but struggle with reality. That is my cry, but there is no echo. I want to dream, and my soul is torn between dreaming and living. Which is better? I am going to think about it.

November 26. I am sitting on a bench. Before me stretches the Hudson, a large sheet of dark-blue water that goes from a misty green to a mournful gray. Today, blue sky lighted by warm sunshine is reflected on the calm and shining water. In the distance, hidden in a light haze, New Jersey appears like a green mountain with little white houses. But when it is clear, one can see many factories with their tall red smokestacks. From time to time a boat whistle breaks the silence. Sometimes, too, the wind carries the murmur of voices, orders called out by workers on the railroad that runs at my feet, for I am on a little rise that overlooks everything I have just described. I am with Thorvald and Joaquinito who are playing noisily around me, but wrapped in my own thoughts, I write and write. My hand moves the pencil swiftly to describe my impressions.

After much hesitation, I have decided to answer the question, Which is better, to live or to dream? Before going to sleep, I went over the general outline of my Life. Almost immediately after I was born I had typhoid fever. Then, as I grew, I suffered in silence each time a concert tour took Papa away for long months at a time. Then, in 1912, I had several attacks of appendicitis that ended with a serious operation which the doctors performed thinking I would die at any moment. I was as afflicted as Maman, seeing her so sad, although she did everything she could to hide it from me. For my convalescence, we went to the Villa of the Ruins in Arcachon. There, there were a few scenes between Maman and Papa that I shall never forget, although I didn't understand them. During that dreary month of June, if I am not mistaken, Papa left on tour and Maman went to Spain. I didn't understand the reason for that trip, which stands out in my memory as the worst time of my life so far, since God seems to want to test me further.

On August 13, 1913, I made my First Communion. That remains a happy memory, although now I can't understand how I could have had a day of happiness when my father was far away from me. But if I was happy, it was in heaven and I couldn't feel the sorrows of this cruel life. After that, my departure from Spain was another sad day, but time has consoled me. In New York, lonely as I am, I have reflected, I have understood, and it was here I knew the hand of misfortune that weighed on me, without understanding why. Life can no longer have any charm for me and I think that dreams, which so far have helped me to live, will be my only guide. And in moments of the deepest distress, I close my eyes and go to faraway lands where nothing can trouble the happy life that, so it seems, carries me to the other side.

December 5. Yesterday Godmother left us, leaving behind her a big empty space and many regrets. She gave me a pretty stationery box as a Christmas present.

Speaking of Christmas, New York is very animated, not with the animation of people running after money or pleasure, but with the animation of people who are preparing for a great day. The shops have luxurious displays that are like fairyland. All kinds of toys, each more beautiful than the other, are displayed in the windows before the envious eyes of the unfortunate and the joyful impatient eyes of the rich. At school, the model classes have become the worst. The tests showed very bad results and the teachers, the Superior, all were angry, but it's no use. Instead of studying, the pupils think about what Santa Claus is going to bring them.

Thorvald and I did quite well and knew our lessons. But that doesn't keep me from dreaming before I fall asleep. Seeing the preparations and everyone's joy, my heart aches and in my mind I can see that dreamed-of Christmas, the family reunion, so sweet, so long awaited. I shall not have it. My Papa is far, far away and he cannot come. Ah, I wish that Christmas would never happen as long as Papa is not with me. Yes, for each Christmas is a sorrow, a Calvary for me, and that memory will never fade.

I know that on Christmas day, reality will be even sadder

than before, but if God sends me this trial, he will also send me the strength to bear it and it will pass like so many others. But I know that for God, everything is possible, and that if He wishes, Papa will be here on Christmas day. To all that, yes and no alternate in my heart in the midst of the storm that rages there. The image of Papa and Maman is like the restless sea that mutters against any restraint. The rocks are like the sky which is deaf to the prayers of the poor sinking ship, failing in its last efforts. I am the one who can hardly hold on in the midst of the tempest. In the distance, hidden by the dark clouds of life, there is a bit of sunshine, intact and pure. It seems to say, Follow me, here is the peace, the happiness you search for. Poor lost sheep, here is the road that you should take; here is the door to the future that you should open. And that bit of sunshine remains in my heart, smiling and pure, although I don't know its name, the name of the one who will be my future, my happiness. Ah, mysterious sun who warms me with his rays at the moment when I weaken, where are you? Are you only in my dreams or do you really exist? Shall I see another such sweet glance on earth? Am I mistaken or is there someone in the world who will be my sun, my future, my happiness, like you, you who in my heart are like the sweet light of happiness? Whom should I follow?

December 9. Today, for a walk, I took Joaquinito's hand and headed toward 93rd Street, where Maman told me there is a statue of Joan of Arc. It was cold outside, very cold, and I hurried. As I walked along with lowered eyes and my head bent, I thought sadly of Papa. Joaquinito was talking to me, but instead of his soft little voice, it seemed I heard the moaning of the wind, a mournful sound. Decidedly, my heart is so sad that it would make the happiest voices sound that way too. The road seemed long. Finally we arrived. Joan of Arc came in sight, bathed in a pale ray of winter sunshine. The statue was new and surrounded by bouquets of flowers. I thought the face full of life, with a clear brow and brave expression, and it seemed to me that I saw her there, resplendent, with her bronze statue's face illuminated with a supernatural light. How long did I stand dreaming? I don't know, but suddenly I heard Joaquinito's voice: Anaïs, is she alive? I couldn't help answering, Ah, if she were only alive, and my heart slowly repeated, Yes, if she were only alive!

But it was cold and Joaquinito dragged me away. I kept saying to myself as I walked on, If she were alive . . . But Joaquinito, naturally, wasn't satisfied with those words which didn't mean anything to him, and I had to tell him her story, finishing with: You can imagine that if she were alive, our enemies would already be repulsed and punished, and France would long since have celebrated her victory! I suppose he didn't understand, but that didn't worry me and I returned home. I opened my books and began to study the table of 8s. 8 times 8 . . . If she were alive, if she were alive! 8 times 9 . . . If she were alive, if she were alive! 8 times 10 . . . If she were alive, if she were alive! I closed my Home Work impatiently, took a pencil and wrote a short poem. Although it doesn't describe what I feel, I could then continue peacefully: 8 times 11 is 88.

Now I know my lessons and can relax with a little chat. I have reread what I wrote about If she were alive and find it mediocre. Only my diary will understand what those words mean to say. When all's said, Joan unfortunately is in heaven and although she may pray to God for her country, she doesn't want to come and she is waiting for someone to rise up and follow in her footsteps. Oh, mysterious shadows that we call the future, will you give us the name of the one who will save France! I call on you with all my heart and I name you from this day forward Sister Joan, or the Sister in Bravery of St. Joan of Arc.

December 18. Today I finished the last volume of L'Ile Mystérieuse[1] by Jules Verne. I have been so absorbed by it that this morning Maman called me twice and I didn't hear her. She touched my shoulder, but I felt nothing. Then Joaquinito shouted Anaïs in my ear and ran away, because he knew he would have caught it. I turned around and was still dreaming because I answered, Captain Nemo, at your orders. When I saw Maman laughing, I smiled, realizing the funny thing I had done. Later, Maman scolded me, but that won't cure me. When I read, I am with the hero, whether it be under water, in chains, or even on the moon. I leave everything behind to follow the hero or the heroes. My heart beats with the same feelings of anguish, sorrow, joy, whatever. It seems as though I myself am on an island volcano that is ready to explode. I follow the labors of the shipwrecked men as though I myself were doing them. A little flame makes my heart pound. I was moved by Captain Nemo's story and his death made me heave a regretful sigh. In that instant I understood that heart, crushed beneath the desire for just Vengeance, I admired

[1] The Mysterious Island.

the place where he went in search of liberty. Captain Nemo's grave must be beautiful. What joy to see the waves caress his tomb like a mother's touch as all the surrounding water seems to weep for him. Nothing can ever soil it or disturb the calm of that undersea grave. When I finished, I stayed staring into space as though I expected to see another marvel, as though Jules Verne would show me other beautiful dreams that he wasn't able to describe. Ah, what a genius. What sweet hours I spend in the company of Jules Verne and his dreams. In my opinion the two greatest geniuses are Jules Verne and Victor Hugo. Those two great men have nothing in common. One has knowledge, the other the sweetest way of expressing himself, together with greatness of soul.

December 25. Since I last left my diary, I have been in a kind of torpor, and while I made calendars for Maman, my aunt and my uncle, I wanted to think but I couldn't. Just one thing, just one word danced in my head, Christmas. But not like a joyful bell. I didn't feel the eager joy, I was afraid of Christmas, I saw it arriving like a new bar for my prison and I kept saying to myself, "I don't know any more than I did before." Why? Because for a moment I had a hope of reuniting Papa and Maman, but, alas, what good are my wishes!

Then I let my mind go blank. I put down my work, closed my eyes, and didn't think any more about being merry. Since I felt nothing, I had to feel something and it was sadness, a dull, dark, mute sadness that was even more painful. Everything went on in my heart, the burning, bitter tears here inside that didn't fall, because God seemed to want to let them dry there by themselves. Nothing could help my deep sadness. Even Kew, where Maman took us for Christmas, even Kew seemed sad. At my aunt's, I laughed and played with my cousins all afternoon, but when I was alone, instead of crying, I sighed, but my sighs couldn't contain all that I felt. For the first time, along with Thorvald and Coquito, I was allowed to help trim the Christmas tree. I enjoyed that, oh yes, and yet with each decoration that I put on, I said to myself, Will Papa see this? When it was time to go to bed, I made a fervent prayer. Need I say that I still felt hope? I didn't dream but slept very well, and in the morning I was almost happy on the outside, for in my heart I felt a terrible pain, a cruel disappointment. Papa wasn't there. And like a blind woman, like a baby, I had hoped for that. I thought I saw a man covered with snow arriving, who asked, Is Anaïs here? and I rushed forward. . . .

Here I am. But the meowing of a cat was the only reply. I almost hadn't noticed that my aunt had given the signal and I was being pulled down the stairs in a mad rush. What cries of joy and admiration from all those hearts. There was just one wish, to thank God, and circling the tree, we sang Adeste Fideles, but Uncle Gilbert's voice was missing. He couldn't come to spend Christmas with us, and all of us thought of the one who was absent. My aunt said we should have breakfast before looking for our gifts and we obeyed. Everyone sat down, including Miss Still, Nuna's nurse and governess. A surprising thing, I found her face attractive and likable. After breakfast, the gifts were distributed. I received a paint box and an embroidered collar and cuff set from my aunt, and Maman had given me, the day before, a scarf and a pink cotton bonnet. I forgot to say that each one had hung his stocking on the fireplace. I won't talk about the gifts for Thorvald and Joaquin. It would take too long. We had a happy day. This evening we came back. But the thought of Papa hasn't left me for a minute. I conclude that God means to send Papa to me next Christmas, with lots of snow, the way I see him in my dreams, and since this Christmas there was no snow . . .

❧ 1 9 1 6 ❧

January 9. It is a new year, and a whole week has gone by without my writing one line. To tell the truth, all these days have slipped by unnoticed. I felt nothing. I thought of nothing, and it was as though I were overwhelmed. I felt only great sadness. Now it is as though I had awakened and today I wonder what it was that made me so sad. Here it is. Like a dreamer, I had hoped that Papa would come, and once Christmas was over, I realized that I mustn't hope for anything. Yesterday evening, in "Oh, Stern Ocean," I poured out the bitterness that filled my heart. In my letter to Papa, I couldn't help saying, speaking of Joaquinito who imitates the sound of bells on the piano, "Joaquinito's bells are like life," because they are sad, sad, and that is what life is like for me. I hate this world, I suffer because of myself and those who are like me: poor, weak, blind, human, deceitful, ungrateful and deceived. I can't explain what I feel. I leave my diary, which I sometimes forget, as I think that I am abandoned on this isle of bitterness with Vanity for a companion.

Oh, Stern Ocean
Saturday, Dec. 8, 1915

Oh, stern ocean
Colored like the angry sky,
You seem to moan day and night
With a slow murmur like a fleeing dream.

Oh, stern ocean
You seem to weep the madness
Of this supposedly lovely world
And you slowly roll and take revenge
With a strange, eternal plaint.

Oh, stern ocean
You rock an impotent force
Against the earth full of endless deceitful joy.

Oh, stern ocean
You lull a smothered ambition
That seems to want to soar
And engulf in eternal forgetting
This earth, cause of your righteous anger.

Then, oh, stern ocean,
Your sad cries and your tears shall dry
And you will be a caress
Instead of a furious sea.

If She Were Alive
Thursday, Dec. 9, 1915

If she were alive, the sweet heroine whom we call
Joan of Arc, girl who incarnated the soul of courage,
Who seems buried under the ruins of ancient Rome,
If she were alive, our angry enemies
Would see and know what Frenchwomen can do.
Alas, why does she not rise from her tomb,
The one we await, for is the fight not strong enough
To break the stone upon the grave,
To revive the celestial soul of the one who is dead?

If she were alive, tears would turn to smiles
And the gardens would be full of flowers

That the people would throw, saying: this done, we can die.
The soldiers would hear the bells ring with the joy of follow-
    ing her,
The fields red with blood would become
A red rose, another vow for her.
If she were alive, then France could shout,
Joan of Arc! Oh, she who saved us once,
Here she is, and to follow her, here we are.
May Frenchmen have just one heart,
Just one glance, one love,
To cry: Oh, no, she did not come too late.

(For my dear little brother Joaquinito)

Here Lies

Here lies I know not what.
For I was nothing,
Leaning only on my faith,
For even joy was not mine.

Here lies I know not what,
Like a rudderless bark
For nothing was for me
A light to follow a voice.

Here lies I know not what.
Like so many others, full of bitterness
I was a little world of too much emotion.

Here lies I know not what.
Who, forever forgotten, will then find faith.
May my fate be a lesson.

January 25. Study and schoolwork have distracted me and kept me
busy during these last weeks. I haven't had the opportunity to
think about things around me. The last thing I wrote was my
poem Here Lies. That day, I didn't want to write anything in my
diary. I felt terribly lonely and unhappy, and my pen was dipped
in bitterness. Ah, that bitterness! It has become my companion. It
seems to want to accompany all the other strong emotions that I
feel all day long, hate for the world, love of solitude, the humilia-
tion I feel at being a human being like the others whose weakness
I despise, the powerlessness I feel and would like to be rid of, since
I long to be powerful enough to swallow up France's barbaric

enemy, Germany!, the ambition I feel to express my sentiments in words so pure that I am unworthy to know their meaning, the anger I feel against myself because of my faults, my wasted feelings, my crazy ideas . . . All that is added to the bitterness, the terrible feeling of being a victim, and bitterness makes me repeat these words, Vanity of vanities, all is vanity! To that, for reasons of my own, I add deceit, hypocrisy, everything is the same human cowardice! I haven't wanted to feel, for my heart aches under the many painful thoughts that weigh upon it. For me, there is no happiness. I am a leaf that isn't in its right place on the tree. I fly, I run, I search, but why keep looking on this tree when my happiness is hidden in another? I shall stop. As my shadow, my diary knows what makes me run away and suffer, "Life." For I am meant for the eternal grave of oblivion, one who can't weep without danger of breaking, who can't feel without risk of getting lost in the shadows whose very heart she would penetrate. I run away from Life.

February 2. I wanted to go over the last few pages that I wrote under the influence of a lot of sadness. The lines that follow will be the same, for if on the outside I seem fairly happy, rather rattle-brained, rather silly, inside I am very unhappy. I think and I forget to be silly. The last time, my last words were, I run away from Life. What did I mean? I think I can explain. For me, life is: noise, madness, amusement or pleasure, bitterness. Since I run away from life, I run away from all that, I long for silence. When there is no sound to be heard, when night covers the great city with her dark cloak, hiding the shining mask, then I feel as though I hear a mysterious voice speaking to me. I suppose the voice comes from me, since it thinks as I do. I stay a long time, half asleep. I don't feel anything, I dream. I forget the earth, I forget everything, and I soar into an infinite without misery and without end. It seems to me I am looking for something, I don't know what, but when my free spirit escapes from the powerful claws of that mortal enemy, the World, it seems to me I find what I wanted. Is it forgetfulness? Silence? I don't know, but that same voice speaks to me, although I think I am alone. I can't understand what it says, but I say to myself that in this world, one can never be alone and forget. I call that voice "my genie." Good or Evil, I don't know which.

These are the thoughts of my heart, the deepest of my somber feelings, of . . . I am looking for a strange name for myself. Ah, of a Philanthropist. Oh, no, I believe that means someone who wants to do good, and I admit I feel more like punishing, avenging, opening human eyes and hearts to the bayonet. What will my bayonet be? My pen. I am out of my mind! But if it's crazy, and I think it is, I promised myself to make a picture of my heart, and there it is.

February 14. I should have written yesterday to describe what Maman laughingly calls my society debut. On Saturday the 12th, Mrs. Pausas[1] and Mr. Jovet[2] took me to the Opera, or rather, the Metropolitan, for the first time. I saw "Prince Igor" in Italian. I was really happy and I liked the music very much. The stage settings were beautiful. I came back about five o'clock with my head full of the music I had just heard.

I haven't had a single letter from Papa in almost a month. That makes me sad, since it is the only thing that gives me a little of the atmosphere of dearest Papa's life.

I would like to write a long while because my heart is very full, but since it is only 7 it seems to me I hear my books calling in English: Stop thinking and come to study! Study! That's what I do all day long, because

1. I study my heart.
2. I study life.
3. I study my lessons.
4. I study Joaquinito (who is really a strange little person)
5. Finally, I study the progress of sadness of which I am the victim (good or bad?)

Now I am going to study my dinner, for when Maman makes it, it's always delicious.

I have finished my homework and now I am sitting down to write. I am going to do my own portrait, because now I am older. I am another *beanstalk,* according to the rules of the family dictionary. My hands are big, with long fingers that Papa said were very well shaped for the piano. I have rather large feet. They say I am thin. My face is white and I think it must be the reflection from the pages of all the books I have read. I have dark-brown eyes. They say my eyes are large. Is that in order to see and understand the horrors, the vices of the world? My mouth is

[1] *Wife of the Catalan painter Francisco Pausas.*
[2] *Unknown. Possibly the Catalan guitarist Miguel Llobet.*

large, my ears rather large also. I am not at all pretty, for even my nose is straight as a ruler, but I dare not admit that I am a monster because my diary wouldn't love me any more. Joaquinito thinks I'm pretty, Thorvald says I am a fish skeleton, and Maman says nothing. My disposition is well known to my diary, who is the only one, I think, who doesn't have to bear my temper, my impatience, my bad humor, sometimes my disdain, and my sharp words, as well as my presence which is detestable for everyone, I'm sure.

February 22. 13 years old! An age when the world gives a glimpse of its abyss of pleasures. 13 years old! An age when the future, which yesterday seemed far away, comes to haunt one's dreams.

13 years old! An age when a locked heart opens, when one that is open becomes locked.

13 years old! An age when a little girl breaks the frail cocoon and becomes a young lady. I am 13 years old!

It seems to me that since yesterday I am newborn or have just died. It seems to me the old Anaïs has nothing to do with the new one. A year ago, 2 years ago, I glimpsed what had just happened like an old remembered story, because memory is like a film, for when the foggy curtain rises, an entire life unrolls before one, all the ups and downs of that long, simple, moving story, "Life." Nonetheless, yesterday is gone. Today I picked up with the same habits, the same routine, and, I confess, the same disposition. Oh, but it's difficult to improve oneself. Yesterday when I did the same things, I scolded myself. I promised to stop. Then someone calls me, I turn around, and Plif! it all disappears and I begin again only to regret again later.

Ah, how unthinking we are! And all-powerful God from His throne on high must certainly smile and say: I must make a soul of iron. . . . I don't think that it would be so frivolous, so forgetful. But then we would be completely useless and I *suppose* that it's better to do something wrong that can be mended than nothing.

But I criticize frivolous people and I am one myself. Here is a proof of that. The same evening, after the little party that Maman gave for that marvelous 13th birthday, I wrote to Papa, and afterward, the next day, to my confidant. Those are the only two (including Maman) to whom I give my heart and my impressions immediately after the fact, for that is the single instant when they are perfect.

February 27. This evening, Joaquinito went to bed very obediently and asked me to listen to his prayers because Maman had gone out. I scolded him for the way he behaved today. Ah, yes, and he promised (as always) not to do it again. Then he said: Anaïs, sing me a song about the angels so that I'll dream I am in heaven. Of course, I had to make one up. I began to invent rhymes, then I let myself be carried along by my inspiration and with my eyes fixed on Joaquinito's white face, I soared off toward what I call the infinite. Here are a few of the lines:

Close your eyes to ugly things,
Open them to heaven's song.
Close your eyes to false lights and things,
Open them to heaven's light so true.
Close your heart to the world,
Let the heavenly angels in.
They will always speak and lead the way.

Sleep, my dear little angel,
Sleep in peace, wearing your heavenly crown
Of innocence and ignorance
Of life's bitterness which you too must learn.
Your little mouth can still say "Hope"
And sorrow cannot yet catch up with you.
Sleep, little angel, mother is watching.
Sleep, little angel, and forget about today.
For you, dear angel, the Past is forgotten
And the Future casts no shadow nor revolt.
Your pale face is like a white wing
That, pure and celestial, holds no blot
On its sweet white cheek and flies away from stain.

Oh, little angel, though mysterious time may hold pitfalls,
Sleep now, rocked by the gentle waves
Of childhood that surround you,
For later on the sea will be angry
And your sole support will be: God.

It isn't poetry nor a poem nor even a draft. It is a cry that escaped from my heart and that found its way into words.

March 7. On rereading these last pages . . . Sleep now, for later on the sea will be angry and your sole support will be: God.

What was I trying to say? That the thought of prayer, of surrender, of trusting in our Lord, came to me very late. Only when I was sick and in pain did I pray to Him to whom I should have prayed during times of joy. Ungrateful one! Later, I prayed, but since I wasn't used to depending on prayer, in my moments of sadness I turned toward humanity where, of course, more than consolation, I found the need to be consoled. In my diary, I unburdened my heart, but nowhere could I find hope. Until now, I felt an emptiness in my heart that I would never have tried to fill, and it was prayer, which still plays a rôle in the human heart, sometimes unrecognized, sometimes splendidly powerful.

From now on, I have two companions: my earthly diary and heavenly prayer. Both of them console, both strengthen, and both know the faults of their Anaïs. In prayer I find hope, in my diary I plant the virtue that I want to imprint forever on my second soul, so as to achieve it . . . if . . . I can . . .

Today it snowed hard all day long, so that there was almost a half-meter of snow, enough to cover a little boy several times over.

Tomorrow, they expect what is called here a "blizzard" and in French, a snowstorm. Through the window I contemplate the whiteness of a landscape covered with its white cloak and I say to myself: Nature is so misleading. What misery and struggle is concealed beneath that calm white blanket. The houses look asleep but are full of animation!

The other day, I went sledding with my little friend, and later she left me. It was 6 o'clock. The deep-blue sky, full of pretty stars, seemed to rival the soft white snow in purity. The snow covered all Riverside Drive. As I looked at a star, I wondered if there is another world up there. Are they happy? Happier than we? Not more unhappy, for that would be impossible. Then I lowered my head and said to myself that God's creations are truly too great, too beautiful not to be mysterious.

March 16. Saturday I felt sick and Sunday I woke up with a slight case of measles. That is why I haven't written, although during the long hours of solitude that one has with illness, I thought constantly of my companion. For two days I couldn't have any light, and on the third day I would have written but my head felt very empty. Today is the 2nd day I am out of bed and I shall risk a long confidential conversation, for more than ever, I need to describe my state of mind.

During these days, I have let myself get carried away with writing fairy tales, but I had difficulty describing the wonderland where my mind was. I traveled to that faraway land where nothing is impossible. Yesterday I came back, to reality, to sadness. I am making fun of myself and I don't want to go on with my stories, which I called Stories of a Mirror. Now that foolishness is past. I have broken my mirror and it is silent. I am only afraid that one fine day the longing for that wonderland may take hold of me again, and then my magic mirror will speak. Why? Because I have a mirror! My diary. Isn't it a mirror that will retell to oblivion the true story of a dreamer who, a long, long time ago, went through life the way one reads a book? Once the book is closed, the reader can go on his way with all the treasures it had to teach.

I shall copy a poem that I wrote during these last few days, one day when my heart made itself heard in the silence. That is to say that in the middle of a fierce battle, a voice is heard, the voice of the angel of peace. I transformed the war in my heart into the war, a hundred times bloodier, that is going on on the other side of the ocean. I transformed the tender voice of Peace into a long lamentation of those who call for her!

The Angel of Peace

Angel of Peace! Lift your voice
And claim your rights.
Take back the ground taken from you by war.
Oh, Angel of Peace! Lift up the oppressed hearts,
Console the weary mothers
And let us pray to you forever.

When the sun sets, your glance is lowered,
Your eyes weep at the sight of life that goes
From all those who fight for their Motherland,
All those who fight for their dear country,
And you tremble at the cannon's sound.
You flee, Oh! Angel of Peace, whom we seek.

Without rest, you shiver in the night,
Sitting in the broken home and hearing the stifled sobs
That escape from the unfortunate homeless ones.
What sadness when you see the towns
Ravaged by the scourge of war.
Oh! Angel of Peace, stay here on earth.

See our hearts on fire,
See what quickens the brave soldiers,
See the heroism of forgiving mothers,
See what makes the cannon sound,
Look with pity on immolated art
And stop the ringing of the bells of war.

Its shadow red with blood that you would flee
And that clings to you as a haven that can't wound,
Bury that blood underground with glory
And let it return to him who shed it with a will.
Breathe on the battlefield
And plant there your flag of peace and work.

But to my powerless voice,
The Angel of Peace replied: What song is this,
Blind selfish human soul,
Who calls on the Angel and gives him a chariot without reins
That can't be guided across any field
Since they are full of blood?

O blind priestess of humanity,
You dare to pray without humility,
For you know not that heroism, once aflame,
Is forever deaf to Peace.
Do you think my voice be raised in lament
When everyone lowers his head without a moan?

My place is not in those embattled hearts;
It is in the souls of workers
Who have not known my mortal enemies:
War, Death, Battle that promise eternal glory.
Pray no more, for I am gone forever,
No hope of ending war for those who work its fires.

March 24. I had a surprise after my walk. Marian Hearn[1] bought
me a bouquet of "Sweet Peas."[2] There is nothing I like more than
flowers. I placed them lovingly on the table in front of me, and
leaning on my elbows, my head over the bouquet and my eyes
closed, I breathed in their fragrance. I dreamed, as is my custom.
I felt intoxicated with the loveliness of each flower. I took the
whitest one between my fingers and, I don't know how, my
lips touched the delicate little flower. Nothing is lovelier than
a rose. To have a shining heart like the buttercup, to be as
sublime as the plain pine tree that casts its shadow, as charitable
as the stalk of wheat that nourishes us, as loving, caressing
and consoling as . . . nature! Alas, that is impossible for us
humans, who must remain part of the vast creation called "being."
Nature must continue to be nature and to keep its own magic.
Since humans and creatures cannot turn into nature, why do they
try? That is a question I ask myself, and now a sardonic smile is
on my lips as I answer: They try because they are never weary of
mixing the pure with the vile, that is to say, nature with what is
human.

Those are the reflections, dreams and impressions that came
from a flower! What kind of reflections, dreams and impressions
will come to me from life? Bitter reflections, sad dreams, the
same impressions that one might feel on a voyage, on a rock,
barefoot, surrounded by tigers and lions, bears and serpents,
eagles and cannibals!

1 *A classmate.*
2 *"Sweet Peace," in the original.*

March 25. I wanted to relive a little the life I had when I was 12, so I have come to Central Park to sit on the same bench where I used to like to sit and dream, facing the big meadow that stretches before me. Nothing has changed. I see again the same trees, the same hills. Only the sky is different; it is light blue. I see it like that because it is that way in my heart. With the song of the birds, the warm sun, and the joy that enlivens spring, hope has come back into my heart. I am no longer unhappy. I am just sad. Along with the flowers, forgetfulness has blossomed in my soul. I have forgotten that I lived to suffer. I have looked the sun in the face and said to it: I want your light. It gave it to me.

I dream. I dream of seeing France glorious and victorious, I dream of seeing Papa and Maman together, I dream of seeing the infinite a tiny bit ajar, I dream that I am strong, embattled, heroic like Joan of Arc, I dream that I live . . . and that I am happy. Why? Why do I dream that? Because I am not happy. I am separated from the one I love the most on this earth: My Father. I feel useless and weak. I want something, but I don't know what. Something is missing in my life. I criticize those who are like me, and afterward I am angry with myself. Also, all those things make me dream that I am happy, for if I don't dream, I am conscious of all that is wrong. When I sit alone on a bench, then I forget myself. This afternoon, I stayed here for quite a while writing all this, then I walked with Joaquinito to the exit from the park, and I am sitting on a bench to finish these few lines. The walk is finished. So is the dream.

April 4. It has been 10 days since I last wrote, and in that time, so much has happened! Death, unexpected and terrible, has struck down Granados[1] and his wife. The waves of the English Channel have swallowed up another genius! Mr. and Mrs. Granados were returning, he full of glory and riches, to see their children, but the Boches fired a torpedo and, like so many other victims of their cruelty, the genius and his wife were drowned. There was great sadness, great consternation here in New York, where he was so applauded.

That night, dreaming of that sad misfortune, I heard the applause coming from the Vaudeville almost next door to us, and I wept silently for a long time. It seems to me that with this new act of barbarism (not to mention all the others), everyone should be

---

[1] *The composer Enrique Granados.*

silent, should not seek pleasure. It seems to me that all the women in black should become shadows to care for and console. It seems to me that all the men, full of strength, should become giants to avenge and punish the tyrant. I wept, too, because for the first time I realized how many people are victims of this bloody war and what misery and what sorrow there is in the family of each victim. The death of one man would allow justice to reign.

Ah! Charlotte Corday, you are the only true woman, for none now dares to seize a dagger and kill the tyrant, as you did. Not even a man!

Let's leave the devastated battlefields and talk about what surrounds me.

Last Saturday, Aunt Anaïs left New York and everything has fallen back into its accustomed way. All three of us go to school and I think that each of our teachers is satisfied with her pupil.

I wrote Papa another long letter and imprinted a little of my soul on each page. When I write, I say everything; if I talk, I say nothing. Writing is my language and my diary knows more about the depths of my soul than any of my confidants, as if I had any, because that's just what I never want to have! I still read a lot and I learn. Thanks to that, I keep writing my "Companion of Oblivion" each month. Papa tells me to persevere in my literary efforts and I dare to do so, calling them scribblings, because literary efforts is really too elegant a name for my kind of literature.

April 8. I dream every night and sometimes the dreams are so pleasant that I can hardly wait for nighttime to find out what I am going to dream.

Tonight it is late and Maman has gone out. It is at times like this that I find the most to say, because then the silence lets me hear that inner voice that always guides my hand.

Nowadays, after school I go to play with Marian at No. 79, in front of her house. We play ball. Day before yesterday, I asked her to come and play a little while at my house. As we were walking, she told me that she keeps a diary and asked me if I keep one. In order not to lie, I said yes, although I hate to do something that everyone else does. It was only then that I understood that many people keep diaries. Only I learned also that most people don't describe their hearts, but their lives. Personally, I don't see much difference, for if I describe my life, I describe the incidents that make my heart beat with impatience, joy, sorrow, passion, misery, etc. If I describe my heart, I also describe the life that makes it beat and also the life that makes it die.

Marian explained that she writes about what she does every day, then she asked me what I write about.

I write everything I do and think, I answered.

About how much do you write a day? asked my friend.

Three or four pages, I said, of course, and she said, Oh! I write half a page, myself; but what do you say?

I say everything! I answered.

When we reached the house, she asked me to show her my diary. I wouldn't do that for anyone, but since she doesn't read French I didn't care. She leafed through one of the "Diaries" for a moment. At that instant Thorvald took it into his head to shout: And she writes poetry, too!

Marian looked at me in astonishment, and Thorvald, seeing the effect of his words, added: And stories!

Marian turned to me and looking right in my face, said: "You'll be an author."

Dear Marian, if it were only true! Unfortunately, not everyone writes well enough to be read by others. Half the writers should write just for themselves, as I do. And what a pleasure it is! One is never flattered, never admired, but always corrected, which means that one improves each time, whereas always admired means: every day one becomes more blind and more a slave.

I hear the breathing of Joaquinito, who is lying next to me, and as I contemplate his innocent face, I wonder if I wouldn't do better to live, rather than philosophize.

April 14. At last. I have taken up my pen again.

In my earthly life, nothing is changed. I am doing good work in school, and I have learned a lot from my teacher, Sister Gertrude, whom I already like a lot. Her moody and rather fussy disposition commands my attention. I study all her actions as though I were looking in a mirror, because except for the religious order, Sister Gertrude's personality is exactly how I shall be when I am grown up.

Often, during an examination, I get to look at the package of papers that contains the students' work. This happens involuntarily because the sister often shows us a paper as an example of what we should or shouldn't do. Often I say to myself, Just the same, these papers are so badly written. If I were the teacher, I would tear them up and make the class take the examination over again. A minute later, Sister Gertrude takes the package and puts it in the wastebasket. Since I also have to do my homework, I often step down from the teacher's place to that of a student and tell myself, just the same, I would take pity on my students and wouldn't make them work so hard for a nasty English paper.

Those are the only little incidents which come along from time to time to trouble a little bit more the stormy waters of my life.

In the life that I lead in the infinite, it's different.

There, all is happiness and sweetness, since it is a dream.

There, there is no school with dark classrooms, but there is God.

There, there is no empty chair in the family circle; it is always complete.

There, there is no noise, but the solitude that gives peace.

There, there is no worry about the future, for it is another dream.

There, there are no tears, for it is a smile.

That is the infinity where I live, for I live twice.

When I die on earth, it will happen, as it sometimes does to two lights that are lighted at the same time: when one goes out, the other burns more brightly. I will be extinguished on earth but will be relighted in infinity. For the moment, I live in both and both are two weak lights, for a soul can't have a harbor, just as it can't have two masters. That is my belief and my doctrine.

April 16. Today, after going to Mass and taking Communion, as I do every Sunday, I am sitting on Riverside Drive with Joaquinito. I feel as though I am reliving the time when we lived in Barcelona.

Here, yesterday was the day before Palm Sunday, nothing.

In Barcelona, yesterday was also the day before Palm Sunday, but what a difference!

Toward 3 o'clock, we went out and walked on the Paseo de Gracia, then afterward on the Diagonal. On both sides of the boulevard there were street merchants, with their wares spread out in front of them, big gilded palm branches 3 or 4 meters long. Maman argued a moment about the price, then Thorvald was given a palm branch and Joaquinito also. I had a banner made of the same material that I carried proudly, letting the cords swing in the breeze. Everyone was buying, everyone was happy. Then we came home about 5 o'clock and I put my banner in water so as to keep it fresh for the great day. We hardly slept, for I kept thinking I heard the bells calling us.

At last the night was over and at 9 o'clock the bells of the great church of the Conception rang the summons. 5 minutes later, the people, each carrying his palm branch, were assembled in front of the church. There was a light wind and the tall palm branches waved in the breeze. It looked like a great wheatfield where God rested his gaze and his mercy. Each time the bells rang, the people raised their palm branches and let them fall to earth with a dull sound that was rather impatient. Only the deep bells never changed tone. Finally they rang 9 and the church doors opened to let the Christians enter. After High Mass came dinner at the home of the elderly grandparents. That is how Palm Sunday is in Spain.

Here, one goes to Mass and receives a thin palm branch one meter in length, one comes home, and the day is spent as usual.

Description of Anaïs Nin by Marian Hearn

Anaïs Nin is very tall for her age, 13. (true) She has pretty dark-brown hair (very ugly) and big brown eyes (very ugly). Her mouth is 2 inches wide (twice that, I think). When she laughs, you can see her white teeth (decayed, unfortunately), which are white as pearls (imitation). She was born in Paris (a great honor for anyone who is born there) and she has traveled almost everywhere in Europe (it's true).

She has been here only a year and she is remarkably intelligent (like a donkey).

She is very gifted at composition and drawing (perhaps). She has a delightful disposition (I say, hum!) and is never angry (except when she flies into a rage). She is very good company because she is very gay and polite everywhere. Everyone likes her (and hates her). The Sisters like her more (I suppose) because she is so good (bad) and so intelligent (I repeat, like a donkey).

Marian Hearn.

P.S. The truth in this tolerable translation is in parentheses.

April 24. I am writing in the streetcar that is taking us to Kew Gardens where we are invited to spend the afternoon with Aunt Edelmira, who is giving a little Easter Party. As I watch the view (the Hudson River[1] or the tall chimneys that stand on each side of the river or the pretty little houses that indicate the beginning of the country), I think and reflect on the days of vacation that are just over.

---

[1] *More likely the East River.*

Yesterday after Mass, we hunted for Easter eggs, as we do every year. Then in the afternoon we went to the cinema and came home pleased and happy to eat our cold supper. That day ended the Lenten season which is full of silence and acts of contrition. But like all Christians, I went to confession and Communion. Then I rose early to go to Mass.

Papa sent me a beautiful big red book entitled "Histoire de France." I read the lives and exploits of the brave ancient Gauls with much joy. I haven't read very far in the book as yet, but I can guess the rest: victories, lessons which lift the spirit, or the lives of all the great men and great women of France. To thank Papa, I wrote him a letter last night. I thanked him also for one of

his large portraits that he sent at the same time. I also told him about the description that Marian did of me, and said: "I think I shall translate it into French and keep it in my diary. When I copy it, I am going to put the truth in parentheses, because that's the place usually assigned to it, unfortunately."

April 29. Marian let me see her diary. This is what she writes every day: "I got up at 7:30; I got dressed, I had breakfast at 8:30 and went to school. Sister was very cross today and I had to stay fifteen minutes after school to repeat my lessons. I came home at 4. I went for a walk with Anaïs and had a nice time. I came home at 6. I did my homework and had dinner at 8. I wrote in my diary. It is already 9. I am going to bed now. Marian."

She does it better than that, but I just want to show how she tells everything, the time of day and the time she took to do a certain thing. That gives me an idea of what a real diary is like and I think I'll do mine like that, although it's very monotonous. All right, let's try it.

So, this morning I got up at 9 because it's Saturday. I got dressed and had breakfast. After breakfast, Jack came to get Thorvald to go and spend the day with him. I helped Maman make the beds, then while she dressed, I read for a little while. Then Maman, Joaquinito and I went out. A friend of Maman's, Mrs. Allen, advised her to get Joaquinito into films to settle his imagination and give him something to do. We went to three different places. They took his name in all of them and soon Maman will know if he is to be hired. After that, we had lunch at Child's and went to Franklin Simon and Lord & Taylor where Maman bought me shoes, stockings, ribbons and some other things. Then we went to have Joaquinito's picture taken. It was 3:30 when we took the streetcar to come home.

I spent the afternoon (or rather the rest of the day) reading, getting my clothes ready for tomorrow, and helping Maman get out our summer clothes, then I set the table and we had supper. Maman had to go to a concert and I stayed with Thorvald and Joaquinito.

That was my day. I forgot to say that the other day, in school, they gave away several half-dead plants that had decorated the altar on Holy Thursday. I got one. With a little care, it has come back to life and now it has started to grow and put out at least 3 or 4 more flowers. I asked Maman what it is called, but she doesn't know. The flower is a sort of white lilac. I call it "my flower" and every morning I like to water it and cut the dry leaves so that the new ones can grow more freely.

I hope that I'll be able to go on keeping a real diary.

April 30. The other day Sister Gertrude, speaking of the end of the world, said: I am afraid it may be soon, because it is written: The nations shall all be at war, brother against brother, father against son, etc. That prophecy has come true, for all the nations are now at war.

The end of the world has caused me to do a lot of thinking. It seems as though I can see the earth covered with shadows, the war coming to a sudden end, people running and crying, houses swallowed up in flames, and finally the sky opening and Jesus appearing, radiant with justice. At that supreme moment, the graves will open, the wicked shall be confounded and the good covered with glory. I feel great fear about the Last Judgment for it makes me think that I have never seen that kind of supreme justice. How great that is, and what will our thoughts be in that moment which determines our eternal happiness! It will be God, the same God who is despised and forgotten, to whom we will turn with prayer and supplication.

May

May! Nature unfolds!
The birds sing. Gone are the long cold nights
Of winter. May is here!
This month blest by joy
Seems to hold the gifts of its Mother:
The Virgin Mary, that Pure Light
Who seems to have touched the sky
With her pale blue mantle that shields our hearts
From bitterness.

May is here; let us be full of joy.
Oh! Tender mother, bless your children
In this month honored by our song.
Hosanna! for the Son of the Virgin Mary.
Hosanna! for his blessed and beloved heart.
Month of May, sing its praises,
Pure and beautiful like nature that blooms.
Oh! Holy joy, fill our hearts with love,
Especially on this month and on this day!
Shout, human hearts, at the sight of these wonders,
Hosanna! for the Son of the Virgin Mary!
Our love and our hearts for Jesus! All for him!
But all our joy
For the refuge of sinners who see
And bless with a loving smile
The Holy Smile of May.

May 13. Again I am writing in the streetcar that is taking me to Kew with Maman and Joaquinito. The weather is beautiful and I am very happy that my aunt has invited us to spend Saturday and Sunday with her. Thorvald has gone to Far Rockaway with his friend Jack [Cosgrove]. Joaquinito and I will have a much better time because Thorvald is cross, Joaquinito is a tease, and they are forever quarreling. This morning at 8:30 we were all up and at 10 we left the house with a cardboard box as baggage.

I have been going over my diary and I am writing now because I am afraid not to have time to write at my aunt's house. Maman told me not to bring my diary so that I might rest, but I asked her to let me bring it because, on the contrary, when I am tired I talk to my diary and the sweet absence of constraint relaxes my mind.

Every few minutes, the streetcar passes a funeral procession going to the Long Island cemetery in Jamaica. Sometimes there are big cars looking sad and melancholy, draped in black, sometimes there are white cars covered with flowers, looking almost happy but carrying tiny little white coffins. Ah! It's so sad! In spite of myself, my eyes are fastened on what represents the end of this great life. How miserable it is! And at the same time that I contemplate the end of this passing shadow, I repeat the words of the "Imitation":[1] "When all is gone, God remains."

I shall disappear, my diary too, for it is the mirror of my soul that I don't want to share with anyone. I am going to dream.

[1] The Imitation of Christ, *by Thomas à Kempis.*

May 17. Today, the little children at school made their First Communion.

I arrived at 8:15 and got in line with the others. We went into the church, which was all lighted, the altar full of flowers. The Mass began, then the organ played and we began to sing hymns. Suddenly, their eyes lowered and hands folded, the little boys and girls who were taking First Communion came in and sat on a bench in the middle of the church. The sweet sounds of the organ were heard again and I closed my eyes. It seemed to me as though little angels were moving toward heaven to receive eternal peace. Then in a moment Father Ryan gave a sermon that I didn't even hear because I still had the enchanting heavenly music in my ears. Then the communicants came forward in a line and knelt before the altar. A little bell rang, the heads were lowered. With closed eyes, I felt as though I were reliving the moment when I gave my soul to the Lord for the first time. I opened my eyes and the vision of little girls in white with their pure crowns and their clasped hands reappeared before me and I felt as though I were with them in heaven. . . . And the tears that I couldn't hold back rolled down my burning cheeks as with one hand I contained the beating of my heart, which seemed to be trying to break.

Oh! sweet and only moment of true happiness!

That was my cry.

Without knowing what I was doing, I followed the girls of my class and 15 minutes later, I was in the classroom in front of Sister Gertrude. Had I been dreaming? Was that sweet vision of First Communion just a dream? No.

I knew my lessons quite well and at 3:20 I left school and went into the church. There, I knelt before the statue of the Holy Virgin and prayed. I asked the Holy Virgin never to let me forget that blessed moment of my First Communion. I prayed for sinners, those at death's door, my country. I asked her to bless my friends, my enemies, my work, my life, my death. I asked her to enlighten me in my vocation and in my work. Then I wept again, saying: Oh! Mary, have pity on me.

I wept because I had a great desire to be consumed in love for our savior. I wept because I am too small and I would like to suffer greatly, like the martyrs.

May 20. Today I have come to sit on a bench on Riverside Drive. The weather is magnificent. Now the trees along the walk are covered with pretty green leaves that hide the beautiful May sunshine. American nursemaids with their baby carriages go by in front of me and happy couples who are enjoying the cool morning air. Lines of automobiles pass in the street, but I am not looking at them because I am thinking. . . . I am remembering the impression that the First Communion of the little ones at school made on me. Only a great rekindled fervor remains. I visit Mary every day and she helps me in my efforts to be orderly, patient and kind. For those are the resolutions that the past caused me to make.

Yesterday I went to the library and brought back "Le Double Jardin"[1] by Maeterlinck. Since Maman allows me to read it, I am going to plunge into philosophy, for Maman tells me that Maeterlinck was a great philosopher. When I find an interesting paragraph, I shall copy it into my diary and discuss it.

May 25. I become more and more sad. My disposition is unbearable and today I have felt like crying more than 6 times because Maman scolds me, Thorvald runs away from me, and Joaquinito makes fun of me. I am ashamed, I am angry with myself, but impatience continues to rule my heart, my actions, my mind and my tongue. Ah! I am so unhappy to be like this!

I am losing my taste for study, the lessons tire me, the teachers seem crabby, stern and unfair. The classroom seems like a black room full of spiderwebs and I feel as though I am seated on a three-legged stool in front of a broken table and learning by candlelight the 6 stone personages: Grammar, Arithmetic, Geography, Physiology, Catechism and History, and they look at me with hatred and haughtiness.

Ah! Why do we have to learn? Don't we know enough? At least I think I know enough because I know only too well about suffering. It seems to me that is all one needs to live this cruel and unpleasant life. I realize that I am lazy, but when I am sad everything looks dark. Perhaps tomorrow I will have forgotten all that and will take up my studies with pleasure. I hope so, but in the meantime I feel that everything in me is breaking . . . except the thread that keeps me on earth. . . .

I write. Two hours have passed and I am changed; it seems as though all the darkness has vanished like a cloud.

Now I think I'll write a description of my schoolmates. There are 10 girls and 12 boys. They are all my friends except Pauline.

Half the boys are rude and completely "tough boy." Only one attracts my attention, John O'Connell. He is 9 years old, has big blue eyes, light-brown hair, and is of medium height. He always

[1] The Double Garden.

knows his lessons and his conduct is perfect, he never talks, he never laughs. He plays quietly and is the most courteous child in the class, always on time and always orderly. Consequently, I feel a little curious about him. I have never known him to do anything wrong and I have decided he is perfect. That's astonishing because I know that nobody is perfect, so I suppose he must do a few bad things at home. The other day Thorvald asked me who is my favorite boy in our class. Without hesitating I answered: John O'Connell, and Thorvald said I was right. For the first time, I realized that one can like one boy better than another. Before, I thought that they were all alike.

May 26. Today Sister Gertrude came back after being absent 4 days. She found the class in a bad state and had to put us back on the right track because we had grown lazy and we spent the day laughing with Miss Stocker, the substitute. Sister still has a bad cough and her face is very pale. She looked weak, and from time to time she closed her eyes and stopped talking as though she felt sick. Today more than ever I realized what a teacher's job is all about. My diary knows my teacher, my schoolmates and classmates, my friends and enemies and the school I go to. It knows me, it knows my thoughts and my tastes, my faults and my qualities, my joys and my sorrows, but there is something new that it doesn't know. I am going to make a drawing of my heart as it used to be and then one of the way it is now.

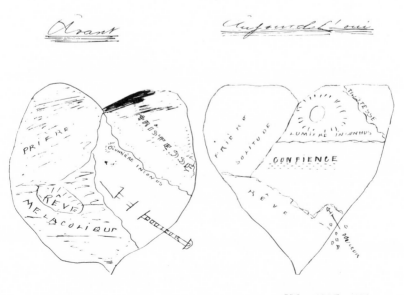

Today, I made a new discovery: I am full of confidence in the future. I have learned that one must not despair and I have confidence in my luck, happiness, the future and life. Until now, I was afraid and I didn't dare look the future in the face. Now I do, because I have put my entire trust in Providence. Life is like a big world where we suffer, enjoy and weep. We live, we work, we discover . . . There are many things to discover, for each person is a mystery, each grain of sand, each flower, each passion is a mystery. One should always discover and always learn. Personally, I have discovered: confidence, solitude, prayer, dreams, misfortune, sadness, pain, distress, lies, hate, friendship, poverty, pride, anger, impatience, kindness, liberty, love of country and respect.

Each discovery is like a staircase that slowly leads to eternity: heaven for those who can learn, hell for those who commit crimes. I still have many steps to climb, and in front of me stretches a long unending desert, full of pitfalls, that is called Life.

la vie est une éternité ?? ?? devant de la vie ? liberté — respect colère pauvreté impatience charité amitié haine douleur orgueil prière solitude confiance tristesse rêve mensonge

June 5. During the last few days we haven't done anything note-worthy except for several little trips to Kew. On one of those trips, we went to the cemetery with Nuna's governess. In a 16-page letter I sent to Papa 2 weeks ago, I talked about the cemetery and told him that as I walked by an ordinary grave, on which there was neither a name nor flowers, I felt compelled to leave on that lonely grave a big bouquet of flowers that I was carrying. Then I told Papa I felt as though someone smiled down at me from heaven. I don't know what impression that visit to the cemetery made on me, but I feel as though it left a great strength in my soul, for at the sight of that calm and gentle sleep, I realized that we must first live and work before we can arrive at the ending that is called "Death."

Well, now, I promised myself not to be sad at the start of the 8th notebook of my life, so I shall try to talk about something else. Because I am a little discouraged about my studies, I promised myself to go to Communion every day during June. And I go. When I kneel in front of the altar, all my worries leave me, and the thought of God, whom I am about to receive, occupies my whole soul. Afterward, during the day, I often say to myself that nuns, locked in a dark convent and subject to severe discipline, must be very happy because they can repeat all day long: "Jesus, I love you."

I would like to be able to live like Sister Theresa. But some-thing tells me that silence and oblivion are not for me. I think that I shall never kneel on a stone to the sound of the sweet bells of the Angelus, nor say the rosary to the sound of my footsteps echoing through long corridors leading to the chapel. Neither do I feel that my head will bend each evening before the dark crucifix as a few late birds pass, beating their wings at the little window that sepa-rates me from the world. No. A voice tells me that I shall serve Jesus by combat in the world.

June 6. At supper Maman talked about Guillermo,[1] who is living with us this month while he looks for a good job, and she said laughingly that when I am grown, she will take me to Cuba and introduce me to society. Then she added with a wink and a laugh: And there, I shall marry her to a millionaire. Everyone at the table laughed and looked at me. Naturally, I didn't blush or feel embar-rassed then, but now I think about that big word "Marriage." It's true, one day I will have to get married.

[1] *The first paying guest, probably recommended by friends in Barcelona.*

So I dream about a tall, strong man with black hair, white teeth, a pale mysterious face, dark melancholy eyes, a dignified walk and a distant smile. Something like the Count of Monte Cristo. Above all, with a soft clear voice. I would like him to tell me about his life, which will be very sad and full of terrible, frightening adventures. I would like him to be rather proud and haughty, fond of books, and able to write or play some kind of musical instrument. We would spend every evening at home, in front of the fire in winter, in the garden in summer, with a book or a pencil, his hand resting on mine! Isn't that the way husbands are?

If ever I should marry, I shall choose a man like that, and we shall write in this same diary together. Then my beloved diary will be the recipient of two great secrets and will have two hearts to watch over. It will know two signatures, A.N. and . . . I would like it to be a fantastic and unknown name like . . . like . . . I don't know. All the same, I shall think about it some more and look for a good name.

June 8. It has rained without stopping all day today. Since I couldn't go for a walk, I studied all my lessons, and then I began to look out the window. The rain kept falling and the drops fell ceaselessly with little "floc floc" sounds. Floc! Floc! the rain continued and this time I looked at the sky. The sky was full of clouds and that made me feel a little sad because it seemed to me those clouds were made expressly for me, as if to announce the clouds in my future life. Then I put those sad thoughts aside and left the window.

The afternoon went by like that and now it is 9:30 and I just thought of my diary. I am writing quickly now, because Maman is calling. Well, Maman says I still have two minutes and I am going to take advantage of them to tell about something that happened in class day before yesterday. Sister Gertrude was talking about the war and said: "Of course, Germany is going to win, because God will punish France and England by counteracting all their efforts. France made the Catholics suffer, dismissed the priests, burned the churches, and disobeyed the Pope. And England became Protestant, so the hand of God will punish them both and lift up Germany, which has been faithful to Him and respectful of His church."

As she talked, my hands clenched into fists, my blood boiled in my head and my lips trembled. From beneath the ruins, I seemed to see the cathedral at Reims and all the other churches that the boches have burned, and a tremulous voice said, "You lie, God is just and He will punish those crimes and forgive those who pray to Him."

No. God knows how to forgive and if one day all of France turns to God and prays with real tears of contrition, God will forgive, for God is just. He will punish the hypocrites, the barbarians who pillage his altars and afterward bring God a cup of the blood of innocents as an offering, while voices from the depths of the shadows cry, "Vengeance!" Vengeance, even though they try to drown them out with heroic deeds that in reality are lying and deceitful.

I thought of all that and didn't pay attention to the lessons which followed that uncharitable speech. In the afternoon, I didn't know any of the lessons and at 4 o'clock I left the classroom without saying good-bye to Sister and came straight home, with a feeling that I am too little to oppose those injustices and too weak to defend my great and beautiful country against false opinions that are based on hatred for a country that now, with all its strength, atones for all its past joys and pleasures.

June 11. Yesterday and today it has rained all day and we didn't go to Riverside as we usually do. Saturday I spent the day sewing, reading, writing and thinking. And while I pulled the needle that I was using to darn my stocking, I counted under my breath: one for Maman, one for Papa, one for Grandmother, etc. It pleased me to name everyone that I know, as well as my family, like a little girl trying to make time pass. I did that because I didn't want to think of anything sad and at the same time because I didn't know what to think about. When I say the rosary, I am accustomed to say before every ten beads, "I offer you this group of ten, O Mary, for such-and-such a thing," and I state my wish.

This morning, I went to Communion and afterward I took pleasure in repeating, "Jesus, I am dust, walk on me." And then it seemed as though I saw a gust of wind blowing and carrying with it a big cloud of dust, and it seemed as though I were running, running toward the end of a mysterious unknown, but in spite of the cloud of dust that surrounded me, I felt as though I saw a brilliant light and I recognized Jesus.

After Mass, I came home to breakfast and I spent the morning helping Maman. Then we had lunch and Maman took us to the cinema. After seeing 3 very nice films, we came home; it was 6. We had a little cold supper of sandwiches, cake and milk. That is how we spent Sunday.

Now I am thinking of tomorrow, Monday, and with sadness I see the school doors opening just enough to let us in, then closing on our dear freedom. Next come serious lessons, punishments, long stern faces, and above all the big blackboard with little chalk marks that dance before my eyes like little demons that are there just to torture the brain and tire the eyes. Then all that disappears and I sit here sadly, looking at the clock. 10½ hours separate me from the studies that I like but that I fear because of the teachers who scold and are so hard to please.

June 19. We have finished our oral tests and tomorrow we have the written ones. I caught myself staring at John O'Connell and afterward I wondered why I looked at him. It's because I find his face attractive, and when he smiles, it seems as though his eyes are like a big book where one can read all his thoughts. He has something, a polite manner, an expression in his eyes, that is different from every other boy in the class. He looks as though he is above his surroundings, and one might think that he has another life elsewhere which gives him that delicate air, and I wonder if he might not be one of the vanished princes mentioned in the legends of Brittany. They had light-brown hair and blue eyes like John O'Connell.

Then afterward I laughed at myself and couldn't help making fun of this silly girl who compares an ordinary little American boy to a legendary prince.

July 4. Here I am again, happy, gay, carefree and dreaming. Of course, my dearest diary is wondering where all these new friends came from, since just two weeks ago I locked the door of my heart against them. Here is the reason. School is over. As soon as I left that cold classroom, not to return for 2 months, I felt so free, so happy, that I wonder how I could have stayed 3 months in that room without dying. At present I don't care about my books or my teacher and her glasses, or my desk or my classes. Free! I am free! From now on, I can get up at 9, have a leisurely breakfast and spend my day reading or playing, just as I wish.

Last year I despised vacation, as I despised everything that everyone else likes, but this year, that is finished and I welcome this dear freedom with the same smile and the same joy as the others. I count the passing days and I would like to live them over, because they go by too quickly. It has been one week, one day and 12 hours since I left school, and what wonderful outings there have been! Sunday to the cinema, Monday a ride in the car, last Friday to the vaudeville, and Saturday on a visit from which we came home laden down with compliments and candy.

This morning at 10 we left home with a package full of provisions and an armful of books. We took a boat called a "Ferry," a boat which crosses the Hudson and takes us to New Jersey. I leaned on the railing and looked at the bright water on which the sun shone, and I wondered if in its delicate sky-blue depths a fairy covered with diamonds might not be hidden, who would appear and ask me if I wouldn't like to follow her, and under my breath I said, "yes, oh yes!"

It would be so sweet to lie on that beautiful golden-blue sheet, without fear of life, which cannot shatter such silence and still-ness. But I didn't dream all the time, because after a short trip we went ashore in front of a magnificent wood that climbed among some enormous scattered rocks. Sometimes they were so high that from their tops, one could see all New York stretched out at one's feet, with only the wide Hudson River in between. We walked for a long time, then settled ourselves on a huge rock that seemed to look out over the whole world, and there we began to eat our lunch of sandwiches and fruit. We spent a lovely afternoon.

Maman has allowed me to read some of the works of George Sand, and on the way back, I looked at the deep water with a new feeling, for I had just learned what is meant by love.

July 19. Maman is invited to a ball given on board the New Hampshire, the battleship Uncle Gilbert is on. She has left and I am staying with Thorvald and Joaquinito. Since I am in bed, I decided to write.

Our vacation goes along happily, in spite of the horrible sick-ness "Infantile Paralysis." This is a children's paralysis that leads to the grave after a week of indescribable suffering. The "Board of Health" here has printed ways of avoiding a continuation of the epidemic. Flies and dirt. One cannot go to the cinema or the beach or out of New York. In the park, the children all play separately. Maman put screens on the windows on account of the flies. I have helped her to keep the house very clean, and I pray to Saint Anne, who has become the patron saint to pray to during this epidemic. I hope there is nothing to fear for Joaquinito and Thorvald or even me, since it appears the sickness is usually found among children under 16.

Here is the prayer I say: Oh! God, deliver us from this plague and above all keep this sickness away from our house. If you want me to die, may your will be done, Lord, but I beg you to let me live so that I may be useful. Cure the sick and receive the dying into your eternal home. Amen.

Every day there are many cases and I wonder sadly how many will be missing at roll call when school opens. Mon Dieu! Death is so sad when it surrounds you without touching you! Isn't it as though it wants to smother you in its clutches without wounding you? I feel each evening as though I haven't the strength to write, for I am sad. Maman does everything she can to entertain us, and I entertain myself, but when evening comes I have a great urge to weep, I don't know exactly why.

When I hear the music from the theatre next door, I close my eyes and utter these bitter words: "How can they go to an entertainment?"

When I see the furtive birds looking for their nests, I weep and wonder, "Why are they searching?"

When I contemplate the stars in the deep and dark blue sky, I say, "What are they doing?"

When all around me I see only darkness and night, I wonder, "What do they hide?"

When, at last, I see myself here, sitting at the window, my head leaning sadly on one shoulder, I think, "Why am I living?"

According to George Sand: to love.

According to the Imitation:[1] to serve God.

According to humanity: to suffer.

According to the bee: to work.

According to the laws of charity: to be useful.

What should one believe? I would like to be useful, but if one day, like everyone else, I happen to fall in love, could I fulfill both of those duties? Or if one day I am obliged to suffer, as everyone is, could I be useful and suffer at the same time? My whole being says yes, but something in me says no, no, no! And a voice tells me: "None of that is good except the first one."

What? to love?

Yes, it's true.

Out of love for my mother, I would be useful. Out of love for my creator, I would work. Out of love for eternal peace, I would

[1] The Imitation of Christ, by *Thomas à Kempis.*

suffer. Out of love for God, I would serve. And out of love for myself, I would do my duty. That's simple. Thank you, little voice, little conscience. If I were like everyone else, I would stop wondering why I am alive, but since I am exactly the opposite, I still ask "why am I living?" For out there, very far away, in the land of the future, it seems as though I see something else that I should add to my everyday duty, and always, until I reach the Future, I am going to wonder: "Why am I living?"

My diary, it is Anaïs speaking and not someone who thinks what everyone should think. My diary, pity me, but listen to me.

July 21. Today we went to see Uncle Gilbert on board the New Hampshire, which is in the "Brooklyn Navy Yard." After an hour on the tramway, we got there. Uncle Gilbert was waiting for us on the deck. We sat on the deck and talked for a while, then Uncle Gilbert asked a sailor to take us on a tour of the ship. We saw the big cannons, the dining rooms, the officers' cabins, the salon, the library, etc. It was lots of fun. While we climbed a sort of iron tower, the sailors laughed and explained life on board to us. We came back on deck and thanked our guide.

On the deck, a little dance was just starting. There were 5 young ladies and 15 officers, and of course they couldn't all dance at once with the 5 young ladies. Maman and I, Uncle Gilbert, Thorvald and Joaquinito, all were watching the dance when two or three officers came over and asked to be introduced. Of course, I don't remember their names any more, but one of them, a tall young man with blue eyes, bowed to me and said with a smile: "May I have a dance?" "I don't know how to dance," I answered shyly, and it was with joy that I heard Maman confirming that I didn't know how. Then he bowed again. "I am awfully sorry," he said, and invited Maman to dance.

Two minutes later, another one came up to me and, with the same ceremony, invited me to dance. This time I smiled and told him politely that I didn't know how to dance. He then invited Maman. But as soon as the dance was finished, here came another one, the third.

"May I have this dance?"

Fortunately, Maman was there, and she told him that I couldn't dance, as I had been very frail and had never been able to learn. As Maman had accepted that dance with Uncle Gilbert, the young man saluted and left. Then I turned my head toward the river and as I gazed at the water shining in the sun, I couldn't help murmuring, "Dance? Already! At 13? What a funny idea!"

"May I have a dance with you?" It was the fourth one! "I don't know how to dance, I'm sorry."

He understood. He offered me a lemonade. I accepted, he saluted and left. But immediately a 5th one came up. When I answered, he offered to teach me. What to say? Maman was dancing, Uncle Gilbert talking with the officers.

"No, thank you," I told him. That wasn't polite. Just then a young lady went by and said to him, "Come on, it's your turn."

So the young man saluted politely and left. That was the last one, because by then they all knew that I didn't know how to dance.

The rest of the afternoon went by. I watched the young men in white dancing with the young ladies in blue or pink, but I didn't feel at all like imitating them. We had dinner at the officers' table, then we left.

"Then, if I had known how to dance, you would have allowed me to, Maman?"

"Of course, why not, my little girl? You would have had a lovely time. They were nice young men who needed partners, and they would have been very glad to have another young lady. You see, that's how the world is. You must learn. At 13, your mother was already a very good dancer."

"At 13?" I said, incredulously.

"Oh, yes. At 7 also."

"Oh, that's funny!"

"But that's how it was."

I said nothing more, but now as I write, I see only white and blue whirling by the million around me, and I repeat: So soon? . . .

September 1. Mrs. Thayer,[1] Jack's mother, invited me to spend a week with her at Cedarhurst, Long Island, but she kept me three weeks. I had an enormously good time there. We went bathing at Far Rockaway Beach. Mrs. Hedrick, a friend of Mrs. Thayer's, taught me to swim, and Thorvald and I swam out quite far. In the evening, we went for rides in the automobile. Often we sang and it made me dream to hear the voices of Mrs. Thayer, Charlie Hayes and myself lifted in the silence of the night, while the big trees seemed to curve in front of us and the road stretched ahead, as though to infinity. In that beauty of sleeping nature, my soul

[1] *Jack Cosgrove's mother, sister-in-law of the family doctor.*

found deep rest, an immense happiness, and above all, complete trust and surrender. Then very late, we came home, silent and dreaming on the way back. We went happily to bed and fell asleep as soon as we were in bed.

I also had a bicycle during the day and Thorvald and I went to the woods to pick flowers, blueberries and wild raspberries. I felt at home in the woods, too. Often I stayed behind, then I stopped and looked around me and thought with a sigh, No, no one understands or ever will understand what I feel when I see the sky, the woods, the countryside and most of all the sea!

Then I broke a green branch, slowly. It was something vague, sad, immense! Bigger than I, bigger than the whole world. I don't know what got into me at that moment but I wept, wept like a pleading child, like a wounded bird, like someone who searches for a place for herself somewhere and can't find it! Then here came Thorvald. "What's the matter with you?" "Nothing, I scratched myself," I had to answer. He slid the result of his work into the big empty basket I was carrying, and while the blueberries fell, I sighed.

Is there anyone who will ever be able to understand me? I don't understand myself!

September 6. I am going to copy here a letter that I wrote to Papa on September 1:

My dear Papa,
Just this morning I received your letter dated August 14, and I notice you say that two weeks ago you had not had any news of us. Only then did I realize how quickly time passes! I spent 3 delightful weeks in Cedarhurst, Long Island, with Mrs. Thayer, Jack's mother, about whom Thorvald wrote you. It's about the same as Kew Gardens but nearer the beach, where we went swimming nearly every day. There was an automobile there and we had some magnificent outings. I rode a bicycle a lot and came home all the time with a good appetite. Everyone was very nice to us and Mrs. Thayer, who doesn't have a daughter, would like me to come back often. I came home much stronger and I gained a little weight, so you see the country and the swimming did me good. My health is fine these days. Thorvald gets a lot of exercise and as he is growing, he isn't much heavier but he is very strong.

Everyone there was delighted with his helpful, quiet, cooperative disposition.

On Tuesday we had the joy of Godmother's arrival, but today she is packing her things to leave tomorrow for Jamestown, Rhode Island, where Aunt Edelmira is. Aunt Antolina will come in a few weeks to spend the winter here and put my cousins in school, and you can imagine how happy I am to have our aunts in New York.

There is less paralysis as winter approaches and we hope the terrible epidemic will soon end. Thanks be to God, we have not had any more in our neighborhood, and let's hope the epidemic will not come again, for a month ago there was one case here, just across the street, but they immediately disinfected the house. I feel very sorry for the families stricken by that plague.

Another thing, next week a very serious strike of all the railways in the United States will begin. Perhaps it will be settled and many people have blind confidence in the government, but prudent people have laid in stocks of provisions, for some who have to do with the strike say it is possible that New York will lack food. We have laid in provisions also.

Life here is becoming terribly expensive. Everything has doubled in price and many people must be dying of hunger in this big city of New York, where everyone minds his own business without thinking of his neighbor. Recently, there was a streetcar strike, and if it hadn't been for the buses, there would have been no means of transportation in the entire city.

If the railway strike takes place, millions of men who live in the country will not be able to come to New York to work.

The opening of school has been delayed by the epidemic, and I suppose school will open on September 25. In the meantime, I am taking arithmetic lessons and trying to catch up.

In your letter you asked me if it is hot in New York. We have had dreadfully hot days when there wasn't a breath of wind. The air was burning hot, and we had to spend the day in the streetcar in order to breathe, for otherwise we would have fallen ill. The only good thing is, after those days of great heat, it begins to rain hard and the weather cools off. Such changes in the weather are very dangerous, but we are always ready for them.

The rumor that we hear about the end of the war fills me with joy. I think I shall not have waited in vain for the outcome, but something tells me that I won't have as much right as others to rejoice, for I am not able to do anything for my beloved country. I am ashamed of the rôle Spain has played in this great European war, and I am very glad not to be obliged to admire and love that country as much as I love France, and above all, like you, I am happy to be French in my heart.

I am still writing, but I would like to know a lot and write very well, in order to help Maman.

Papa, someone told me that men are very selfish. Is that true, Papa? If it's true, why is it necessary for them to be like that? Isn't there a single man on earth who isn't selfish? In any case, if they are all selfish, do you think I shall have to get married when I am grown up? Answer very soon. I hug you very tight for Thorvald and Joaquin and myself.

Anaïs.

P.S. A week has gone by and I haven't mailed this letter, because I forgot. I was quite sure that it was already covering the distance that separates us, then, in looking for something in the library, I found it. In a way I am glad, because I can give you the news and I hope you haven't been worried by my silence. There hasn't been a railway strike, for Wilson agreed to sign the law for the 8-hour day.

But yesterday the newspapers announced that on Monday there will be a strike of the subways, elevators and streetcars, but it isn't definite and probably it will be settled. You realize that in a big city like this, there always has to be something wrong.

Today we are expecting Aunt Antolina, but she hasn't yet arrived and I hope she will come tomorrow. Aunt Juana has already left.

Joaquin's 8th birthday was celebrated yesterday, September 5, by just the family. In spite of being 8, he hasn't changed at all and it looks as though he will be a wild little fellow and full of the devil all his life, but I would like him to improve, just the same.

I see autumn slowly coming on. I watch the yellow leaves fall from the trees, and sadly I see the trees become black shadows and I say to myself that nature changes, but my heart and my life don't change. There is no spring nor summer nor autumn nor winter for me, but only sadness. Why is my destiny so different from that of others?

Everyone has some sadness, some trouble, I know, but it seems to me there is a remedy for them, while for my sadness there is a cure that so far I think is impossible and I see it only in my dreams. You know what I mean, Papa, don't you? You know what else I miss, Papa, and you know that you are the only one who can make it come true. Do I have to say it? No! I have said it so often!

Papa dearest, it is your daughter who speaks to you and asks you!

September 7. It is 8:20. Maman is reading, as is Thorvald; Joaquin is asleep. I can't hear anything except the music from the theatre next door, but that doesn't bother me. I am a little stunned by the sudden quiet after so many days when I didn't stop for a moment and hardly had an instant to think a little.

Yesterday evening I didn't have anything to say and I copied the letter I wrote to Papa, in which I said briefly how I spent the last month. Then, suddenly, I had to wipe away the dust that covered my "Companions of Oblivion"[1] in order to show it to God-mother, who was very much interested. She promised to subscribe for 50 cents a month, and we agreed that after I read the monthly journal to Thorvald and Joaquin, I am to send it to her, so that I don't have to write the paper twice. I would spend the day writing happily and without getting tired, but Maman watches over my health and won't let me do that, saying: "Don't hurry so much, fifille,[2] you have time."

Miss Mary Devlin, a friend of Maman's, came over yesterday in the evening and I had to read her my latest poem, "Birth," and it seems to me she said it was very good. She told Maman that I could write for "Le Courrier des Etats Unis." Ah, if I could! My goodness! what a joy for me if I could make use of my chicken tracks and earn a little money for Maman! But alas, I haven't much hope.

Maman went calling this afternoon and she came back de-scribing how nice her friend's children were. "One plays the piano very, very well, and when I told him that you write, he said he would be very pleased if you would write something in his album." Oh! If it hadn't been Maman, I wouldn't have said any-thing, but since it was she, I asked, "But what shall I write?"

"Write something nice. That isn't so difficult, is it?"

"Perhaps not, when I know him."

I searched and thought about it. Would this be all right?

> What good will they be,
> A few words from me
> That will perhaps make you smile.

[1] *A.N.'s magazine,* Compagnons de l'Oublie.
[2] *Little girl.*

But no matter, if I must say
What I think, I shall say,
Fame awaits him who seeks it.

I just read it aloud and Maman says it isn't bad. I shall write some others, but in the meantime, I am ready.

Emilia Quintero also asked me to write something in her album, but that was easier. I hope I won't have to do this too often because at times I find it very difficult to write in albums; that is, to write a kind of compliment, especially when I have never done it. Oh! My diary, I am very glad that you have no album, but if you ever have one, I shall write:

My soul belongs to you,
Oh! mute companion of my life,
Who keeps all my tears enclosed
In your humble destiny.

September 27. Monday I entered school, to learn that beginning that day, I would be in a new grade, 7A. The classroom doesn't look out on the street, but gets its light from three windows in the ceiling through which I can see the beautiful blue sky. The desks are a dark yellow, as in the other classrooms. The room is decorated with pictures, and in front of us are a crucifix and two large statues, one of the Holy Virgin and the other of the Sacred Heart of Jesus. Rising above the entire classroom is the teacher's big desk.

But instead of a sister, I saw a lady about 30 years old—a Cuban, Miss Pomares. She is a lady of medium height with very large black eyes, an aquiline nose, a rather small mouth, very thick black hair. Her complexion is tanned by the sun. Her entire face expresses kindness and indulgence. She is rather thin and when she smiles, one sees her very white teeth, but it seems to me she looks rather melancholy. When I said that she looked very kind, I was right, for until now I have found her very patient and very indulgent.

She explained to us that in her class we would study a great deal of geography because we are getting ready to take the government examination in geography. Immediately I made good resolutions about the future, and after looking at the large map of the world that hangs on the wall, I looked at the crucifix, then didn't take my eyes off the teacher during the whole time she talked. So far I have had 100 percent and I hope to continue like that.

October 1. Beginning next month, I shall have 25 cents a month from Godmother, 25 from Uncle Gilbert, 25 from Aunt Edelmira and 25 from Uncle Thorvald, which will give me 1 dollar a month and 12 dollars a year. My goodness! if it continues like that!

Aunt Antolina came today to take her trunks, because she is going to move from the Hotel St. Andrew into an apartment on 119th Street or somewhere like that. She made me a present of a muff, a pretty statue of the Holy Virgin, and a box full of type-writer paper, more than 500 sheets. After having thanked her, I went out with Godmother for a little walk on Broadway in the weak autumn sun, for the house was freezing. It is very cold and since the heat is not yet turned on in the house and the rugs are not laid, we freeze all day long.

Maman has decided to take another apartment on the same floor but which looks out on the street and where the sun comes in and warms everything.

October 22. We are already settled in our new apartment, and by working hard, Maman has made everything very comfortable the way we like it, that is to say, we now have a very pretty buffet in the dining room and a magnificent brass bed and a dresser in the bedroom. Aunt Antolina left Maman a very pretty rug that Maman put in the living room.

Yesterday we went to Kew to celebrate Nunita's birthday, but Aunt Edelmira wasn't feeling well and we had just a little family party.

We are going to school as usual. Each morning when I arrive and see the same faces of Miss Pomares and my classmates, I wonder if time doesn't have any effect on my companions. No! They always have the same disposition, the same smile. The boys don't change either. The lazy ones still don't know their lessons and the ones that work hard do.

And yet, for me, each day is something new and it seems as though my disposition is always changing. I always get up at the same time, but every day I have a different impression. Even if I wear the same dress all week, it seems different to me every day. Even if I repeat the same prayers during an entire year, each time I say them differently and each time I understand them in a new way. Why? I don't know. But I imagine that it is thanks to this trait that I don't notice that my life right now is monotonous, the reality of it, for of course the life I live inside me is always full of different incidents, and since I have read George Sand and Pêcheur d'Islande[1] by Pierre Loti, I dream about an ideal love, and a beloved face which will always be my dream is engraved on my mind. But I am afraid it doesn't exist, for it is too delicate, too frail, too faint and distant to be real.

In my dream his name is André, for I don't know anyone with that name.

October 26. Today I began another story called "Heart of Gold," into which I want to introduce a lot of mystery, because that is my only amusement. When I come home from school I feel like talking, but Thorvald is too cross, Joaquinito too little, and Maman too busy, so now every afternoon I sit down and write or read, and that is a great pleasure for me. The public library is open and yesterday after school I borrowed a book about Egypt, The Song of the Bells, and "Turgenev" from Selected Pages by Great Writers.

And now I am sorry that I read it, because "Spring Torrents" has spoiled the idea of love that one of George Sand's books gave me. I find Turgenev cold and dry. His heroes are common. He violates the rules for a good novel by imagining a man who falls out of love in three days. I detest him for that and find him simply dumb. To console myself a little for the sadness that reading his book gave me, I tell myself that it's only a story. I am sure I shall never again read anything by Turgenev and I continue to believe in plain happiness, and also I still believe that the soul cannot have more than one way of making us behave, because the soul does not change.

In the book "The Song of the Bells," I found my idea of a heroine in all her beauty and naïveté. Yes, that's how I imagine a little spirit who is always near me and whispers in my ear: "To dream is to live, to live is to dream."

And I dream . . . and I dream. . . .

In front of me there is a bottomless pit and I wonder, if I continue falling this way, how long will it take me to reach the bottom? I imagine that the bottomless pit is life, and the day I reach bottom will be the day I am through suffering. One of these days, I should be able to say: My diary, I have reached the bottom. Then my diary will cover the pit to protect me from the light and I shall not be covered with dust. In the meantime, I plunge into the light.

November 4. I am starting to write, but I don't know if Joaquin will leave me in peace. Each day he becomes more impossible and

[1] An Iceland Fisherman.

I am out of patience with him. He badgered me to have the colored crayons that I was using to draw with, and after I gave them to him, he took them and put them in hot water in the wash basin because he wanted to watch them melt. At last he is sitting down doing cutouts and although he is filling the dining room with paper, I have decided to let him go ahead . . . and I am writing.

I am seated at the table in the dining room. In front of me is a vase full of roses. I breathe the fragrance with pleasure. I lift my head from time to time to look at them. I notice also that from time to time a few petals detach themselves from a rose and fall on the lace doily. Moved by a feeling of love for the dead petals, I pick them up and keep them. Then I think that my life drops its petals in the same way, and I wonder who will pick up those that fall from my heart?

November 11. I am sad, on edge, and my head feels heavy. After having spent all day reading three volumes of "Le Collier de la Reine"[1] by Alexandre Dumas, I wish I hadn't read it. My head is too full of mysteries, intrigues, pursuits and different personages who whirl around in my brain and overheat it. Marie Antoinette makes me dream, the cardinal wears me out, the Countess de la Motte frightens me, the Count of Calisteo or something like that seems like a ghost. I read it so quickly that my eyes hurt, but I said to myself that nonetheless I must tell my diary what I think of my first novel by Dumas.

Maman says they are cheap novels, and yet, after thinking it over, I am enthusiastic about the book, which in truth is my first real novel. I suppose that in time I shall become more difficult, but in the meantime George Sand and Dumas are the first to open for me the door of the unknown garden of "Love"! George Sand showed it to me behind the mask of a man, and Alexandre Dumas behind the mask of a woman. Well, both are sublime!

Oh, I have let myself get carried away! I am afraid so much reading has gone to my head. So I'll dream.

November 23. Today I am sad and in a bad humor. I am mean, really very mean. When Maman scolds me, I am sorry and I cry inside, but an insufferable pride makes me wear such a nasty air of indifference that Maman calls me "a bad lot." And heaven knows I suffer. A long time later I ask Maman to forgive me, but a voice still whispers in my ear that I was right.

I know that I am disorderly, lying, hypocritical, nasty and

[1] The Queen's Necklace.

every bad thing there is in the world. I know I am the worst creature there is. I know that I deserve every imaginable suffering. I know that nobody loves me. I know that everyone criticizes me and scolds me, and then I feel this indescribable shame come over me. When I think about it, I hate myself and pour out a flood of tears, and yet my cruel pride holds me back and Maman never knows the regrets that I hide from her out of pride.

I would like to die right there when I see that Maman is angry with me, Thorvald runs away from me, Joaquinito makes fun of me, Godmother scolds me, and all that because I am bad, so so bad! I struggle with myself and I know I can't control myself, because Maman is right when she calls me "Your father's own daughter"! I remember Papa's strong, unshakable, even stern disposition. There is something in me that gives me an impatience and anger that I can't combat, and it hurts me terribly, oh! yes, it hurts me so much!

Sometimes I feel as though I am 40 years old because I think I have already suffered so much. I am ashamed of myself when I let myself dream of happiness, because I know, I understand that I deserve only misfortune, yet how much I have suffered and still suffer when evening comes. I have only one true friend left and that is my diary, which forces me to understand part of myself.

November 25. I am going to copy here the letter I wrote to Papa this morning.

Dearest Papa,
I just received your letter dated November 8 and I hasten to answer, knowing that you will receive this letter when you return from your concert tour in Spain. I am happy to know you are there for I can guess ahead of time the great joy it will give my dear little Grandmother. I see that the fall you had is still giving you trouble and that it has weakened your health, and I promise not to write too long a letter so as not to take away moments that are very precious to you just now, for I know the amount of time you need to have for your students and for the rest of your work.

Alas! I am very lazy these days, because all the time I would like to devote to reading and the study of French literature must be given to school. I feel as though the road I intend to follow will be difficult, full of thorns. I know that one must work hard, tire one's eyes and fill one's head with learning in order to express in writing all that one thinks, one's impressions, one's ideas exactly as one conceives them. And yet, that is what I want to do. I shall never be anything special, I know, but I console myself by thinking that even if I don't become famous or rich, I shall be and can be happy with a pen and a morsel of bread, daily bread.

What does the rest matter, what do I care what people say? If I want to earn money, it certainly is not for myself. You see, Papa, how I take things.

I have heard very little about Rousseau, the great philosopher, but I have read a few lines about his life: "He let the rain fall without taking notice, then he became thunder and lightning, powerful and destructive."

He was right. Only I shall let the rain of events fall, but I shall never become thunder. What good would that do, Papa, since I am nothing but dust, made to be walked on. Only I am a little bit ambitious, and I who am dust, I want to spread myself on a lot of paper, turn into lots of sentences, lots of words so that I won't be walked on.

Oh! Papa! from a distance, I see you smile and lift your head to breathe a little fresh air, because you certainly must wonder if I am going crazy, and that's quite natural, for I am afraid that's what everyone thinks about me.

In a few words, I want to say what I would like, and that is to be able to write and see my name in print at the end of something good, rather well written. And that's why I am telling you all kinds of things that you must find *stupid*. That's why I sometimes stop myself from dreaming and thinking, in order to take my head in my hands, close my eyes, and say to myself: "What good are all these impressions, all these thoughts, since nobody, nobody understands me!"

Sometimes I have feelings that I can't explain, impulses that I can't control, impressions that I can't sort out, dreams, thoughts that are different from everything that has gone before. When I read a book, I discuss it with myself, I criticize it, find its faults, its qualities, and I begin to think about things that are so deep that I get lost, get tired, and I don't understand myself any more. Then I become angry and wonder why I don't think like everyone else, why I don't read books as other people do, that is, without exploring them deeply, without playing with them; why I start thinking of things that don't exist instead of taking life simply and innocently, as it comes, without trying to understand its mysteries, its windings and its depths. Ah, I ask myself so many "whys" and I can never answer, since I don't know either.

Now I stop and am embarrassed, because I have just written you my most frequent impressions, my deepest thoughts, and I am afraid you will smile again when you read these lines that I have written quickly, all in one fell swoop, holding my breath a little so as better to hear the noise of my pen scratching across the paper, but always, always writing. It has already written a lot and it will write much, much more . . .

December 3. All these last evenings, I have forgotten to write because I was devouring La Comtesse de Charny,[1] Joseph Balsamo, Le Collier de La Reine and Les Deux Reines.[2] And I have had a great deal of pleasure in reading those books, which are so ardent and romantic that immediately I was consumed in their flame. Especially Joseph Balsamo, where I found the man of my dreams, the mysterious man with the distant smile, infinite power, tall and strong, a man that perhaps existed once but who doesn't exist any more for me.

I have suddenly been seized with a great love for medicine. I tried to hypnotize the cat, the only poor victim of my experiments, who doesn't even belong to me since he is the neighbor's cat. The result of my love for medicine: I made up a poison and have kept the recipe. To see if it worked, I dipped a bit of bread in the result of my long research and threw it to the birds. A bird took the bread that I had kept my eye on, and swallowed it. He flew up to a tree and jumped on several branches, then he came back for another crumb. Then, to my great surprise, I saw him hesitate, throw his head back a little, then he fell down dead before my eyes. I was so astonished, frightened, surprised and also sorry about this effect, this misunderstanding, in fact, of my concoction that I took Joaquinito's hand and began to run, and it was only when I knew I was quite far from my victim that I calmed down a bit. Out of shame or out of fear, I am sure I shall never return to that place.

So much for medicine. In trying to hypnotize the cat, I stared at him so long that my eyes got tired. Then, in spite of my gaze and my extended finger, he refused to move and fall asleep, as I was trying to get him to do with all the strength of my soul and my body. In a word, in trying to draw him to me with my gesture, all I got was a deep scratch on the hand. Thorvald made fun of me and he was right.

[1] The Countess of Charny.
[2] The Two Queens.

I took a glass of water and tried to see something in it. This time, I had a good scare because, either by a hallucination or my imagination, I saw a large spot of blood. I looked at the glass and the water, but I realized that it was in my head that I had the spot of blood. I don't want to try again, for since I know that I have no power, I would have to attribute the cause to my disordered mind and I don't want to find out again that I am crazy. Now I laugh at my foolishness and promise myself not to try to imitate Joseph Balsamo in any way. Just the same, I would really like to be able to hypnotize everyone, beginning with myself.

December 16. Yesterday morning when we woke up, we found everything white, because it had snowed all night long. On the way to school, we played in the snow, and more than ever, I regretted having to be shut in a dark classroom and all day long I couldn't keep my mind on my studies. I didn't know my lessons, to my teacher's great surprise, and everything I did was badly done. The teacher caught me two or three times with my head raised, staring out the window where I could see the blue sky and the beautiful snow that was still falling.

At 3, I was the first one out of the room, and in spite of my impatience, I resolved to make my daily visit to the church. I was kneeling in front of the altar of the Holy Virgin and was beginning to pray when the organ began playing. It was a Christmas carol that several boys were rehearsing, but I listened only to the organ and I fell into a deep reverie. Suddenly, I noticed that John O'Connell was there in front of me, also praying, with clasped hands and his eyes fixed on the statue of the Holy Virgin. At the moment that I saw him, he turned his head and our eyes met. I thought he looked very much like de Charny, whose portrait I carry in my dreams ever since I read the book. He didn't turn around again, he continued to pray, and I stayed there dreaming a long time with my eyes on him, and my vague prayers were accompanied by the sound of the organ that seemed to come from far, far away. Yesterday, I didn't even touch the snow, for my wish to do so had melted away, but I spent the rest of the day thinking of John O'Connell! . . .

Everything foretells the great holiday that is approaching. Excitement and joy are on every face, and I love the beauty of the display windows. For my part, I have worked a lot because I have painted six calendars, I have painted and made four memorandums, and also I have drawn and painted four Christmas cards. I have made a little workbag for Mrs. Thayer and painted several little cards for the family.

We went to the stores this morning and Maman bought me a dress made of dark-red velvet and a hat. Maman bought a little lace purse for Godmother and several other little things. She took me to the oculist to have my eyes examined because recently I have been tiring my eyes with reading. He examined me and told Maman that I am near-sighted, and he made glasses that I shall go to pick up at 5 o'clock. I wanted to write once more in my diary before putting on my glasses, which I am supposed to keep for about 3 years. Now I can read and read and read, and Maman can't say anything to me. I am going to read Dumas again, for now I know whom to put in place of all the heroes.

December 17. This morning at Mass, all my classmates kept looking at me on account of my glasses and after they had satisfied their natural curiosity, I began to reflect. I feel strangely sad with glasses because it seems to me it isn't I who am looking at the things that come through my glasses. Also, I don't really know why, I think I am twice as ugly as before; that is, now, I am ashamed to put myself in place of the heroines in the books I read.

This morning at table, speaking of me, Maman said: "My daughter was really very pretty when she was a very little girl, and it doesn't matter if she isn't as pretty now, for in 3 years or so, she will take off her glasses, her hair will be arranged, and she will turn back into my dainty little doll from Saint Cloud."

I smiled and I have dreamed a lot, wondering if that will happen one day. Little by little, that idea has taken shape in the little brain that I have, and all of a sudden, I told myself that if some day I become pretty, then I . . . I don't know how to explain what I shall do, but then perhaps the man whose shadow is all that I know will appear, will stop being afraid of me, and then I shall be happy when I can walk under the beautiful sky, amidst the flowers, my diary under my arm, murmuring the beloved name, whatever it may be.

Ah, but one has to be pretty to be loved like Marie Antoinette, like Catherine Baillot and so many others who have been loved in the books I've read. Maman says that being kind is enough to bring happiness, but alas! I don't have even a speck of kindness. I know that everything in me is bad, and more than ever I understand that if I want to live, I must safeguard that corner of the infinite that I have opened with the key of dreams, that corner of the infinite where all is love, happiness, union and beauty.

Right now, up there, I see a little house covered with snow, and when I look in at the window, I see myself, who has become pretty, sitting near a handsome young man with deep-blue eyes, with a dreamy and distant smile, holding my hand in his. Across from me, Papa and Maman are sitting on a sofa, happy and together. Maman is still young and beautiful, Papa too. Thorvald is playing in a corner with lots of toys, so is Joaquinito, and they aren't quarreling. There is a beautiful tall Christmas tree, and since no one is watching, I squeeze the young man's hand and he returns the pressure. His beautiful blue eyes look at me with an expression of great sweetness, for he loves me because I am beautiful and I love him because he is handsomer than de Charny, nobler than Athos, braver than d'Artagnan, and he loves me with a love truer than all the books, all the stories, all the tales of the whole world. That's what I am living right now, but when I come down from there and see the big red house covered with mud, Thorvald and Joaquinito quarreling, Maman working and looking so tired, and when I remember that Papa is far away, and that I am so ugly and mean, that there is no young man with deep-blue eyes, then I lay down my pen and ask God to let me die because *I don't know how* to be happy and I don't know how to use His gifts. He never answers me, oh! no, He punishes me because I deserve it and I know that I am obliged to look again for my cloudless sky where so many happy events occur. That is why they have nicknamed me "Miss Absent-Minded." I go through the day putting salt instead of sugar in my coffee, hanging my dresses in the kitchen, answering yes to any question or not answering at all, making the beds all wrong, putting the plates in the oven instead of in the cupboard, putting three cups of sugar in the potatoes instead of in the applesauce, sewing things backward, putting the books under the bed instead of on the table, putting the silverware in a flowerpot, passing the potatoes when someone asks me for salt or my plate when they wanted my spoon, carrying my red parasol when it snows, putting the inkwell in the drawer, sitting on the floor when I meant to sit on a chair, and so forth. Then, only then, do I feel happy, because I am dreaming.

❧ *1 9 1 7* ❧

January 17. A new year full of hope has begun, but alas, in spite of all my resolutions, all my wishes, all my prayers and all the vows I made, I find that nothing in my disposition or my life has changed.

On New Year's Day, I promised myself to be joyful, not to feel sorry for myself, not to suffer without any reason during the entire year. And so here I am again with my "black thoughts"! Black as ink, for it has been a long time since my pen has set them down on the white paper of my dear diary, which consoles me by taking them away.

On December 21, I left school for 2 weeks. Miss Pomares seemed very happy to leave us and I am afraid *we* were not at all sorry. For all of us, it certainly was a pleasure not to have to come back for two weeks to that dark, cold classroom. For two weeks we wouldn't have to open a single book, for two weeks we wouldn't have to hear Miss Pomares' rather sharp voice which scolds, which punishes, which carries out, in a word, her duty as a teacher. In my joy, I remembered that she also might be spending the Christmas holiday with her family. So as I left, I said to her in English, "I hope you will have a Merry Christmas." For the first time, she smiled, dropped the stern mask that her position requires, and answered in a soft voice, not sharply but nicely: "A Merry Christmas to you too, Anaïs."

At that moment, I understood the true nature of Miss Pomares and I thought how difficult it must be for her to act angry when she is not, to speak sharply when her voice is gentle, to cast stern glances when she would like to caress. And that's what the poor teachers, who are often thought to be mean, must do. I wished each one of my classmates a Merry Christmas, and then, with a light step, came home. Since December 21, all I have done is sew, paint and draw, write and dream.

After lunch on the 24th, we went to Kew. In the evening, Joaquinito, Nuna, Coqui and Thorvald went to bed and I stayed up to help trim the tree. I made little boxes out of colored cardboard for the table and several other things, then at 10 I went to bed, leaving Maman and Aunt Edelmira to spread out the big stack of different-sized boxes that I had glimpsed.

In the morning, the same scene as last year. Only I wasn't expecting anyone. Isn't the little experience that I have had enough to rid me of that blind hope that fills me with dreams . . . and disappointments?

We circled the tree singing "Venite Adoremus" and since this time I knew it, I sang it right out loud, my eyes fixed on a beautiful gold star, which instead of hanging on the tree, seemed a long, long way off, at the end of a long, barren road that I have promised myself to walk. Afterward, we had breakfast without touching our toys, for Aunt Edelmira had asked us to wait until Aunt Antolina, Antolinita, Rafael and Carlos arrived with Godmother. We went to Mass, then when we got home, we found them all waiting for us. Godmother called me, spoke to me for a moment, and I went upstairs with her. A few minutes later I came back dressed as Santa Claus, and I took all the presents off the tree to give each one his gifts. We sang Venite Adoremus again and then, since everyone recognized me, I took off the mask and the red suit, and I could then take my time looking at my gifts.

Afterward, we had a delicious big dinner. The table was very pretty; there was a big snowball hanging over the table. Since we were 14 at table and everyone was happy, we laughed and talked the whole time. At the end of dinner, everyone rose, and then Aunt Edelmira announced that each one should take hold of one of the red ribbons hanging from the big cotton snowball and pull. It was a joyful surprise, for each one pulled out a pretty little souvenir at the end of the red ribbon.

The rest of the day, we all played together with all the games. In the evening, after a cold supper, we went home, each to his own house. Surely if everyone had as merry a Christmas, what prayers and thanks would have risen to All-powerful God before whom we kneel each day, calling him Our Father! . . . But alas! Far away, on this beautiful day, what tears will have fallen in memory of those who were not there to give this great festival the double happiness of joy and a complete family circle, united with father as king, mother as guardian angel and the children as little lambs.

I thought about that and said to myself that I would like to be able to sacrifice my happiness (yes, my happiness, for the only thing lacking was my Father) in order to give a little happiness to others. But once Christmas Day was over, I stopped weeping for those who suffer, and leaving this earth again, I settled myself again "up there," where every day is Christmas Day for me!

January 18. I resume my conversation by telling about the few days of vacation we had after Christmas. I went several times to the cinema with Antolinita and almost every afternoon I went to play with her. In general my little cousin feels rather lonely and doesn't like to be with friends and classmates, but she has developed a friendship for me, and not once did we quarrel. She is very nice as long as one plays games she likes.

On New Year's Day, we didn't go to Kew because it had snowed and the cold was so intense that everyone stayed peacefully at home. I had time to think and to make a thousand resolutions, of which I have tried to keep only one: to control my temper. Goodness, it's so difficult! During the next two days, Joaquinito seemed to have guessed my resolution, and as though to thwart it, he behaved impossibly. One time he hid my shoes under the dresser and I looked for them in vain for half an hour. When he suddenly said, hypocritically, that perhaps they might be under the dresser, I would have liked to grab him and hit him. I contained myself by a great effort, but I couldn't keep from turning red in the face, and my eyes filled with tears that I wiped away furtively. He played a few other tricks during the rest of the day, but in the evening when he came to say goodnight, he said: "A kiss, Anaïs." I couldn't help pushing him violently away and calling him "naughty boy!"

When he had fallen asleep, I slipped noiselessly close to his bed, and looking down at him for a moment, I thought: "Ah, Joaquinito! How you make me suffer! It's so difficult to contain oneself when you are naughty." But I think that was the only time I have been able to hold my temper, because in spite of myself a great anger is always ready to rule me, and alas! its power over me is so great that I always have an insult on the tip of my tongue and a big black spot in my heart. At the slightest teasing, my whole body trembles with impatience.

But enough about my temper. Two weeks went by like that and it was only on Wednesday of the third week that we went back to school. Miss Pomares had already put on her cold, stern mask and I found it very difficult to look at her after having got used to joyful faces.

Until Tuesday the 16th, there was nothing new. But I am going to tell how I spent Tuesday evening.

For some time now Maman has known Mrs. Sarlabous,[1] and knowing that Mrs. Sarlabous writes very well, she showed her my

[1] *Wife of Dr. Sarlabous, who was an ear-and-throat specialist for Metropolitan Opera singers.*

poems. Mrs. Sarlabous said that I had ideas and that if I would come over Tuesday at 8, she would show me how to write. Happy and eager to be able to learn something that I couldn't learn all by myself, like so many other things, I went there with Thorvald Tuesday at 8 o'clock. It was the first time I have felt what is called timidity. That timidity that Thorvald has always tried to make clear to me and that I have always made fun of. I wondered how Mrs. Sarlabous would receive me and I wondered also if I would be able to explain myself if she asked me something. But I didn't have to wait long, for in a few minutes, Mrs. Sarlabous herself came to me with a pleasant smile and shook my hand. I noticed that she is a very pretty lady with a very sweet expression. She had me go upstairs to the library and within a few minutes I felt completely at ease with her. I didn't worry any more about standing up straight or making blunders. In listening to her explanations about the rhythm of poetry, I found myself in what I call my milieu. After a clear explanation of certain rules of poetry, she showed me what was wrong with my poems, which "contain ideas but don't follow the rules."

Afterward, we talked about books. Miss Sarlabous joined us in the library, as did Mrs. Sarlabous' mother, and we talked. Mrs. Sarlabous named all the famous authors: Hugo, Verne, Dumas, Daudet, etc., and when I told what I have read, she said I have read a great deal for my age. I gave her my opinion of certain books. We both admire Shakespeare, almost all of whose works I know by heart. After that, since I found in Mrs. Sarlabous the first person who understands a great many of my ideas and impressions, I talked to her about my diary, my tastes, my thoughts in general, my opinions, my impressions and everything.

When I saw that she understood me and approved, I could hardly contain my joy. I told her that I like legends better than anything. She then said to me: "But you like legends because you have a poetic soul, my dear child!" Ah, it pleased me so much to hear that! I admitted to her that I dislike New York, that I find it cold. And while I talked, I couldn't help casting an admiring glance at the beautiful books. Their colored bindings and titles printed in gold made me want to own them all. Mrs. Sarlabous followed my glance, and to my great pleasure, she rose and opened the big bookcases and showed me several books.

Well, to tell the truth, I have never revealed so much of that world of dreams, thoughts and impressions to anyone as I did to Mrs. Sarlabous. I felt like dancing with joy, for I saw that she didn't make fun of me, she didn't say, as Maman does, "Now you are being dramatic!" with that mocking accent and tone that almost everyone uses with me when I say just a few words. I saw that I was saying thousands of words to Mrs. Sarlabous and that she was not mocking.

Only at 11 o'clock, when I saw Thorvald yawning, did I realize I must leave, and with what regret! That night I couldn't fall asleep before almost 1, saying to myself: "I am not crazy, I don't think impossible things, I am not too stupid, perhaps I shall be good for something. Ah, what happiness!" And I fell asleep by dreaming that Thorvald and Joaquinito wouldn't make fun of me anymore, that Maman wouldn't tell me that I was becoming "dramatic."

Next day in school I felt like laughing at everything and nothing, and it seemed to me that the entire class, and even Miss Pomares, should be as happy as I, and yet nothing had changed! Since then, I see everything through rose-colored glasses, because I am happy to be able to say: someone understands me.

Ah, it's so difficult to have to admit to oneself that one thinks wrong, that one is crazy, that one does everything backward, and I have tried, I have been trying to get myself to understand that I thought very badly and that I was incorrigible. Then Mrs. Sarlabous came along. She set everything straight, put everything in order in my poor mixed-up head. She made me understand that each person can have his own opinions if they are well-founded. Without saying it directly, she made me understand that I could continue to think the way I do, because it isn't "crazy," as I thought it was. And now, it seems to me that instead of a black hole, confused, disordered, incomprehensible, I see a well-lighted room, clean, orderly, with everything in its place. I get so much good out of what I read, I don't mix up my reading with my own ideas, and so on.

There is a lot in myself that I don't understand, but there are other things that I understand now. If I feel sad about nothing, it is because a "dramatic soul," as Maman says, is struggling within me, and it surrenders to sadness more easily than to joy. If I love poetry, it's because I have a soul made for poetry. My habitual dreaminess, my impatience have nothing to do with my intelligence, but rather with my disposition. One of these days, I shall talk about the things in myself that I don't understand.

January 26. It is very cold today. Since Maman has allowed me to stay home, I am going to write as much as possible.

On January 24 I took the government tests in geography. I got to school at 8 in the morning, and the teacher, after a few last recommendations, took us to the sister. Two by two, we left school and began to walk toward the Elevated.[1] My friend Catherine Coughlin talked to me a lot, but I barely answered her for I was thinking of everything that Miss Pomares had taught us. As the Elevated was already full, we had to separate, and suddenly, without realizing how, I found myself next to John O'Connell. After a moment, it was he who spoke first to say to me: "If each of us were on his own, I would have taken the streetcar."

I answered that I would have, too.

"Do you know your geography?"

"A little."

"I know it quite well. It isn't difficult."

While he was saying those few words to me and looking at me, I felt myself getting red, very red, so I was very glad to see Thorvald and several other boys come up and start talking to John O'Connell. At the same time Catherine Coughlin came looking for me to tell me that there were two seats empty behind me, so I sat there with her. From my place, I could see John O'Connell without being seen by him, so I began to compare him to de Charny, whom I admired so much. Suddenly, Catherine raised her voice to say to me: "Anaïs, you are the only girl who hasn't named your 'boy' in the class. Do you have one?"

"I don't think so," I answered, beginning to enjoy the conversation.

"Is it Jack Cosgrove?"

"Oh, no!" I answered, almost angry at such an absurd and improbable idea.

"Michael Huff?" my friend continued.

"Oh, no!"

"John O'Connell?"

I blushed without intending to and didn't answer. I should have said no, but my friend had noticed my embarrassment and got up to tell another girl that my "boy" was John O'Connell. And when I left the Elevated, I surprised a few smiles in my direction, because the girls had been teasing me for a long time, saying that I was the only one who didn't have a "boy." Truthfully, until now I hadn't thought of John O'Connell except as the living portrait of the hero I admire, de Charny. Now he is two things to me, the

---

[1] *The elevated railroad, or the "El."*

living portrait of a great hero in my favorite chapter of the history of the French Revolution, and my "boy," according to the class.

January 29. It was at Eleanor Flynn's house that I went to spend the day on Saturday, and I am going to tell what I did and who Eleanor is.

Eleanor Flynn is a little girl, 12 years old. She has very blond hair, worn in long curls, blue eyes, and a trim slender waist. She is sweet, nice, patient and neat, and I think she is the most charming and the best friend that I have ever had. She is very modest and very unaffected, and all the teachers like her very much, as do her friends. Above all, her tastes are very much in harmony with mine.

Saturday morning we went skating together, and she showed me how to skate and held me up. As it was my second lesson, little by little I began to skate without leaning on her, and we talked while we skated. Her conversation was so different from that of other girls I had heard up till now that I listened to her with pleasure. She told me what she thought about certain girls and seeing her so frank, so kind, I admitted that I too had had very bad and false friends.

Finally one o'clock arrived and we hadn't stopped talking because we had so much in common, so I went back to her house for lunch. Her father came in and during the entire lunch he told us very scary stories. Eleanor held my hand in both of hers and in the dangerous and terrible parts, she squeezed it. After Mr. Flynn left, we began to do play-acting. Just what I like! I was glad to introduce all that I have read about plays and the theatre, so that Eleanor was delighted with me, almost as much as I was with her. We played like that all day long, and if Thorvald and Joaquinito could have seen their "serious one" laughing with all her heart and playing like a little girl, they would certainly have thought that Eleanor was a magician.

Today school began again and I became again the "serious one." But I discovered something: Thorvald and Joaquinito love stories. Now, when I want to keep them quiet, I begin to tell stories. I make up mysterious automobiles, trips to the moon, haunted castles, because that's what they like, and when I find that they obey my slightest suggestion, I understand that the only way to rule hearts is by the charm of words or actions, and I have chosen words (without the charm). I have made up so many stories that Emilia, who rents a room here from Maman, says that my mind is like Niagara Falls, because of its power and continual movement.

February 13. Saturday at 5 o'clock Mr. and Mrs. Sentenat came to see us on Papa's behalf. They brought several gifts: a stamp collection and a billfold with 3 dollars for Thorvald, a coin purse containing 2 dollars for Joaquin, and 5 dollars for me with a beautiful prayer book, a little patriotic rosary, and a letter from Papa. I was happy to get this present, thinking that even if Papa is far away, he still thinks of us.

February 17. My birthday is coming on the 21st. There are only a few days left until then, and as I see the beginning of another age for me drawing near, I reflect, I feel sad at times, and other times I am happy. I am sad when I think that time goes by so quickly and that I don't do anything. I feel happy sometimes when I think that this 14th birthday brings me a little closer to being a young lady, which is the theme of all the beautiful stories of adventure, real misfortunes, love. Because I hope that in growing up, I am going to find the young man of my dreams.

It has been very cold these last days and it has snowed twice. Emilia Quintero, who rents a room from mother, took our pictures in the snow-covered park, and I think I shall send one to Papa to give him an idea of how I look.

March 4. I had my illustrious birthday on February 21. I had an enormous amount of fun because all my cousins were there, also Eleanor and her sister and Marian, Jack, Godmother and Aunt Edelmira. We had a magnificent tea and I received many gifts. Everyone was so kind to me and I felt so happy that it made Aunt Edelmira say I had a "heavenly smile."

Now I am fourteen! The noise is finished, the celebration is over and everything is calm once again. But I am trying to improve my disposition and I have taken sweet Eleanor, my best friend, as my model, because in her I find all the qualities that I lack. When I am with her, I feel a great longing to become good. When her beautiful blue eyes look at me and plunge into my soul, I earnestly want to be able to look at people as directly as that, for her eyes hide nothing. In her gaze, one can read her mind like an open book, and I love to read it because of its beauty.

People who want or intend to please me say that perhaps I shall become famous, because I have inspiration, I have a natural

taste for poetry, for writing. Eleanor doesn't have that, and no one tells her that she may become famous. She is modest, calm, and so kind that I would willingly change all that I may have later on for a little bit of her goodness.

Let's not count our chickens. I am not a genius, I don't write anything, I am not useful, and on top of that I am mean. Perhaps, later on, I shall write well. I shall be inspired. But what good does that do me now? It doesn't make me any better, and I judge by the present and not by the future.

I am going to make a drawing here of a staircase. On the left I shall put my failures, on the right my victories, and that way my diary will be able to follow the rocky road on which I am going to walk and see whether in a year I acquire a speck of kindness.

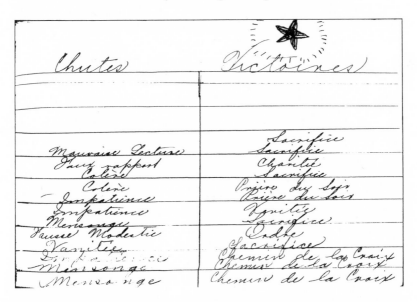

March 13. Sister Dolorita, our new teacher, has discouraged me terribly by her severity. It's not really the first time this has happened to me, but I feel as though I hate her. She is very unfair with me, and since on top of that, arithmetic, which is my worst enemy, is the main thing we study in this grade, I am tired and downhearted. Sometimes I work such a long time on a problem that my head becomes so heavy and full, I am afraid it will burst. Ah, I certainly will not describe my years in school as the best years of my life!

If I can study in my own way, I find it pleasant and interesting, but in our school and in almost all schools here, study has become a heavy burden, an endless nightmare, an obligation, a tyranny. I hate that, and it is with joy that I see a day coming when I can again learn everything by reading and not by rules, threats, cruel and useless punishments. Now we are taught things as though we were donkeys, but personally I prefer to learn like a person, without being struck, without being tyrannized.

Two or three times I have started to think and wonder why it is that we are born to obey. Why must our whole life be a long, heavy chain of obedience? I often have wondered why God created us only to obey. The entire world always obeys. The laws of God, the laws of Nature, etc. Nothing but laws, commandments. Why? We could have been created free, so why was it that our original parents, by their fault, caused us to come under the yoke, the slavery of obedience?

One must obey, obey now, obey later, obey always, obey everywhere, on earth as in heaven. Couldn't the world exist without obedience? Without kings obeying God, man obeying a leader, the animal obeying man, Nature obeying its laws, and millions of humans always obeying someone above them? Why not? What would happen? I wish I could find someone who would enlighten me and take away my doubts. I shall search for an answer.

April 30. [Two weeks ago,] I was sick, I had a bad cold and the way I was coughing frightened me. I was thin, really very thin, and I wasn't hungry. Maman kept me home, took care of me, spoiled me. At the end of the first week I felt better, but then something happened to take my mind off myself. I saw Maman looking anxious and sad, which doesn't often happen to her, and I realized things were not going well. One day Maman pulled her big little girl onto her lap and said: "Fifille, I have an idea. I am tired of working without anything to show for it, and especially without any rest, so do you know what I've done? I looked for a house and I found one on 75th Street, a big house with a little garden in back of it. I am going to rent rooms and perhaps by doing that your mother can make money. At least she is going to try. What do you think of that, my fifille?"

Of course, I haven't given here the exact words that Maman used to tell me that, with her sweet voice full of calm and hope. Maman talked to me a long time, and seeing her so courageous, so full of hope, I remembered the book "L'Idée de Jean Têterol,"[1] which I had just read and which said, "Ideas make men." Maman

[1] Jean Têterol's Idea.

certainly was more than a man at that moment, for joining energy and kindness, courage and beauty, strength and gentleness, she was more than a man in conceiving that idea which would feed her children. She was a guardian angel, an incomparable woman.

Well, the contract was signed, the trunks were packed. I ran from one trunk to the other. I hugged Maman, for I was very happy, just as happy as Maman herself. Saturday, April 28, after having said good-bye to our old apartment, after having tipped all the people who had done things for us, we took possession of the new house. And what a house! There are five floors. Everything is big, clean, with big closets everywhere, mirrors, wonderful lamps, enormous rugs. Several rooms are already furnished with very expensive and very beautiful pieces of furniture.

Joaquin was crazy! He climbed up and down, touching everything and shrieking with joy, unable to sit down and stay in one place. Thorvald kept saying, with a dazed expression: "It's pretty." I couldn't leave the garden. I kept looking at it happily and I was already making plans for planting, raking, cleaning and arranging everything.

We had "lunch" in the kitchen; a lunch of cold meat, jam, cheese, cakes, bread and butter. All the rest of the day was spent unpacking and putting things in place, and when evening came, Maman and I were exhausted. We made up a few beds any old way and went to bed.

The next day, Sunday, we all went to Mass and when we came back, we found a beautiful bouquet of carnations from Mrs. Lynes[1] to wish Maman good luck and happiness in her dear old house. At this last kind and thoughtful gesture, Maman wept. We put the flowers on the table in a pretty earthenware pot. Just then Godmother arrived and we showed her our house of which we are so proud. I worked in the garden a good part of the day, watering and transplanting my geraniums that Maman bought me when I was sick.

Thus Sunday went peacefully by and when we went to bed, that calm day had given all of us a little hope for the future of Maman's idea. As though with heaven's approval, the weather during those two days was beautiful and almost warm.

Today I went to school. I saw once more my teacher's unbearably cross face and I resumed that school life which sickens me because it is nothing but scoldings, shouts and requirements. We have changed schools, though, and are now going to Holy

[1] *Former owner of the house.*

Trinity School on 83rd Street because they are tearing down our school to build a beautiful big church there, and a new school will be built on 70th Street.

I was dizzy with so many changes and that is why I haven't written in my diary, but now I want to, I want very much to write and I am ready to promise that from now on I shall write every day. Isn't that natural? With a big house like this, my thoughts will become vaster and lighter, since they won't have so many walls to go through.

May 1. What miserable weather! It has rained ceaselessly all day. The garden is soaked, the sky is dark, and the rain keeps falling. I went to school as usual. Twice Sister Dolorita scolded me unfairly, without noticing my sudden flush and my impatient gesture, a gesture that I couldn't hold back. For a long time now, that impatient gesture escapes me each time she scolds me unjustly. The truth is that every day I find her more unbearable, more crabby and more unjust. Even though I work as well as I used to, she is never satisfied. Even though I watch my deportment, she still scolds me. Maman tells me that if I don't want to, I don't have to go to school, but I don't want to leave before passing my examination in arithmetic, so I am patient, or rather I am impatient, to tell the truth.

Yesterday I forgot to tell my diary that Uncle Henry[1] is here. He has been exiled from Cuba for having conspired against the government, and Maman told him that he could stay with us. He occupies one of the little rooms on the fifth floor. Emilia Quintero has the other one. Speaking of Emilia Quintero, I must introduce this strange person to my diary. She has a mixture of genius and madness in her life.

Emilia is old, I believe, and since I don't have to be polite in my diary, I shall add that she is ugly. She is very good-hearted and very generous, but she is also very demanding and rather envious. She has one bad fault: she talks too much. She talks to everyone, she talks all the time. She makes one dizzy, she drives one crazy and, to begin with, everyone puts up with her, but after a little while everyone avoids her, mocks her and criticizes her. She is to be pitied. Nothing suits her and she always has something to complain about. She is never happy, never contented with her fate. She plays the piano very well, though, and she also writes. She keeps a diary, writes her impressions and everything else that one can write, writes very well, too, but other than that,

1 *Enrique Culmell.*

she is a bit mad. She talks about her early death and makes us feel sorry for her, then she exaggerates the beauty of the least thing. Well, that's how she is, but it seems to me that a person could very well change his personality so as not to give others the impression that he is crazy.

That's enough for this evening. A nice bed and a kiss from Maman are waiting for me.

May 2. The weather today was beautiful. I got up late, I had breakfast and I spent the morning sewing, reading and getting ready for school, for I went after lunch. Each time the sister scolds me without any reason, I am satisfied to shrug my shoulders and to say to myself: I don't care! Afterward, you can't stop me from having fun!

When the clock struck 4 and I left school, I met Eleanor, whom I hadn't seen since I was sick. As we talked, we came to our house and I invited her to come in. After having a bite to eat, I showed Eleanor the house, and then we went to the garden to play on the swing that Uncle Henry has put up for us there. We played until half past five, when she left. Then I started to work in my garden. The first thing I discovered is that ¾ of my land is made up of earthworms. Here is how I remedied that: I took a pail, I turned the earth over for an hour, and in an hour and a half the pail was full of earthworms that twisted and turned in vain. Five minutes later, all those poor worms were in the garbage can. Then I learned that earthworms are good for the soil. Too late!

My soil is nice and clean now. I took out the rocks and other trash, then I used little stones to divide it into clean little squares of the same size that now are ready to receive seeds of every kind. From time to time I find an earthworm that escaped the massacre and I leave him in peace; they are good for something, I just found out, although it's hard for me to believe. They are stupid and disgusting; but if they hadn't been right under my shovel, I wouldn't have thrown them out.

I ate dinner with a keen appetite and after dinner I sat down to write, because I promised myself to write every day. If I don't find anything to say about myself, little diary, I shall talk to you about my earthworms. Isn't that a good subject? And a very interesting one?

May 5. I decided that when I have only a few minutes to write in my diary, I shall write like a telegram. Today I should have written: Godmother arrived. Cinema with Antolinita. Planted tomatoes, radishes, cabbages in garden. Maman has a headache. Good night.

May 8. Too busy writing to Papa, from whom I just received a letter. Changed teachers in school. Went for a walk with Eleanor. More and more disgusted with school. Pupils these days are stupefied by punishment. No one has laid a hand on me, but just let them dare; the blood of the poilu[1] flows in my veins, since I am French!

May 11.
Dearest Papa,
I have waited a long time for a letter from you, but in vain. Why don't you write? It is exactly a month and a half since I have had news from you, and each day I have been saying to myself: I'll write tomorrow, because this evening there may be a letter from Papa.

Tonight I decided to go ahead, but before you receive this letter, I hope that one will come from you.

The effect of the declaration of war is felt everywhere here. At the two great words "Justice" and "Liberty," all of America has risen up and all hearts here are joined as one to the heart of France which suffers over there. Everywhere there are red crosses, soldiers, appeals and above all, the most beautiful thing, flags everywhere. And especially, Papa, think of my immense joy, my pride, when I see our noble flag entwined with the American flag, the two floating together in the air, fluttering in the sweet breeze of hope that moves all hearts. And the beautiful Belgian flag! Just as glorious, just as noble, it always finds its place between my flag and that of the New World, if that is how one should call this great country which is going to take part in the war that has already shaken, crucified almost the entire universe.

The newspapers say dreadful things about the Kaiser and make fun of the boches. The children here avoid the German children, at school they are looked on with suspicion and all the games are at their expense. The girls who jump rope sing: "One, two, three. How many shots will it take to kill the Kaiser. Four, five, six. And bury him in China."

In a word, the little friendly feeling that he enjoyed here has vanished.

[1] *Term used for the French soldier in World War I.*

But enough of war. In a week we shall be at a new address. I haven't yet seen the house (for we shall no longer be living in an apartment), but I believe it is very big, and also there is a little garden in back of the house, something like the one where we lived in Brussels. The address is 158 West 75th Street. When I see the house, I shall describe it for you.

One of Maman's friends told me that in the big public library on 42nd Street, he saw a new book written by you, and the greatest pleasure you could give me would be to send me a copy.

I had to interrupt my letter. Since we started getting ready to move, I haven't had a moment to write.

Saturday, April 28, according to the description that I wrote in my diary, the house is . . . etc. etc. (here I gave the description of the house).

That is how I described the house for my diary and I have copied it here for you to give you my first impression of it. Don't you think it's time that success, good luck and happiness come along for dearest Maman? As you can tell, she always keeps on trying without giving up, without getting tired, always with the same energy and the same kindness.

We admire her, Papa, but not enough. For me, Maman is peerless, but how can I show her what I feel? Just to say it is nothing. That's how it is, many people admire Maman, but not many of them show her the way they feel.

I shall change the subject, Papa, for if I let myself go I could fill a notebook talking just about Maman.

I announce with joy that I just received your letter dated April 16, followed immediately by a package of 3 [issues of] Qui? Pourquoi? Comment? [magazine].

About the newspapers, Papa, I should ask you not to send me any more of them, because for Christmas Maman gave us her entire collection of newspapers in English and I am sorry to have them twice, although it gives me pleasure to reread all those things in French.

In your letter you say that my letter was wet with sea water when you received it and that made me feel bad, for it reminded me of the way things are these days. As for the photograph, please forgive me, dear Papa, for that omission. I found it on the table after having posted my letter.

You also mention that Grandmother told you about Joaquin-ito's First Communion. He hasn't changed, but for a few days before and after the great day, he seemed very impressed and full of respect that he had been taught for the great and wonderful experience he was about to have.

His First Communion was very beautiful and the sweet memory of that day will give him pleasure later on.

But he quickly resumed his usual ways, which consist of living as madly and excitedly as possible. He does everything without thinking, although without meanness. His great intelligence is always dedicated to finding ways of teasing and trying one's patience.

The only thing that keeps him quiet has always been, is, and always will be the piano. The instrument is too small for him. He plays with all the liveliness and strength in his make-up. To see him sitting there, untaught as he is, with his head thrown back, fire in his eye and his light hands flying, almost compels respect. For him it is no effort at all. Everything is noise to him, and for him the piano is transformed into a big impressive orchestra. There is never any discord in what he plays and one could sit listening to him for a long time, if he would allow it. Two days ago we had this conversation:

"Anaïs, do you like what I play?"

"Oh, yes!"

"Well then," he said, remembering the explanation I had given him about a certain opera, "we'll write an opera. Make up something and I shall write the music."

So I started writing and wrote for two hours, putting my pen down only long enough to tap my fingers on the table as I searched for the meter. Well, Papa, if you had been there, you would have been surprised. Imagine Joaquinito sitting at the piano with that proud look he has, and next to him your Anaïs who turned into an actress, playing all the roles in a kind of opera. From time to time I whispered to Joaquinito, "Sad," and his music became so sad that I felt I could hear the moans of the person I was playing.

At the end I was a prince, I had to take poison, and I whispered to Joaquin, "Death!" He understood. Something like thunder happened, quickly, a real description of the soul leaving the body. I drank the poison, Joaquin paused, and at the moment when I swallowed it, he played a note like a tiny high-pitched bell.

As I fell down, silence. Then my agony began, and the piano replaced all the moans that escape one at a time like that. I only made the gestures.

I died, and Joaquinito, who had finished playing, was crying when he turned around: "I thought you were really dead!"

And it goes on like that all the time. Joaquinito and I become as one when our ideas express themselves in gestures and music, in a word: artistic.

Of course, I am nothing. I can't do anything without Joaquinito, whereas he can get along nicely without me. In your next letter, tell me what you think of all this. I will let you make fun of me, but you must admire Joaquinito, do you see?

I had the good fortune to see the great French marshal, General Joffre, who was received here with shouts of joy. In his honor, the United States put on the greatest and most beautiful demonstration ever.

When I saw him, so noble and handsome, dressed in that beautiful French uniform, my heart thrilled. I saw all of France, beautiful, noble and brave, which has such a large place in my heart, personified in that great man. I have only a small French flag, but I don't need anything to remind me that mine is the most beautiful country of all.

Do I need a great enormous flag, when there is not one as great as the love I feel for that France so far away? No. I don't need one, I have more than the emblem, I have the motherland itself, her sorrows, her joys; all of that is in my heart and will never leave it!

You may have guessed all that, Papa dearest, but it does me good to say it. With that I shall stop or the envelope will be too full. The letter isn't as long, however, as the kisses sent tenderly to you by your daughter.

May 13. All week long I thought, I wracked my brains. Why? I don't really know myself, but it came about through a blunt question that I asked myself: "What do I do?" The first word that came to me was: nothing. Then after a moment's thought, I replied: I help Maman with the house, I take care of Joaquinito, I write, I read, I learn, I do my schoolwork. . . .

And then?

There was a great silence within me, I could almost have thought that even my heart had stopped beating with that "And then?" so short, so brief, which meant so much.

In that moment, I was like a traveler who after having traveled a long time, suddenly asks himself: "Where am I going?"

I walked a long time in the street, looking for the end, and suddenly asked myself: "Where am I going? What is my goal?"

That is absolutely the truth. I had never asked myself whether I had an idea, some kind of purpose, serious and strong enough to guide my conduct. And I searched.

In a word, I gave some serious thought to my vocation, and at present I am face to face with the void of "the Future." I can't see anything; it's dark, dark, an unending tunnel, without a wall to guide me, without a ceiling to protect me, without solid ground to walk on.

And suddenly, a little light appears, weak and distant. Little by little, it draws near and a vision appears. It's something white, pure, sublime, beautiful, admirable: it is a nun. An ideal nun, a true nun, of which there are few, surrounded by light, smiling in her sacrifice.

The light moves off, the nun disappears, and then I see a young girl, with a laurel wreath on her head, her left hand leaning on a stack of books and a pen in her right hand. She smiles sweetly, her eyes shine with glory, and from time to time one sees a gleam of bitterness in them, that gleam of people who know, that gleam of those who have learned! . . .

Then nothing else comes, and I wait, I wait, and I hesitate.

Then I understand that those are the only two things I can be. My two destinies and I must choose.

I am going to read a nun's life, I am going to study the results of a struggle for fame, and on January 1, 1918, dearest diary, I promise you that I shall make a decision. If I take so long, the reason is that if I am going to make the sacrifice, I want to examine my conscience, and if I am going to undertake the struggle, I want to test my strength of character.

There is a part of me that says I shall never have a companion in my struggle and I understand *that there are two people in me.*

If I don't find my dream, my de Charny or my Joseph Balsamo, and if I ever announce to you that I am going to marry someone who isn't like them, then, dearest diary, it will be because I shall no longer be Anaïs Nin, the girl whose soul you know at present, who gives you her promise never to commit such a foolish act.

May 19. I am writing at a lovely desk that Maman bought me and I have only to raise my head to see a row of beautiful geraniums, red, pink, a variety of light colors, on the windowsill.

I have read straight through Horace by Corneille, Après Fortune Faite[1] by Cherbuliez, Le Château des Airelles[2] and L'Ami des Mauvais Jours.[3]

As for "Horace," I don't dare pass judgment on it, but I don't like it. The second book made me realize for the second time that Cherbuliez is vague and monotonous. Since I just read "L'Idée de Jean Têterol" I might add that he writes the same story twice.

[1] With Fortune Made.
[2] Castle in the Air.
[3] A Friend in Need.

There must be a man like Jean Têterol and Monsieur de Frayaz in his family because he thinks too much about that character, and having it described to me twice, I no longer admire it.

In Le Château des Airelles, I rediscovered the same old story that I read every day, although it was very well written. I confused Olivier with de Charny and that's all. I thought about it a long time and it made me sad, but I didn't learn anything.

As for L'Ami des Mauvais Jours, I kicked it against the wall. I wept at Napoleon's death, I pitied him with all my heart, but I was furious with the men around him, his jailers, those who held him prisoner, and pushing away like a nightmare the heartbreaking story of his exile, which is too sad and which I admire, I told the book bitterly: "Who are you to dare to talk about something as beautiful as that?"

Looking at the little black letters on the white paper, I thought: "He is dead, since his story is here in the book," and I added, "All the great men are gone!" Later, I remembered the glimpse that I had of a great man wearing the French uniform, of whom someone said to me, "He is a hero, a great man of our time." And still thinking about Napoleon, whose entire life I know, I added: "Their shadows remain." And opening my closet, I found myself face to face with a portrait of "Papa Joffre" in all his splendor and next to him a French flag. I remembered what I had just said and, changing my opinion suddenly, in a burst of "modern" heroism, I said to myself: "No, there still are heroes . . ."

May 22. At half past five this afternoon, I was on the swing. My hair, which Maman had curled, sometimes covered my face, sometimes danced around my head. I wasn't thinking of much of anything when suddenly Thorvald called to me. He was sitting not far from the swing, busily whittling a boat with his knife.

"Anaïs!"

"What?"

"I have something important to tell you."

"Well, tell me, I'm listening."

"Do you think you're pretty?"

"Ah, Thorvald, are you by any chance making fun of me? You know very well I don't, and on top of that I've convinced *you* that I'm not pretty. What more do you want?"

"I know someone who thinks you're pretty, though," said Thorvald with a little teasing air.

"Who?"

"John O'Connell."

I turned red, and Thorvald, who was watching me, added: "And he also told me that he wants you for his girl." At that point I almost fell off the swing and if Thorvald hadn't stopped it, I would have taken a tumble. He had to repeat what he had said three times and I couldn't believe him. There. I preferred John O'Connell to the other boys in my class, and now he tells my brother that he wants me for his "girl." As I write that, I smile, I smile serenely, happily, but a bit mockingly. My goodness, what a little girl I still am!

Is it possible! A girl of 14? Yes, my little diary, it's true! Your crazy little confidante has found her knight, her tiny and nice little knight (American). . . . But he has beautiful blue eyes, nice manners, he is brave, and that's all that I want. If I build castles in Spain, if I dream of magic voyages, etc., it's John O'Connell that I'm thinking of.

Let happen what will happen! It's a school game, a bit of foolishness for girls like me who read too much, and who, alas! search too eagerly for the living image of the heroes whose lives they have read about. And I am still smiling. . . . I smile as I shall always smile at those games, which later on will become serious.

June 3. Since the last time I wrote, that is, May 22, an event has taken place, an event that awakened a new feeling in me. I am very impatient, but I shall hold myself in check and tell it in the proper order.

May 23: I was busy with my garden, I read, worked, but didn't write since I was in a bad humor with myself. I felt afraid of the blank pages of my dear diary.

Same thing on May 24 and 25.

On May 26, I went to the public library and took out a book on housekeeping. I was seized with a sudden love of order, of cooking, a sudden wish to be useful and to stop dreaming. I put down my books, made myself an apron, and shut myself in the kitchen: I made biscuits and they were successful. Thorvald and Joaquinito tried them, and soon Maman did too. I feel a new pleasure at hearing myself called a cook and in knowing how to do something. There it is! I am becoming orderly, calm and useful. Each morning, I promise myself to spend the day thinking of something which will make me happy. Maman smiles and calls me her little housekeeper, and I think she imagines that this won't last long.

May 27: I went to school, as usual. I read the life of Jean de La Fontaine and I saw that he felt the same way I do about school.

But I understand why: he was a dreamer, he couldn't always keep his mind on the silly things one learns in those places, and being gentle and sensitive, he suffered. I am a dreamer, I suffer, but it isn't because I am sensitive and gentle; I have too much pride, I have too many ideals and the brutality used by the teachers hurts and offends me and I suffer because of that.

May 31: Mrs. Carlo Polifeme telephoned Maman and asked her to bring me to her house the next evening at 8:30. I remember that lady very well; a year and a half ago, she dedicated her book to me like this:

"Bless me, Mother, I kneel before you."

To Miss Anaïs Nin

I am ready and I am happy.

June 1: I went there. We sang and danced. I am to appear as a dancer in Jeanne d'Arc à Domrémy.

June 2: I went again. We had the dress rehearsal. I am rather nervous when I think that I am going to appear in front of an audience for the first time. Maman bought me some beautiful patent-leather shoes and silk stockings and gloves.

June 3: It's over, all finished, but here is how it went: At 2:30, Godmother came because Maman was obliged to go out. We took the subway and reached 14th Street at ten minutes to 3. We went into the Union Square Theatre by a little low door on which swung a sign marked "Stage Entrance." Godmother and I found ourselves in a large hall; half-dressed women were seated everywhere, smoking and talking. In a word, we had before us people of the worst kind who act in vaudeville. However, we didn't look at them for long. Mrs. Polifeme came over to us, gave me my costume, and led us to a little room with a low ceiling, full of unpainted wooden tables, some without legs. There were already several girls there getting dressed. With the odor of wine and cigarettes, everyone found the place disgusting.

Godmother helped me to get dressed. After taking off my dress, I put on a little white blouse, a long dark-green skirt with a little black velvet ribbon near the hem, and a black velvet bodice that laced in front. A little black apron made me look like a peasant from Lorraine, which was how I was supposed to look. I let my hair down and put on a white bonnet with a little black velvet ribbon. Just then Maman arrived with Mrs. de Sola.[1] Also just then, one of the ladies came in with a little brush and a box of red paste, another box of blue paste, and offered to paint me because she told me laughingly I would look like a ghost under the very strong lights of the theatre. She put rouge on my cheeks and lips and blue on my eyes to lengthen them. I had to laugh because I looked very funny. At least I thought I looked funny, but Emilia, who had just arrived, told me I was very pretty. Maman smiled with an expression that seemed to say "Perhaps." Godmother and also Mrs. de Sola said that I was really very pretty.

Oh! my diary, what would you have thought if you had seen me blush suddenly and, above all, smile in a way that meant: "I would like to be." Do you know of whom I was thinking? John O'Connell! There, that's out. I have said the most difficult thing, so let's go on.

Once I was dressed, it was only 3:30 and the play was to begin at 4:30. We went for a walk with a girl who had beautiful hair as long as her dress and with the singing teacher, Miss Victor. After walking for a moment, we found ourselves backstage. They were playing a little comedy. Imagine, diary, an enormous dirty curtain, faded paint on the side away from the audience. And at the back of the stage, which looks so pretty from a distance, there was a frightful painting, full of holes, old and faded. The furniture was old and the silk torn, but none of that is visible from out front.

A lady burst into tears, as the play called for, and left the stage; she was hardly off stage before she burst out laughing in the most unaffected way. The rushing about of the man who raises and lowers the curtain at a signal from the one who directs, the different costumes going back and forth off stage, the low, unintelligible murmurs that doubtless represent what the actors are going to say in a few minutes, the comings and goings of those in charge, and when the curtain is lowered, when the men hurry to change the scenery, when something breaks and the carpenter is called in a rush, the times when suddenly the lights go out because the man in charge of the lights makes a mistake, the excitement, all those different noises, the hurrying people who think only of themselves and what they are going to do—all that fills me with a strange sensation, a mixture of astonishment, admiration and confusion.

I kept my eyes wide open, looking at that place, backstage,

[1] *Candelaria de Sola, a family friend.*

where perhaps I would never return, and all of a sudden I was seized by the same fever, the same general excitement that animates everyone behind the scenes. Sometimes I leaned forward a little and I could see part of the audience laughing and applauding, but in a relaxed way, for they were far from feeling that fever that takes hold of those who work at making them laugh, weep and applaud. I said to myself that I too had often applauded and laughed in the same way, finding everything simple, imagining that it was all easy to do; but in that instant I promised myself never again to applaud only what I could see, but to think of what I couldn't see, behind the scenes. Well, that's it, I now know the different secrets of backstage and it seems to me it will be impossible for me to listen to a long lecture in the theatre, now that I realize how much work that lecture required, and I know that instead of listening to the speech, I would be backstage where, a few minutes earlier, the speaker was murmuring his speech, tapping his foot feverishly on something.

It's impossible for me to write here all that I thought about at that instant as I looked at the audience, listened to a bit of a play, heard close to me the varied, mysterious backstage noises! . . .

"Young ladies, get ready!"

It was Mrs. Polifeme's voice, also a little excited.

Then we got ready. A green skirt, a red skirt, etc., and we were also murmuring excitedly the words of our song. I reminded myself not to look at the audience while I danced because I was afraid of having "le trac,"[1] as Maman calls it.

Joan of Arc entered; what she said reached my ears as a confused sound. I couldn't hear anything; it seemed as though I couldn't see, either. I only knew that in that instant I felt myself being carried along in the dance.

> "Je ne suis pas si vilaine
> Avec mes sabots
> Puisque le fils de roi m'aime,"[2] etc.

I sang but didn't look at anything; I sang but I heard nothing, I sang but I had no idea where I was. I realized we had made a mistake, but no one noticed. Then, there we were again, offstage! I felt completely dizzy. If anyone had asked me for my impression

[1] *Stagefright.*
[2] *French folk song:*

> *I am not so ugly in my wooden shoes*
> *Since the king's son loves me.*

of that moment, I would have answered: Complete blank! Nothing! Absolutely nothing!

However, it seems to me that at one moment I dared to raise my eyes and where the audience was I saw . . . a big black hole and just a few faces. That's all. The second time, I was braver and I looked: I saw hands applauding. When we left the stage after the Angelus, that vague sound of applause haunted me for a long time. It wasn't for me, it was for all of us, and yet a voice whispered, "You would like that applause for yourself."

And once again I realized that I was born to hear applause. I liked it, and a doubt crossed my mind. Is it fame that I want? It seems that it's over, but I am still dreaming of that moment when all I could see was hands applauding and some lights, and as audience only a vague, mysterious and indefinite darkness.

Godmother, Felo, Thorvald, Joaquinito, Uncle Henry, Mrs. de Sola, all were there. People said hello, people congratulated me. Felo shook hands, Godmother kissed me, Joaquinito stroked my hair, Thorvald tried on my little apron, but I was still dreaming. . . .

It was only in the silence of the little room, as I changed my clothes, that I woke up. It was a happy awakening because I had been afraid that it wasn't real. . . . I took off my costume, I said good-bye to Mrs. Polifeme and the other girls, and I left with Maman, who called it my debut.

"Did you have a good time, fifille?"

"Oh! Yes!"

I said that vaguely; I was thinking of the moment when I found myself onstage for the first time, dizzy, deaf, blind, and aware only of that big black hole with hands that applauded!

Dearest diary, isn't that one more sign which should convince me that my vocation is to seek applause? I think so, and I begin to dream again. . . .

June 7. When I had finished describing for my diary that event which for a moment disturbed the housekeeper who didn't want to dream anymore, I wanted to say something else, but Maman called me to dinner and after dinner a friend of Maman's came to see us.

Yesterday: School in the morning; in the afternoon I sewed on buttons, finished mending my stockings, then I went upstairs.[1]

---

[1] *There was a large room on the third floor where the Nin children often played.*

I am thinking about a play that I would like to put on up there and I keep my things in the drawers there. I have a Communion veil that I have covered with a pretty gold net, a hat covered with the same gold netting which is very shiny, also a golden scepter for the queen, a white lace dress, a wide pink ribbon for the belt, a hat in the style worn by Catherine de Medici, with black lace which falls from the top of the hat clear to the floor, another white dress, a blue ribbon for the waist and a black hat covered with pearls for another queen; a hat trimmed with feathers for the page, a black cloak for the prince, a wooden sword, a wooden dagger for the prince, a white lace dress covered with pink pearls for the princess, and a cardboard crown, also for the princess.

I wrote the play; the idea came from Eleanor. I painted the programs and the invitations. We plan to put it on a few days after school closes, as a surprise for Maman.

But enough about the theatre. I am going to talk a little about my garden. I counted my corn stalks: I have 156 and about the same numer of peas; I have 102 lettuce plants, 10 carrots, a lilac bush, 4 geraniums, a climbing plant whose name I don't know, a hyacinth, about 200 radishes, 11 cabbages, a rose bush and 3 Chinese lilies.

June 10.

Dear little Papa:

What has happened? Why don't you write?

I assure you that I am more and more worried about you. I have never gone such a long time without news from you, and this is the 3rd letter that I have written you in 3 months. The first two went unanswered and after having waited three weeks since I sent the last one, I am writing again, hoping to receive a letter before this one is posted.

The way things are now, I think that perhaps you write and your letters don't reach me. That only increases my hatred for the ferocious beast that is the cause of it all, all that is happening and all that will happen.

I am resigned, then, to await your letters, which are the only thing that still gives me hope that the dream of having you near me may come true.

I have something else to tell you, Papa dearest, something which took place just a week ago. It wouldn't have interested me so much if it were not that just now, when I am thinking about my vocation, everything is a sign and a help.

You know that I write everything in my diary, so I would rather just copy here the description of it all from beginning to end.

*   *   *

In copying that [description of the performance of *Jeanne d'Arc à Domrémy*] for you, Papa, and in rereading that description, I feel exactly the same way that I did then. It seems to me that you will understand those feelings and impressions. In your opinion, isn't the work that you do the kind of work I would like to do? In working at your profession, don't you work as I would like to work, out of love for your art, love for all that is beautiful, in the name of that other thing which is behind all life, that thing which is seen by those whose imagination lets them go beyond ordinary life, beyond everyday life, those who have seen the other side of the world, life's other face, which is known to so few?

I think so, Papa, and I am sure that the first time you heard applause that was a little bit for you, you too felt a wish to hear it again, because it told you that you had worked well; and if there was applause, it was because you were giving those people a bit of happiness, a bit of heaven, that you had insight into the wonderful voyage; and also because it told you that in giving those people a bit of the happiness you had managed to glimpse, they wanted more, they would follow you, and thus you would win more disciples, more soldiers to work in the cause of art and to widen the narrow road that leads to the wonderland where all is beautiful, pure and unknown.

Please, Papa, correct me if my ideas aren't right, correct me if my thinking is wrong, if I don't understand clearly the purpose of your work and of that which I would like to engage in.

If I am mistaken, you will explain to me how it is, won't you, Papa? Because these are my ideas, this is what I think, and perhaps I don't know enough and am mistaken.

I have a very faint recollection of your "Pro Arte,"[1] but it seems to me you said that art is everything that is beautiful. I think you also said that you work in the name of art, that you want to make it known, that you want people to understand it and believe in it.

Halt! I see my letter getting longer and I have so many other things to say: each time I write you, I forget to ask if you think I am too talkative. Does that bother you, Papa dearest?

I am afraid the answer is yes, but if it is, the only thing I can

[1] *Published in 1909.*

do is write letters like telegrams, because I can't keep myself from writing a great deal about the least little thing to those I love. The longer my letters are, the more I love the person I am writing to.

You and Grandmother, Papa dearest, are the only ones to whom I love to write long letters, but I am very much afraid they may bore you and I wish you would tell me if they do; I will make them shorter.

*   *   *

All of a sudden I have been seized with a great fondness for cooking, for orderliness, in a word, for everything that has to do with housekeeping. While I await the day when I can be useful in another way, I make myself a little bit useful and I have fun making desserts, mending stockings, looking after the linens and other things of which I used to know nothing because I was always dreaming.

I don't dream any more now, for I realized that by dreaming all the time, I would never do anything. Nothing prevents me, though, while I am mixing the cake dough, from thinking of many things, and above all I always remember that you will not be eating that cake with us.

As you see, it's sometimes very difficult not to be absent-minded, and yet I try, and when I think of you, I always say to myself: "See you soon." That "soon" means many things. If you would come soon, I would soon be *perfectly* happy, but also that "soon" seems very far away. Don't you think, Papa, that one day or another, that "soon" will arrive? I wait for it, and since my letter is getting so long it will never end, I kiss you a thousand times with much tenderness, and I leave you, loving you always.

Anaïs

P.S. I have learned of the death of Mrs. Carreño[1] and also of Mr. Granados. That great void called death has come very close to us, giving me a vague feeling of pity for this world where so many people weep.

June 28. As I took my poor dust-covered notebook from the bookshelf, I made a promise never again to neglect you for such a long time. But I wiped that shameful dust away, dearest diary, with my housekeeper's apron and it's that apron I am talking about when I remind you that it isn't Anaïs Nin who has neglected you, but the new housekeeper, Maman's new cook, who has exchanged her pen for a feather duster, her notebook for cake dough.

[1] *Teresa Carreño, Venezuelan concert pianist.*

The effort I am making to make myself useful, not to dream, not to be idle a single minute, has been very difficult for me. My diary has seemed like a forbidden country that I didn't have the right to enter until I could say to myself: the work is all done.

I have fought so hard, I have worked so hard that the moment has finally come. Right now, there is nothing to do in the house that hasn't been done. The stockings are mended, the backyard is clean, the garden is all in order, there isn't a single hole in the linen, my closet is neat, my ribbons and collars are washed and ironed, my books are all straight, the whole house is clean, Maman has a dressing gown to wear, the dessert is prepared for this evening, I have work ready for when I go to the park, peace reigns with Joaquinito, my letters are written and sent, etc.

So now I can sit down to write.

July 13. On July 6 Aunt Edelmira came to New York and asked Maman to let me go to Kew. I went and I came home last night so tired that I couldn't write. I had a lovely time, but the thing that gives me the most pleasure is that I came back with an idea for a cinema plot. The idea came to me while I was sitting on a bench waiting for the streetcar, across from a little old wooden house that looked abandoned.

I am going to write it right away. I want it to be well done, because for a long time I have been waking up each morning promising myself to take one step toward . . . becoming an author.

July 14. It is rather late. I have been working hard on my story, which is coming along, and I have shown it to Maman, who encourages me. By correcting me and criticizing, Maman helps me. I write quickly, without stopping, without getting tired, with a fever that I can't describe. I have made myself a promise to finish it with one idea in my head, a goal of producing something, and above all, I want it to be "good for something." . . . I feel that I must wake up, must work, for my 15th birthday is drawing near and I haven't yet done anything to climb the first step that leads toward the "goal."

Something unexpected has disturbed me a lot these last few days.

About 2 weeks ago Maman had a visit from Mr. Francisco Pausas, a Catalan painter introduced to her by Emilia Quintero. It was the first time I had seen him. Maman was very busy, and after a moment she told me to take Mr. Pausas out and show him the garden. I showed him my corn, but he looked at me; I showed him my peas, but he looked at me; and during the entire time that I talked to him, he still looked at me. I wasn't embarrassed, but surprised: I didn't understand what was so extraordinary about me. When he left, he told Maman that I am the "Byzantine" or Catalan type, and after looking at me again, he added that I would look nice on canvas.

Yesterday evening he came over again. We were sitting on the stoop and Maman invited him to sit down too. I was telling Joaquinito a story, but I knew that Mr. Pausas was looking at me again. It didn't bother me because I supposed that perhaps he was studying my Catalan type, as Maman had told me that painters often study different types. Suddenly the conversation turned to painting and Mr. Pausas said he had an idea for a painting.

Later, before he left, he asked Maman to let me pose for him. Maman said yes. He told Maman to dress me simply as I always dress and to bring me over Monday morning. I am impatient for Monday to come, and I don't know why, I am happy. It seems to me it must be something strange to sit for a painting and I dream of doing it. Two weeks ago, I certainly would never have thought of it. The idea that I am a special type had never crossed my mind, although I was always proud to hear that I look like my dearest father. I didn't understand how, though, because to my eyes my father is handsome with the proud and magnificent beauty of my dreams. If I say I felt proud, it's because that is the correct word for what I feel when someone tells me that. I am proud just to think that I look like something. Being the Catalan type pleases me, for I think and suppose that Papa would be happy. I know he is proud of his origin.

July 15. I was so impatient for Monday to come! Then Mr. Pausas came to lunch with us and said that since he was leaving for the country, the painting would be put off until later. Now I am going out with Maman and we are going to the cinema, so I shall quickly forget about it.

July 16. Thorvald wrote. He says that we can go to see him on Thursday. I am very glad, because now that Thorvald is away, I miss him terribly and recognize his worth. I miss his sweetness, his gentleness and kindness toward me, compared to Joaquin who is so impatient and naughty with me.

July 17. I am still busy being a perfect housekeeper, but my goodness, it's difficult! It certainly isn't my custom to worry if I leave a closet door open, and it isn't my custom either to think always of putting my ribbon where it belongs when I take it off or of picking up an ordinary pin. But take heart! Each day it seems to me that I do better.

July 18. It is so hot I haven't the energy to write. I think I shall go and sit outside the door, but it is impossible for me to write in my diary by moonlight.

July 19. We went to Far Rockaway to see Thorvald. He is all sunburned, but he has a lot of fun swimming in the ocean with his friend Jack. On the way there, Maman tried to get me by in the train with a half-price ticket, which I believe is only for children under 12 and I got by. Maman told that to Mrs. Thayer, who said perhaps it was Maman who got by on the half-fare. We laughed a lot at that.

Maman and I would have liked to bring Thorvald home with us, but when Maman saw how happy he was, she said it would be better for us to make the sacrifice and leave him there to have a good time. The house seems a little sad with Thorvald away and we all miss him very much. When I have just seen Thorvald, who is calm and smiling, with such a kind air, and then I come home to see Joaquinito, who was sick a few days, with his peevishness, his wailing and his whims, I can't hold back a sigh because the difference between them is certainly very great: Joaquinito's dark eyes shine with mischief, whereas Thorvald's eyes are blue and candid. They seem like two completely different pairs of lights that illuminate my life in two different ways.

July 31. The hottest day I have ever known in my life. People are stupefied, prostrate. Everyone suffers terribly.

August 1. Dreadful heat continues. My head aches and I can hardly think.

August 2. We put ice wrapped in cloths on our foreheads and spend the day fanning ourselves.

August 3. It's over! That horrible nightmare, that killing heat, has ended. It rained this morning and the weather cooled off. The result of the heat wave is 200 people and 377 horses dead, 407 people prostrate. We went to the beach on Tuesday to try to breathe. The crowds leaped on the tramways while they were moving, without giving people time to get off. When we got to the beach, the sand was burning hot. Only in the water could one realize that one was still alive. In the cabins where we undressed, our clothing was hot to the touch. People sat on the benches, their expression vague and stupid, sweat running ceaselessly down their faces. People fought to get drinks from the orangeade and lemonade stands; water cost 5 cents a glass and there wasn't much of it; a man had his head in a bucket full of pieces of ice; and on the way back, the crowd walked on people who had fainted in the struggle to get on the tramways. Even on the boat, at full speed, there was hardly enough air to breathe. Maman took a vow never to go back to Midland Beach, and everyone said the same thing. Men found room by pushing the women and children, who were forced to wait for another tramway. Many people spent the night in the park, lying on the grass.

Everyone blessed the change in the weather today, and the cooling off must have saved a good many lives.

Maman was very sick and I was quite frightened, for these days of great heat cause her to suffer horribly.

It's over! If it comes again, we will suffer again, but for the moment we live. My head really hurt and my hand trembled when I picked up my pen to write.

It's over! I am going to sleep for the first time in 3 nights.

August 4. I went to see Eleanor. We have a club now which is called the Secret Service Club. Gertrude[1] founded it and I immediately became a member, then president. I then took advantage of that to add many things and make it more interesting. We are supposed to do one good action every day; otherwise we are punished and lose the right to give our opinion in the next two meetings. We have a meeting each week. I found a motto: Let's live in order to be useful and let's be useful in order to live.

We are going to have a "magazine" every month, full of stories, pictures, poems and other things. We pay two cents at every meeting and with that money we buy paper for the magazine and the things we need when we put on a play. With the money from the magazine and the plays, we plan to go on outings and give to charities.

[1] *Eleanor Flynn's young sister.*

August 5. The weather continues to be bearable. We don't plan to go out today and I have begun to write.

I forgot to tell my diary how I earn $1.50 each week. Miss Nooman, the lady who has the big room on the 3rd floor, overlooking the garden, came here 5 weeks ago to learn Spanish in a summer school. She asked me one day if I would like to earn $1.50 by giving her half an hour of conversation 3 days a week. She has already taken 6 lessons from me and I have earned $3, which makes me very happy.

I am still working on my story, the one that is supposed to be "good for something."

August 7. I went to Riverside with Joaquinito and Thorvald, who is back from Far Rockaway; but Joaquinito, who gets worse every day, started in with his unbearable whims and I was obliged to come back.

We have a kitten now, cute as anything, just a few weeks old.

August 8. I don't feel very well. As I felt one of my attacks of sickness coming on, I went to the public library and picked up a supply of books.

August 9. I knew it! I had to stay in bed today, but I can't complain. I put on a dressing gown for breakfast, then when I came back, I settled in with lots of pillows, the bed covered with books, and the cat. Stroking the cat, I began to read. According to Maman, I "went away"; according to Thorvald, I "stuck my nose in a book"; and according to Joaquinito, I was "Miss Boring."

I read until noon and Monsita, the maid, brought me a nice big "lunch" on a tray, because my indisposition never affects my appetite. At quarter to six, Maman allowed me to get up for a while, and I begged so hard that she let me go up and give my lesson. By the way, I earned $2 this week.

Maman received a letter from Aunt Antolina announcing that she will arrive on Sunday. I shall be very happy to see my aunt again and very happy also to see Antolinita, whom I like very much in spite of her capricious disposition. She says that she is bringing a surprise for me and some candies and Cuban desserts for the whole family. As always, her arrival will mean a thousand generous gifts. Maman is arranging the rooms on the 2nd floor for them. We are waiting.

Mr. Pausas came, I believe it was night before last, but he

said, speaking of the painting, that he is going to wait until it is cooler. He says I look so delicate that he is afraid it will be too tiring for me. If I had a mustache I would have laughed in my mustache, as they say in Spanish, but since that ornament doesn't belong to my sex, I smiled politely.

After that gentleman had left, Maman looked at me and said: "You're your father's own daughter, you always look as though you're at death's door." I laughed a long time at that and Maman too, because that's one of the family jokes we make about "Miss Asparagus."

Hoping to feel better tomorrow, the mustached Asparagus bows before her dear Majesty.

August 10. I promised Maman I would write only a few lines so as not to keep her waiting to sit in front on the "stoop."

I got out of bed today and since I felt better, I even worked a little while in my garden. The corn is magnificent and in a week and a half will be ready to eat. I enjoy looking at everything and taking care of everything. The little cat follows me everywhere as I work and one time he slid into a hole I had dug to plant a rosebush. I have arranged everything so that when Aunt Antolina gets here, she will find my garden in perfect condition.

August 16. Sunday at 4:30 Aunt Antolina arrived. Maman put her on the second floor in the room that overlooks the garden. We eat downstairs.

Aunt Antolina brought me a pretty bracelet. The only thing is, I am supposed to take care of Antolinita almost all day and I can't do anything worthwhile. For the first time, I understand the sweetness that comes from freedom and I suffer at having to play and waste my time with Antolinita. My aunt is very kind to me and I don't say anything, but I confess that I was better off when Antolinita wasn't here. I have hardly been able to find time to write these few lines and a short letter to Eleanor, who is at Far Rockaway. Farewell! I shall try to find another moment of the freedom that is so dear to me and without which I fear I couldn't live very long.

August 17. You are my only friend right now, dear little diary, because out of pure meanness, ingratitude and nasty lies, Joaquinito has managed to make Maman believe whatever he wants and

Maman is angry with me. Thorvald too. Godmother must think that I am naughtier than Joaquinito, and Charlie and Antolinita are mad because I don't want to play cards. Besides my diary, which fortunately doesn't believe Joaquinito's lies, I have only the little cat. Dearest diary, consider yourself lucky not to know the willful, lying, ungrateful and *mean* devil who is my brother. Another day I shall talk to you calmly about myself, because right now indignation and anger make my hands tremble.

August 19. Maman, Joaquinito, Antolinita and I all went to the cinema. The story was about a romantic girl who is criticized, unhappy, rejected and misunderstood by everyone, mocked by everyone, and it made a great impression on me. I understood her feelings and I felt sorry for her, but when at the end she found her dream and her ideal, I admired her sincerely and promised myself to do the same.

It taught me a lesson, though. If by romantic they mean someone who dreams, I am a romantic, but I shall keep it a secret and never dream except with my diary. The two of us, all alone, will dream peacefully when it is time for dreams. Except for that precious moment, I shall not leave the kitchen for those other places where one is supposed to be realistic, solemn, serious or perhaps cranky. When I dream, I shall be glad or sad. I don't want them to say of me: "She is always dreaming!"

No. I came along a little too late, and one can't *always* dream. In the century in which I live, people who dream should take their dreams, write about them, sell them and make money. Idle fancies? One takes them, calls them an "idea" and they become a "thing." So that *my* dreams and my idle fancies may belong to me, so that they never turn into fact, so that I may always call them back to keep me company, to make me alive, I shall keep them in the depths of my soul or in the most secret pages of my diary.

Let's quickly take off our crown of dreams, our coat of "what I believe" and put on the dirty apron of "what is happening."

My anger at Joaquinito has cooled and I am ashamed when I reread what I wrote about him at that time. Once again I understand how little control I have over myself, but instead of tearing out that page, I am going to leave it in as evidence of my hot temper that even leads me to write bad things about my brother. Alas! My temper may even lead me to do more serious things, but I shall remember when I see that page and watch myself.

I reread my diary a few days ago, but instead of being

pleased, very often I was angry with myself for the silly things I wrote and I wanted to tear out the pages where those things appeared, but Maman saw my gesture and asked me why. When I explained, she told me not to tear them out, that later on those silly things would make me laugh and I would learn not to do them any more. Perhaps what I have just said is one of the silly things that I shall recognize in a few years, but if I tore them all out, what would be left of my diary, of my life which is silly itself in its eternal monotony? I shall pardon my past stupidities and read them again when I want to laugh.

What was it that made me believe what I wrote 2 years ago, that Papa was coming on Christmas Day? My hope? No. My faith? No. I think I was naïve in those days, and I thought that Christmas should truly be marked by a wonderful event just as in stories, those fairy stories that I believe in. I was sure that my life was like the lives of people in the storybooks, and I thought it was natural that something like that should happen. What has happened now? I have understood the beauty, the wonder, the dreams, with which those stories were made, and I have understood that nothing beautiful, nothing wonderful, nothing, not even a speck of a dream can happen to me, just an ordinary mortal, who can only *believe* in those stories.

The result is simple. I shall do like everyone else: the day that I see my dearest father again, I shall say stupidly: "That's life," instead of saying joyfully, as they do in stories: "It's a dream!"

August 31.
Dear little Papa,
Since I see that I have no news from you, I am going to write to you anyhow so that you won't be worried, as I am, because of your long, interminable silence. Are you ill? If that is the reason for your silence, I beg you, send me just a few words.

Because I have waited a long time to write this letter, I have many things to tell you, but I would rather you guessed them because I lose heart when I tell you about me and about what is happening here, then realize that I know nothing, absolutely nothing, about you. . . .

I had to interrupt this letter for one day, and what joy this morning when I received your postcard!

I am very happy to learn that you are not sick, as I thought you were, and that your silence was due to your being busy. When you write me, tell me about your concert tour, your success, and what happened. Do you think you will have to travel some more?

To keep me from worrying, write me a very long letter to take the place of all those that I should have received.

By coincidence, at the same time I had no news from Grandmother. It has been a long time since Maman and I have heard what is happening there.

What do you think of the Americans who came to see you? If you judge them all by those you met, you surely will be mistaken because they send the best ones from here over there. When they left, I envied them sincerely. They were going to see my country, they were going to fight for her, while I hardly know her and can do nothing to help. But never, never will they love her as I do. . . .

In my letter you will find two poems, "To Die on the Battlefield" and "Maman."

Notice that little by little I am succeeding with the rhyme, and it is thanks to Mrs. Sarlabous that I feel I can justly refer to them as "poems."

I wrote a short story and when it is typed on the machine, I am going to try to have it published in a children's paper.

I keep trying because I want to take advantage of the fact that I am in this great country, where there is room for everyone to "learn" to make [his] way.

I pick my letter up after an interruption of one week.

Today, September 7, Godmother and I have come back from a week of vacation in Norwalk, Connecticut. Godmother invited me to go, and you have no idea what a pleasant week it was and how much good it did us.

I would like to describe Norwalk, which is very beautiful, for you; but I realize it is impossible to put everything in a letter.

Only now do I realize how many things I have to tell you, because for 3 months, always waiting, I didn't write anything.

We have started back to school, but to another school, a public school, while they are building the new Catholic school. The change of school has been very good for us and once again Maman's mind is at rest concerning our education.

In this school, I am studying seriously and very well: drawing, gymnastics, cooking, sewing, and many other things, of course. The other day I was very happy when my English teacher complimented me on a composition I wrote.

She had me read it to the class, which applauded politely, and then she said that she would be very happy if, when I become famous, I would remember to let her read what I write, that I should be proud of my name, etc. And this accomplishment, which has made my name famous at school, gave me a lot of encouragement. It was also a reason for all the girls to learn to pronounce my name correctly, to please me. But, dearest Papa, I immediately noticed that success, however small, always attracts a procession of flatterers, who cluster around me now like flies, but there is a remedy, "flypaper" to catch them, and here is what I did: I let them talk, talk, talk, then I smiled in a rather sarcastic way and said good-bye, thanking them politely. But I didn't take it seriously and I was much amused when, for example, a girl of 15, who is in a higher grade than I, was named by her teacher to be president in charge of "demerits," and taking advantage of her rank, was haughty and unfair to all the other girls. One day I accidentally dropped a book and she gave me 5 demerits. I didn't say anything. When my composition made my name known to the whole school 3 days later, that same girl, the haughty and unfair president, came up to me when she saw me at recess with my shoelace untied, and knelt down with a smile to tie it for me. Her action left me speechless for a long time. Poor girl! I laughed about it heartily afterward and when she asked to apologize for the 5 demerits, I forgave her immediately, and on top of that, when my turn came to be president, I made her a present of 2 *merit* points. Since that day. I have begun to pay attention, and in that school, which often seems exactly the same, I have noticed many small incidents, acts and differences of disposition which are subjects of meditations and strange thoughts for me. Now I observe, I listen, and I shall talk about it later when I am grown up. . . .

Once again I had to interrupt my letter, but thanks to that delay, your letter, your long letter, Papa dearest, had time to arrive, full of good news that made me infinitely happy.

You wrote a great deal, the good moment lasted a long time, and I thank you a thousand times for the trouble you took to write that long letter between lessons or during your only time to rest.

Now let's talk joyfully, without care, almost happy because you are not sick.

I see that you have been able to rest, enjoy yourself a little and build your health up to begin again. Bravo for the orchestra of Cámara Valenciana which at last has recognized Mr. J. J. Nin as more than worthy to be engaged as soloist. You understand that I hope with all my heart that your success, which I don't doubt for a moment, will be twice as great as usual.

You say that the project of coming here has been put off indefinitely, since the fees are not large enough. Ah! if I could become a manager, fill New York with announcements, shout from the rooftops who you are, make you earn millions of dollars, then . . . whatever else you want, so that you might come and stay with us.

Don't smile, it isn't funny, I assure you, and it is the only intelligent thing I have said up till now, even if it's impossible. But since I can't do anything, I shall just send you some snapshots that Mrs. Quintero took. Your daughter is growing fast, isn't she? What do you think of Thorvald, who is the one who thought of the military salute that we are making for you?

You spoke of the rise in prices in Paris, and I understand that. Here we are astonished at the price of butter, 50 cents a pound, and 49 cents for a dozen eggs. I wonder what it must be like in Paris. Don't speak of gifts, Papa, and don't worry about it, because it would not give me pleasure to have you spend money on souvenirs when I would prefer you to give my France the money that you would otherwise spend on all of us.

You have probably heard of the American "Liberty Bond," sales of which amount to about 5 billion dollars. Bravely and nobly, Maman gave 100 dollars and bought one. Recently she bought a $50 bond for Joaquinito, a $50 bond for Thorvald and a $50 bond for me. Our duty has been done and well done, don't you think?

To reply to what you said about my "epistles," I must make a promise and it is: not to go so long without writing you, but you must promise me not to think that I have stopped writing when you yourself don't write. You say that it is in those moments that you need letters the most, and I shall remember that instead of waiting for your letters. But you mustn't think that I hold it against you, my little Papa. I realize only now how little time you have to write, and I would like you to write only a few lines . . . but often!

You spoke about your hair turning gray; it makes you sad and you find it distressing. Alas! No one avoids old age, but try to forget about it, Papa dearest, for someone else counts the passing years, those years that strengthen my filial devotion, these sad years during which the long days of separation pass slowly and sadly.

I may not have expressed myself very well and what I wrote you made you think I was considering a career in the theatre, but that appearance was only to please Mrs. Polifeme, who wanted

her "Jeanne d'Arc" to be a success, so that a manager might be interested in putting on the play. Far be it from me to make a career in the theatre.

I can't send you the grades I got in school. They were not very satisfactory last month because I didn't know the school rules and the way they teach. This month there are only two subjects that are difficult for me and in which I am not doing very well: arithmetic and English grammar. I have to work hard to satisfy my arithmetic and grammar teachers, but the teachers are very kind, very patient, and I shall manage to pass my examinations in June.

Too bad! My letter has become terribly long, but it has been such a long time that I haven't talked to you.

Write me a few lines when you can and tell me what you think of the little photograph.
                    Epilog.
I hug you very close and for a long time.

Your fifille,

Anaïs.

December 1.[1]

Dearest Papa,[2]

The first thing that inspires me to write is that I want to wish you a Merry Christmas with all my heart!

The noise, the excitement and all the other turbulent emotions that surround me subside slowly into a vague murmur when I come face to face with you. My pen longs to write my heart's most ardent wishes here, but it hesitates. . . . Ah! it is so difficult to bring your face close to me, to try to remember your gestures, your smile, so as to forget that you are not here!

There is an emptiness somewhere that no one can fill but you, and the joyous, magnificent Christmas season, when everyone kneels to turn their eyes and their hearts toward heaven, instead of making me forget you, makes me feel your eternal painful absence even more than I do during the rest of the year.

Instead of flinging my arms around your neck, hugging you, sitting on your knee, I have to guide my pen across this dreadful paper to write you, "Merry Christmas!"

Do you think those two words on the paper mean anything?

---

[1] *An unexplained lapse of time, possibly caused by a lost notebook.*
[2] *Apparently a letter that was not sent.*

No. I detest them, I look at them with a haughty air, those two words that my whole being would like to be able to shout, out of a heart overflowing with joy and gratitude.

Since you can't do anything about it, read those words, Papa, and try to understand that they are sincere, very sincere.

You have friends, good friends, who will say them to you, but they won't say them as I would.

You will celebrate Christmas with them and perhaps you will be happy, but don't you think it would be better if you were with your daughter, your sons?

No. I can't imagine that you are happy. Every time I try to see your dear face, I can't make you smile. On the contrary, your gaze is sad, your lips contract when you try to smile, and you have tears in your eyes. . . .

Answer me, tell if it is true that this Christmas you are going to weep, forsaken, alone, sad and perhaps unhappy?

If that is the case, don't you think you could come and be consoled, for wishes often work miracles.

Why must it be that because of a misunderstanding, a word spoken at the wrong moment or some other reason, one must suffer such a long time, and sometimes forever?

Forgive me, Papa, for what I have just written, but I am a big girl, I understand, and I would give my life without caring if I could bring about your happiness and perhaps Maman's.

Life is so short, so thankless, so bitter, why not make an effort and make it sweet and joyful for others and for oneself?

The vague murmur is gone, little by little the happy excitement, the various noises have begun again, and slowly your serious face disappears and is lost in the shadows.

Our conversation is over. Dearest Papa, Merry Christmas!

I wait for your answer—since you take me seriously, I hope.

December 16. I was standing at the window, looking at the tree, the houses across the street and the garden, completely disguised and transformed by a beautiful blanket of snow: the first snowfall of the season! In spite of myself, my thoughts went back to another scene, a scene of misery, or suffering and desolation: The War. The newspaper was lying on a chair beside me and I could easily read the large print, the news headlines.

> Save sugar, there is a shortage!
> Coal supply exhausted!
> Eggs are 5 cents higher!

Germans invade Italy!
Buy a "Liberty Loan"!
English troops thrown back!
French lose 20 cannons!

And after all that, a single consoling line, ablaze with victory: "Jerusalem taken by the British!" Jerusalem! That name which seems to rise up from the years and the centuries, shaking off the dust of history, and appears, surrounded by light, to suffering civilization. The rest of the paper, rumpled, read and reread, is on the floor.

I sigh, thousands of melancholy thoughts, sad memories, trouble my mind and clutch at my heart. I turn away from the newspaper and my glance falls on the bookcase. The sun, which had been hidden behind a cloud, appears again and one of its rays strikes the bookcase, causing the red and gold covers of my books to shine. As though I were reciting the alphabet, I murmur the titles of my books. At the fifth one, I stop between "Les Grandes Femmes de France"[1] and "La Belle Nivernaise,"[2] and I see my diary, the mirror of my life. The same feelings that the English must have had at finding Jerusalem comes over me when I see "My Diary," which, like Jerusalem, seems to rise up suddenly out of the grave of years, and I add, without hesitating: of centuries.

In a few seconds I am settled at *my* desk, my diary open, my pen wet, and my inkwell (where I borrow my ideas) all ready to lend me its wisdom.

First and Last Chapter

My diary is not blind but shut up in a bookcase between two selfish neighbors. I suppose it has no idea about people, circumstances, the state of affairs, the time and place where we are.

Something in the "people" has changed, for Godmother left us to return to Cuba, leaving a great emptiness behind her.

The circumstances haven't changed. The state of affairs right now is sad, too sad to describe. We are still in New York, but the fact that it is December 16, one week before Christmas, is very important (especially for my brothers).

A great feeling of sadness inspired my imaginary letter to Papa. It says what I feel, but says it so frankly that, dismayed by my effrontery, I have left it in its cradle and its grave: My Diary.

I must tell my diary about Miss Storms, about Gertrude,

[1] Great Women of France.
[2] The Beautiful Nivernaise.

Eleanor's sister, and finally about *my* desk. So I shall begin: To give you a better idea, let's imagine that you are suddenly transformed into a girl and that we are going hand in hand to school. In a word, this is a description of school and of the teachers. But before reaching the school, let's walk along Broadway on a December day, like today, for example, at 8:30. A bag full of books under one arm, a tin box which contains a few thin sandwiches for our lunch under the other. It is cold, the wind blows and buffets us on all sides, but we keep moving forward. Generally we walk happily, we run into friends, we talk and laugh the whole way, but when school comes in view, we stop. . . .

That big red brick building with its great enormous doors standing open has a stern look, as unforgettable as a prison; and although many girls (the unfortunate victims of scoldings) don't realize it, it is the gloomy appearance of the building that strikes them dumb and frequently erases the smile that tries to light up their faces. But you and I, dear Diary, we always, always laugh. What does that school matter to me? I go there to learn, but soon I shall leave it and learn what I want to know with my friends, my best companions: my books.

Let's go in through one of those doors. How surprised we are to find that laughter returns and that the atmosphere has changed. Why? Because we see the teachers, who are smiling, joyful and in a good humor (as they always are in the morning). In addition to the teachers, we see big, well-lighted classrooms, very well decorated, with yellow desks. We aren't frightened any more, so I shall begin.

At twenty to nine, we are seated at our desks in the classroom with a book in our hands. Our teacher of geography, history, sewing and penmanship is named Martha Jackson, a name they tell me she is proud of and bears with a dignity worthy of her ancestors, who apparently have a place in a certain but unknown history book about celebrated men and women. Mischievous blue eyes full of kindness, abundant graying hair, a mouth that is neither ugly nor pretty, very white teeth that we often have occasion to admire because she laughs frequently, these are the external characteristics of this interesting lady. As for her inner qualities, they are a thousand times better, for the stamp of character that gives her face an agreeable and interesting expression is multiplied in her actions, which show great strength of intelligence and a great heart. Although we aren't acquainted with her ancestors and although she is a schoolteacher, complete with ruler, we all like her very much because she is never cross, except when she really gets angry, and then we really admire her. In a word, Martha Jackson could very well have filled the position of President of the United States because she combines great strength of mind with a constitution sturdy enough to let her, single-handed, wage a war to wipe out the Germans (seriously). She's a funny teacher, but I am very glad to have her.

Our teacher of composition, dictation and reading is Miss Estelle Storms. If I were another girl, perhaps I wouldn't like her as much, for she is serious and difficult to understand, but since it is the Lord's will that the pen shall have no secrets for me, I like her very much, I understand her, and I am grateful to her for her great kindness to me. Since she discovered what she generously calls my talent, we get along very well.

She often calls on me, we talk together a great deal, and above all, we talk about books. In view of her deep understanding of everything I have read, I feel sorry for her, because I realize how difficult it is for her to talk to her classes all day in a way that is simple enough for everyone to understand, while more difficult words dance on the tip of her tongue, eager to find someone who will listen to them. Without trying to, she has made me think, and those thoughts have made me feel a great pride in my name and a confidence in myself which has often done me good and has brought about a noticeable change in my disposition and my opinion of myself. It isn't really pride, but something which has lifted me in my own eyes and which, if it had remained unrecognized, would have seriously damaged my ambition. I can't describe her, her face has something that I can't define, her eyes hold a light that I didn't know before, she is too reserved, her actions too strained for me to describe her clearly.

The other teachers are like those in the other school, just teachers, nothing more; machines that stop running and become women only when they are at home.

There is nothing else to say about school except about the bell. It's a marvelous little bell in the middle of the school which rings every 40 minutes and reminds us that it's time for a change of subject. How many times at the terrible instant when the grammar teacher, Miss McClave, has asked me a question, that beloved bell rings, and since we have to change classrooms quickly, her question remains without an answer, which I didn't know anyhow. It rings at three o'clock also and we leave school. It rings frequently, and always for a good reason. I assure you, I really like that bell and think it's wonderful. That's all. For me, school seems different every day, according to events and my impressions. I study the girls, my schoolmates, in another special little notebook, because it would take too long to describe all the girls, among whom I now have only *sincere* and devoted friends.

I promised my diary to talk about Gertrude. Gertrude is 10 years old. She is a wonderfully intelligent and very pretty little girl. I noticed her because of her great sensitivity and her skill in singing and dramatic dancing. It seems that I made a great impression on Gertrude, who is very romantic and told her sister that she had never seen anyone like me, that I am someone quite different, and I was very happy to hear that. She seems to like me a lot, and on my side, I also like her a great deal. I don't understand why, when she looks at me, her eyes shine with a lively but astonished light, and sometimes her glance is full of admiration, the reason for which I don't understand. She is ambitious; I can see that she has an idea, a definite ideal, but she talks very little and never about herself, unless we are alone. Then she is naïve and opens her heart to me completely, and I see in her only a loving, sensitive nature, a fertile imagination, and, as I said before, a great intelligence. The other day she tried to explain to me why she was sad. Here is what she said:

"I don't know what comes over me when I see all the beautiful gifts in the shops and I see people buying. Even Eleanor has money, but I don't have any and yet I would like so much to be able to give gifts to everyone, to make everyone happy, and I would like so much to be rich. At night in my bed, I think about that and I cry and would like to die and I feel so bad. I don't understand why. . . ."

She looked at me and I saw tears in her beautiful blue eyes, shining tears that came from deep down in her heart, more eloquent than everything she had just said. So I talked to her and explained that I also often felt like that, and I brought into play all my powers of consolation, talking to her the way I talk to myself; then I gave her 25 cents. Here is how she answered: "Anaïs, I feel better, you are so kind and so wonderful. No one understands me the way you do."

And I smiled, because isn't it natural that I should know how to console her for a sadness that *sometimes* has the same cause as my own?

My Desk

When Godmother went away, she left me her little desk, and Thorvald brought it downstairs for me. I quickly moved it in front of my window, next to Maman's. I put my papers in the big drawer, my letters in their place, and I was delighted when Maman gave me, as a Christmas present, a pink blotter, a calendar, a pen-wiper, an inkwell, a penholder, etc., everything in pink.

Mrs. Quintero had the good idea of giving me a very beautiful book for my diary; I am going to start it on January 1.

December 27. Christmas is over. We had just as nice a time as last year, and I am not going to undertake a description of how we spent that beautiful day. I received a silver purse from Aunt Edelmira and that completed the list of things I wanted; right now I don't want anything else, absolutely nothing.

I amused myself by rereading my diary almost from the beginning, and from time to time I am going to stop and pass judgment. I have just read a few pages written in those days when I was seized by religious fervor, and at those words of love for our Lord and that blind confidence in the power of prayer, I sighed deeply. Alas! Why must I change? I feel nothing. I am cold and just now I don't understand religion, and I know, I understand that it's my excitable nature that causes me to cool suddenly toward something I used to adore and into which I put all the strength of my passion. I am ashamed, I suffer, but God understands that I love Him. I respect Him as much as before, and He will pardon me, poor frail creature who doesn't know what to say to Him, how to pray. Yes, I am frivolous, I am not steadfast, I am fervent, but I trust in the mercy of the Lord to whom, just now, I don't know how to pray.

I said that when I read George Sand I learned the meaning of love. Since then, I have changed my mind. I think that I still don't understand what it is, or else I must believe that I shall always be immune to that feeling. I imagine that I am a philosopher and I think that I shall feel love only for my pen and my books, because my heart is very small and doesn't have room for "anything" else. I say anything, because I consider a man an "object."

I smile when I reread the pages in which I described my adventure on Uncle Gilbert's ship, when I didn't know how to dance. Without realizing it, I learned to dance at school, and little by little the idea of knowing how to dance at the age of 14 seemed perfectly natural. To Maman's great joy, I explained that to her, and gently, with that angelic voice and that expression, so sweet and so beautiful, which belongs only to her, she said, "You are becoming civilized, my daughter, and you will be much happier for it when you are grown up."

The rest of the notebook is full of dreams and reflections on

Dumas' novels. Little by little the fires of admiration for those stories, which broke the daily monotony, have died out, and it seems to me that I am becoming more sensible as I get older. I dream less and I think much more, and I analyze and discuss with myself the ordinary little events that, with a bit of good will, I can call interesting and that *seem* to make my life much less monotonous. By the way, when I am in a good humor, I begin to think that my life isn't monotonous at all and that I know how to get something out of the least little event, which I didn't do when I spent my days lamenting and trying to console myself for my "attacks of sadness."

In this notebook, I notice I talk about many stories that were begun with a fixed aim of "making them good for something," and that makes me want to laugh, for those poor little stories are now in my big drawer to be used as scratch paper.

December 28. Last night I ended the reading of my diary with a sigh. As I grow up, as the years pass, I seem to change many of my opinions. It's all for the best, however, because I am sure that those "opinions" will settle down and become a little more reasonable (I hope).

We are on vacation this week and my diary can imagine that I feel like enjoying myself. I am in a very good humor and am going to try to be like that always, for I can see that it does me as much good as it does others.

A week ago, I read, in English, "The Autocrat of the Breakfast Table" by Oliver Wendell Holmes, an American author whom I admire very much. The way he described the people at the breakfast table seemed very interesting to me and extremely amusing, and it gave me a good idea. Since I *want* to write in my diary every day beginning January 1, let's suppose that every day I write a small part of the conversation at supper, because like the real American citizens we are becoming, it is only at that time that we eat calmly.

Jack came to see Thorvald for a little while today and I suddenly remembered that I have never talked to my friend about that little person who is Thorvald's best friend. To begin with, he isn't little. He is fifteen and yet he seems taller than I. Blue eyes, red hair, and a face covered with freckles; in a word, an agreeable face. He learned French in Brussels and speaks it quite well. By a strange coincidence, one year after we left, his father, who is a painter, rented the house that belongs to Maman's singing teacher.

He has two faults—he is clumsy and shy—but they are easy to forgive, especially by me. But his shyness is really becoming worse and worse. When he talks to me, he never looks at me, and even if he says a few words to me, he blushes immediately. If I look at him, he never fails to drop whatever he has in his hand, or else he makes a mistake in what he is doing, and I am beginning to think he is afraid of me. On Christmas Eve, he came to bring us our gifts. He gave Thorvald and Joaquinito their gifts, then he said good-bye because he had to go and visit his aunt. I saw him to the door and at the last minute, he took a little square box out of his pocket, gave it to me and said, "Oh! I'm sorry, I forgot to give this to you. I hope you will like it. I picked it out and I hope very much that . . ."

He stopped, turned red, then said "Good-bye!" and went out. Jack had never talked that much to me before and I was very much surprised, although I would like to know what it is he hopes I will do. The gift is a very pretty little brooch decorated with a little blue butterfly, and of course when he came back the next day, I thanked him. He didn't answer, but he dared to look at me, a little astonished. Poor Jack! I don't understand what has happened to him.

Conversation

Maman: Joaquinito, was it you who took a razor or something like that and cut the curtain and bedspread and scratched the table in the upstairs bedroom?

Joaquinito: Yes, Maman.

Thorvald: Oh, that's great.

Anaïs: Marvelous.

Maman: You will be punished, as you deserve to be. You get naughtier every day and perhaps later on the good Lord will punish you.

Joaquinito (mocking): Since Jesus forgave the men who crucified him, won't he forgive me, since I don't do anything *very* bad, do I?

(General astonishment. Thorvald is the first to come to himself and expose the false logic.): The men who crucified Jesus Christ didn't know what they were doing, but you know perfectly well!

Joaquinito (calmly): I don't know perfectly well, I'm too little.

Anaïs: Joaquinito, you are very stupid.

No one has an answer to that. Silence for two minutes, then the conversation takes another tack, quieter and more interesting. Joaquinito, who can't think of anything else to do, puts salt into Maman's glass; she doesn't notice. Tragi-comic result: Joaquinito goes without dessert.

So as not to have to fold his napkin, he hides it under the table. Monsita finds it and doesn't say anything; she is really too nice. . . .

For dessert we have "Turrón,"[1] and I like it enormously.

Maman: "You can't deny your Catalan blood, my daughter."

Everyone laughs. I don't answer, I just take another piece.

The telephone rings and we leave the table, each one going about his business. After answering the phone, which was for one of the roomers, I sit down to write. It is only 9:30, but everyone is sound asleep.

December 29. Maman doesn't feel well and has gone to bed. I spent the day reading, then we had supper downstairs, in the kitchen, so the conversation wasn't very interesting, especially since Maman wasn't there.

This evening, we went up to the empty room and played "Theatre." Then since we couldn't think of a play to put on, I told my two little devils a story. When I tell them a story, I amuse myself by letting my face represent what I am describing, and at the same time I watch their faces for signs of attention and interest. Sometimes I succeed, other times their faces look tired, but today they were interested the whole time and I was very pleased.

I went out for just a moment today, and without the help of a barometer, I could feel the intense dampness and terrible cold. The temperature on the American scale was between zero and 1 or 2 degrees all day long, according to the newspaper that I have just spent a moment reading.

Tomorrow I am going to Communion. I am trying very hard to make my soul as religious and as pious as it used to be, and that is how I go about it. Tomorrow I shall ask God to stop the "thing" that I just read a description of in the newspaper. I shall pray for the end of this war, this time of misfortune.

I have only 2 days left to think because I promised my diary to say, on January 1, which vocation I plan to follow, to say in which role and which dress I am going to make my pilgrimage, to

[1] *Almond paste, hard or soft, traditional at Christmas in Spain and Spanish-speaking countries.*

say how I shall fill the passing years, which become the past and which must be filled.

December 31. What cold weather! We have a few logs burning in the fireplace and we spend the day sitting around the fire. And we think we are very lucky to have coal, as there is a scarcity of that precious substance and the misery that prevails in many places is pitiful to see—people die of the cold—people leave their homes where they can't live and walk the streets or try to find lodging with their families, families burn their furniture in the fireplaces to keep the children warm, and at the same time they are poor and have almost nothing to eat.

It's dreadful. It's so sad.

They say that millions of people, with tears running down their faces, have begged God to take pity on their misery.

And the cold continues in spite of everything. The newspapers are full of news of fires everywhere, of the war, of death. . . . We shall remember always! always!

Tomorrow a new year begins: 1918. What will our destiny be?

1918

We turn toward you,
New Year!
We listen to your voice,
New Year!
Let your eyes bring,
New Year,
A look of hope, never too old,
New Year,
Full of light for us,
New Year,
Of happiness so dear to us,
New Year.
Give us, give us victory,
New Year,
And to our enemies, a black hell,
New Year!
May you be
The last they ever see;
May your joyful songs
Let us laugh at them,

And may death smile at them,
New Year!

Yesterday, the day it was so cold, the conversation at supper wasn't interesting. We had almost nothing to say, as the cold obliged us to eat in silence to try to keep warm, to look like living creatures.

Tomorrow I shall write in my new diary, my new friend, and today is the last day that I have the right to say silly things. My pencil goes from one side of the paper to the other, stops from time to time, to make little drawings on the blotter, and sometimes to plunge head first into the inkwell. But what's the matter? What a funny pencil! . . . Ah, I understand. Suiting the gesture to the phrase, I just dipped it in the inkwell. Should I laugh? I think so. Let's go on: I was talking about my pencil which wanders around, writing in my diary all the silly things that go through my head.

Ah, that head! Right now it's empty, at other times it's full. It's the strangest thing that the Good Lord could have put on my shoulders. A long face that gets longer according to circumstances, that gets shorter while one side of it turns red, or blue, or green, as the case may be. A head partly covered with brown hair that should have been located somewhere else so that it would be easier to comb.

There is nothing to say about the nose that emerges too abruptly from the changeable side, nor about the two rabbit eyes which, like all shameless ones, seem to have made their neighbors move over to make room for them, nor about the mouth which is always opening (to yawn); and still in the same hemisphere, about the two ears, always alert, half open, and always ready to learn, who behave like two well brought up little girls wearing an interested expression, but strangely silent.

Ah, that head! All the rest is nothing when one tries to look inside. It isn't the nose nor the mouth nor the eyes nor the ears nor the hair that frighten you, but that brain! That brain! made of an unknown substance, afflicted with a sickness, as unknown as the patient, who lies on a bed, miserably empty and deprived of her four portable instruments.

Alas! The chaos is too dark, let's close the eyes and not look any more. . . .

Ah, that head! Why must we have that capricious little world set on our honest shoulders, our poor honest shoulders which struggle with their neighbors (kicking).

Mon chat
130
110
100
700
800
$18.40
Pain!!
notre Maison
ICE
Joachim
Grand Mère
ou
Anaïs
ma tasse de lait
ma maison
Joachim
Ecole
L'Etude
Les leçons

Ah, that head! Always awake, never asleep, tomb of words, cradle of ideas, like a poor bird without wings! Ah, that head!

I certainly am taking advantage of my last "intimate conversation" with my diary.

Now, I take my old, old notebook, my old friend, and kiss it once, twice, then close it gently, letting an artificial tear fall on its pages. . . .

And I take leave of it!

Your devoted, memorable, affectionate friend

Anaïs

Tomorrow, I shall come face to face with my frightfully serious new friend. My hand trembles. . . .

❧ *1 9 1 8* ❧

January 8.

Dearest Papa,

I really don't know how to begin my letter, because once again I am going to talk to you about myself, and I do that when I don't know anything about you.

I received the two beautiful books that you sent us, Les Contes de Ma Grand-mère[1] and Japon,[2] for which I thank you very, very much. Then I waited a few days for a letter from you, but nothing came. I shall console myself by writing to you.

Did you receive my last letter, written at Christmas?

How did you spend Christmas?

I thought about you often over the holidays; more often, to be exact, for I think about you every day of the year.

I am not going to tell you about our Christmas. We had just as nice a time as last year, we received many presents, everything was the same, but in spite of everything, we were very happy.

January 19.

Dearest Papa,

It is with a great deal of joy that I start this letter over in answer to your postcard, a little proof of my gratitude for the books that

[1] Grandmother's Stories, *probably* Contes d'une Grand'mere, *by George Sand.*
[2] Japan.

we received and shared, but above all as a proof that I don't forget you.

I shall begin by talking about the books. Your choice was excellent, the books are beautiful and very interesting. For myself, I thank you very much. Your picture gave me a lot of pleasure too, and the little card which said, "Forward, Frenchmen!" made me smile with pride and hope.

How did you spend Christmas?

In answer to the question that I imagine I hear, I shall tell you that our Christmas was just as pleasant, just as enjoyable as last year's. No need to describe the big lighted tree laden down with pretty things, the tree that we have never failed to have since we were born, nor the happy faces, the shining eyes, the happiness that filled us all, nor the many beautiful gifts given and received, for that would be a description of the same beautiful picture where you are the only one missing, and perhaps your imagination provides a better picture of Christmas than any I can draw.

Here are the events that have taken place on our battlefield (school): 1. Battle of examinations and the Germans won, leaving all of us in bad shape. 2. Battle against the coal shortage, in which the general told his soldiers that there is a faint hope of Peace (Vacation). Result: three truckloads of coal arrive, the battle is won by the Germans (teachers), and school continues.

Oh! Papa, what do you think of me? But that's really what happened, described exactly as it seems to me. But so you will know that I don't always say silly things, I am going to talk to you very, very seriously. I am going to tell you a little story that you must believe, but first there is a preface.

Will you please look back a few years and try to remember your schooldays? Did you always behave perfectly? Did you always know your lessons? Did you always feel like studying? I don't know what you answered. If you weren't always good, you won't care, but if you were always a "model" student, you will be ashamed of what I am going to tell you. Joaquinito and I leave the perfect lessons and the "model" conduct to Thorvald, the studious one. I don't know how it happens, but I don't always know my lessons (nor does Joaquinito) and frequently I feel like turning into a problem child and playing mean tricks on my teachers, who with their impassibility and their eternal sermons, sometimes seem like cardboard dolls. But I refrain and, as you see, I am considered a very well-behaved girl who studies hard and does very well. Only, as you see, I am sincere and I don't mind if my

Papa knows that his daughter is a model of good conduct, kindness, and above all, sweetness.

Speaking of sweetness, Papa, does it please you to know that I resemble you very, very much and, to be precise, in almost everything?

But don't pass judgment yet, Papa. I can't help it, the connection between my pen and my brain is too good. My pen follows all the detours in my thinking.

But let's return to my little story. You already know the kind of work I do in school, and really, you have no idea how much good it does me; later I shall explain why. This month I had a "C" (that's the kind of grade they give in public school, A, B, C). Well, there are two letters ahead of "C" that are much better for several different reasons, and since "C" is the easiest grade to get, 2/3 of the class got it.

One of the girls came up to me after school and asked me what grade I had. I answered proudly, with a little regret: "C." She then wiped the tears which were dripping from the end of her nose and said, with a smile spreading across her face, "If you have a C, I don't mind having one. I'll tell my mama and she won't scold me, since *you* got one too."

Now comes the explanation. I had noticed that the girls who received A enjoyed the admiration of the cardboard dolls, but they are a small group, set apart from the rest of the class because they are serious, even grumpy, and disliked by the other girls, as all model children always are. Take a class and think of it as a country; those girls are the kings, the rulers who enjoy the respect of the crowd, sometimes the friendship and fear of the populace. If you study a king, he has nothing but his intelligence and his sword, his title and perhaps his patriotism. That's all.

Turn to the crowd, and there you can study tears and laughter, suffering, ignorance, poverty and riches, the struggle of ambitious men, the failure of the good-for-nothing, real true life, the true soul of the country, the child who must be raised, the people.

With whom would you rather live? For my part, I prefer to live with the people, and since I want to tell them something, I shall help to raise them up, but I shall be careful not to act like a king.

You are wondering what that has to do with school. A "C" puts me in with most of the class, makes me a sister, and I gently win the confidence of my little "people," I help them without their being aware of it, they think I know as little as they and they are right, but slowly I shall rise above them and they will follow; and when I arrive where I want to arrive, they will think: "There's a girl who got 'C' and yet, if she were still in school, she would get an 'A.' She was no more intelligent than we, so I can do the same thing and I will."

And I shall pour words into the ears of my friends, whereas if I had an "A," the people would say: "She was the brightest one in the class, that's why." That's not surprising and they wouldn't listen to me, they would treat me as if I were a king, who has only his intelligence and his sword, his title and perhaps his patriotism.

Don't be afraid, Papa, it isn't my funeral oration that I am chanting.

Socrates said, "The heart's logic is not in harmony with that of the mind." But the logic I gave you is in harmony with both faculties, I assure you, even if it took the form of a funeral oration. But enough silliness.

Day before yesterday, we went to Aeolian Hall to hear Joseph Bonnet[1] play the organ. When I came home from school, I found your letter and put it in my pocket (don't be angry). After hearing Mr. Bonnet, who played magnificently, we were obliged to put up with a singer who had a sore throat and an accompanist who had rheumatism in both arms, so without making any noise, I took out your letter. I opened it and read it, and in that way I spent an agreeable quarter of an hour, then I put it back in my pocket when Mr. Bonnet and a group of violinists appeared. Afterward, we went backstage and Maman introduced us to Mr. Bonnet, who said to Joaquinito, "Do you like Catalan songs?" And Joaquinito, who always has an answer said yes.

This letter is getting too long and yet I have written only foolishness, so I hug you tight and promise to write you seriously very soon.

Sincerely, yours truly, with her head in a very bad state,

Anaïs.

[A manuscript volume of the diary covering the period from January 1918 to March 1919 was lost. The next volume resumes one month after A.N.'s sixteenth birthday.]

---

[1] *Famous French organist, composer of organ pieces based on Catalan folk songs.*

❧ *1 9 1 9* ❧

March 22. I have just opened a new notebook and made a new friend. I have just closed a notebook which is already full, and here I am face to face with one with blank pages to fill, and I hope with all my heart to be able to write things in it that I shall never be ashamed of. After a few days, dear new notebook, you will know me very well and will become acquainted with my ideas and the meanderings of my mad imagination. I shall try to write faithfully and sincerely every day and you will take your place with my other diaries, filed under the same name and written with the same pen, next to the old red notebook that I have just finished. I should begin by telling you the state of things around me today and my occupations. Monsita, who has been sick these last days with a bad cold, got out of bed today for the first time and the house is running smoothly again. The weather today was beautiful; Thorvald and I went to the park and walked in the warm sunshine and talked together for a good fifty minutes.

After lunch we took Joaquinito to the cinema, and the rest of the afternoon I played with my little canary. After dinner I sat down to write, as I do every evening. Frances[1] just called me. We are going out together on Tuesday, which will be a holiday because the 27th Regiment of American soldiers is going to parade on 5th Avenue in front of millions of spectators. She also wants to start a correspondence in verse and that idea strikes me as very amusing. This evening she is going to write to me. I shall let you see my reply.

I notice that it is now only 7:15 and I am going to take advantage of the time to write Papa.

Dearest Papa,
After having written you several times without an answer, I have gone two months without writing, as your continued silence seems unexplainable and disheartening. Sometimes I am afraid that you have forgotten us a little bit, and yet you say yourself, in the last letter that I had from you, which dates back to Christmas, that you are working and traveling. Grandmother makes me feel even

---

[1] *Frances Schiff, a classmate.*

more worried when she writes us long letters and never talks about you. So you will understand that it is with a heavy heart that I am going to try to tell you about the things we are doing these days.

To begin with, my elementary schooling has come to an end. After passing the examinations that I was so afraid of, I changed schools, and from now on I am called Miss Nin and I am a young lady. The school I go to now is Wadleigh High School. It is a huge brick building with big classrooms and many teachers. We have been given many books and I am starting to study French, science, literature and composition, the inevitable algebra, and other things. No doubt, knowing that I am studying French will please you very much, also knowing that I have a marvelous teacher, Mrs. Cavalier, from whom I expect to learn a lot. Even as I write this, I am thinking about my verbs and trying to write them as I should, but please don't smile, Papa, because I know that I still make terrible mistakes.

Thorvald does very well in school. He has grown a lot, but he is still strong and healthy. Both boys are going to write you this very minute and tell you all they are doing.

February 21 was my birthday, and I would like to tell you about it in just the same way that I described it in my diary. Here is how I was dressed: "A pretty light-blue dress, the shoulders covered with a big piece of blue tulle that made a charming effect. I wore silk stockings and narrow little shoes, also a coral necklace that Maman had given me for the occasion, and my hair was pulled back in a chignon of curls with a narrow blue ribbon around my head. As guests, we had my friends from school and, for the first time, a few young men. Among other things, we pretended to know how to dance and the rest of the party turned into a real dance. I was delighted and I danced a lot. I was spoiled, I received a large number of gifts and compliments."

But that wasn't my only dance in two months. I have been to 2 or 3 little dances since then and had a lovely time. In just a short time, I have met very nice young men of my age. Once I met one who is an artist. He wants to study in the Latin Quarter of Paris, and he seemed very interesting. Of course we talked about books, art, etc.

Along with those evenings of pleasure, there are days of misery when my poor tired imagination in its harsh prison is tortured by that awful algebra. Do you like algebra, Papa dear? One day the teacher took me aside and announced calmly something that I already knew: that I have no common sense! At first I was very unhappy and said to myself: "Without that, I might as well jump in the river." But afterward, I thought: "Who ever heard of a philosopher or poet who had common sense?" So I am content.

The other day I read "Un Philosophe Sous les Toits"[1] and I hope you will read it, it's wonderful. But I'm sure that you must have read it already.

Before finishing this letter, I want to beg you to write to me, even if only a few lines. They would give me such great pleasure and would let me stop thinking that you have forgotten your little girl who loves you with all her heart.

March 23. I have just spent a terribly monotonous day. The weather outside is beautiful but I can't go out because there is an advertisement in the newspaper and people are coming to see the rooms. I am reading a book by Charles Dickens, "Hard Times," but I don't like it.

This morning we went to Mass and took Communion; then we read the newspapers, which are terribly stupid and uninteresting. I learned that Maeterlinck has remarried and other things of that sort, and all that put me in a bad humor; at any rate I had better not write any more so as not to write disagreeable things.

March 27. At exactly 3 o'clock, it began to rain buckets. The steady rain lasted all the rest of the day and even now, as I write, at 10 at night, I hear the wind rattling the windows and the dripping of the rain. The day went as usual. Only I mustered my little bit of courage to put one of the poems that I wrote during the algebra lesson into an envelope. Tomorrow, I believe I'll *try* to put it into the letterbox of the Editor of our school's "Owl." I can already see myself with my pitiful verses, enduring all the tortures of shyness and fear of ridicule that are felt by a poor bluestocking who tries to astonish the world with her genius. It's comical! Maman hasn't read it and I wish she were here right now to give me advice on a case such as this.[2] I shall let you know what happens.

Tomorrow I also have my dancing lesson, the 4th one, and I am thinking about it a little, very little, almost not at all. That doesn't keep me, however, from being continually embarrassed

[1] A Garret Philosopher.
[2] *Mrs. Nin was on a trip to Cuba.*

because somebody in the family saw me as I danced with myself all around the house, accompanying myself with songs and also acting as the orchestra. Just the same, I don't like it too much when I think about it, because I am no longer Anaïs Nin but "Miss Nin." That makes a big difference, you know!

March 28. There was an assembly at school, as there is every Friday, at which we got a long lecture about our health and cleanliness.

The dancing lesson was very funny. I was only sorry that a boy I often dance with and like very much wasn't there. Perhaps it was because of the weather, as it is snowing hard outside and the wind howls and blows the snow into our faces. An umbrella does no good. But I didn't miss going. I know the fox trot, the waltz, the one-step, the two-step and several other dances very well. I danced with one fellow who kept saying: "What the deuce!" which means something worse than "Que diable!" in French. Another one danced very badly, another came from Oklahoma and detests New York, but they are all very dumb. When we rest, the conversation is horribly stupid. When we dance, it's better not to talk for fear of making a mistake.

I walked Frances to the Subway, struggling to keep my umbrella open, and people must have thought that under the umbrella there was one person with four feet. Natalie [Lederer] didn't come and we decided to take away her title of Musketeer because she isn't brave enough to keep on trying to learn to dance. So there are 2 musketeers instead of 3 who keep up a mad correspondence to the great joy of the postmen (I think).

Instead of reading all the time, I now take more pleasure in writing my own silly things. I confided in Eleanor about my lack of nerve and she saw to it that I put the lamentable poem in the box where it belonged. Now I am waiting!

I am still class president, but I fear I shall never get rid of my shyness, my way of blushing deeply whenever I hear anything vulgar, and my fear of being severe and unfair. Recently I discovered a new flaw in my nature and my disposition: I can't make people obey and respect me, I don't know how to command a crowd or a class, which is the same thing. That makes me very sad. Each day I feel more uncomfortable with the atmosphere of independence which reigns in the whole school, the lack of respect for the teachers, the disobedience, and especially with how little the teachers have to say, how little their ideas weigh compared to the weight of the ideas of an entire class of ignorant girls. I learn things that I don't want to learn, and sometimes I am afraid of losing entirely the delicate and exquisite mental picture that I have of the beauty of things around me, because I find myself in contact with the ugliest side of life . . .

That's why I often dream, or when I'm not dreaming, I listen in silence, I smile ironically, I write face to face with reality disguised in a costume that disfigures it and turns it to ridicule. Some lessons are very hard to learn and cost a lot, and yet, although I know I am paying the price, I can't learn the lesson. What to do?

Oh, I wish Maman would come home soon, soon! When she is here, I don't think of all those things. When she is happy, I wear rose-colored glasses, I think as she thinks, I imitate the way she has of accepting things as they come, I never worry about tomorrow. But when she goes away! . . . Patience, I know she will be back in 2 weeks. Two weeks! I might as well say two centuries, two eternities! Oh, what a life it is without Maman!!!

March 29. I have just done my homework very carefully, summoning all the patience that I need each time that I do it, and now I have a few minutes of peace. I want to describe here a tiny battle with myself because it shows better than anything what my disposition is like and the kind of struggle that I have with my conscience.

It was this morning. I had just taken out of my dear bookcase one of the books that I bought for ten cents, "Silas Marner," and with all the joy that I always feel at the idea of being able to savor a book, I had settled down comfortably at the living room window. Then I noticed that Thorvald's bed wasn't made. At first I sat down without worrying about it and tried to read, but the unmade bed kept going through my mind. I told myself it didn't matter, that the maid could make it, that it wasn't my bed, etc., but all the time I went on knowing that I should make that bed. Finally, with a sigh of regret at having to put off my reading, I got up and made the bed as well as I could. Then when I sat down to read, I was satisfied. Alas! Why did I hesitate between duty and pleasure? It was only a book and an unmade bed, and yet, I hesitated.

March 30. Today all the clocks were set ahead one hour, in order to economize light. By the new time, we got up at 9 o'clock to go to Mass at 10. On the way back, we bought some newspapers to help pass the time, the long hours of Sunday. We had lunch at one o'clock and half an hour later I left to meet Frances, with whom I had an appointment. First we walked from 112th Street to 77th Street, where there was a very good film. We walked fast and there weren't many people on Broadway at that time of day. About 6 we came out of the theatre and once again walked up Broadway as far as her house, and this time Broadway was full of people of every kind. That's what I want to try to describe.

It was cold and rather windy but the sun shone on the wide avenue, which presented an absolutely comical spectacle. There were many, many people. I can't describe the men, who were of all ages and dressed in every possible way, but the *women!* Heavens! The fashion these days looks a little like this:

We saw all those ladies walking with little tiny steps. They almost all looked like painted dolls. Each was surrounded by several men and they looked terribly artificial. The more extravagantly they were dressed, the more attention they got from the opposite sex, which would stop walking to admire them. Some of the men stroll around on the street corners and stand there to watch the people go by. Then when a "lady" comes along, they follow her. It was all very funny and very dumb at the same time. Broadway looked like a parade of dolls on the stage of the Grand Theatre. Just as onstage, everyone was artificial and silly, each one playing his rôle on Broadway and walking the way people walk in a big city like New York, aimlessly and going nowhere, made up for the play and disguised for the eternal masquerade.

March 31. Today I had the good news that I have been promoted to a higher French class. After three o'clock, we played basketball, and the desperate struggle to catch that silly ball, the whole game in all its stupidity absolutely disgusted me. I came out of it with bruises and the memory of the unbearable behavior of some of the girls. I came home at 5:30 and found a letter from Frances to console me. This evening she telephoned me to ask me for an outing with her tomorrow. Tomorrow we are also going to have an examination in algebra.

April 1. We had the examination. It was unavoidable. I know all too well the miserable grade that I am going to get on that big sheet of yellow paper full of numbers and unintelligible letters. The worst of all was having to write my poor and honorable name on that shameful paper. But an hour later, I had forgotten all about it, I was walking near the stream in the park with my friend Frances, talking and walking happily. The weather was beautiful. After having walked through the park, we strolled along Broadway. At that hour there were many young men carrying books, students, no doubt. During the entire walk, whenever we met them, I lowered my eyes, as I am accustomed to do, which made Frances laugh. Afterward, we danced at her house, just the two of us, and then I came home, very happy.

April 2. A lovely day tempted Eleanor and me to do our lessons in the park. The wind, or rather the warm breeze, kept blowing our papers away and it was funny to have to run after them. Eleanor helped me do, or rather, did my algebra lesson, while I watched her instead of thinking about my lesson. She made such a pretty picture, with her pretty golden hair shining in the sunlight and her clear blue eyes worrying over the problem she was trying to work.

Just today I was put into the second term of French by Mrs. Cavalier, who thinks that I can be advanced. I now have a teacher named Miss Gelbach and I am prepared to study hard. Notice the improvement in my spelling, if you please.

April 3. Eleanor and I have decided that we would do better to give up the dancing class that is given every Thursday after school, because it deprives us of one of our few hours of freedom. Furthermore, by that time of day we are very tired. After having given some sort of excuse, we left school and took a leisurely walk home.

Right now I am thinking about that dancing lesson. I am also thinking of something else. Do you remember Mr. Walker? I hope so. Although I have seen him only once, he is an artist and a friend of mine (who doesn't know it). I remember he told me he danced one dance in a musical comedy called "Maytime," and yesterday for the first time I noticed big placards announcing "Maytime," and that made my heart flutter. It's strange to know someone who is on the stage, which apparently is full of actors who don't have at all the same kind of life as we.

April 4. Today's dancing lesson was very amusing, as it always is. I couldn't dance very often with Frances because I suddenly found myself continually invited by the opposite sex. I tried to discover the reason. I thought it might be my nationality, because a Parisian is always fussed over here as an object of curiosity. Frances completed the confusion that I felt all over by referring to my popularity and saying it was because I was the prettiest girl there. That was very nice, but my mirror doesn't lie and always reflects an image that I recognize as mine, and whose lack of charm I know only too well. When we left, the young men were standing on the street corner and as Frances, Dorothy Eddins and I went by, they raised their hats as though they were gentlemen and not just youngsters.

Oh no, dearest diary, I am not afraid of gentlemen. When I think of those I know, with their glances and childish grins, I am filled with a great feeling of tenderness, as if they were all just my little brothers who need smiles and loving care. They aren't ogres but princes as in the fairy tales, and they are all looking for princesses because their father, the king, wants them to marry. The world is full of those princes, although they aren't all brave and handsome. The world is full, too, of princesses who are waiting. Oh, if the world were really like that, a big garden full of flowers eternally in bloom, beautiful juicy fruits, with a lovely pink and blue sky above! A garden full of birds and butterflies, music and dreams, where everything is beautiful and pure! A garden full of princes and princesses who can love each other faithfully and rule like kings over their own hearts! Under a sun that shines all day long and a moon that lights the night, while a thousand stars twinkle in endless space!

April 5. As it has been raining monotonously since I opened my eyes at 9 this morning, the day was spent like certain rainy days. After breakfast, I read in a way that I never read; that is, I read the first book I found at hand, and it was a very badly written book. At 1:30 we went to the cinema. When we came home, I sat down to write. I just got up now and left my diary for a moment because Mrs. Carreno,[1] or Mrs. Blois, who are the same person, was playing music that made me want to dance all by myself, as I often do; but she changes every minute (which proves she has no perseverance) and after having danced madly to a Spanish dance with imaginary castanettes, a rose in my teeth, a twirling skirt and a mantilla, also imaginary, like Carmen, I am sitting down again, worn out from dancing, and now I have nothing more to say.

9 o'clock: I have just done my lessons, which reminds me that on that yellow paper I mentioned the other day, I got a grade of 25%. Well done, eh?

When I thought of that, I started to walk from one end of our big room to the other, my hands behind my back and my head down, as I often do when I am preoccupied. What would Papa say? What would all my friends say, and what would everyone who knows me say if they knew that? Because it's truly shameful! 25%!!! Someone once said that when you are dumb, it's for life. If that's true, I don't know what will become of me.

I who was talking a few days ago about princes and princesses! Does a princess have the right to be dumb? But the more I thought about it, the angrier I became with myself, and finally I stopped in front of my bookcase to look for a book to read or reread. I was provoked because it seems to me that I am getting blasé about reading, and I can't find anything that is well written that I haven't already read. So I started to write.

I have just counted the days that Maman has been away from us and according to my calculations she should come back soon because she has been gone a long time; also I think about all the naughty things that Joaquinito, taking advantage of her absence, has done lately. Sometimes he is so naughty that I suddenly run out of strength and patience and I can't help crying; I cry in a way that puts to shame all my resolutions not to give in to tears, which are so weak, and I don't want to cry. Thorvald is often my ally when Maman isn't with me. He is a prankster, but I can do exactly what I want with him, whereas with Joaquinito I give up.

Today, like certain other days, they were selling pretty bouquets of violets in the street. That always makes me dream a little, because I love violets so much but I never have any.

---

[1] *Teresita Carreño, daughter of the Venezuelan pianist, who came to live with the Nins after the death of her mother.*

April 6. Belica [Tallet] came to see her mother[1] and we decided that we would go together to visit Mrs. Godoy,[2] who has just come back from Cuba. Among other things, I learned that she is expecting Maman on the train this evening and I am terribly happy. The rest of the afternoon I walked with Belica on Riverside Drive. We sat on a bench and saw a whole baseball game played by some sailors, who played exactly like children. They played while the sun slowly sank behind the hills on the other side of the river. Then when the great ball of fire had disappeared completely below the horizon and the sky was covered with the most marvelous colors imaginable, suddenly, from an American warship in the middle of the river, came the clear sound of a trumpet. Immediately all the sailors stopped playing, turned as one man toward the flag which floated at the prow of the ship, and saluted as it was lowered. A few minutes later, while the sound of the trumpet still floated lightly in the air, they resumed their game.

On the way home we saw an automobile accident. A beautiful young woman, covered with blood, was placed in the ambulance right in front of us. I almost fainted at the sight of her.

Oh, how many things one sees in the course of a day! How many sublime and beautiful things, how many sad and dreadful things!

April 7. I stayed up late waiting for Maman, but she wasn't here when I woke up. It was only at four o'clock when I came home from school that I found her. During dinner, she told us with great enthusiasm about all the things she did in Havana. We listened open-mouthed, hardly finding time to eat and to ask as many questions as we wanted to. But of course Maman was tired, and all the chatter had to stop when she went to bed, while we did our lessons for tomorrow.

April 8. At school we are going to put on a play from Roman times and I had to stay after school to study my part. It is a very small part because the director, Dorothy Eddins, discovered that I can't act mean and cruel or speak harshly to anyone; it's absolutely impossible! So finally I have the part of an old woman. I, who am such a good actress when I am alone in front of the mirror, find I am a mediocre good-for-nothing in a real play.

French is going well, algebra worse than bad, and as for the rest, who cares?

[1] *Isabel Duarte.*
[2] *Julia Cordovés de Godoy, wife of the poet Armand Godoy.*

Ah, yesterday in my haste I forgot to write that I received a gift from Godmother: a delightful yellow, brown and black canary who sings very well. Right now he is singing an accompaniment to the scratching noise of my pen.

Everything seems beautiful to me today. Maman is back with us.

April 9. Maman took me downtown and bought me a pretty serge cape, patent-leather shoes, black silk stockings and gloves, and we came home very happy. As for school, I am in despair. To be surrounded by so many people, so many teachers, who are hard-hearted and have neither delicacy nor anything human, puts me in a horrible state. But why talk about a nightmare?

April 11. I wore my cape and my beautiful new shoes for the first time, which meant that I went to my dancing lesson putting on more airs than usual. Frances doesn't go any more, alas, but Dorothy was there and the two of us were pleased to find that we could dance together only once. I danced with Mr. Duryea[1] himself, who dances wonderfully, of course. Afterward, I left with Dorothy, who invited me to dinner, and it was raining when we left school. I met Dorothy's charming mother and nice brother; to be brief, I thought it was a very nice evening. We went to the theatre, where one thing almost spoiled our good time: we saw a poor man with an attack of "epilepsy."

I am going to bed, happy at the idea that vacation begins tomorrow.

April 15. If I wasn't able to write yesterday because of the uproar from Thorvald and Joaquinito, today I can hardly write for almost the same reason. Joaquinito is practicing the piano, which means that from time to time the listener hears discords and unbearable sounds coming from the unfortunate instrument.

Maman has resumed her routine: she left this morning about 10 and didn't come back until the midday meal. While she was gone, I tried to surprise her by making her a hat with all kinds of things that I found, but after looking at it critically, Maman consoled me by saying that although it was well done, the hat was too old to be refurbished.

Joaquinito wasn't feeling very good and since he was in bed, I had to satisfy all his requests and demands. On top of that, it was raining, so the day was rather fruitless.

[1] *The dance teacher.*

April 17. I went to the library and brought back several books. The rest of the day I took care of Joaquinito, who is still pretending to be sick. I keep making plans for the future without school, because Maman will allow me to leave. Oh! how glad, how glad, how glad I am! To leave all those teachers who are about as human as blocks of marble, leave that school full of unaccountable and inexcusably grotesque girls, leave the routine of a coarse education, leave the lessons, algebra and all the rest that goes with Wadleigh High School! Happy? I am more than happy, I am dizzy, overcome with so much good fortune!

April 18. Maman took Frances, Joaquinito and me downtown to lunch and then to the cinema. We wanted to go to the Barnum and Bailey Circus, but there were no seats, so we had to content ourselves with Mae Murray in "A Delicious Little Devil" and the inevitable Charlie Chaplin in one of his ridiculous comedies. On the way home, Joaquinito and I stopped at church to pray for a moment, then walked slowly home because the weather was beautiful today and I took pleasure in letting my cape float in the breeze. It's a feeling that always makes me think of poets. And then a cape can make you believe that you are someone powerful like Napoleon, or a queen with a cloak of diamonds and rubies, or just a girl dressed "in the fashion of France" (as the song says).

April 19. At 10 o'clock I was at Frances's house. We went rowing for an hour, and in the remaining time before lunch we walked peacefully in the park, which was very beautiful today with all the trees budding and some of them covered with flowers. After lunch we went to a theatre that, as Frances explained, is very popular with "youth," that is, for example, the girls and boys who were at the dance she gave and at Albert Rosette's party. Also she told me in advance that we were going to see a "matinee idol," a dancer that *several* of her friends (even Natalie) are in love with. Heavens! How can I write the silly things she told me! Fortunately, to make up for all this, which will lead you to believe I am having one of my attacks of frivolity, I can admit quite sincerely that I thought the show abominable. Natalie had opera glasses through which I could view George White,[1] the favorite, very clearly, and I saw that he is only very handsome but dances rather badly. However, he had a thousand times more applause than a young man who followed him, who danced much better but didn't have such an agreeable face. Which proves . . . You can guess.

[1] *Producer of* George White's Scandals.

After that silly thing, we did another by walking up Broadway listening to Natalie talk about it! Finally I came home, very glad to find my calm house in its usual place, after so much vanity and uproar and feminine foolishness.

Among other things, this morning, when we were serious, I talked to Frances about my diary, after she told me that there are often things she would like to tell to a good listener. She is interested in the idea and on the way home, she bought a notebook. That's a good sign!

April 20. Easter Sunday! After a fervent Communion, an ample breakfast, an Easter egg hunt, a walk in the park and lunch, I was alone with Maman and Sunday went by, slow and melancholy. From time to time I looked out the window to see the people walking by, as it was a wonderful day, fair and warm. But it was impossible to go out. I didn't want to leave Maman alone, and there was Monsita to be cared for, Monsita who has been in bed for 6 or 7 days, looking so little and thin, with tonsillitis. She is having a lot of pain. This very day, Dr. Murray had to come and lance an abscess which was making it hard for her to breathe.

In the street, all the ladies have new hats, pretty straw hats with flowers, like mine. As for the gentlemen, I don't know and didn't notice. I also read "Lucrezia Borgia," "Marie Tudor," and "Angelo" [in one volume] by Victor Hugo. It wasn't a cheerful book, of course, but I liked it a lot and I didn't know what to do when I got to the last page, when all those people that I liked—Lucrezia, Tisbe and Gennaro—had been killed.

Maman has written the letter that will give me my freedom. Here is a copy:

My dear Miss Hart (the algebra teacher)
  Wishing that my daughter Anaïs may continue her studies at home, she will not attend school hereafter.
                              Sincerely
                                R. C. Nin

Tomorrow I go for the last time. I won't miss anyone except Mrs. Cavalier, Miss Gelbach, Mr. Cornich and perhaps Miss Hart herself, but not what she teaches. I leave the rest of it with the greatest pleasure in the world, the pleasure that a prisoner feels on leaving his prison after a sentence of a thousand years.

April 21. It's done! Everything went calmly. I met Eleanor as usual, and once we reached school, I presented my letter, feeling rather moved. Each teacher said something, sometimes nice, sometimes disagreeable, about the dubious success of my education at home. At 9:40 I was on my way home in the subway. The weather was warm, I was happy. Today I had to take care of Monsita, so I could only straighten up a few cupboards and put my things in order to please Maman. I also painted a flowerpot and planted some flowers in it.

Mrs. Madriguera and her daughter Paquita[1] have come back from Spain and are staying here with us, which means that Enrique Madriguera often comes over. He always has the air of an artist in search of a bluebird. . . .

Godmother writes that she is sailing on May 8. Such a lot of good news for one day!

April 22.
Dear little Papa,
Your letter came at last. If you knew how I waited for it and all the pleasure it gave me, you would understand why my letters were becoming infrequent. The only way I had of knowing more or less where you were was by Grandmother's letters from Liège, but now I also know that you weren't able to go back to Paris, as well as your plans for the future. You seem to be very busy and I am very proud of all the engagements that you have these days.

Thorvald and Joaquinito read your letter. I don't mean that Joaquinito *read* it; he doesn't read French very well and, like almost all artists, he is too stubborn to study it. As for Thorvald, he always gets mixed up in speaking French; when he had finished your letter, he wanted to talk about the part where you spoke of Grandfather's "indisposition" and he called it "indigestion."

Just now we have no pictures to send you; later I shall take some, as the weather outside is starting to be very nice, long spring days that are turning into summer.

You spoke about our studies. I have a bit of news to give you that is going to surprise you: I have left school. Now, as the philosophers say, everything has a cause, a reason for being. It's a long story. The school was dreadful. You will answer, no doubt, that has nothing to do with education; but the education was as bad as

---

[1] *A student of Enrique Granados who later married Andrés Segovia. Enrique Madriguera was her brother.*

the rest. Alas! We had some teachers who had been teaching for 18 or 20 years and who had lost, or never had, *all* the sensitivity, kindness, patience and humanity that a woman needs to be a good teacher, of whom sensitive people aren't afraid; for when I received a reprimand, deserved or not, just or unjust, I trembled like a leaf and felt very bad. The idea of that school, in general, was independence. Well, what prevailed everywhere was the kind of independence that produces anarchists, Bolsheviks, etc. Everything was ordinary. I was president of my class, and when the teacher left the room, those girls didn't have enough pride or feeling of honor to be quiet. That alone made me terribly indignant. Maman understood it all. I was progressing slowly in French and learning to translate and do other things instead of learning to write, which was what I needed. Algebra was a nightmare for me. In literature, we studied books that I know by heart because I have been reading them ever since I learned to read English easily, and almost all of the other girls were as slow to understand them as I was to understand algebra, which is something just as interesting as literature. Only science was very good. Drawing was merely making rather bad copies, and gymnastics was horrible. I repeat, Maman understood it all, and on Monday I left school forever. There are some people who don't say anything but think a lot and I know they all believe I shall be a dunce. But Maman, who knows me, and you, Papa, who understand me. and all those who know that there are no dunces in my family or among the families of my ancestors, I hope they realize that I shall not be ignorant. I know how to learn and I like to read and study. Maman is going to find a French teacher for me; and as for the rest, I shall be able to manage it very well. Tell me what you think of these arguments.

You ask Thorvald and Joaquinito to write you and they are going to do it. Well, there is nothing more for me to do except hug you tenderly and beg you to continue to write me.

Your fifille who loves you,

Anaïs

April 23. Monsita still hasn't recovered, so I am taking care of her and doing a thousand other things at the same time. There are times when I escape for a moment and run into the garden, where I dig and take care of the soil so that I can plant vegetables and flowers as soon as the frost is completely gone. Among other things, I continue painting in the 20 volumes of the "Book of Knowledge," which amuses me immensely. Enrique Madriguera comes over several times a day, and like the practical joker that he is (like all the Catalans), he tells me that he comes as often as he does because I am the one who opens the door for him. I mend a lot of stockings (stockings that look like sieves) and I sew buttons on everything that needs them.

April 24. Monsita finally got out of bed today for the first time, but she is still very weak. Aunt Edelmira, Nuna and Coquito arrived from New Orleans because Uncle Gilbert has been sent to Mexico. That makes nine at the table, including Nuna's nurse. She is going to stay with us a few days and we are very glad, even if there is a little too much noise and a lot more work.

This morning I got up very early (because Dolly, the other maid, doesn't come before 8:30 or 9) and I made breakfast. I make very bad coffee and I know that the family swallows it out of politeness.

Joaquinito came home today with tears in his eyes because he was so naughty that they made him sit with the girls. And he tells us this, using the polite language of his little friends, who are all real little bandits, frighteningly rude and dirty.

April 25. Yesterday evening, after spending all day from 9 in the morning until 10 at night packing a trunk that Maman has to send to Cuba, she and I were so tired we couldn't fall asleep. So she began to talk to Monsita and me, and little by little she began to talk about herself and about Papa, and she told us a marvelous story, a story of her mad youth when she was beautiful and romantic. A story that convinced me that Maman wasn't always the serious businesswoman she is now, who laughs when someone talks to her about marriage and makes fun of what I take seriously. And here it is: Maman in those days (Maman didn't mention the date) was young, beautiful and admired, and because of Grandfather Culmell's success in business, very much sought after in Cuban society. One day she was out walking with Aunt Edelmira when she wanted to go into a music store belonging to Anselmo Lopez to buy some sheet music. Papa, who was young too in those days, had come to Havana with his mother, after having been obliged to leave Barcelona because he had fallen in love with a young girl who was his pupil and wanted to run away with her, when her brother, who now is married to Papa's sister, had wanted to kill him. At that time, he tried to give concerts in Havana. When Maman came into the store, Mr. Lopez introduced

Papa to her as a young pianist to whom the influence of a young woman of society would be very helpful. Maman and Aunt Edelmira then asked him to play, and after a lot of coaxing, which it still takes (Maman says), he played. Here, I interrupted to ask if he played well. "I'll say," said Maman, with conviction. Then the story continued. Papa was invited to Maman's home and introduced to her friends. He then began to write her in the morning, to come to see her in the afternoon, and to telephone her all the time. Maman left for Matanzas for a while and he continued to write to her. When she returned, he proposed, and Maman, looking at his threadbare coat and trousers, his hair and his blue eyes . . . accepted, to the great distress of the entire family. But it was done.

And then? I asked. They were married and everyone regretted it. And then? But Maman wouldn't say any more.

Then we fell asleep. And I dreamed, a dream that makes me laugh now. I dreamed, and I hardly dare to write it, that I married Enrique. I woke up just at the moment when Maman was telling me that all artists are delightful, but that they don't make good husbands.

Before that, Maman had told us a funny story. It was about her grandparents, Mr. and Mrs. Vaurigaud.[1] Mrs. Vaurigaud had brown hair, blue eyes, and fine-grained, delicate, fair skin. Being so beautiful, she was very much pampered by her husband. He used to get up early in the morning to make coffee for her. It would take him a long time and at last he would bring it to her in bed. Then she would start in:

"Mr. Vaurigaud! What coffee!"

"Mrs. Vaurigaud, I do the best I can. Is it very bad?"

And so on every day:

"Mr. Vaurigaud! What coffee! Mon Dieu . . ."

"But Mrs. Vaurigaud! . . ."

So this morning I carried in the coffee I had made for Maman, saying:

"Mrs. Vaurigaud, here is your coffee."

And Maman answered: "Oh, this coffee is terrible, Mr. Vaurigaud, really terrible!"

But that's not all that I am going to write about today. You know that today was the day of my dancing class. I curled my hair, which looked really very nice, and I put on powder and a tiny bit of rouge because I was so pale—and my blue dress, my new hat, etc.

[1] *Théodore Vaurigaud and his wife Catherine.*

When I arrived, I met Dorothy Eddins and Frances. The dance was very lively. The young man, the only one that I find nice, was back and he danced very often with me. At one point they gave us half of a post card and we had to find the matching half. And it was he who had the other half of mine, so we had to dance together. He told me that he is studying to be a lawyer and asked me if I would bring my cases to him. But it was his last lesson and I don't know his name. He had just told me that he was leaving when we noticed that the piece they were playing was called: "Frenchie, Frenchie, Don't Cry." And that made us laugh.

I came home, walking part of the way with Frances and the rest with two young men. One of them was deaf, or almost, and the other came from Texas. That's all I know about them, and it isn't much.

April 26. Eleanor and Gertrude went to the cinema with us. We saw Mae Murray in "What Am I Bid" and Tom Moore in "A Man and His Money." On the way home, I saw Enrique Madriguera and availed myself of the opportunity to invite him to the reception next Saturday at the home of Duryea, our dancing teacher. The rest of the evening I read a delightful book, "Les Musardises"[1] by Edmond Rostand.

April 27. This morning I got up at 8 to get the breakfast and at 10 Maman and I decided we would go to the cinema together. Just as we went out, we saw the inevitable Enrique who was driving an automobile that he had borrowed from a friend and he invited us to go for a ride. It was magnificent the way he tried to go very fast when anyone got in his way, and the way he managed as soon as possible to drive fast, very fast, as I like to. He was very funny, too, and did nothing but talk and laugh. So far, he does everything that all the other artists do. That's their specialty, I imagine.

At 4:30 he left us at the theatre on 81st Street, and there, Maman and I spent the rest of the afternoon watching a stupid vaudeville and the famous William Hart in "The Poppy Girl's Husband." At 8 o'clock we reached the house to find everyone waiting for us for supper.

April 28. After lunch, I went to the cinema with Eleanor and Gertrude and we saw Sessue Hayakawa in "A Courageous Coward" and Billie Burke in "Good Gracious Annabella," which was very funny. And now I haven't yet had dinner, but I started to write for

[1] Idle Times.

a few minutes to pass the time. I have nothing to read because Maman doesn't want to let me go to the library; it's too late for that. And while I am writing, Maman and Enrique are talking about marriage, so please don't be surprised if I don't write exactly what I am trying to say.

April 30. At 10 o'clock I went to my first French lesson, which was very interesting. I worked in my garden again and read a lot. My life right now is like good weather after a storm. Even if I voluntarily get up very early, the entire day goes by like a delightful dream. I have my freedom, I have my birds, flowers, candy (which sometimes is beautiful . . . to look at), books, drawings to make, a garden to take care of, and lots of ideas. There are no lessons to do in the evening, and I have only one task, that of helping Maman as much as possible with everything. Mrs. Beaulac advised me that one of my weaknesses in French (and there are so many that my poor French can hardly stand on two feet, it limps, and I am very sad) is that I have a very bad way of reading aloud. That comes from my habit of always reading to myself. But in my enthusiasm, I am learning new words. Here is one that I am going to tell you apropos of nothing: Je m'esclaffe;[1] another: tonitruant.[2] I'll use the others I have learned when the time is right. One day my French will be triumphantly resuscitated, because even if it is dead, I haven't buried it yet, you see?

May 1. I got up very early this morning to work in the garden, but it was raining buckets. At 2 o'clock I went to the cinema with Frances and saw Montague Love in "Four Green Eyes" and a very good actress whose name I can't remember in "Totou." When I got home, I was soaked, but afterward I settled down to read and forgot where I was until dinner.

I have just done my French lessons, which are very pleasant, and opened the door for the twentieth time to Mr. Madriguera, who always strikes me as a madman. I would like to see him serious just once, but I begin to think that's impossible for him. I suppose he has already forgotten about the dance on Saturday, whereas I am thinking constantly of that day. But I suppose that I have nothing else to do, while he . . . is an artist.

Emilia Quintero, the famous pianist and old friend of the family, always comes to visit us with a hurricane of compliments;

[1] *I guffaw.*
[2] *Thunderous, noisy.*

she is the only one who thinks I am beautiful, Joaquinito calm, and Thorvald everything that he isn't. She reminded me that it has been a long time since I wrote any poetry, and now I have an idea.

May 2. If I begin to write just now, it isn't exactly because I have anything to say, but I feel a bit lonely. Maman and I have been sitting in the living room, powdered and dressed because we are expecting a visitor, a gentleman whom I don't know. And the living room is "arranged." That is, the chairs, armchairs and sofas are placed in their irrevocable position, looking as though they were waiting for someone to sit on them, and also they look so theatrical and so unnatural when everything is exactly in its proper place, and the fireplace looks like a museum, while the pictures, which never move, give me something or other, a stomachache, no doubt. And since the visitor hasn't appeared, I shall go on . . .

This morning at 10 I went again to Mrs. Beaulac's house for another French lesson. Everything is going well on that front. My garden is almost ready to receive the seeds that I am going to plant

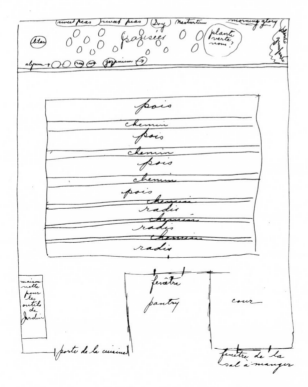

in it. Today I had the painful job of putting fertilizer on the soil; the odor almost made me sick, and now on top of that the whole family shrieks when I walk through the house with a handkerchief "soaked" in Houbigant, my favorite perfume. Well! "This is the life!" as they say here in New York.

The other day I asked Frances, whom I persuaded to start a diary, how it was going. To my surprise, and it was a surprise that made me sad, she told me it wasn't going at all. And suddenly I began to wonder what *I* would do without my diary. Can you answer me that, my faithful confidant? You know who I am, must I tell you again? A poet with a cracked and muddled head, a philosopher who doesn't know anything, a bad pupil and many other things like that. How and to whom could I say everything that goes through my mind? When I am angry, I write and my anger cools; when I am sad, I write and my melancholy wears off; when I am happy, I write, and I am happy every time I reread what I write; when I have no friends, I write, and you are there; when everyone calls me an ignoramus, I write and am consoled; when I bungle a poem, I write and am comforted.

The visitor hasn't come . . . I shall continue. I just discovered that I am still a child. Can you believe that *all day long* I thought about tomorrow's dance? My blue dress is pressed and swinging peacefully on a hanger while I, with my imagination soaring, put myself inside the dress, leave for Duryea's, and dance, dance, dance . . . and yet the dress is still there, perched on the hanger and looking at me, I suppose, the way fools look at an airplane. And the shoes are in my closet, but the same thing happens to them as to the dress. It's unexplainable, laughable, comical, and (here's my new word) "je m'esclaffe"! You see, I am a child, 16 years old!

The visitor hasn't come, Maman makes a face and stands up to go to bed, and I am going to do the same, I think.

May 3. After having thought and dreamed for so long about the dance, as soon as I got there, I relapsed into my "natural" state.

Frances and two young friends of hers came to pick me up at 4:20. The dance was nice, but it seemed long and silly. I don't know if I told you this already, but I had invited Mr. Madriguera to come with me, but he couldn't come today and I was very glad because I don't think he would have had a good time.

Although I put on a lot of powder and rouge, I couldn't hide the big dark circles under my eyes and I was terribly pale, which made me think, because I realize how right Maman is when she says I am not outside enough. And to explain how I looked, I have to mention that Frances said that when she dances with me, she is always afraid of losing me. And a young man said he felt as though he were dancing by himself, because I was so light. And a lot of people look at me as though they think I might evaporate from one moment to the next.

I worked a little in my garden and after dinner I went to confession. One thing weighed heavily on me: I have been very *pleased* about receiving compliments. But the good priest laughed heartily and told me it was nothing at all. On the contrary, he added, it's quite natural. . . .

Now I am going to bed because I am very tired. Without meaning to, sitting here in the living room, I saw myself in the mirror and was surprised to see how pale I am. Yes, I really must go outside and become rosy like Frances.

May 5. The heat continued today and I managed to forget it by reading a book by Jules Verne that described glaciers and the North Pole. Then Mr. Madriguera invited Joaquinito, Coquito and me to go for a ride in the automobile. It was very amusing because he went so fast. We had to return very quickly because the rain came along to spoil things. But it didn't rain long and right now the weather, although cooler, is beautiful again. Now I must leave you to get ready for the concert that Paquita Madriguera is giving this evening.

May 6. The concert last night was memorable. Not only because Paquita played wonderfully and brought down the house, but also because the audience at the Aeolian Concert Hall was made up almost entirely of Catalans and Spaniards, so that it was more like a social gathering than anything. We were in a box with Emilia, Vicente de Sola[1] and Mrs. Pausas. I wore the same dress that I wore the evening of Frances's dance, and everyone kept telling me that I look more like Maman than ever. Last night I was surprised myself at how seldom I blushed and at the calmness and tact with which I greeted all kinds of people who were introduced to me.

After the concert, everyone met in the artists' reception room, where the conversation was a general mixture of rather silly things. We wanted to leave before they turned out the lights, but Emilia's conversation flowed in an interminable stream. At the last minute, I had an opportunity to relax and laugh a lot because

[1] *A family friend, son of Candelaria de Sola.*

when I tried to put on my cape, there were three Catalan gallants who wanted to help me. One of the three acted as spectator while the other two struggled in vain to find the sleeves of a cape that doesn't have any, and it was only after several minutes of mad laughter that I was ready to leave. Paquita's friends assured me that they would do a much better job of helping me next time.

I again saw Mrs. Sarlabous, her husband[1] and her daughter Germaine. I met Mrs. Fitzu,[2] who sings the Goyescas of Granados, and other people whose names I can't recall right now. Enrique Madriguera was there, of course, always laughing and making fun of everything. We had come in a taxi, but an extravagance like that couldn't happen more than once, and to go home we peacefully took the Broadway tramway.

When I left home, I was powdered, painted and curled, and in the mirror I saw Maman's image. When I came back, I was pale, serious, pensive and tired, and my hair was disarranged, and in the mirror I saw Papa's image. It's strange, but I have two different faces and two personalities, also very different. The face that looks like Maman goes with the personality that is sociable, gay, full of the pleasures of dancing and society; and the other one, that of a poet (mediocre), goes with the personality of a philosopher (unsuccessful). You know which one I prefer, everyone knows except the opposite sex, to whom I appear with Maman's face. And I begin really to believe that everyone has two natures, two faces, two personalities, but only one soul and only one conscience. It's curious, and I am going to examine myself carefully to see which one is generally the more pleasing.

Today I went to the cinema with Maman and Joaquinito, and afterward I walked on Riverside until 6 o'clock. We have just had dinner and Joaquinito is taking his piano lesson with Emilia while I write. Enrique Madriguera just went through here like a hurricane, but he took time to make us laugh by having us guess what was missing from his "toilette," and I saw immediately that it was a flower in his buttonhole. Then he said that I should give him one, and I had to decorate him with one of the beautiful red roses that Paquita gave us this morning out of all those that she received last night. And now they have all gone out in the little automobile. And I am smiling as I write all this, knowing very well that every time I talk about Mr. Madriguera, it will be about the crazy things he does and the crazy things he says, because he is nothing but an artist.

[1] *See footnote p. 152.*
[2] *Anna Fitzu replaced Lucrezia Bori in the premiere of Granados's Goyescas.*

P.S. At the cinema, I saw Vivian Martin in "Little Comrade" and "The Test of Honor" with another actor, John Barrymore.

May 9. To my sincere sorrow, I just remembered that we are going to a dance today. That is, I am going to Duryea's, and after having prepared everything joylessly, I sat down to write with a feverish impatience that I can't control. I'm not happy, for you already know that those dances are nothing but child's play that I give in to sometimes when I am like Maman. Sometimes I tell myself that I shouldn't go because it's raining, but something in my economical conscience impels me to take advantage of my last lesson, since I need it.

This morning at 10 I was at Mrs. Beaulac's; she told me she is very pleased to see that I never look at the clock. Thus each day I take great pleasure in seeing my French revive. Little by little, from beneath the dust of memory and many long years, I triumphantly discover a word . . . another word that I shall never forget again. And each word brings back delightful memories of the time when we spoke only French, in Brussels, in Arcachon, etc. I have learned that the tree growing in our garden is called a "frêne."[1] I am reading "Maître Pierre" by Edmond About and the Revue des Deux Mondes.[2] I dream in French, I am speaking better, I am becoming a Parisienne!

May 15. It's a little difficult to explain what I have been thinking about the last few days. I have been living in a strange world, in an attack of reverie, with a change in my character that astonishes me a little. This is the result of the long hours that I spend alone thinking, I suppose. I couldn't write because when I tried to discover what I was dreaming about, I found only a bottomless chasm the depths of which I couldn't sound.

Last night it was hot and I was leaning on the sill of the open window in the living room. Then my imagination got the better of me. A single idea had taken possession of my dreams, a thing I had never, never thought of, an emptiness that I had never felt. I was alone and something was missing. It wasn't the love of my mother, my brothers or the rest of my family; I knew that I wanted someone very strong, very powerful, very handsome who would love me and whom I could love with all my heart. It is an image or an idol that my dreams have created and that I am searching for in mortal form. Does he exist? And there, under the starry sky, the

[1] *Elm tree.*
[2] Two Worlds Review.

smiling moon, face to face with a horizon that doesn't go further than the end of the street, with my head in my hands, I sent a very sad prayer into infinite space: Love me, someone!

I don't understand it at all. I had never been aware of that immense empty space that can only be filled by a Shadow that my mind has created, that my dreams have given a soul.

Then, with a calm smile, thinking no doubt of all the novels I have read, I took a large armchair and set it very close to my chair, and looking into the eyes of the one that my imagination placed there, I talked with him.

May 16. Perhaps it's true that I sometimes seem crazy because I dream a little too much, but there are other days, like today, when I get up in the same state of mind as all the practical and plain people, and spend the rest of the day in a useful and very natural way.

At 10 o'clock I was at Mrs. Beaulac's house with my head full of worries, such as: the price of the eggs I had to buy, the place where I could get the best buy on fruit, etc. At 11 o'clock I came home to find Maman ready to go out to work and I received permission to go with her. I chose one of her purchases, a beautiful sky-blue cape for a customer my age, so I was able to help Maman. At 5 we were home again. I washed my hair because I am going to the theatre tomorrow with Godmother (that doesn't mean that's the only time I wash my hair, quite the contrary). I had dinner, I transplanted a big box of pansies that Maman bought me, and at last I started to write, very pleased with myself because I didn't let my imagination run away with me, as it has been doing lately.

But oh, it's so much more amusing to dream all day, to read . . . and yet, I know very well that dreaming is good for nothing, absolutely nothing. I have decided that the unknown person who is going to fill the empty space that I felt the other night will be called my "Shadow" and from here on that is how I shall speak of him. I don't know why I think about that now, when such an idea has never entered my head before, but I think that it's because I am 16 years old now and becoming a woman.

May 22. I would never have believed that ideas could really move out, just like ordinary furniture, but it has happened. The reason was simply that they didn't have enough room and they were jostling around in my head in a manner that didn't please me. So I took a big sheet of paper, pen and ink, and I wrote a long time, arranging my ideas carefully on that big blank page. In that way my ideas slowly emerged from the disorder and found themselves, with pleasure, in the light of day. When they had all come out, in the form of the beginning of a book, I was satisfied and could throw myself again into the tasks that preoccupied me before.

During all that time, I wrote only a few words here because the kind of ideas that were troubling me were not the kind that I usually write in this notebook. It was impossible for me to write both things at once. So now that the moving is over, here I am. The book isn't finished, not even half-finished, not even a quarter, but the ideas are coming more slowly and my writing can keep up with them. . . .

It has been raining since Saturday and I have long hours to think about what is going to happen on June 5. Emilia Quintero, whom you know, I'm sure, wants to get enough money to go back to France to see her brother, her only relative. She left Europe 7 years ago. Maman offered her "studio" and Mrs. Quintero is going to give a concert, a performance, with the help of Paquita and Enrique Madriguera, and Miss Cholet, who has a very pretty voice. The tickets are $2 and so far everyone who is coming is a millionaire, or almost, which means the same thing.

The ladies will go upstairs and leave their coats and powder their noses in Mrs. Madriguera's room. Dolly, our maid, will be there. The gentlemen will go somewhere else for the same thing and there the man who takes care of our cellar and the fire to heat the house will stand guard, dressed in his best. He looks like Caruso (but Caruso would like to be as handsome as he). The living room furniture is going to disappear to make room for a few hundred chairs. The entrance hall and our dining room, also decorated, will complete the concert hall. And then—here is the surprise—it will all be followed by a dance!

Suddenly, to my astonishment, because I didn't expect it any more, my "attack" has struck again, struck with all the strength of its magic, perhaps because of my age of 16, and that dance, that dance that I might have wanted to avoid, that dance seems delightful, magnificent! All the romantic stories about dances, you know, I dream continually about them. And yet, it's 3 weeks away! Such a long time to wait!

All this foolishness reminds me of the place where I went last night with Godmother. It was in the home of Mr. and Mrs. Villemin, who gave a "Montmartre" party. The French I heard there was adorable. It was slang, and by a very natural miracle, since I am Parisian, I understood everything, absolutely everything. There were songs that made us double up with laughter, puns, piano playing, singing. . . . And the event that made the humorous evening complete occurred when we took the tramway. Emilia, that marvelous woman, had to stay downtown for supper and she didn't want to leave us until she had put us on the tramway. When it came, to the conductor's great surprise, to my speechless astonishment (for I was holding the money in my hand, ready to put it in the box), she leaped on the tramway, put 10 cents in the box, and explained to the conductor in her terrible English that it was to pay for the two ladies; then she jumped off. All this took only a second, but we laughed for 10 minutes at this unexpected leap, which Mrs. Quintero probably did out of pure politeness.

When I got home, Maman was not yet asleep, so I understood that the same thing happens to her as happened to me when she went out in the evening. Her absence used to keep me from sleeping, and mine had the same effect on her.

There is something else that I want to write, since I am so chatty today. Apropos of Elsie de Sola's appendicitis attack, Maman told me the story of my second abscess: I was still in the hospital, waiting for healing that was very slow to come, and the doctor was mystified. Maman had tried everything, tears, prayers, vows, and yet I was still bedridden, frighteningly thin, and white as a sheet. Then Maman obtained the doctor's permission to take me on a tour of the entire hospital in a wheelchair, so that I could offer fruit and cakes to the patients. The nurse tried not to bump me, but the movement of the wheelchair tired me terribly; however, the joy I had from the thankful smiles of the patients and the handclasps of all the people who were visiting the less fortunate were an ample reward, and I can remember feeling very happy. Some friends followed me with trays full of things that I went on distributing until the end of the visit, when they took me back to my own bed. It was God's will that this effort saved my life, for the movement of the wheelchair caused the second abscess to burst, and otherwise it would have had to be operated on at great risk. After that, I quickly got better and one day was able to return to our little house full of flowers. The street was decorated too, and everyone in the street welcomed me back with shouts of joy. I shall always remember the kind friendship of the people of Brussels for all of us.

May 23. It wasn't just in fun that I once told you I learn something new every day. These days, since I have been learning only insignificant things, I decided to try something original. This whole day long, I have spoken only 14 1/2 words. Only 14 1/2! Not counting, of course, those in the conversation that I am always having with . . . myself. Those aren't words, those are thoughts spoken aloud, and in that way I am sure that they enter my head. The half-word was an indignant exclamation at one of the fables Joaquinito takes pleasure in inventing, of which I was the victim. But my indignation was controlled in time, and instead of exclaiming "Liar!" I said "Li——." The other words were absolutely necessary and consisted chiefly of "yes" or "no." The longest sentence I said all day long was: "Please pass the salt," to Thorvald, who pretended that he didn't understand what I wanted.

I can assure you that it isn't necessary to say more than 14 1/2 words per day. It's much simpler, much easier, much wiser, much more intelligent to listen to others talking and to *think* about what they say, instead of saying something stupid. First, there is less noise in the house, and second I had time to analyze all the conversations that I heard and to "ruminate" like a cow about what was said.

Also, this gave me a great desire to write, and last, I guessed that everyone around me was very happy about my silence, because I never open my mouth except to say silly things. There is only one drawback. Today by chance I didn't see the person to whom I would find it impossible to say only 14 1/2 words in a day. I mean Mr. Madriguera.

May 24. I opened my eyes at 8, remembered that today was Saturday, and before I got up, I thought a moment of the great joy I used to feel, not long ago, when I went to school, when I remembered that. Now every day is Saturday for me, except Sunday; that is, tomorrow.

After breakfast, the garden took all my attention. After lunch, I went to the cinema by myself because Maman had many letters to write, Thorvald was with his Boy Scout troop, and Joaquinito had gone on a picnic with his friends. I saw Harold Lockwood in "Shadows of Suspicion" and Dorothy Gish in "Peppy Polly." Once I got home, it began to rain torrents and I was sitting near the window, talking with myself, when suddenly, in the midst of the downpour, the majestic sun shone through in all its splendor, so that the drops of water, which previously looked gray, were transformed into diamonds. And just now, when I went to confession, I saw another marvelous scene: on the big sheets of water left by the rain, the red sky was reflected like a flame of fire.

To complete a day like today, I read, from cover to cover, Alphonse Daudet's superb book, "Trente Ans de Paris,"[1] which shows so well what it is like. And also I wrote two poems, one right after the other. Am I industrious? Oh, yes, but the result is that my eyes are very bad and every day my color looks more like the paper I am writing on.

May 26. Book after book. Gardening when my eyes *refuse* to read. Dream and dreams. Zounds!

May 27. I am still in the midst of the intrigues at the court of Henry IV and the sons of Catherine de Médicis. Enraptured by de la Mole, Coconnas, Mme. de Nevers and Marguerite, Queen of Navarre. Impossible to return to New York when I am living in the Louvre and the Bastille.

May 28. With difficulty and sincere regrets, I tore myself away from the lovely kingdom of France and came back to platonic, noisy New York with its Presidents and its ideas of liberty, a city full of police and prisons that prevent the murders and poisonings that need to exist to stimulate our imagination. And the only reason for this awakening was the end of the book, when I found myself face to face with the back cover following the epilog, and I had to close it as one closes a door. And as a change of occupations, I mended stockings, etc., to make myself useful. Now, as I write, I am listening to four concerts: Teresita Carreño-Blois at the piano, Paquita Madriguera at the piano, Joaquinito composing at the piano, Enrique Madriguera playing the violin. It's very funny, but very difficult to follow. The weakest is the violin, which comes down from the top floor.

It's hot now, very hot, and twenty times a day I think how lucky I am to have so many beautiful days ahead of me in which to be joyful. Truly, I have never been so happy. The proof is that when I'm not reading, I sing, dance, run up and down the stairs, talk to my birds, and play with my flowers as though they were dolls. And since the day when I said only 14 1/2 words, I talk less, I listen a lot, and naturally I learn a great deal. I have never had

[1] Thirty Years in Paris.

time before to study all the people around me and I am making some splendid discoveries.

Also I can take care of Maman as I never could do before. I get up at 8 o'clock and take Maman's breakfast to her in bed. The rest of the day I do all I can. Meanwhile, Maman, who is invincible, energetic and intrepid, has started another business. For $500 she bought the furniture for an entire 10-room house from one of her friends, Mrs. Mantilla, and now she is looking for a house that she can furnish, fill and sell for a lot more. So on top of running around looking for a house in an overpopulated city full of people who don't know where to go and where all the houses are selling for an exorbitant price, she continues working with tremendous energy at her buying. It's true that there are times when she is very, very tired, that she sometimes goes to bed and can't sleep for thinking, that stomach pains caused by nervous indigestion lay low this woman who is not discouraged by hard work or anything else. When that happens, I don't sing any more and I am sad. When I see Maman sick, I wander around the house like a lost soul. Fortunately, Maman is almost never sick.

May 29. Last night, knowing how much I admire everything French, Emilia Quintero took me to hear Mme. Eugénie Buffet. She spoke on the subject of French songs and sang several songs beautifully. The songs were very French, full of wit and emotion. Chiefly in honor of the Poilus and mocking the Boches. I came home at midnight singing the chorus of "Madelon" and feeling more Parisian than ever.

May 30. Today I went again to early Mass, but I try in vain to pray. During the entire Mass, I looked at the altar without feeling a single pious thought or a single prayer coming into my heart. I was indifferent to everything, even to the organ which always used to melt my heart and help my soul to pray. Thus it was coldly, ashamed of myself, that I came back from Mass as from an unsuccessful outing.

I have been invited to go horseback riding with Paquita and her "following." I am mad with joy! This is one of my dearest dreams come true. I am going to run, gallop, and I know I won't be afraid. Oh, no! Aunt Edelmira has a riding habit. It will begin Sunday at ten o'clock and will finish who cares when!

Yes! I can really say that I am happy, even spoiled. Right now I have perhaps everything that a 16-year-old girl could want—everything apart from the great emptiness in my heart, in my dreams, in my whole life, the name of which I don't know.

May 31. Today is a rather memorable day for the simple reason that Maman bought a tiny little house at Edgemere, Long Island, near Far Rockaway. The day began with Maman's decision that we would take the eleven o'clock train to go there. Once there, in forty-five minutes we had bought sandwiches, cookies, cheese and bananas, and we ate our lunch on the white sand beach with the blue sky and the sea spread out before our eyes like a beautiful painting. Afterward, while I read and Coquito and Joaquinito ran barefoot, collecting shells, Maman left us to look for a house. An hour later she came back, smiling, her eyes full of surprise, and we went to visit the bungalow which I shall describe for you when we go there.

At 7 o'clock we were home, but as I have an enormous headache, I hardly ate, but I wanted to write in order to go to bed with a feeling of satisfaction. But above all, tomorrow, oh! tomorrow! I found that Aunt Edelmira's boots are a thousand times too small, and I hardly dare believe that they will turn out all right.

June 1. I opened my eyes at 7 after having the kind of night one has when one goes to sleep with a problem, thinking: I'll sleep on it. My first thought was the weather. By the pink reflections from the house across the street, I could see that the sun was already up. On top of that, it wasn't too hot, with a welcome breeze, and I decided it was a perfect day. Next I thought about my boots. But since I had to go to Mass and absolutely had to have breakfast, I decided not to think about them until later. I had done everything possible to find a pair. Impossible! Paquita told me that perhaps I could find some at the Academy where they rent the horses, and I ran there an hour ahead of time to see what I could do. Fortunately, I met a nice French lady who for a dollar (5 francs) let me borrow a pair of boots that I took for lack of anything better. At 9:30 I was back home, out of breath. Maman and Aunt Edelmira helped me to dress. First I put on a linen blouse with a big collar and a black ribbon tied in a bow, then a jacket of light gray "crash," almost white. A pretty little cane completed my disguise. I hardly had time to look at myself in the mirror, because Maman was tying my hair into a bun and putting powder on my face at the same time. But when I was ready, a murmur of admiration ran through the entire family, Mrs. Madriguera and the others, so

I thought that my costume must be nice. Mr. Madriguera (or Enrique, since I already know him) came for me. At the door, we found another gentleman and Paquita.

The four of us walked to 66th Street, where I had already been. There we met Mr. de Alba, a young lady, Emilia Fernandez, and another young man whose name was Macaya. We took the horses that were reserved for us from among many others. Like good Christians, they all had names. Mine, a beautiful brown horse, very easy and lightfooted, was called Browny. Then we left.

The ride was very amusing. I was almost the only one who didn't have to change horses. Enrique had one at first who was full of fire. He wanted to gallop all the time, and if he couldn't, he reared up on his hind legs. After a while Enric was tired and traded with one of the other gentlemen. In exchange, he got one whose name he had to change from "Happiness" to "Mule," because it stubbornly insisted on going at a walk.

As for my own experiences, I am rather ashamed, even though they were quite funny. At first I couldn't go at a run because I was jumping around more than the horse itself, but little by little I corrected that. Also I held the reins too loosely, so that I was obliged to go wherever the horse wanted. Although he was very obedient, sometimes he broke into a trot or a gallop at the most unexpected time. Not once could I choose with whom I would ride; it was my good old horse who chose for me. We walked with Paquita, trotted with Mr. Macaya, walked again with Emilia and Enric. Just once, my horse assumed that graceful position, very uncomfortable for me, of rearing back on his hind legs, and only by patting him could I get him to calm down.

The ride lasted 2 hours. Out of all that, I made a choice. What I liked best was to gallop by myself and to go at a walk while talking with the violinist, because he is 17 and was the only one about my age. In addition, he is very amusing.

After leaving the horses where we rented them, we walked home slowly, stopping at a shop on Broadway to drink an orangeade. It was only when I got home that I realized how tired I was. I didn't eat; I just let Aunt Edelmira take a picture of me and then I fell asleep on Maman's bed.

It's all over, but I won't soon forget it. A horseback ride is like a trip to fairyland, except of course for the fatigue and soreness in every bone that comes afterward. But it's worth the soreness in order to enjoy a few hours of pleasure. There are no roses without thorns, no horseback rides without a painful aftermath. But I'm ready to begin again this very minute.

June 2. Today I couldn't do very much because I am still very tired from yesterday's wonderful horseback ride. I read a lot, and in spite of the terrible pain in all my bones, I found a little time to work in my garden. When I was tired of reading, I had only to raise my head and listen to Enric's violin. That's about what I did a good part of the day because he practiced enormously. There's no doubt that he is a great artist. He plays in the most wonderful way, and once one starts to listen, there's no use trying to do anything else. And although he lives "in a garret" like a philosopher, every time his delicate notes pierce the walls and resound throughout the house, I see his young face and his eternal smile above the violin that he plays so well.

After closing my notebook, I saw that I had forgotten to write something that I thought about for a long time several days ago. From reading, from the conversation of those around me, perhaps by instinct, I know that the older people get and the more they know, the more they think before doing anything. Above all, they lose that blind trust in the honesty and goodness of their friends in good times or bad. A child's glance is frank, clear, open. An older person's is rather closed, a little cynical, shadowed by hidden thoughts and the tears of disillusionment. All that is natural.

I myself am neither a child nor on the wrong side of forty. I am 16. I used to think that everything was beautiful and everyone good. If my eyes met a pair of eyes in which I could clearly read profound irony, malice and despair, I turned my eyes away and thought for only a short while of the strange way those eyes made me feel, without ever trying to probe the heart, the thoughts or the actions that were reflected in the mirrors of the soul. If someone mentioned "bad" people, I thought it was because they didn't go to confession or to church. And yet, in spite of myself, as I grew up I slowly lost that wonderful trust. I have often tried to think of people as perfect. But to my great distress, after getting to know those people, in the light of all their feelings, their desires, their goals, I always saw them changed as day changes into night, and I found myself face to face with a human body, a heart and a conscience of stone. People to whom I had given noble aspirations, lofty sentiments and very few faults.

It's true that I consider myself the worst of all. I know myself well enough to realize that all the disillusionments that I find in others, I also find in myself, but it's so nice when one is sick to be surrounded by healthy people, instead of others who are just as sick as I am. O sad Fate of those who search for Bluebirds, or Perfection, in this human world.

Now I have faith in only a few people, those whom I can put on an altar in my heart and keep there, for in the time I have known them, amidst the most terrible misfortunes, they have always been the same: angels on earth. But they are very few in number. Although there are others I can't help loving, I know them too well, I have seen them fail, they have made me lose the trust that I kept like a beautiful diamond of immeasurable value. But that's all over, and it was inevitable.

I knew that by the time I was 40, I would have no illusions left; I would know everything. But I never thought that at 16 I would know the bottom of the human heart, in whose depths, after having explored the fragrant surface, I found only mud. But perhaps I myself may have caused another to lose faith and robbed him of his illusions! When I think of that, I shudder!

June 5. The day of Emilia's concert. There is still work to do! Having removed the furniture from the living room, we arranged the chairs. The same thing was done with the hall and our bedroom, which is really a dining room. I wasn't afraid of getting too tired, since it was necessary, but from time to time I thought of the dance as something distant and impossible.

I am writing because I have a few free moments. I am already dressed. I have on my pretty blue dress, white shoes and stockings, a coral necklace, my hair is in a chignon with curls, and to complete my ensemble I have a pretty bouquet of pink carnations that Emilia sent me. But more than ever, when I look at myself in the mirror, I think I look sad because I'm not pretty, and sometimes I would really like to be pretty. Also, as I write, I notice that the things I have been doing lately to help Maman haven't beautified my hands the least bit. I look pale and tired, and Maman's rouge doesn't do a thing. Fortunately, to go with all the discoveries I am making every day that I am turning into a very stupid girl, I have certain philosophical ideas and quite a lot of resignation. After all, here is a poem that I keep in mind to forget my lack of beauty:

> Never you mind the crowd, lad,
> Nor fancy your work won't tell;

The work is done for all that, lad,
To him that doth it well.

Fancy the world is a hill, lad
Look where the millions stop;
You'll find the crowd at the base, lad,
There's always room at the top.

Perhaps right now you don't understand why I worry about being pretty, something about which I had never given a thought. Someday I'll have enough courage to tell you a little secret, the secret that I dream about at the windowsill at night, in the garden during the day, the secret that I sing about when I am alone and which has put a smile on a face that usually is serious. Finally, it's a secret that I don't write because I don't dare because it would make me blush. Suffice it to say that it is the only reason why I would like not to be ugly.

But here's Emilia and it will soon be 8 o'clock, so I leave you to plunge into the momentary delights of a concert and a dance.

Studio of Rosa C. Nin, 158 West 75th Street

Thursday, June 5th, 1919, at 8:30 p. m.

Evening Musical

by

EMILIA QUINTERO

assisted by eminent artists

RENEE CHOLLET . . . . Soprano
PAQUITA MADRIGUERA . Pianist
ENRIC MADRIGUERA . . Violinist

Programme

Sonata XIV . . . . *Beethoven*
Emilia Quintero
Slavonic Dance . . . . *Dvorak-Kreisler*
Serenata . . . . *Lalo*
Enric Madriguera
La Boheme (l'addio) . . . . *Puccini*
Renee Chollet
Ballade III.
Nocturne }
Valse } . . . . *Chopin*
Emilia Quintero
Allegro . . . . *Saint Saens*
Enric Madriguera
Triana . . . . *Albeniz*
Danza espanola . . . . *Granados*
Paquita Madriguera
Le Nil . . . . *Lerroux*
Renee Chollet
Rhapsodie XII . . . . *Liszt*
Emilia Quintero

Arranged by Miss Anais Nin

June 6. One of the most beautiful things in the world is memory. Is there anything more beautiful than to be able to relive happy moments as many times as one wishes? That's what I have been doing with last night's party; it has unfolded before my eyes more than twenty times, down to the smallest details.

At 8:30 everyone began arriving and taking places. There were old ladies, thin, fat, ugly, little and big; men, young and old, girls and young women, which formed a curious mixture. Everything was brightly lighted and joyful.

When Mrs. Schiff and Frances arrived, I seated them very close to the piano and I sat next to Frances. Later, one of the three Bermudez brothers (the ones who came to call one evening and from whom I hid in a closet) came over to sit there and talk to me. Then the program began. There were funny moments when Mrs. Quintero gave a speech in her terrible English; dull moments when everyone nearly fell asleep because of a Beethoven sonata which, added to the stifling heat, lulled the audience; pleasurable moments when Mr. Diaz of the Metropolitan sang Massenet's "Elégie" and "Tes Yeux," in addition to a piece from "Romeo and Juliet"; moments of admiration when Paquita, with her great talent, played the wonderful "Triana" and other pieces; and finally, moments that for me (here I dare not speak for the crowd) were full of unexplainable emotion, when, with shining eyes and my soul full of dreams, I heard floating on the air the delightful and inimitable sound of a seventeen-year-old violinist.

Everyone was well received, but it seemed to me that he deserved it more than all the others. Never has a violin seemed as full of magic as that one. He stood under the very strong lights in the living room, which clearly illuminated his serious face and agile hands that nimbly moved the bow. And I listened, holding my breath for fear of missing a single note, but my heart was beating so hard that I thought it suddenly would stop, which wouldn't have displeased me, because it was a moment when I was afraid my heart would leave me in spite of myself, but in a different way.

Here I stop a moment to smile and also to tell you that right now, you can read that heart like an open book. But you must know that to you alone, out of the whole world, I dare give that book, because it's really to myself that I am saying once more all that I am thinking.

But to continue! The concert finished about midnight, I think, and after a few minutes of general conversation, most of the audience scattered to the four winds. Then there were left in all: Maman, Aunt Edelmira, Godmother, Thorvald, Coquito (Joaquinito and Nuna had gone to bed), Mrs. Sarlabous and her daughter Germaine, Paquita, her mother and brother, Mr. Mendirichega, the three Bermudez brothers, Frances and her mother, several other young men, two or three old ladies, Miss Williams, and I believe that was all. Maman had paid $5 to a lady who then began to play the piano for dancing, and I recognized many of the pieces that they used to play at dancing school. My first dance was with Enric, who made me very happy by telling me that I am a good dancer. He had the second dance with Paquita, and then he disappeared for the rest of the evening, as he was doubtless very tired. The dance continued for about an hour. I danced with the Bermudez brothers and Mr. Mendirichega, but I didn't have a good time at all. Germaine Sarlabous left me speechless with astonishment; she is a terrible flirt, and I would never have thought that anyone could make so many faces and say so many silly things by the dozen to win masculine attention so successfully.

Finally, it all ended. Little by little, everyone filed out of the house and little by little the music stopped, the lights went out one by one, and a great silence reigned in the whole house, which a short time earlier was full of laughter, music and gaiety. But I couldn't go to sleep. I lay for hours with my eyes wide open in the dim light, too tired to fall asleep.

This morning I could hardly open my eyes. However, little by little the familiar noises brought me back to reality and the thought of Maman's breakfast. Last night she received a telegram asking her to go to see Thorvald Sanchez in Newburgh, where he was operated on for appendicitis, and Maman left to come back this evening or tomorrow morning. I read two books because it was raining, and the rest of the day I did a little of everything.

Emilia came this evening while I was writing and I had to confess that I was thinking of the concert; and then, with a guilelessness that stabbed me through the heart, she told me she would like very much to know everything I had said about her. But even now, I can't do that. There are people and things that one can't write about without being mocking, severe, hypocritical or humorous, because they are so peculiar. In a diary which sounds the depths of one's soul, what is needed above all is the pure unvarnished truth. And you who know how unfeeling and cold I am in my affection, you will understand that before I could talk about someone who is a dear friend of the whole family, I would rather let you think the best, as you will surely do, since you are nicer than I. She is leaving for Paris, she is going to see Papa to tell him about us, and to me falls the task of acquainting him with the personality of this lady whom he will meet as one of our best friends.

Now I leave you. Yes, I am very ugly, not very interesting, really crazy, it's true that I dream too much, that I'm not practical, that I'm not an angel, it's true that when I go to Mass, I can't pray, and when I write I hold back secrets that make me blush. But O beloved diary, I shall change in a wonderful way when I find my shadow. Now I am going to talk with the stars, who wink their eyes eternally because of their wisdom. One day you will know what I tell them. But it's nothing sad, I assure you, because . . . A little more and I would tell you everything . . . Alas! Women are so indiscreet!

June 8.
Dearest Papa,

If I recall correctly, you should have received a letter from me not long ago, but this one will prepare you for a visitor who will tell you many more things about us than I can write in a letter.

Among my earlier letters, in speaking of the little snapshots I sent or Joaquinito's piano lessons, I must have mentioned more than once the name of Mrs. Emilia Quintero. She is leaving for Paris and is going to keep a promise made a long time ago to go to see you. And I want to introduce her to you ahead of time so that you won't be too surprised. When we came to New York 5 years ago, we met her at Aunt Antolina's house as a poor piano teacher, and since then she has become an old friend of the family, one of those people who drop in at any time of day, someone we are happy and comfortable to invite to dinner, someone we know we can count on in case of need.

She is neither young nor beautiful, but she has a very good heart. I can't judge her as a performer; you will see for yourself. But she deserves a lot of credit because her life in New York is like that of many artists all over the world, a life of poverty, sometimes of hunger, hope, lost dreams, and sometimes of unhoped-for joys and pleasures that come unexpectedly and never last long enough. In a word, a sad poem that deservedly is called "Destiny" and that everyone knows by heart.

One thing she has always known is solitude; I mean, she has

no family, and that is the reason for a small fault, otherwise unexplainable, her great love of conversation. But that will probably give you pleasure, for if you let her talk, you will find her very amusing and I am sure she will talk constantly of us, since that is why she is going to see you, she says.

Her other activities are a bit bizarre, but you know that's how it is with artists. Her opinions, her philosophy, her conversation and ideas are tinged with romanticism and a little exaggeration. She is given to flattery, too, because her kind heart has figured out that flattery and compliments give pleasure to everyone. Many people think as she does. I have to tell you all this because one has to know her for a long time not to find her, at first glance, a little mad. So don't be offended if she invites herself to dinner, especially if you have fish, soup and rice. You see how well I know her tastes!

Let her take pictures of you, of your house; don't laugh too loudly when she puts her nose against the things on the mantel, the pictures, your books, etc., and uses a lorgnette to help her see, because she is very nearsighted. But don't tell her that, because she doesn't believe it, or pretends not to believe it, which is the same thing.

You don't need to listen to everything she says, and if you can keep all your patience and remember the things I have told you, the visit will go very well.

Now I still have to tell you how she is managing to go to Paris, and why. She has a notion, which nothing can change, that she is going to die soon, and she doesn't want to be buried in prosaic New York; in addition, she wants to see her only relative, a brother, before she dies. So Maman offered her our studio, her friends bought tickets, people gave her gifts of money, and one fine day, the 5th of June, the living room, hall and dining room, where we had put chairs, were filled with people who came to hear the concert, the program of which I enclose. Emilia will give you a thousand details about all this.

Now you know everything, and I hope you will forgive me for such an uninteresting letter. I'll write you again in a few days to tell you about something else. So good luck and write to me soon to tell me what you think about all this.

With all the tenderness, dearest Papa,

of your fifille

Anaïs

P.S. The real importance of this visit is that so far, Emilia is

Joaquinito's piano teacher. A wonderful teacher for a little boy who can learn only with an angel who has superhuman patience and a gentleness that overcomes all obstacles, particularly the obstacles raised by an impulsive boy who is full of life, foolishness and unquenchable caprice.

Mrs. Quintero is going to give you a picture of me taken a few days ago. I hope you will like it. Believe the picture and not Emilia's descriptions. No doubt on account of her myopia, she is the only person in the world who thinks I am pretty.

June 9. Copied from La Prensa, Society Notes
The Departure of Emilia Quintero
In view of the future trip to Spain of the celebrated pianist Emilia Quintero, many of her friends suggested the idea of a farewell concert before her departure. The artist accepted this suggestion with pleasure, making plans immediately to present the concert in the studio of Mrs. Rosa C. de Nin, with the kind cooperation of this noble lady, whose charming children are the pianist's pupils.

A select public made up of artists from the Opera, music lovers, bankers, journalists, writers, poets and professional people, both Yankee and Hispano-American, filled the salon of the charming Mrs. Nin. The musical fiesta began with words appropriate to the occasion spoken gracefully and wittily by the mistress of the house, then Emilia appeared, dressed in black with red roses on her breast. As always, she was affable, urbane, elegant, distributing smiles and greetings to all who were present to bid her a fond and sincere farewell. . . .

What can we say about Emilia, so good, so endowed with lofty qualities, and such a fine artist, that we haven't already said on other occasions?

There was one surprise that drove the audience at this pleasant evening mad with joy: the appearance in the hall, close to the piano, of the Spanish tenor Rafael Diaz of the Opera, an elegant young man with an attractive face and a voice that we hope God will grant him for many years. He sang, and sang very well: the Partida which moved everyone earlier, and we also remember an aria from Gounod's Romeo and Juliet and two French songs. Another surprise: the celebrated Yankee pianist Oliver Denton played a Barcarolle by the great French critic Rubinstein, and also other works.

*   *   *

. . . More than 300 persons filled the three rooms of the elegant Mrs. Rosa C. de Nin, who was very attentive to her guests and welcomed them all affectionately. At the end of the evening, all the guests signed their names in an album. Many expressed thoughts dedicated to the artist who is so well loved in New York and to whom this reporter sends best wishes for a pleasant trip to France and the mother country.

P.S. It isn't exactly because I admire that description in Spanish of the evening of June 5 that I copied it, but rather because Maman bought me a new diary, a very beautiful book bound in black leather, and I am eager to begin writing in it as soon as possible.

June 11. Something miraculous happened to me today. You know that I go to Mass every day with the firm intention of *trying* to be pious, but without any success. Today, I got up early and went to the small church. The little group of women that is always there was there, and among them a few gray-haired men with patriarchal beards. I was on my knees, distracted, feeling anything but prayerful, my heart closed to pious sentiments. Since I was like that, I even dared to turn my head and glance at my neighbors, as I would do at the theatre. No one was looking at me, and I could see that they *all* were praying fervently, with their eyes riveted on the cross, their hands clasped and heads bowed with respectful love. All at once, my heart melted. A flood of emotion and repentance swept over me. I lowered my head with great shame, I closed my eyes to drive away the miserable distractions, and I did what I haven't been able to do for a long time: I prayed.

The rest of the Mass was nothing but fervent and real spiritual communion with Almighty God, whose existence and grandeur I had forgotten. Finally, when I stood up to leave, regretting that I can't always pray as I did in that brief half-hour, I was changed, transformed. No more sarcasm, philosophy of my own, pessimism. On the way home, I promised myself to become once more a simple girl, always happy, with just one goal: to give pleasure to everyone and to find everyone better than I, instead of treating my family selfishly and thinking that I am above their simple ideas, which make people much happier than the other kind of ideas. Oh! please God that I may always stay like that!

But how can I change in one day the mask that I have been wearing for 16 years? Tomorrow, perhaps, the delicious calm that I found in prayer will seem like bigotry and the resolutions that I made like foolishness. I'll feel morose again, I'll read book after book without any emotion, like an old woman who knows life so well that nothing astonishes her, and I'll believe that I know everything that anyone can know, that I have reached the end of the road after a great deal of suffering, instead of trusting in heaven, believing that I don't know much and that I have suffered very little compared to what I deserve, as I believe today.

O sad Fate to be an actor who can't change his rôle because he knows it too well, who is too old to learn a new one, and who understands, but much too late, that the part isn't right for him.

But pray, let's pray, and the actor will be able to change his part a little, without anyone knowing.

June 11. I'm still a little girl. Mass this morning was a victory over my distraction, and I am proud of that.

Today, Maman and I worked hard from 9 in the morning until 9 this evening, straightening up the cupboards and putting everything in order. We are very tired but very happy.

Emilia just arrived, a hurricane of words to express her ideas. Finally, out of the chaos, I understood that she is thinking of giving a little party at her house on Friday, and that we are invited. The Madrigueras are going. Apropos of them, I am seized with a great yearning to learn to speak Catalan, but Maman doesn't want to help me. She says that she *knows* how to speak it, but as she adamantly refuses to do so, I begin to think that she can't. She makes fun of me and to tease me, she says I should go and ask Enric. She knows very well that I won't do it and thinks in that way that I'll give up the idea, but I won't at all; I'm still looking for a teacher. She has condescended to teach me one thing, but hasn't condescended to tell me what it means: "T'estimo molt, noia." I suppose that it's "I esteem you very much, my child."[1] That's all that I know.

June 12. Maman says that I don't have much confidence in myself. What that means, I don't know. She said that apropos of a heavy package that I lifted with great difficulty, and when she told me not to do that ever again, I replied that everyone except me can do it easily and that I don't want always to be useless. My lack of strength and endurance worries me, because I can't help Maman as much as I would like. It's true that I stay home all day, opening the door and answering the telephone every two minutes, but

[1] T'estimo *means "I love you."*

afterward I have circles under my eyes and Maman never fails to see that I am tired, when I wish she wouldn't notice.

Another thing I think about a lot, and always as one thinks about life's problems, is the road that I am going to follow. Nothing guides me in my choice, but everything makes it more difficult: my lack of talent, my lack of dexterity, of common sense, of initiative; and no advice, no scolding can interrupt the dead calm that confronts me each time that I look for a way to launch my bark in the midst of the tempest. Sometimes it seems as though I shall always remain on the wrong side of the ocean that one has to cross to reach the other side, cross it or drown.

June 13. It's this evening that I am going to Emilia's and even if it's only one o'clock and we aren't going until 8:30, being a Nin I can't help getting ready well ahead of time. That's why my pink checked gingham dress is swinging on a hanger, my patent-leather shoes are set out next to my pair of black silk stockings, my white gloves are washed, my handkerchief is perfumed (already) and I have in front of me a little pink hat, very soft and very pretty, that Maman bought me a few days ago. My dress and hat are being worn for the first time, and as the proverb says, "tout nouveau, tout beau."[1]

I wonder what is going to happen this evening. To please Emilia, I copied the program she has planned, but while I was copying a funny program that didn't even make me smile, I thought deep thoughts. Once at a certain age, very old people decidedly begin to think the way they thought in their childhood. Emilia is the person and the program is the fall from old age to infancy. They say "History repeats itself." Well, fine, Emilia is starting life over. I suppose that she hasn't time to begin *everything* over, but I wonder if she is going to die at the age of 5 or at the age of 16? It's sad to die so young!

There are times when I feel as though I have already been an old, old woman and that I am now in second childhood (without anyone knowing it, of course) and with some ideas still remaining with me from the time of my old age.

Two hours ago I closed a notebook and put it on the bookshelf between Don Quixote and a novel of Sir Walter Scott's. I thought I wouldn't write any more today or at least not any more about myself, but I can't resist the temptation. During the last two hours, I have been busy rereading several of my diaries, from the

[1] *Brand new is beautiful.*

one I began in 1914 on the ship that was to carry me far away from Spain, down to the lines I wrote two hours ago.

I have gone through so many impressions. At first I couldn't read the dreadful handwriting and horrible spelling, for I was only eleven years old. But I could read my character, and with the help of memory, I could follow with breathless interest the changes that events have made on my personality. I arrived in New York with my mind made up to detest it. I was ignorant, shy, naïve, like a country girl. Slowly I grew up; I wrote things that I found unexplainable at the time and that now I understand. I am sad and happy. Around me, the natural and inevitable tragedy of life unfolds. My personality is developing, my handwriting is changing, my spelling is a little better, my ideas are becoming clear and precise. I am neither naïve nor shy, and am less ignorant. At 16 I have changed so much that right now, when I analyze my feelings, I understand that the little eleven-year-old girl and *her* character exist only in the notebooks.

This transformation, which is so normal, is like an abyss that makes me dizzy. It is a deep mystery of nature that takes my breath away. Even now, I may be on the threshold of another transformation, on the threshold of another being that will be added to or will replace the one I am about to leave behind, as one gets rid of an old worn coat. What food for thought. From the time I was born until 5 or 6 years of age, no doubt I was a baby. Then until 10 years of age, a little girl. From ten until 13 or 14, I don't know. At that time, I didn't know myself. I must have been a young girl, but the change was extremely subtle and prepared me for a sudden transformation, at 14 or 15, into a young lady. I feel more certain about what follows, as one is of a reflection that is closer to him. On February 21, when I was 16, I became a young lady. That's what I still am. What does the future hold for me? The feelings of a young woman, of a mature woman, of an old woman, feelings which will suddenly end in the grave, as rivers do in the sea.

So many faces, so many changes, so many preparations, to end by being forgotten! Each of us is a book without an Epilogue, an unfinished book whose Author reserves the right to write the ending, since He wrote the beginning. Perhaps that is why modern books little by little remain unfinished, indefinite and vague in their purpose and their reason for being, because men have begun to understand they can't write "The End" because they don't know it and would have to make it up. Perhaps that's why also a few philosophers have said that Life is the beginning of something much greater.

Well, if I have got off the subject, it's because I am traveling in a country that has no landmarks.

June 14. Even if I am impatient to talk about today, I must take things in order. Yesterday, then, in the afternoon, after having written my very serious thoughts in one fell swoop, I read until dinner time. Maman came home late and extremely tired, but she told me that since she was already dressed, she would go [to Emilia's party] in order to give me pleasure. So after dinner I got dressed in the things that I had carefully prepared earlier. I combed my hair in long curls and put on a tiny bit of rouge because I was pale, but I don't want you to think I like to use paint, except when it's necessary.

Later I helped Emilia to carry several bottles of Sarsaparilla and Ginger Ale to her house. Also I had to carry glasses, spoons and 3 cakes in a little satchel.

At 8:30 we were at her house. People arrived little by little, but when everyone was there, we were: Maman, Godmother, Emilia, Miss Cholet and her father, a young lady, Mrs. Madriguera, Paquita, Mr. Diaz and Enric. I don't count myself. At first it seemed as though it was going to be terribly boring, then later it was only a little boring, and finally everyone pretended not to be bored at all. It's always like that in society.

We teased Emilia, we did and said silly things, we danced the Tango and the Waltz, we sang off-key, we ate and drank, and in a word we did all the things that crazy people can do. Maman, who had told me she was afraid she would fall asleep, was the funniest one of all, along with Rafael Diaz. At eleven o'clock we began to leave. Emilia played a wedding march and everyone paired off, pretending to be married couples, Maman with Mr. Diaz (Emilia wanted to separate them) and others. Enric wanted to walk with me, but Maman made things even funnier by separating us.

Enric's little automobile was waiting at the door, and since Paquita and Mrs. Madriguera preferred to walk, Enric invited us to go for a short ride in his automobile. He was seated in front in the driver's seat, with me beside him. Maman and Godmother were in back. First Enric took Maman home because she was tired, and then he drove us along Riverside for a few minutes. I didn't want to talk at all, for that ride under the stars, very close to the dark river with many lights along the shore, fascinated and delighted me, and the conversation broke the spell. But I talked from time to time, taking care in the way I spoke Spanish, which embarrasses me only when I talk to Enric. That was the nicest moment of the entire evening. But it soon ended.

There is one little thing that I forgot to write and I don't want to forget it because it gave me so much pleasure, even if it's not true. I am going to write it in Spanish because that's how Enric said it:

"¡Eres guapa, ya!"[1]

But there are only two people who believe that and only because they are nice. Because Enric is very nice with everyone.

Now I omit the details of my restless sleep, getting up, breakfast, taking care of my garden, and the violin solo that came from the room on the upper floor to accompany my work; Maman's plans and how they were carried out, the reunion of the Nin family in the dusty Subway, the ride in the rusty train, the arrival at Edgemere and lunch in a modest hotel, and I begin my record in detail with the time when we were all together in the cottage.

The old furniture that was there the first day we came has been removed and I can see the real size of the house. I shall describe it in detail later. Our furniture will arrive this evening, so we are going to wait for it and spend the night here. Maman left us in the cottage and went to take care of the gas, water and electricity, and the three of us went out to "explore." When she came back at 4 o'clock she told us to go to the beach so Thorvald and Joaquinito could go swimming. I am writing all this sitting on the sand, not without stopping frequently to raise my head and search out Joaquinito to be sure that he is all right. Now they have come out of the water and are drying in the sun, getting ready to go back to the house. So I shall leave you for the moment. What a heavenly inspiration it was to bring you with me! With you I am never alone and never bored.

6:30—We have just "dined" (?). On a bottle of milk, cookies and sandwiches.

We are very satisfied with our little house and we think we will enjoy ourselves here. The furniture has not yet come and there will be no gas or electricity until Monday. Maman bought candles, matches, 10-cent knives and forks, a bar of soap, a 10-cent towel, and other necessities. I wonder if Monsita will remember to send my brush and comb, because my hair is all tangled. We have no toothbrushes either. On top of that I think my fountain pen is

[1] *You're really pretty!*

going to run out of ink, so our situation is really very odd. Just the same, I shall write as much as possible.

7—Maman has just discovered that she hasn't much money, so we are going to have to get along on a shoestring. It's like being at war.

7:20—A terrible phonograph is squawking away much too close to us and I am praying that it won't squawk too long.

8—There is just one very old armchair in the house which was left for us because of its infirmities and we are taking turns sitting in it. I don't want to admit it, but I am very tired.

8:30—I decided to forget about being tired and I have just gone walking with Thorvald across the sand and through the tall grass that surrounds the Bay. It's wonderful. Right now the sun is setting and for the first time in a long while I can let my gaze wander over a view that stretches to the horizon, with no chimneys and no houses. Just trees, meadows, beaches, grass, water, and a rainbow-colored sky.

The furniture is still not here! And there is still some ink in my fountain pen.

8:45—We are all sitting on the porch which is built on the back of our little house. It is so cool that we have to wear sweaters.

Thorvald is building a little fire just for fun, and Joaquinito is trying to put it out. That's characteristic of him. I am astonished that my ink is holding out, so I'll take advantage of it. But soon I'll run out of light instead of ink and will have to resign myself to silence.

10:45—What a funny mess! After having waited in vain for the furniture, Maman stayed at the cottage, sleeping on an old, old bed that was there by chance, and Thorvald, Joaquinito and I are in the train that is taking us back to New York. I am writing this in the train, as can be seen by my penmanship. Poor Joaquinito is half-asleep with his head on my shoulder. Thorvald too. Good-night! I must watch over their sleep.

June 16. Everything went perfectly. The furniture is installed in the little house at No. 4 Delmar Court or 43 Edgemere Street, Long Island. We spent the night there. We breakfasted on cookies and milk, lunched on cookies, cheese and milk, dined on cookies, sandwiches and strawberries. Between meals, we went walking along the sea and along the edge of the bay. Now I am writing in New York, at 4 o'clock on a beautiful afternoon. I found my garden a little dry but very well and my birds very gay. In the garden where I am writing, I hear Enric's violin and Paquita's piano, which forces me to realize that I am really in New York and not at the seashore. But right this minute, I can't decide which I prefer, because down there, there is no music. But there is the ocean which is so beautiful and so wonderful. I haven't much to write, but I can't bear to leave my garden, so I shall leave you open in my lap so that I can write when I feel like it and listen to the music at the same time.

June 18. Aunt Anaïs and her children arrived. Cuca,[1] whom I wanted desperately to get to know, was with them, but since it was at the dock where they debarked that we met them, we couldn't even talk together. Aunt Lolita[2] also arrived.

June 19. 1:30. In half an hour I am going horseback riding with Paquita. I am half-dressed and am writing, because it's the only way that I can keep calm. Now I am writing again because Paquita isn't ready. I have just learned that Enric isn't coming with us and I begin to think that I am not going to enjoy myself

[1] *Caridad Sánchez, A.N.'s cousin.*
[2] *First wife of Thorvald Culmell.*

very much because the other gentlemen are too old and also I hardly know them. Just the same, I am dressed, and since Maman isn't here, it's Godmother who had passed judgment on my appearance: Good. Here they are.

8 o'clock—After a fine ride on a nice but spirited gray-and-white horse named Dandy, we took a taxi to go downtown on an errand for Paquita. We got home in time for dinner.

I have just seen Enric. He wants me to give him French lessons, but Maman says that she will do it. General laughter! He says that he has finally received his passport and will be leaving soon.

This morning I went to Communion, but today I couldn't collect my thoughts, in spite of all my efforts. For once, I confess that I don't understand myself at all. I am disturbed by ideas that aren't vain or frivolous and that I have never had. I have reached the threshold of a new era in my life, I believe. But which one? From the girl that I am now, I am going to become a young woman, but I shall never do that while there are so many things that I don't know. And yet for unexplainable reasons, I prefer a chignon to my eternal long hair and I keep letting my dresses down a little at a time. But Maman watches me, mocks me, and pleading in favor of my 16 years, chases away my attack of worldliness for a little while. But I think that I shall always remain serious, uncommunicative, even sullen, unwilling to accept the compliments that I am so far from deserving (and that I never receive), never interested in frills and never trying to improve my long sad face.

Would you like to know how I am these days? Serious? I sing all day long. Uncommunicative? I am as talkative as an old parrot, even if my head isn't logical. Unwilling to accept compliments? That I can't yet say; I don't know very well whether compliments are given as they are in books. Not interested in frills? Consult the contents of my "wardrobe." Improving my face? That is really impossible! Oh, dearest diary!

But I am straying from the subject. They say I haven't enough confidence in myself, but if they knew what "myself" means! As well to put your trust in a glass house built on sand, at the mercy of wind and waves. Might as well say: put your trust in a representative of humanity, a rather overdone imitation of the human personality. All that is myself. So if I put my trust in *that*, my hopes, my faith, my illusions will be struck down by the future, which can so easily demolish my glass house.

So I keep my trust for my Shadow, the day that I find him. Long ago, I liked to think of my shadow as a strong, stern, severe figure, full of wisdom, with nobly graying hair and steely eyes. Now I like to think that he is very young, quite mad, with very little wisdom, of course, but a lot of talent.

June 26. Since I last wrote, I have done several things that I am going to try to recall. The day after I went horseback riding, I went with Maman, Thorvald, Joaquinito and Aunt Lolita to Edgemere. We spent Saturday and Sunday there. Sunday afternoon, Godmother and Aunt Anaïs appeared on the scene with all my little cousins and with provisions for a picnic. I came back to New York with them in the automobile, and Maman and the rest of my family came back later on the train.

After a party, about 8:30 Mrs. Madriguera and Enric invited Maman and me to go for a ride in the Chevrolet. Mr. Macaya was there too and he rode in back with the two ladies, Enric and I in front. The outing lasted until eleven o'clock. We drove first through the park and then up Riverside.

On Riverside, we went as far as "Inspiration Point," which Enric insisted was poetic. All along the way, the conversation was very amusing. At one time, Enric even showed me a little gold ring he was wearing and told me with a straight face that this meant he had a fiancée in Spain, and I believed him, but I calmly asked him for details. Then he started to laugh, saying that he plays that joke on everyone to see if one day someone will faint. In the meantime, Maman slipped me her wedding ring and I put it on. Then I told him that I too have a fiancé. He became very serious, believed or pretended to believe me, and wanted to see the name engraved on the ring. When we got to Inspiration Point, he struck a match and saw that it was Maman's ring. On the way back, it was Mrs. Madriguera who drove the car.

Tuesday morning I went horseback riding again. We lunched in a restaurant, and for the first time I tasted claret and Italian vermouth. Also I was very embarrassed when they asked me if I wanted a "demi-tasse," and I refused without having the slightest idea what it was. But I was sorry to be so ignorant and I am still wondering what Mr. J. de Alba, Mr. Nacher, Paquita, Mrs. Madriguera and Enric must have thought of me. I had always thought that books had prepared me not to make social blunders, but my friends didn't help me in this case.

The same day, as it was the saint's day of St. John, we gave a little party here in honor of Juan de Alba, Juana Culmell, and Juan Macaya, the brother of the Mr. Macaya who was with us the evening we went for a ride in the automobile. As for Juan Macaya, he is a young man who strikes me as very nice. We shouted, danced, made music, etc. Enric played the violin, Paquita and Emilia the piano. Cuca was there and she seemed to have a very good time. Everyone said it was a wonderful party. We have to take their word for it.

Personally, I had a "Nin" kind of attack. Everything seemed to me to be a terrible chore. Apropos of which, Aunt Lolita made me a present of a bit of philosophy: don't ask more of life than it gives you. From that I understand that I have been going down the wrong road. My reading has given me an idealized notion of the world. Although I think I am not romantic, I have to admit that I am, a little too much. I take one person after another in my entourage and make heroes of them. As soon as I get to know them, they become more like the villains in my books than anything else.

It has always been said and rightly so that comparisons are fatal, and I always compare. Even right now, I am sad. I just made a discovery. With my head full of romance, I am looking for the embodiment of an illusion. I thought I had found it. It's no use to give his name. I thought he had all the virtues of my greatest heroes, the qualities I am forever seeking. He has talent, goodness, youth, enthusiasm, beauty, etc. etc. I was going to put him in a book. Impossible! He is so human that he is just like all the others. Perhaps perfect heroes don't exist any more, after all, and I should abandon all hope of finding one and shouldn't think about it any more. I am not going to read so many books, I am going to read people. But oh, what a contrast!

I have started to write again because I understand that sometimes I write cynical and pessimistic things, things I would have no right to write if I were a little wiser and had a better disposition. But it is purely the fault of Mother Nature and my artistic temperament.

It was raining outside today and I was in a frightful humor, but sometimes the sun is shining outside and inside it is stormy. And my artistic temperament isn't the cause of my different moods, and I beg you not to have too bad an opinion of me, because it runs in the family. You see, as I grow old (and at present I am 16 years into old age) I understand many things I had never thought about before. And today, as I meditated on my inexplicable changes of mood and their results, I had a brilliant insight. My disposition is a faithful copy of Papa's. With one single difference: his is noble in its weakness and wonderful even with all his faults, while mine is like that of a child who has been badly brought up because of a change of teachers, and is ruled by feminine weakness instead of masculine severity. But I try so often to be reasonable, to be lighthearted, to look the world in the face instead of from a high mountain of sand with my eyes shut, and with ideas that are so numerous and so easily blown away by a light breeze, so transparent, as trivial and useless as the sand.

In a book I read, they said that the pen is as mighty as the sword and that whoever wields the pen as a weapon must learn to prefer single combat in the dark of night. Perhaps that is why this evening I have fled from the room where my family is gathered to laugh and talk, far away from the living room which is full of visits from the Madriguera family and where I hear above all the other voices that of Enric, far from the garden inundated by rain, to the kitchen where I have the company of culinary insects, a mournful light, and the delicate fragrance of the lotion that I always use to bathe my hands as the only pleasant sensation.

Literature has rules about the way things should be written in logical order, but here I want you to know that I write my diary in violation of all the rules of the universe. That's why, since I am now tired of reflecting on my nasty disposition, I shall change the subject abruptly.

In studying people as one studies animals and plants, I am making discoveries. Thus, like certain flowers that have no fragrance to give them away, there is someone who had never attracted my attention as an object of study and now, by her beauty, I have discovered her worth.

This is Monsita,[1] our maid, who has revolutionized and completely destroyed the prejudices I didn't think I had against certain races. I take so much pleasure in listening to her serious opinions about the books she has read, about people, that although her skin is a different color from mine, I can't help respecting her, admiring her noble character and a vast intelligence such as one doesn't often find even in the race of white people (among whom there are so many scoundrels), which has been able to make itself the strongest because of its large numbers. And now I observe her. One of the things that delights me the most is to see the lightning speed with which her anger rises—and falls, the effect of her rapid

[1] *Monsita (Montserrat) had been a schoolteacher in Puerto Rico.*

expression of indignation that is like a powerful discharge of electricity, the pride and dignity that flow from her smallest gestures, and the soundness of even her slightest reasoning. Thus she is one of the most striking proofs of the nobility of work, which no servitude can humble. How dare anyone, in the face of a maid who has better manners than a great lady, how dare anyone in these times of modern liberty still place a social and moral barrier between noble work and the ignoble idleness of a pretended aristocracy?

June 27. A person with enough curiosity and lots of time to waste could have sat on the highest tower among the New York buildings and witnessed the following spectacle: several millions of umbrellas moving, tramways and automobiles trickling water, and all the roofs shining clean under the shower. From time to time, the streets that have been deserted by the crowd are transformed into mirrors sparkling with streams of various sizes.

Among the crowd of umbrellas that were not acquainted with one another, there were two umbrellas whose owners you know. Those two umbrellas left their homes at 9 this morning, one more or less protecting Maman and her sister Anaïs, the other Cuca and insignificant me.

They walked very quickly along Fifth Avenue and each time they passed a large store, they closed, and with a sigh of satisfaction the 4 people walked in among the counters where a thousand different kinds of merchandise were spread out. And so on from one store to another. Once the two umbrellas had half an hour's rest under a table, while above the table lunch was eaten. Little by little their task became more difficult, because in addition to covering fashionable hats (badly), those dignified umbrellas had to cover dozens of packages of various sizes. Finally, as their services were not at all satisfactory, they were closed and put in the corner of a taxi. That taxi transported one of the umbrellas to the Hotel Netherlands and the other to 158 West 75th Street. The latter was greatly distracted when it was put in a difficult and shameful position to get rid of its wet coat, while its two masters examined the things that had been purchased. A pink ball gown with a great deal of tulle and a big rose at the waist, a navy-blue taffeta dress with funnel- or bell-shaped sleeves, an adorable black velvet jacket, two blouses, one made of georgette and the other of pink net, a pink silk skirt to go with the blouses and the jacket, silk stockings, and—I think that's all; no, I mean that's all the umbrella saw.

If the umbrella had been curious, it would have learned that for those unaccountable frivolities for a spoiled girl, Maman spent the fabulous sum of $113.75. And an amazing thing! she has no regrets at all. She consoles herself by saying that this amount, which prepares me to spend one or two weeks in the mountains with Aunt Anaïs and one or two years in New York, would buy Cuca just *one* dress. There, that's human consolation! But since I don't believe an umbrella can think like that, I shall disappear (I mean that I put the umbrella back in its place). After becoming *un*wet, it returned to its place in the umbrella stand. But outside the rain is still falling, as money falls from the pockets of rich folk and tears from the eyes of the poor and the pessimistic philosophers. (That's me. That's how I cry—when I cry!)

But here, I must put in a personal word, because the umbrella doesn't know anything about what goes on when the weather is fine. I am leaving Tuesday for Lake Placid. That outlay of money is to fill my trunk, because my closets are almost empty. I am going for just a short time. Aunt Anaïs says I am going to gain weight, Cuca says it's to enjoy myself, Maman says it's to gain weight and enjoy myself, and as for myself, I withhold my opinion.

June 28. Yesterday Thorvald and Joaquinito finished school for the summer, but in my feminine egotism among my frills, I didn't think it was important enough to mention. They are delighted, however! That makes me think of that faraway time when I also celebrated vacations with many smiles and great satisfaction. For the moment, my life is an eternal vacation. There are times when I think with tears in my eyes and despair in my heart of how useless I am. I wait in vain for a literary inspiration, an idea for a book that would simultaneously make me rich for Maman's sake and a member of the French Académie for my own. But every day I wait for my book and it doesn't come. I have often begun and moved forward without hesitation until the story reaches the tragedy or comedy of passion and love. Once there, I hesitate, I get mixed up, I stop writing and start to cry. How, oh, how to describe a feeling that I don't know, an art that is unknown, inexplicable, and not very real? I who can write endless chapters about the personalities of children and grownups who are not married or are widowed, about birds, animals, geography, travels, discoveries, inventions, etc. etc., I am confronted with a problem when I want there to be a little bit of love in my stories, for without that, it seems to me that nobody will read them. But I can't imitate the things that Dumas or George Sand or Pierre Loti or James Allen or Scott write on this subject, which they seem to know thoroughly. Yet if I keep waiting, my book won't be written until I am 40 or perhaps never, who knows!

My family has always been very patient with my taste for literature, like all families who hope to see Fame arrive in their midst and aren't yet sure on whose head it will descend. At present, Joaquinito doesn't feel he has to call me a poet, nor does Thorvald, because I have changed so much since the days when Maman did the mending and I the writing (that was when they respected me). Now I do the mending of stockings and shirts and I write only in notebooks that they are not allowed to read. And Maman, having no substantial proof of my progress, no longer considers me a poet or an author who will be famous one day, but rather a daughter to be married off. That's more natural, more down-to-earth. And please God that before she tries the latter and fails shamefully, may I find my place in front of a desk covered with papers and a pen in my hand to write not my first book but the twentieth, and may I already be a member of the Academy, etc.

As if it were possible to run out of breath from writing, I shall pause for a moment to pant.

It's for the future that I make plans. And what a future! If I live long enough, I'll see—as the fly must have said, once it was stuck to the flypaper.

I have just noticed that the more I write, the more my birds sing, until they nearly deafen me. But it's pleasant to be deafened by the songs of two canaries.

You must be wondering why I write so much in one day. I am alone, all alone in our big room, because Maman, Thorvald and Joaquinito have gone to Edgemere to spend Saturday and Sunday. I didn't go because I have so many preparations to make. It is 4 and I have done all that I can do today, so now I can enjoy talking to you. It's really the only time that I can really enjoy chatting, I who talk so little and with such difficulty. Sometimes I really savor the pleasure that my diary gives me, and I have often wondered if it isn't out of unbounded egotism, since I am continually talking about myself. Perhaps it may be that, but also the real reason is that I understand how much good you do me.

My entire stack of books [diaries], which represents a stack that has been accumulating for years, acts as a strainer. Not the kind of strainer that one uses in the kitchen to strain the soup, but a mental strainer that has a certain charm. All that I say, all that I think, is put slowly through that strainer and spread out on your pages without any artistic preparation. And there, I study it and I see that by going through the strainer, all of it is improved, purified, filtered. I can remember things that I haven't done so that I wouldn't have the shame of writing them down; but if I did them, I find them written straight out, spread out here with all the love of the truth which is *not* in my character but which *you* have forced me to cultivate.

So it isn't all egotism, it's also a way of acting as my own teacher.

June 29. I was very surprised and very sad last night to go to bed all alone in the big oak bed. I brushed my hair in silence, a thing that never happens when we are all together. But I discovered that if I remain alone like that for several days, I'll be able to write a book with amazing ease. Last night I was already inspired, but Maman had made me promise to go to bed at 9:30, and although they say that bluestockings never keep promises, I kept mine. But as Maman hadn't ordered me to fall asleep at 9:30, I thought until our clock had sighed midnight.

This morning I got up at 8 and I was going to Communion. But I am going through a cooling-off period and it still hasn't passed.

Aunt Lolita, Godmother and I had lunch together.

At 2 Aunt Anaïs came with Cuca and Ana Maria.[1] We went to visit Rita Allie[2] at the Hotel Majestic. She is as beautiful as ever but very much changed. The conversation turned to dance and the theatre, things to which she used to attach no importance, but perhaps that's because, like me, she is growing up. But someday I shall put her beauty in a story, as I shall put Monsita's anger, Joaquinito's mischief, Thorvald's love of good things to eat, and many other things as I discover them.

We have just had a cold dinner, and Godmother and Aunt Lolita are reading the newspapers. I am taking advantage of the long hours of daylight to write, because I feel very lonely, not materially but spiritually. Today I found out that Godmother knows an infinite number of details about the lives of Maman and Papa, long ago when they were happy. I shall use them when I

[1] *Ana María Sánchez, A.N.'s cousin.*
[2] *A Cuban girl attending convent school in New York.*

begin to write "Maman's memoirs," because Maman herself never goes further than his declaration of love, in spite of my enthusiasm to know more. I begin to think that the best part of love is the declaration, and this upsets the little bit that I know about that tragedy in which everyone takes part. I myself thought it was what came *after* the declaration of love that counted. How can I write a book in the midst of all these changes!

But one thing is true: the love described by poets and writers, the kind you find in books, is one thing, and love in real life is another. I don't yet know the difference, but one day I shall know. I don't want to deceive the public like that, even if it's only to make them happy. I shall write a book that describes Life exactly as it appears to my curious gaze, and that way, the generation that reads it will be ready to live when it has finished the book, whereas I have used books as my teachers, have let them fill my soul with poetry, my heart with romance, my eyes with illusions, and at present when I leave them behind, I have to begin to learn to live.

Now I am going to climb into the big oak bed and think a little. There is one thing I would like so much to know! Since I am so frank with you, couldn't you give me the same kind of answer to my question? Oh, tell me: Am I really very—ugly?

June 30. An entire day spent in the stores has tired me terribly. But I forget my fatigue when I look at my purchases: a pair of white satin shoes with Louis XV heels, a pair of tennis shoes, a pretty comb, hairpins, handkerchiefs, a black velvet tam-o'-shanter, and blue slippers. My trunk is almost packed, but I am almost asleep.

July 1. Still in New York. My trunk has just left. I have run so much all over the house getting my things ready to go that God-mother and Aunt Lolita say I look like a bride on the eve of her wedding. My suitcase is ready, everything is in except you. Yesterday Godmother bought me a bag called a "Vanity Case," which contains my powder and rouge, jewelry, and also a pen and a perfumed handkerchief.

Until just now I haven't had time to think about the things and people that I will miss during these weeks. It isn't for long and it isn't very far away, but still! I made everyone promise to write. I'll miss Maman more than all the rest. Then Thorvald and Joa-quinito. Also my birds, my garden, Monsita, the living room window and the little armchair in which I never sit like everyone else, Godmother right after Joaquinito and Thorvald, and finally, in the same category with my birds, Enric Madriguera. He will fly off on July 9 and will come back in September. Yesterday in the evening, I returned his books to him with a little note, thinking that I wouldn't see him again, but this morning while I was on the telephone, he pulled my hair as he went up the stairs. That was his last gesture, because by September he will have forgotten me, and I him.

I received a letter from Papa that gave me food for thought. Among other things, in speaking of the idea that Thorvald and Joaquinito have forgotten him, he said, "they will be sorry to have been so lacking in courtesy toward their father, who has never done anything wrong in his relationship with them. I underline those words to emphasize them. Don't forget them."

Those words weren't at all a riddle for me. Without anyone having told me anything, I have understood something about the silent drama that separated my parents. That isn't a riddle, it's an overwhelming misfortune that tears me apart. It's that part of Life that I don't understand.

I shall put off answering that letter for a long time.

July 2. (In the train) It is so early that the sun hasn't yet risen. I am writing in a little bed which is in a compartment, with Cuca in the bed above me. But let's take things in order.

Yesterday at 7 o'clock I said good-bye to Maman, who went with me to Grand Central Station. Once in the train, the family was separated. Bernabecito and Eduardo[1] came into our compartment. We talked merrily until it was time to go to bed. We even discussed which came first, the chicken or the egg, as we ate a box of cherries and ice cream. I am beginning to be better acquainted with my cousins, but I shall leave their portraits until later. The heat was suffocating.

At 9:20 a Negro made up our berths and we went to bed. I had accepted, or chosen, the lower berth because of the view from the two windows.

Cuca had a great deal of difficulty climbing into her berth but was rewarded by being close to a cooling electric fan. Since I was exclaiming about the beautiful river, bridges and trees, Cuca came down to sleep with me. At first we tried the natural position, but she was too warm because one of the windows, the one closest to

[1] *Bernabé and Eduardo Sánchez, A.N.'s cousins.*

my head, was closed. Then she put her pillows at the foot of the bed and settled herself in that direction, but the open window let in so much black dust that it threatened to change her color, and if she shut it she was too warm, so she made the difficult climb back up above and I believe she fell asleep.

But we had time to talk and since we were already around to confidences, we broached the inevitable subject: "men" of our age. Cuca told me that of all her friends, there is a special one she prefers. I forgot myself so far as to tell her that of all those I know, even Mr. Walker, I prefer Enric Madriguera. And yet I completely forgot to tell him good-bye yesterday because I was so excited!

A "nuit blanche"[1] then began. I, who always sleep so well and dream so sweetly, didn't sleep the whole night long. I saw the stars and the moon, and the rest of the night the telegraph poles and trees, telegraph poles and trees, telegraph poles and trees, etc. Sometimes I dreamed awake, and then a strong bump, bells, the noise of steam escaping from a smokestack would come along and the train would stop in a station. One of them was Newburgh, but there were 4 or 5 others that I didn't know. Little by little, the stars disappeared, all except one. I watched the day break, and with daylight a wintry cold set in. Only now, the sun is beginning to appear through the mist that covers the low hills and lakes.

Two automobiles were waiting for us. In a quarter of an hour, we were at the house. We went to have breakfast at the Club. Cuca and I have been given our room, one of the nicest: large, white, simply furnished, and with a view from the windows fit for all the kings. There are mountains, valleys, fields full of flowers and wild strawberries, a beautiful lake called Mirror Lake that reflects the pine trees and cottages. Everything is natural splendor, majestic scenery, incomparable! In just a few minutes I picked bunches of flowers as I used to do in my dearest dreams; there are daisies, bluebells, little golden flowers, wild roses, lilies of the valley, lavender flowers.

Close to the house there is a nest with four little eggs in it, and a strange thing: it isn't perched in a tree but is simply on the grass.

The house itself is lovely to see. Everything is new and white.

We are waiting for our trunks so that we can change our clothes, and I am writing while Cuca takes a bath.

But the day has only begun.

[1] *Sleepless night.*

July 5. It is morning, about 6. I made an effort to get up before the others and having combed my hair and put on my sky-blue kimono, I am hurrying to write in my diary. Since the day I arrived here, I haven't been idle for a minute and it has really been impossible for me to write. But I knew you would be very glad to hear that I am undergoing a transformation: I have rosy cheeks and my whole face clearly shows the kind of thing I have been doing.

The walks that we have been taking together (generally Cuca, my [other] cousins Anaïs,[1] Graziella,[2] Eduardo, and I) last for hours and hours. Without worrying about spoiling our old clothes and old shoes, we have climbed a mountain, walked around Lake Placid, explored fields, little lakes and pine forests. Who can describe the joy of climbing a mountain! The excitement in the places that are dangerous, the pleasure of breathing the pure air fragrant with pines, the general merriment as each one tries to take the lead.

Yesterday in the evening we went to see a Venetian Festival on the big lake. All the boats were decorated with lanterns and several had flags, flowers and ribbons. In the dark, one could see only the lanterns reflected in the lake and the scene had an irresistible appeal. As it was the 4th of July, Independence Day, there were firecrackers and fireworks, which often took the form of many colored stars that opened to release a thousand sparks, like a shower of gold and silver.

A Club automobile brought us back to the house, and that ride also gave me pleasure. It's the only way to get home because the roads are so dark!

We take all our meals at the Club, at a big table, and we get a great deal of amusement from the grammar on the menu.

July 6. We went to Mass at the village church. It rained heavily and there was a noticeable change in the temperature from summer heat to winter cold. Right now, as I write, my hands feel as though they are made of ice.

Yesterday evening Cuca, Eduardo and I went rowing by moonlight. A very beautiful happening turned the outing into something truly magical. The clouds settled on the mountains, partly covering them, and the fog, doubtless caused by the contrast between warmth and cold, covered the lake. We rowed along among those fairy-tale clouds as though in a dream. I had my

1 *Anaïs Sánchez.*
2 *Graziella Sánchez.*

hand in the warm lake water and I was enchanted by it all. We only came back because the boat was slowly taking water.

Another thing that makes me very happy, besides all these wonderful things, is Cuca's friendship. It is a friendship that has a great deal of charm and value because the person who gives it is a remarkable girl.

Yesterday we visited the Club library and took out several books. Cuca is going to read "La Neuvaine"[1] by Colette, which I recommended to her, and I, "Lorna Doone" by [R. D.] Blackmore.

July 8. My day never ends when I go to bed, it begins again. In the silence of the chilly night, in a room lighted by the soft rays of Pierrot's moon, the gentle murmur of two soft voices rises from the two white beds, separated by a narrow strip of floor. The murmur begins when the lights go out and ends when the talkers fall asleep. Secrets are told, the kind of secrets that I have never told, that I never felt the need to tell. They come from the hearts of two bemused girls, not very serious and a little bit romantic. But Cuca has a lot of common sense. And if in the depths of the drawer you hear the murmur, you will know that I am learning what Cuca teaches me without knowing it.

An extraordinary thing: placing my trust in Cuca and knowing that her opinion would help me, I let her read a few pages of my diary. I acted happy, but deep down I was anxious, and very satisfied when she told me she liked it.

Since I have been here, out of whim or because of my unaccountable temperament, I have thought more than once of the violinist who remained behind me in New York and was going to leave for Spain on July 9. I wanted to write him a postcard, only a card, thinking that perhaps it would give him a tiny little bit of pleasure, since I forgot to say good-bye to him. But I didn't get around to it until the day he left because I had lost track of the days and thought it was a day earlier—so I sent it, but too late. Now he has gone. Gone until the month of September, and I miss him very much. No one will read this, for only my diary understands—will always understand—the delicacy, the fragility, but the sincerity of a young girl's romanticism that I can't overcome—and don't want to overcome.

Today we all carried our lunch in a little box and we climbed the mountain, carrying the boxes on our backs. Halfway up, after many detours and comical gymnastics among the rocks and minia-

[1] The Novena.

ture precipices, we separated two by two to eat lunch. Cuca and I found a nice hollow among the rocks and trees and had lunch together. It was a very jolly picnic.

July 14. I had to break my unspoken promise to write every day because it has been impossible. I hardly manage to write to Maman from time to time, giving her a mad description of my activities, because sometimes I feel with a great deal of sadness the number of miles that separate us.

Since July 8 I have done many things. But they are more or less a repetition of the pleasures I have already had. Saturday evening we danced. I danced with Bernabecito, who told me I am a good dancer, and with Mr. Bruzon, a friend of Cuca's. Also with Eduardo, who dances like Mr. Walker and Enric Madriguera. We have a wonderful time together, Eduardo and I. Our tastes are very similar and the influence we have on each other is truly comical, for each one sees in the other a counterpart of his own madness and fantastic leanings. If he is reading a book, I have already read it; if I say something, he was going to say it; he feels romantic (in the moonlight) and so do I; he is writing a composition and I am too; he wants to build a little theatre, which is just what I love; I am ecstatic about music, it makes him dreamy; he feels enthusiastic, I feel more enthusiastic than he does; I want to be someone different and so does he. And I could go on like this for several pages.

Watching over the mad moments brought on by the blending of two artistic temperaments is a wonderful kindly smile, so full of pity for the two lunatics, so full of good sense and patience— Cuca's smile. Of the three of us, she is the nicest, and for her the future holds the kind of happiness it knows how to give to those who make careful plans. Eduardo says he wants to bury his money and run away to become an actor. He wants an adventurous life. But there I am different. I have no money to bury and I don't need to run away. Also I want to be a bluestocking and turn people into actors, rather than being one myself.

Today I am writing because it is raining torrents. We are all in the living room with a fire in the big fireplace, and since none of us can go forever without talking, no doubt the conversation will be the cause of a little disorder in the way I write, but in my diary it doesn't matter!

First, I must copy a letter that I wrote to Papa, answering the one that upset me before I left.

Dearest Papa:

I received your letter in the midst of the great disorder that preceded my trip to the mountains, and it's only several days after arriving here that I can answer you.

The news you gave me about Grandfather[1] makes me very sad and I think of him often with regret. The only memory I have of him is of a venerable, stern, reserved and solemn person!

However, if I feel sorry about one paragraph, what can I say when I read the one following? I feel an infinite sadness that merely opens the wound in a heart which is already marked by Destiny. You complain. And what about? O Papa darling, if you could only see your two sons right now, you would understand why they, with their silence, are only behaving very naturally. I remember you, I love you more than other girls love their fathers, I am old enough to understand, to follow my inclinations and my heart; old enough, too, to suffer and to sympathize with the suffering of others.

One of the boys is just a child who hardly knows how to write, who doesn't remember you, who has inherited an incorrigible egotism and who can only love those who are devoted to him; he can't love out of duty. The other, a practical little fellow who respects those he loves, can only love real people, those he sees, and not the memory of a father whom he hardly remembers. He isn't hurt and doesn't understand why someone should feel pain about something he doesn't understand.

Neither of them has ever thought of you as one of Life's problems. You are their father. That is enough for them. Do you believe they have ever thought about whether you are in the wrong or not? It's not because the little one doesn't write well and the older one doesn't like to write, for if Maman is away for a few days, both of them write at length and sometimes so much that Maman can't answer it all. It all depends on you, you see. You have to win their love and when they love you, they will write to you, not out of politeness, which would be an ignoble reason, but out of their need, with joy, as they write to Maman. If the things I am writing here hurt your feelings, forgive me, because what you said called for a direct explanation. You say you are in excellent health, so you will have time to rebuild your lost happiness.

My love will never fail you, you can always count on your fifille, and later, when they relearn what they have forgotten, on your sons.

[1] *A.N.'s paternal grandfather, Joaquin Maria Nin y Tudó, had died.*

This is a long answer to your few words, but it's all that I have to say.

Now you must be curious to know how and why I am here. Aunt Anaïs . . . etc. etc.

In a word, I am in the midst of a whirlwind of pleasures . . . etc. etc.

All the love of your linotte,

Anaïs

After having written so much, I think I don't have anything more to say. Oh, yes! As this is the most important thing and something I have been thinking about the whole time, I'll put it in a P.S. [to my diary].

P.S. Something unexplainable is happening to me. I thought that I had outgrown this kind of childish caprice. When I was in New York in my garden or my room and the sound of a violin obliged me to think of the violinist all the time, I didn't think about him the way I do now. I said to myself that it was the violin that was magical. And now, at any time of the day or night, without there being a violin to remind me, I think about the violinist without seeing him. And when I think of him, sometimes I'm happy, sometimes sad. Happy to have so many things about him to remember, and sad because he has gone away. Could it be the violinist who is magical? And what is happening to me? I am sure that he has already forgotten me, that he only thought of me when he saw me from his window, working in the garden while I listened to him practicing. I remember what he did the day of my 16th birthday, the dance on the evening of Emilia Quintero's recital, the wedding march the night of the little party, the rides in the automobile and especially the one on Riverside, the horseback rides—Oh, heavens!

Cuca has just tried to read all this. What will she say? If she knew what I have written, she would never want to speak to me nor be my friend. She wouldn't understand—it's on account of all the books I've read. But, oh! how I would like to know if books affect her the same way—

And also there's something I don't understand. I always think of him at the same time that I think of my canaries and my garden. When I am boating by moonlight, I think regretfully of my canaries, my garden, and Enric. Which category does he belong in? I never read *that* in a book!

Perhaps I'll know what all this means when I am old, very

old, and that's the only reason I am writing it down. So that I can understand it someday! I wish I were already old!

Aunt Anaïs is still sick and Cuca is very worried, as she is the little mother of a very large family. And I wander around like a lost soul. I wish with all my heart that I could be home again. I knew that would happen, but not that I would wish it so hard. Tonight, I'm sure I will cry myself to sleep, and heaven only knows how homesick I am!

July 15. Aunt Anaïs is not any better, but as the weather is beautiful, we often go out. Cuca is sad. At first I did what silly people do, I tried to find out why; but after a while I realized that I am not the only one who has "attacks." And by coincidence, the two of us found in a book a very simple description of the reason, which neither of us knew:

The Lost World
by Henry Van Dyke

There is a sadness of youth into which the old cannot enter. It seems to them unreal and causeless. But it is even more bitter and burdensome than the sadness of age. There is a sting of resentment in it, a fever of angry surprise that the world should so soon be a disappointment, and life so early take on the look of failure. It has little reason in it, perhaps, but it has all the more weariness and gloom, because the man who is oppressed by it feels dimly that it is an unnatural and an unreasonable thing, that he should be separated from the joy of his companions and tired of living before he has fairly begun to live.

Hermas had fallen in the very depths of this strange self-pity. He was out of tune with everything around him.

July 16. Amidst so much natural beauty and thoughts of certain bygone days that I can't drive away from my memory, my thoughts had to turn toward a different light and open a new subject. Is it my age? The intoxication of Nature? The charm of novelty? Alas! I hardly know myself anymore! Everything around me sings in an unknown language, the same unexplainable and mysterious song that books and older people talk about. And I listen and think and . . . don't understand. Everything is transformed into music, which can be grand and solemn or light as a fairy.

The other day, in the midst of a musicale, a comparison came to me, and as soon as I was outside, I wrote it on the envelope of a telegram. Here it is:

Love must be like music, intoxicating, gay at times and infinitely sad at others. Perhaps, after having drunk of music and love, one could lie down and die.

Dearest diary, you know very well that I have never talked to you about romance—as I thought myself a very wise philosopher, a very serious girl, the result of a sudden transformation from little girl into old woman. I thought that my ideas were above an illusion which is only a little rose and gold amidst Life's solemn scene. And all that has left me like a damp storm cloud that stood between me and the sun. Yes, dear God, I am only a girl of 16 and like all the others, those that I looked down on with sarcasm and disdain—before all this happened. It's Nature's spell . . . it will pass. The rose and gold shine for a short time compared to the dark colors, which last like all real things, while the others live just the days of illusion and dreams—one day—like butterflies.

July 18. The Bruzon family, friends of Cuca's, took us for a ride in their automobile that lasted from four until seven o'clock. It was like visiting a gallery full of wonderful paintings, but a thousand times more beautiful. In the background there were mountains, clad in dark forests. And all around us, fields carpeted with flowers, little houses covered with wisteria and other climbing plants, fields golden with the harvest, and from time to time, haystacks drying peacefully in the sun. The road was like a rollercoaster, sometimes running through meadows and valleys, sometimes through dark woods with their majestic trees growing toward the sky. I saw things that I had never seen except in pictures and paintings: small herds of cows with little bells around their necks, chickens, and wheat-fields. I was full of enthusiasm, giddy with pleasure, when suddenly something terribly platonic, stupid and inevitable happened: the car ran out of gas. It was like a cold shower on my imagination. After having waited in the sun a long time for gas, we came back at a speed of 40 miles an hour.

One of the things we saw was Upper Saranac Lake, which is nine miles long. It stretched out there among the mountains like a long wide river as blue as the sky, reflecting the golden rays of the sun.

This morning very early, Bernabecito came back from New York with Billin, my other cousin, so now everyone is here. We now have a car and it's funny to see how we all crowd in to go everywhere.

July 19. The place where I am writing is worthy of a little description. Imagine a big lake, a real blue mirror, with mountains and forests all around; silence that is only broken from time to time by the light sound of the oars of other boats passing by. We are in a fragile little green boat in the shade of a big tree whose branches have grown out over the lake, and I am writing while Cuca reads a thick book. I can see the bottom of the lake covered with stones and leaves, and I often raise my head to look at Cuca a little while, for a narrow beam of sunlight slips through the branches and shines on her hair, which looks full of light.

But there are other things to see as well. Through an invisible crack, water is leaking very slowly into the bottom of the boat. It makes me think that this is the way slander and flattery enter our hearts.

There is something else I want to write about that came to me yesterday: the prudence of older people, the imprudence of the young. Two elderly ladies were frightened by the speed of the car, while three young people wanted to go faster still. It seems as though the elderly hate to see the end of the Great Ride and wish that time would not pass so quickly, for they are very close to the End; but the young rush into everything with the enthusiasm of youth, without fear and without hesitation. What a difference! What a contrast! Both can lack only one thing: gasoline . . . or Life. Then both must come to a stop. It can't be avoided!

These last few days I have caught a terrible cold which keeps me from breathing and talking in my natural voice. We are waiting for the time of the bath—four o'clock. At that time a comical procession begins, and then the whole family is ready for the dinner hour in the supreme elegance of cleanliness. And this evening we think we'll go to the dance.

Cuca has a headache and is stretched out on her bed, while Ana Maria jumps from one bed to the other, laughing and shrieking with joy. As to Ana Maria, she is a little angel, 6 years old, in the style of Joaquinito. If I do her portrait here, I'll be able to reread it with pleasure later on. She is a real little Cuban doll. The first thing one notices is her brilliant eyes, two big black eyes shining with the same light as Joaquinito's: intelligence, childish mischief, innocence, and almost always happiness. She has a little turned-up nose, a pink heart-shaped mouth, little pearly teeth, golden hair; in a word, this little girl is as pretty as an angel. She is very lively, with adorable manners and caprices that no one can ignore.

But since you know Ana Maria, you should also meet all my cousins. There is Graziella, who is 12 years old, a nice little girl with all the faults that children have at that age. There is Anaïs, whose depths I haven't yet been able to sound, but the surface is something that causes her family a lot of sorrow: extreme selfishness. She hides her smile, her feelings, and only lets one see her capricious side. I always feel like taking her and turning her inside out, as I am sure there is good within. There is Eduardo, whom I have already described a little, and I consider him a linotte in masculine form. Thorvald and Bernabecito are two magnificent examples of well-brought-up, honorable, perfect young men.

To be sure, I should have started with Cuca. But I hardly dare write the things that I have in mind, because if by chance she took my diary and read it without my permission, she might believe them and swell up with pride. In my cottage, far away, I shall introduce you to Cuca, aided by unforgettable memories. Suffice it to say that if I turned Cuca inside out, I would always find myself face to face with an ideal disposition.

Four o'clock is drawing near. But I feel very bad, both as to health and as to emotions. I look at my little family in this little bungalow with feelings of infinite tenderness and the sadness of our separation to come. Another kind of tenderness always comes over me like music when I think of the sunny days at 158 W. 75th Street, which won't be there when I go back. Why is it that we recognize joy only when it is gone? And why must the memory of happy days be sad? When I scold myself about it, it's even worse; so I write in order to make it pass, knowing that you and I understand. Enric will come back in September, but will it all be the same?

I have just read a thin little book that contains the diary of a little Japanese girl. It's like a storybook. There is a tiny little resemblance between her thoughts and mine, and I almost wept out of sympathy—something that would never happen to me if my mind were not disposed for such things.

July 20. Everything is silent. Only from time to time I cough and the cough hurts a lot. I am alone in the house with Anaïs, who also has a cold, but outside the weather is splendid. Since I feel sick, I also feel sad, but my thoughts are not in harmony with my surroundings.

Last night after dinner I felt so sick that I didn't go to the dance. Everyone left, and Anaïs and I stayed home. We read and made tea. This morning everyone has gone to Mass. I wouldn't care if I were at home and sick, but here I feel very sorry about it. I am so afraid to cause work for the family and to make my visit a burden rather than a pleasure. There are some things the good Lord sends us that we can't explain. And naturally, all this makes me feel even more homesick. I have explained all this to Cuca and I think I will leave soon. Oh, I think with such tenderness of the little house at the seashore! I have been trying in vain to shake off my melancholy. Just now, I hear everyone coming back. And they are laughing so hard that I have to smile.

3 o'clock. One might say, and rightly so, that one's feelings change like the weather. As soon as Cuca arrived, the effect of her clear gaze was instantaneous. Now I am happy, and yet it is raining outside. We had lunch, after which we went for a little walk. Now we are waiting for 4 o'clock to go rowing. Sundays are very calm here. All the entertainments are closed to the public and there are very few things to do. Cuca and I are sitting under a little canopy near the house and we can see the mountains and fields. Extremely clear air completes this pleasant scene. As Cuca is very much absorbed in her book, I can write what I am thinking without being distracted.

From here I can hear Thorvald playing the mandolin, which he does very well. He is playing "Madelon," "I Told My Love to the Stars," "Won't You Help Me Out," "Hindustan," "Beautiful Ohio," "How're You Going to Keep Them Down on the Farm?" etc. etc. I know why they say that one shouldn't make comparisons. Especially when I compare the dance music of the mandolin with the classical music and studies for the violin.

Cuca just interrupted me to tell me that she spoke about my trip to Aunt Anaïs, and I can leave on Tuesday by myself. Oh, the thrill of a long trip all alone! But everything is very prosaic and heaven knows when my thirst for a Great Adventure will be satisfied. But I keep that thirst alive in little ways, as in always choosing danger and looking for it everywhere.

July 21. It's very true that I will remember these three weeks at Lake Placid as the best vacation I have had in a long time. But I have also learned the great value that I attach to my own little family and how I suffer when I am far away from them. Yes, it's absence that helps us to understand!

Last night, after Cuca and I went to bed, the murmur began.

But the finale of the symphony was different. Generally sleep over-takes us and we just say good night, but last night we hugged each other and promised to be friends forever. I can't remember another friendship that has grown so rapidly and with so much sincerity. Cuca says she was always afraid to meet me because Godmother had talked so much about my good qualities, and it was exactly the same with me. The result was not a failure, but very funny, human discoveries. I have found in Cuca everything I hoped to find, and in 3 weeks I understand her better than Godmother will ever understand her. And I hope with all my heart that Cuca will forgive my tastes and my whims, so different from her own, as different as the temperament must always be between sensible people and crazy ones.

I wrote yesterday to Maman and am waiting for a telegram to know if I should leave. I shall leave with regret, and it's not because I know I have to leave. I have a secret, a secret that I want you to know. Do you remember the strange pain in my side that I had a long time ago and that worried Dr. Murray?

Sometimes it came back, but no one knew it. There is no point in worrying Maman about such an insignificant thing. And now it has come back and is very bad, and I am the only one who knows. But I don't want to be sick here on top of being homesick and make work for Aunt Anaïs, who is so kind, and for Cuca, who deserves to have a wonderful, wonderful time without anything getting in her way.

When we go out in the canoe, Cuca dreams about a castle with palm trees on the banks of a river. She will have cows and brown horses. Then I describe the splendid castle of my dreams, on the ocean shore with golden sand dunes and pine forests. I will have black and white horses but no cows, because I am very much afraid of them.

There are several things that I don't care to talk about, like the inevitable violin that always accompanies my dreams, canaries in golden cages, big dogs, little white cats with blue eyes, rooms full of books; and my bedroom, which is going to be all in sky blue, the furniture and everything, with large windows overlook-ing the sea. The forest will be my garden. And my Shadow will be there, he who will write in my diary with me, and also the chil-dren that I am going to adopt, who will have black curls and black eyes and will know how to speak French and Catalan. There will be a girl whom I shall marry to Joaquinito's son, if he is an artist, and a son whom I shall marry to Thorvald's daughter, who will have a lot of common sense, I am sure.

But what good does it do to dream like this? Am I such a child that I still build castles in the sand?

Cuca is upset because I forgot myself and made a little fun of Cubans. Now I am terribly sorry but I don't dare tell her so. We have settled down in our room and she is reading.

It is still raining. Ana Maria has just been given a bath and she is walking around in her little sky-blue kimono, babbling. It makes me think of Joaquinito when he goes around after his bath without any clothes on and nobody in the world is able to make him get dressed.

It goes on raining—I think I won't make fun of Cubans any more. It isn't very nice. I think also that I don't very much want to go to heaven because three people have already said to me, "Good-bye, I suppose that we shall meet again in heaven . . ." The third one was Ana Maria's very ugly governess who left this morning. Unfortunately, she is French, and I was not very proud of that fellow countryman, I can tell you!

Ten o'clock. Our bedtime. We have just had a family discussion about people's diaries, and everyone thinks that they cannot be absolutely sincere. But mine is the most sincere thing about me, don't you agree?

July 22. It is raining again today. We are not very active. I am waiting patiently for the telegram to arrive.

This evening we were assembled in the living room and Aunt Lolita turned the conversation toward the inexhaustible subject: girls and love. She said a lot of really sad things that have left me very thoughtful. She is only telling the bitter truth, I suppose, but I refuse to believe it. I am going to refuse until the day that I can find out for myself about what she said.

July 23. Lake Placid. I woke up in Maman's arms! That was the answer to my letter. Maman darling, if you knew how quickly all my sadness flew away, you would understand how dear you are to me.

She spent the day with us and I am leaving with her this evening. I am hurrying to pack my trunk.

July 24. Edgemere. From the mountains and the shores of a lake, you have traveled to the seashore, to a cottage. And I with you!

Last night at 8:10, the dark train left the station at Lake Placid and began its long trip, leaving behind my cousins and Cuca, who was with me until the last minute. The memory of

Cuca's face is still with me and I am so sorry to have left her behind.

Instead of traveling in a compartment like a millionaire, Maman and I were merely seated in a little corner of the train. I was looking forward with secret pleasure to the moment when I could write in my diary, and when the moment came, I hurried to get out my pen and write a few words when—(like the day of the gasoline) I ran out of ink. Despair! I looked for a pencil, no pencil, and then I sighed and resigned myself because there was nothing else to do.

A strange thing, I didn't spend a "nuit blanche." On the contrary! I began to look at the stars from the depths of my pillow, with my eyes wide open, but Maman, who slept in the same bed, made me lower the shade and—sleep. After all, it was more beautiful to watch the stars, but more comfortable to sleep.

Very early, toward 7, the train stopped in New York, that same dusty New York that I left 3 weeks, 3 months, perhaps 3 years ago. I didn't feel any emotion worth analyzing, except for the great urge I had to stop everyone and exclaim: "I've been to Lake Placid!" But how can one analyze a feeling controlled by the fear of being shut up in a lunatic asylum!

I can truthfully say that my heart ached when I came face to face with my old house. It hadn't changed, but I had, and very clearly. First, when we went in, no one whistled to me from the second floor. Once inside the house, everything was silent; no laughter, no violin. No one came running down the stairs. Twice, while I was in the living room, people came in and the sound of their key in the lock, the familiar noise that always followed the entrance of a shadow that I could still sense behind the door, made me put my hand to my heart.

Without meaning to, I climbed to the top floor, went into the little room and saw, sadly, the indications of the presence of someone new—not a violinist but an *old maid!* Absurd! On the living room mantel, there is a new photograph. It's a picture of Enric with his arms crossed and his head thrown slightly back; it looks very noble, very young, very handsome, and very far away. And I am keeping the best for the last, the saddest part. It's a note that he wrote Maman, and he said something in it for me. I know it by heart; it's already a little worn from having been in my pocket all day long.

What Aunt Lolita said haunts me: "When girls are 16, they often idealize someone during his absence."

And she added that one shouldn't do that. But since I do it

without meaning to, how can I stop myself when my heart aches or beats very hard, or stops beating?

And so wrapped in the supreme egotism of a dream, I can't write here about the simpler, happier, more prosaic things in life. I'll put that off until tomorrow.

July 25. Today was the beginning of a series of unbearable days. Aunt Antolina is here; she has a cottage very near ours, and Charlie[1] and Antolinita spend the day with Thorvald and Joaquin. They have many things to do, many wild little friends, and they spend the day all together, yelling, laughing and playing. They are children, but I avoid them like the plague because I don't feel like playing.

One of my chief occupations is hunting down flies. I give them names—Miss Hart and others—I track them carefully and bang! I flatten them with a sigh of satisfaction, for the good of mankind.

But I dream more than anything else and am learning to dive into the water.

July 26. Yesterday afternoon we were all together for dinner in Aunt Antolina's cottage when Maman arrived from New York. Her absence makes me just as homesick as when I was at Lake Placid.

Today, a few minutes after breakfast, we went to swim in the bay. At noon we were starving and we ate like wolves. Later we went to the beach to play in the big waves. But all day long, I fled from people, wanting only to be alone because of an unexplainable melancholy. I suppose that it's only a whim. So I spent most of the day lying in the hammock and letting my dreams swing on the sea breeze—my dreams!

I laughed a lot one time when I was taking a sunbath in the sand after swimming; distractedly, I had written Enric's name in the sand and Maman caught me. Usually when she makes fun of something that I do, that's enough, but what could be stranger: after mocking me, she left for a moment, came back, and caught me a second time! That time, I ran like mad and dived into the waves, feeling truly sorry not to be able to fall asleep at the bottom of the sea and not think of anything any more!

While I am writing, I can't help thinking of Lake Placid and its pleasures, and my little pine-needle pillow gives off a delicious

[1] *Carlos de Cárdenas.*

fragrance. At the same time, I have to hear the entire conversation between Maman and Godmother, for although I am in Maman's room, the walls are probably made of paper. There are other more or less pleasant noises, too: a baby crying, a phonograph, a player piano, a dog, trains, etc., and I wonder how I can write a book in such surroundings.

I am really in the position of a poet who had the bad idea of getting married and is attacked by a great big, very cumbersome family. There are children everywhere, friends of Joaquinito and Thorvald, whom I refuse even to meet. There is only one little boy whom I like very much: our little neighbor, Arthur. He is a little Irish boy, I believe, with blue eyes and an irresistible smile. He and Thorvald can make me smile in spite of myself. He has only to look at me and the joy in his eyes and his infectious smile are enough. I was almost angry with myself, today especially, because I felt so unsociable, so serious and solitary.

One thing has added to my sadness: the very heavy rain that broke the calm of a superb day, and I am still writing, as I so often do, to see if that will make the feeling go away.

My cold is better except that it has settled in my chest and Maman is very worried. And all day long the whole family exclaims that I am thin as an asparagus stalk, as though they had just discovered something new.

July 27. Swimming in the ocean all day long has made me very weak and Maman is taking care of me as though I were a little baby. Little by little, I'll get my strength back.

I don't swim very well but I am not at all afraid, so I go far out, away from the beach and the people. I love to be alone among the waves and in the midst of danger.

Maman is very happy but very tired because every 5 minutes the cottage is full of sand and swimming gives us an appetite that calls for a lot of cooking. What upsets me the most is the noise here. Even now, every imaginable kind of noise is coming from the other cottages, while in our own there is the singing of my canaries and Joaquinito's whistling.

I am still having an "attack" of unsociability and I make a big effort to smile from time to time. But I haven't written anything in the sand.

July 28. During the night we were all awakened by a terrible storm which seemed to want to tear the cottage from its foundation. The wind carried a strong odor of salt water, and that, on top

of flashes of lightning, thunder and the shaking of the cottage, gave us quite a scare because it felt as though we were in the middle of the ocean.

Maman got up very early this morning, and after having breakfast without making any noise, she left for New York, left for work. Thorvald and Joaquinito played all day long. Maman came back at 5:30, had a bath, then ate with us. That's the sort of life we expect to have all summer. Maman will spend only Saturday and Sunday entirely with us.

July 29. It's noon. Maman left long ago. I have discovered that it pleases her if I get breakfast for her. Thorvald, Charlie and some other boys have gone fishing and will eat their lunch right in the boat. Joaquinito is playing with Arthur. I just went swimming in the bay with Antolinita and now I am writing in an old armchair while my hair dries in the sun.

The amount of salt water that I have swallowed while learning to dive is beyond belief, but that doesn't kill my appetite. I can swim a little better and a little longer, too. Before leaving Edgemere, I want to swim across the bay, because Thorvald has already done it more than once.

Yesterday Maman brought me a picture of me on horseback that Enric gave her before he left, and once again that reminded me of many things and I fell into a reverie. I have only a little sense of humor, but even I had to laugh when the minute my "attack" returned, everyone thought I had caught another cold and offered me advice.

Aunt Edelmira wrote me a long letter that I am going to answer as soon as I am in a normal frame of mind.

I went to Far Rockaway with Antolinita and we went to the cinema together. When we got home, Maman was there and we had dinner. Then I walked around for a long time, so now I feel very tired and sick. It's a strange thing what an effect my state of mind has on my health. In order to get better, I try in vain to drive all the ideas out of my head so as to keep it as empty as the heads of all the other people who are always so happy.

I was thinking the other day that I would much rather be a bird than a girl, because I like the way they love much better than the way people do. They sing to one another all day long and never quarrel. What an example!

But someone who is sick should go to bed early and get a good night's sleep—*I* go to bed to reflect, think, dream, and get up in the morning to do the same thing during the day. I like the night better, because during the day one has to talk and laugh, even play sometimes—play at the age of 16!

July 30. A workman is painting our little cottage. Almost everything is green, except the windowsills, which are very clean and white. Right now it truly looks like a little doll house. To transform the interior, I have only to sweep every day and dust the furniture. It's our dishes that are funny. Can you imagine that all we have is two big soupspoons and two soup plates, so that Maman, Godmother and I have to eat our soup in cups, using teaspoons? We have four plates; the fifth one is only half a plate. There are enough glasses, but we make coffee in a little teapot. Maman will buy other things later on, but for the moment there's no need to spend the money.

My canaries are extremely happy here and one of them sings constantly. The other day, from I don't know where, Joaquinito brought home an ugly little black cat with green eyes. Later, when I surprised it on top of the canary cage, I asked Thorvald to take it away; so today when Joaquinito let go of it for a few minutes, Thorvald hid it in his sweater and lost it a long way from here. Joaquinito cried a lot and I was ready to bring it back, but Thorvald had more strength of character than I and refused.

July 31. A loud crash, a few dishes and pans falling, the table overturned, chairs thrown up in the air, windows broken, the house shaking, and from under the wreckage the calm and peaceful voice of some member of the family:

I killed a fly!

That's life at the cottage. C'est la guerre!

August 1. Maman said yesterday that she is disgusted with life, so I am too. It's no fun at all to be disgusted with life, especially when nothing comes along to make you feel better. The reason is very complicated, and since the day I understood it, I know that it's because I am 16 and am beginning to understand life. Do you know when one understands life? When one discovers all the things it involves: hypocrisy and selfishness, and after one has lost faith in real people. It's simple!

It's Godmother's fault. Here I want you to get to know Godmother. And without the slightest remorse, even though she is seated practically next to me, I am going to write the naked truth. But it isn't easy and I don't know where to begin.

Godmother is Maman's sister, and that name was given her the day she held me in her arms at my baptism. I don't remember that, but I've heard them talk about it. When I was very small, there were four adults in our large family who were extremely important to my happiness: Maman, Papa, Grandmother and Godmother. They spoiled me, took care of me, and I grew up in their midst. But little by little, first Grandmother, then Godmother, drifted away from us as everyone does, carried off by Fate. I heard almost nothing about Grandmother until I saw her during our trip to Spain, but like the fairy godmother in stories, Godmother always sent letters and gifts. I thought she was perfect, as I used to think people were. When I was little, I always used to pray that my hair would become ash-blond like hers and my eyes blue. I prayed to be tall and thin like her and to live as she does in a little house at the edge of the sea in Havana, with no husband and no children, sewing and reading all day long. Godmother was my model for the future. It was from her that I received my most beautiful dolls, and when I played with them in those days, my ambitions were like a doll's ideas about her doll house.

But it wasn't only because she spoiled me that I am grateful to Godmother. As I became aware of the world, I understood how devoted she was when Maman had need of her, and her sacrifices for our betterment. So I loved her first for her presents, afterward for her kindness toward Maman, later for all the useful things she showed me when Maman needed my help, still later for the illusion that I tried not to lose of the Godmother that used to be.

My aunts and cousins always criticized Godmother, destroying my illusions, and I defended her, I cried, and I always wound up believing that my aunts and cousins were very mean and that Godmother was still—Godmother.

And today—I can't hold onto the pen; I haven't the strength. I have just called up the past, which was so beautiful, and the present seems unworthy of being compared to it. And yet you have to know why Maman and I are sick and tired of it all: Godmother isn't a fairy godmother any more, she is a woman, just a woman like all other women. She has as many faults as everyone else; everything that Aunt Antolina and Aunt Anaïs said about her is true, alas! To be sure, Maman knew all that all along and that's why she has been disgusted with her for a long time, but she never said anything to me. Now Maman begins to see that I am old enough to understand. Among other things, Godmother makes our lives miserable by interfering continually with Joaquinito and Thorvald. Maman comes home from work tired, and instead of finding peace and quiet, she has to hear an avalanche of stories about quarrels with Charlie, quarrels with Antolinita, and many other things that are just as disagreeable and that make me terribly indignant.

Maman gets angry with Godmother, Godmother gets angry with Maman; Joaquinito gets a scolding, gets angry with Thorvald, Thorvald sulks; Maman goes to bed sadly, feeling almost sick. Godmother shuts herself in her room, she who is the cause of it all; Thorvald and Joaquinito cry themselves to sleep, and I am disgusted with life. That's not all. We have been talking about this for a week in the Cuban fashion; that is, exaggerating everything and making a scene. It's disgusting!

Once again one of my sand castles has collapsed, ruined. I have only a few left and the day that I don't have any, I shall go and fall asleep among the waves. But fortunately, there is one that nothing can demolish, the most beautiful one of all: my faith in Maman. And that castle is very strong because it's more than an illusion, it's a real, unchangeable truth!

August 2. Godmother has left. The whole family is peaceful, as though after a storm. Joaquinito is sick, probably with indigestion, but Maman is with us today and all is well.

August 3. Mass at 10. I am still having an attack, but little by little I am breaking the ice between Thorvald's friends and my unsociability. But it's very difficult to do. I have just this minute come back from a little dance at Antolinita's, and I could hardly bear to stay for half an hour. I know that they all wonder why I'm not more sociable, and I can hardly analyze my feelings myself; I only know that I'm sad.

August 4. Maman left at 8. I got breakfast, washed the dishes, made the beds, took care of my birds, sewed, ironed, washed, made lunch, washed the dishes again, and knitted. I have just had a bath and am lying in the hammock to let my hair dry. Each time I open my diary, a little paper written in pencil falls out, and I never fail to reread it. I don't know if you understand exactly why, but it makes me happy. It is to feel the same way I do when I am alone on the beach and can sing everything that goes through my head.

I was going to write more to explain my whims a little, but I remembered my duties as cook and since then I have had various things to do. Lucy, one of Antolinita's little friends, invited all the other children to a dance at her house, but I fled. . . . I shall let you know as soon as I become myself again, but I beg you not to be angry, not to grow impatient, because it's only my usual "attack" which is lasting a little longer than usual. And you know that I am never nice in a case like that.

I have discovered that I don't exactly get great pleasure from cooking. It's much nicer to put books in order rather than plates and silver, and the grease on dishes is unbearable. Pots and pans cause me to despair; Thorvald and Joaquinito laughed for half an hour at the faces I made while I was cleaning them today. I understand now why nobody believes in the housewifely talents of bluestockings.

August 5. It's raining. Everything is perfectly in harmony with my thoughts.

I have just reread my diary, as I do so often, and it seems to me I used to write better, a few weeks ago. I suppose that it depends on my mood and I wonder why I have changed so much. Sometimes I think it's the things I learned recently which make me so serious, but keep on being patient and soon I'll be myself again. Perhaps the rain will stop, too.

I have just discovered another reason for the way I am writing in my diary: I am responsible for the house, and every two minutes I jump out of my chair to see if the rice is burning or if the potatoes are cooked, so you understand that I can't go into any of the subjects that I used to discuss with you. I have to take care of so many prosaic things, like the menu, etc., and so the other ideas, a poet's useless ideas, fly away, apparently furious at finding themselves in the company of practical ideas in a head which previously was their domain alone. You see, it's already time to set the table and I must go.

The day is over; that is, the kitchen is in order, the dinner dishes are washed and there is nothing more to do. I am terribly tired and the broom hurt my hands, but I am very happy because the clean house pleased Maman.

Unfortunately, although Maman never says anything, I understand that she is always worried about my cooking and that's why she looks after everything as soon as she gets home. I feel very sorry to see her come home so tired and start to work again. We are thinking of hiring a maid soon.

Maman intends to stay here for the whole month of September and perhaps October, in spite of the cold, because life at 158 West 75th St. will be unbearable if the whole family is there together. Thorvald will go to school as usual in New York, but Joaquinito could go to Far Rockaway. We'll see.

August 6. Today I have made as many resolutions as on New Year's Day: I'm going to be nice, I'm going to be very happy, I'm not going to run away from people any more, I'm going to smile all day long and sing when I am alone, even if it rains forever. I'm very happy, very contented and—oh, but it's difficult to act happy! Forgive me, oh, forgive me, but it's impossible! Give me a few days more and I'll behave as well as I used to.

This morning after Maman left, I served breakfast and washed the dishes. After I mended a lot of stockings, I made the beds, made lunch, did the dishes, and that's all. Thorvald and

Joaquinito spent the day outside in spite of the rain. Now I am going swimming with Antolinita and Joaquinito.

It's very pleasant to see the peace that follows the day's work. When Maman has no more buying to do, when Thorvald doesn't want to play any more, when Joaquinito is tired of running, when my dishes are clean, we all settle down around the hammock where Maman is resting and we breathe the pure air.

We have just come in after three-quarters of an hour of silent pleasure because it has started to rain again. So Maman went to bed very tired, and Thorvald, Joaquinito and I began dancing in the kitchen to the sound of a phonograph in our neighbor's cottage. There was all the music from my dancing school and I could give them a few lessons, but Thorvald was able to show me a new dance that he is very proud of.

A very unimportant thing made me smile. I was dancing in an old worn pair of little shoes that I am wearing just to wear them out. Those ugly little shoes were once pretty little white leather slippers with crêpe georgette pompons and I wore them with a blue dance dress and my chignon of curls that I was so proud of. They were ruined forever the evening that I danced with Enric at Emilia's house. The fate of a pair of dancing shoes is very interesting, very odd, after all. . . .

August 7. Here are drawings of our cottage and its interior. I'm the one who drew them, so please don't judge my talent as an artist too severely.

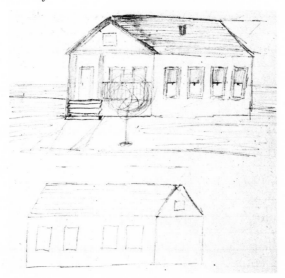

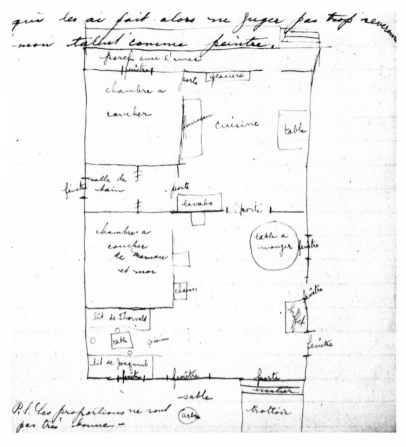

P.S. The proportions are not drawn too well.

I have just been having a good time, since I am alone, singing a waltz that I like a lot. When I finished, someone applauded a long time and I don't know who it was. I don't dare sing any more, but after a while I'll begin again because today I am very happy. And yet it's raining outside, raining torrents, but my "attack" is over. All alone in the cottage, I have a continual smile on my lips, like Enric, and the reason is my own thoughts. My canaries are singing along with a phonograph and I stop what I'm doing to dance from one end of the house to the other, carried away by an invisible someone, as I used to do at 158 [West 75th St.] when the hand organ went by.

Here, there are many peddlers. They almost frighten me because they are all so surly, especially their voices when they call their wares at the top of their lungs. There are also wagons full of vegetables and fruits, a man with baskets full of fish, a man carrying ice, another with a basket of bread, and finally the postman with his little whistle and his package of letters.

Every day Maman leaves me 1 dollar and I do the marketing. Little by little I am learning to say a brave "no" to bad goods and I am also learning to select good ones. In addition to that, I have other amusements. One of the things that really fascinates me is the group of fishermen: big, bearded, suntanned men with eyes almost always the color of the sea, wearing shirts of very coarse material and high boots.

At the beach, there are women exactly like the pictures in the New York magazines that advertise bathing suits; there are many children, sunburned and covered with freckles, without shoes and stockings, sometimes without blouses, wearing pants as full of holes as a sieve, or little girls wearing old dresses, their hair tangled from running and playing games; there are the men who save the swimmers' lives, big men, also very tan, in bathing suits, their eyes always watching the sea, ready to dash out at the slightest cry of distress. And many others.

Maman, who is always looking for things that will entertain me, who is always afraid that I need parties and the cinema so as not to be bored, Maman should see all the pleasure that I get from the simple task of examining and studying all that I see, like people who spend their lives studying plants through a microscope.

Yesterday I wrote a name in the sand again, but I am beginning to forget a bit to think about my little romance as I used to think about it, like the little Japanese girl whose story almost made me cry. Sometimes I wonder if that will be the fate of all my illusions!

But as long as the sun shines, let's not cry.

The potatoes are on the fire. That's the kind of occupation that drives away my melancholy. Thorvald came home with about fifty fish. Poor little fish! They are stretched out, giving off a fragrance of salt water, their eyes open, dead! And Thorvald dares to ask me if I can clean them! I? He might as well ask me for the moon. We won't eat them, since I haven't the courage to clean them. Thorvald is going to sell them.

It's just not fair, after I wrote a beautiful poem about fish, that Fate should ask me to undertake something so detestable, so unpoetic as cleaning them!

Joaquinito bought some modeling clay and since he let me borrow a big piece of clay, I began modeling heads. I worked a long time and Joaquinito saw a resemblance to Maman in my work. Afterward I worked still longer, stopping from time to time to consult my memories, and when I put my work on the table, Thorvald and Joaquinito cried out together in admiration: "Enric Madriguera!"

And it really looked like him. The statuette in front of me was a perfect resemblance, the best thing I have ever done in clay. I would have given a lot not to destroy it, to keep it for a long time; but Joaquinito, who doesn't understand anything and isn't very generous, took the bust and began to model it into something else. He made a pear out of it and the speed with which the chunk of clay lost its charm for me made me pensive.

Yesterday Maman showed me how to cook a Catalan recipe and when she finished, she said: "That will be very good."

And I answered: "Anything Catalan is good!"

Maman laughed. Maman always laughs when I talk about marriage, about my ambitions and about Catalans. Sometimes I think Maman must have thought the same as I about those three things when she was my age, and she knows that after a while it all blows over.

August 8. Maman stayed home with us today to rest and we are very happy. It's always like that: when Maman is with us, everything is fine.

We are all going swimming in the ocean. The weather is splendid, but there is a lot of wind and the cottage still shakes a bit. This morning I saw a little old boat that had been filled with geranium plants, and that original idea for a flower pot struck me as a fine invention. I would have liked to let the boat slide into the water to see the effect, but everyone laughed. I have saved that plan and will carry it out when I have my castle beside the sea.

P.S. Last night we came home from the little [going-away] party for Antolinita at 11. We danced. For my part, I danced a lot with Thorvald, a little with Ernesto, a Cuban friend of Charlie's; and a little less with Alfonso Bermudez. After the dance we had ice cream and cake. It was afterward especially that we had a very good time. We played a game called "Spin the Bottle." Everyone sits in a circle and someone takes a bottle and makes it spin around. The one who makes it spin has the right to kiss the person the bottle points to when it stops turning. We played a long time amidst much laughter. Everyone had a turn, and one of the funniest things is when a boy has to kiss another boy. Thorvald often

had to kiss Letty, a little girl he admires a great deal, and Charlie had to kiss Ethel, the girl he likes best. Charlie and Ernesto had to kiss me several times and that reminded me of the day of my birthday. I wish that Enric had been there last night.

August 9. Today I am in a wonderful humor. It was a big house-cleaning day and I sang all day as we worked. I beat time to the music with a stick, on the mattresses and cushions. Now the cottage is very clean, everything looks pretty, and I am overflowing with the joy that comes from the deep peace of workers at rest.

August 10. There was Mass and the sermon, which made me think of yesterday's cleaning. The priest said: a very rich man built a magnificent house far from the city and one fine day he decided to go and live there. He sent all his servants, his cooks, his soldiers, his carpenters, his decorators, etc. to make arrangements for a hotel on the road where he would travel and spend the night, so that he might be well received. Naturally, after the trip, when he reached his beautiful house, there was no one there to welcome him.

The hotel is our world, the beautiful house is heaven, and the rich man is us. We sacrifice our life for a "night" on earth, and afterward we lose our right to heaven. I have been thinking a lot about that since, and if it's possible for me to be even more serious, I am, because I have learned something else.

P.S. While I was writing that, the noodles proceeded to burn. How many things can happen in one day!

August 11. It's a few minutes after 8 o'clock and I am writing in the train on the way to New York, where Maman, Joaquinito and I are going to do some shopping. The train is very full and I can hardly write because of the motion. This is just to say I am glad to see you again.

August 12. In the morning I went shopping with Joaquinito and we rode on the bus. The bus trip, which costs only ten cents, gives us a great deal of pleasure because we try to see which one of us can find the funniest thing in the street, which we see very well from the top of the bus. There were many ridiculous people and many funny things that made us laugh throughout the trip.

In the afternoon I went to the movie theatre on 77th Street where we used to go so often with Antolinita and Joaquinito. During that time Maman was working. She came back from the shops at 5 o'clock and the three of us left to catch the 5:18 train. Once we were back on the beach at Edgemere, we all commented on how lucky we are to spend the summer here instead of in New York, where it was suffocating today.

Thorvald had cooked lunch very nicely and made the beds as well as a boy can make them all by himself. It was funny!

Today, disguised in my blue apron, I have resumed my domestic occupations. On her return Maman found the house clean, the children's appetites fed, only *one* burned pot and everything in order. In addition, I spent several hours by the sea, under a parasol or in the waves, where I swallowed a lot of water.

When Maman came home, she brought me a surprise: a post card. Can you guess who it was from? Enric Madriguera. He wanted to make fun of the little bit of Catalan I know and sent me three words, as I did in my card: Molts recorts d'Enric.[1] With the single difference that he knows how to spell them, whereas I made a mistake. It was very nice of him because the card made me very happy.

I said in the month of July that when September came, I would have forgotten Enric and he would have forgotten me, and yet we are already almost in the middle of August and we remember each other. There are so few days left to forget that it's going to be almost impossible. Next door a phonograph is playing a piece by Schubert that Enric often played and of course when I hear the piece, I think about the violin and a sweet thought of Enric also comes stealing in. I don't really know why I wanted to forget him, but I suppose it was because I had him on my mind too much at Lake Placid, a long time ago. And I know that if Maman knew that, she would call me a little scatterbrain, etc.

Here, in order to complete my study of the masculine sex a bit at a time, I should write that Maman says men are very selfish. If I took seriously all that Maman thinks about men, I would certainly turn into a suffragette and an old maid. But what puzzles me terribly is that after saying something like that, if I ask Maman whether she doesn't regret having been married, she answers quietly but firmly, "No!"

You must admit that at 16 there are some absolutely inexplicable things that one has to try to understand.

Two minutes later. Thorvald and Joaquinito went to the cinema especially to see the famous Charlie Chaplin, an actor in the style of Max Linder, and after having seen him, all the chil-

[1] *Many greetings from Enric. A.N. misspelled it* records.

dren begin imitating him, to the family's great distress. So Maman, who was very tired, went to bed and let me go on writing, because when I write I don't make any noise and she knows that I am entertaining myself.

I just thought of Antolinita, who was having a wonderful time at Edgemere but had to go back to New York because her Maman was too bored here. She is truly a poor little rich girl. Now, in New York, she will spend long, sad, boring hours because she doesn't know how to have a good time by herself.

I am never bored; I realize I don't need people to be happy and that all my friends are only pleasant memories that I have no wish to meet again in real life. Where does this loneliness of the soul come from? This happiness far from pleasure? This perfect contentment with my fate? If Maman talks about buying a house, I can tell her and tell her truly that it doesn't matter at all to me, absolutely not at all, whatever place or country that she wants. Nothing matters; as long as I have Maman and my little brothers with me, I am happy. If I have attacks, sometimes it's because my illusions disappear too suddenly and that hurts me, sometimes it's because my faith in the beauties of life seems to be disappearing, but otherwise I am perfectly contented. When my friends are far away, I love them more. But I don't miss them. I suppose that kind of coldness is another Nin fault, but that supreme satisfaction with solitude belongs to me alone, as long as I have my own family and Maman's relatives. Perhaps it's because we know a lot about life, Maman and I, that we are becoming older and more serious. We know how to appreciate the joy of a little house that belongs to us, and a thousand other things which are unimportant in the eyes of people who don't understand them, and they are many, unfortunately.

August 13. 8 o'clock. Another post card with three words written on it: Molts recorts d'Enric! I suppose he laughs every time he writes those same words, thinking of my poor Catalan, and I laugh when I receive them. Just the same, I would like him to write something else. The post cards are from Paris and I think he is going to come back soon. It's very strange, but when Maman brought me the post card a little while before dinner, it took my appetite away. I wonder if I am going to get any more cards.

9 o'clock. Joaquinito and I have just been playing Spin the Bottle, substituting the table and chairs for the little girls and little boys. I thought we'd die laughing.

Of my two brothers, Joaquinito is the one who gives me the most trouble, but there are times when the resemblance between us brings us together and attaches us to each other more than anything else could. He has the same way of finding pleasure in the least little thing and in imaginary things, and I think that together, using only our imagination, we have a better time than any children in the whole world could with the most beautiful toys imaginable. It's an Art which has its own delights, and God knows that in my pious moments I never fail to thank heaven for having given it to me.

Papa sent me a post card. He is waiting impatiently for Emilia Quintero so as to have "live" news of us. Sometimes I am sorry to have told him so truthfully why Thorvald and Joaquinito don't write to him, but Papa should know the truth, even if it's sad.

Today Maman came home at 6 o'clock and found dinner almost ready. I think that it pleased her. I also swept the house, but I am not very brave; there are times when I would like to stop because the broom hurts my hands, but I never stop. The pots and pans are still my despair, but I am learning many useful things that I badly needed to know. Little by little, in taking care of the house, I recognize the value of order, which is as important as cleanliness. All day long I have many occasions to be patient and persevering, painstaking and practical. I am improving, changing noticeably, and Maman is delighted to see the pride that I take in our little house. Maman didn't know that I have enough energy to make up for my lack of strength, didn't know that my practical sense needed only an occasion to be awakened, didn't know that I could put in long days without dreaming, almost without writing, and without reading at all. It's the war that makes the heroes.

But I would like to be more useful. I am still waiting for the book that never comes. I dream every night, all in vain, that I have become a member of the French Academy. I have enough characters to fill a library, but not enough experience for 2 chapters. But if I live long enough, we'll see.

If I didn't receive post cards from Paris, if I didn't cook, if there weren't so many phonographs and babies here, perhaps my book would have been started over. But I expect too much. I'm going to try to write in spite of all the obstacles.

August 14. 10:00 [A.M.]. Edgemere. I am going to begin my book.

9:30 [P.M.]. Too many things to do today to waste my time

writing. And what I can say, finally, is that I was useful all day long. Not a single minute of daydreaming, not a second of laziness. The result of my work was astounding. Maman was as happy as if I had won a prize in composition. There's no need to write here all the things that I did; they are things that every little girl in the world has known how to do for ages, but for me they are the beginning of a new career. Et voilà! I am contented, satisfied, pleased with myself, surprised to find so much pleasure in being good for something, and rewarded a thousand times over by Maman's goodness to me, she who is blind only to my faults and always ready to encourage me. I am tired, of course, but that's a secret between you and me, although I guess that Maman knows it on account of my eyes, which always give me away.

In spite of the fog and wind, Thorvald, Charlie and Joaquinito went to the beach today to collect a cargo of coconuts that the tide brought in from a shipwreck. After collecting them, the boys sold them, the same way they sell fish and crabs, and right now they are counting their money and the remaining coconuts.

I don't know what the neighbors think, but I spend my day singing, imitating the way my canary expresses his joy. And when Maman comes home tired from New York, with her head full of the worries and fusses at 158 W. 75 where everybody argues, when she reaches her clean little cottage and sits down to dinner while the three children and I entertain her with long meandering stories about how brave and smart Joaquinito is, how much Thorvald helped me, and even if she knows that Joaquinito probably didn't behave too well and Thorvald wasn't a great help, those happy fibs can only do her good. That mental and physical change of atmosphere, that peace after the daily struggle, are enough to keep us happy and to put Maman back in her sweet good humor of other days. Her whole face relaxes and her brain has a complete rest from her other occupations. Only someone who has never known pain can fail to appreciate the wonderful feeling one has when it stops. That's all I can say about that.

9:40. Charlie is hanging around the table where I am writing. He has already asked me very curiously several times if I was writing anything about him, and with the bravery of a knight wearing a suit of armor, I am going to write whatever I please about him right under his nose, without letting him read it. But all the things I can say about him are good things. He is not at all ignorant, he is very nice, very quiet, and above all very polite. Imagine a boy used to all the comforts of wealth who makes his own bed every morning, knowing that otherwise I will have to make it, who always helps me with the table and in a thousand other ways that even my brother Thorvald neglects to think of. Charlie always thinks that everything I cook is very good (no doubt to encourage me), whereas Thorvald is forever mocking and cares only whether I have fixed enough.

Although they are nice, my two little brothers have inherited the Nin egotism and have accustomed me to spoil them a little (without their spoiling me in return) and to think always of their comfort, their happiness. Sometimes they forget I am their sister and they think of me as a second mother whose sole duty is to take care of them. And I, who am immeasurably delighted to be spoiled myself, who am so happy when someone is a little thoughtful of me or likes me a little, when I complain a tiny little bit about their selfishness, Maman answers that all men are selfish and lazy. Even if that isn't a consolation, it's a kind of excuse that I accept for all of my two little brothers' faults.

August 15. I had finished with the breakfast, the beds and the housecleaning, and while I waited for lunch to cook, I was sweeping the front porch when suddenly a gypsy appeared. She was rather an old woman with glittering eyes and a wrinkled face framed by a faded kerchief. As she walked, she swung her wide skirt and several petticoats which imitated the effect of a hoop skirt. I stopped sweeping to watch her beg at my neighbors' houses. No doubt she saw the curiosity in my eyes and she came up to ask if I wanted my fortune told. The impulse was irresistible; I nodded my head in acceptance and she promptly came up on the porch. I set down the broom, got out the 25 cents she asked for and put it in her hand; she then began some mysterious hocus-pocus. She made magic signs with the coins, then noiselessly slipped them into her pocket. Then she told me to make a wish, so I did but I am ashamed to write it—no, since I always tell you everything, I am going to tell you the silly thing I wished in the surprise of the moment: that Enric would come back very soon.

And here is all she told me: first, that I would always have good health, I would live to a ripe old age, and there was someone who was on a trip whose return I desired and that person would soon come back. That I would be married three times, the first time out of love for a young man, who would be as romantic and have as little head for business as I, and that first marriage would be a failure but after being divorced I would marry a man who would be young but very rich and always very successful in business, who would make me very happy and would make me forget every day that I used to be poor and had to live on love. She pretended to know very little about the third marriage but said it would be to a millionaire seventy-nine years old. She said she was very sure of the initial of my first husband's first name, but not very sure about the last name, and she only knew that he is a foreigner.

Then she wished me good luck and left me there, dazed, astonished, confused and troubled by her stories, which made Maman laugh all evening. I believed them all and wondered where that woman had learned so much magic. I could think of nothing else—and all this is a good lesson, first to rid me of my naïveté and credulity, and also because Maman, who knows me so well, had forbidden me to have my fortune told and I disobeyed her. The broom standing in a corner, the wind that shook the leaves on the tree, the beautiful sunlight that reflected off the Bay, the whining children and phonographs, Joaquinito's voice asking for his lunch, the smell of burning toast from the kitchen—only these brought me back to reality, to the life of pots, broom and the blue apron of Edgemere.

Oh, that gypsy! I who thought that deceitful people wore that label written across their faces, how am I to know when I should be on guard?

A very heavy storm came at the end of the beautiful day—rumbling thunder and a violent pounding rain. It's a little bit like the echo of the moral conflict going on in my head as the result of a new experience with the world and its strange beings. But I say only a little bit, because the storm is solemn and sublime, while my thoughts about that lesson are ridiculous and even funny. I am in the best possible humor and do nothing but smile.

Thorvald and Charlie are at a friend's house and Maman is letting me write until they come home. Tonight after dinner, Maman lay in the hammock and I sat at her feet, knitting without watching what I was doing because it was already rather dark. We began to make plans. Maman's dream, which is as dear to me as it is to her: a house of our own. If Maman sells her business at 158 W. 75 for three or four thousand dollars, she can buy a little house in Kew on the mortgage plan. This is me speaking: "And what will you use to furnish it?" Maman, energetically, her eyes full of dreams: "Everything will be new and to my taste. You will have your little white bedroom and I will have mine. There will be à library for you, and a white kitchen too. We will have a car to go into town, you can entertain your little friends, and you will go to the theatre in New York. Would you like that?"

"Would I like it? There is nothing in the world more wonderful than a little house! And also it's only fair that you shouldn't always have to think about the future, that with what you have earned you should be able to have the satisfaction of realizing your ambition. Thorvald is growing up, and with his good education and his fine character, he will be able to work."

"But daughter, don't you think that buying a house is also thinking of the future? Anyhow, Thorvald is too young and won't be able to take my place until he is 21. I don't spend all the money I earn on the necessities, we have Liberty Bonds, War Stamps, the cottage and money in the bank."

While I was writing all this, the storm redoubled in fury and then after several terribly strong flashes of lightning, the lights went out. Maman was in bed and Joaquinito and I felt our way into her room and lay on her bed, very quiet, very calm, probably frightened without knowing it, full of emotion. Finally the storm died down a bit, the lights came back on and the family resumed its normal state. Just then Thorvald and Charlie came back from their visit soaked to the skin and I stopped again to hear them tell the story of the streets full of water, people crossing them without shoes and stockings. Also how the mother of one of the little girls started to say the rosary in front of all the children during the storm, and when she struck her breast, murmuring incoherently with her eyes shut, one of the little boys, who didn't understand what was happening, said: "What's the matter with her, is she crazy?"

August 16. I was sick today. But although I was really sick, I took care of myself like someone who was half-sick, helping Maman as much as I could and pretending that all the signs that Maman knows so well were nothing but the result of a swim this morning which had tired me out. But when there was nothing else to do, I lay in the hammock in front of the house and knitted. I spent the whole afternoon like that.

Once we had a good laugh. I was daydreaming, which I hadn't done for several days, and my knitting slipped to the bottom of the hammock. Suddenly I heard Thorvald in the living room, swearing in English (which isn't as bad as in French). Then he said, "Who in the devil mended this pair of socks for me?" And I answered in surprise: "I did. Why?"

"Why? Because I can't wear them. They're awful, they feel

like cardboard. I knew it was you. Maman would have done them better than this."

So I called Maman and asked: "Maman, don't you think it's very difficult to darn the big, big holes that Thorvald makes, and that you couldn't even do it better yourself?" And to console me, Maman answered, "Yes."

Then Thorvald said mockingly, "You'll make a marvelous wife and I feel sorry for your husband. Every time he gets a hole in his socks, he'll have to buy a new pair."

"But I won't let him do that!" I answered.

Then Maman said laughingly: "Thorvald, you know very well the gypsy told your sister she is going to be married three times."

"That's because every time you give them a pair of socks darned like this, they'll commit suicide. That's why you'll have to get married three times."

I have written all this down to show you, first, what Thorvald thinks of me; and second, how I darn socks. (Very badly, I admit.)

Today Thorvald found 7 or 8 things wrong with the soup, such as not enough salt, no taste, too many onions, too hot, etc., etc., after which he discovered that it was Maman who had made it, instead of me! And also Maman found a cup that had been very badly washed, thought I had done it, and then found out that it was Thorvald who had washed the breakfast dishes. Such discoveries! This is the kind of life that bored rich people ought to lead! We are never bored.

This evening I felt better, or almost, and once again Maman and I talked, like last night. I brought up the subject of my trip to Havana. Maman says she will take me there when I am 18, to introduce me to my family and present me to Cuban society, in which she was such a belle. So I asked her how one manages in society when one is poor and very ugly. I added that I am not very lively and am quite different from the Cubans. Maman says that money doesn't matter and that I should simply be *myself*.

Then I tried something else. I asked Maman very calmly, if I am successful with my pen within the next 2 years and have begun to make my way in my career, whether she will still want to introduce me to Cuban society (which I dislike in advance) to marry me off. And Maman, as usual, arranged everything with her own kind of logic: she says being introduced into society doesn't mean that one is there to be married. It's clear, it's simple, it's stupid, but true. So let's not talk about it any more, since Maman says that in 2 years I will never be able to make enough progress to begin a career. And she winks.

As I have already said, who can talk to Maman about Catalans, ambitions or marriage? It's impossible.

August 17. When we came back from ten-o'clock Mass this morning, we found that Maman had cleaned the whole house during our short absence. I was very upset that Maman had tired herself out like that on the only day she has to rest, but the fact that the house was so clean, so clean (because Maman knows how to do everything well) gave me a lot of pleasure. But afterward, she hardly did anything all day because I followed her everywhere, helping her with everything and begging her every 5 minutes to come and rest, read the paper or something. So much so that once when Maman was trying to iron but couldn't get rid of me, she told me to go lie down in the hammock and she would join me immediately. So I left with my knitting, but came back after three or four seconds and surprised her. We had a good laugh, it was so funny to see Maman trying to fool me and me not wanting to let myself be taken in.

Now it is 9. Maman went to bed half an hour ago. She says she feels so good and so happy. She gave me the menu for tomorrow and told me what things I could sew and mend. I have just finished knitting a scarf for Joaquinito and Maman says Joaquinito should behave like me because I am so "good." And I am so happy, so happy.

To imitate me, Joaquinito has started to keep a diary. It's a diary more or less like every diary in the world, full of events. I explained to him that he should write a little bit the way I do, telling what he thinks; but he answered, "That's too much work!" He writes in English. That's natural; he doesn't know how to write in French. The days that I don't feel like writing (which never happens), I'll just copy what Joaquinito writes and let you judge the interest of a 10-year-old boy's diary. His mistakes in spelling are part of its charm. Today, for example, he writes:

Sun. 17, 1919, Aug. This morning I went to church with my sister and Arthur. In church in the seat in front of ours was a little girl about 5 or 6 years which made us laugh during the service, once I stoped as I turned around the little girl was laughing and so I giggled like a fool.

After lunch we had a game of baseball and our side won by the score of 5 to 3 or 4. I don't know exactly the score.

After dinner I and Arthur and other friend of mine went to the open air movies, in the middle of an interesting story it began to rain: we went out and got our rain checks and went home.

August 18. How it is raining! Ever since I opened my eyes, I have been hearing the monotonous murmur of the rain. Maman had many difficulties traveling because the roadbed of the train was flooded, as were the streets. And she didn't come home until 7 this evening. Fortunately, the dinner was ready. It's very funny to see Maman trying to explain to me about something that isn't really well done, smiling all the while and trying to find very kind words—and I have to help her!

I have a little notebook in which I write what I spend each day, and every evening Maman and I have a conference about expenses. The other day I served a dessert that cost 38 cents, not counting the gas, and a half-dozen peaches—and Maman showed me how to serve one just as good for 15 cents, not counting the jam. It's simple! A little common sense (which I didn't have in Algebra) and that's all!

This evening is as calm as usual. I can hear only the crickets and some people discussing the difficulties they had reaching Edgemere on account of the rain and the strike.

Everyone is a little astonished at the number of lines I write per day, and I have just noticed that every day I write more. I suppose that the number of my experiences grows with age, but also I notice that my enjoyment of writing increases every day.

Today I made a pleasant discovery: I didn't make a single mistake in the long letter I wrote to Emilia in Spanish. I am very sure of myself in English, so it's only French that isn't good. But I wouldn't give up studying it on my own and using it in the only thing I write—my diary—for anything in the world.

Joaquinito's diary amuses me greatly and I am going to take advantage of the time I have each evening to copy it as we go along, because some day during one of his fits of anger, which tend to be destructive, he is going to tear it up or throw it out the window. I am copying it exactly as he wrote it:

Mond. 18, 1919, Aug. When I woke up my mother was dressing to go to the city. I dressed and ate, then I said goodbye to my mother and she went to catch her train that was leaving at 8:15. My cousin Charles went with her.

Then I called Aruther to play cards with me we played many amsuing (amusing) games, for it has been raining all morning and I have not been able to go out.

After lunch it cleared up and so we had a game of baseball. At 6 o'clock I went to meet my mother at the station, instead of coming in a train she had to come in a truck the strick (strike) was the cause of this.

No post card! I would like very much to receive another one, even with molts recorts! I don't know why.

August 19. This morning after Maman left, we had breakfast, as we do every day, but this breakfast was marked by a long discussion among Thorvald, Charlie and me that lasted until we had finished washing the dishes. It began with politics and migrated to individuals. I don't want to start it up again and I will write only the facts: Charlie said that like all idealists, I want to reform the world. Thorvald ate and didn't say much, and I thought, Charlie is as much a realist as anyone can be.

I spoke of the poor and he told me a bad thing: their lack of gratitude. He said that one time his mother used her influence to return a prisoner to his family, gave his daughter an education, took his wife into her household, and while she was on a trip, the wife stole dozens of things in the house. I told Charlie that charity had come too late for that woman and that misfortune had hardened her and made her unable to feel gratitude, but such isn't always the case. Charlie continued to maintain his cruel theory, which is so ugly, so horribly human and true, and I wouldn't change mine, which is based, as Charlie said, "not on logic but only on pity and a heart that is much too idealistic." Those were his words. He didn't convince me nor I him, but he caused a lot of confusion in my mind because his way of thinking is that of people who are old, wise and wrinkled by years of experience. Could he by any chance be right?

Today, besides the pots, I cleaned the stove. It was a little worse than the pots and I got black dirt on me from head to foot. And my hands! The saddest part of the whole business was that when I finished, there was only a tiny little improvement. Of course, I didn't expect the stove to turn white, since black is its natural color, but I thought I could make it nice and shiny.

At dinner there wasn't enough salt on the rice and the cabbage, but to make up for that, the potatoes and dessert were quite good. This evening Maman gave me a lesson about tomorrow's menu, told me that she was pleased with me, and explained to me why she is running away from 158 W. 75. It's the kind of story that Charlie probably would like, the unbearable life that pessimists discovered, the ugly side of the Night, the sort of happening that destroys one's dreams, the kind of thing I refuse to believe. Why write about it? I would only be saying bad things about poor people who probably are better than I, after all, whom I can't judge, but whose acts, which bring worry to my darling Maman, make me feel angry and indignant.

August 20. Faced with a flood of stockings to darn, I had enough will power to refuse myself permission to write in my diary until I had finished. From 10 o'clock until lunchtime I mended, and from 1 o'clock until 3, I mended again. Now all the stockings are laid out in order on the bed for Maman to see. The procession reaches from the head of the bed to the foot. And I am still wondering why Thorvald and Joaquinito get such big holes in their socks! Maman's stockings are all very old, very worn, because Maman never wants to think of herself. Mine are all new and almost all silk. The stockings alone can tell the family story.

This morning after I made breakfast and the beds, I raked the Autumn leaves that are already falling from the trees onto the golden sand. Autumn! It's Nature's melancholy, like tears and sighs, a sublime Elegy that touches the hearts of poets. All of Autumn's beauty is in harmony with the last lines of the song of Love, when it withers and dies away . . . in harmony, too, with old age and its gentle sadness, and everything speaks to me of sadness . . . the dry leaves of my heart. . . . This morning when I was raking, I felt as though I were crushing my vanished illusions. There have been so many of them! Those golden, scarlet and russet leaves driven before the wind were so much like my illusions, which had barely left the nest and were to die so soon . . . So many leaves! So many dreams! So many cruel iron teeth to carry them away! But some still remain! Look at the trees still full of leaves! Look at the shining sun! Listen to Summer's voices which still are not far away! Take heart! It's only when all the golden leaves are gone that I can weep with the winds of Autumn, weep as the Poets weep and the leaves too. And after Autumn comes Winter—a long, never-ending story, all that beauty that we don't deserve!

This outburst came to me in the middle of a daydream in the hammock, and I didn't expect to be able to write down my impressions of the moment; but now, after having written them, I have stopped to dream a long while, carried away by my own words. I am still writing in the hammock. All our neighbors left for the beach a long time ago amid much noise and shouting, and all the cottages are wrapped in silence. Although ours is usually quiet, today there is not a sound because Thorvald, Joaquinito and Charlie are also at the beach. I am glad to be alone, to feel myself mistress of the house, alone with the trees, the bay, the sky, my ideas, a pen and my diary. I have loosed my hair to the sun and the wind makes it fly. Sometimes it covers what I am writing. I never knew that my hair was so golden, so full of light and so long. It's the first time I have paid attention. . . .

But now, in just a few minutes, the weather has changed. I can see dark clouds coming up from the Bay and sometimes the sun is hidden for a few minutes, to come out again a little less brilliant. I wonder if a storm is coming, and that makes me think how changeable everything is, in addition to people. Fortunately, even if it rains Maman won't get wet because Thorvald and Joaquinito will go to meet her at the railway station with an umbrella. And when she arrives, dinner will be ready. If that is to be true, I must go.

9 o'clock: Maman came home today feeling a little happier. The family quarrels are relatively settled and she received the good news that Uncle Thorvald is coming soon. As soon as Maman came home, she bathed and then we had dinner. There wasn't enough salt on the potatoes and carrots, the meat was a little rare, and the dessert, which was chosen by Thorvald and Charlie, was a bit too much to their boyish bad taste. But Maman insisted that I was a real chef because I succeeded in making white sauce!

After dinner, which was interrupted by frequent requests for salt, compliments (?) from Thorvald and Maman's defense of me, the boys went out and Maman and I settled in the hammock, Maman to rest and I to entertain her. And if ever I make an effort to make entertaining conversation so as to give Maman pleasure, it's then. And I succeed remarkably well. I am animated, I change the subject every two minutes, and I talk, talk, talk until Maman relaxes, forgets her troubles and her worries. That's the way!

Today Charles insisted that I wouldn't find a single person in the world like the Vicar in Victor Hugo's "Les Miserables" and I got almost angry. So much realism in one so young is horrible. And I am absolutely the opposite! Once I said to him that since he has such cruel ideas, no doubt he shares Maman's bad opinion of marriage, and he assured me that he *does*. At the moment I didn't know what to say. I was angry for fun, but astonished for real. What is there left for him to believe in? Fortunately, although Maman mocks the institution of marriage, at least she says that she can find hundreds of people like the Vicar, which I also believe with great energy and assurance. And the day that I introduce my ideal husband to Charles, he will see, he will see *us* helping thousands of poor people without expecting any thanks and giving each of all those "miserable ones" a chance to be as happy as we are. Then we shall see if kind treatment and happiness don't melt all those hearts hardened by misfortune.

August 21. One day I talked to Maman about the past and, as usual, it was I who asked the questions and Maman who answered. I wanted to know, after one has loved, whether there is still something to live for, whether there is any other wonderful thing to wish for. Maman told me the two important things that she would always wish for: good health and success. Love was the most important thing only when she was young. I wanted to know what Maman thinks about Love, but Maman said she never thinks about it. I just remembered this because I am lying in the hammock as I was yesterday, with my hair loose and my pen in hand, and for quite a little while I have been dreaming about love as it's described in books, forgetting to write. It must be the magic of silence, of solitude . . .

When the wind passes the trees tremble, bending before its mighty breath, and the leaves fall . . . the ground is covered with them. My birds are singing, and just as at Lake Placid, I have a wonderful impression that all this murmur around me, all those vague sounds are voices, voices that speak to me—and I understand them. They remind me of stories in books, of heroes and heroines . . . and I wonder why, oh, why is there such a difference between the people I have read about and those that I know! The voices speak and make me dream. I dream about the prince who is going to come for me, and then at the same time I think about what Maman said. And then I stop writing and I think, but I can't dream any more. Oh, how I would like to know the truth, to know if the people who tell me that Life is cruel are right, or if books, which say that Life is the way I think it is, are mistaken. The people who already seem to know the answer all have wrinkles, gray hair, a sad look in their eyes, and can be compared to Autumn after Summer. Are those the results of the Great Discovery, the ravages made by wisdom and experience? So then what is the answer to my question? Are the books wrong? Are people like Charles right?

But even if I sometimes have doubts, I am going to believe just the same in my Land of Princes and Princesses, and people like the Vicar will always exist in . . . my heart. And when the wrinkles come and my hair is gray, instead of being full of light as it is today, when my eyes are sad, if my Prince has come, if I have loved and published, if like Maman I have nothing more to wish for except two things that are as useless, in my opinion, as good health and money, then who cares! since I will have all my memories!

And the leaves are still falling, the sun disappears, giving way to the cloud that precedes a storm, the sand flies away along with the leaves, carried on the wind. Everything changes, but nothing can change the Country in my heart. I swing in the hammock with the enthusiasm of a poet who has succeeded in writing a description of paradise, without a care. . . .

And I shall wait for my Prince, even if the entire universe assures me that he doesn't exist!

9 o'clock: I really admit that I must be a little scatterbrain or something of the sort. Can you believe that as soon as Maman came home, I ran to her, barely took time to hug her, and immediately asked: "Do you have a post card for me?" Maman answered no. And I am so sorry not to get a card that it makes me ashamed. Maman thinks that I am expecting post cards from Eleanor or Frances, and she could never guess the truth. I begin to believe that it's because I had absolutely decided to forget Enric that this is happening.

Tonight at dinner there was too much salt in the rice, not enough on the meat, and I cooked the corn in salt water, which made it turn yellow and a little tough. Oh, salt! What a mystery. But we had beautiful fruit for dessert and everyone was satisfied just the same. Charles says that when he is grown up, he will have the best cook in Havana on his staff, and I told him that would doubtless help him to forget the days when I was the cook, but he said no.

After the dishes were done and the boys had gone out, as they do every evening, Maman lay down in the hammock, and partly to please her and partly for my own pleasure I put on the blue organdy dress that I often wore to dancing school, with a blue ribbon in my hair in the Roman style. Dressed like that, I sat down and talked to Maman as I do every evening. I can only explain my dressing up like that by the numbers of hours when I wear such an ugly, ugly blue apron!

Just the same, Maman says that when we get back to New York, I will be able to help her a great deal with her work. I believe we are going to have to leave Edgemere soon because Maman is going to be too busy to come out here every day and she doesn't want to leave me alone, even if I explain to her that I am already grown-up. I would like to know at what age one is "grown-up"!

I have just been entertaining myself watching Joaquinito, who is sitting across from me. He opens his Diary and holding his head in his hands, a pencil between his teeth, he struggles to remember what he has done since lunch. He just asked me and since I didn't know, he heaved a deep sigh and said: "Well, I'll have to make it up." But no, now he has remembered and he is writing very, very fast, only stopping to ask me how to spell "invitation" and "accept." He wets the pencil with his tongue to make it write darker, and that boyish stunt seems so funny to me! What would you say if I wrote half in ink and half in saliva? Terrible! He has almost finished and asks me, as usual, whether he writes as much as I do, and I answer, "almost." At the same time, Maman tells him every two minutes, "Joaquinito, go to bed." And Joaquinito, not moving, answers: "Just a minute!" And this goes on for an hour and a half every evening. Besides everything else, Joaquinito is very disobedient.

But if I write Joaquinito's faults in here, I can tell you that when Thorvald gets up from the table after having eaten, he wanders around the kitchen filling his pockets with bread, bananas and candy and eats them a few seconds later on the pretext that he is "hungry"! Oh, men!

August 22. Oh, guess, guess what I received! A letter from Enric with Molts Recorts d'Enric, and his address. I was sitting at the foot of the hammock when Maman remembered she had a letter for me. While I looked for it, I thought it must be from Frances or Eleanor but I *knew* by the funny way my heart was beating that it was from Enric. After having opened it and read it twice, because I didn't recognize the handwriting, I wasn't tired any more at all, at all. . . .

And with the letter in my pocket, I took my place again at the foot of the hammock, changed in some way that I can't explain.

And with his address, I think I am going to reply to beg him to change his molts recorts, because I now know how to spell them perfectly.

I have forgotten all the things I was going to write about the house, the dinner, the cleaning and the blue apron. Right now all that seems quite uninteresting to me.

Maman says that we will leave here whenever I want to and that I must tell her as soon as I am bored, and I always give her the same answer: I could stay here all winter and never be bored.

Joaquinito writes:

I had breakfast and went to Farroxaway with my sister and bought a hammer and a pair of henges, we came back and had lunch. I went to the Ocean and when I came back my mother came home.

(He stopped here because writing *bores* him and he would rather play cards.)

You must be the one to keep my letter safe—it's one of my happy experiences. . . .

August 25. I can't explain very well what has happened to me, but I have lost my enthusiasm, my energy, my gaiety. I don't have too much energy, after all, and I can't be "good" for very long at a time. Today I didn't have enough energy to sing while I worked, nor even to smile. And to think that there is so little work in a little cottage like this one, and yet I am so terribly, terribly tired and that's why I am sad. Maman doesn't know it and I want to write a little bit about it here so that it will go away.

It's only 8 o'clock and I don't want to go to bed; that would be an admission and would worry Maman.

Saturday went the way I thought it would. I devoted my efforts to entertaining Belica [Tallet], who is so nice and whom I like very much. We went to the beach in the afternoon with Aunt Antolina, Godmother and Antolinita, who also came to spend the day. But Aunt very soon went away, and Belica and I went to the cinema in Far Rockaway. Before that we went to visit a little friend of Belica's who is in a convent. She told us about her homesickness and that she can't stop crying because she feels so alone. She says she is afraid to be sick in the convent because she would have to be alone in a room where the wind whistles at night. While she talked, I could read real sadness, timidity and fear of solitude in her eyes—and also her dreams. She told me that she would like so much to leave the convent to learn about life and "especially, especially," she said, "about romance, about love. . . ."

On Sunday Elsie de Sola and her mother came for the day and left after supper. Elsie has changed a lot, and for the better. It seems that all the girls are changing—and for the better. She managed to regain my attention, which was really very far away during our conversation, when she said that she loves to ride horseback. Their visit contributed a great deal to the golden dream that Maman and I have of a house in Kew, because they live there.

Belica left very early this morning with Maman. And then after lunch Charlie also left and will only come back from time to time, with Antolinita. So now there are just the four of us. Maman is both Papa and Mama, Thorvald and Joaquinito are the children, and I am the maid. But I understand now, during these visits, why maids don't have much fun: they're too tired.

Once I told you that I would write down all my faults (I have so many!) but to break the monotony, I will combine them with the compliments that I get, whenever I get any. And you can see from this that I occasionally have good ideas, because compliments are usually nothing but polite phrases, and personally I never believe them, so I couldn't be vain even if I tried.

Elsie said that she had been noticing my hands all day long and that . . . oh! hang it! It's so difficult to explain—so—I'll try. Well, it seems that a sculptor made a cast of the hand of one of Papa's aunts, after she died. And Grandfather had very beautiful hands, and Papa too: the "Nin" hand; and luckily, without knowing it or trying to, I inherited the hand or hands of the Nin family. You see how important heredity is. And since conversation about ancestors always goes on and on, I learned that my almond-shaped eyes also come from the Nin side, etc., etc.,—the gestures, the walk, the expression.

I would very much like to know what I inherited from Maman but I suppose that's asking too much, because Maman was so beautiful, so beautiful, and I should be happy to look really very much like a girl whose ancestors were—Catalan.

Just now, by some miracle, I smiled . . . and like the sunshine after the rain, I am happy again and have forgotten my fatigue.

It's really funny to see how Anaïs Nin can amuse Anaïs Nin, without either of them having a single speck of sense of humor.

I just remembered the last conversation that I had with Charles this morning, still on the same subject that we never manage to finish. It's really funny to explore ideas with Charles, who always exposes them to the X rays of logic. But on another subject, he once told me that he can't understand how a handsome man can marry an ugly woman or vice versa, or how an ignorant man can marry an intelligent woman, etc. From the depths of my brain, a place from which I had doubtless never brought anything forth, having never thought of marriage but only of Love, I told him that in marriage, I think one almost always searches for one's opposite. It's quite natural to admire something that we ourselves don't have, whether it's good or bad.

But for myself, I knew deep in my heart that was not a principle that I would follow. That doesn't mean because I am ugly that I want a husband who is very handsome, because that absolutely doesn't count for me; but I would like him to be superior to me in literary talent and intelligence, and above all I would like him to be an idealist, understanding of my dreams, able to live that other, inner life which is so beautiful but which so many people refuse to believe is as important as this life, and also I would like him to be full of faith in the poor people of this poor little world!

Oh, but I always say so many foolish things when I talk about my Shadow.

August 26. I am at the beach with Thorvald. It is about 2 o'clock and we made plans to spend the afternoon here. A big strong woman is at the house to wash the sheets and clean the cottage thoroughly, so I went calmly away, because when I come back everything will be clean. Since Thorvald has gone to play with some other boys, I am alone; I am very happy to have come here with my diary. There are very few people and I am sitting so comfortably in the sun with my hair hanging down that I feel very much like dreaming.

Enric's letter and post card almost blew away forever, but I caught them in time. And everything is flying around me; each day the wind gets stronger. My diary is full of sand and all the beach umbrellas are blowing away while each family runs after its own umbrella. But now the sky is suddenly full of clouds and I am just waiting for Thorvald's return to leave before it rains. Little by little everyone is leaving the beach. I am alone with the sand and the gray sea. The sky is very, very dark, and I would like to stay here forever. Everything seems so beautiful!

August 28. Yesterday I went into New York. Maman left me in the stores and I bought a little black velvet hat to go with my jacket. Also a very plain pair of black pumps and that's all.

I had lunch with Antolinita and Charles in the house at 158, which seemed terribly gloomy and very much changed. My cousin wanted me to spend the night there so that we could go horseback riding today, but I wanted so much, so much to run away from the strange dark house to the sunny cottage so near the sea, and immediately after the Hippodrome, where the three of us went, I met Maman and we ran to catch the train.

When we got home, we promptly prepared an uneventful dinner, except for the moment that Thorvald sat on a dozen eggs. Thorvald had made the beds with almost everything upside down and everything was in a state of disorder. But I couldn't expect anything more of a boy, as Maman says.

Today it was Thorvald's turn to go into the city to get ready for school, which begins much too soon. However, we have decided to spend the month of September here and afterward we'll see.

I was so pleased and happy with my new shoes and hat that my conscience troubled me and I asked Maman if I was too extravagant. Maman said that my "extravagance worries her terribly," but she said it in such a funny way and added afterward that I am a little bird, so I don't believe Maman thinks I am too extravagant. In any case, I should have known that Maman never believes me when I tell her the truth and I shouldn't even have asked her.

We had a marvelous dessert: 4 exquisite little cakes that are known as Danish pastry. Before we ate them, each of us, as a game, picked the one he wanted: Thorvald the only one decorated with a red cherry, Joaquinito the sugared raisins, Maman the one with blueberry jam in the center. I was left the plain cake and the juice, but I like the "beauty" of the dessert a thousand times better than the taste. Everyone laughed when I said that. There are times when my whole family laughs at things I say in all seriousness. It's funny that they make that mistake. I told them about a poor girl in my class who managed to spend 5 cents that she borrowed from somebody, without ever paying it back. First she borrowed it from me, for instance, and the next day she borrowed it from Eleanor to pay me, then the next day from Dorothy to pay Eleanor, and on all around the class like that. Then when there weren't any more girls, she went away and didn't come back again until the last unlucky girl had forgotten about the loan of 5 cents.

And everyone began to laugh—and after all it was a *sad* story . . . for the last girl!

Oh, dearest diary, I have kept the best for the last page. Look out! I'm going to break the monotony with my faults and qualities again. One evening I was talking to Maman about the three things that make her smile (read further back and you'll know what they are) and I told Maman, among other things, that I am ugly, etc. etc. And Maman winked one eye, smiled for a few minutes without saying anything and said: "Fifille, you're not at all ugly, you're improving all the time, and every year you get prettier!" Those were Maman's words. But they don't count, because Maman is always mistaken when she talks about me. I think she always says the things that she would like me to be or say or know. That's quite different! quite different! So this page doesn't count—cancel it, cancel it!

I suppose that I should tell you what I saw at the Hippodrome: dancing elephants, a scene in which all the fairies, heroes and heroines came out of great big books, songs, dances, clowns, wonderfully trained horses, the Golden City, with the whole set painted gold and the people dressed in gold, with a big lake in the center covered with little boats, and other things that were fantastic and very pretty. When I go to the theatre, I always have an irresistible urge to become an actress. But I suppose that's because I am a scatterbrain, so I console myself by demonstrating everything I saw as soon as I get home. Joaquinito is always a very enthusiastic spectator and claps as loud all by himself as a very large audience.

August 31. Maman put me to bed Friday night because I was really sick and I told Maman about the pain in my right side. I spent a very, very bad night, with my eyes wide open all the time and in pain. But in the morning when I got up I was cured.

It was Maman's name day. And since on Friday, in spite of being sick, I had cleaned the cottage thoroughly, Maman didn't have to tire herself out. It was a delightful day. While I wrote a story, Maman made meringue and Floating Island. Thorvald and Joaquinito were out all day until dinner time, when they came back full of amusing stories. And in the evening we were at the cinema until 9:30, which is when it always begins to rain. I was very glad to go to the cinema, if only because I could wear my little velvet hat embroidered with a red rose and my black jacket, which made a stunning outfit. That shows how extravagant I am.

As I didn't have a penny, for Maman's name day I made her a clothespin bag. I drew a funny design on it and Maman thought it very pretty and also very useful, which made me feel better.

Today we all went to Mass together. Maman seemed very thoughtful and very preoccupied. On the way home, she told us that she had made a vow to build a little church in Kew Gardens if she closes a good piece of business that she is hoping for in October.

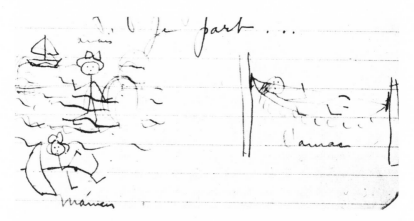

After lunch we went to the beach. The waves were very big, which made the swim so pleasant that we didn't come home until dinner-time.

It may be because of the calm, orderly life that we lead or it may be because of our dispositions, but we are always in a good humor. I always knew that Thorvald had a very American sense of humor and Joaquinito a little bit too, but Maman could never get hold of that sense of humor. And I? Oh, it's inconceivable, unheard of, but I am really funny!

September 1. Today is an American holiday and Maman stayed home with us. We cleaned the house.

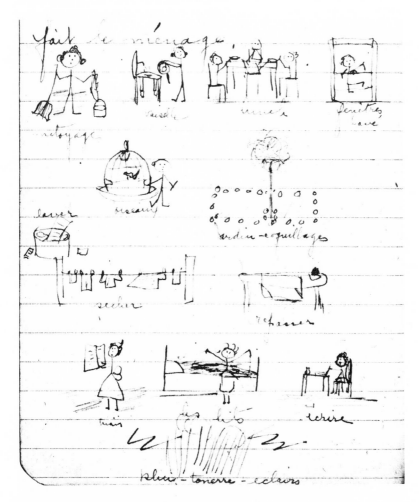

Yesterday afternoon I wrote a short story. Suddenly, unexpectedly, a great many ideas have come to me and I receive them with pleasure, as this doesn't often happen. When the story was finished, I got busy and copied it carefully. I fell asleep last night dreaming that I had taken it to a publisher who frightened me terribly and told me that I could do better. And now today, obsessed by that dream, I wrote another one that *is* much better. I am a tiny little bit discouraged because I write rather like a child, not like a lady, and I haven't yet been able to correct that. I have only one aim: as soon as I am in New York, I will type my story on the machine and putting all my sensitiveness and especially my fear of being ridiculous to one side, I will really go to see that terrible publisher. Oh, I absolutely have to help Maman! I can see in advance the sarcastic smiles of those important men, who know so many things, when they read my stories, and I am already covered with shame. But no, it doesn't matter, I am going to try in spite of everything. Perhaps they'll make allowances for my 16 years, and perhaps they'll understand why I want so much to sell them, even for 10 cents! I am going to take advantage of the month that we will still be here to write, write, always better, better and better.

It's strange how this real ambition has suddenly come to life. For a long time I have written nothing except my diary, and I had somewhat lost hope of ever becoming an author. It's my French that worries me, but lo and behold, I have English at my disposition now, and I can write it better than any other language! Furthermore, I am here in the great country of opportunity, so I can try. And what enthusiasm is tied to this dream of hope and ambition! I have never taken lessons in how to write stories, I never went very far in school, and yes, there is a lot of discouragement, things that make me feel doubts about my career, but also there is that inexplicable something that I was born with. One doesn't learn to write, one is born with it, and little by little experience will teach me all the things that I lack.

But there is one thing that gives me food for thought. When I read what I write to my brothers, they make fun, and Maman doesn't really listen and her enthusiasm is terribly doubtful—I don't know what to believe—I have to go forward, counting only on my own confidence, and how can I do that? I don't have any! And especially there is such a difference between Frances's stories and mine! I suffer a great deal by comparison. My stories are so poetic and imaginary, I could just as well write them as poems. And also when I write something that I mean to make amusing, people don't understand and remain perfectly serious.

What do you think? It's sad but true that if I don't make a good bluestocking, perhaps I will have to get married, because I don't know how to do anything else. When I think that one day I will have to make my living, I feel so small, so small, and so weak. That's the reason I am afraid—a little bit—of Life. It's not lack of courage or fear of suffering at all, but there are so many little details that still offend my sensibilities and that are found only in real Life, which is rough, incomprehensible and selfish, and which I sometimes see only too clearly, in spite of my fortress of ideals. And when I talk to you about marriage in those cases, it's because to me marriage is something grand and ideal; it seems to me it's like putting all the best that I have under the protection, the nobility, the grandeur of a man. Marriage is the noblest thing there is. If it's sometimes sad and withered, that's because either the husband or the wife hasn't understood that, doesn't understand it. This is another house of cards . . . which will never be shattered.

Just the same, I always compare my career as a bluestocking to a victory and marriage to a defeat. It would be so wonderful, so wonderful, not to have to depend on a man for my own good fortune! Maman has such a bad opinion of the masculine sex, and even my brothers are examples of supreme selfishness, in spite of their good qualities.

Oh, I have a new idea about my Shadow. He could be a great writer and I would help him a tiny little bit in the fantastic, poetic, imaginary chapters, when he is writing about illusions and poets and Autumn, birds, flowers, the sea, against the government, to defend unfortunate prisoners and the poor. . . . Perhaps I would do better to write the book myself, and he could correct it. No. Perhaps I would get angry, after all, and it would be better for my husband to be a shoemaker—or an Icelandic fisherman. But would the latter love Sir Walter Scott as much as I do? And would he fall asleep when I read my poetry to him? In that case I would also get angry. Oh, what a lot of nonsense! If I am very critical of a certain kind of man, the same thing will happen to me as happened to Grandmother and Maman, who always said bad things about Catalans and who both married Catalans. Fortunately, I never say anything bad about them, so that will never happen to me. But why write about it so much since, after all, I am going to be a bluestocking?

I just made a sensible decision: to write only one page a day as soon as I catch up on the dates in this Diary. It will be difficult to get used to being that exact after having had time enough to write everything that goes through my head and to waste as many pages a day as I like. That's really too extravagant. But for example, this evening I have been left to my own resources to entertain myself and in the entire house there is only one little book to read, Shakespeare's Othello, which I have already read 3 or 4 times. So I sit down and write, write, write, until it's time to go to bed. Then Maman asks me if I am bored and I always answer truthfully: "Oh, no! I'm having a wonderful, wonderful time!"

A few days ago I read something in English: a little story in which there was a woman who said a lot of mean things and then immediately afterward was sorry and didn't mean them. So her husband told her that even if she didn't mean them, she said them when she was angry and at the moment, she believed them and said them to hurt others . . . etc. etc. Is that a Nin trait? Things said in anger which wound the person they are meant for, and feeling sorry afterward doesn't help at all. I write that so that you will get to know the Nin family better, and they all have a very peculiar disposition.

September 5. If someone came to me right now and asked me for a prescription for happiness, I would answer: Run a thousand leagues away from all your aunts and cousins. Do you notice how many days it has been since I last wrote? Only the first day has a reasonable excuse: I was sick, because I am sick almost every day recently; but the next day I went to New York with Maman, Thorvald and Joaquinito. Then I let Thursday go by because I was afraid to write because of the shock I had. More houses of cards that fall and keep on falling. I was going to let today go by, too, because I am still pensive and preoccupied, but I thought after all there's no use waiting for a change of heart that will never come. What I should do is not write anything, which would be telling the truth without intending to, and sometimes the truth is a harsh judgment of another's faults. After all, this is *my* Diary. Maman and my brothers are in it and the people I love who occupy large or small houses in my village of Illusion. As for the others, I am putting them aside for my books, and there will be a long chapter on the encumbrance of Aunts and Cousins and Godmothers. Those poor people haven't done anything to me, but they try to run Maman's life, they pester her to death, they worry and weary her, and only half of all this would be enough to make them criminals as far as I'm concerned. Maman always says, and rightly so, that I exaggerate everything. But my exaggeration is more like the Philosopher's enthusiasm or deep despair after a marvelous or stupid discovery. No more of that.

Today I am sick again, but that isn't keeping me from making preparations for Maman's arrival with Aunt Lolita and Uncle Thorvald (who are total exceptions to the prescription for "Happiness"). The garden has been raked and the shells rearranged. The entire house is shining clean and in order and their future room is neat as a pin.

Maman wanted to take me to the doctor because I never want to eat lunch and eat very little, even with Maman there, at dinner. But I begged, pleaded and promised that I would take care of myself—so she let me stay home. It certainly isn't an emotional upset like the last time. It's true that although I am worried when Maman is worried, that has very little effect on my present state of happiness. There are times when I have nothing more in the world to wish for! And that's an unprecedented feeling. My ambitions don't disturb me at times like that. I think I am not yet old enough to realize them and that's that.

Dearest diary, you must already have noticed that I am full of foolish and excessive whims. And they have all been satisfied sooner or later in a way that is sometimes rather odd. For a long time I have wanted to have a dog, a beautiful big dog. But Maman said that my brother (Joaquinito) and dogs don't go together. Now I have taken to looking out for all the dogs in the neighborhood, the poor animals that no one feeds, and I give them the leftovers from our dinner and sometimes my entire dinner. (That is, I simply leave my meat and afterward ask permission to give it to the dog.) Contrary to human beings, they are all faithful to the law of gratitude, and 4 big dogs of every color follow me everywhere, whether I go to the market or to the beach. But since I usually stay home, crocheting in the hammock, they all sit around me and sometimes fall asleep in the sun. Four dogs! And all the while my birds sing at the top of their voices! Two wishes wonderfully satisfied, don't you think?

Yesterday and today I have been making myself a silk sweater the color of the sea when it is rather blue—and I only need to have a vision of white silk instead of spray to imagine that I am crocheting with the waves! And since my imagination is easily kindled, or rather is always on fire, that image seems delightful to me. As I was daydreaming, the idea came to me to keep that sweater and not wear it until the Day . . . No, that's another whim and I won't write about it until the day it comes true. And then you won't be able to do anything but forgive me.

I forgot to write that today is Joaquinito's birthday. He is eleven, and yet I can only think of him as a continual torment, a mountain of whims and selfishness. As far as I'm concerned, Joaquinito's only quality is perhaps his Talent, and even that hope seems to evaporate before the evidence of a complete lack of perseverance. To celebrate, no doubt Maman will bring a cake with 11 little candles. But it is only four o'clock and I don't know what we will do afterward.

I have found a delightful way to do the dishes when I have a great deal of time, when I am happy and when there is no one in the kitchen to mock me. While I wash the plates, I sing, and while I dry them I talk to them and tell them stories. Then I make the silver bow to the plates as I put them away, and needless to say, I dance all around the kitchen. And when everything is finished, I make a deep bow, like an actress at the end of the act, and then I turn out the lights of my kitchen theatre. It's crazy, but during that time I forget that I am in the kitchen and the silver and plates seem like little fairies who are my children. Sometimes I think that I believe in fairies; I can imagine them and sense them everywhere in the house. Whenever we get angry, it seems to me I see a sad little procession of fairies leaving the house with their heads bowed, not to return until we are happy. That's like my Shadow!

9 o'clock—Uncle Thorvald is exactly as I remember him, very, very nice. Maman says that he is as like Grandfather as two peas in a pod and that makes me think that Maman must have been very proud of her father. We had a very happy dinner together, with Joaquinito's cake for dessert. The little devil was very much spoiled by everyone, with toys and candy all over the place. He was so happy, he even managed to be good. Later they all went to the cinema, while Maman and I stayed home to crochet and talk. Maman was too tired to go out and I always stay to keep her company, without her realizing it, of course.

September 8. As Maman was really worried about my illness and my lack of appetite and sleep, she took me into the city. We took the train very early and Belica left us at the station in New York. The visit to [Dr. Murray] was very long and very tiring. He examined me thoroughly, thinking that there was something wrong with my chest or my liver. When he finished, he said there is nothing seriously wrong: I don't assimilate my dinner carefully enough because of being nervous and worried. He also said the pain in my side will come back every time I worry too much, because I am not very strong.

After the doctor, we visited Mrs. Murray, who told us that Jack is already wearing long pants, and the mere idea seemed so funny that I often thought of Jack all the rest of the day.

Ah! I forgot something. Before going to the doctor, we went to the house and I looked through a big package of letters on Maman's desk. And I found a little blue envelope—for me. This time I recognized the handwriting. It was a "telegram" from Enric with those three very original words that you know as well as I. He always gives his address but Maman told me not to reply, so I'll wait for his return to laugh at him.

I telephoned Eleanor, who was in school, and Frances, who wasn't at home. Later we went to lunch in a Chinese restaurant where they cooked the rice the way I do, without salt. Joaquinito and I went downtown and I bought a camera. Then we met Maman at the door to McCreery's and left for Edgemere, where Thorvald had been since about three o'clock. For dinner we had something new, hot "Tamales" and a delicious ham (not all of it, of course). Both things were presents from the wife of the President of Cuba, who is one of Maman's customers. To show you how little attention Maman pays to clothes, today was the first time she has noticed, because of visiting the President's wife, that she hasn't bought herself a pair of gloves for a long time!

But that visit to the city made me appreciate the beauty of our vacation more than ever, especially since yesterday was one of the hottest days of the whole summer. Tomorrow Thorvald and Joaquinito start school. At first Maman didn't want to leave me alone, but I managed to calm her by making her laugh.

September 9. This morning I saw Thorvald leave very early with his books under his arm, I saw Maman leave with her little black leather case that is full of business papers, I saw Joaquinito leave with his cap over his eyes and his sandwiches tied to his books, and I remained behind, the only lazy one in the family! But I didn't waste a minute, especially to be worthy of Maman, and it's only now that I have stopped working very, very hard. Maman had forbidden me to clean thoroughly and "wear myself out," but there are times when I have to be disobedient. That's why Maman says that I have *a very hard head*. (Maman says that to me, but to other people she expresses it more elegantly: she says I have a great deal of will power.) I ate a tiny, tiny little lunch instead of nothing, because Maman said she was going to ask me whether I had eaten.

Thorvald just came back from school with the good news that tomorrow is a holiday and I am delighted to have cleaned, because this way Maman will be able to enjoy herself and rest. Joaquinito also came home. The stack of books reminds me of Wadleigh and I think with enormous pleasure that I haven't regretted for one second having left school.

The other day I read that there are three reasons for avoiding people and wanting solitude: bitterness, indifference or sensitivity. I have too many illusions to be bitter, I feel too much pity and sympathy to be indifferent, but I know that I am extremely sensitive. Sometimes I have the impression that I see the world upside down and that's why millions of things upset and shock me— things that don't have the least effect on other people. My idea of religion, for instance, so far seems to be the opposite of most people's. For me, religion is simply beauty. Sometimes it's the chanting in church, sometimes it's the incense, the bell, the lights, the other people on their knees, the gilded statues, the flowers, the rays of the sun through the rainbow-colored windows, or the silence of the vaulted roof when the church is empty, the little red flame that burns day and night, the mysteries that move me, fill me with emotions that are impossible to describe and that make up my idea of religion. I pray most to what seems to me the most beautiful thing in church, instead of to the altar itself. As for other people's ideas, I have a vague impression that they find religion a duty, a visit during which one kneels on a wooden bench, or a way of covering up acts that are not very charitable or generous. There are some who say that it's a consolation, a comfort, and others who never think about it, who do everything out of habit. Above all, what I don't understand is the people who read the words in the prayer book. Haven't they ever tried to talk, to meditate? Last Sunday at the end of Mass, Maman asked me why I never bring my prayer book or my rosary, and I almost explained this to her, but instead of that I only answered what the question required.

Really, during the Mass, I was busy thinking about the pretty climbing plants that had entered the church through the open window and whose shadows were waving behind the windows that were closed. I was so absorbed in the beauty of the scene, in my reflections on the supreme Art of the creator of the Universe, that I didn't "pray" one single time during the entire Mass. But would God have understood the prayer that was in my profound admiration of something beautiful which belonged to him like all the other beautiful things in the whole world? So you see, I don't know if I see religion inside out, but even if that is the case, the wrong side of everything is the more beautiful side! I have just discovered the answer to the question of a prescription for happiness: turn the world inside out!

Emilia Quintero wrote me a very long and interesting letter. She had not yet seen Papa because he had left Paris when she finally arrived there. She is very proud of a letter that he wrote her. She is disappointed to find that Molière's house is rented to a *butcher.* She visited the grave of her "adorable Chopin" and took a few laurel leaves as a souvenir. Emilia saw Thorvald's violin teacher and says that he had a surprise from his patron: a wonderful new violin. Her letter seemed as long as her conversation and just as interesting. This is a case of another person whose value and worth I recognize when the person is far away. But I always knew that I was fond of Emilia.

So many pages! But soon I will have caught up and will be able to write only a little, so I am taking advantage now.

4:30. After I have written something, I sometimes think about it a little and I want to illustrate what I thought.

September 11. Yesterday while Maman and I were getting lunch, Antolinita arrived with her French governess. We all spent the day at the beach and I brought back some very beautiful shells, fish in the form of a star, and 8 rusty cents that I found when I was digging in the sand. Thorvald dug up 26 cents and Joaquinito 13. I don't know who discovered that by digging in the sand, one finds money that people have lost, but everyone spent yesterday afternoon looking. It's curious to study the things that are most often lost in the sand: a great deal of money, dozens of hairpins, and a few rings. One lady found a ring with three real opals, another found a wedding ring. It was very exciting.

In the evening, Antolinita missed the 5 o'clock train. When I telephoned, Aunt Antolina gave permission for Baby to spend the night with us, as the next train would have reached New York very late. This morning she left with Maman, and once again I was left alone with "Sport," one of *my* dogs.

It's 4:30 and I have finished working only now. I made great changes in the arrangement of the furniture and I'm waiting impatiently for Maman's return to see if my idea was a good one. One of my greatest joys, I believe, is to see that Maman is pleased with me and proud of my work, and my whole day is spent in thinking of millions of things for "her." Maman says as a joke that I earn 15 dollars a week, but I tell her that I spend 100—also as a joke.

5:00 The other day Joaquinito and Thorvald spoke crudely, and after they left, I talked to Maman. "Is it from Papa that I inherited an almost excessive love of good manners and refined language—in a word, all the qualities he has of a 'born gentleman'?"

"My fifille, on the outside your father looked like a prince. As a man of the world, he was wonderfully courteous and his manners, too, were as noble as possible. But at home, *en famille,* he was rather crude—very different and too Catalan. That is not to say that he wasn't a gentleman, but he learned his manners as he took his place in society."

"But then where do my 'good family' and my aristocratic lineage come from?"

Maman then explained that the Nins were a very well bred family, and when I mentioned the bad taste, the vulgar things Grandfather did, Maman added that those things were only "an old Spanish custom." That even the King of Spain was vulgar because it was a little bit bred into the country and into the character of the people. And I have nothing more to say. A house of cards has just crumbled in my heart: the illusion I had of Papa's perfect nobility. I always saw him as a true Prince of an aristocrat from whom I had inherited a love of good manners and polished language.

September 13. More than ever, I firmly believe that my best friend and companion in the whole world is Maman.

Today we were expecting Belica, but she didn't come so Maman and I spent all day alone together, because Joaquinito and Thorvald were playing in the neighborhood. While we did the housework in the morning, Maman talked to me and I remembered a little girl I knew at school who said that *her* mother's conversation bored her. I remembered that with my heart full of happiness at the contrast, comparing my mother to all the other mothers in the world! In the afternoon we went swimming and after the swim we bought two red apples dipped in caramel and stuck on a little stick and ate them like two schoolgirls. For dinner, Maman made little corn cakes, but I only watched her make them.

After dinner, Maman sat in an armchair in the house because it was cool outside. She began crocheting her orchid-colored sweater and from time to time helped me to finish mine. Yes, it's finished. And when I tried it on in front of the mirror, it was so becoming it made me forget I am ugly. But when Maman told me to wear it tomorrow, I wasn't brave enough to tell her that I would like to wear it for the first time on a certain day, and I said yes.

September 14. Belica didn't come. We all went to Mass together. This was one of the most beautiful days we have had all summer, and finally I was able to take the snapshots I have been wanting to take. I have really been bitten by the camera bug—twelve pictures are already being developed. I took the snapshots at the beach— and for one of them I absent-mindedly walked into the water with my shoes and stockings on. Maman finally let me take a picture of her; she always refuses. I also let Joaquinito take one of me in the new sweater, which I wore all day long.

September 16. Several days ago when I went to the doctor, he said that I am sick with worry, etc. I think the real reason is my poor brothers. Last night when everything was quiet and everyone in bed, I cried myself to sleep, soaking my pillow and my hair with tears. And I wouldn't let myself write for fear I would say things that weren't nice, as I do when I am angry. Now that so many hours have gone by, I see things more clearly and I am more reasonable.

The problem is their teasing, which exasperates me, and they never understand me: if I want to help them, they get angry because I "meddle." And they tell me such bad, bad things that I know they can't possibly mean what they say, but still they hurt me very much. When I cry, Maman comforts me and explains to me very gently that they are only children and that they don't torment me out of wickedness. Then Thorvald and Joaquin start to yell that all I have to do is cry for "Maman to believe all my lies." Today I manage to see their teasing and their ugly words in a different light: they are children, still little boys, and although I certainly won't tell them this, I forgive them from the bottom of my heart. Perhaps when they are all grown up, I'll forget all the nights I have cried myself to sleep.

This morning after Joaquinito and the whole family left, I went to Far Rockaway to do the shopping and to pick up my 12 snapshots, which are wonderful! When I came back, I found the only remaining neighbor walking all around looking for me because she thought something had happened to me.

Edgemere is almost empty. Since the 1st of September, the cottages and stores have closed one by one. The trains stop much farther on and only from time to time. The beach is almost always empty and the street, which was always full of screaming children, baby carriages and automobiles, seems very empty now—all the better. The days are shorter and colder—there is often fog and wind, the sea is always very cold and very angry. It's beautiful! Sometimes the sun appears only at the time of sunset and it seems to want to redouble its splendor then to make up for it.

The housecleaning is done. To keep me busy, I am making a tam-o'-shanter with the same silk that I used in my sweater, and I have a pair of stockings to mend—but I prefer to write.

Once I put on a floppy black bow tie, which is one of the things I love enthusiastically, and Maman told me that Papa never wore anything else—always a floppy black bow tie. That seemed such an amusing discovery, and such a plausible reason for the liking I have for a black bow, that I was delighted. The whole world can make fun of me, even Cuca, but if Papa could wear a big floppy black bow tie, I am proud to share his taste and do the same!!! Hurray for the artist's bow tie!

And next to the black bow tie, the black velvet tam-o'-shanter is the thing I like best, and then my black velvet jacket, because those three things are artists' garments—but what I like next best must have come from Maman, because silk stockings are neither artistic nor masculine! And my sweater? That doesn't count.

Maman said when we go back to New York in two weeks, we are going to occupy the entire second floor, the two millionaire rooms! And also Antolinita is leaving on September 26, but Aunt Lolita and Uncle Thorvald are going to spend the winter here. Maman said that if I helped her with her business, I would make more money than I would writing stories. I accept the first idea and am holding onto the second one. Both are good.

Wanting to try an experiment with my camera, I took a picture of the beautiful sun, and I was already imagining a magnificent frame with a picture of the golden ball and the blue sky full of white clouds that look so much like snow. But my family promptly and scientifically explained the disastrous results of my experiment, with smiles that seemed to say: tête de linotte!

Tonight we are going to the cinema. Thorvald is staying in New York for a Boy Scout meeting. We expected him late last night but this morning his bed was empty, so I went to the village to telephone Monsita, but Thorvald hadn't spent the night there. At that moment, I realized what an important place my little brother has in my heart—I who thought I didn't love him any more because he made me cry with his teasing. During that moment when I was looking for his friend Jack's phone number, I had horrible doubts about the reasons for his absence and I had only one wish: for him to return, even if he teased me the rest of my life. Fortunately, it was a false alarm, and Maman and I forgot our anxious moments when we learned he had spent the night at Jack's because they were going somewhere today. He had telephoned but we were at the cinema. One learns many things in a day—and I must already have one gray hair!

September 21. The wife of the President of Cuba made Maman a present of a big box of chocolates. Joaquinito always asks for a family: a great big piece of candy is the papa, another big one is the mama, and a handful of little ones are the children. He doesn't dare take the aunts and cousins because they would give him indigestion, like real aunts and cousins. (That isn't kind, but I said it as a joke.) When Thorvald puts his hand into the box, he puts it in without a word. That's Thorvald. I don't do that, I choose carefully, taste them, and give them to Thorvald in secret. That's my way of civilizing him a little.

At the cinema, we laughed at these funny things: A man stops in front of a window where two human skeletons are on display. One is very big, the other is a small one. Then the man goes into the store and asks: "Whose skeletons are those?" "The big one is George Washington and the little one is George Washington when he was a boy." Also a little girl asks a minister: "Is God everywhere?" "Yes, everywhere," says the minister. "Is he in this room?" "Yes, he is in this room." "Is he in the cellar too?" "Yes, he is in the cellar too." "Is he in the attic?" "Certainly he is in the attic." "Well, then, you're a liar because we don't have any attic."

September 23. Sunday, after I finished writing and had put on my blue apron to help Maman with the lunch, Ramona Ortega, a friend of Maman's, came. The smell of the meat and saffron rice had already announced that it was lunchtime and I had just set the table for 5 when Aunt Antolina arrived in an automobile with Felo, Antolinita, Charles and the two young Bermudez boys—and a big box of provisions. Lunch was a Bolshevik banquet because of the noise and the appetites. Afterward the others went out to play while Maman and I did the dishes. Oh, so many dishes. But Maman goes fast and makes the dishes shine with just a drop of water, so it didn't matter. And anyhow, whatever I do in Maman's company, even mending stockings and entertaining certain visitors, is transformed from a bore into a pleasant occupation just because Maman is there. All that on the subject of dishes!

Later we all went to the beach. I had a terrible headache and saw everything through a strange light. Everyone seemed so dull, so stupid! A little 14-year-old coquette named Ethel caught my attention. I had never noticed her, but I distinctly remember wondering if I could ever imitate her. The idea was so funny that I watched her for several minutes with the special smile that Maman calls "the Philosopher's smile."

When everyone was good and wet and had swallowed enough salt water, we decided to come back home to dry off. Then when everyone was dressed, they attacked the provisions again. If someone had asked me just then what people live for, I would have answered simply: to swim and to eat. Fortunately my headache went away before the family left and I could see people in a better light.

While I was combing my hair, Felo put his head around the door that was standing ajar and cried out in surprise that I was "componiéndome" (Spanish or Cuban).[1] I thought that was funny and we had a good laugh together.

[1] *Putting myself together.*

Then Aunt Antolina said that Rafael Bermudez, the little Spaniard who brought me roses the day of my birthday, had worn a new suit in my honor and I hadn't noticed it. I thought that was funny too! I am not mocking anyone, I'm just writing as I always do. But finally everyone left and I could say as they do in books: "A deep silence followed the uproar, the lights went out, and only the night was still awake."

Monday I didn't write because I felt indignant about people. Yet I had worked all day long, the house was shining clean, laundry was hanging on the line, the dinner was ready, appetizing and well salted, so that when Maman came home she could feel contented the rest of the evening. But she arrived with the "family" worries that I dread. Nothing was said during the dinner hour as we have a tacit agreement to keep it sacred and happy. But later Maman sat down to crochet, while I wrapped my arms around my knees and rested my chin between my knees. That's my listening position.

I want to write as few unkind things as possible in my diary—I feel so much pity for that group of human beings around me who aren't happy because they are materialistic—but since I made you a silent promise to show you the whole world exactly as it looks to me, I shall simply describe it without beating around the bush.

Human nature, with its faults and qualities, is a mystery. At 16 I have made certain discoveries and I will continue to do so until the day I die, because the mystery is bottomless. Up until now, I have always discovered a quality and at the same time a corresponding fault. It's only in my Dream Country that the qualities eclipse the faults; in Real Life, alas, the faults seem to be more numerous!

Maman has struggled bravely in Life to support herself and her three children. She has rich sisters who, at the beginning of her struggle, lent her or gave her money—after all, none of them needed the money and Maman was their sister. They should have laid down their lives, if necessary, if only because Maman was their sister. But human nature is such that the money given or lent to Maman is considered an action worthy of gratitude. Ask Godmother to whom Maman owes her advancement and the answer would be: to me. Ask Aunt Antolina the same thing—same answer. Therefore, Maman's hard work, her energy, her courage, her constancy, her faith don't count. Now, just at the time when Maman is beginning to expand her business, Aunt Antolina tells her that she should *give* Godmother the house at 158—the thing that pays for the food and rent—*give it to her out of gratitude for all that Godmother did for her*. Aunt Antolina also passes herself off as Maman's benefactor.

Gratitude? Doesn't the recital of favors *kill* gratitude? And Maman suffers. Last night, sublime in her indignation, she told me yes, she would repay *all those favors* one day, but there would be no gratitude *left*. Little by little, her indignation faded away; the struggle was too hard. But all her words pierced my heart and it was I who suffered terribly. My gratitude is gone too, and what I shall do from here on is what Maman will do—*only our duty*. It will be money for money, favor for favor. No more affection in return for favors, gratitude in return for money. The heart is overwhelmed by the terrible reality. Oh, human nature, human beings, who do good in return for *gratitude!* Can it be true? Is it possible? So much cynicism, such a matter-of-fact attitude?

That may be overstated—I always overstate everything, and I know it. If Maman comes home happy today and tells me about a kind act of Godmother's, a nice thing that Aunt Antolina did, I will say: "I can forgive and forget everything, no matter what, no matter who, no matter when, wherever and whatever the circumstances." Who can deny the strength of such a perfect rule? Who can be hurt with a maxim like that to guide him? Pain comes when one hesitates to forgive, when one doesn't forget, when one can never forget!

Last night during our conversation, Maman crocheted my black silk tam-o'-shanter to go with my velvet jacket. As she finished, she saw that she had done it wrong, so she silently undid what she had done. When we went to bed, she stroked my hair and said in a rather strange voice, very sweetly, calmly, and sadly: "That's how one goes through life, my little Philosopher: doing and undoing!" It was splendid. I looked at Maman, trying to read in her face how she accepts life. The answer was there: a smile!

There was a storm during the night, and Maman and I were awake quite a long time, each one thinking that the other was asleep. But after discovering the truth, we realized it wasn't exactly the storm that was keeping us awake but worry, the fear of another kind of moral, human storm!

In the morning it was all over, with only the damp sand as a reminder of the night's rain. The sun was shining brightly. I am sure that Maman had the same thought as I—at the end of every storm the sunshine follows the rain, in Nature and also in Life. Hope? Yes, hope and forgetting, forgiveness and still more hope, that's the secret of happiness.

I said that this morning the sun came out, but right now, at about 4 o'clock, a big cloud covered it and rain began falling in torrents on the roof, the street and the trees. The more the rain fell, the more I wrote, as if each drop of water brought me a word.

But now I'm going to let the raindrops and the words vanish into space and take up the broom, which I put down to write "a few lines." Only 17 pages! If only I could write a book as easily as I write my diary! I would be a millionaire and we would never have to wash dishes again!

September 24. We have only three days left at Edgemere. Never in my whole life have I seen a summer go by so quickly—and so well.

Today as I did the housekeeping, I thought that soon I won't be able to be Maman's "maid" and I'll have to find a new way to help her. Maman is often cross with me and says that I am disobedient when I wash the clothes that Thorvald and Joaquinito need. Then I try to joke about it and I pretend that sweeping puts on weight and strengthens the arms, washing keeps the nails clean, and as I told Maman, I have to learn to do everything so as to be helpful to my future husband, who will be very poor. Every day Maman makes a long list of things that she forbids me to do and every day I do all of them. But strangely enough, that kind of disobedience doesn't disturb my conscience in the least.

I found time to read Stevenson's beautiful book, Kidnapped. I would like to write a few pages in my diary in that pleasant language: "nae, nae my lass, ye kenn, that is no lee ye are telling naow. . . ."

Apropos of a maid who walked out of the house at 158 without a second's notice, Maman said angrily: "The world is rotten!" And I answered with a smile, "It isn't the world that is rotten, but people." And I was right. I hear everyone say so many bad things about the world and human beings that I am used to it, but I don't believe a word of what I say. I love poor little humanity and this funny old world, I love the poor people and I sympathize with their sorrows and their joys and I think that the predominant feeling in my heart when I am not melancholy is tenderness and pity for the whole world. That doesn't prevent me from being afraid of it.

Thorvald just shocked me and a heavy discussion just took place in which he admitted that he is a *donkey*. One of the books he is going to study in school is George Eliot's wonderful story

"Silas Marner," a book that I bought with great good luck for 10 cents and the conviction that I had found a treasure. Now he shows me the book and tells me calmly that the author is a teacher at his school. I explained to him with great indignation the fact that he is a donkey! And finally, stubborn as a real donkey, he wanted to have the last word and said stupidly: "Well, they have the same name!" O Thorvald! I wouldn't be surprised someday to hear you say that Sir Walter Scott was your geography teacher, or worse still, arithmetic teacher, or that Charles Dickens sells cookies for $.07 to the boys in your school. Thorvald never knows whether it was Othello who wrote a book called "Shakespeare" or the other way around. A badly written book that describes 3 or 4 boys of his type, "roughnecks" as they say here, interests him a thousand times more than a well-written book about Napoleon, for example. It's disgraceful!

September 25. It's one o'clock. I have just eaten lunch—an egg, a piece of bread and butter, and an orange. And I have absolutely nothing more to do in the house, except read or write. There was a great revolution in beds because of Mrs. de Sola's arrival this afternoon. We had to change all the mattresses, vacate Maman's room and settle ourselves in the room that belonged to Charles. Once I was carrying one of the mattresses that was rather big and heavy, and I fell down with the mattress on top of me. Just at that moment the bread man came along shouting: "Bread, bread! Fifteen cents!" Every day I call him and buy bread from him. As I didn't call him today—or rather I called him, but the mattress smothered the sound—I had to run after him. Naturally everything that I did was an act of disobedience, and when Maman came home she was angry at first and afterward she hugged me and called me "Chérie," "Fifille" or "mon Coco." That happens every day. Our little world is a nice place, after all, when one has a Maman like mine. I want you to know that half the silly things I do come from the fact that I am so, so spoiled. The other half I inherited.

Mrs. de Sola is bringing a maid. So today I am not the maid any more, I am a young lady. Perhaps when I think of the season spent at Edgemere, it won't be especially because of the superficial pleasures, to which I am more or less indifferent, but because of the great Lesson that I learned here. Perhaps never before in my life did I realize Maman's great burden and her courage. No, I am sure that I never thought to help her by making her burden lighter. I was absorbed in my own pleasures, I was disorderly, selfish in the way I spent my time. Lake Placid was the cause of my moral awakening. My character actually changed, and that is what my two brothers noticed when they said that I was sweeter and nicer than before. And the good Lord was kind enough to give me an opportunity to fulfill my resolutions. From Maman's happiness when she noticed the change, from my brothers' few words of thanks, who were perhaps surprised that I took an interest in their clothes, their games, I know that I have won my battle. Before, one of the most difficult things, perhaps, was not to pick up my diary until all the stockings were darned and all the other work done. Now it's a habit.

And it's with all my heart that I want to stay this way, my brothers loving me more, Maman loving me more, and what would I live for if it weren't just for my little family's happiness? This morning, for the first time in a long while, Joaquinito kissed me good morning. I was happily surprised. When he kissed me again before he left for school, I couldn't help asking him why. "Because you are much nicer." Do I discover, then, that my happiness depends on the happiness of other Egoisms? That doesn't exist any more in me. I have two great aims in life from now on. Make my family happy. Make my family proud of me. When I have made my family happy and proud, then I'll take everyone else as my family and begin over. I see so many roads ahead of me and they are all beautiful. I am so happy, so changed that I would like to see the whole world changed and happy as I am. My little family and my big Family—and I need to love all of them!

What is happening to me? Is it the sunshine, the magic of the silence, the clouds overhead, and the water so near me? I could almost promise that I was born an optimist, if I didn't know that it will rain one day and I will turn back into a disagreeable pessimist.

September 26. I am transformed by the spirit of Washington Irving—his book "Sketches" seems to me like the rising of a theatre curtain on another of Life's scenes, the Great Drama. And what a scene! There is an incredible charm in the choice and style of his sentences that one never tires of, and the beauty of the scene inspires still more lofty ideas, marvelous impressions, because of their strange and original aspect. All that refreshes a Poet's heart and easily convinces me that I am not yet blasé. The richness of his vocabulary almost blinds me. That is the magic and that is the ability that I want to subjugate, to set free one day and give a little pleasure to the world.

I interrupted my reading because I suddenly received the long-awaited visit of Inspiration and I began My Book. I can really say, like Washington Irving, in speaking of my literary spirit: "I have no command of my talents, such as they are, and have to watch the varyings of my mind as I would those of a weather-cock." The weather-cock turned in a favorable direction—it's the beginning of my harvest-time. Courage!

4 o'clock. Mrs. de Sola and her daughter arrived last night. Elisita has cut her hair short in the current fashion. She looked so strange—as though she had only a few locks of hair, and I caught myself looking at her often with surprise and astonishment. At bedtime, I was brushing my hair in front of the mirror and the same thing happened as happens every evening: the brush giving it even more electricity and the hair falling over my back and shoulders in a mass of colors. Maman stopped a moment to watch me and I asked her mischievously: "Would you like me to cut my hair like Elsie?" Maman looked at me with an expression on her face that is special to her and that I have learned to interpret as an unspoken: scatterbrain! Then I had to hug her to show that I was only teasing, and I was very glad to see that she was as sure as I that even if I am a scatterbrain, my hair is firmly in place on my head, for I will never cut it of my own free will. I am like the man who never thought about his castle until the day he discovered that his neighbor was living in a wooden house. Then he was as proud as he could be!

5 o'clock. I am waiting for Elsie, who went to the city, so that we can go to the beach together. I take care of my duties as hostess when Maman isn't here, but I would very much like to find myself alone again. That's why Maman says that I am an unsociable little one.

I am going to work on my book, which has a very original title, I hope—"Polaris."

September 27. Guess what occupation you are sharing with me? Fishing. There are three of us in a little boat—Elsie, Thorvald and you—and as we are inseparable, that means that I am there too. The anchor is dropped and the boat is motionless between the two shores. Knowing that fishing consists mainly of silence and waiting, Elsie brought a book and I a slightly different book, isn't that so? Around us there is a large sheet of water and on the shores there are little houses and great mansions, even a castle, many trees, and the tall grass that is characteristic of the Bay. Before settling down in silence, each with a long line on the end of which an unfortunate earthworm is hanging, we went to get provisions to feed the fish.

I always had a romantic vision of fishermen and their houses and I didn't lose the illusion by satisfying my curiosity, a curiosity which Thorvald has mocked for a long time and is still mocking. We were met at the door by a pretty dog that wagged its tail constantly and licked our hands. The house itself was very old and badly built, in addition to being not very big, but even if the windows had no panes and the house was falling to pieces, in contrast, it was surrounded by great fields of high grass that the wind shook and bent down and the tiny waves lapped gently at the foot of the house, making everything charming and picturesque. Several small old boats were lying half on the shore, half in the water, with their anchors buried in the sand but still swaying a little with the waves. I noticed a big crab nailed to the door.

The interior was what I expected. The room looked like an attic—and while Thorvald did the marketing, I looked all around. I saw an antique stove in the middle of the room, lighted, although I don't know why because it isn't cold yet. There was a line across the room from which hung pairs of stockings like those I used to make for the soldiers, some big, big red handkerchiefs, as in Spain, and a pair of tattered pants. A bottle of milk and a loaf of black bread were on the table, which certainly seemed very clean. There was also a pair of boots that reminded me of the story of Hop O' My Thumb, and many big jars full of crabs, worms, eels, preserved in mud and sand. Many dead crabs were nailed on the wall, with a picture of a sailboat such as one sees in little children's ABC books.

Only the fisherman was a little like all men. He didn't have a beard or long hair and his skin was a little darker than Thorvald's is this summer. But he was wearing a heavy woolen shirt, brown trousers and big black boots, not very clean. He always kept his hands in his pockets but had no pipe, and this last seemed to me terribly lacking. Fortunately his eyes were the color of the sea and his expression was so open and honest that it was a pleasure to see. He was polite and spoke without swearing and seemed to love his dog very much. All told, it was easy for me to forgive the missing beard and pipe.

From where we are, we can still see the house and the crab

nailed to the door and the man sitting on the threshold with his dog's head resting on his knee and—a pipe between his teeth.

A few minutes ago Thorvald caught an inedible sort of little fish, and as he was trying to throw it back into the water, he lost his little sinker stone. So I pretended that I don't like to fish and I gave my pole to Thorvald. An hour later no one had caught anything except that one little fish. Elsie is hysterically afraid of the poor earthworms, and everything Thorvald does with them disgusts me a little. Once to test my courage, he took one and said: "You don't dare pull that, I'll bet." "Don't I?" So I closed my eyes after taking the "tail" in my fingers, and I pulled . . . feeling sick but with a smile on my lips. Thorvald, who listened to Elsie's shrieks and could compare us, seemed proud of me. You have to make your brothers proud of you, even if it takes a great effort.

September 28. 2:00. Our last day here! To add to our regret, the weather is more beautiful than ever, but the trunk is packed . . . we must leave. I am sitting on the porch with Maman and Mrs. de Sola, who are reading. I was so tired from the struggle between my politeness and my disgust that I refused to go fishing with Elsie and Joaquinito. All my old dislike for Elsie has come back, in spite of my efforts to contain myself. Everything she does is revolting and perhaps my only consolation is that Maman admits that she wouldn't like to have a daughter like Elsie.

After all, I am glad to leave. In New York I am going to see Cuca, who is back from Lake Placid, and Antolinita, whom we are expecting today by automobile. And also I am glad to go back to 158 so changed.

The other day I thought about the approach of my 17th birthday and of all the progress that I have made since my 16th birthday, the kind of spiritual and physical progress that makes me think that I was a little girl until yesterday, and since I think of this every day, I keep trying to grow up in the way I think and act.

2:30—Mrs. de Sola has a maid, Emilia, for whom I felt an immediate liking and that strange pity that I feel for everyone. She is Catalan, not Spanish—and so sweet, so obliging, with sad eyes rimmed with curly lashes, very fine chestnut-colored hair which is always adorably mussed, very pale and thin, with hands that are chapped and deformed by housework. If I were rich, I would keep her near me for the pleasure of hearing her speak Spanish in the charming way of everyone I knew in Barcelona; she wouldn't ever have to work and I would spoil her. I would like so much for her not to have those eyes that are so sad, and her smile is so beautiful it makes me want to cry. And it always seems to me that her hands hurt her, the way mine did the day I washed the sheets. I always want to help her and would gladly do her work while she rested—if Maman would let me. She knows Paquita Madriguera and she listened to me saying the famous message: "Molts Recorts" with a vastly amused smile.

Yesterday when we came back from fishing, we met our young Jewish neighbor, Mr. Bob Aftstein. I am always charmed by his conversation, which indicates such a good education, and I regret a little the race prejudice that prevented me from making friends with his sister, who is 14 years old and seems just as nice and well brought-up as he. And on this subject: our Catholic neighbor, little Arthur's uncle, left without paying their rent. Maman borrowed coffee from Mr. Bob's mama, and Maman made her a special dessert because she was sick, but we never got beyond: Good morning! and Good evening! Only because they are Jewish!

8 o'clock. We are all assembled in the dining room. Thorvald is doing his lessons with a worried and studious expression on his face. Mrs. de Sola and Maman are rocking back and forth with relaxed faces, talking about the old days, and sometimes I stop to listen to strange stories about the lives of many people whom I don't know. Fortunately, Maman seldom talks about those things and I am proud of her. She even listens with an amused look, like me when I hear dreadful gossip that I don't believe. But when she lowers her voice, I stop listening and write.

I have tried in every way to think of things to entertain Elsie, but each time I am more discouraged by her bored air, the kind people have who don't know how to find pleasure within themselves. Finally, with a resigned expression, she decided to draw—and I might add that she draws very well.

Sometimes I feel sorry for the unrelenting distaste that Elsie inspires in me, and at times I wonder if it isn't my fault. No, I am not nice, not patient and charitable enough, and I am going to try again—but luckily I am leaving tomorrow morning. When I think that Elsie's mother has been such a good friend to my Maman, I can forgive her, and I hope she forgives me for everything that I have thought and written. We don't understand each other.

September 30. What a change! I have never noticed such a difference, such a contrast. Sometimes I think that I am the one who is changing, not other people and things.

Yesterday we were up before sunrise. After much running around, many farewells, arranging of packages, etc., we were finally settled in the train which took us, to our regret, back to New York.

I found 158 so dark, so solemn! We are living in our old bedroom. All afternoon, I could entertain myself only by rereading Scott's Quentin Durward. We have lunch and dinner in a restaurant very near here which is already famous because of its old clientele: Mr. Tagliapietra,[1] Emilia Quintero and the Madriguera family. We do that so as not to cause an upheaval in the house.

I am going to help Maman in her business. I even have a little notebook to write down the things I should do. I am going to try to be a good businesswoman, without sacrificing my literary ambitions.

October 3. Wednesday morning I did some buying for Maman and in the afternoon I went to see Frances. It was raining miserably and we stayed in the house to talk. Frances has made plans for us to go together to the first dance at my Dancing School, from 8 in the evening until midnight because we are older now. So Thursday I spent my day "preparing," with the care and the impatience that I always feel on such occasions.

Before leaving for Lake Placid, one of my extravagances was an adorable pink dance dress with a lot of tulle and a beautiful rose at the waist, but really as simple as it is beautiful and original. I wore it last night with silk stockings and black shoes, and a little piece of pink tulle with fringes of little white pearls, but not a single piece of jewelry because it seemed to me the rose was perfect by itself. My hair, which I fixed with Monsita's help, was artistically arranged in a chignon of curls, like the night of Emilia's concert but even better. My dress was so pretty that the whole family and the people in the house came to the room to see it and exclaim over it. Even Charlie, who usually is very indifferent, was very nice and offered to accompany me to Duryea's.

At 8:30 I was there, waiting for Frances in the little room where one puts on still more powder. At 9 I was dancing, and I didn't stop until midnight as I had every dance taken. The first 9 are also taken for next week. Everyone seemed to have as good a time as I did. There were dancers of every age, principally on the other side of 20 and a few in the neighborhood of 100. But it didn't matter because they dance better than young boys and we learned

[1] *Husband of Teresa Carreño.*

a great deal. Fortunately I know how to dance, and at the end I even knew how to do the new dance from London, "The Rocker."

In looking after the cages, I discovered my little bird, the one who sang so well, lying in the bottom of the cage, almost dead. We gave him castor oil, brandy and warm water, and wrapped him in cotton, but he died anyhow and Joaquinito buried him next to the other one, beneath the same lilac tree.

When I think about the picture that I took of him, about his songs that gladdened the silence of my solitude at Edgemere, I feel sad with thoughts of the things that pass. . . . It's only a bird who has gone from my life, but I am aware of that strange Law that forces us to separate, that causes such emptiness and breaks so many hearts when its fatal power is felt.

October 4. Aunt Antolina has moved to the house at 172 W. 86 Street, which Maman is also going to rent. All morning there was so much work to do! Our trunk finally arrived and everything had to be put away. We can't live there yet because my admirable family continues with their misunderstandings.

Godmother is unrecognizable. She is even bitter against me for unexplained reasons, and I understand why there are people who think the world is so ugly and so sad: a single person like Godmother can destroy all the fairy castles. But although my disillusionment makes me very sad and I have lost faith in Godmother, I am looking for other people to love and admire. I admire my Uncle Thorvald very much; he is so good, so jolly, and he is very much like Maman. I am expecting him this evening as he is going to read me the manuscript of a story he has written for the cinema.

We are living so much the way we did before that it seems to me I've never left 158. The day that Eleanor came to see me, I found she has grown as tall as I, but she is still the same, just as nice and studious, with a big package of books under her arm.

This afternoon I went to the theatre with Antolinita. We saw the supposed magic of "Thurston," which was strange and amusing, but Charles can explain all the tricks.

Until now the beginning of my book has been in the trunk and this evening I want to go on with it. But really, the day's events, which I always think about so much, have affected the mood of my pen, in contrast to the peaceful happiness at the cottage. Before leaving you, I want to give you the good news that I have finally adopted the serious chignon as my coiffure. I inherited a great facility for dressing my hair from Maman, and even Maman, who fortunately is always so indifferent to useless things, takes pleasure in the compliments that I get from Aunt Antolina and from everyone in general about the way I do my hair. It's to break the monotony of pages covered with my faults that from time to time I put in the good things that I inherited without intending to.

October 5. 9 o'clock. Since Aunt Antolina left, the room that used to belong to the Madriguera family is empty, and as it's the prettiest room in the house, I have come up here to write. I also have the silence that I want when I am writing. But there is no desk here. I am writing at the dresser, and because I am wearing my blue sweater, sometimes I am distracted by the image reflected in the three little mirrors.

This morning we went to ten o'clock Mass and I ran into Mr. J. de Alba. As we chatted, I asked him if he had news of Paquita. He thinks she is coming back in November, but he says Enric sailed a long time ago and probably has already arrived without anyone knowing it. Mr. de Alba received a post card from him from Paris—like mine, I suppose. By coincidence, when I got home I was looking for some papers for Maman and I found Mr. Madriguera's picture—so I put it on the mantel in the living room, and it seemed really as though I should beg his pardon for having left him so long in a drawer.

After lunch Uncle Thorvald came with his story for the cinema, which he calls "The Artist." I promised to type it on the machine for him and to shorten the description of the characters. I became so enthusiastic that I was at the typewriter all afternoon, even though the weather outside was beautiful. When the time came to get dinner, I regretted Thorvald's and Joaquinito's appetites, as otherwise I wouldn't have eaten anything. Afterward Maman went to bed so tired that I left the machine to write a little by hand.

I would like to write Papa, but I like to be able to tell him good things about everyone and today Joaquinito drove me to despair with his terrible naughtiness. There are times when I think I will never be able to forgive him, especially when he lies and is deceitful with Maman. I believe that Joaquinito is the naughtiest boy in the whole world.

I see that I soon must buy a new notebook. I am surprised at the speed with which I fill them up. Perhaps I write too many details, but I think I will write less now because I'm not as happy as I was during the summer. I wanted so much, oh, so much, so much, to live over there! But Maman is sacrificing everything for her business and I never can talk to her as I did at the cottage because she is always busy, so I feel lonely, very, very lonely in this big house which doesn't seem to belong to us. Perhaps this evening I am going to let fall a few very sad tears, without knowing why. I feel so unhappy. This is only an attack—but no one understands.

Maman promised to let me work and I have nothing to do, but when I talk about it, Maman becomes strangely impatient, and I think it must be because she is sick. But my ambitions, concerning which I need advice and help so badly, seem not to matter to anyone but me. Oh, if Maman knew how lonely I feel here, she would take pity on me, but I shut it all up in silence and in my Diary.

With a big family all around me, I am going to have to make a decision absolutely on my own and without any help. No one realizes that I am grown up and that I am ambitious. Maman suggests that I work seriously with her, but when I ask her: "How can I help you today?" she says: "Go and pick up some rat poison for me and put your things away."

My "things" are one dress and sometimes a few hairpins.

Let's not talk about it any more.

October 6. It's funny to see where I have settled down to write, just where I used to be so often—in the living room, next to the window.

One of the things that I bought this morning is a new Diary, because this one will soon be finished. I have been dreaming for a long time about the things that may happen next year, and I've dreamed about it so much that I almost believe something wonderful will happen the day that I write the first page. Perhaps it will be Papa's return, or my visit to Cuba, or maybe a tiny literary success. The only sure thing is that I am going to be 17 next year. . . .

I think, too, that I would like to receive a post card from Enric in order to be sure he is back. I had such a funny dream last night: Enric arrived here very, very poor and asked for the little room under the eaves, but Maman told him she couldn't give it to him because he hadn't any money. Enric then looked so sad, like the last time I saw him, that in my dream I went up to him and told him to stay, that the rest of it would work out. Then I talked to Maman and told her that I would pay her for the room under the eaves with the money that I earned by writing books. Still in my dream, I became a member of the French Académie and I became very rich and gave all my money to the poor violinist without his knowing anything about it. But one day it was he who became rich and Maman told him everything, in spite of her promise, and just as I heard Enric calling me to say thank you— Joaquinito woke me up. I was very pleased because it's fun to do something nice, but it's not fun when someone says thank you.

October 7. The family is going to bed, but I have permission to write and until now I have been working on "The Artist." I am very much absorbed in the story—the characters seem so real to me. Every time Uncle Thorvald comes over, we enjoy talking about the personages as though they were real people whose fate we have to decide. Sometimes I feel sympathy for one of them, or pity, and then I plead and Uncle Thorvald makes a solemn judgment and changes a few lines. The hero, the Artist, is magnificent, and the heroine, Thelma, is so noble that my entire interest is taken by the ending and I am very glad to know that they are happy. There is a violinist, a painter, and a very selfish woman, Clarine, who dies in a dramatic fashion at the end. And a studio, with pathetic and artistic scenes. I hope with all my heart that Uncle Thorvald will be a success.

As soon as I have finished with the manuscript, I am going to begin my own work. Before turning seventeen, I want to have earned some money to help Maman. Perhaps if Maman were rich, I wouldn't be so ambitious, because my only thought is helping her.

October 8.
Dear Little Papa:
You must be surprised not to have received any letters since the one I wrote in July, but I was so delighted with Emilia's visit, which was such a good substitute for all the letters that I might write you, that I waited from one day to the next for a letter from you giving me the details. Then I got your post card, I waited some more, and a long letter from Emilia came to take away all my illusions.

It's such a pity [that she missed you]! But there was a tiny little bit of amusement mixed with my regret at this new evidence of one of Emilia's characteristics: she is always late.

So now I will tell you all I can about the three of us, since that gives you pleasure. We have just spent a perfect summer, and I hope with all my heart that you have been as happy as we all were. Maman bought a cottage at the beach, and Thorvald and Joaquinito were mad with joy. From the first day on, they spent their days outside, swimming, fishing, busy with all kinds of exercises and vigorous amusing games.

When I came back from the mountains, I finally had a little house to take care of and all the delights of housekeeping.

At dinner, we were all together after the day's activities. We have never appreciated so much the joy of having our own house, just for the family, and away from the big city.

It was there that I caught the pleasant fever of photography. Do you like the results? You will easily recognize us, even if we have grown and are quite changed. When you write, tell us who we look like, for the opinions vary greatly—the only unquestionable thing being that Joaquinito is the image of you, in spite of his big dark eyes, and so am I when I am serious and inspired, but not when I go to dances, etc. And Papa, if you will, and even if you make fun of me, stop reading and look at your hands, because it seems I have the "Nin hands" exactly. As for the other things, you will see them in the pictures.

The season at the beach ended a week ago when we came back to the same house in New York. Now Thorvald and Joaquinito are going sedately to school and I am going to begin again working on my French and on the dance. I spend the rest of my time writing on the machine, most of it to help Maman with her business, which is prospering admirably. She lets me think that I am her secretary.

The other day Thorvald arranged his courses at school so as to become an Engineer, so his career is already decided by the classes he is taking. Since Emilia Quintero left, Joaquinito has not had a teacher, but his talent seems more prodigious than ever. I wish I could explain the qualities that he was born with—all the things that other people study a thousand years to acquire, while he has them simply and naturally in his magical hands. I can't define his technique, I don't know enough about it, but I am artist enough to understand the genius of this little 11-year-old boy, a little devil at school and at home—but many things can be forgiven in a real artist! But if you can hope to find in Joaquinito the heir to your talent, you won't find the same thing in Thorvald. Because his young violin teacher is away on a trip, Thorvald considers his violin an antique piece of furniture, suitable only for viewing. He is absorbed in mathematics, in that dreadful algebra, and in the baseball championship—American style.

Mrs. Quintero herself couldn't have told you more than I have written. If you felt like demonstrating your pleasure with a letter, I wouldn't be so sad as I sometimes am when I feel that you don't think very much about us. Write, please do, and receive a thousand tender kisses from your

Linotte

October 8. An Autumn evening.

It is cold for the first time, after the beautiful days of summer.

The trees are already dry, the leaves have all flown away, all of Nature is withered, dying, to turn green again later on. . . . There are people who are older, who have aged with the passing months—like faded flowers—and so for them life is going to be a continual Autumn.

There are others who are still young, who weep with Nature and also smile with her in Spring. There are even dreams that are born in Autumn because there is much Beauty in melancholy, and Autumn is too beautiful to be sad.

But when cold knocks at the door (a little elf dressed in blue, covered with little drops of ice water and wearing a cap of yellow and red leaves), then we are all very happy, all of us sitting around a fire that crackles in the big fireplace.

Everyone thinks his own thoughts. Maman has a determined look on her wonderful face. No doubt she is dreaming of great projects in the future, of her business, of the obligations she has imposed on herself for the good of her children. She is a study in courage—a heroine!

Thorvald is ruminating again on a difficult problem—he looks so serious, so perplexed and so intelligent. He is a study in the model boy.

Joaquinito's eyes are full of mystery and mischief—a study in depth.

As for me, what do I see in the flames that seem to fly upward from the logs, fragrant with pine resin? First, the logs, and the great forests of fragrant pines, then the fall of those trees that were so proud, so straight and so magnificent! The flames enveloping the crackling wood—very strong to begin with, very hot and full of light while the log is still whole.

I see fairies dancing, wearing veils of every color. I see their long golden hair moving in the wind that comes down the chimney. It is the wind that speaks. Then the fairies in the flames are animated and dance higher, higher, faster, still faster. They are mad, their dance is Madness and Youth. That goes on for a long time, a long time!

Then a log breaks in two with a shivering moaning sound. The dance stops. The fairies let go of their veils, which fly up the chimney to meet the clouds. There is a moment of silence when the fairies dance no more; the flames seem to go out and lose their bright colors.

Little by little, the tiny flames that hover around the crumbling log give off their last gleams, while the fairies surround them and weep. Little by little, very gently, the log that was so strong at the beginning of the struggle succumbs and falls into a little heap of embers. The flames die and the fairies fade away into space. The embers are still full of light; it's so beautiful! Perhaps it is the death of Madness. After the beautiful scarlet, azure and golden flames, the embers are transparent with light at first, then later they turn to ashes and it is finished.

So much life, so much beauty, so much madness, so much

enthusiasm, and then everything fades away and dies—so much melancholy!

Suddenly the wind blows, trembling cold knocks again at the door, and realizing the disappearance of the fairies, the departure of the flames, the death of the log, breathing the air still impregnated with pine, we sigh a little sadly. After a few minutes, the wind sighs mournfully and calls to us, as it called the warm light from our fireplace, but no one hears it. The cold calls again more loudly, but no one opens the door because—we are all asleep, while the stars above watch over us. We are dreaming of the Autumn evening and the magic dance of the Flames and the Fairies. An Autumn evening is the cradle of mad, fantastic dreams. It is a study in Fantasy.

In the flames I saw smiles and tears, rain and sunshine—I saw Life! I saw the people I love and the people I ought to love.

I saw the Human Race!

I saw illusions, a million beautiful things, a castle suspended in the clouds.

I saw the country of my Dreams.

But I didn't see Love in the flames, and after looking for it sadly, I found it in the ashes—a long time after the fire went out.

October 9. Last night I was positively perplexed by my strange way of beginning a new notebook, but I had no control over my imagination and my pen. I can't tell you at all how those ideas came to me, and especially the surprising effect that those pages, and above all the ending, had on Maman, who wept.

And yet there were men in the living room, discussing business with Maman in their loud voices, Joaquinito and Thorvald were squabbling, and Monsita was very close to me, typing on the machine. As for me, I was far away from it all—and one of the surprising things is that when I finished, I who have so little confidence in myself (as Maman says), I cried out: "Oh, Thorvald, what I just wrote is so pretty!"

Fortunately, I don't deserve the credit because the words came all by themselves.

With tears in her eyes, Maman said: "My little philosopher."

Perhaps without knowing it, I had rekindled the embers in her heart, and at that moment I was such a visionary that I could see the flames in Maman's heart. Today I have transformed all of it into an "Essay" in English and it's a thousand times more beautiful. It's someone else who was acting for me—I recognize neither my French nor the ideas. As for today's English version, Washington Irving would have thought he was reading his own words.

I have dreamed so much of the surprising and thrilling things that might happen while I was writing this notebook that I am truly delighted to have started it by writing prose and philosophizing. Perhaps something interesting will happen every day.

Let's see, today I went to the library, where I discovered a magazine that helps writers to sell their literary merchandise, and I was delighted by the descriptions and the classification of the work. I understand that my style can only be printed in a "magazine for young inexperienced writers, which pays nothing for manuscripts but promises a great deal for their future renown."

Hm! Hm!

So I corrected and wrote, punishing my typewriter, and interrupting my work only to answer the telephone and the doorbell. (All of New York may have remembered us today!) At present my poor efforts are under the critical eye of Miss Stockbridge, who lives at our house and is a bluestocking. I expect to hang myself (when I have finished reading the Légendes d'Ingoldsby[1] by T. Ingoldsby). Today I learned about the doubts that assail an author when he writes something that people read with joy.

P.S. I forgot to say that Thorvald and Joaquinito put two little dead mice in my slippers this morning. But they were cowards and made me promise not to say anything to Maman (their conscience bothered them) and I have to wear my slippers as usual because I haven't any others.

October 10. It's only two o'clock and I am alone in the house. I am writing in the living room so as to watch for packages that are going to come for me—the result of my purchases this morning. The stores are like fairyland, full of things that we will never be able to own!

As Maman couldn't come with me, I went with Monsita, and we had 2 coats and 4 velvet dresses sent out. From those, Maman is going to select a dress and a winter coat. But the prices made me feel guilty.

I was in a fitting room, which is another name for a modern torture chamber, because I was supposed to choose one dress. As Maman knows I am quite reasonable, she didn't set a price limit, and I walked around the room, surrounded by all the pretty

[1] The Ingoldsby Legends.

dresses imaginable, trying them all on, listening enthusiastically to Monsita's exclamations, astonished by the beautiful reflections that I saw in the mirrors.

Choose one! Oh! I wanted them all! They were so different and all at different prices. Luckily, the least expensive seemed to me the most beautiful! (Next to one that cost 100 dollars.)

If you like, I will frighten you with the price of my new ensemble. Look:

1 Ermine	$40
1 Velvet Dress	29.50
1 coat	49.50
	$119.00

It's 10 but Thorvald and Joaquinito are at a Scout meeting and when I asked Maman for permission to write while I wait for them, she answered yes in her sleep.

This afternoon I straightened up the bookshelves and Maman's desk, running to the window rather often, but nothing has come yet and won't come now. The ermine won't be ready, but all that is the kind of thing we are used to from events these days and the dreadful politics. It's the Bolshevik routine.

It was so warm and beautiful after dinner that Godmother and I walked along Broadway, which was very animated and brightly lighted.

I thought I was going to be able to write something very long and serious, but alas! Thorvald and Joaquinito are already back.

Today I learned that even philosophers take pleasure in a new outfit when they have a nice Maman to spoil them.

P.S. Thorvald can't understand why Maman won't approve of a purchase that he made all by himself of two pairs of stockings at 2 dollars each, whereas the price of my silk stockings at 2 dollars a pair has always struck her as perfectly normal. I suppose that's one of the differences between the sexes, the weaker one (according to ancient laws, not modern ones) having its privileges.

October 11. This morning I tried on the 4 dresses in front of Maman, trying to make her believe that the least expensive was to my taste, but Maman has much better taste than I and she told me I would wear the black velvet dress at 55 dollars or nothing.

It certainly is a lovely dress—when I had it on, I felt like a Princess. Simplicity, in fact, is its greatest quality—and also it is long and narrow and makes me look like a young lady. I wore it to go to the theatre with Cuca and when I came home, I could hardly make up my mind to take it off.

At the theatre we saw "Roly Poly Eyes" and I am not even sure of the name because I was feeling serious today and it all seemed idiotic and frivolous. Cuca is so changed that our conversation was limited to the play and to clothes. Never was there so little resemblance between two people who became friends because of their similar tastes. And I don't know at all what it is that separates us, besides the diversity of our interests. It is as though the secrets we shared at Lake Placid never existed, and her behavior forces me to contain my enthusiasm. I am afraid I was mistaken about Cuca, as I so often am. Oh, but this time it's a pity!

Maman and I talked about my French and I explained to her that I would like not to continue studying with Madame Beaulac, for although she knows all the verbs in the grammar to perfection, she is sadly ignorant on certain indispensable subjects and I can't work well with a teacher who I know is inferior to me and whose opinions I can't admire and respect. Maman dictated the fable of the Grasshopper and the Ant to me and I wrote it with only 4 mistakes. I looked up 12 words in the dictionary and wrote my verbs. I have made a resolution to study like that every day.

I take great delight in the dictionary. It's truly a book full of keys which open the doors to stories, dreams, and history—a book woven with the threads of imagination. It's strange that until now, no one I know has advised me to read the dictionary as a masterpiece.

October 12. Last night before going to bed, I stayed a long time in front of the pantry window to watch what was happening in one of the houses across the street. All the curtains were raised, and I saw the apartment lighted and full of elegantly dressed people. It was the music that first attracted me, a piano and a violin attacking the same wedding march that Emilia played so often. While they played, the guests walked around the living room, and it was then that I realized it was a wedding. They danced all the rest of the evening and the music was so beautiful that right there, in my nightgown and my blue slippers, with my hair hanging down and the brush in my hand (for I had been brushing my hair), I started to dance. Much later I fell asleep to the sound of faraway dance music, dreaming of the wedding.

This morning it was as cold as in winter. I wore my coat and went to ten o'clock Mass with Maman and Godmother. To my great joy, Godmother has become the person she used to be in the old days, the Godmother I love with all my heart, who was like a second mother to us, so sweet and so generous in spite of her bad luck in financial matters.

Uncle Gilbert and Coquito came to dinner. Godmother dined with us also. The table looked very nice and I was already feeling proud of my success, when catastrophe struck. I was serving hot chocolate, which I had made with great care and pride, when suddenly Joaquinito tasted it and uttered an exclamation of disgust. Then Godmother tried it too and made a face. I had put in salt instead of sugar! There was general laughter that lasted a long time. I was very sorry about my ruined chocolate, but the humor of it outweighed the regrets.

After dinner, everyone settled down in the living room to talk. Then without making any noise, I shut the door so that Maman wouldn't know what I was going to do and I washed the dishes. A long time later, everything was done and I went into the living room. At that instant, they were talking about me. My uncle, wearing his uniform with many decorations, said in his calm voice, looking at me with his sea-blue eyes: "Anaïs is definitely the Parisian type. She has a very 'spiritual' face."

"Anaïs seems to like compliments," Godmother added with a laugh.

"She isn't the only one," Maman replied, "but she will soon get used to them because she receives so many!"

Then I asked everyone to change the subject and talk about something more interesting. They did, and I then slipped away to write while they were talking "business."

Joaquin worries me terribly of late. Sometimes his devilish naughtiness reminds me of stories I have read in which the Devil takes on human form to shock the family and everyone else. Perhaps Joaquinito's mission is to make even angels lose their patience.

Today I learned to taste the salt and sugar before using them.

October 14. Outside, Nature is glum and is expressing it with continual showers, so my thoughts were like the weather and I kept busy straightening up my closet and throwing away all the little souvenirs of the old days which take up so much room, but which aren't really very useful. It was a very delicate operation, and finally I didn't throw out anything at all. One of the letters I reread was from Papa, and by coincidence it reminded me of the

13th of October 7 years ago, which was the first day of my long sickness with appendicitis.

Apropos of Papa, Emilia Quintero wrote me a long letter, because she saw him. She sent two little pictures of his house and of the street. The house looks very pretty and the neighborhood very French. Emilia says that Papa is elegant and handsome. It seems that all my gestures are like him, the way I walk, talk, my profile, etc., etc. Emilia writes profusely, in a way that completely satisfies all of one's wishes, a charming and very characteristic way. I had written to Papa just a few days earlier and now I am going to write again, in spite of the sorrow that I feel because of his silence.

I am going to do my French lessons and read a book that Mrs. Clarke[1] lent me: Colette Baudoche by M. Barrès of the French Academy. Eureka! That means, I have found, and I add: I have found a good book!

October 16. Yesterday morning Maman sent me to the Hotel Astor to see Mrs. Casteleiro. That means that I started to work, because Mrs. Casteleiro is making purchases. She left me about one o'clock, when I went to see Cuca for a few minutes, and afterward I had a little lunch in a modest restaurant. I was amazed to be there alone, obliged to decide everything for myself. Amazed and pleased, for responsibility is a sign of age.

The rest of the afternoon I shopped for the things that a Mrs. Núñez had ordered, and once I got home, I found that the total of my purchases was $103.20, which means that I earned $10.32 in one day. Maman was very pleased and so was I, although I was excessively tired because I am not very energetic, as you know.

Today I stayed home until 2. Then I went to see Frances and we spent the afternoon together. She told me some of her new stories, which I thought were very good, and I dared to read her the Essay on the "Autumn Evening," which I have subtitled "Visions in the Flames."

Fortunately Frances is delightfully frank and I understood immediately that she didn't like it very much. Also it was something profound and she says there is something in it that "strikes her sense of humor." When I read: I saw the faces of people I love and those that I ought to love, she exclaimed: "Yes, that you ought to love, but you can't, specially relatives!" And I wondered if she had had the same experience as I with aunts and cousins, etc. etc.

[1] *Adele Van Name Clarke.*

Frances says that I wasn't born with the gift of writing little stories of the kind that she writes and that sell so well these days. She says the kind of literature that I write is the kind that doesn't sell, doesn't amuse or entertain 3/4 of the people, but is instructive and does good morally to the other 1/4 that reads philosophy and "dry" literature, in the style of Washington Irving and Emerson. So ahead of me, when I examine the horizon, I see the pleasant prospect of making money in business and publishing my books when I am rich . . . and old.

October 19. A pessimist would say at the end of this beautiful Autumn day, "We bought an old house." But I say: "We bought a palace in Fairyland."

I knew that a lot of good things would happen in this diary because it seems as though, after having deprived us of many good things, the good Lord suddenly wants to spoil us.

Let's ignore Friday to Sunday, which are unimportant just now, and talk about today. Maman left yesterday for Kew without a word, but with the fire that I always see in her eye when she is going to do something grand. She came home in the evening, mysterious and flustered with happiness. She talked to us about the house she looked at in Kew and almost took our appetites away telling us about it. That dinner was too funny for me to forget.

Since I am the oldest, Maman asked me first to name the things that I like in Kew and in a house. First: Close neighbors. Maman looked delighted. . . . Second: A big, big house. Maman smiled and assured me that I would be pleased. The things that Thorvald and Joaquinito mentioned were too numerous and too silly to waste time writing them down.

We decided to go and see it today. I almost couldn't sleep and Maman couldn't sleep at all. Finally morning came. After Mass and breakfast, Aunt Antolina came in her automobile to pick us up and we were on our way to Kew Gardens. After about forty minutes, having passed Ti Coco's familiar house, the station and the Club and driven along a beautiful street lined with big trees, we stopped in front of the House.

It is surrounded by a big garden covered with dry leaves and by big trees. I will tell you about the house itself later on. Before leaving, Maman wrote the owner a check, the beginning of payment of $14,000, which is the price of the house—our house.

We came back in a state of merriment. Except for me. I was

ecstatic, and during the drive back I smiled at the countryside, at the trees, the sky, the passersby, reflecting on the goodness of God, and when I thought about myself, I wondered what I had done to deserve so many joys.

October 20. I went out this morning with Leocadia Menocal,[1] and as she made $128.10 worth of purchases, I earned $12.81. But I have a headache because Maman and I spent a sleepless night on account of the house. Maman seems happy to see me enjoy working at something practical, and since it's the best way to resolve the problem of my future, I have already sacrificed my literary ambitions to business, in the American way.

October 21. In my little notebook, on which I have written "assistant secretary to Mrs. Nin" underneath my name and address, I entered the sum of $7.51 today. This time I went with Cuca, who had called me about 8 in the morning so that I wouldn't get away from her.

There are times when I regret that Maman bought the house in Kew, because she is so worried. And then the house of our dreams couldn't be as beautiful as we imagine it, because everything is fine as long as the dream is far away, but it seems as though as soon as Time brings it closer and one has to acquire it with money, it's the money that becomes a dream. How can my furniture be a pleasure for me if I think that Maman is anxious about the price?

My ermine just came. I will always be a child, I suppose, in my childish pleasure, effusively expressed, when a dream comes true.

Maman has gone to bed. She asked us not to talk to her, because her head is too full of worries.[2] So if yesterday I was glad to be alive, today I feel different. I only wish that all the bad things could happen to me, if in that way Maman could be happy.

I am remembering, with a tiny little bit of sadness, the lunch at the Waldorf Hotel given by Uncle Bernabé.[3] I say sadness because I was upset about my manners and it was really just my lack of self-confidence, because Maman has often told me that good manners are in my blood and also that I have the manners of

---

[1] *A relative of the Cuban president, Menocal.*
[2] *During the economic recession following World War I Mrs. Nin's Cuban clients began to delay their payments for purchases she had made.*
[3] *Bernabé Sánchez.*

a princess, but that day it seemed to me I did everything wrong. I would like to have more pride, after all, because I see many people who lack certain qualities but who say that they have them and everyone believes them.

Bernabecito came this morning, as he took Maman at her word when she asked him to come and help her. And he worked. Now that I think of it, I believe that of all my cousins I like Eduardo and Bernabé best. Charles is also very nice.

Oh, what a life! Godmother came in to talk to Maman for a moment and as Maman was telling her about her last discussion with Aunt Antolina, who is so unjust and willful, Maman "broke down" and started to cry. And Maman cries so seldom! The three of us were around her bed, distressed, with tears in our eyes, and it was a relief to see that the crying did her good. Yes, the storm is over. Maman is calm, very quiet; but that scene had a very sad effect on us.

I no longer feel like studying my French, I hate my ermine— Oh! I must go to bed to be able to think and think about the things that happen. How often our hearts go off course, in the midst of so many tempests. Will we ever reach the end of this long Voyage?

October 22. As I was sick all day, I stayed home and took advantage of that to type Maman's accounts on the machine. Bernabecito helped Isabel and me until twelve-thirty.

Maman was very pleased with the work we had done when she came home. She just told me that tomorrow we would go together to look at furniture.

I was much amused by the articles bought by our Cuban clientele and I can assure you that the items sent to Cuban women consist chiefly of:

> 24 boxes of rouge
> 36 boxes of powder
> 12 jars of cream
> 6 negligées
> 12 brassieres
> 12 corsets
> 12 blouses
> and 3 pearl necklaces

P.S. Mr. Mendirichega came to see Maman because he is going to take a little room under the eaves at 172 W. 86th, and among other things, he announced the arrival of Mr. Madriguera in 10 days—he is coming on the steamboat "La France." To tease me, Maman said she is glad he is coming because he owes her money. Anyhow, we will be in Kew Gardens[1] by then.

Frances just called to say that we can't go to Dancing School on Thursday and I am delighted. That means that I am in my natural state. All is well!

October 29. A mountain of pillows on a big bed which is also covered by an immense comforter, books and writing paper everywhere, a mirror. Under the bed on the left, a pair of slippers; at the foot of the bed, a dressing gown; on the right a chair holding cotton, a medicine bottle and a glass of water.

Have you guessed? Yes, I am sick. Sick? Oh! I have been in pain since the last time I wrote in your pages. I had an abscess on the lip, a strange infection. Every day I saw Dr. Murray arrive with his little bag full of instruments, and every day I cried in Maman's arms, completely spent, because of the operations. Finally, after the abscess went from the upper lip to the lower lip, after sleepless nights that were like torture, the pain stopped and I am on the road to recovery.

I was spoiled, although I don't deserve it. Every day someone came to see me and brought me candy, to Thorvald and Joaquinito's great delight. Today I am convalescing amidst loving care and smiles, with the bedroom full of sunshine, while the men move all our things to Kew.

I am still very weak, too weak to write all that I would like to. I am going to ask Thorvald to copy my letter to Papa in here because it made Maman laugh a lot.

Dearest little Papa:
Don't be surprised at the pencil nor at the ugly appearance of this letter, because I am still in bed, recovering from an illness that lasted a week, but which promises to end with a pleasant convalescence. I had a great deal of pain, but since the Doctor (a big, nice Irish-American, who always came with his little black bag and a kindly smile) comes every morning and tells me that I am getting better, I am as happy as a lark. So this letter won't show any signs of being written in unusual circumstances, except for the pencil.

Last night I received your letter of October 15, and with so much pleasure! I really thought at the time that joy would cure me, but I now begin to think that such things only happen in

1 *Actually, the house was in Richmond Hill.*

books. In real life it's the Big Doctor and the little doctor . . . and Patience.

Mrs. Quintero wrote me a few days before you did, giving a very detailed description of you and of events that made me very proud, happy and grateful. She sent me two little snapshots, no doubt taken with the same little camera that used to photograph us so often. One was of your house in Paris, which I think is very nice, and the other of the street, showing trees, a horse's head, and a little boy's leg. It was very Parisian, but I like the house better. . . .

It's very funny that you have a Corona typewriter, because that nice little machine is fabulously well known here, where a typewriter is indispensable to modern authors. They no longer use the old-fashioned pen, and the Corona suits their pocketbook. The latter, at least, is unchanged and as modest as ever.

No doubt you have noticed that no one ever gets sick at the right time, but always when good health is most needed. It's my experience that justifies that remark. A few days before I fell sick, Maman bought a house in Kew Gardens, outside New York. She was inspired by our lack of comfort, by the detestable life one leads in a big city, and by her wish to see our dearest dream become a reality. In telling you about Aunt Edelmira, I must have described the beautiful countryside around Kew, which shares both the riches of Nature and the charm of many houses surrounded by gardens. I will give you enthusiastic praises and a detailed description of our house when we have moved in. It seems to us the most beautiful house of all. That dream is one of the rare ones that has crystallized without being destroyed: Our House!

Each of us will have his own room (mine will have white furniture and all the rest will be light blue), and with pride in the things that belong to us, we will be able to turn the house into a happy nest for the family. Uncle Thorvald and Aunt Lolita are going to live with us. I explained about my illness because the family is waiting for me to get better in order to move. And perhaps I am more impatient than the whole family put together, because I have a bad habit of going into everything with the enthusiasm typical of a lunatic or a poet (which is the same thing). The address I will send you later will show that our property is in Richmond Hill; it is located just beyond the line separating Kew Gardens from Richmond. In the meantime, I am a thousand times more spoiled than I deserve to be, which always happens to me, anyhow.

A "chimère,"[1] it seems to me, is something far away and difficult to reach. That's how it is with my French. But I have too much will power, too much enthusiasm to give up my dream, so I pursue it. They have "Illustration" and the "Revue des Deux Mondes" at the public library, and I am always the first to take them when they appear. They are a little old, but in any case more advanced than I am. I have also been delighted with a book by Maurice Barrès of the Académie Française, of which I hope to be a member some day. (Shh! Don't laugh too hard because I might hear you.) I have made a long list of words to use in the future, but up to now I haven't had any use for words like "chiper,"[2] for instance. I wanted terribly to keep M. Barrès's book, but I don't admire him enough to risk going to prison on his account, and anyhow they wouldn't let me have the book once I was in prison nor even after I got out, so some day I will write a better book than "Colette Baudoche." (That time I heard you laughing.)

I forgot to say that I am going to buy a copy. That will be easier.

I am very grateful to you for comparing my letters to sunshine and happiness, which are such good things. I must have inherited your courage, because during my illness, I answered everyone who asked me how I was with "All right." And the worse I felt, the more it hurt, the more stubbornly I answered: "All right." Fortunately, the doctor didn't ask, he operated.

They tell me that I am brave, but it's only to please me.

Your paragraph about the kind of love people feel for you is sublime. The line or procession of those who love you must be a long one! I can see it, and I hope you will let me put myself at the head of the whole line. Also I thank heaven for filling your life with Art, to take the place of the other great happiness that you are missing. Send me your books so that I can share in your successes, your failures, your happiness and your solitude.

A thousand kisses from your

Linotte

November 4. 620 Audley Street & Curzon Place, Richmond Hill.

Oh, dearest diary, what changes, what events have occurred! Since last I wrote in here, so many things have changed, I don't know what to tell you first.

From Wednesday to Saturday, I did my best to get well

[1] *Chimera, vision.*
[2] *French slang for "to steal."*

quickly. I noticed in the mirror the continual progress that each hour made in my lips and when Friday came I felt well enough to get up, but was too weak to walk. But Saturday morning I was seized by the wonderful energy that comes when I need it. That, together with my enthusiasm, gave me the necessary strength to do everything.

At 10 Aunt Antolina's car came and the funniest moment of the day occurred. We filled the car with boxes of every size, pots and pans picked up at the last minute, suitcases and little packages, besides Maman, Joaquinito and me. At the last minute Monsita was crying so hard that to console her, Maman told her to come along in the car and spend the day with us. Once we were in, each one held something on his lap so as to take care of it. I had my little bird, and all along the way the water from his cage dripped slowly onto my dress and underclothes, ran down my stockings and finished its strange trip inside my shoes.

The trip was relatively silent. We couldn't help thinking about our new life, and the only conversation consisted of exclamations each time we thought of things we had forgotten at the house.

It was a beautiful day at the start, and when the automobile stopped in front of *our house*, it seemed more beautiful than ever. Monsita, Joaquinito, the packages and I all went into the house, while Maman went on in the car to go and buy provisions. Just then a man came to fix the electricity. Everything was fine.

In the evening we lost a little of our enthusiasm when we discovered that the man hadn't fixed the lights after all and it was raining torrents outside, which meant that it was dark at 5. We ate our dinner very silently by the light of a few candles that threw our shadows on the walls and added a fantastic fear of witches to the mystery of a big, silent, unfamiliar house. At 6 we were all in bed, without light, listening to the dripping rain, and unable to sleep because of thinking, thinking, thinking.

The next day we were awake very early. We fixed our breakfast over little alcohol lamps, since we had no gas. Sunday was spent arranging the house, which little by little assumed a pleasant aspect. In the afternoon Uncle Thorvald and Aunt Lolita came to get their things, because a few days before, they had come here, thinking to live with us, but they were immediately discouraged by the lack of light and heat, the cold, no maid, and once they got back to New York they decided to stay there. Fortunately after so many years of traveling, privations, and the habit of not

letting anything discourage us, we can live anywhere and anyhow, without losing heart immediately, or ever.

That night we went to bed again at 6. Maman had a bad
headache and seemed so worried, so discouraged—she who is
always so brave—that I fell asleep with tears in my eyes.

Very early Monday morning, Maman left for work and
Thorvald for school. Joaquinito had a bad cold and was supposed to
stay with me anyhow. Monsita had promised to come during the
morning and take care of us.

I felt much stronger and took advantage of that to put many,
many things away. I had the joy of seeing my furniture delivered.
(I will tell you about it later.) At the same time, the brooms,
which we were awaiting impatiently, came—so I was able to
sweep the whole house. When Monsita arrived, she hurried to
make lunch, then ran down to the little town, which is very close
to here, to arrange about the light and gas.

The man came back during the afternoon and afterward we
happily tried all the lights, which worked perfectly. No more
candles, no more dark, no more sadness!

Toward 5 it was already dark. That was when Maman arrived and found a happy family and had the heart to listen to our
chatter while a thousand worries wrinkled her brow, while her sad
thoughts put circles under her eyes and gave her smile an infinite
sadness that breaks my heart. While Monsita lighted the big coal
stove and prepared a lovely dinner, setting the table in the dining
room, I took care of Maman's headache and let her talk to me as I
used to do at Edgemere, listening with a sarcastic smile (because
the reality continues to shatter my illusions) to the results of
Godmother's sour disposition, the struggle with the house on 86th
Street, without servants, the struggle with 75th Street, also without
servants, the worry of the many things she has to buy.

Finally her spirits recovered and she came downstairs to try
to have dinner. It was a strange dinner. Thorvald and Joaquinito
didn't understand Maman's problems, and Monsita and I treated
the conversation like an elastic band, pulling it here and there to
try to amuse Maman, who smiled at everything and everyone in a
sad, vague way. So even though we had electricity, we all went to
bed about 7 so as not to disturb Maman with our noise.

Our yard is very pretty. Just now it is covered with leaves
and acorns. All around the house are traces of flowers and climbing plants. Perhaps they will grow during the winter and flower in
spring. We are surrounded by trees; every window frames a scene

prettier than any painting. The houses are built on hills, so ours is quite high and from the second floor windows we have a very good view of the countryside. Behind the house is a large garden which ends with one of those lovely roads built entirely by Nature, so that it doesn't have the symmetry and straight lines of human workmanship. The left side of the house faces the garden and a large lot which is for sale. Dearest Maman has set her hopes on that and the two of us have a vision of adding that beautiful lot to Our House.

November 5. We were up at 7 this morning, swallowing our breakfast in haste, walking hurriedly toward the station to catch the 8:13 train which took us to New York. Thorvald had left long before. Arriving at 158, I noticed the strange silence of the house, its sad and deserted appearance, although it was full of strangers. I helped Maman the best I could and when everything was finished, she asked me to go to the cinema with Joaquinito.

We were going to leave the house to catch the 5:37 train when an accident happened which left us with the sad impression that our presence is necessary to the preservation of our poor house. The hot water heater almost burst because the gas was left on all day, without anyone thinking to turn it off. I saw that the accident worried Maman terribly. No doubt she was thinking of the unpleasant result if the accident happened again—a house that might blow up for lack of care!

We talked about it a long time, going over the situation in our heads and how to take care of it, and the only answer seems to be our return to New York until Maman can find servants. Maman ran an advertisement and we will see first what results it brings. I realize that I am writing facts without using any imagination or sense of humor, but it is through that lens that I see everything today, to the point where I worry about coal because it is cold and about the windows because the wind is blowing. In my normal state I would have put all my enthusiasm into describing my feelings for you, telling you about the falling leaves . . . but today I don't have the heart to joke. All around me I see only serious things, critical situations, people who suffer because of their sour disposition, and others, like Maman, who suffer unjustly because of other people's selfishness. I can really say that the worst torture in the world for me is to see Maman unhappy, for her happiness is mine and her sufferings break my heart.

The wind is blowing hard outside; I have the feeling we are surrounded by moral and physical tempests. When will the sun shine as before? Cold and wind! The cold penetrates my soul, the wind shakes me. . . . I don't feel like thinking and reflecting any more about the things that happen—I don't understand them.

Courage! Courage! Yes, it's true that there is a storm outside, but we are under cover. Aren't we fortunate? From here I can hear Maman and Joaquinito talking while they get ready for bed. Thorvald is sitting across from me, doing his lessons on the dining-room table. And I lose heart at the time when I should be so happy!

Even if tomorrow we have to return to the city, this evening we are in our home, the family is together, as happy as poor human beings can be. . . . That's why it does me good to write. I see more clearly and straighten out my ideas, and in that way I always discover the chief rule that guides my thinking: the philosophy that I have inherited from Maman.

November 6. We are real soldiers of fortune. The house at Richmond Hill is dark and silent right now, while we are installed once more for a few days at 158 W. 75. Heaven knows!

About eleven o'clock this morning I was sweeping my room when Monsita arrived with orders from Maman to pack our suitcases. We waited for Thorvald to come home, then after a long walk in the delightful cold (which turned our cheeks unbelievably rosy), we caught the 5:03 train. It was the best way of solving our domestic problem.

We had dinner (oh, such a peppery, detestable dinner in a restaurant) and as we are always at home almost everywhere, each one calmly resumed his daily occupations: Thorvald is studying, Maman is thinking in her big bed, Joaquinito is torturing the family, and I, oh, you know what I am doing. I was terribly sorry to leave Richmond Hill, even for a few days. I love the quiet house, the peaceful view, the life we lead there.

Here, while I wrote those few lines, I had to stop 6 or 7 times to open the door and answer the telephone. But, without wanting to, we love this house, having lived here so long. That's why Maman refuses to sell it, to keep a base of operations for her business.

One of the things I did this evening was to answer the advertisements of people looking for work as servants.

I don't know why, when I started this diary, I thought it would be the most entertaining one of all, and up until now my opinion has been justified by the variety of things I have written each day. Maman's ambitions are beginning to be fulfilled; soon we will have an automobile, and I will be like Cuca. I wonder if my diary will be more interesting than when our fortunes and happiness were suspended from the cloud of Illusions.

November 7. The day went by so quietly, although not without work, that I want to make room here for a conversation Maman and I had. It took place when I was sick and to please me, Maman was lying down near me.

I had just received a wordy letter from Papa, full of innuendos, which he uses so often in speaking of the past. That past has troubled me painfully for a long time and I wanted to know the truth, although I knew in the depths of my heart that the truth would be still more painful than my uncertainty. This time Papa said that there were many things he *wanted* to tell us and *ought* to tell us. . . .

Maman was calm, so I took my courage in both hands and began very slowly, as the questions I had always wanted to ask came to mind.

"Maman, why does Papa say that there are things he ought to tell us but can't?"

I was astonished by the strange bitterness with which Maman talked to me the rest of the time. She answered briskly:

"Doubtless he would like to tell you bad things about your mother."

"And do you imagine that I would believe him?"

"Oh, daughter, you don't know your father's skill at writing. He can make anyone believe whatever he wants, even lies."

There was a silence.

"Can Papa ever ask us to live with him?"

"Oh no, he has lost all his rights over you. He can ask nothing of you, absolutely nothing, since he deserted you."

"He deserted us? Oh, but I thought it was you who took us away from Arcachon. Tell me how it happened, will you?"

"It wasn't anything. Your father never loved his home, he was always with his friends and with strangers. Also he made our life very unhappy because he was very brutal. He would lock me up in one room so as to be able to beat you, and he only came home to scold and criticize. So one day at Arcachon he wrote a letter and he left. I returned to Brussels and sold our furniture to get a little money, then I left the house and came back for you to take you all to Spain. You must remember many scenes of brutality, don't you?"

I nodded my head weakly to say yes.

"Maman," I said, "Could you ever forgive Papa?"

Then Maman mocked me and said sarcastically:

"Fifille, do you really think that one day Papa might come back and that we could be happy and all that? Those are romantic illusions, my daughter, which are good for nothing in life."

"But Maman," I said, trying to defend my poor illusions, "at my age, you would have believed the same thing. Fortunately, until now I have been a little girl, but now, alas, I have changed! I will use your 40 years of experience as my own!"

"Yes, you see, that's how one learns. But you shouldn't think that all men are like your father. He will never come here, he will die alone because of his selfishness—and one day I will be gone too, so you will be left to do the same foolish things that I did."

"That's true," I said thoughtfully. "I'm sure that if right now a man like Papa came along and asked me to marry him, I would forget his faults and I would do it, so the same story would begin over. But whatever Papa may say, I have understood the truth. Besides, isn't my faith in you stronger than the whole world?"

Maman hugged me, but when she asked me not to talk about

it any more, her voice was still very changed. And I had suffered enough, I had seen my poor little Papa as he is, I had seen a sarcasm and bitterness in Maman that I had never seen before and there must have been a reason for them; I understood Thorvald's and Joaquinito's personalities. My childish illusions, the cherished dream of a reunion, the vision of a father in our home, the mysterious charm with which my imagination had surrounded the name "Papa"—all that was in ruins, all that was dead. My romantic dream had become one of those real and terribly sad dramas such as we see all around us.

Oh, can you understand why I cried for long hours in the silent night, my hands joined in prayer to God not to shatter everything in my heart at once! During the night I had a terrible fever and horrible nightmares—only cocaine could calm me and soothe what Maman thought was physical pain. For Maman didn't know what store I set by my illusions. Perhaps that's the only thing that she can't understand.

I wanted to write this, although it was difficult, because one day perhaps that sad event which deprived me of a father, whose talent is the only thing I can cherish, will influence my ideas and some of my acts. Maman says that I know a great deal for my age. Yes, I understand only too well. Perhaps that's why I don't cry any more.

Poor Papa! Poor Maman!

During the move I found some boxes full of old letters and when I asked Maman where I should put them, she replied: "Put them in my room and one day I'll burn them all." It seemed as though they were letters full of promises that Papa had broken! I carried the boxes reverently, in fear and melancholy. I wish that Maman wouldn't burn them!

Oh! let's not talk any more about the past. Only the future counts, and yet the Future is born of the Past. Will the future inherit all of the miseries of the past? No, the laws of inheritance are too unjust to be the law that rules our Happiness.

It is half past ten. I am leaving to go and dream a little, in spite of knowing that tomorrow will bring the shock of waking, the anguish of reality.

Courage! Courage!

November 8. Today I went with Charles to the Standard to see "Molière." It was superb! Very profound, happy and sad all at the same time. Godmother saw it earlier and had told us that we were going to cry at the death of the great man; so, as Charles makes fun of what he calls "sentimentality," I was very careful not to cry. In spite of that, a furtive tear escaped, and Charles was amused.

Time goes very fast when Charles and I are together. I don't know why we always find so many things to talk about. He has spoken to me so often of Lord [Bulwer-]Lytton's books that I am soon going to try to read them in order to be "up to date"! On my side I urged him to read Dumas' "Ascanio." To complete an American afternoon, we ate a "sundae." and that was it!

I wanted to stay with Maman, who was not feeling well, but she ordered me to leave on the pretext that she was glad to get rid of me. That's the best way to make me go. This morning Maman's parlor looked like a doctor's consultation room. All the armchairs were occupied by servants, because of the advertisements that Maman ran. I was the page and secretary, very much amused by all the different kinds of women and Maman's choice. We have one woman, Mrs. Thuma, for 86th Street, Mrs. Holt for 158 W. 75, and a very young woman with a little girl 3 years old for Richmond Hill.

Godmother is also sick. I went upstairs many times with tea and soups, hot water bottles, etc. etc. I would like Godmother to realize that my attitude toward her will never change, in spite of what everyone says about her and in spite of her poor sour disposition, which I attribute to her state of being an old maid. I like her very much just the way she is.

Today I was very worried by an article I read on the usefulness in the world of people who make others laugh. Mr. Frank Crane, the author, expressed his belief that everyone should do his best to be merry. He said, what would we do with a world full of Ibsens and without Charlie Chaplin?

There was food for a whole stack of thoughts in his lines, which led me to the idea I already have that everyone around me would be happier if I were merry, because melancholy is selfish and absorbs our entire interest, although it can come from indifference, bitterness . . . and a liver attack.

Let's be happy! And when we are sad, let's write in our diaries instead of tiring everyone with a recital of our imaginary miseries.

November 9. The newspapers are dedicating many pages to an absorbing scientific discussion. A professor has expressed his belief

mon nouveau
chapeau

mon peignoir

Madame Montespan

garde-malade (Une servante qui
veut plus d'argent (La servante qui
qu'un banquier) veut prendre
deux bains par
jour et ne pas
faire du travail
"fatiguant" $60 par
mois.) (Moderne)

paquerettes
et Thorvald

Dimanche 9 Novembre 1919
A 10 heure Thorvald, paquerettes

that from December 17 to December 20, we are going to have
volcanic eruptions, floods, tempests, deadly wind and cold, because
of a disturbance between the planets and the sun, a deviation in
their normal path. To reassure us, the scientists in the government
have announced that none of these accidents will happen and that
the unusual movements of the planets will take place without
causing things "worse than the end of the world." We have talked
a lot about this, about the end of the world and the human race,
and I have discovered that in many things Thorvald has very little
discernment, so that after a few minutes he gives up the discussion
and leaves Maman and me to talk a long while about the interesting subject. I have often noticed that Thorvald doesn't want to
know other people's opinions, and Maman and I are the only ones
who enjoy talking. Maybe that's because we are only women!

We are still eating in the restaurant, with pepper and all. We will be very glad to eat at home—perhaps tomorrow, if Maman is better.

November 10. Maman was only a little better today, so when Mrs. J. Menocal telephoned her to do some buying, it was I who went. I spent the morning downtown and earned $4.73.

At present I am sporting my new dressing gown and writing for my own pleasure, but not very quickly, because "business" seems to kill my usual torrent of foolishness. In the stores one doesn't have time to observe and entertain oneself. During the trips in the elevated train I am enormously amused, not only because people push me, but because they push grumpy people. The trip is spent hanging on to a leather strap and standing on the poor neighbors' feet. One can look out the window at the houses and shops. Today during the stop at one station, I had time to read an advertisement that made me smile because it was very comforting:

"Undertaking with pomp and elegance for 75 dollars. Comfortable cars."

I say it was comforting because these days life is so expensive that burial is relatively cheap, considering the comfort and elegance!!

Another advertisement offered false teeth for 2 dollars a dozen!

If everyone read the advertisements that go by, they wouldn't all have long "desperado" faces during the trip, even if they are obliged, being only women, to hang on to the straps in order to leave the seats to the men. The strap would be very comfortable if the train were always at a stop, but otherwise—

Enough foolishness!

Maman and I have discussed our point of view about life. Maman is very contented, happy to be able to earn her own living, to be independent, to have children; she is glad to see that her business is going well, and past privations lend added charm to the comfort of the present. She is glad about her energy, her good disposition, her philosophy—about everything. She finds difficulties interesting and believes that every problem has a solution. It's a wonderful point of view, a pink room in the middle of the ruins, a star in the desert—and food for thought for me. . . .

I notice that I am writing a great deal every evening. I suppose that as I grow older, I will discover new developments in my ideas, more observations, more nonsense, because as someone said: "What an old fool Age really is!"

Perhaps instead of being interesting, this diary is getting boring, but it doesn't matter since I am my own severest critic!

November 11. A year ago we were celebrating the Armistice! I remember that day as though it were yesterday—a wonderful day!

Patriotisme

Today I performed my role as Maman's secretary very well. I wrote letters and checks, receipts and bills, on the machine, and when the machine became ill (I suspect it of neurasthenia and of trying to live with just the memory of its former splendor), I "took my pen in hand." In adding the sums of money in the bills, I followed the American motto, "Slow but sure."

Maman is in bed, still worrying about the house because the maid she hired for 158 appeared only to give us a sample of her bad disposition and then immediately disappeared. So we are staying here with the other young servant, Alfareta, and her little girl, Anita, until further notice.

Godmother is well again.

I had a serious talk with myself and scolded myself until I cried. I sat myself down in front of the window to think and make resolutions . . . all this because of my pessimistic leanings at a time when the opposite is needed. I have had an opportunity to remark this bad fault in myself of late, but I am going to cure myself of it—I am cured.

November 14. Oh, what a life! Pessimism? Optimism? Neither one. It's face to face with life, life that we have to accept the way it is, which sometimes is horrible. Today I had to bear the worst pain in the world: the torture of seeing Maman suffer.

It was just yesterday that we worked all day from 9 to 5, straightening out the accounts and sending letters. Then after dinner, feeling very peaceful and proud of our work, we went to the cinema. There we laughed for 2 1/2 hours, forgetting and enjoying. When we came out, it was very cold and we ran home, glad to share that happy moment. Before going to the cinema, we had stopped in front of a furniture store to admire the lamps and talk about our house! That evening gave us the illusion of living a happy life.

And today!

This morning Maman was sitting at her desk and I was reading the letters to her while she made comments and I took notes. At that moment Godmother arrived. Oh, no! I refuse to call her Godmother. From now on, she will only be Aunt Juana, just a legal relative.

Aunt Juana has the unhappy knack of saying almost everything in a cutting way. The conversation was about a fur coat, but apropos of nothing at all, Aunt Juana began saying that Maman treats her like a dog, after she has sacrificed for Maman all her life, giving her more than half of all she had, working outside all day for her, even when she was sick. . . . She even brought up one time when Maman heard someone come in the house, and thinking it was her poor old friend, who doesn't even have enough money to buy an umbrella (it was raining), Maman said: "Oh, it's you, Isabel. I'm so sorry you got wet!" But when Maman saw it was Godmother, she didn't bother to say a thing.

In a word, she has that dreadful way of throwing her kindness up to you and humiliating you with her demands for gratitude. Maman had been sick because of all her worries, sick from working and struggling, and those words were like a slap in the face. Her anger was perfectly justified, but I thought I would cry, watching her walk from one end of the parlor to the other like a caged lion, her face transformed by the sharp pain of the open wound. Then her nerves seemed to crack as she let go. Her last words were more like a cry, uttered with frightening sincerity: "I will give you back everything, everything that you gave me, penny for penny, and you will *never again* be able to throw in my face the things you have done for me."

Then she turned to me, as if the truth depended on my answer: "Oh yes! fifille, we will give it *all* back, won't we?"

I was brave enough to answer "yes" with all my heart. For a moment I had the terrible idea that Maman had lost her mind, she was so transformed by her anger and I read so much suffering in her eyes. I realized that it wasn't just that particular moment that made Maman suffer, but also the past. . . .

I ran to her and tried to calm her with caresses, but the only thing I was able to accomplish was to lead her toward her room. It was then that I did something that I suppose Aunt Juana will never forget. I saw that her presence was a torture for Maman and that the quarrel had to end if I didn't want Maman to go mad; so when Godmother wanted to follow her, I stopped her from coming into the room and I tried to shut the door. The look that I saw in her eyes was enough to make me understand: it was only then she realized that I wasn't on her side and also that she had suddenly lost all the gratitude that she might have hoped for from me. When I tried to shut the door, she said: "Then you don't remember all the things I have done for you?"

"Yes, but look what you've done to Maman."

Then Aunt Juana left, while Maman dropped into a chair, without a tear, as though she were dazed. She brushed aside our caresses and seemed not to notice our presence. Once again the terrible fear seized me, but suddenly Maman put her head down on my arms and wept. . . .

Joaquinito was frightened and cried too, while with my eyes also filled with bitter tears, I stroked Maman's burning brow. Finally she opened her eyes and with a sad smile she said: "Poor fifille!" Did she know that I was suffering almost as much as she?

I put her in an armchair, with a pillow, and until almost time for lunch I sat near her to caress her and calm her, while she wept and murmured that it was her fault, her lack of patience. But when I told Maman that she should have told Aunt Juana the truth a long time ago and that it was much better to have done so, she seemed to believe me and little by little began giving orders to Monsita and having me telephone about other matters.

At lunch I couldn't eat for seeing Maman so weak and looking so old.

Maman rested on the sofa all day while Isabel and I did the accounts. She was suffering from mental fatigue, her head was heavy, her hands shook, and she had all the signs of a "nervous breakdown."

Luckily Aunt Juana is leaving us completely alone. Today I thought more than ever, but not at all about my poor dreams and tender illusions. I thought that if ever we lost Maman before she had been able to repay everything, I wouldn't be able to live happily until I had repaid it *all*, to get away from those *false benefactors*, even if I had to beg. I would work to feed Joaquinito and Thorvald. But without Maman, we are really *alone in the world*, in spite of all our aunts!

Aunt Juana often tried to make me believe that Maman did too many things to do any of them well and that she was very "fuguillas" (short-tempered). Maman, Maman who is the noblest mother in the entire universe, the only perfect and sublime woman, who never is wrong, who having sacrificed everything and suffered so much for *us*, never told us about it. We will be that much more grateful to her, and if I could have spared her today's scene by giving my life, I would have done it with a smile, proud to be able to give it. But that isn't how things are done now.

Maman is in bed. I have been so zealous in caring for her that she just asked me to leave her alone, jokingly, for her spirits have risen, in spite of the traces on her face of the recent wound. Right now she is thinking of Mrs. de Sola, who just telephoned that she is freezing at the cottage. Maman is making plans to let her come here and pay her maid for taking care of the house, so that we can leave for Richmond Hill and Maman can have a day of rest that might heal her nerves and weakness and save her health, which is so precious to us!

Forgive me if I give in to pessimism and melancholy, but I am writing all this to comfort myself and to see if I feel ashamed to tell all that happened; but since I am proud, in spite of not being brave, I know that poor Aunt Juana is at fault. I have started a thousand times to write the name I used to have for her . . . used to have, but never will again. The Godmother that I loved is dead, and the Aunt to whom we owe *money* will stay with me until the day the debt is paid. Now I am beginning to know what life really is. What will I think at 40 of this life I am afraid of at 16!

But the world can't be full of people like my aunt, and we don't owe money to everyone! There is always Japan, where we could go and live one day, and Thorvald will soon be a man and able to help Maman. I will be able to work too, so someday we can send all the Cubans to the devil and be proud to be civilized, French or Catalan! What does it matter! But we won't go to Cuba to live and I refuse to be presented to society or to marry a Cuban millionaire, because the further we are from our family, the more peace and happiness Maman will have.

I have written enough foolishness for this evening, putting aside the fact that I am impulsive and get carried away. I let my indignation guide my pen. But if ever I regret having written this, I will no longer be a Nin, who has her pride, who adores her mother, who, at the bottom of her poet's heart, keeps her damaged illusions for mending the day that she gets to heaven.

November 16. Yesterday morning Maman seemed sicker than ever and I was in despair. It was Maman herself who knew how to save the situation.

"If I get out of this house, I will be better immediately," she admitted, and I hung onto her words as though my life depended on them. Mrs. de Sola came to talk to Maman while she ate a little lunch that I took her on a tray. Now everything is settled, as Mrs. de Sola will stay in Maman's room and her maid will help Alfareta to take care of the house until Monday.

An hour later, almost cured by the mere idea of leaving that house, Maman called a taxi and we departed with all our packages to rejoin Thorvald and Joaquinito, who had left in the morning. Dinner was calm and happy. We forgot to bring our old friend the alarm clock, so we ate when we were hungry, went to bed when we were sleepy, and today (Sunday) we got up when we woke up, had breakfast, and were right on time for ten-o'clock Mass.

It was an especially beautiful day, with the kind of cold that made us feel gay and vigorous. The return home was a long walk. Lunch consisted of a chicken that Maman roasted in the big oven because we had no gas, and many other good things. To sum up, I don't really know why, but the day was ideally peaceful. I felt immense happiness to see Maman's expression change, and she forgot her troubles enough to take pleasure in caring for her hair and her hands, while I revolved around her like a parrot, talking

to her about movies, the future, our house, Christmas, etc. etc.
Two or three times we talked about the infernal situation, but in a
house full of sunshine, one can almost forget the dark clouds.

November 17.
Dear Frances: [1]
If you only knew how sorry I am to have been away the one day
that the Postman came with your letter. He thought that we had
gone away definitely and kept your letter until now. Surely you
must have been as surprised at my silence as I was of yours, but
now, here is my answer, although it would be 20,000 times better
if we could have spoken about it.

*   *   *

Yes, it does pay to explore human nature, unless you want to
go blindfolded through Life and fall into a Precipice of astonishment at the end. If you explore you will find *tinsel* and *silver* in
great quantity, but it will make you love the *gold* for its true value
and scarcity.

But promise me, oh, promise me *not* to *believe what you are
told,* because this is a world of prejudices and envy; if you find out
for yourself you will know the *truth.* Of this I am sure, oh! so very
sure!

Do you fear to meet disillusionment? Yes, that is the fear of
the Dreamer. You and I have illusions, infinitely beautiful
dreams, unbounded confidence in the beauty of the World,
Faith—but here is where I have stumbled too. Can we keep all
these things through Life?

Why is there sadness in the eyes of aged people? Why is
there doubt in their words, lack of Faith in their advice? Why?
Why?

I sometimes think that *we expect too much of Life,* a great
deal *too much* and that is the reason of our shattered dreams, that
our natures are too weak to be worthy or capable of perfect happiness, that everything almost that causes loss of faith in *others* is
the lack of *faith* in *ourselves.* I think that if you yourself are not
up to your ideals, that others cannot be.

I have found out that I am *selfish* because I *find selfishness* in
others, while Mother is generous and believes that everyone else is
also.

It will be with anxiety that I will expect an answer. Tell me

[1] *Written in English.*

if I have understood, if I have not wandered from the subject (I know I did but I wanted to write all this to you long ago), if you understand what I mean— What you will say will mean a great deal to me because everything I have said comes from the very depths of my heart and these thoughts had never seen the light before. I had to gather vague dreams a-floating and tie them to Earth with a string of words.

Love,

Anaïs

November 21. I haven't been able to write for almost a week for various reasons, although the past days have been like fair weather after a terrible storm.

Maman and Thorvald leave very early every morning. Then Joaquinito, who goes to a Catholic school. Then I wash the breakfast dishes, I sweep, I make the beds, singing at the top of my lungs so as to forget that I am all alone. It's funny! And above all there is all the time I waste looking out the windows, dreaming. . . .

I worked at everything in the house, took pleasure in arranging the closets, etc. I used the light-blue silk to make a cord with a long pompon on the end and attached it to my light cord, which is very short, to make it easier for Joaquinito to reach and also to beautify my room.

Maman got home at 6 and could sit right down to dinner. The nicest hours of the day are in the evening. Thorvald and Joaquinito are busy with their lessons and Maman and I sit in my room. I brush her hair while she gets ready for bed, then I take care of her clothes and after she is in bed I read to her.

Tonight Maman said: "Guess who came to the house today."

I began to blush and I *knew* it was the violinist! But like the true woman that I am, I asked, "Who?"

Maman told me I am a hypocrite and said that Mr. de Sola had opened the door to Enric Madriguera, but that he (Mr. de Sola) is so dumb, he couldn't tell Enric when he could see Maman. I don't know why I am so excited, but I know I'm glad that the violinist is back, because I want to find out if he is angry at me for not answering his postcards.

While Maman was doing the dishes tonight, we talked about the habit that Thorvald and Joaquinito have of looking elsewhere for their pleasure, always outside the house. I asked her why I am not the one who does that, why I love the quiet evenings at home.

"It's because you're a woman, fifille. It takes very little to make a woman happy, and it's only very bad women who spend their lives away from their home."

Last night Thorvald helped us by taking off the tablecloth and this morning I found it thrown in a heap on a chair. Oh! Boys!

Maman is resting. There is no table in my room, so I am sitting on a cushion and using a chair for a desk. I wrote a letter to Frances before writing in my diary and I confess I am very much interested in this strange correspondence, because her letters are wonderful, and it's at Maman's suggestion that I copy my own in here.

Since I was at Lake Placid, I have changed a great deal in one respect. For example, today on the way to Richmond Hill, I stopped a moment to thrill at the view of the sun setting behind the trees in the forest. And my whole being felt only one emotion. I trembled with happiness, and I felt my heart calling Romance with all its strength. It was so strange, so unworthy of me, that for a moment I was shocked, but afterward I realized it's that way in Life, just as in books.

Oh how I am waiting for a Great Adventure, to be full of feeling for something, to *know* the wonderful Romance which seems to be everywhere, in all beautiful places underneath the vast reaches of clouds and of Dreams.

I wrote Frances that it seems to me our dreams are selfish, because we think only of ourselves, of our own happiness. And since I think too much of my family, I don't want to be selfish and dream—but I'm not dreaming, for Reality is as beautiful as a dream just now, reality which is renewed each moment, which prepares my future and my Great Adventure!

Without opening her eyes, Maman just asked me if I was going to write all night. She hears the scratching of my rusty pen and probably knows that I need to wipe the rust away.

I wrote Eleanor that my room is a mixture of white and light blue, which made me think of a little bit of sky. My electric light is a solitary star and I am a Poet who, as Frances says, "walks with my head in the clouds until the day that I stumble and fall, never to stand so tall again." A bit of sky, a star and a Poet—those three things could make a melodrama that only Mr. Nin could set to music, because Papa is a terrific composer!

Maman just opened an eye to see if I am not getting as sleepy as she is, but I am more wide-awake than ever, so she closes it in a discouraged fashion and pretends to be asleep. Thorvald and Joaquinito went to a Scout meeting and I wanted to wait for them; but never mind, Maman's sleep is more important than that of the King of France, in the days when it was worth a lot.

November 22. The thing I most want to tell you about is the few hours that I spent outside. Thorvald has always said that all of his friends' sisters are very jolly, whereas I never "play" with him. Today I was making the beds and when I opened the window to air the room, I became absorbed in watching Thorvald and Joaquinito playing ball, falling onto the piles of dry leaves, running hard, and making the air ring with their shouts and laughter. I started to think how young they are, how much fun they have, and that I would like to do the same. Suddenly the idea struck me that at 16, I am not yet old! So I made the beds in a few seconds and ran into my room to put on a sweater and a tam-o'-shanter. Before going out, I had time to notice that I was very pale. Once outside, I took part in all their crazy games, and I have never laughed so much or run so much. I played like a little girl! When I was tired of playing, I got on the swing and swung clear up to the branches of the big trees. I had to go in because I was hungry and all three of us had a snack of fruit and cookies.

When I went upstairs to take off my sweater, I was astonished at the transformation I saw in the mirror. Thorvald was extremely pleased as well!

I dread Sundays because of going to Mass in that subterranean church! Luckily Sunday comes but once a week.

November 24. Sunday morning Maman seemed so tired and Joaquinito so lazy that Thorvald and I went to Mass alone. And unfortunately, in spite of all the Good Lord's kindnesses to me of late, I found it impossible to pray, impossible to come upon a single thought that would make an impression on my heart of stone. That coldness is almost impossible to drive away.

I don't know why, but this morning I woke up with the idea that something extraordinary was going to happen today. I wasn't very far from the truth, because I came home with a maid—something that in these modern times is almost as strange as it is impossible. Her name is Annie; she is an elderly Irishwoman, clean, orderly and respectful. I am charmed to hear her call me "Miss Anaïs" and to have her listen to my orders just as she does

Maman's. (I was so used to being tyrannized by Monsita!) But really the most important thing that happened was the sale of the house on 86th Street.

One of the things that I really discovered today is my aversion to the city! Perhaps the only thing that attaches me a little to New York City is memories. . . .

There is one thing that Maman must never know. Sometimes the decision I made troubles me and I wonder if I did the right thing. I had the occasion, the opportunity, to take a course in Literature at Columbia University, through the help of Mrs. Clarke, a friend of Maman's. But suddenly I realized that Maman needs me, needs me to help her, needs me to *bury* my literary ambitions *absolutely*. And it is done! I didn't go to see the Professor I was supposed to see, I let slip through my fingers the key to the door which sometimes leads to physical misery, but which always enriches the mind—my vocation, in a word—and the key has fallen into an abyss. It is already decided that I shall be a poet only when I am no longer able to sing of youth and love, smiling through eyes that are veiled, not by tears, but by age, old age.

Thorvald's education has to be perfect because after all, since I am only a girl I don't really count, and all Maman's hopes are in Thorvald. I am very glad to recognize that if I want to, I can be good for something. So here I am, ready to work, to forget about myself a little to make up for all the selfish things I have always done until now. Maman always says that men are selfish, but personally I think that women who walk around with their heads in the clouds are guilty of incredible selfishness, because one lives only to give pleasure to others, not to find ways of forgetting all the real miseries and, by ignoring them, to let them grow. I did that, but I won't do it any more.

November 25. Tonight I feel terribly unhappy. Oh, what wouldn't I give not to see Maman in the state she is in today. Sometimes I am afraid she will never get better, and then a bitterness I have never known till now takes hold of me and what I suffer is unimaginable. Right now she is in bed, looking old, painfully changed by the pain in her head and by her sick nerves.

Aunt Antolina added to my distress by taking me aside today to tell me that if Maman doesn't take care of herself, she might die. Die? Oh! My God, if I don't die at the same time as Maman, I will go mad!

We had so many packages to carry that when Maman became sick, without any strength, I called a taxi and we came home in silence. The route we took was also the route to the cemetery, and carriages with coffins passed us at every moment. And today I have lost all my nerve, to the point where I think I would like to die!

Oh! Can you believe that I had to interrupt this to stop Thorvald and Joaquinito from quarreling? Then Joaquinito, who is always the naughtier of the two, yelled so loud that Maman came downstairs. I could hardly persuade her to go back up to bed. This evidence that my brothers don't understand anything at all, not even that Maman is really sick, hurts me terribly.

I am crying as I write and have been crying for a long time. Last night I also cried. Why must there be times when God lets us think He is going to make us happy, only to make us suffer again and again and always? In our whole lives there are so few happy days, so many privations, so much misery, and when the misery stops, we lose our health—I can't see any more through my tears! I can't write any more! I should be braver, but it's too much. Oh, it's too much, too much—

November 26. I am really puzzled when I think of all the various ways Life looks to all of us! Yesterday I was in despair. Never have I felt so weak in the struggle against bad times, never have I seen Maman overcome by events, and my last words last night were a cry of distress: Oh! It's too much!

But today, by contrast, everything went as though God had heard my prayer last night. Maman was afraid that the lady who was going to buy the house on 86th Street, or rather the deal, might fall through at the last minute, but the contract was signed at one o'clock and everything went well. Then the lady who owns the house at 158 W. 75, Miss Lynes, sent us a certain Miss Healy who wants to buy that house. One burden less. We have until January 15 to move out, so no doubt Maman will take a little office on Fifth Avenue and put all her energy into her work as "Purchasing Agent."

Monsita has also been one of Maman's worries because she is so changed, probably by the Bolshevik spirit, that she is good for nothing any more. But Maman talked to her today and the problem will be settled by Monsita's leaving the first of December.

When we came home, we found dinner ready, the house nicely in order, and nothing to do but rest. So Maman and I are once again filled with hopes and dreams!

November 27. Uncle Thorvald and Aunt Lolita were with us for Thanksgiving dinner, which was very good and very nicely served by the old Irishwoman, who is a first-class cook.

We all went to the cinema together, where we saw one of the best stories ever, called "Lombardi Ltd." The hero was Mr. Bert Lytell.

We had supper alone and now we are together in my room. I just read a little story to Joaquinito called "On ne Prend pas des Mouches avec du Vinaigre."[1]

Thorvald is reading too, while Maman rests. And when I contemplate so many peaceful hours, so much calm, compared to the torments of these last days, I don't know what to think or what to write. I have discovered that it's much easier to describe the tempests in life than the beautiful days. The latter are beyond us, extraordinarily rare and indefinite!

Maman invited Aunt Juana to have dinner with us on the holiday, too, but she refused categorically. She spent the day all alone in New York, and it was the first in a series of similar days, because she has decided to take a room in Uncle Thorvald's boarding house. Poor Aunt Juana!

I am scolding myself and arguing with myself because I haven't written to Cuca, but without knowing it, she ended my friendship with her to a certain extent. She has always been reserved, but I believed during those days at Lake Placid that I understood her and had discovered her good qualities under the aloof exterior. The door was partly open then, but suddenly it has closed again—and in exchange for my expansiveness (for my demonstrative nature gets the upper hand when I love someone) I had only a strange silence in return, like a judgment that my lack of self-confidence easily took for an accusation. She made me feel that I am poor, as though poverty were a fault, and she doesn't know that certain riches are far from being noble. Without meaning to, she wounded the inherent pride that I have by right from my ancestors, as I have their noble blood and their richness of spirit. The latter is the goal of my ambitions, the riches that I want to attain. Poor Cuca! If she could understand!

I notice that she is the second person I have felt sorry for this evening. It's just that sometimes the whole world seems pitiful.

One of the careers that I have come to feel sorry for is that state of being an "old maid." If I used to contemplate that terrible prospect with pleasure, these days I am quite decided to marry so

1 *"You Don't Catch Flies with Vinegar."*

as not to become *sour*. I have noticed, too, that old maids have time to complain to everyone about their troubles and illnesses, things that married women forget because they are occupied with house-keeping. Finally, for a thousand reasons, I am going to pray every night for My Great Adventure! From here on, I won't paint my Prince's portrait for you until I have found him, because I change every day. That's why I am a woman.

One of the things that I think I am discovering in myself is the truth in what Maman says about women: they have the more difficult role, the more serious task.

Time will tell.

November 29. Out of devotion to my French, I read to Joaquinito every evening. You can add to that devotion my love for Maman's peace, and you will understand why I never want to refuse the Young Master, when he is ready to listen to me.

Yesterday I went to the library. I started a study of Lytton.

I finished something I have been knitting for Maman, and since I am listing my different occupations for you, I will add that we have hung the pictures in the parlor. Also I bought a little can of white paint and touched up several pictures that seemed incurably ugly.

I have discovered that I can make hats. Last Saturday I took a little black tulle from an old ball gown of Maman's, the helmet of an old hat of Aunt Antolina's, and a blue flower, and I made a hat that I wore to go to Mass. To my great surprise, first Maman, then Aunt Antolina, Aunt Lolita, the neighbors, etc. etc., all told me that it was very pretty and added that they would like to know where I bought it. Ha! ha! Maman amused me with stories of her younger days, which add to my conviction that I inherited all the good things from Maman.

December 1. Yesterday, after Mass, after a walk, after lunch, I wrote a dozen letters, I made another hat and I read. I was so absorbed in E. Lytton's book that the hours flew by, and I found myself in bed with my heart and my imagination on the Moon, abode of Romance. That shows that I feel Romance is far away from me and difficult to attain.

For the first time in a long while, Maman was obliged to accept an invitation to dinner. Among the telephone calls today, a masculine voice asked for Mrs. Nin, and as soon as I answered that she had gone out, before I could offer to take a message, the owner of the voice thanked me and hung up. I remained pensive for several minutes, trying to remember who belonged to that familiar voice. And suddenly I knew. It was Enric. He had already come again on Saturday to look for a room. Probably his little room under the eaves—but dear old house where we spent so many days, you will soon belong to new masters!

Life is like that, and so Maman will no longer be a "Rooming house keeper."

> Cut your cloth, sir,
> According to your calling.

And Horace says the same thing:

> A labore reclinat otium.[1]

Perhaps one day the violinist won't have to take a room under the eaves, where it is too hot in summer and where he freezes when it is cold outside; but before that happens, everyone must go through difficulties and climb slowly, slowly, so as not to fall!

About an hour ago I finished the book "Night and Morning," which I admired very much because of the language and the magnificent portraits of the characters, who were human, alive, and all of whom I loved, from the ugliest one to the hero, but I liked Sydney the least of all on account of his selfishness. Perhaps Lytton doesn't know women too well, because his heroine is deplorable—but to make up for it, Fanny, Mrs. Morton and Catherine are much better drawn than Camilla. But I am going to read another book before including E. Lytton among my favorite authors. It's thanks to Charles that I made the acquaintance of that author—delighted, I'm sure. . . .

Poor Maman! I can imagine her, seeming to be gay and taking an animated part in the conversation, but secretly wishing for the peace and quiet of home, that is, when Thorvald and Joaquinito give her any!

P.S. I bought a Diary for Frances to encourage her a little.

December 3. Monday night I read Lytton until Maman came home, so I was able to finish "Night and Morning" and "Leila." I liked the second, a historical novel, very much.

Today I spent the morning straightening up my room, and later Maman telephoned me to go to New York and to the theatre

1 *The complete quotation is* "Nullum ab labore reclinat otium"—"*No period of rest releases me from my labors.*"

with Rita Betancourt.[1] It wasn't the play "Irene" that delighted me, but Rita's presence. It's astonishing that I love so many people who hardly pay attention to me, and sometimes I would like to be nicer so that people might love me a little.

I am writing in bed, although Maman has asked me not to for fear of spotting the bedspread! But I love so to do it! I am thinking of Sunday. I have never liked Sunday, but this week I see a very pleasant day ahead. Mother has invited Mr. Macaya and Enric for that day, and Rita too. And as I find almost everything amusing, the idea pleases me of entertaining at home the best girl and the nicest boy I know, except my two little devils (my brothers). I would like to have Frances here, and Mr. Walker (whom I still haven't forgotten).

I don't know why, but suddenly I am sad. Lately I have read romances, seen them at the cinema, in the theatre, in the street, everywhere in the whole world. I would like so much, oh, so much, to be worthy of receiving their golden rays! Must I always dream in vain? What must I do to make my dream come true?

No doubt: be beautiful!

December 4. I have read so much these last days, I have been so much alone. free to think, that I have again become the horrible Serious One of the old days! I thought I had changed for always, but I find I have not and I am sorry. When I go to the market, I always stop at the library. I linger there, I stay, feeling remorse as I furtively watch the hours slip away, but without making an effort to put down my book. After "Leila," I have read in succession Pausanias, Lytton's life in various encyclopedias, Le Grand Meaulnes[2] by Alain-Fournier, and a small volume on problems in Philosophy. The rest of the time, I distractedly decorate my room, with my imagination in the clouds—

In Le Grand Meaulnes, as in Colette Baudoche, it is the language that surprises, charms and intoxicates me. . . . Expressions like "ridé comme une pomme,"[3] "bonnets tuyautés,"[4] etc., are stored in my memory like treasures. I also found a phrase that I have needed for a long time to describe my position when I read or write on a chair: "accroupie devant une chaise"![5]

---

1 *Rita Allie Betancourt. See footnote 2, p. 263.*
2 *Published in English* as The Wanderer.
3 *"Wrinkled as an apple."*
4 *"Goffered bonnets."*
5 *"Crouching in front of a chair."*

December 6. Last night I lost myself in finishing Le Grand Meaulnes. I persisted in admiring only the style, but from now on I must admire the whole, including the author. It is precisely that enchanted, light yet accurate and exquisite manner of telling the most ordinary things that I have searched for so long in the country of my books. Alain-Fournier, I salute you! Since authors let us glimpse their own characters, through the golden cloud of a light breeze, with a pen lighter still, they make us see the truth drop by drop . . . drops of sweet water!

If I had to give today a title, it would certainly be "My Musical Day."

It began early, to the sound of an alarm clock dancing on the chair. The reason for this early-morning rising was another move. The furniture from our old house arrived, and soon after Maman came with the news that Rita had invited me to the Opera today. I dressed the way I did when I went to school, but this time it was to catch a real train. It was "Il Trovatore" by Verdi, with Madame [Claudia] Muzio in the role of Leonora and [Pasquale] Amato in that of the count. It was beautiful! Maman told me afterward that she doesn't like it, but I have seen too few operas to compare. I like it especially when they all sing together! (However, I didn't like Amato's voice.) But I am enthusiastic about almost everything, and I was very well pleased with all of it in general.

When we came out, a different kind of music surprised us: the monotonous sound of raindrops on the pavement. It was the beginning of a rainstorm, and I was very glad to get home. A long run from the station, with no light because of the fog, tripping over every stone in the road, and with the fear of dogs who might be prowling about—so I was delighted when I saw the lights of our house through the trees, only a few steps away.

After dinner, Maman sang for us, to celebrate the arrival of the piano. Now she is reading in my room and I am writing in the dining room, with Thorvald near me. Annie is working in the kitchen and that forces me to think of the blessings that we have received lately. No more dishes after dinner, and I used to dread the dishes. And so many other things! Some day I will tell you about my room, about Maman's room, and about the entire house, so that you can understand why I say that I am much luckier than I deserve to be.

Annie treats me like a princess. She doesn't know me very well and thinks that I am nice. . . . I hope she will think so for a long time—it's very funny to see other people with so much faith in my inadequate Goodness! . . .

One of the pictures that I mounted on a very delicate-blue paper in my room is a drawing of a child who seems to be waiting in despair in front of a heavy closed door. I like the drawing very much, but the author called it: "Love Locked Out." I don't like the title. I like to think that the door hasn't been opened yet, and that love is waiting sadly for it to open. I like the heavy door and the distress of the visitor who hasn't been made welcome, and I never go to sleep without letting my glance wander over the picture, which is illuminated every night by a little ray of light, half moonlight and half streetlight.

Tomorrow is Sunday, but none of the expected Visitors is going to come. Rita has to do something else, and Enric is going to see Mr. de Alva and Mr. Macaya off for Spain. Perhaps when I am grown up, I won't go to Mass any more, unless I get better as I get older. But I am still very young and very bad!

Rita loves Browning. It's a pity, because I don't like him at all, or almost not at all when I think of Shelley. Some day I will tell you the poems that I like. They are not all written down. I still see many all around me, unpublished poems of life. My favorite poet is Nature.

Bobby Foerster, the funny little friend whom I can't forget, wrote me today. I am going to put her into a book some day, but I'll have to think about which sex she should be. She should have been born a boy, as I would have liked to be a cloud, or a fairy, or perhaps a nice little girl.

December 9.

Dearest Papa:

Apparently it is my destiny to write long epistles to all those I love and to receive only short replies. That's how it is with you, with Maman when she goes away, and with others. I am ready to believe that all the grownups are always busy, and I am beginning (for I am already grown-up) to want to imitate you and I can find very little time to write.

But you once said that my letters give you pleasure, so I keep that in mind . . . and if sometime you want to dissipate the doubt that makes me think my Papa is only a beautiful dream, write me a few words.

You know that Shakespeare said we are actors and Life a stage. I consider the past years as Act I. The curtain goes up to show you a country villa. In the background, trees, etc. etc. In spite of the cold season, the gloomy rain—in a word, the winter which reigns in these parts—the scene is one of peaceful, indescribable charm.

The house is large, with harmonious proportions, as beautiful as it is comfortable. I won't tire you with a complete description. No doubt the room that will interest you most is the Study, which adjoins the parlor. In it we have our books, photographs of artists, with yours among them, and the piano. Do you remember that big, big picture of you that was, I believe, in the children's room? I put it into a very beautiful frame and you seem like the King among all the other artists: Granados, Carreño, the Barcelona Trio, violinists and singers.

Thorvald's room is full of signs of a different kind of Study: Algebra books, a globe of the world, notebooks of problems.

Joaquinito has busts of Mozart and Wagner, which he inherited from Mrs. Quintero, books of fairy stories (although he already gives signs of having an amazing memory and a marked taste for the same books that I like, which aren't more beautiful but more difficult to understand than fairy stories), and photographs of artists.

If you wish, you need not read this paragraph, but I can't resist the temptation to tell you about my room. My Domain is large, full of sunshine (except on rainy days) and light. The furniture is ivory color. The walls, of a very delicate blue, are sparsely decorated with my favorite drawings, pictures of the people who are essential to my happiness and of those who are essential to the education of my intellect (which is also essential to my happiness). There are a few books of philosophy and poetry on the mantel (no Algebra), two or three knick-knacks that remind me of Brussels . . . a few things made of ivory with my initials in pale blue on my dressing table—and since I am the princess in my Kingdom, I have a page, a little canary that hops about all the time and delights me in my brief moments of solitude.

Thus everything is blue, white and gold, the sky, the clouds, the sun! Do you blame me for believing in fairies, believing in everything that is like my Kingdom? For believing in dreams that may come true?

Every day I get letters from my girl friends, and sometimes I go to New York and to the theatre or the Opera with them.

A sweet old Irishwoman, who cooks like twenty "cordon bleu" chefs, is our housekeeper.

Christmas is coming. I can already send you my most tender greetings and my wishes for your happiness. If you are a little bit alone that day, remember that there are three children thinking of you in the midst of their happiness, three children who are going to dream on Christmas Eve of your dear presence around the tree. Also on Christmas morning and all the rest of the day, even more than the rest of the year, because it's a special happiness that must be shared, there is never enough of it. . . .

The curtain will always be up for you, because I will write you often.

Sometimes I wonder if you realize how much we have all changed. Joaquinito is so big now that it's impossible to consider him the baby of the family. Thorvald is a man in spite of being only 15—strong, as tall as I, jolly and rather fond of teasing. And I am a young lady. I already wear my hair in a bun, because I feel so serious. When I arrived here I was anemic, timid and so ignorant that when I reread the pages of my diary written 5 years ago, it frightens me. Now I am not thin any more, but slender, still a little shy at times with strangers and gentlemen, but otherwise very talkative with people who arouse my enthusiasm.

And my features are a strange mixture of yours and Maman's, with a result that is rather artistic. That is, I should be a lady painter because I was born to wear a black velvet coat and the artist's floppy bow tie. My taste for the latter caused my Sánchez cousins a great deal of amusement during the Summer. One day you will be surprised by my traveling to Havana to be presented to Cuban society. But you know I am only making fun of myself.

But enough of these foolish ideas. In a word, the most precious part of this long letter is simply all my best wishes for Christmas and all the tenderness of your

Linotte

December 10. I have been sick, and every day I tired myself with so much reading that I hadn't the energy or the strength to write. I was very much absorbed in my study of Lytton, perplexed for a long time before arriving at a judgment of him, and finally I abandoned him without regrets. He gives me the impression of fireworks, because his exterior and his style are very boisterous and attract attention at first. Then when the sparks are changed into ashes, one arrives at his basic ideas. . . . As for virtues: he knows the world, in spite of the impression of lack of sincerity that is typical of his characters! Farewell Lytton! Bon voyage! And may the dust of the library weigh lightly on your mediocre books!

It's real madness that takes hold of me: when I read a book, I am hungry for another, then another—I forget myself, I forget my family, I am the Anaïs of former times, concentrated in another's life—pure selfishness.

Last night I was brought back from a trip by the mute reproaches of my brothers, who didn't have one pair of darned socks.

I kissed my books and put them on the mantel, promising not to let myself be tempted like that any more. But I couldn't stop looking at them all day long, as though I could read them without opening their covers!

There are times when I fear that reading so much may harm me, morally. I have a strange sensation of being asleep, and my imagination is so wrapped up in the pages I am reading that I walk and talk in my sleep. I *live* the books that I am reading at present. I suffer, I am happy, all my senses are at the Author's command. This trance lasts a long time after I have stopped reading, while I think and think. . . .

The return to real Life is always a shock, and sometimes it hurts.

I would like to be able to read with the same carefree attitude as Thorvald, who never thinks about it, is never upset. But also, by dint of thinking, something is developing in me. I don't know its name, but every day I feel this power growing in me, a Thing that governs my ideas, my acts and my words, always clearer, an elevation, the discovery of the *good* side of my nature. Oh! Books are wonderful teachers! For instance, tonight I am going to fall asleep with one of Pascal's thoughts about religion and the heart. Tomorrow I will be a little better, a little bit changed.

I can always read, but I must live for *others*, and live with my heart and my imagination joined.

Pascal says: "Do you want people to think well of you? Do not speak well of yourself."

December 14. The first snowy day! And something unexpected arrived with the white flakes: *Godmother* came to see us, and suddenly a miracle happened, because by trying, we love her again as we used to and a silent reconciliation has taken place on all sides. She spent the afternoon with us, talking peacefully with Mother, had dinner here, and at 7 Thorvald and I accompanied her to the station. O lovely day, which saw a new castle rise up on the ruins of the old one!

Since Maman can forget so easily, so can I, dear Godmother. Maman said correctly that everyone has his faults, and when she asked me if I would stop loving her if ever she turned out to have a fault, I answered with all my heart: never. I am so happy!

Last night we went to a bazaar for the benefit of our church and I bought a beautiful big picture of Sister Theresa of the Little Flower. I put it in a beautiful frame, and since she is up there in my room, I feel her gentle influence, I feel that her beautiful face, so full of heavenly sweetness, is going to inspire me to better feelings and better behavior. Oh, I will be nicer, I am sure, for as soon as I look at that picture, I lose my indifference, coldness and lack of faith—which are signs of a lack of feeling! I am going to be better for your sake, Little Flower!

It seems that everyone has seen E. Madriguera these days, except me. But Godmother told a funny story! It seems that the whole "crowd" was in the parlor over there to celebrate Mr. de Alva's departure for Spain (and he is taking a gift for Grandmother). Godmother was going by the parlor and was going to say good evening when she heard Enric say a very bad word, so she hurried out without saying anything. That incident, which shocked Godmother, pleased me because it's just that kind of childishness, that foolishness, which amuses me so much in Enric! He is so much like Joaquinito!

I often think of Aunt Lolita's words about "idealizing people during their absence." Because sometimes I compare my opinion of him with everyone else's opinion, and I fear that Enric may not be at all what I think he is. Anyhow, I don't understand why I talk so much about him. All those ideas are so unreasonable— there must be a sorcerer who has bewitched me. (I have a very vague idea of what bewitched means.)

December 24. Christmas Eve! I have done so much sewing, embroidering, knitting, crocheting and buying that I haven't had time to think, much less to write!

I received three books from Papa! He will be all alone, without a family, on Christmas Day! How sad it is! . . .

There are many things that I can't forgive the Cubans. They hurt Maman so often, those mean people! They have the heart to make Maman go to New York on Christmas Eve and to wear her out with their whims and demands.

I have discovered the two ways to enjoy the cold: in an armchair near the heater, but frozen just the same by inactivity, and on sleigh rides under the stars. The second way is delightful!

Amidst all these revolutions and preparations, I let December 22 go by, the memorable date when the keys to 158 W. 75th changed hands. I have thought of it often, though. So many years spent in a house can never fail to endear it to one, because of the memories. . . . In the space of a few seconds, all the events have passed before my eyes, and I regretted some but relived others rather happily.

I still have a few things left to do, in spite of the huge drawer full of presents, and I can't take too much time to rest. It is only 2 o'clock and I will be so happy to see Maman come home!

Tomorrow for the first time I am wearing shoes with Louis XV heels. Think of my bun, my long dress, my serious thoughts—and you will realize that I am a young lady . . . already. . . ! Furthermore, I shall soon be 17!

December 26. After having waited for Maman on Christmas Eve with great impatience, I had the joy of seeing her arrive with a dozen little packages containing a few small details to decorate the tree. After dinner we began to trim the tree—a tall fir, with its topmost branch kissing the lofty ceiling, as though to wish it a Merry Christmas too. The four of us were busy, happily placing the little candles, balls of every color, snowflakes, stars, little dolls, little bags of candy, and all the other charming things that traditionally disguise a solemn evergreen to make it more human—that is, more attractive to man's gaze and all his senses. That was quickly done. Then came the moment to place the gifts, the packages nicely wrapped in tissue paper and red ribbon, and crowned with a little tag with a name. What mysteries, what smiles!

Joaquinito's eyes were worthy of study. Thorvald's were not quite so big, but almost as expressive. My curiosity, which had been dormant a long time, was also awake but less noisy, like Maman's. Once again I had the impression of being much older in my ideas, very far away from Thorvald and Joaquinito, unable to share their happy-go-lucky nature, and because of that, closer to Maman, closer to the more serious things in Life.

The time came to go to bed. I took one last look at the holly which I had used to decorate the mantels, lamps, windows, and banister, and the mistletoe hanging on a red ribbon. The tree shone at the end of the dark parlor. Do you believe that I thought only of the beauty of the scene? No, mixed with my somewhat poetic impressions were thoughts that responsibility has taught me. I was thinking also that everything was clean and in order. A woman has to be a *practical* poet!

The night was disturbed by dreams. The doors were open and I heard all of my dear family rolling over and over, each in his own bed. It wasn't just the excitement of Christmas night, it was also the cold and the wind.

At dawn I was awakened by a strange feeling of rain on my face. It was snow that the wind invited into my room and onto my bed, through the open window. I got up to close it and saw the result of the silent work accomplished in the night by the Great Painter. The landscape was majestic! I was so thrilled I couldn't go back to sleep, so I thought. I must have looked funny, half sitting up in bed, staring out of the window, thinking of many different things, while the dim light of early morning filtered slowly into my room. Of course I was the first one dressed. But the snowstorm had been so violent that I didn't go to Mass.

Before Thorvald and Joaquinito left, we lighted the tree and sang "Venite Adoremus," accompanied on the piano by Joaquinito. The packages were opened and immediately the cries of joy began.

Breakfast was a little quieter, for Maman wasn't feeling well. Afterward, while the boys went out, Maman and I dressed with great care. I had made a big tulle bow for my black velvet dress. Sometimes it amuses me to be a coquette. Not always, and *never* as much as Germaine Sarlabous.

The visitors arrived a little while before dinner. The dinner was a success, as almost all dinners are. It's not very difficult to talk, eat, laugh, talk, eat, laugh until it's over. Some people talk very little and eat a lot. Others only talk and laugh, but several eat well, talk delightfully and laugh at the same time. That must be a characteristic of a "woman of the world." Doubtless it's a good quality! By trying hard, I succeeded in talking a good deal in order to be pleasant. I am not unsociable any more! To avoid being unsociable, one must tell lies and act like a clown, which is very simple for liars (or flatterers—same thing) and for clowns!

After dinner we talked. There must be a reason for this old custom. I think it's because a starving man is not very pleasant, so after dinner everyone has an opportunity to be agreeable, in order to make up for past mistakes.

To complete the celebration of this beautiful day, I went sledding with Thorvald and Joaquin after dinner. There are always many children and it's a real party. Even now I can see the hill and the sleds going by, overflowing with children. I can hear the shouts clear into Maman's room, where I am keeping her company, as she is in bed.

They nicknamed me "White Cap" because of my white beret, and since Joaquinito answers all their questions every time I go, yesterday a few of the boys called "au revoir" and other words that they murdered with the worst American accent. I don't know why, but the few girls who go there can't stand me, and while I was wondering why all of them were giving me such unkind looks, I heard three girls talking near me as a sled full of boys went by, shouting (the boys, not the sled): "Hello, White Cap!" "Want to ride on our sled?" One girl said: "See that girl with the white tam-o'-shanter? Well, she is the biggest flirt!"

And the other one added: "Most of the boys behave like fools since she comes here."

Decidedly, I will have to change my hair style!

December 28. Maman is still sick in bed. I don't leave her for a single minute, so I have read 2 books. But the silence weighs on me terribly and I am invaded by a strange melancholy that betrays itself by the four words that I murmur very, very often: I am so alone. . . .

Maman forced me to go out for a few minutes after dinner to get a little fresh air. Lately my eyes hurt me when I read a book in a few hours, and last night I had a headache—so I would have been glad to go sledding—but no, I keep thinking of Maman, Maman, always Maman, and I came back promptly.

These last days I met the boy who lives next door. His name is Raymond, he is 16, and he seems very nice.

Jack [Cosgrove] has already spent several days here. I have known him for a long time and one might say that we grew up together because each time we meet, the two mothers, his and mine, invariably make us pass a test by putting us side by side. At first we were the same height, then suddenly he grew and grew, like Alice in Wonderland, and he is already wearing long trousers. He still has red hair, but he isn't afraid of me any more. However, he doesn't know how to dance and he seems funny to me, as though he had only grown physically while mentally he remained very young. Which proves that boys don't know how to be grown-up, and that's why they impress me as big children—even if I am a little afraid of them because they are such noisy children!

Apropos of children, I haven't thought about Mr. Madriguera for a long time now. It is as though during the summer, since Lake Placid, I became someone else; then when winter came I wrote all that terrible nonsense, and I turned back into the Serious One.

It's very hard to explain without saying bad things about my brothers, but I have really lost my faith in . . . men! That's strange, isn't it? All of a sudden, just like that. But I told Maman the truth the day I said that I will never marry, because not all men are as nice as girls. I took my girl friends as an example, and the comparison was made with a smile that made Maman laugh hilariously.

But perhaps all this is going through my head because I feel so alone, so alone. . . . Especially when I look out of my window and see everyone having a good time. . . .

Last night Thorvald and Joaquinito made me cry with their selfish attitude. Maman was sad because neither one of them has come to her room for a second, even though they know she is sick. All their noisy, heedless pleasures, hiding their inheritance of selfishness under the cloak of childishness!

As for myself, I certainly know I don't count for much, but sometimes I compare the open, frank attitude of the boys I meet everywhere with the ungracious way that Thorvald has of offering me a ride on his sled, after he has had it all day long. Added to those things, so insignificant in themselves, is the excessive sensitivity which is one of my faults, and the deep impression that the least little thing makes on me. I should correct that. Perhaps it's my fault. . . .

If I rebel against indifference, it's because I feel that I give away a big part of my heart to be hurt for nothing. If I am against selfishness, it's not for myself but for the mother whom I adore with all my big, ugly heart. One brother is 10 years old, the other almost 15, but as the twig is bent, so the tree is inclined, unless the faults are corrected.

No doubt I have more faults than I can imagine, but I *know* that I really love those who love me, and I *know* that for a long time now, I am not always thinking of myself. A very great effort was required to manage the latter, especially, because of the inheritance of selfishness, of which I had my share, and I had to fight against it and not put up with it.

6 o'clock: I feel gay. Do you know why? Simply because I looked at myself in the mirror and I looked so sad for so little reason that I just felt like laughing, and I laughed. I have been singing and dancing. In a word, to be cured I need only look at my face.

December 29. I received a letter from my old friend Natalie Lederer. I used to tell you enthusiastically about her, and it is only the long separation, with no answer to my letters, which has made me forget several of my friends. But I am glad to have news of her. I must have changed enormously, as my enthusiasm was easily kindled and I sincerely admired many people, but so ardently that at present the little flame has gone out and can only rarely be relighted. It's strange how often I was wrong in my judgment of people. I always begin by thinking they are angels—and the ending is sad. It is as though I were walking through an endless gallery, with little idols on the right and on the left, each one on a pedestal. I stop before each one, and at first glance, I cry out: "What a beautiful idol!" And when I study it, I think it must be carved in gold. Then suddenly it falls and breaks into little pieces, and when I bend down to take a closer look, I find only pieces of painted clay. Then I turn away and look at another one. It falls at my feet, a little pile of clay. And so on until all the idols are broken. Behind me, the gallery is a sad spectacle of ruin; before me are many more idols, shining and drawing me on. At the end of the gallery is an immense, wonderful statue of pure gold. As I move forward, watching the false treasures fall at my feet, I draw near the statue and recognize its value.

I hardly have time to name them, there have been so many! Not long ago one of the most beautiful idols was Miss Storms, and after her many other unimportant people, then some others that I hardly dare to name for you, but you can guess that the violinist, Godmother, and many, many others are among them. . . .

No doubt everyone has his own gallery. Maman must be well ahead of me, as she must already know the name of the great Statue.

December 30.

Dear little Papa:

Do you think the first thing I am going to thank you for is the books? Not at all—it's for your letter! It seemed like a Christmas gift that arrived a little late, but was a delightful surprise. Thank you a thousand times for the books also. I was rather surprised at how different they are from the books I am used to reading. They have a "certain something" that is very modern and Parisian. I was too bewitched by the language to notice the only thing that is very difficult for me to forgive: the realism.

I like your article for the Courrier very much. It expresses in words what the situation is like everywhere right now, and I know it. I can give a small example—you have no idea how disappointed I was by the Opera, of which I used to have such a good opinion. Everywhere one finds what you describe as the betrayal of true art. But it isn't only the concert halls that are "full of people and empty of perfection," it's all of life. But I am not yet a cynic, quite the contrary. However, I am full of contradictions because I never stop idealizing all the people around me and at the same time, while I idealize them, I realize regretfully that it is in vain. . . .

However, Papa dearest, don't you think that there is a touch of pessimism in your opinions? Haven't there always been the masses that abase Art and a small group that elevates and supports it? Don't you think there is nothing that can change that conflict of contemptible ideas and ideals that are fragile but of inestimable value, which no doubt will exist as long as the Cause does? And since the Cause is above all else, nothing can harm it. Art is too powerful, even if it seems weak in comparison with its brutal opponent.

But remember, Papa dearest, I am only 16 and I know very, very little, so forgive these ideas that only Time and Experience can correct. You just have to smile at the things I write—you can even mock me. . . .

You are someone who forces people to think and, accidentally, to write what they think—but I still have so many things to tell you! Simple things, because life is rather simple, after all, and it's our life I want to write you about.

We had a delightful Christmas. Just imagine, we are "chez nous," in our own house! No doubt you can imagine that we had a tree, so tall it reached the ceiling, which the whole family trimmed—as well as tons of packages, with such pretty gifts for everyone! We had Visitors—Uncle Thorvald, Aunt Lolita and

Godmother, as well as several friends. To celebrate, Nature was wearing white of a matchless beauty. I decorated the house with holly, etc., etc. There was dinner on Christmas Day, etc. Mocking like that is one of my many faults!

One of the loveliest things about Richmond Hill is the snow-covered hills that lend themselves so well to sledding. I can hardly describe the great pleasure that I generally take in such games, which Thorvald calls Sport. I go every afternoon. There are many children there, and from the beginning Joaquin answered all their questions, which has allowed the boys to murder a few words of French, apparently to please me. And the girls say, or rather whisper, that I am a "flirt," which isn't true at all, at all. Perhaps that's the reason wise men say that it's difficult to be liked by everyone! . . .

I love the country so much that I go to New York only from time to time. Last night I went to a dance; and again, in a crowd of boys, I found only one with whom I enjoyed talking. I assure you, Papa dearest, that it's funny how easy it is to tell the difference! But I am so often wrong that I doubt my own judgment and wait for people to reveal themselves. One has to wait a long time!

On rereading your letter, I find you asked about my health. The last time I had just a little abscess on my lip. It may have been caused by anemia. I went through a little pain in order not to be disfigured. At the time I thought I had a lot of pain—it's always like that—but I have forgotten it long since. . . . I assure you that my health is excellent; living in the country, in particular, has transformed me. You mustn't think we are in bad health because we are thin, as none of us has the slightest tendency toward weight, except perhaps Thorvald, who bears a great resemblance to his Uncle Thorvald. I haven't had to use rouge for a long time now, not even when I go to dances! It's too bad, though, that everyone takes my paleness as a sign of bad health, and the same is true of Joaquin.

I laughed a lot at some of the sentences in your letter, which were too Parisian for someone who is only half French to understand. But please go on writing like that, because Maman can easily explain all of it and that way I learn. . . .

How happy I am that you like the snapshots! I wasn't sad in the one where I am sitting on a bench; I have a somewhat perplexed expression because I had just made a philosophical observation. I am often perplexed, you know. . . . I'm only sixteen!

*   *   *

Linotte

P.S. I have been advised to send you several dozen aren't's, r's, s's and t's so that you can put them anywhere they are missing in my French spelling. I hope you will have enough to go around and you can send the excess back to me to use in my next letter.

December 31. It is 11. Maman is in bed; so are Thorvald and Joaquinito. I am writing—the two of us are waiting for the New Year!

How many things there are that no one can write, no one understand! Tonight I am troubled by many different feelings, for as I realize a New Year is about to begin, I have been going over the old one. . . . Many people generally spend the few hours before midnight making resolutions and promises. I promise nothing; I have such a weak character that I can't *promise* to be better, but God knows how much I want to be, with what enthusiasm and will power. I want what is *best* in me to *live*. But I know that I have very few things to ask for just now, compared to the infinite number of things for which I should give thanks. What do we lack?

It's about my gratitude that I can't write; it's too lofty, too strange, too vague. My feelings are too sincere to be expressed in mere words!

I can confide my wishes to you—you know that I want to become better and better, you know that Maman's happiness is above all else for me, you know that my little brothers' happiness is as important to me as my own, you know my love for the perfection of our home, my search for the most beautiful books, everything from my tiniest whim, my ambitions, up to the simplest prayer, and my regrets—you know all that . . . and more!

The pettiest and most childish thing in other people's opinion, but the thing that I consider a real treasure, is the little bit of my heart and the sweep of my imagination which await the stranger. . . . Will it be this year that I find the sweet light that people call—I am almost ashamed to name it, it's my only secret—I am thinking about love. . . .

If I didn't dream so much, I would never have thought of that, but everything beautiful appears in my dreams, and love is so beautiful!

I haven't told you anything about the dance. But there are times when I fear the immense influence of my impressionable imagination. I know that I am too easily impressed, and sometimes I suffer, for my imagination is like a violin; it lends itself easily to letting sounds be drawn from it, but sometimes a string is too taut and breaks. . . .

I met a boy there whose name I don't know. It was the same thing as with Mr. Walker; we were attracted to each other because of a strong resemblance in our tastes, opinions and ideas, even in the midst of many other people. And everything went very well, I was very happy to talk with him and dance with him. But at one point another boy swept me away, far away from him, and he looked at me in such a strange way, with so much regret and I don't know what else, that it made me thoughtful. I couldn't dance with him after that, but he kept his eyes continually fixed on me and I was both troubled and perplexed.

When it was time to leave, he looked at me again with regret and gave me a smile that reminded me of all the artists I have known, for artists do everything in a different way from other men—Eduardo Sanchez, Henry Walker, Enric. . . .

I have thought so often of his intelligent face and his dreamy expression that I didn't want to write about it, thinking that my violin had been touched by an unworthy master. . . .

If only I were like everyone else, I wouldn't be so silly!

I learned the last name of my little neighbor, Raymond McCormick, because he lends me books. He says he doesn't like Scott's books "because they are too slow, too dry. I like books like the Rover Boys, with excitement all over and easy to read."

I laughed quietly, but I wasn't at all angry.

But here I am, waiting for the New Year and talking about little boys, about children! I who am always so serious—no, not serious, I mean calm and indifferent about gentlemen.

The year 1919 had the honor of curing Anaïs Nin of her unsociableness, teaching her to dance and receive compliments without being too embarrassed, to be amiable and sociable. In short, to be a "woman of the world."

It will soon be midnight. My little "Love" has been weeping at the door for a long time without being able to come in, and I look at the picture with a smile. If he doesn't come in this year, I won't be able to bear the sorrow and I'll give the picture to someone else. . . .

I also see Sister Thérèse, my guardian angel. . . . She never seems angry with me and her serenity does me so much good!

I see Belica's little calendar. That little package of paper represents a year—but few things except Time are so full of strange comparisons. A year, many years, a lifetime—a lifetime is always long, and after life, Eternity. It's always Time, the hours that pass and can never be recalled, the hours that we count while we are alive, that we stop counting when we die, whose value on the other side probably is useless and unable to change anything, while it controls man's life here below.

What a quiet way to await the beginning of another year!

There must be many other things to think about that are more important than the passage of time, since so many other things stir our enthusiasm and drive us to act. That proves that Time doesn't rule through the power of the Inevitable, and that the Inevitable isn't Life.

There are the bells, the whistles. Happy New Year! Happy New Year!

❧ *1 9 2 0* ❧

January 4. I remember very clearly what I did when I heard the bells and whistles announcing midnight. First I ran to Maman, who already had Thorvald and Joaquinito with her, to hug her and wish her a Happy New Year. Then when Maman had sent us back to our rooms to sleep, I stood a long time at the window, not thinking of anything, murmuring, "O God, make me good!"

Once in bed, I fell asleep immediately and the first hours of 1920 were only full of dreams. . . .

On New Year's Day we went to the cinema, and although Thorvald and Joaquinito didn't behave too well, quite the contrary, the day passed peacefully enough.

All these last days, Maman and I have spent our time doing the accounts, with our heads full of all kinds of names and numbers. I make a funny Secretary, for no amount of scolding has been able to rid me of the habit of counting on my fingers. "Practice makes perfect," and I succeed in handling the numbers with surprising speed, not to mention the accuracy of my method!

Tomorrow I am going to New York to help Maman, and do you believe that I am already thinking happily about the dress that Maman is going to buy me for my birthday? For just think, on February 21 I will be seventeen! It's a year since someone turned me into a *coquette* by a mad kiss!

Annie has moved out. This morning Maman criticized the coffee, which is always terrible, and the old Irishwoman demonstrated the hot temper which is traditional with the Irish. Farewell, Madam Annie! The Nin family is always difficult, because they are aristocrats who have never had much money but who have princely tastes, even where coffee is concerned.

My poor cousin [Cuca]! Only to [my diary] and to Maman

do I dare confide the fall of another idol! I can write hundreds of letters if they give pleasure to those who receive them, but it's very sad to write one (the equivalent of one of those enthusiastic conversations in which I give so much and get nothing in return) and not to receive an answer—especially when the whole family knows that Cuca is in perfect health and goes to parties day and night. Twice I wrote her with pleasure, frankly, as I write only to those I love; afterwards I selected the prettiest of my Christmas cards and sent it, then a book by Maeterlinck that I kissed two or three times before letting go of it. Then a week after Christmas, I received a very formal little card—with Cuca's name. So that strange Kingdom of Sensitivity, which takes up a great deal of room in Myself, was hurt—as though I had lost something dear, the true friendship that I usually give to my invisible heroes (and *rightly so*), the tender trust that hurts one when it is rebuffed like that. . . . Really I don't know why or how, but Cuca has wounded me.

Maman shrugs her shoulders at such things and hardly pays them any attention. But I am still a Pupil, and my Teacher is very hard on me—sometimes. . . .

This morning I went to Communion and I found that I haven't changed. The ritual of the Mass absolutely does not touch my heart. I understand the Creator and his Wonders much better when I listen to music or when I watch the sun setting behind the trees in the forest which are still covered with snow crystals. . . .

January 5. Today was a tiring day. We went to New York and came back only at 4:06, having spent the day in the stores. At one point I lost Maman, and at the age of 16 1/2, I wanted to cry; then when I found her again I felt a childish joy. O *little* girl of 16, you are a long way from the gravity, or the wisdom, of Age. When I am 17, I will change.

I received the funniest letter from Natalie Lederer! Her French is deliciously dreadful!

While Maman and I were doing the dishes, we talked about the little dance that I will have on February 21. What interests me the most, besides the names of the guests and the music, is the dress I will wear! Which of all the dresses hanging in the immense closets in the stores will be mine? Among so many colors, flowers, laces and ribbons, so much silk and tulle that make up the dresses, I must choose a little fairylike material for the day of my 17th birthday, and the only thing I am sure of is the color: blue.

Franklin Simon's windows were interesting today, for to celebrate the production of Maeterlinck's Bluebird, they have put a new shade of blue on the market, a Bluebird blue, lovely to see and to own!

What strange faces I saw today—besides my own, of course. The intense cold (five degrees below 0 Fahrenheit) transformed the prettiest faces into clown faces (rouged cheeks, white powder, red ears and noses) popping out of fur collars with startled and frozen expressions.

We saw the famous film actor, Jack Pickford, on 5th Avenue, and Maman and I were much amused. However, [pictures] are changing a great deal and keep improving.

I have just been playing the violin on an elastic band, which reminds me that Maman was obliged to name E. Madriguera when I was making a list of my guests, as I had completely forgotten him.

"Woman is fickle. . . ."

My imagination is like Joaquinito's, so diabolical that I used to think I was "in love" with Enric—something so absurd, so ridiculous and so impossible that after one Summer I have forgotten it, and at present I look at his picture as indifferently as I do that of Robert Imandt, for example—another violinist whom I knew only when I was baby. But I was so ashamed of the tricks my imagination played on me that at confession, I asked the priest, hesitantly: "Is it a sin to think a great deal about one boy?"

"No," said the priest, "if the boy is kind, good in every respect, you must not worry if you think about him."

Fortunately I will soon be 17, and at that age one doesn't think about such silly things. I am writing all this to punish myself, for I am blushing as I write.

January 8. Knowing how impulsive I am, I haven't written these last days in order to have time to think about what happened. The funniest part is that for Maman and everyone else, it's a very simple thing, but I am very troubled, as troubled as I was yesterday.

Late yesterday afternoon, Maman and I came back from New York, where we had worked hard, and I was looking through the mail when I saw a letter addressed to me in an unknown handwriting. I opened it quickly and as I read the first words I felt my cheeks growing hot with the "blush" that happens to me so often and so easily.

The letter was from the boy I told you about, the one I met at Dorothy's dance: Marcus Anderson. Never have I received such a strange letter! I have so little pride, so little, that I never thought for a minute that he would think of me, would remember my tastes and my words. He begged me not to be offended—he was trying the only way he knew not to lose sight of me, because he found me interesting, pretty, charming. Oh, my goodness! I am blushing again!

Well, how can I explain the tone of the letter? No one has ever thought that my friendship was of such value—I was embarrassed, surprised, happy, rather touched, and my imagination was flying, flying—while I set the table and ate dinner, while I dried the dishes. . . .

You see, I knew that if I didn't wait a month to tell you about this, I would overdo it the way I always do. Oh, what a foolish way of looking at things!

Well, let's be serious and sober. Maman gave me permission to answer the letter, which was written with sincerity. And this morning I put in the letter box a letter just as sincere and a little longer than his. I hurried because he wrote that he would be waiting anxiously for my answer.

Maman has been making fun of both of us. She tries to make me believe that "everyone does the same thing," and I try to laugh, but I keep thinking of Marcus Anderson's serious face, his dreamy eyes, his artist's smile, and I am waiting more impatiently than I dare to admit to Maman or to . . . myself . . . for his answer. Be forgiving, dearest diary. Just think, this is the first boy to play the rôle of Prince, because Enric was never sincere—and I am not yet 17! And Mr. Anderson loves books, writes poetry, seems to understand about Art and Dreams—that's enough to make me interested in our correspondence.

But I am truly the most egotistical of daughters!

Is it possible that I was carried away and told you first about a caprice, instead of about the most important thing in the world? Maman! I was with her yesterday when she went to call on a businessman who proposed that she make a trip to Cuba to display from 20 to 30 thousand dollars' worth of merchandise from the Bonwit Teller store. And Maman is already planning it for the beginning of February.

I was able to study the gentleman and could sense the admiration and sympathy that he has for Maman, and I was proud to have the right to love her, the wonderful Queen of Mothers!

January 10. Yesterday I worked on the books with Maman all day. Once in a while we stopped to cook or wash dishes. Our hands are very sore and Maman herself admits that she doesn't like to do the dishes. Oh, those pots! Then in the evening we were so tired mentally that we went to the cinema to see "The Country Cousin."

Today it was our turn to do the housekeeping. I cleaned my canary's cage and after lunch Maman and I went to market. Right now Maman is in bed with a bad headache. I took a little dinner to her on a little tray. It seemed very sad to do the dishes in silence, all by myself. Usually Maman and I talk and forget what we are doing.

Today a fat lady and gentleman came to see our house, for you have no doubt guessed that Maman already has another business deal in mind. She has been offered $18,000 for a house that cost $14,000! You will soon see us clearing out with suitcases and furniture, for we are Wandering Christians! Only Heaven will be our home, and Maman will have to be our guide to get up there. I hope there will be gardens in heaven! No, I am not mocking, I just always say things that don't make sense.

I don't know why, but I reread this diary before writing tonight. I can assure you that the Future is wonderful! The things that I never foresee, the way that events come about, the way that people leave, come back, leave again, and whose existence I so soon forget. What I observe fascinates me—sometimes makes me feel sorry, sometimes glad. And each day I know a little more, a little more. Do you know that my eyes change as I learn? They are sadder, I am sure. When I smile at the mirror, my eyes don't smile. . . . I have often looked at the reflection of my eyes in the glass and sometimes I wonder why they look as though they are asking a question. It's strange, isn't it, that I can't understand what my eyes are saying.

9 o'clock: I received a letter from Cuca. If it's true that I am easily offended, it's also true that I am quick to forgive. Five minutes after reading her letter, I answered her.

No letter yet from Mr. Anderson.

January 11. Godmother spent the afternoon with us; then when the snowflakes began to fall, she hurried off. After dinner I went sledding. It was delightful and the keen cold, the shouts of joy, the "thrill" of the ride down combined to cure an unreasonable, unbearable melancholy that had seized me because I didn't want to complain of the pain in my side and Maman wanted me to go skating. But fortunately by dinner-time I felt better and could go sledding, which I really love! I have to go to New York tomorrow with Maman. It's a pity! I prefer to stay here.

The other day we talked about patriotism. Like the true Artist's children that we are, we realize that we aren't really attached to any country. I discovered that my love for France existed purely in my imagination, not in my heart. I would like to explain to you the confusion that reigns between those two kingdoms, for each considers itself the All-Powerful Ruler, but in truth, imagination is the real victor, a thousand to one!

It's thanks to my imagination that I am so often mistaken, that I sometimes suffer, for in its splendor and independence, its rule is almost tyrannical, but I love it for lack of anything better.

January 13. I received another long, interesting letter from Mr. Anderson. He has a gift for expressing himself, he is intelligent, and he has really good taste in poetry. Sometimes I try to remember how he looks, for I hardly remember his features. I have made the acquaintance of Alfred de Musset, thanks to him. It seems unbelievable that I had never read the poems of that admirable poet, but remember that I am alone to choose my books, and lately, for lack of French books, I have been exploring English literature.

I answered Mr. Anderson's nice letter, explaining that to him, and talked to him about W. Scott and asked him to send me a few of his poems. Oh, how I love those that he loves so much too, such as Rappelle-toi,[1] La Nuit de Décembre,[2] and the answer to "Qu'est-ce la poésie?"[3] Musset's poems are so sad they make one weep. . . .

I never thought that a boy could have such delicate feelings, and I'm sure he is a poet. . . . Oh, how wonderful it is to find someone I can talk to about things that make such an impression on me. I have always suspected Frances of having tastes that are good, but a little too modern. No doubt Mr. Anderson and I are "old fashioned"!

Last night after dinner and the dishes, I went skating with Thorvald and Raymond. I had Mr. Anderson's letter in my pocket, and as I listened to Raymond's very simple conversation, I wondered why I enjoy the cultivated mind and refined manners of the

[1] *"Remember."*
[2] *"December Night."*
[3] *"What is poetry?"*

one almost as much as the simple speech, childish ideas, open and loyal deeds—something sincere about the kind heart and mind—of the other. You see, I think that both are of almost equal value—the qualities of mind . . . and those of the heart. But of course I greatly prefer Mr. Anderson, for there are many things which delight the two of us that Raymond doesn't understand. The same thing happened so often with Enric, whereas Eduardo was rather like Mr. Anderson.

Once when Raymond and I were skating together, he told me that Thorvald skates the same way with his "fiancée."

"Which one is she?" I asked with a great deal of curiosity.

"She isn't here."

"And your own fiancée?" I said laughingly.

"I don't have one," he said, looking at me very seriously. I was troubled, remembering that Cuca said that I am a great "flirt." Just think of the terrible thing that it seems I am *without ever realizing it!*

I think I understand why Aunt Lolita said that soon I wouldn't write in my diary any more.

January 16. Yesterday I was very sick and spent a sleepless night, listening to the hours strike, my head sick and full of thoughts, my soul restless and my nerves painfully overexcited, without any apparent reason. I didn't want to admit that I wasn't up to getting out of bed and I dragged all day behind Maman, as I always do of late, but usually instead of dragging, I hop like my canary. I even wrote long letters to Mr. Anderson, to Frances, Eleanor, Natalie and Ti Coco and I think that's all. Toward 5 Maman put me to bed with a book and sat down near me to read. The prospect was too appealing for me to protest, even if it spoiled my happiness and hurt my conscience to hear Maman washing the dishes all by herself!

Today I was still a little dizzy, but all right. This morning when Maman went shopping in the village, she forbade me to touch anything or do anything, so I amused myself writing my name in the dust on the furniture while reflecting on the inconvenience of the vanity of modern servants. I hate politics and dust, but not other things.

The other things consist chiefly of the beautiful ball gown that came for me, which Maman selected in secret. Oh! It's so, so . . . divine! It's made of tulle, as light as a feather, with a few bits of old rose ribbon and little roses. It is turquoise in color, like the blue of the sky at sunrise or on a beautiful Autumn day. It suits me perfectly and I would like to be as pretty as Emilia thinks I am, to be worthy of it. I think a dress like mine is the kind that the Fairy Queen might wear, or the Clouds on the day that they wed the horizon, at the end of the desert, beyond the ocean, beyond the forest. . . .

Maman received an answer from Enric. He has been sick, poor boy, but his letter is funny. The only P.S. consists of: "Diga a Anaïs que me escriba!!!!!"[1] Notice the number of exclamation points.

8 o'clock. Maman and I are settled in front of a nice little fire in the parlor fireplace. We are hoping that no visitor will come to interrupt our peaceful evening. And while I write sitting on the carpet, Maman is seated in her little armchair, reading the newspaper stories on crime and politics, gossip and Society chatter. You will always see Maman sitting correctly like that, but as for me, look for me on the back of the armchairs, among cushions, on the rug, perched on a table, kneeling in front of the fireplace, or stretched out full-length on my stomach with my head bent over a book. As for sitting calmly and correctly in a chair, I reserve that torture for visits and dances and church. At dinner, I manage to balance my chair on one or two legs. It's more "thrilling"!

"Anaïs, Anaïs, what do you make of Life?" my Maman and my optimistic canary, who follows my every gesture, seem to ask. What shall I answer? Everyone lives his life as he wishes, like the chairs, and up until now I don't put them to their proper use. I certainly know exactly what a chair is meant for, but Life—not yet!

You remember that I have seen Mr. Anderson only once, between dances, among many people, so that's why I hardly remember him! You know me well enough to understand that after each of his letters, I devote 5 or 6 minutes to painting a portrait of him on a mysterious canvas. The canvas is half finished, but it is done in the most brilliant colors. I imagine that he is a true poet, loyal, intelligent, cultivated and not at all realistic, but that last color is inseparable from the richness of the color of poets, I am sure.

Today I tried on my Princess costume and felt such pleasure imagining the parlor happily full of all that little group, my girl friends, my boy friends . . . and one of the things that I did, to get used to the idea, was to go up to Mr. Anderson and talk to him

1 *"Tell Anaïs to write me."*

the way Maman talks to visitors, easily, effortlessly, with gaiety and charm. Oh! I can always talk like that when I am alone!

I could also see Enric flirting (as usual) with everyone, but I know that wouldn't bother me at all, on the contrary. A few months ago I took a strong dislike to Germaine Sarlabous, because by flirting *on purpose*, she forced Enric to kiss her, and now I have the consolation of knowing that I didn't have to force him! But oh! I am becoming terrible! Terrible. I had never thought of such silly things, but I read a book that put ideas into my head. Fortunately, all I have to do is contemplate the fire, almost burned out, to become philosophical again and forget about banter by thinking deep thoughts.

I am almost at the end of another notebook. But oh! how few adventures I will have written if nothing else happens before the last page! To be sure, Maman is definitely leaving for Cuba, but that is rather sad, and I always feel gloomy when she is going away.

Also, if I write so much every day, I will not be able to tell you in here about my 17th birthday! I ought to shorten my chats, but I was born with a terribly long pen instead of a long tongue, and the dozens of letters I write seem like a drop in the water—I always want to write more!

If only you had a tongue, my little diary! You know that there was a sculptor who created a statue that came to life, and people who made a snow-child that also came to life! From one moment to the next, I expect a little movement, a smile. I created you. Oh, become somebody!

January 19. It's snowing again! It is so beautiful that I am tempted to spend my day looking out the window. A terrible thing, when there is so much housekeeping to be done!

Last night we went sledding from 7 to 9:30. Thorvald and Raymond make horrible fun of poor Elsie, and once they made fun of me for wearing lip rouge. I pretended to be vexed, but I laughed with all my heart a few seconds afterward when I saw how upset Raymond was.

Thorvald is just going out to skate. I can see him from here, walking like a man, which makes me think about his long trousers!

Today Maman began to select the things that she will take to Cuba. I would have liked to go with her to have a good time, but I had the sad and ridiculous idea that the stores and all the pretty things in them were causing my attacks of frivolity—and I don't want to have any more of them!

January 20.
Dearest Frances:[1]
I accuse you of something really wicked! You take one of my greatest faults, lack of sense of humor, and disguise it so well that I am now inclined to accept it without trace of dissatisfaction, instead of eagerly pursuing my cure of it. What am I to do if you do not criticize me very severely now and then?

But I have things more serious to talk about than my numerous faults. Frances dear, no, I mean, Dick,[2] what did you ever find out about what is termed the "difference in classes of people?"

(Diff. bet. educated boy and kind hearted boy.)

I have thought long and often on their difference, not taking them personally but generally, because that contrast is so often repeated; and I am a little confused. I would like to know what you know and think about it all. Although it seems so unimportant and useless, it is food for thoughtful ideas, Dick, and it is pleasant to observe the ships that pass in the night, not merely to greet them on the way, but to endeavor to understand the object of their voyage.

Most lovingly,
Linotte

January 22.
Dear Natalie:[3]
If I were near you at this moment I would just stare and stare, and stare—Your Po-Ums are so foolish! Are you offended? No. Remember the fable of the fox and the grapes.

Etc. etc. etc.

I wonder if you could create a poem with the material on hand. (I have not done it before, or ever will, because as Frances says, "I have no sense of humor.")

I have a canary bird. He invariably chirrups about the events of life in the most lighthearted fashion. While he watches all my movements, he seems to be thinking that I am a very amusing person; in fact, my canary bird can be said to be an "Optimist."

[1] *Written in English.*
[2] *Apparently Frances's nom de plume.*
[3] *Written in English.*

I also own a pussy cat. He is always very grave, rather proud and vindictive; all his evil designs on my miniature Caruso are cleverly frustrated, which causes his temper to be of no pleasant sort, naturally. He seems to be saying all day: "I will never catch this infamous bird!" I believe he is a pessimist.

Now, which of the two is the most happy? Which should be imitated by anyone in search of a model for the moulding of his own character? Would you like to be my canary bird, or my cat?

I wonder which of the two is most useful to Society?

I will be delighted if you will answer this with a Po-Um. The person (or thing) to whom it will be dedicated will be allowed to peruse it. A "chirrup" will be the sign of satisfaction from the first party, but I must yet study the signs of a cat's phraseology.

Hoping this confused "Tale of Two Animals" (one of which is a bird) will not cause you any trouble,

I am, most lovingly,

Anaïs

Yesterday I received a letter from Mr. Anderson, or rather Marcus, as he asks me to call him. I read it with immense pleasure, and I was "thrilled" by several very nice phrases: "It remains with you to smite my lips into fuller music, Anaïs."

Only a poet expresses himself like that! I have received four of his poems, and there are three that I like especially. I answered today and Thorvald put my letter in the post box. No other boy has ever written me like Marcus, and please remember that when you judge my enthusiasm!

Thorvald is a bad sort. Can you believe that he had the diabolical idea of showing my letter to Raymond, adding the meanest details to make fun of me. I don't know why, but Raymond got angry.

Tonight we went sledding. Raymond wasn't angry anymore, but he was continually out of sorts when the other boys shouted funny things to me. I am truly "bewildered" by all this banter, all these things that other girls have known about for a long time. I am just discovering them, and it's natural that I should take them quite seriously and philosophically at first, instead of lightly and foolishly, as one is supposed to take them.

And dearest diary, how, oh, how can I explain to you the discovery I made? I am already blushing, but when I think of the wonderful way you keep my secrets, I can tell you this one.

Dearest diary, I am sure, I know by a million signs, that I am not ugly any more! I have left behind the period of straight hair, unruly locks, shiny nose, sallow skin—in a word, all the horrors and horrible features of a schoolgirl—all that is past. At Lake Placid, I began wanting not to be ugly anymore and a little before Lake Placid, I was awakened by Enric—afterward, during the Summer, I don't know what else!

At Dorothy's dance, Martha Boynton told me so, and I over-heard Dorothy Sanders and Dorothy Eddins talking about it. Marcus told me with his eyes! Afterward, "roughly," but it's true, the boys at sledding, Raymond when I go skating, and I don't know who else! I have changed without realizing it. When I was little, I heard Papa say that I was ugly and the idea never left me. I didn't even try to see if it wasn't true until now. It's a miracle of Nature, it's the air and sun, and happiness! And I don't feel an ounce of pride. On the contrary, it's simply another gift from the Good Lord that I don't deserve.

Do you want to know what I see in the mirror when I brush my hair? It's a secret. My eyes are almond-shaped, big and brown,[1] with very dark long lashes. My features are regular, my face a very narrow oval, with a certain something like all the faces in paintings. My lips are very sensitive, but not very red when I don't feel well. The only thing that I like a little is my hair, because it is very, very fine, very smooth, very light and shiny, and it falls to my waist. As for its color, I never know. Rather brown, with red and golden lights, or something. My skin is too white and my cheeks are pink only when I am outside.

It's the pure truth when I tell Maman that, personally, I don't think I'm pretty, and I don't understand people's taste. But it's that strange kindness that everyone shows toward me that puzzles me enormously. What do people think I am? I would like them not to think I am so good, and they would only have to read my Diary to understand all my shortcomings! If they could see me when I have been crying, with tear-streaks in my rouge, they would know I am not beautiful. And yet what pleasure I, a little philosopher, take in the unspoken compliments and the rowdy compliments! It's unfathomable!

I hope with all my heart that this inundation of "worldly thoughts" will pass without doing any damage, and will pass quickly. And yet if I were ugly, I could never know the Great Adventure, my Romance and my Dream! I must still pretend to be beautiful, so that my little "Love" can come in.

January 23.
Little Papa:
I received a letter from Mrs. Quintero. She never fails to refer to the visit to you that she had "the honor" of making, but this time the news she gave me made me sad. She had a post card from you which told her that you were sick. That's how your life is spent— sometimes sick, sometimes carried away in an overwhelming avalanche of work, leading a nomadic life, an artist's life, and always alone; and without meaning to, without realizing it, you

[1] *See footnote p. 65.*

leave those who love you without news most of the time, in sad and vague anxiety about unexpected things and events!

These days, we lead an entirely different kind of life, which lets us devote many hours to writing those who enjoy getting our letters.

I am sending you some other snapshots, one of which will give you an idea of the beauty that surrounds us, and the others an idea of Thorvald's and Joaquinito's games. In my next letter, I will send you others, not yet developed, of me.

One day, quite soon, you will receive an amusing piece of news: perhaps in March Thorvald is going to have his first pair of long trousers! He is so big, as tall as I am, and physically capable of looking like a man. His mental outlook is still childish, and it's his way never to stop his teasing, his practical jokes, his rather gay and lighthearted way of facing life and of living. I smile when I think of *your* first long trousers, *your* first cigarette, your childhood. I used to listen to Grandmother talk about those things with the same enthusiasm I had at that time for fairy tales and stories. Thorvald already knows how to smoke, having no doubt tried it in secret many times, with the enthusiasm of all the little boys in the world! He is already demonstrating a vague ambition to learn to dance, which formerly he mocked abominably, tries to talk to his friends' sisters with a debonaire attitude, without success. It's a metamorphosis, still incomplete, but certain and necessary! And I assure you that my observations about him are rather amusing.

Sometimes I call him a "fop," mostly to see him run to look that word up in the dictionary, but he is far from being one. His head is full of precise reasoning, of normal concepts, just like his Algebra books. He is not endowed with a wonderful imagination, like Joaquinito's; his mind is rather practical and down-to-earth. The result of this bent is his ambition, and you know what it is.

Joaquinito succeeded in writing down one of his compositions. He can't practice very regularly, but his superb talent develops from one day to the next in an astonishing way.

When I try to explain all this to you, I can feel my French lagging behind my ideas, clop-clop. Recently I have come to think that my knowledge of the English language far exceeds my knowledge of French. This is a bit because of my explorations in English literature, which is wonderful. It is much easier for me to obtain English books that satisfy my needs, and rarely do I find books in French, to the point where I have just been introduced to Alfred de Musset by a young American poet! I think in my last letter that

I talked to you vaguely about a young man who is different from the others. Do you remember? Now I receive nice letters from him, and his poems—and thanks to this charming correspondence, we are making the most beautiful trip together through the incomparable land of poets, idealistic dreamers, writers of every kind and of every kind of talent. There is much pleasure in this exchange of thoughts, and he has taught me many new and wonderful things, such as Alfred de Musset, while on my side I have introduced him to Rostand.

I spend a large part of my days answering letters! I discuss philosophical problems with a bluestocking, the horrors of school with a student, and dances, the masculine sex, etc., with my other girl friends. I don't like this last kind of correspondence, you know, but I have to choose between "woman of the world" and what I was before: an unsociable little creature.

I hope I haven't wearied you too much with my commentary. I don't use any Parisian expressions, such as "s'excrimer contre sa trotinette,"[1] because I can't find them in the dictionary. When you have time, Papa darling, write me one of those letters which force me to ask: Why don't they make you a member of the Académie? There are people who all their life have wanted to work in a candy store or become a coachman, a Napoleon or a Turenne,[2] but I have always wanted to become a member of the Académie. But one mustn't regret the Past!

Tell me also if I sent you enough extra letters in my last letter to take care of my spelling mistakes in this one.

In closing, I kiss you with all my heart and whisper a secret: Don't send any more postcards to Mrs. Quintero without sending a dozen to me, for brown-eyed people are very jealous, did you know?

More kisses and love from your

Linotte

I am in bed, feeling very bad. . . . After the letter to Papa, I plunged into the prose and poetry of Francis Thompson, to whom Marcus introduced me; then I read the life of Shelley and reread his poems. When dinner-time came, I was in that strange "trance," like an oppression, inattentive and absolutely transported into another life. Afterward I went up to one of the windows without realizing it, and saw the crowd of carefree children

---

[1] *The modern equivalent might be "to knock oneself out" (with effort).*
[2] *French marshal during the reign of Louis XIV.*

on their sleds. They were shouting with joy and I could hear their laughter clear in here. The contrast between their gaiety and my senseless melancholy wounded me deeply. . . . I shut myself in my room without a twinge of remorse, because Maman had asked us to let her sleep, and Thorvald and Joaquinito are at a Scout meeting.

Marcus once wrote a phrase written by a poet: "Oh! for a life of emotion instead of thoughts!"

But tonight I am more afraid of my emotions than I am of my thoughts. I am so sad I could cry. Perhaps my imagination is overburdened, as this morning I was absorbed by [Martin] Tupper's philosophy. But oh, how precious to me are the hours of solitude. How I love those moments of meditation and dreams!

If I sometimes seem frivolous and gay, it's because I am a woman, but underneath all that, my soul is very serious and very deep! My true nature shows itself in my impressions this evening, my facility for sympathizing with Shelley's idealism, my melancholy because my ideas are based on some terribly sad poems—what do I know? Right now, it would be absolutely impossible for me to go sledding and to behave in that superficial and normal manner, as I have done recently because my passionate emotions were dormant, lulled by the false melodies of apparent happiness. I am full of contradictions; my dreams, my Fantasy are as powerful as my philosophy, my ideas and my ideals.

"My mind is my kingdom." says Tupper, and my kingdom is so big that it has contrasts and discussions, such as there are in every kingdom. This evening all my emotions and my thoughts are united in one vague and powerful sadness.

Yet I already feel the influence of solitude and silence. Little by little, this sensitive spiritual suffering is becoming sweet and beautiful in its bitterness. I can look at the volume of Shelley's works without being blinded by tears. It's true that the wonderful poet is dead and no longer suffers, but what touches the strings of my soul is that I find in his soul the echo of my dearest and most secret thoughts! And it's there, in that echo, that I find the greatest bitterness, an exquisite bitterness!

Oh, Marcus, without knowing it, you have taught me two wonders on the road that I want to travel and know completely. Thank you, thank you!

I have wept with Alfred de Musset and Shelley, and as I dry my tears, I feel that I have learned something and that a few sublime thoughts are worth a few tears!

The irrevocable Today will soon end in deep sleep, and tomorrow morning I will begin to live again. What will I do with that superb day? I don't know. But if I can suffer deeply, then drive away my sorrow, if I can dream, relive my emotions, come out of ecstasy only to fall into confusion and puzzlement, and learn to love yet another poet, as I did today—then I won't regret that day!

January 24. Can you believe that I wrote two poems today: To Fancy. I have been wanting for a long time to write something to explain the delicious charm, the sublime power of enjoying the most beautiful of dreams, the lightest of fancies!

Today the branches of the trees were heavy with drops of frozen rain. Everything was snow and ice, as the rain mixed with snow and hail, an interminable avalanche that fell from a pearl-gray sky. I was ecstatic, dazzled by so much beauty, but happy not to have to go out and struggle against the wind and the cold.

To bring me down out of the clouds, Maman suggested that I do the books, address envelopes and mend socks. Yes, I came down, alas, and a little fleeting idea, a little dream light as tulle, dissolved into needle pricks and ink blots!

One day I ought to write a poem about my feelings when the postman goes by. What waiting behind the curtain, what impatience, what disenchantment! In imitation of my Sir Walter Scott, I have a strange habit of answering the letters I receive with exaggerated promptness. But my friends don't hurry—and I am left sighing every day . . . in vain!

But to tell the truth, I take surprising pleasure in writing letters! I say surprising, because I have noticed that correspondence always seems a boring task for many people. I am sorry when I hear someone say: "Oh, goodness! I have to write a letter!" In almost all my letters, I put a great many little pieces of myself, and I much prefer the distance that separates me from the people I love, because it gives me the right to idealize them, to make them suit my taste—

I notice with pleasure that Marcus answers my letters the day he gets them, but now I am disturbed and I must let a few days go by before answering. If not, our correspondence will come down to a letter every two or three days, and I am always afraid to distract him from his studies, since he is in school. And yet I would be very sorry if it were to come to an end. But why stop? We will write for a long time. Perhaps I will see him again only at dances from time to time, but we can always write and our friendship will become a very sweet and sincere thing, like a special little star in an immense firmament . . . of unknown stars.

I have got into the habit of writing in bed, while everyone is asleep. First, because I am not always very sleepy, and also because I can take advantage of every minute before my little Maman murmurs, through her sleep and dreams: "Turn out the light, fifille!" And fifille turns out the light, obediently, but regretfully!

Sometimes I stop to idle away the time and admire my little Nest. Just this evening, while I was brushing my hair, I philosophized about how easily we have accepted all this comfort which was unknown to us before. I forgot to tell you that we have another maid, Marguerite, and we live like civilized people.

It wasn't very long ago that we had only one little mirror for combing our hair. Now I have four big ones. We used to comb our hair standing up, but now there is a little bench. I had always had just one comb and brush, and now I have the nicest toilet things spread out on my dressing table. What can I say? But oh, how I appreciate those things! That's the difference, the joy of having what we never had! The wealth of the poor!

Goodnight: "Turn out the light, fifille!"

January 25. It's a little late, and I expect the reminder from my little conscience, and from my little mother—but how can I sleep without telling you about the change that is happening to me?

Until now, something, several things, have held closed the golden door of my soul and kept all my poems prisoner inside. No doubt it was cares, the life I led, perturbation; then suddenly, amidst ineffable and peaceful beauty, real happiness, the door has opened—and the world has become a perpetual subject for the most natural expression for me: poetry. Poetry? Yes, I wrote a poem "To Fancy" yesterday—and today another that has no title. And the strangest emotions, the most fantastic ideas flutter around in my kingdom, waiting for my pen's good pleasure!

Just today, I read F. Thompson's definition of what a child is: "little enough so that elves can whisper in his ears."

Dearest diary, I am sure, sure, that if I seem to be almost a woman, I am still only a child! I believe in so many things, I spend an eternity in a moment, and above all, although I seem grown-up, oh, yes! I still hear the fairies murmur. Everything speaks to me, everything is alive—and sublimely simple and beautiful! More than ever, at such moments my heart is a beautiful song. . . .

I am a visionary, impressionable, perhaps peculiar, but I am happy this way—a child in my dreams and my ideals—for how long?

All the strength of my emotions thus awakened will flow into clear little streams, each one murmuring its song through the solemn forests of my deepest thoughts, to brighten, caress, bedew, refresh— It's an exquisite flood, which runs on like that until something stops it—

The night is so still! It seems as though the world is sleeping, while I stay awake, Waiting for Something Wonderful!

January 26. Tonight I am in the grip of an attack of melancholy, and as usual for no apparent reason. So don't be surprised at any of my thoughts . . . it's your way of comforting me.

I had a great longing, an irresistible desire to go out—to brave the cold and wind and go sledding. And I told this to Thorvald, without thinking that his indifference always hurts me. He shrugged his shoulders. Seized all of a sudden by an indefinable sadness, realizing how alone I am because of my unsociable disposition, I fled to my room, like the other evening.

My room is full of books. All afternoon I traveled. . . . I became acquainted with the lives of Coleridge, Burns, De Quincey, Tennyson, Lamb; I fluttered around Tupper, Shelley and Thompson again. Then Keats. It's true that I am unreasonably sad this evening, but I appreciate the Providence that allows me so many peaceful hours to myself. Never have I been able to read so much, write so much, dream so much. To tell the truth, these days seem the happiest of our life. . . . And I can't help smiling at Society's ideas. Maman ran into Mrs. Sarlabous—told her about our moving, and she exclaimed: "But poor little Anaïs, it must be very dull for her out there!"

And Mrs. Madriguera said almost the same thing when Maman telephoned her this evening. Superficial opinion has it that I am isolated. Of course, in the real sense of the word, I have been isolated all my life, through my own fault, and by my own choice—and I haven't yet been able to find a single perfect Friendship, except yours, dearest diary. Here in the country, just as in New York, I flee from people because I haven't the strength to put up with them, but why can't people understand that I am a thousand times happier here? I have no idea!

As Maman's departure draws near, I am becoming positively mournful. Maman attributes my state to every reason except the real one, and I say nothing, for no one can understand my strange feelings and my moods. I don't even understand them myself! No,

I am not joking. I know my faults only too well to joke about them.

I keep seeing the pages disappear and it looks as though nothing "thrilling" is going to happen. I should nickname you simply the Preface to the wonderful contents of another little volume.

I read that Heller said that "true artists are all a little pagan." And I am glad of it. Not that I am an artist, but Papa is, and I have inherited almost all his . . . faults!

Oh, may tomorrow bring me something to dissipate the fog that hides my sun! I am going to pretend to sleep and pretend to wake up soon—for the more I think and listen to the shouts of joy and the bells that proclaim the delight of good health and a light heart, the more alone I feel—terribly alone and to be blamed! I call my dreams with all my heart—here they are!

January 27.
My most Honorable Françoise (Frances): [1]
A foolish girl stood behind a pair of blue curtains, watching the slow movements of a postman as he climbed the slippery hill toward No. 620.

Would he bring the expected letter? The question, personally considered more important than all the phlegmatic politics of this world, was answered most joyfully by the arrival of a blue envelope, rather heavy. . . . The foolish girl was ecstatic and uncontrollably enthusiastic—what not, why not?

O for a letter like yours every day!

I remember once you said that it was when you were saddest that you wrote the "funniest things." All's well as to the description of your book. Wonderful!

You have excited all my curiosity, and that incurable enthusiasm of mine! If you could tell me a little more, just in that spontaneous, inimitable way of yours, just to retain the spell, the fun of it! The illustrations are ravishing!

In exchange for your "raving," I enclose material with unlimited space for improvements. Please put on your spectacles and the gravest of your expressions, and peruse my poetry; please use severity, and all the inhuman qualities of the English critic who at one time accused every great poet of every possible fault. No, seriously, Dicky darling, name the faults and I will be happy. One is needless to repeat, of course, the meter is abominable; but it has always been so with me.

Something in my life, in my surroundings, has awakened the

1 *Written in English.*

dormant emotions. In sunny Spain, I was forever writing, but since I came to New York, something shut the golden door, and my daily impressions were the results of Imagination, but not feeling. Now, dazzled by natural and picturesque country life, with endless peaceful hours of my own to dispose of, I read incessantly, and consequently cover page after page with the thoughts and fancies that flow so easily under the touch of solitude. And yet, such are the ways of the world, that a few days ago Mother was informing a lovely lady-friend of the change in our life and she exclaimed: "Poor Anaïs! It must be lonely for her there!" At this I wrote in my diary: "(Solitude d'hier)."[1]

But you write about melancholy too, so I am wondering if this strange emotion is just a crisis, at our age—and it may pass away.

But here I am, speaking of sadness, when I began my letter with the spirit of an optimistic canary, who spends his day exclaiming: Chirrup! Cheer Up!

I can tell you little more about my poet-boy; but he *does* exist, and a few days ago I was allowed to peruse his poetry and found it very beautiful. He presents me Musset, and I in exchange give him Rostand. Later, I am charmed by Francis Thompson, for which I shall make known to him Alfred Noyes.

You would find a great deal of material and scenery here for a book. This neighborhood is a colony of Youth, devoted to Sport. If this is thought to be a secluded prison, a group of persons should visit it at the hour chosen for sleigh-riding—the moonlit snowhills, and the census would be confronted with endless lists of boys, boys, boys, from fifteen to twenty years, myriads of them!

*   *   *

I must now confess something. Will you tell me if our friendship is endangered by the fact (disgraceful O Shame) that my youngest brother has been expelled from school for mischief?[2] His eyes are a very deep pool of uncertainties; he is now astonishing his family with incredibly beautiful poems! What Fatality seems to unite to Genius such an insufferable capacity for mischief? I know not.

On the other hand, we are seriously contemplating to disguise Thorvald into a deferential pair of long pants! Such a grave step must be celebrated, naturally, and as soon as Mother returns from Cuba, a dance will be created in honor of this, and the arrival of my seventeen years!

[1] *Yesterday's loneliness.*
[2] *For having ridiculed the janitor's Italian accent.*

Then you will meet personally the young poet, the cousin who deciphered your character from your handwriting, the boy who has the education of kindness, the transformation or metamorphose [sic] of a Brother!

*   *   *

With all the love of your absurd, obscure, and abstracted

Linotte

P.S. Do not forget the microscopic criticism of my poetry, with a dash of severity, a dash of truth, and none of kindness or pity.

Dearest diary! Dearest diary! My Romance has come! Seeing my little Love sorrowing in front of the closed door, someone sent him to me with his precious message and I am the one who forbids him to enter. But I can open the door when I want to.

I had written to Frances, I had read and mended stockings, also taken care of Thorvald's and Joaquinito's colds, when toward 3 o'clock the postman arrived with the letter I had been waiting for since Monday—a letter from Marcus. He says that he loves me, O little diary! And his letter is so beautiful, like a poem. . . . Never have I been so deeply troubled, shaken and touched. Still a child in my emotions! But he asks me if I love him—heavens, I don't know—I don't think so, I don't know the meaning of the Love he talks about and in my answer I offer him all that I can give him, *my* love, which is a sincere and deep friendship. He says that I seem to have stepped out of a book of fairy tales, so I call him my Prince, Prince Marcus. Maman liked my letter very much, and I don't know why, she had just the very slightest trace of tears in her eyes. . . .

Marcus is going to become a poet later on, he says—that and many other things, but the last page, in which he writes my romance in letters of gold, that is the one I have reread a hundred times. He is just a boy, perhaps, but what sweetness in those words: "I love you, Anaïs."

It's "My first love"—O my diary—can you understand why my heart is beating so hard? No, I certainly didn't reach your last page without my adventure beginning—the one I dream about with the stars, the clouds, the flowers, the wind, the night—everything and always—Prince Marcus!

January 28. It is always with regret that I give up an old notebook. I put so much of myself into each word and each page. But here is the first page of a new notebook, and yet . . . My diary, I have managed to confide all my thoughts freely to you; you are my best friend on this earth, the most faithful, the most sincere.

On the last page of the other notebook my Romance began! No doubt you will know how it turns out, and yet in this moment the Future is impenetrable. I am troubled by the strangest emotions. I feel as though I have just crossed the threshold of a new world, ever since the moment when I was so deliciously "thrilled" by the Stranger. O dearest diary, if I were allowed to answer the letter from Prince Marcus all over again, I wouldn't know what to say. The tone, the sincerity, the beauty of his letter touched not only my imagination but, in a hazy way, my heart. Never have I been so aware of the presence of that heart that I thought was made of snow and ice. Yes, thanks to my unsociable nature and my reticence, I thought I was far from the emotions that I see in the sufferings of the people around me. I thought I was cold and indifferent. A little philosopher, already wise, and only occupied with observing the passions and dreams of others.

And now my fortress has almost come tumbling down at the first sigh of the breeze that causes so many hearts to tremble! How could I write last night: "I do not love you"? I don't know, because suddenly today the thought came to me that my Prince combines all the qualities of my Ideal. I had never thought of that, never.

And yet something always destroys my dreams. Maman mocks me, Maman says I am a child and that Marcus is a madman. So when I am plunged into grave reflections, Maman's laughter echoes in my ears. In order not to think any more, not to count the hours between posting my letter and the reply, I plunged into the works of Plato and read 100 pages without understanding one word.

I don't recognize myself, and I would give a great deal not to be so susceptible and impressionable. But how beautiful it is to find the keys to Fairyland like this. I have only to murmur very softly: Prince Marcus—and the wonderful stories, the enchanting landscapes, the mystery and inexpressible charm of the Thousand and One Nights unfold before me in a superb and divine procession.

It was warmer today and the snow was all transformed into drops of water. The sun shone very brightly and the beauty of the day gave a faint illusion of the end of winter. I went to the village to do the marketing and dust off Plato's books, out of pity for their inactivity in that nice country library. I did a lot of typing on the machine for Maman the rest of the day. On the subject of Maman's business, she has taken Vicente de Sola as her secretary. At one time I accused Vicente de Sola of being stupid, but as I have become better acquainted with him, I have learned the stern lesson of the injustice of opinions quickly formed. If I don't write any more the things I learn each day, it's surely because I learn too many things. Besides, you will hear about those lessons, as I grow up and perhaps . . . improve because of them.

I am writing tonight to calm myself a little, but it is only 7:30, and so as not to wear your patience thin, I shall go back to Plato. Till tomorrow.

I start out by writing 5 pages. What will become of me at this rate? Without knowing a bit of arithmetic, I still can see that my observations are multiplying.

January 29. How wonderful to read a simple and beautiful book! It was as though I were thirsty and suddenly found a deliciously cool and joyful brook to refresh me. The book is "John Halifax, Gentleman"—a simple book, I repeat, but infinitely sincere. It paints a picture that is neither too ideal to be possible nor a frightful realism and positivism. It depicts the world and human character in general, hearts that are warm and light, healthy sentiments. A certain something that is natural and beautiful. Such a book could convert me to optimism and common sense, even without poetry. Then that same day I read a book sent me by Marcus, Prince Marcus: Poems by Alan Seeger, and the two together form a tableau toward which I feel myself strongly attracted: youth, beauty, the wonders of this little world, love of life.

The other day Thorvald preached me a sermon about how little exercise I get. Walk to the village and back. I told him that in my opinion my health isn't worth two cents and that it's the same to me whether I am weak or strong. I shall never forget his answer, which was unexpected: "Well then," he said, "you should never get married and have children."

I was shaken. I had never thought of that and it was my brother, the more uncomplicated of my two brothers, who lifted the curtain on a world that I had never suspected. . . . Life as a duty, health as a pleasure and for the happiness of others! Oh, how I fear the "Nin" traits! How I struggle against my inclinations. What a powerful force guides my deeds, and how I have been able to overcome the most terrible faults in my nature! And yet here is another one appearing on my horizon, a heavy dark cloud: another form of selfishness.

So I should believe in youth and in physical and moral

health. In life, which is a truly sublime task, since it asks only that one understand and love it. I have a strong tendency toward melancholy, observation, philosophy, toward being shut up in my shell, physically powerless and morally sick. For my mind is unhealthy when it is mournful, always looking out for a strong emotion to make it alive.

Oh, look at the world, made immaculate by the snow and bathed in the sun's rays! Look at my 17 years shining in the Future, a fresh young star! Look at Life, as beautiful as I want to make it! Everything sings, everything murmurs, everything seems glad to be alive. One must laugh or make others laugh. I can hear the laughter of Raymond, who has put on his first pair of long trousers, Thorvald's shouts. They are young, and so happy.

I am young too. I will be happy some day when I have learned how. Just think, who will teach a little philosopher, poet, and linotte to laugh?

Sometimes I think the thing that moves me the most, that makes my whole being sing, that always remains stamped on my heart and soul, is not love but Beauty. That is why I believe that Marcus, like a true poet, loves the Love and Romance in me, and that's all. Perhaps he has already found another girl, because I told him that I do not love him, and perhaps She, the other one, is as much in love with the Beauty of the emotion called: Love. What can I say? I can't think about those things, I can only feel them.

Last night I asked Maman half in jest, half because I didn't know, what Prince Marcus would have done if I had said yes. Maman said that he would have asked me to wait for him. . . . Wait! At that I became so far-away and pensive that Maman had to laugh and break the spell.

We talked about Papa. I wanted to know if Maman still loves him. "Good heavens, no." The indifference of her tone hurt me. I wondered what I would have done in her place. Then with the sincerity that I have inherited from her, I hope, I told Maman that I would have tried to die.

"Ah, no, fifille! What about my little ones?"

Duty again. Oh, heavens, I had never thought about that. Everything on earth seems to turn around a center, the center of the Circle. Apparently, anyone who loses his way loses his balance. Then in spite of what the poets say, Life is scientific? A circle, with a point in the center: Duty. We revolve around it, to the end. Then we leave the circle noiselessly, while the others keep on turning.

February 1. This morning, I put on my Princess dress, not the Fairy Queen dress which is for dances, but the black velvet one. Oh, I looked so pretty, thanks to the dress, that I took it off tonight with regret. Maman was very elegant too, and so beautiful. All this for a visit from Mrs. Thayer, Jack's mother. I hadn't seen her since those days of distress and ugliness, and I saw immediately in her eyes an expression that I catch so often lately . . . and I smiled philosophically, for I mock my "beauty" a little and only believe in it a tiny bit. Mrs. Thayer is going to take Maman's place while she is on her trip, and while they talked together about housekeeping details and about Joaquinito, I let myself have some very sad thoughts. Oh, these absences of Maman's!

The only time all day that I felt like laughing was when my incorrigible little mother talked about Prince Marcus and I saw Mrs. Thayer look almost serious as she asked me not to give Jack up altogether. That tall little fellow who still today doesn't dare to look at me!—just because Maman told him to give me the box of chocolates that he had bought for me and that he tried to leave on a corner of the table without saying a word. Yes, I laughed a long time over that. We spent the afternoon in front of a bright fire in the parlor fireplace, interrupting the conversation for a glass of I-don't-know-what and cookies.

Last night and tonight Maman sat down at the piano and composed waltzes so that Thorvald and I could dance. Thorvald is very strong and dances very well—he picks me up like a feather, and we make up dances that are as fantastic as they are comical. Thorvald is too much a Nin to be a pleasant and friendly companion for his sister, but in some things we are brought together like that by our age and our tastes.

I have been rereading my diary with great amusement, rereading the strange passages in which I tried to explain about waiting for romance, when I believed that everything the books are full of would never happen to me. Oh, it's so strange, the unexpected things the future holds . . . perhaps the greatest mystery of all, since it is made up of the smallest events of each minute, each instant . . . Sometimes I stop and look at a blank page in here and dream about what I am going to write on it some day, in this funny little handwriting of mine. . . . O wonderful future, so strange and impenetrable!

February 2. What a full day. I must begin at the end, to make an excuse for my pessimism. I am sick in bed. It's funny, this sensation that I sometimes have of being so tired, so very tired, to the point that I want to die. That great fatigue is really always the beginning and the end of my illnesses. However, this morning I got up, for it takes a lot to make me admit that I am sick (another of my faults), and Maman and I took the train to New York. Once there, we separated to gain time and get through the long list of purchases. Then at 11 I met a friend of Mrs. Madriguera's, Mrs. José Marti, whose only words in English are "very well," and naturally she needed an interpreter. Instead of Maman, it was I this time who was present during an endless dress-fitting. Finally, when I thought I was free to rejoin Maman, the nice lady invited me to lunch at the Hotel Estrella. I went with her, heavy-hearted, because I was feeling so unsociable that I wanted terribly to run away to Japan. And above all, I knew that I would run into the Madrigueras there.

At 1:30 we were a few steps from the dining room and my heart started to beat and beat like the wings of a frightened bird. I knew before we went in that I was going to see Enric (I am writing all this to punish myself, you see). Sure enough, at my first glance around the room, my eyes met those of Enric. He was so surprised, and so was I! I had wondered so often where and how I would see him again for the first time, Enric whom I had idealized so during his absence. What a disillusionment, that meeting in the dining room of a wretched hotel full of coarse Spaniards, with a family that I had just met!

Oh, but if you could have seen poor Enric! He looked so sad, so unhealthy, so changed! I don't know exactly why, but we were both troubled and apparently unaware of our surroundings. He forgot to let go of my hand, I forgot to take it back. I would have wished him not to look at me like that. I would have preferred his old indifference and carelessness to the renewal of that "softened" glance that remained in my memory when I left for Lake Placid. The lunch took us to separate tables. A headache had taken away my appetite, and more than ever I felt like running away—

After lunch, Enric came to speak to us again. I hope that he didn't notice my impulsive and sincere regret when he told us that he is going to have a throat operation and that he had almost broken his arm in a "boxing" match. I don't think any other boy has ever inspired such pity in me, such a wish to be his sister, to take care of him and protect him, because he really seems like a lost child, with no family and no home. Poor crazy boy, whose bohemian life so many people envy! Suddenly, without realizing it, we were separated, for the Marti family was leading me toward their room. As we went up the stairs, I remembered Enric and turning around, I waved good-bye. He answered: good-bye!—It was over—a prosaic meeting, normal, like everyone else's, all other meetings.

I put into the mail box an answer to Prince Marcus's letter. He says that before sealing his lips on this subject (love), he asks me just one question: Am I in love with someone else? The idea was so impossible that I smiled when I read it and answered that I am in love with Beauty. Instead of separating us, that unites us, doesn't it?

I am very glad that my Prince doesn't want to talk about Love any more, because the other day I read: Love creates love! And I have decided *very* firmly only to love boys as little brothers.

February 3.
Beloved Dick [Frances]:[1]
By my quick answer you can well imagine how eagerly I was waiting to hear from you. I am oh! so sorry about school. But school days are only a passing nightmare for some, and if instead of being a good scholar, you are the most lovable girl in the world, you should not care a whit about your knowledge of the thousand useless and abominable things taught in the so-called buildings of Education. Fiddlesticks are of greater use in the world than any examination!

You may be shocked by my doctrines but I am a living example of the truant's life. Do they teach you the beauties of Nature in school? The indescribable, most wonderful science of the study of human nature? Do they teach you to feel, observe, think, sympathize, love—dream? The rest are nonentities! Oh, Dick, how wicked I am when I talk like this, but even my wickedness is true and unchangeable, and I want you to know the things of which one can really be ashamed. By contrast, your bravery, your efforts, your control over your love of liberty, stand out clear and beautiful! I am so proud of you! Promise you are not ashamed any more, you failed only *once*, once against a long record of good work—

We should go for a walk through Riverside, and we should talk, talk, talk, while the wind would talk too, and the sun shine on the dancing waves of the dark, long River—

I should never forgive you, if by only placing yourself in "corners" of your book, you would exclude one of your greatest gifts (sense of humor).

As to a nom-de-plume, I am sorely perplexed. I beg a little

1 *Written in English.*

time to find one, but meanwhile it would be safer for you to create one—as my imagination often lags behind my good intentions.

*   *   *

Could I but fly with Mother to Cuba, to escape [Mrs. Thayer's] intended reformation in our habits, because, as the kind lady says, "Children, girls like Anaïs, need plenty of house-parties, dances, theatre, outdoor exercise!" And Mother agrees. Pity me, Dick, who love my indoor life, my shelves of philosophy and poetry and nothing else. Will this gay person leave me any time to write? I know not, but I am sure it will take a much longer period than 3 or 4 weeks to rouse me from the ecstasy of peaceful observations and reading.

You ask about my book. You remember all my trials. But now I am quite positive that nearly all my literary ambition has melted into the thrill of actual romance. Oh! Dick—this is a secret—a beautiful dream perhaps, but you know me well enough to know that to me it is True, and I take it gravely. Two boys, both in every way my ideal, have said that they love me. And though both have touched my imagination and form a part of fantastic dreams—my head is just made of snow—which makes Mother say that I am fickle! That is how I think I have discovered that Love is *not* the Great Adventure. Dick, please answer me soon, and keep my secret until you find out what the Adventure is.

Your ever-loving, unchangeable

Linotte

February 4. In a moment like this, I am overflowing with enthusiasm and reflection. I would like to be able to talk with someone, to express what is going through my head. I feel the need to expand. But Thorvald is doing his lessons, Joaquin is sleeping, Maman has her head full of business and preoccupations. And yet I can really say that these days are perhaps the happiest in my Life! Even if no one can plunge with me into a labyrinth of marvels such as Italian Romanticism, and even if I am alone to contemplate that "pageant" of passionate romance, violence, enthusiasm, "throbbing life," "picturesqueness," and the heroism of History, I consecrate these precious hours to those travels and I can unbosom myself in your faithful pages.

It isn't only because of my literary discoveries that I feel the sincerest gratitude to Heaven and to the God who guides my Destiny, but also to my House! I thought of that this evening, for outside the wind is blowing with unusual violence and the snow and cold are more and more severe. And I thought of those unfortunates who have no roof, no fire, no clothing, who are perhaps dying of cold. Oh, heavens, I, who am so weak, so selfish, so unworthy of the kindness that I receive, was reading [Alessandro] Manzoni and [Ippolito] Nievo, huddled over a book of Treasures, holding my breath lest I miss a word, a pearl of an idea, surrounded by comfort and calm.

What shall I tell you about this trip through Italian literature? I think I was as surprised as I was delighted. I discovered that in me there is an Echo of the most diverse thoughts. I learned to analyze my feelings and those of other people. I learned to think, meditate, to try to judge myself, and I learned the names of many of the strange, vague things that in the past only troubled me. Always after a long conversation or discussion, especially with Charlie, I wondered what was lacking in me. That is what used to make Charlie stop suddenly, as though he realized that it was useless to argue certain questions with me. And now here is Manzoni who speaks and illuminates a thing that used to be shadowy and inexplicable: "The visionary as well as the irresolute man are useless participants in a conversation which aims at practical conclusions. That which is possible I generally do not like; that which I like would seem extravagant and untimely to others and would distress me if changed from a fond dream into a concrete action, weighing by its consequences on my conscience. My part in many important conversations can be resumed thus: I object to everything, I propose nothing."

Charlie and I used to talk about criminals and prisoners. I wanted them to be treated differently. But how? I didn't know. Here my impulsive nature gets the upper hand and I would like to write Charlie and tell him what I have discovered. I wonder if, like me, he tries to throw light on the minor problems of human nature. By deciphering like this, by analyzing, I understand myself better, and consequently I understand others better. Thus by uncovering the idea that I am a visionary, I realize at exactly the same moment that Charlie is not! Like a two-sided image.

I have fallen into the habit of "soliloquizing" about such things, and it's about the way I spend my evenings—without feelings of remorse, however, because the rest of the day I perform the tasks of a daughter, a sister, and a secretary.

Another discovery: "As so often happens with men who live intensely the intellectual life, Manzoni was peculiarly helpless in practical matters."

As for my lack of gaiety: "Nievo's idea of greatness is too high, his love of beauty too real, his emotions too genuine for him to joke about them—"

I could go on writing like this all evening. There are times when I would sincerely like to have Marcus near me, to share with him the "ecstasies" that slumber in all these closed books, which awake splendid, illuminated, crystalline at the first touch of light and of our gaze. Literature is so slow, and so quickly turns long and heavy! If one can say of certain people: they talk too much, how is it that no one has ever said: he writes too much! It may be just as great a fault, but such a delightful one! I am convinced that these "Confessions" are like a channel for a flood of emotions that are too powerful to be imprisoned or held back.

In a little while, when I turn out the light, you will go on the foot of my bed with "Writers of Italian Romance." A more worthy companion for a notebook that represents the nature of a "worshipper of Romanticism" would be hard to find!

Oh! I think that Maman's departure is going to be a horrible despair! In the midst of everything I do, her absence is my predominating thought. Then I shall be poorer than the beggar dying of hunger and cold on a winter night, poorer than the poorest of the poor, deprived of sun, light, air—Life—without Maman! I know that if ever her absence went on longer than 4 weeks, 4 months, 4 years, I would die of sorrow. There now, I am crying. All alone in my Nest, my eyes full of tears. Where does so much weakness come from? The Little Flower seems to understand and comfort me.

February 5. For the second time I have written a poem based on an idea developed in my diary. And I really think that "Your Life and Mine" is the best one in my little collection.

The snowstorm which has already lasted two days and two nights is even more violent this evening. The snow and hail fall ceaselessly and the wind is incorrigibly mischievous in the way it makes fun of people and especially old maids, who are horribly embarrassed about things that happen to their hats and skirts. One can only walk slowly, sinking into the snow at every step. A splendid sight. To my great despair, the postman cannot reach the house, and the day passed rather slowly. We went to the cinema and the program was atrocious, so as a consolation I plunged back into my Italian Romanticism and I wrote to Charlie.

Fortunately Maman has delayed her trip until Sunday evening. She has her head full of numbers, my little mother does! I found out today that she is 48 years old. I thought she was at the most 38! I have never seen so much vitality, energy, courage and beauty combined as they are in her!—

Perhaps one of the things that I love the most in Maman is that she is always mocking me. For instance, today I was telling her that when I try to be funny, I become sarcastic, and Maman said that I spend my life like a tragedienne. She didn't want to explain that statement and I have to be content with trying not to think any more about it, but I would really like to know what I am. One day I wrote that I thought the home of Romance is the moon, which shows how far away I thought it was. And I still haven't changed my mind. For me it's simple to reach the moon and look at my cherished dream, but sometimes, oh! dearest diary, I think that I am unworthy of loving and being loved! Prince Marcus is mistaken, but how can I destroy his dream of idealization when I know how attached a poet is to his dreams! Oh, just as I would suffer if he were not what I think he is!

A tragedienne, yes, an actress—if I make people *think* that I am good. How can I present myself before the public without a disguise, since they wouldn't recognize me like that!

February 6.
Beloved Dick:[1]
Joaquin and I are both stretched lengthwise on a carpet, before a cheerful fire, and similarly occupied. You see, in this preference of indoor quietness we are both foolishly alike. But you can well understand why we like to watch these flames! The fire is so warm, just like some friendships! As dazzling as beautiful words, and just as short-lived as dreams! The greater the heat it gives, the shorter the hours of its existence. So very much like the death of a soul that has spent itself in unreturned sympathy or condemned enthusiasm!

I would be very unhappy if you would cease telling me how you feel, just because you seem to be complaining all the time. Oh! Dick, if you always wrote that you are forever placidly happy, I would know that such a life is unnatural for a—poet. And I would not care to tell you how often your emotions are echoed in my heart—I cannot really imagine what is the matter with us *both.* By this poor little poem you can see—it is my life—

But I wish you could share my consolation. Sometimes I

1 *Written in English.*

wonder at its very singularity. For instance, a day passes with the predominant lack of interest, and although, as perhaps you remember, Van Dyke says that such a state of mind is the result of disillusionment, I sometimes think we create ourselves those disappointments, do you, Dick? Well, at the time my little family sleeps quietly, I sit up for hours amidst my pillows and allow all my emotions to flow freely into my little book—unconsciously comparing the happiness of my physical life with the intensity of the imaginary sorrows of my intellectual world. Dick, I have often tried to understand why this seems to reproduce my thoughts and actions into what they truly are, and can only accept the fact that by this analysis I mock myself out of every childish despair and child-like mistake. Then, when the tears come to your eyes, stand before your mirror—this is what I whisper: "Why am I weeping, why? For such a little thing, such big tears!" And then I look so funny, when the tears drop on the pages of the guilty book, I see so much pathos in my eyes for so *little* a reason that I smile—half a little smile, like the unhappy beggar when given a penny, like an artist (very hungry) invited to dinner—or a foolish little girl trying earnestly to be reasonable. (In vain.)

*   *   *

Oh! Dick! I love your "Thru Snow"! You cannot imagine how I can divine your thoughts, the feelings that trace those songs of yours! If I am made, to your belief, as the expression of a *thought,* then you—oh! you, I cannot tell you what you are—you always make me think of action, sincerity, something indefinite . . . as if I had been seeking an author, a poet, and I find it united with a girl, real and lovable. You are as different in your hope—even in this little thing, *you* have a *call* in the midst of your most desolate solitude. *I* am *lulled* by the present sorrow, whatever it may be, just like this:

Your Life and Mine[1]

etc. etc.

Always odd rhythm, but the harmony between my ideas and the correct way to express them is always weaker than the mere necessity which brings them together.

With all the love of your true

Linotte

[1] *A.N. did not quote the poem here.*

Mrs. Thayer is coming tomorrow. I am in despair and feel like running away. Run away? It isn't very easy, for the snowstorm has turned dangerous; they are even afraid of famine.

I am sick, but nonetheless I wrote another poem, perhaps the best one of all. Joaquinito "played" it on the piano and I sang. It was so beautiful that I could hardly recognize the modest poem set to the lovely music!

I was very sad because nothing came from Prince Marcus, although the postman was here, and I thought a long time about the foolishness of answering letters so promptly. The one to Frances is on its way already, with one to Charlie.

I have never seen Maman so tired and yet so happy. And her "goodnight" was much more tender, if such a thing could be possible, as if the two of us realized in that moment that we are going to be separated.

February 7. Oh! I am so sad I could die! Maman is not leaving until tomorrow, but Mrs. Thayer's presence reminds me every minute of what I would like to forget. Outside the snow is so beautiful that I would love to lie in it and go to sleep—

The postman added a tiny bit to my despair and Maman tells me that perhaps Prince Marcus is sick!

Joaquinito is playing my Elegy and Mother sings the words:

> All my lovely dreams are dead.
> Ask the strange strange world today
> Just how or why . . .[1]

And when my dreams cease to exist, so shall I, because I am entirely made of dreams.

8:30. We spent such a pleasant and happy evening that I forgot my sorrow a little and now, while Thorvald resuscitates his violin to give a concert to our little family, I slipped noiselessly out of the parlor to tell you how Mrs. Thayer has entertained us by telling our fortunes with cards. When my turn came, I whispered a silent wish to receive the expected letter from Prince Marcus. Then Mrs. Thayer began by saying that there is a young man who loves me very much and is making me sad without meaning to because he has been very sick, and also is going through a crisis because of his studies or something like that (no doubt his exami-

---

[1] *Written in English.*

nations). That my wish would come true later on, that I would receive another "love-letter," that I would be invited to a dance far away from here. Also that I would receive bad news about Papa and a letter from an old friend across the ocean.

I am not superstitious, but my imagination always is caught by extravagance, madness, and fantastic inventions, like those cards, for example. Then my *mind* (not me) becomes pensive and preoccupied. A little because of that, a little because I am always glad to fly away from conversation and laughter, I came upstairs to chat. And face to face with all the personages in my kingdom, I am surprised to find them so sick—please don't get tired of always hearing me complain. I will get better some day—when Maman comes back. For the moment, everything makes tears come to my eyes, even the devilishness of my little brothers—and when I try to scold myself in front of the mirror, trying to find something funny in the strange depths of my eyes, which are big, so big, with the lashes all wet, and a tear in the palm of my hand. . . . Oh! I know that you understand. That's why I am writing, why I lay open my poor little heart of a tragedienne and a poet.

And my Elegy keeps floating in the air, followed at times by Gounod's Ave Maria, the song that is most like a prayer, my only prayer. I must really be different from everyone else if I prefer a song to a prayer and tears to laughter. . . .

Someone is coming up. I can't think any more, I have to talk—and laugh.

"What are you doing, fifille?"

"I'm writing."

"You write too much, darling."

"No, Maman, I'm finished."

February 8. Maman has gone! The last time I saw her, I was behind a window and she was outside, happy, beautiful, confident. I smiled to see her so gay, and betrayed my emotion only by a quaver in my voice. She had just announced the arrival of a surprise: a phonograph for us to dance to, and her last words (as she traced a circle in the air with her hands) were: "Dance a lot!"

My wonderful little mother! Joaquin was in tears, the poor boy. As Maman left at 5 o'clock, we had dinner quietly by ourselves. Until the moment when she phoned to say just one more Good-bye, good-bye!

But Mrs. Thayer is very nice. She thought of taking us to the cinema to console us. Now we are all in bed and nothing seems different except that Mrs. Thayer is in Maman's bed. Joaquin is very nice, very much impressed by all this, and very calm; he is like me in his way of feeling things deeply, whereas Thorvald laughed and repeated that Maman was going to Cuba to "have a good time."

4 weeks to wait for her to come back. I wonder if I will be as sad and lonely every day—and I promised Maman to be strong. Mrs. Thayer is going to have me have my picture taken to send over there, and I can already hear my large family's comments on the terrible question: "¿Es bonita? ¡No es bonita!"[1]—

I remember having said to Maman that I would rather be poor than have her work so hard, and today she remembered that, saying that she was going to Cuba to make millions for her children, without having to do much work.

February 11. Since Maman's departure, I have replaced my diary a little bit by writing daily letters. But this evening I have a few minutes to myself and want to write. The other day I received a letter from Marcus. The cards were wrong, as he isn't sick but worried about his examination in—Algebra. He had 24%. Oh! how much alike we are. But he knows much more than I, and I can't keep from mixing a little deference and admiration in with my friendship.

I look so funny. I have glasses, like Thorvald and Joaquin— not for myopia but because of a tiny little defect inherited from Papa. However, I was very surprised to see that I am not ugly with big glasses, and I laughed especially when the oculist said that it was a pity to find something wrong with such *beautiful* eyes!!!!!!!!

We all went into town to make some purchases and among other things, I bought a lovely little silk dress the same color as my hair. Mrs. Thayer said that she would like to have a daughter, but it was a consolation to think that I might soon be her daughter! Then I asked what Jack would say to that, and we laughed together. I like Jack enough to think that I would like to have a sister so that he could marry *her*, and then we would be good friends, but as for myself, I will only be the wife of my Shadow, my Ideal.

In the middle of so much care and kindness, I don't feel so alone and sad.

St. Valentine's is drawing near. It's a very gay, very Ameri-

[1] *"Is she pretty? She's not pretty!"*

can, very nice holiday. I am sending cards to: Maman, Frances, Prince Marcus, E. Madriguera and—no one else. I wonder if anyone will think of me—like that, for fun.

For the first time, my glasses hurt me a little, and instead of writing, writing, writing, I am going to think and sleep.

Without glasses

Mrs. Thayer says that the space between my eyes, which is so wide, resembles the statues of the Virgin Mary. To write the bad things along with the good, Thorvald says that I look horrible in glasses! And that I am going to lose all my "sweethearts"! And that I have red hair! Oh, Thorvald doesn't mind saying what he thinks, ever!

On the subject of compliments, dearest diary, I am a horrible girl. I am so ashamed of my feelings that I don't understand how *anyone* can love me—I feel real, sincere pleasure when Prince Marcus writes of Joaquin: "I am sure he is only less beautiful than his sister!"

I feel as though I were a flower and that such words are like the sun, which warms me and makes me grow, live, smile! It's so beautiful to hear something nice about yourself, to see that others believe in you—and I am so ashamed, so ashamed to be happy because of it. Instead of always withdrawing into myself, there are times when I come out of my shell, when I expand, because of kind words, compliments, sympathy. And I am happier outside my shell and I wish that there would always be enough sunshine outside so that I could come out often and stay a long time.

It will soon be my birthday. Ah! I have waited so long to be 17! You will find that I am still a child in millions of things, serious only because my shell is so deep, but ready to dance like the specks of dust in the slightest little sunbeam that manages to slip in. . . .

February 13. I have no one with whom to share my excitement and joy, because both are completely unreasonable. But here it is, dearest diary, the résumé of my day: We had photographs made of my crazy little self—yes, of *me!* They did my hair, posed me and arranged me so well that I was beautiful. I wonder if the portraits will come out well. Just think that they will be the answer to the traditional question asked by Papa, Grandmother, all my friends, cousins and aunts. And they will see what a grown-up young lady I am. Prince Marcus has already told me the strange secret with his eyes, with his pen—he and others. But today I was more em-

Avec toute la tendresse
de ta fiffille Anaïs

Avril 1920

barrassed than ever. They turned me this way and that, measured my lashes and my eyes to judge my profile, the color of my hair and I don't know what else. And to my great despair they kept saying, out loud, in front of me, all the time: that I was beautiful—?!!! Especially that I looked nice in the little blue dress with ruffles, the one I have worn so much, and my chignon of curls. At one point they gave me a bouquet of roses, another time a piece of tulle, and a rose in my hair, another time they wanted me standing with my hands behind my head. The hardest thing for me, because of my timidity, is to smile and look animated. It's really easier for me to be sad and pensive. Perhaps the thing that gave me most pleasure was when Miss Levins[1] said that she could tell, from the expression on my face, that I love reading and writing, and when they said that I look a little like the poet I love as much: Shelley.

I am always very disturbed when someone says something nice, as though I didn't deserve to have people think I am good, I who know so well that I am silly and childish, and scatterbrained and vain and frivolous and mean and spoiled and extravagant—etc. etc. I can't write what Mrs. Thayer said to me today, it was so unexpected and I was so embarrassed! But in truth I realize that in spite of my appearance and my efforts to look like a "young woman of the world," alas, I am not at all blasé and am very "old fashioned," as if in reading all the books I have read there had developed in me a strange mixture of all the qualities and faults of little girls of other centuries, which have become a part of myself. I have often felt that difference, which is the greatest cause of my sudden retreats into my shell . . . and Nature has played its little part as well by adding to my scatterbrain the traits of the little girls in paintings. . . .

What will Papa say? Will he think that I am still his "ugly" little girl?

Frances says that her diary is not going anywhere, because she finds it amusing to laugh about things that happen, but not about what one thinks—whereas I mock everything about myself and all that I think, if a linotte can think, and I entertain myself, I entertain myself—Oh! I laugh all by myself—I am happy, but so alone, so alone—I who would like always to share my troubles and my joys with someone, and for lack of someone, I accept the company of some *thing*, like you.

Tomorrow is Valentine's Day! I wonder how many people

[1] *A friend who accompanied A.N. to the studio.*

will think of Miss Linotte. I think that I talk and think so much about myself because I haven't found someone who will do that, while I think about someone else. Oh! Life is entertaining when one is timid and not blasé, when one's head and heart are full of questions at 17, and full of answers at 40—I have hope, and later I will have certainty—rather sad, I'm afraid.

February 14. This evening I hurt, I hurt. Oh! so much, so much! Once again it's a feeling of sad and absolute loneliness—and without any reason. I can't sleep and would rather write.

I answered Marcus's letter. I wanted so much to talk to him as I talk to you. Oh! I am sure he would understand, but since I can't, I sent him two poems.

My photographs came. I can't explain the feeling they gave me. All those pictures are not me. I only see someone who looks pretty, charming, and strangely like everyone else—just a girl. My profile is clear-cut and perfect—Mrs. Thayer says so; but now suddenly I think: that's the way I look to everyone. Everyone sees me as I am in my photographs, not my ideas, my fantasies, my dreams, my observations. Another day I wouldn't have thought of that, but tonight I am bad and I see things wrong side out, so I smile, almost mocking— And yet a few minutes ago I was writing almost joyfully to Maman to let her select the picture she likes, and I looked with a feeling of pleasure I had never felt before at the strange "me" who is not myself. But it's always like that; at present the things I do during the day change me, but when evening comes, I think, and when I think—I weep.

I received a very pretty blue Valentine, a very nice one. Mrs. Thayer says it's from Jack. But it was the only one, and today more than ever, I would have liked so much to have someone else think of me, as if that would have healed the pain in my heart! I want to die, yes, for I am ashamed of myself and my thoughts, which are always so useless and egotistical—and I feel so small, so weak and so alone without Maman. Yet everyone is nice, and happy—and that's just why I feel out of place everywhere, except in my shell.

February 17. I was going to write last night but my eyes were full of tears and I preferred to think. Tonight I was the same way—so alone and so "friendless." So I went close to Mrs. Thayer and asked her to let me kiss her goodnight because I felt so sad without Maman. Mrs. Thayer kissed me so willingly that I went away almost comforted. It was she, too, who gave me the idea of writing a poem for Maman on my birthday, and I wrote one of the best things I have ever written or will ever be able to write. Mrs. Thayer cried, and I noticed again the strange power in what I write to touch someone to the point of tears. I wonder why.

Doubtless you have noticed the long time that I have let go by before I answered Marcus—and today, while my letter is on its way, I received a letter from him asking why his Princess is silent. With the outgoing nature and the confidence that I feel with certain people, I explained all that to Mrs. Thayer. She told me that she has been worried about the letters I receive because they are going to do me harm—and that it's all "rot." Yes, there is the difference between grownups and children: she doesn't believe in them and I *do*—

However, I told her that none of Marcus's letters could change me—that I will always remain what she calls me: "a little old lady"—and a little old lady can't be romantic, isn't that so? That made her laugh, because she means that I am old in my occupations and my ideas, my little responsibilities—and my childishness.

There are two new things in our family—a phonograph and Jack. (Remember my birds and Enric, and you will understand that combinations like that are a habit!)

The phonograph is a gift from Maman! It's wonderful for dancing, dearest diary, although much, much too modern to be artistic—and dancing has the wonderful power of making me human—that is, happy! Jack is here with us for a while. Now he often dares to look at me—and we dance together—but I still can't get used to the color of his hair!!

I have talked so much to Mrs. Thayer about Eddie Sanchez and Charles that she asked me if I would ever marry one of my cousins. Good heavens, no! But I am very glad that Eddie especially is my cousin because this way I can love him very much and I don't have to marry him. Oh, Lord! I who have so little interest in getting married!!!!

Dearest diary, I am writing nonsense to try to be gay, but really, really, I am so miserable! I hope Maman will understand that I put my whole heart into "Mother Darling"—but I wouldn't want her to weep. I wrote it so simply with so few changes to make, so little thinking to do, that it's very natural. If someone else had written it, I would like it even more. Luckily, I am very severe with myself.

I am very upset by the opinion Mrs. Thayer has of me. And when I told her that I don't want any gifts for my birthday because I don't deserve them, she answered that by being so modest, I am not being truthful!

If people could read my diary, eh! What would they do to me? Would I be hanged, or decapitated?

Dearest diary, do you think if Marcus knew me better, he would stop loving me? (or *thinking* that he loves me)??

For this evening—

Exit Princess whom no one can make laugh. She will be given in marriage, with half the kingdom, to him who can cure her.

Triumphant entrance of the hero: Anonymous!!

February 18. Do I feel like laughing? Not at all. I spent my day writing, then wanting to have someone near me to read what I had written. I would like to be Dickens to draw you a picture of Mrs. Thayer. I like her very much, and yet I am afraid of her. She mocks a little cynically—she doesn't like what I like—to me, she represents a "woman of the world." What disturbs me is that she was once like me, a young girl who believed in almost everything; then suffering, her experience with the world and with people changed her. She told me that I too will grow up and learn—

"Is the world really full of bad people?" I asked her.

"Unfortunately, yes! But keep your dreams as long as possible."

"Don't you have dreams any more?"

"Oh, yes! We have different dreams at my age, dreams that guide our actions."

We talked for a long time. I learned that people are different outside, indifferent and cynical, to protect their sensitive feelings and their impulses.

Mrs. Thayer is still young, inclined to be stout, and has a florid complexion; she has very beautiful red hair; her eyes, which are almond-shaped, dance and sparkle; sometimes they are green, sometimes brown. She is affectionate and generous, with amazing powers of observation and discernment; stubborn and sure of herself, capable and well educated. But I never know when she is going to mock me, for she is gifted in the same way Frances is—and I don't dare argue with her because she dissects everything with bits of logic and reasoning that she offers me slowly but surely, and the result is that I am forever perplexed, the way I was when I studied algebra.

So today I wrote letters to Marcus that I will never dare to send, but which calm me, as if he could really understand my strange Desert, my moral solitude—and could cure me. I think I have never respected any boy so much, except perhaps Enric, and yet 20 times a day Mrs. Thayer tries to lower him in my opinion. She doesn't like the poets he likes, and tells me why, nor the poetry that I showed her one day with pride: "God's Handiwork."

But I am a young girl—she is a woman. . . . Ah! How sad it must be not to believe in anything! And yet I suffer so much, so much, every day with the destruction of my idols. But while they are still standing, I adore them—

I feel great and true happiness in the "fellowship of those who feel"—and why reason, and think, since nothing can change an emotion except its complete destruction.

Maman wrote us a few hurried, tired lines. It seems as though she has been gone a year.

February 19. Little surprises are being prepared for my birthday—and I enjoy that. For the second time in my life, I went into town to the hairdresser, who made me as beautiful as a fairy. . . . Then we had lunch at Macy's, where I saw Eleanor's mother in a "waitress's" uniform. She looked very sad and very tired—and I wanted to hug her and tell her something very nice—only I am too afraid of my impulses to let them rule me, never knowing whether I am crazy or purely "linotte."

I guessed from the way Joaquin looks—an incredible mixture of fun, mystery, and . . . regret—that he has spent his money on me. I heard him tell Mrs. Thayer to buy me a little cardboard theatre so that he could play with it too!!!

As all the desks are occupied, I am writing in front of my three mirrors—and after every other word I look at myself with surprise. Really, this time, I look like my photographs, not like myself: not dreamy, distracted, very useless, and melancholy, but simply Miss Seventeen, superficially agreeable, with a fashionable hairdo and the features of a "little old-fashioned girl"—and the "linotte" that everyone thinks is so well behaved!!!

All right, no more coquettishness! I am becoming impossible, and vain to boot!!!!! It's the hairdresser's fault!

I would have liked to take you over there, for fun. Listen:

Act I

Enter a small fat lady with an unattractive hairdo, no powder at all, white hair, etc.

Hubbub of curling iron, bottles, pots of cream, electric machine, etc. etc.

Intermission

Act II

Exit a young woman. slender, tall, red-haired, curled, powdered and painted—

The End

That is called a "Beauty Parlor." And if ever anyone said that beauty is skin-deep, they could also have said, quite truthfully, that certain kinds of beauty are cream- and powder-deep.

Joaquin turns the bed into a battlefield, so if I stop suddenly in the middle of a tragedy, you will understand. It won't be for lack of ink, for I am using an antique inkwell instead of a fountain pen, as the latter's attacks of paralysis disturb my most fantastic ecstasies!

I could really write a book about the people I see on my little trips. But I am not Dickens—not even myself. I often have the feeling of being alone on a mountain-top, detached from other people, as I observe them. But I often mock myself, too, when I feel so very young and when I think that everyone mocks me!!

Here is an old lady whose faded hat flies away in a gust of wind and snow. She cries out, runs after it, then stops, runs in front of an automobile, draws back, cries out again, stamps her foot. A young man decides to help her, and bravely fishes out the hat, two feet away from a car, and brings it back with a smile.

You are expecting: Thank you, sir! Not at all.

"Good gracious, man—couldn't you pick it up when it first fell down? Look at it now, all mucked up and muddy! Oh, dear! Oh, dear!"[1]

And she goes off muttering, while the young hero scratches his head, then puts his hat back on and goes into a shop to console himself with an "ice cream soda."

Here is a lady who is buying shirts and neckties! A young man who is embarrassed in asking for a "boudoir cap" and silk stockings. And a little girl who yells out in the middle of the store: "Mommy, do *you* want a doll for yourself, too?"

There are always angry people who make everyone else angry too, people who hold the door open and those who let it slam

[1] *Written in English.*

in their neighbor's face, at the risk of making a moon of their visage by flattening the nasal promontory—and there are sales-ladies who sell nothing because they want so much to sell some-thing, and the people who don't buy anything but touch every-thing. I have noticed that smiles are as rare as sugar was during the war, and rebukes as numerous as the "hand grenades."

There is a little man at the station from whom all the people want to buy their tickets, because he seems so happy, as though he were having a good time. Someone asks him a stupid question: he smiles. They repeat it: he smiles. They get angry and insult him: he smiles. He says "good morning" all day long in such a positive way that everyone is sure that it is really a "*good* morning," even at 9 at night.

There are always those in the crowd whose glance I fear—students who look at you as though you were a clown, who look back after you have passed, who follow you, smiling— Then I fix my eyes on the pavement. If I look up after a long time, there they are, sometimes, often, the same ones—frighteningly *stupid!!!* What I can't explain and don't like is the way they look at you—even after I straighten my hat and look at myself quickly in my little mirror, where I see that I look all right, really all right. Poor people! They want to be so friendly and pleasant that I avoid them like the plague.

For example, I go into a store: a strange creature holds the door, looking as though he had been cut out of a catalogue showing the latest fashion for men. I walk by. "Thank you very much."

"You're quite welcome, Miss. Is there anything else I can do for you?"

"No, thank you." I walk away. He bows deeply.

"Good-bye, Miss."

"Good-bye." And all that just to walk through a door!

February 20. I was surprised today by a letter from Marcus in which, to my great joy, he corrected my poetry. Yes, I would have regretted it if he had been blinded by indulgence. But I am always surprised by his letters—they are always different, and I am never finished asking myself what he is like.

I came out of my shell to dance with Raymond, and Jack, and Thorvald—but I went back in immediately to rejoin Tennyson, Pope, Coleridge, Cowper and Milton. You know me well enough to understand that I preferred the hours of reading and study. . . .

I have been forbidden to go downstairs for lunch until I am

given permission. Everyone looks mysterious—and I smile several times a day—

I was going to write more, but there is a poem floating in the air. Quickly!

February 25. These days of silence mean that I exhausted my gaiety in daily letters to Maman and my energy in a sudden attack of absent-mindedness and its *results*. It's true that I am 17 (and we celebrated my birthday with lunch in the city, theatre— "Mamma's Affairs"—beautiful gifts, and joy), but if I thought my age would make a difference—oh, despair! I have been very unhappy because yesterday, out of a check for 40 dollars . . . I lost half. Think of my *shame!* I *vaguely* remember having been to the village and walking from one shop to another with my mind somewhere else—dreaming of something—my head full of a poem that I had just learned, "Ode to Tennyson," and of Marcus —deep in thought—and I lost 20 dollars, just like that, like a handkerchief. I was almost sick with shame—my cheeks burned all day long and I didn't dare to stop being busy for a second lest I think about it again. Oh, heavens! to be so heedless, at Seventeen! I worked like mad that day—sad, repentant—unrecognizable, in a word—

Then this morning, I was given 5 dollars to do the marketing and I left, holding my pocketbook in both hands with all my strength. I went to the butcher's—scolded him in my own way (an absurd reproof) for having given me mutton the other day instead of something else—and he answered that he wouldn't do that because "I was too nice." Picture: I was embarrassed! Besides, when I was ready to leave, he said to Joaquin (and I heard him!): "Some kid, your sister!" I was even more embarrassed, went out (still holding onto the pocketbook tightly, tightly!), and when I went to pay for something, there was the pocketbook in plain sight, but the *money* had disappeared! *Twice!* 25 dollars! At seventeen! I thought that I would really go crazy. Joaquin, with his kind heart and incomparable imagination, suggested saying that it was *he* who had lost it. And at first, in my confusion and despair, I agreed to the diabolical idea of asking the vegetable man to lend it to me and pay it back another day. Then the phantom of the "Nin lies" rose up before my tear-blinded eyes—and I led Joaquin home. He ran ahead and began the story, I rushed in and my lips blurted out the truth like lightning! "I lost the 5 Dollars!"

Surprise! Heavens! Then I *cried*—and Mrs. Thayer stopped

her work to give me a lecture and confessed that I had dropped the money in the house before leaving.

Again today, I worked furiously in the house, thinking frequently of how fortunate it was that I had told the truth, and of Mrs. Thayer's words, so sweet, so patient. She says that the world is practical and that dreams don't serve any purpose! Perhaps the only thing that I can't forgive her is that she says that Marcus and his letters do me harm and turn my head! They make fun of him, my brothers—Jack . . . and perhaps because I am not used to it, perhaps also because I take everything so seriously, their ridicule hurts me very much—very, very much.

In the evenings I write in my little room, using the rhythm of a poem to drown out my eternal prayer for love, sympathy, advice, an audience for my poor poems . . . all of which I deserve so little but need so badly. I find in books everything I need to delight my solitude, but they don't teach me to live. Rather they help me to enlarge the scope of my other life of fantasies and perfect beauty—and they don't *love* me, for all my love for *them* —and at my age, my heart seems more than ever like a sunflower, always turning toward the light and warmth for more strength and force of character, for more beauty and wisdom.

On an impulse to confide in something, I wrote two poems about . . . Love. But I would never dare to show them, lest I make myself ridiculous.

February 26. They are forecasting a huge snowstorm, and I stood at my window a long time, in a state of ecstasy at the sight of the sky. Oh, what a scene! Great silver clouds floating on a pink background, and a few soft gleams of turquoise-blue joined with the last fiery rays that follow the setting sun in its glorious departure!

It is still very early, but I am allowed to choose what I want to do because I was very industrious (that is, *almost* industrious) at my tasks, so I am curled up on my bed. My bed is a veritable kingdom where I love to take refuge. It is so white and so blue, so soft, and it serves as my observatory because from here I can see all my surroundings. . . .

Yesterday I forgot to mention the letter from Charles. Words to express what I think of him fail me. This is an idol which is breaking with a great crash! I knew he was materialistic, absolutely lacking in imagination, but not indifferent and bitter. Also he classifies poets and idealists in with the bolsheviks, socialists, radicals and other horrors!

After dinner. This evening Papa's spirit is in me. I know intuitively that Papa is sometimes sarcastic, skeptical, pessimistic and sullen without any reason. . . . Well, I am in the midst of an "attack." Let's try to work through it together—

I looked at myself in the mirror but didn't see anything to laugh about. . . . Only my eyes showed, immense and somber, mysterious and grave. Then I scolded myself: "Now, Anaïs, what is the reason for this state of things? Let's see, they make fun of Marcus—well, that's the fate of all my poor friends! And then? Maman is so far away! Yes, but that's necessary, and she will be back soon. And then? Nothing."

So I am writing in my diary to cure myself. Thorvald is getting so strong! As a game, he carried me from his room to mine as though I were a feather. Also he dances as well as Eddy, Enric and Marcus—and together we make a very good "couple." Jack is learning to dance and I often dance with him, and with Joaquin. Dance has a magical power to make me happy, and tonight I was fine until we were all together around Mrs. Thayer's bed to talk, and I wanted suddenly to run away. Also a great desire, a "longing for a little bit of love," as the song says.

I am reading "True Love" by Shakespeare and "True Love" by Cowper, and having many thoughts about the beautiful lines. I feel all alone on my Observation post. A long time ago, I thought that observing and judging was my only choice, my preference. But now I feel alone and selfish at my post and I prefer to mix with the crowd, and to live, suffer, cry, laugh, love, die with it, and above all, above all, to alleviate people's miseries—increase their happiness. Oh, if I marry my Ideal whom I have not yet found, I want him to think as I do about my beautiful dreams of charity . . . and not have a speck of selfishness in him!

February 27.
Dearest Papa:

*   *   *   *

There is a dreadful invention, very modern in its *profanation* of Art, but indispensable to the gaiety of a young family. It is very squeaky and not very gifted for harmony, but universally admired—an invention, in a word, that Maman has always hated but that we have finally introduced into the family circle as a toy. It isn't beautiful but it is fun. I mean a Phonograph!! I am going to give you time to recover. . . .

I can assure you that it is very amusing to see the effect of the years on all of us. 5 years ago, Thorvald, Jack and I all went to the same school; we were always together on the same bench, in front of the same desk, scolded, or complimented and praised in the same breath by the same teacher. In those days, I was anemic and ugly, Jack was shy and awkward, Thorvald clumsy. What a picture! Five years later! Thorvald and Jack distribute compliments without blushing, dance without destroying my pretty shoes, talk about girls with a knowing air. It's enough to make you laugh a long, long time!

However, we are not always mad. We dance just a little after . . . (reading, sitting around the fire, lessons). I write poetry in English and my poet friend corrects them, for his talent, it seems to me, comes very close to being that of a genius, although you can imagine that he is very young! If you understood English I would send you my little collection, but it isn't very good, you know, and I prefer you to imagine me simply as a young woman and not as a poet—a young woman without talent, who writes poetry between the lines of her "Menu"—at seventeen!

At night before I go to sleep, I always write in my well-known little Diary—my observations about people—but not at all, as Charles says, as a *spectator*. Oh, no! I am too fond of my little world and the little people in it to mock, to avoid sharing their miseries with all my weak intuition, with all my sympathy and tenderness. No cynicism and doubt at seventeen! I believe in almost everything, so I write what I believe and I write about what destroys my beliefs—and that's life.

Dearest Papa, you seem like a distant dream, etc. Sometimes I dream that you are very lonely in your little house, with no gaiety, no noise, and no one to share your worries or your joys, no one to take care of you, little Papa, and I feel the doubt, the sad realization that I know you very, very little.

That and many other things I don't understand, and won't be able to understand for a long time. Sometimes I think that if I got married and such a misfortune happened to me, I would want to die. But I know I am not brave—never am, and that such things are inevitable and unexplainable.

But even if an Ocean separates us, a letter has wings to tell you that I love you, my little Papa—and the one who sends you a kiss is your daughter, as well as your

Linotte

P.S. Write a little bit. It is the only proof I have that you are real, and I need that so much.

A.

February 29. The days that have passed without my writing were days of "attack." I went to bed early so that I would sleep instead of think. I keep very busy all day long so as not to think. It's unbelievable how much I miss Maman! And Joaquin, oh! Joaquin is so naughty! He is always good with and in front of Mrs. Thayer, but later he and Thorvald tease me until I cry. Then when evening comes, I am nervous, sick and unhappy. Maman doesn't write; I can imagine how much work she has and I hope twenty times a day that everything will go well for her.

Last night we went sledding with a young friend of Mrs. Thayer's and Jack's, and there wasn't enough room, so one person always had to stay at the top of the hill and wait. I was so detached that I enjoyed staying up there more than the ride down. Afterward we danced.

Several times during the evening Mrs. Thayer told her goddaughter that I am crazy about clothes, but it was not as a joke, and that hurt me so much, so much! That made me remember the opinions of the Sánchez family and Godmother—yes, with bitterness. A few years ago I didn't care at all about my appearance—luckily, since Maman couldn't always give me pretty dresses. Then everyone complained that I was so ugly, so countrified. I always took pleasure in observing "stylish" people, well dressed women. . . . Then one day, I can't say exactly when, I began to take pleasure in being well dressed, and I discovered that I could wear my hair like a picture. It's true that Maman spoils me with dresses and hats, and I am learning very suddenly that I am no longer ugly. Now people are angry, as though it were a fault, and criticize my "coquettishness."

Perhaps it's because I am in this state of mind that a simple accusation seems to me so unjust, but I know, oh! I know that it isn't *bad* to take a few minutes to put on one's hat, to glance in my little mirror from time to time, to consider it a pleasure to be carefully dressed and agreeable, in order to please others. Why should it be a fault? All the girls I know, all of them, are like this, and much worse than I, a thousand times worse . . . and no one criticizes them—and besides, if I can't have a little fun now, I will never be seventeen again, never again. I think that grownups don't ever understand those little things, and I am sure that they were like me when they were my age, but now they want us to have their virtues, their cynicisms, their indifference. Oh! I don't care what everybody thinks! They call me a coquette? They do, eh? Well, fine, a coquette I am. I must tell that to—to Marcus. It's another fault that I am afraid he doesn't know, and perhaps because of it, he won't love me any more. But I will not have false modesty, no, no, no, and as long as I can *look* pretty, I will pretend to be pretty, and I will always be happy to have a new hat and a new dress—

Oh! heavens, how bad I am today. And that's not all. Marcus may write "rot," may be a scoundrel, a bandit, etc. etc., but I, Miss Linotte, I don't believe a word of it and I count the days between the departure of my letter and the arrival of his. Yes, I count the days, and I am not a bit ashamed, and if I knew that I were going to see him the next minute, I would run to my room to put on *powder* and arrange my little curl on my cheek, and I would wear the perfume I like even if the whole world considers it detestable. Bad . . . Oh, yes! From now on I am going to be as bad as possible. "What's the use of trying to be good?" They call you coquette, etc. etc.!!

And do you know what I did today? I went to Mass and didn't pray because Raymond was sitting in front of me and kept turning around to smile. Never mind, never mind. Oh, yes! When we were walking home, I gave him a very coquettish Good-bye.

From now on, I will write down all the crimes I commit and that way you will know the kind of little baggage that I am. Poor Linotte! Now I really feel like crying, only it may be just coquettishness—and the funniest part of the whole thing is that I haven't the slightest idea what coquettishness is!

I vaguely remember Germaine, who kissed her fan and used it to give a little slap to an insect called "Lover." I know that she was always dropping her handkerchief and her fan, and she fluttered her eyelids and used a voice completely different from her usual voice during the entire dance. Whereas I have never done such things, and the whole business bores me. . . .

To pass the time, we have started a terrible newspaper: "The Snowbound Chronicle." I am going to keep busy with that now, instead of with all my worries. After all, the world is an amusing place, isn't it? Especially when one is a "coquette"!

March 3. I have just reread these last pages and am astonished by my cynicism. But I think that I sometimes become grumpy when I am sick without realizing it. Mrs. Thayer admitted to me that I haven't been myself these days, but said it was perfectly natural and that many people are on edge every day of their lives, whereas that very seldom happens to me. At present I feel nicer.

Yesterday I received a little letter from Marcus. I am a little bit put out with him because, by delaying like that, he made me do something that I am now ashamed of. Oh! If Maman had been here, I would have asked her and would have learned to control my impulses. But Monday when I came back from New York, I saw there was no letter for me and since I count the days, I thought that Marcus was sick, so I hurriedly wrote a note and, without thinking for a minute, I sent Joaquin to put it in the postbox. It was only later that I dared to ask Mrs. Thayer if I had done right. To my great distress, she explained that Marcus was going to mock me and that I would lose his respect! I was miserable during the night, thinking that perhaps I might be able to get the letter back. But the next day brought me a letter, and the news that mine had already gone. I always regret the scatterbrained things I do!

Yesterday was a wonderfully full day. We made some purchases, we had a soda, went to the Rivoli, had dinner at the Riggs, saw the show at Daly's, then had another soda and took the train! Mrs. Thayer told me the history of the Daly Theatre—how in her day the richest people went there and walked about the galleries in evening clothes. Now it is old and badly kept up. The whole theatre will soon be torn down because it is in the way.

Today we were quieter. Only a visit to the village, a ride on the sled, taking snapshots because the day was divine, like a spring day; received a letter from Frances, wrote letters to Maman, Godmother and Aunt Anaïs, and ordered only six photographs, to my great sorrow. It is quite cold this evening, however, and that is why I am not writing in bed. We have little kerosene stoves to give a little extra heat, because our coal is almost gone.

I can't read anything at all. I sew on curtains the whole blessed day and take great pleasure in seeing how pretty the house is becoming. Aunt Helen (Mrs. Thayer) asked me to read Marcus's letter to her and she judged it very seriously: he is a "gentleman," writes very well, but the tone of his letter shows that he is very pleased with himself. That is one of the things that I admire in others, because it contrasts with my own self-doubts. Then Mrs. Thayer told me that she would be very sad if I became Marcus's fiancée without getting to know other young men, without traveling, without taking time to grow up and learn. I tried to reassure her on this point. Oh! I am too romantic not to dream, not to be "thrilled" by every word, and not to want with all my heart to see Marcus again— Yes, I like him even better than Enric, I think, but I don't love him—and that's all there is to it! Yet I feel growing in me a great desire to love and be loved, as in stories and books! Always that Ideal, that Phantom that I have created—I am still waiting for him, although I don't know his name; but that doesn't comfort me at all, and I often wonder what it is makes me want to love anything at all, anyone at all, and to be loved. I have Maman, little Maman, but besides her, I always seem to love more deeply than the others love me—and to suffer when they change and turn their backs on me.

Oh! How I regret that confession that let Marcus know that I count the days and that his letters please me. He is going to mock me—and yet, I believe he isn't like all the other boys, and perhaps he takes those things as seriously as I do.

March 7. I received the letter I was expecting from Marcus and a book for my birthday—it was the book I wanted most and that he bought for 10 cents in that little old bookstore. I don't think that he mocked me for my impatience, but he was surprised. I have already answered. My poem for Maman was very carefully corrected and I am very proud.

We have published the second issue of our newspaper, "The Icicle Chronicle." A superb issue!

A telegram came from Maman which upset us a little. She has had no news from us, although I write every day and so does Aunt Helen. No doubt the mail is slower than ever because of the snowstorm. For the cold continues, with outings to go sledding and a few visits to New York. I went to the Strand, to Daly's, to the Rivoli and the Rialto. I almost always accept candy and other things, and really, little by little, I am becoming civilized.

And then, do you know that Aunt Helen says she is sure that Marcus is going to come to see us during Easter vacation? That's what everyone does. And I am very happy. However, they make fun of me a lot because of him, but I have discovered that as I accept the pleasantries with so much good humor, they soon grow tired of mocking and then I am the one who has the last laugh!

March 14. All these last days have been a series of culinary preparations and other preparations for last night's party. Yes, we gave a little dance to celebrate Thorvald's 15th birthday.

Marguerite, the maid, went off the other day and you can imagine that there has been enough to do! Today I have found a few quiet hours before dinner to give you a detailed account of the events of these last days, but I feel so frivolous that I have forgotten almost all the work, the difficulties, the discouragements and the fatigue, and all that appears before me is a shining picture of pleasure.

Yesterday at 4 I had done so much that I thought I wouldn't have the strength to dance. Aunt Helen was very tired, too. Thorvald and Jack had chopped wood, and since we have no more coal, they had to go and "borrow a bit from his neighbor the ant, a little something to keep himself alive"[1]—or a sack of coal. Then after getting dressed for the dance, they went to the basement to light the fire. Joaquin, I believe, kept busy going through a stack of dance music which had been prepared for the evening. The rugs were rolled back, the furniture moved against the walls, and the floor "waxed."

Toward 6:30, after a light dinner, we started to get dressed, each in his own room. We had two friends of Aunt Helen's with us: a young lady, Miss Casey, who is her goddaughter, and a Mrs. Gray, who is nice and fat.

I don't know how Aunt Helen dressed—I wasn't in her room—so I shall take you to my "nest." I put my hair up in the chignon of curls that Maman likes, and to you alone, little Diary, I dare confess that last night I was pretty—that's funny, isn't it? But it was true. I wore a very light dress of Prussian-blue georgette crêpe and taffeta with transparent sleeves, embroidered black silk stockings, and my "young lady" shoes. A little flower in my hair with a tiny bit of perfume, several poses in front of the mirror—and Miss Linotte was ready. Aunt Helen put a little coral necklace around my neck. Joaquin wore a sailor suit and a very mischievous look in his eyes. Thorvald and Jack were like two elegant young gentlemen. Aunt Helen had done her wonderful red hair beautifully. That's all!

There were many things to take care of, but a little before the guests arrived the fire in the basement took hold and then everything seemed to go better. At 7:30 we were waiting in the parlor, talking. Joaquin had invited our neighbors, whom we didn't know, and we were talking gaily about them.

Toward 8—doorbell. Enter our neighbors! There were two young girls about my age, very nice, and their brother, to whom I didn't pay much attention at first. Little by little everyone arrived: two boys, friends of Thorvald's, and Elsie and Vicente de Sola. The phonograph filled the air with music and we began to enjoy ourselves. Jack danced very well with everyone, and I was proud

[1] *Quotation from La Fontaine's fable of the grasshopper and the ant.*

and delighted to see Thorvald perfectly happy and Joaquin not too devilish. I would like to tell you what everyone did, but something very strange happened: I was enjoying myself so sincerely, with all my heart, that I didn't have time to notice the others the way I used to at dances in the old days, when I was an eternal "wall-flower."

Now I must tell you about my neighbor, because he played a very important rôle last night. His name is Jim, a name like any other, practical and "business-like." He is 16, very tall, neither ugly nor handsome. That's Jim. We saw immediately that he is terribly gallant, a dreadful flirt, a modern young man. I was so afraid to be called a "coquette" that I fled from him. I flashed distress signals to Jack and he danced with me, then to Joaquin and Vicente. But Mr. Jim watched me and once he rushed forward so quickly that I had to dance with him. Then it began. He danced in a very original style, but I could follow everything he did. We talked a little, but we were very much absorbed in dancing. When the music stopped, Mr. Jim kept on whistling and dancing until the music began again, and everyone thought that very funny. I danced once with Elsie, who said she would like to dance with him—so I introduced him. He danced once with her and then came back to Miss Linotte. But he held me too tightly and I was almost angry—also he sang: "I love you, I adore you," in every key and said he would have left the party long since but had stayed just to dance with—Miss Linotte!

Once, by accident, all the young gentlemen were around me, so Elsie dragged me away from them and said, almost angrily, that the biggest flirt at the party was—Miss Linotte!

Well, I was monopolized by Mr. Jim all evening, even at table! And I tried, I tried so hard, not to be a coquette! It seemed to me that I was going to be punished for every gesture, every glance! Poor Elsie was angry, I think, while Mr. Jim continued dancing, talking with and complimenting—Miss Linotte!

Toward 11 we were tired—so the guests started to leave, and I pretended not to know my neighbor's name, after I had taught him how to pronounce mine. Before leaving, he looked at me like—Enric, I think; and I heaved a sigh of relief when the party ended. Ended? Oh, no! Half was still to come, the amusing part. We straightened up the kitchen, did piles of dishes, put away the piles of sandwiches that were left, then said a pile of silly things before going to bed. Of course, the subject of the conversation was Jim—and his behavior. I was forced to confess some of his compliments, and I had to decide a very simple thing: did I prefer him to Marcus?

A thousand times: NO!

Then everything went fine, everyone said terrible things about him and about—Miss Linotte! Do you know what? They say that I am a *natural* coquette, that I can no more avoid it than I can avoid breathing. They say that! And out of pity at my despair, Aunt Helen added:

"But that's not a fault, it becomes you. Have a good time while you're young—"

"But I don't want my girl friends to be angry with me," answered Miss Linotte. "It seems very bad in their eyes to be a coquette and to please others." (I was thinking of Elsie.)

"Almost all women are cats, Ninise," replied Aunt Helen, "and as long as you make a hit with the boys, other girls will be envious and will tell you things that aren't very nice."

Toward midnight everyone was asleep, except—Miss Linotte!

I thought about the horrible fault that I was born with and that I can't help, I thought about Jim and his way of holding me so tight and singing, "I love you," about Marcus and his way of dancing that is so different, the way he talked to me with his eyes, and the way he held me as though he were afraid of hurting me, and about the things Aunt Helen said about my neighbor, that he doesn't love me at all except to have a good time with. At breakfast this morning we talked again about all that, but last night I fell asleep thinking of Maman and what *she* would think about it all.

We spent the day putting out our newspaper, which this time is called "Frolic Weekly" and I drew a pair of dancers, silhouettes, underneath two lanterns. Jack made fun of everyone (especially of Mr. Jim), and on the whole we listened to the contents of the paper with a great deal of pleasure.

Tomorrow I am going to answer Marcus, whose image does me good amidst the disturbance caused by my first party in the company of a modern young man. For I am disturbed, with a strange vague feeling of shame to think that Jim dared to treat me as though I were—Germaine Sarlabous, and also of astonishment, for not long ago I was left very much alone at dances, and suddenly I am sought after and surrounded by flattery—I, Miss Linotte!!!

Oh, dearest diary! I am not writing any very wonderful adventures in these pages, simply the very small events in a young girl's life, and no doubt one day I will burn them (the pages). But in the meantime, I find that taking the ideas that pass through my scatterbrain and putting them down in black and white gives me a bit of the common sense that I need so much!

From now on, I will try again to write every day. I wonder if you like Mr. Jim! I am going to make a study of him and mock him a little to pass the time. "All right?" Yes, yes, you always say yes, and you don't help me to dis-coquette myself!! Oh, Incurable Sickness, Hypochondria! Oh, Jim!—Oh, Linotte!—Oh, goodnight!

March 16. Little Diary! Another adventure! This morning I received a letter from Marcus: he has his Easter vacation, two weeks, and Saturday we are going to the Opera together in the afternoon; this is the beginning of several days that we are going to spend together.

I had often wondered when I would see Marcus, and now suddenly I am going to see him—the boy I prefer above all others!

Aunt Helen wants to make me even happier, so after the Opera, Marcus will come to dinner with us, then we will dance a little, with our neighbors and among ourselves. Oh, how I thought today about all this! Now I am ashamed of my enthusiasm—oh! how can I be such a child—tonight I am sorry and sad and alone.

If Maman were here, she would tell me that I am not as bad as I think and I would be able to smile—but at present I can only think of all the things that I have done and thought—she is so, so crazy, your poor little Linotte! I am glad to be able to write you how bad I am; someone should know that I am coquettish and vain and—etc. etc. etc.

I wrote 10 pages to Maman, from whom I had a little letter today—and I told her everything. Oh, I want you to know how I am! Everything!

Today I wanted with all my heart to have *a new hat*—with all the hats that are in my closet, all my extravagances! (And after that I looked at myself in the mirror for 5 or 10 minutes.) Also, Mr. Jim "throws kisses at me," and I am very much amused.

What else? That's enough, I think—at 17!!!!

I have interrupted this two or three times to hide my head in my pillow and—cry. Is that funny? Oh, yes, poor Linotte—how much she needs her little Mother—and when I think how little I deserve to have such a wonderful little mother—I cry. It's simple.

I would like to be good and not to be pretty—not to want to see Marcus again on Saturday and not to think of the joy that friendship gives me—all this is horrible—and the tears flow!

It's funny that I am "fickle"—that I change the name of my Prince so often. I am afraid if Marcus knew me better, the ideal that he has built around Miss Linotte would be ruined!

Oh, Saturday, Saturday! Crazy little girl, you and me, let's go and dream!

March 17. Mrs. Thayer is angry with me—and I with her. I was naughty: for once my pride, which I had succeeded in controlling up until now, refused to be humiliated. Sometimes I am afraid that I am too pliant—when they call me coquette, I am sad and try to improve; or extravagant, and I try to smother the least desire for the prettiest little thing, and so on, for I haven't much confidence in Miss Linotte, I know that she is ignorant and silly and all that. I know that I write French with millions of mistakes, but as for speaking it, I know that I can speak it better than—Mrs. Thayer. I have always said that Mrs. T. speaks French very well, but I told her that I don't like to speak French with her because half the time "she misunderstands me." But what good does it do to explain that? She said that I was disagreeable, I was surprised by her bad humor and—I am angry with her and she is angry with me. The End!

And I have a mad desire to cry, but I am too proud and no one but Maman knows "my wretchedness," because I wrote her this evening. No, no one has the right to hurt me like that; everyone seems to have a right to be mean and disagreeable, but I am always supposed to be angelic and as soon as I am a little bit human, everyone is horrified! Oh! how I want to be bad, to paint my face, to dress like an actress, to be a coquette, to tell everyone the truth about my "niceness" (?), not to take care of my little brothers' clothes any more, not to sew any more, nor clean nor make the beds—when people are angry with me—

Oh, what a joke! Mrs. Thayer just came and talked to me as if nothing had happened, as if she had forgotten it, and I was going to write 100 or 200 pages about my distress. I will continue to be good, I suppose, and this is a lesson: I make mountains out of molehills.

I have learned that on Saturday I am going to hear the famous Caruso and Amato. Caruso for the first time! Happy? No—I miss Maman too much to be happy.

March 21. Oh, what a quiet day, after yesterday's excitement! I have had a little time to think, and now I have found a few minutes to write. For the first time, I would like not to write. I would like to keep the emotions I felt yesterday like a secret treasure, and I feel them again as I tell you about them. I am going to *try* to tell you—in the right order.

Toward 1 o'clock I took a last look at myself in the mirror, then the whole family examined me with apparent satisfaction, and I was delighted. Do you think I wore rouge? No, I was rosy enough from emotion.

I ran to the station. I got there early and was obliged to take a train that got to New York too early. Once at Pennsylvania Station, I spent 15 minutes walking from one end to the other of a long corridor that leads from the trains to the street, asking myself 100 times if I would recognize Marcus Anderson and what he looks like. When the time came, I took a taxi to the Opera. I got out, paid, and as I turned around to look for a way through the crowd, I met Marcus's eyes. I forget what we said. I was happy to see him, little Diary.

We found our seats and the Opera began. At the first intermission, we slipped out to have a demitasse and cake. After that, I preferred the intermissions a thousandfold to even the songs of the famous Caruso and Rosa Ponselle and Amato, because Marcus talked to me and I listened. At times we talked of poets, at times about Lake Placid, and a thousand other things. The Marcus whom I knew yesterday is very different from the one I knew through his letters. I like the *real* Marcus better.

Afterward we wanted to have tea at the McAlpin but it was too crowded, so we went directly to the station in a taxi, and I saw that I had half an hour to wait. Marcus couldn't come to dinner, for he had to return early to his aunt's house in Greenwich, Connecticut. But he wanted to wait with me. So we walked around Pennsylvania, talking; Marcus gave me his arm, and that half-hour was much too short. He talked to me about his career, about his school—about poets. Until a moment came when the two of us, very moved, suddenly stopped talking. I have almost forgotten everything that happened, but I know that Marcus spoke to me of love and that I didn't have the strength to interrupt him. Never have I been so moved. I know that I said "Please—please," very often, that I explained to him that we could only be friends. The prosaic railway station, the people, *nothing* mattered except that we were talking together. I barely glanced at the clock and saw that I must leave, and when I said "good-bye" and offered my hand, Marcus took it and kissed it like a Prince; then—I fled.

During the trip, I didn't think very much, I was too "thrilled," and I kept looking at my gloved hand, remembering the look in the eyes of "my first Love."

When I reached home, I had to eat next to an empty chair, Marcus's chair, since we had been expecting him for dinner. The dinner was so nicely served, so perfect, and I felt terribly grateful for all the work Aunt Helen had done, in vain, in honor of our "guest." We had invited our neighbors for a little dance, so we spent the evening dancing, until midnight. Thorvald has fallen in love with Jimmy's little sister, Christine, and Mr. Jimmy flirted with Miss Linotte in the most terrible way, in spite of how little I felt like dancing and flirting.

By telegram, we learn that Maman will embark today! Oh! What happiness, what happiness!

March 22. The house is ready for Maman's return. There are roses in her room—the bed is made, and we are so joyful!

Aunt Helen and I have done more painting and cleaning. In the midst of struggles with a bucket of paint, Marcus telephoned, and I had to refuse to see him Wednesday because Maman will arrive from one day to the next; but Saturday we will go together to see "Hamlet."

When our work was finished, we went to the village to buy

seeds and a few plants, and we worked almost all afternoon in *my* Garden. And Mr. Jimmy was working in his. And apropos of Mr. Jimmy, during the dance I complimented him on his "pussy willow," so Sunday, enter the triumphant hero, whom I had seen attacking the tree with a pair of scissors, carrying a superb bouquet of "pussy willow" for Miss Linotte. I realized that this was my opportunity to play the rôle of a young lady, so I talked, talked, talked like a real "woman of the world"—tra la la la, tra la la—

Sunday evening we published our newspaper as a sort of Farewell to Aunt Helen. Jack has left us too, to everyone's regret.

That's all, I think, but I would like to have a magic pen to describe the beauty of a Spring day for you . . . that strange hope which seems to be born in the soul with the birth of a new season—that quiet happiness which grows as the days grow longer. . . . Oh! No words can explain that divine mystery.

And Maman who is coming home with the spring and the flowers.

Oh! Life is sometimes so beautiful, so beautiful that one wonders why it has to change—like the seasons!

March 27. Maman came back on Tuesday! We were still asleep, and what a joyful awakening! Maman didn't come back a millionaire, of course. She started right back to work—Aunt Helen will stay with us until Easter. I received a bottle of toilet water, my favorite Royal Begonia by Houbigant! and two canaries. But by accident one of my little singers, along with the one belonging to Aunt Edelmira, was put on the heater and asphyxiated, to my great sorrow. Another day I would have wept over the death of my little favorites, but not today.

At 2 I was with Marcus at the entrance to the Lyric to see "Hamlet" and afterward we met Maman and Mrs. Thayer in the Hotel Pennsylvania, across from the station. Maman and Aunt Helen wanted absolutely to *see* Marcus, and the result of the examination was that Marcus is a "little gentleman." Only more than ever I noticed that he is so young, so young—

I have always talked to you about Marcus the poet, the author of the package of letters in my drawer, but not about his physique, etc. You know me well enough to know that I base my judgments very little on physical beauty and give it very little importance.

My girl friends say about a boy, "He is handsome—he is not handsome." I, poor crazy little Linotte, think of everything except that. I can't try to describe Marcus as other people would. Here is my way: He is a "gentleman." I *think* his eyes are blue, but I am sure that they are kind and gentle. He isn't sturdy and not any taller than I, but he is like a Prince in everything. His only fault (and this is because I am really me, even if I am a "little old lady") is that he is still a boy.

These days, only two in number, that I have spent with Marcus have been like adventures in fairyland, because everything that he says surprises me, everything that he does surprises and "thrills" me. When I say that this is "my first Love," Aunt Helen protests in Jack's name. Jack? Oh! That's so funny, but it's true that Jack is starting to give me compliments, like the other young gentlemen. And if Maman says that I am very "fickle," it's just that I have the right to love many people at once, and to change my Prince often. You remember about poor Enric, and Edward, and Jack, and Jim, who came after little Henri in Brussels, and others. But now I prefer Prince Marcus.

Oh! I forgot, Prince Marcus has curly hair—An Artist, in a word.

April 2. I went to see "Monsieur Beaucaire" with Marcus. It was our last day together until June, but we found it even more delightful than before, I think. Oh! little Diary, he asked me, begged me for my picture—he calls me "Sweet Princess," and he gave me a poem, such a pretty one, written for me. Our talks make the hours pass like a dream—although the ending is very prosaic: the station and the train! I really regret this separation, and I can say that it's only today that I came to my senses and remembered that on Monday we are going to have a *big* dance.

As I wash the dishes and the pots, I can't help smiling at the thought that Marcus says my hands are whiter than new-fallen snow, and that I look like the Empress Eugénie. But I don't always think about the things my Prince said, for one must be practical, isn't that so? And there are so many socks to mend!

Aunt Helen is working with Maman at present. She still teases me terribly, for she doesn't like Marcus, but I forgive her for that. I think he is more perfect than ever!

I think it's because it's Spring, but there are times when I have a mad desire to run through the fields—and laugh! I am really happy and strangely good; that is, I don't read at all and I write only business letters and just a few lines in my diary instead of sleeping. But the alarm clock is going to ring at 7:30, and if I don't sleep now, I won't have the time to finish my dream. And I have to dream at night for lack of another time—because during the day, we work.

April 4. Easter Sunday! It is raining, and I am not good. We spent the day at Edgemere, having put our cottage up for sale, but no one came. Mrs. Thayer, for her part, is trying to sell her house at Far Rockaway.

I have several reasons for saying I am not good. Yesterday I received a short letter from Marcus, a very sad letter—and after I showed it to Maman, Mrs. Thayer acted so offended that I showed it to her, too, and she said so many dreadful things that in that moment I realized (although her teasing never makes me angry) that everything Mrs. Thayer says about everyone else, except Jack, is something mean. Perhaps it is my fault too, the dislike I feel for people who are critical, who condemn, and who are themselves full of faults. Perhaps it is my fault that I feel old enough to refuse to be dominated by anyone else but Maman—and my husband. But since I was very small I have never been able to like Mrs. Thayer. Yet, during Maman's absence, I thought at times that I could succeed, succeed in giving her faults different names, like good will, good intentions. But my former "dislike" came back so strongly today—that's that. I had a dreadful headache at table; I was silent and sad. And Mrs. Thayer says things that sting like needles. I shall never be able to like her again.

I realize, anyhow, that I am unreasonable. But do you know who I think Mrs. Thayer looks like? The "typical," rather sad pictures drawn of mothers-in-law. She *dominates,* she puts her nose into everything, she condemns and criticizes, cynically— Oh, it's shameful that I can think such things about a woman who took such good care of us during Maman's absence—but what can I do? Tell you that I love everyone? Or tell the truth?

April 9. How much I have to tell you! Where to begin? The party! When does a party begin? At the first ring of the doorbell? No, no! It's when one is getting dressed. I don't speak of the work, the preparations to be beautiful. One sleeps a few minutes, and after great exhaustion—the miracle happens!

Maman looked very beautiful in a black dress—Thorvald delightful in his first long trousers—a proud young man, that famous little kid. I have nothing to say about Joaquin's good looks, except that fortunately he is still too young to break *all* my friends' hearts with his pretty speeches. For, my goodness, he is gallant! Mrs. Thayer, poor Mrs. Thayer, took a long time getting dressed, but her hair spoils her appearance—it is too red for my taste! I wore my fairytale dress, a crown of flowers on a gold ribbon, my shoes with the Louis XV heels—and it's a miracle how I am able to do my hair. But I think what made everyone say I looked like a picture is just that I was happy, happy! Because I am not yet blasé and a dance is the realization of one of my dearest dreams. You have to be happy when a dream comes true!

Queen Mother—red hair—long trousers—mischievous eyes—and turquoise tulle came downstairs together. The doorbell rang for the first time, then little by little the guests arrived.

Here I must confess that I am ashamed of my conduct, because I was having such a wonderful time that I didn't notice anything. It seems that Elsie almost fainted and that the salad was bad—I couldn't say!

I only remember that Jimmy began to monopolize Miss Linotte but that Macaya and Homer Eddins surpassed him, so he turned around and fell madly in love with Dorothy. Jack wasn't quick enough and I danced only a quarter of a dance with him. Elsie had forbidden me to flirt with her boy friend, but "I couldn't help it." He then danced once with me, and I think it was then that Elsie fainted.

If everyone had as good a time as I, the party was a success. But Paquita is blasé—and I'm afraid Frances was wearing a dress that was not becoming.

I am using my dressing table as a desk, and without meaning to, I see myself in the mirror every time I lift my eyes. With my glasses on, I look like a school teacher. That reminds me that the speed with which I remove them when someone rings the doorbell has become a family joke. A thing like that makes me think dismally of how much I need to reform. The other day someone was talking about face powder (a very modern subject of conversation!) and Maman told everyone that I had not worn any until I was 16. (I remember having worn it then, on Sundays, as a reward.) Then Thorvald yelled, "She's making up for it now!" His opinion of Miss Linotte is a calamity!

April 12. Maman is in bed, very sick and provoked about it. But she has been writing in bed and had a dispute over the telephone—now she is reading. Until now I have acted very happy, but to you, little diary, I can admit that I am quite sad and discouraged. It's

always like that when Maman is sick and a thousand little responsibilities assail me in which I have to be practical. Practical?
Oh, there are so many qualities that I don't have!

This morning I spent two delightful hours raking the dry
leaves in the garden. The weather was warm and I would have
liked to rake for a long, long time. As I raked the leaves into piles
for burning, I thought, I sang, I dreamed— Sometimes I suddenly
dropped my rake to let my eyes follow the flight of a bird or the
passage of a cloud. I must be crazy—heaven only knows—but I
had a better time outside today than at the most wonderful cinema
show. And what a surprise to see the image reflected in my
mirror: pink cheeks and shining eyes. My appetite was keen, too,
and I enjoyed fixing a little lunch for my dear invalid and for
Joaquin, who is going to school now.

While I was working in the garden, the postman brought me
a letter from Marcus that made me terribly sad. He had not yet
received my letter and asked me why I was making him unhappy
by not writing. Every proof of my Prince's love makes me feel
more upset and ashamed. Ashamed because I wouldn't intention-
ally make someone unhappy for anything in the world, and if I
can't learn to love Marcus, he is going to be unhappy when I have
to tell him that. I don't want to think about it any more.

April 16. Maman has spent the best part of these last few days in
bed, still feeling very weak and worried. She had me bring her
paper and ink and has worked enormously. In the mornings, I go
to her office in New York, a little room at 1929 Broadway, to get
the mail. Also to do some buying. One of these last days, before
going to the city, I received a letter from Marcus. I answered
today.

Tonight I am writing in front of my three mirrors, which
explains my distracted way of writing—because I look at myself
in the mirror and scold myself because I was unbearable today. It
was raining, so I wasn't particularly gay, and I began to read . . .
a little party in my little armchair. I was reading with all my
heart, happy and deeply absorbed. Suddenly I remembered the
socks that needed mending. I looked at my watch—another five
minutes, I still have time—and I read, I read—looked at my
watch—all right, five minutes more, then five minutes after that,
five minutes—for a whole hour. What a temptation! Do you think
I mended the socks? Can you guess? Well, I did. After an hour
passed, I got up resolutely and went to look for the execrable,

stupid old socks. And while I darned them, I dreamed so much that I forgot what I was doing. Oh, it's a gift to be able to dream while one is pricking one's fingers! But there's no use talking, one is very happy after performing a difficult task. The chapters of my story seemed even more interesting than before. Still, that hour of weakness weighs a little on my conscience and I was ashamed to see that it took me a whole hour to make up my mind to behave properly!

April 21. I am here with two fixed ideas in mind: write until I become reasonable (for I am morbid and unhappy), and tell you what is happening. When I have accomplished the latter, the former will take care of itself.

A few days ago, Ti Coco arrived from New Orleans with Gilbert and Nunita. Mother went to see Dr. Murray and decided that she would obey him and take a week's rest, for her most serious illness is *lack of rest*, the eternal race from 8 in the morning until evening—her worries—and the "nerve-racking strain of her work." So my little mother is spending her days in my bed and the nights too, because Ti Coco is sleeping in her room.

While I was straightening up the kitchen, Thorvald played the phonograph, so I danced by myself as I put the things away. It was semicomical, because I would stop all at once, suddenly seized by my former attacks of disapproval of frivolity—the Anaïs of the old days, pensive and detached from the world, between the moon and the clouds, perhaps.

This evening I am slow to get better, really, but I want to tell you about the tiny bit of optimism that I discovered the other day. It was on a sunny morning, on Fifth Avenue. I was moving with the crowd, slowly, in front of the Hotel Waldorf. Out of curiosity, I looked through the big window at the rich people having lunch. They looked supremely bored, disgusted, and about as interesting as blotting paper. In that same moment, I remembered our breakfast. It was cold this morning and each of us took his plate so as to eat close to the fire in the fireplace. You should have seen us! And heard us! It was so warm, so comfortable, that breakfast tasted delicious and everyone was happy—yet after breakfast we were going to have to wash the dishes and the pots and pans. . . .

The other day I told Maman that I have learned to *love* New York. It's a strange affection that one feels for this big City. One flees from the dust, the lack of light, of sun, air and space—and especially the lack of poetry—and yet, a little emotion stays in your heart, and you feel a "thrill" when you stop a moment to realize the splendor, the incomprehensible charm of New York. There is the little hand organ, the kids, the crowd, in a hurry, yes, but it's a humanity that one loves just the same—the stores, big and small, the carriages, the automobiles—the big department stores—it's Life, pulsating and fascinating, which unfolds in the greatest theatre imaginable, the superb City. Yet New York doesn't always seem sunny to me—there aren't many Spring days—but perhaps the saddest days can be spent just as well in New York and one loves it just as much—for affection only flourishes better when it grows in sadness and misery! I love New York, I, the little Parisian. But the best reason for that is no doubt that—I don't know Paris!!!

I received a letter in *French* from Marcus! I am going to answer soon. But one can hardly write to clients about their expenditures and write to a poet the same day!

April 27.
Dearest Dick:[1]

I now understand your poem very well; and am not a whit alarmed by your letter. Only I wish you would not analyze yourself and your impulses so continually. Will you be plagued if I tell you what I think about your two selves? Then skip this paragraph, for I cannot help but tell you.

I do not believe there is exactly such a thing as two selves, as you say. They say that the *mind* is a great kingdom. Well, in every kingdom there are dissension, dualisms, wars and peace—wars caused by the active creators of differences, and peace to rest between the wars. Stop laughing! I can just hear you, but I am quite in earnest though all this may sound like pedagogism and pedantry.

You are just one "self": the "self" that all those around you know so well. Only your *mind* is full of dualism. Your impulses, all of them, are good, but when you begin analyzing them and doubting them, then you doubt all your thoughts, your deeds, and your dreams. You go as far as doubting whether you still have a soul, you think that routine can make a machine of you. A machine has no soul; you are not a machine because if you once had a soul, you still have it. No routine, or in other words, no machine-life, can kill a soul. I hope you understand me. I do not quite understand myself because I fear all this is logic and com-

[1] *Written in English.*

mon sense. And you know how far I am from possessing either quality.

Oh! Dick, your poor dreams are not dead! Do you know what has happened to them? They have fled, like the birds who fear the cold and fly to warmer lands until the Spring. You cannot grasp them, or ever hope to reach them while they have to live side by side with lessons, for example. But wait until the summer comes, the freedom to recreate new dreams, the peace and quiet, with no other roof than clouds over your head, no thoughts of "how to spend money, how to dress, how to exercise."

Oh! I could write forever to keep the "inside" of you from disappearing. That is the most priceless part, Dick—though it is true that one seems almost forced to look forward to only tangible things nowadays—just because people forget the mere color of the sky and the smell of the woods and the fields, living in a large City, reading and discussing politics, the H.C. of L. [High Cost of Living], while Tennyson's poems, Shelley's poems, millions of poems lie under coats of dust, neglected in the old libraries.

      *   *   *

Your letter is not mad, it is just that you can write as you think, instead of according to the amount of time you have, as most people do. Please always write as you please to me instead of your diary. We can travel through great labyrinths of wonder together. Only do not look inside of you too much, there is nothing as unfathomable as our own minds and hearts, and there is a source of great fun in the observance of other people's "outsides." If you like, we can send each other portraits of all the funny and queer people we know, and guess at their innermost thoughts, tho' by judging through facial expressions, generally most people do not think at all.

      *   *   *

                                                Anaïs

April 30. These past days I have been to the City with Maman; I am almost a businesswoman, after numerous painful experiences. In my moments of leisure, I soliloquize on my timidity, my lack of "self-reliance," and other disagreeable subjects. Until now, by strength of will, I succeed perfectly in making my purchases with assurance; I do not hesitate, I trust my own opinion, I stay calm and "lady-like."

The only thing that I can't control is the ease with which I blush, and also I cannot scold and look really angry. There are still some people who think I am a little girl; they can hardly manage to call me "Little lady" from time to time.

After a whole day with all my common sense on the surface, after having banished absolutely the slightest eccentric ideas and useless thoughts on various observations, I reward myself by reading Shelley and Keats, and especially Tennyson, in my little bedroom. At the same time I open all the doors very wide to my poor ideas, and my common sense leaves me abruptly with indescribable indignation.

Mentally, I am always a bit tired from all this fuss, and physically, I am almost dead. And yet, I find a bit of "pep," I don't know where, to dance a little with Thorvald every evening. We are soon going to wear a hole in the carpet!

May 3. Saturday evening I went with Thorvald and his friend Gerald (?) to see an amateur company massacre Shakespeare's "Comedy of Errors." It was at De Witt Clinton, Thorvald's school, a huge red brick building. I will never forget the grimaces of the two Brownies and the wigs of the Antipholus'es, as well as the characteristics of various other personages who were very well played.

Maman and I go into the city almost every day. And today my little Maman bought me a dress of blue gingham! At lunchtime I was so happy that I wasn't hungry. Just think, little Diary, how much fun it is to have a new dress, a "plaid" skirt, and also—listen—a pair of very small shoes from Paris, with Louis XV heels and a ribbon bow!

Sometimes I think that I am changing, that I am becoming trivial, like the other girls—and I am glad; but immediately some little accident shows me that I am still very much the Serious One. Sunday I had a great desire to go out and walk for just a little while. I always dread so much the long, heavy hours on Sundays, I don't know why. When I asked Joaquin to come with me, he answered: "Not now, I am having a good time."

Thorvald didn't want to; my little Maman was tired. So instead of starting to read peacefully, I stood at the window, feeling terribly sad for no reason, and I cried. . . .

I could have gone to pick up Lucy, or Martha, or Wilhelmina, whoever. And that is the question that discourages me—why I react with so much "dislike" to the idea of going for a walk with girls my own age? Because they are going to talk to me about "handsome boys," the latest musical comedy, or one of the modern novels about which I am ridiculously ignorant. Why at present can I not like the world of "those things," just like everyone else?

It is really absolutely my fault when I realize so often that I am very isolated, very much alone, very "lonesome." And yet I don't understand, if I am happier when I am alone, why I am sad because I am too much so. I am a little like the man "who hates noise and is afraid of silence." I prefer Springtime (notice that logic!). But it's true that there are times during these wonderful days when I marvel at so much beauty and am surprised that I am happy *only because of that!*

And I am the one who writes Frances to stop probing her own nature! What a strange doctrine for a Linotte, who worries her head over the problems of everyday life, and for a "failure" as a poet. . . .

This evening I did nothing but reflect about my "faults." No doubt it's for that reason that I feel so terribly morbid. With good reason! I am discouraged, after so much, much effort and continual self-control and "will-power," to have so many failures. I want so much to be good, and sociable, and sweet, and gay— What do you think? Oh, Little Diary! I wonder what you would be like if, like Pygmalion's Statue, you came to life— I think I would love you so much, because when I reread you, I notice that in spite of all my confessions, you seem always to reflect my best "self"—a completely strange person in spite of my efforts to write nothing but the whole truth!

May 11. What perfect days! They have all passed so swiftly that as I went to bed, I was surprised by the number of things still to be done. I have neglected you a little—but I am really living up in the clouds since Spring came. Maman leaves for New York at 9, Joaquin and Thorvald go to school, and instead of the clouds, I have just this big house all to myself. Some day Maman will come back and find the house empty—I will have gone to the insane asylum, for to chase away the chill of silence which weighs on all the empty rooms, sometimes I sing at the top of my lungs in a scandalous fashion, and when I have exhausted my repertoire, I wind up the phonograph. But one should be systematic, even to relate the life of a poet, and I am going to try to tell it in order. I can't think of the right order, but what does it matter?

At 7 o'clock the alarm clock dances on the chair near my bed. I give a start and leave the delightful places that I always frequent in my dreams (gardens and castles, etc.). I get breakfast for

Thorvald. He leaves, and then it is Joaquin's turn. Naturally, two boys never get dressed without banging doors, using bad language as they put on their collars, and they always wake Maman.

Toward 9 I am alone and I begin my lovely days by the absorbing, upsetting, semitragic wait for the postman. Sometimes it's funny, as for example the day I received a letter from Eduardo! (he wants to sell his manuscripts) and soon after, one from Marcus. On those days I deceive myself a little by doing the accounts, but otherwise I am not very bad, I haven't got time!

I spend my morning doing the housekeeping, with all the windows (and the doors) wide open to let in waves of sunshine and the "twittering" of the birds. I do a lot of silly things because I insist on trying to write poetry while I wash the pots and pans.

Joaquin arrives at 12—thirty minutes for lunch. I spend the afternoon doing the accounts, and I go to the market. Then suddenly it's time for dinner. I think that in heaven they must not have dinner, because who would wash the dishes? No doubt there is a "dumb waiter" between heaven and hell, and at the end of dinner the angels send the dishes off to hell—

One of the things that is sometimes hardest to explain is the reason for our gaiety, for our happiness. We have been like that this week, not daring to think too much, knowing that deep down, alas, there is something to be sad about. Despite my apparent lightheartedness, I understand very well the state of affairs for Maman. There came a time when she found herself face to face with the terrible fear that all her efforts, all her sacrifices and courage were going to be in vain, and that her plans were going to be reduced to ashes. It's lack of capital, of money to pay the bills that the Cubans settle with Maman only months and years later, and sometimes never. Half on account of the inevitable delay, half because of the mysterious fears and doubts that exist about finances as one of the natural causes of war, James McCreery, one of the biggest stores in New York, has withdrawn the 10% commission. As I write, that doesn't represent a real misfortune: it's what their action portends for the future. If all the stores withdraw their commission, all of Maman's plans are destroyed, and she will have to give up. In that case, only God knows whether Thorvald and I will go to work to help. We will be poor again— But this is only the dark side—

War always turns a country's finances upside down, as during the administration of the American President Van Buren, when the banks didn't have a cent to pay the unfortunates who had deposited all their money. There are "swindlers" and "forgers"—so that one is rich one day, penniless the day after. But the government was weaker then, it seems to me—at present such catastrophes cannot be so frequent, and if there are fears and doubts, they will be momentary, until affairs in the country return to normal. Perhaps McCreery is also going through a crisis of debts, despairs about its money and takes extreme measures to collect it, and perhaps the other stores will change absolutely nothing.

Just the same, it's fortunate that we are older and capable of helping Maman, which we couldn't do five years ago when she began the brave struggle.

May 14. 11 o'clock. Paquita Madriguera leaves for Cuba tomorrow and is taking a trunk full of things for Maman. It's unbelievable how my little Mother has worked these last few days! She comes home at dinner-time and spends her evening writing important letters. Almost every day I trot behind her, because Jenny, the maid, has reappeared. Last night I typed the bills on the machine and today Maman went to make final preparations; I was obliged to stay home because this evening I am going to a dance with Thorvald. I have done all kinds of things, and I still have a long afternoon to myself. No, my dress isn't hanging on a stand as in the past. I don't know what is happening to me. I am not blasé, oh, no! but I am not excited and impatient—I fear that I have relapsed into my normal state of feeling lukewarm about worldly things. I stand at the window and fall into a state of ecstasy and absent-mindedness, I laugh when I see the squirrels playing—but as soon as Jimmy, or Gerald, or Edward, etc. appear, I want to vanish into the air. They are just as interesting to me as matchsticks!

I am worried about Marcus's silence. I wrote to him the same day I wrote to Eduardo—Eduardo has already answered and I am ready to write him again from one day to the next. It's true that I was forced to confess to Marcus that I do not love him, and I can't imagine the effect this may have on the regularity of our correspondence. Oh! I begin to think that love causes more sadness than joy, even though I know nothing about it, but I never think of Marcus without a feeling of sadness. I was a thousand times more carefree when no one thought of me, when the arrival of the postman didn't make a bit of difference in the beauty of my day. I don't want to think about it any more.

Maman made me laugh yesterday. She ran into Germaine Sarlabous at Paquita's and Germaine told her she had heard through the Madrigueras that I have become very pretty and am having a wonderful time. She also wanted to know if it is true that I am going to marry a rich Cuban!!!!!!

Just imagine, Mrs. Madriguera told Maman she is glad to see that I am not a recluse any more, the way I was last year. Oh, how people get everything upside down! Luckily, Maman thought that was very funny, and when I think of the way one year has transformed my person, I am "tickled to death."

Pretty? My face is exactly the same, isn't it? So people are silly—simply because I wear my hair as in a picture and am fashionably dressed the miracle takes place. Believe me, there are a lot of funny things in this life! And one of them is the remarkable opinions that people have about the state of affairs.

4:30. Oh, la la—I was reading a newspaper very peacefully when suddenly I stumbled across this:

"Absurd"

"We were talking to a librarian the other day who said it was more important for boys to read a book in which the characters all speak perfect grammar than one in which the characters talk as folks really talk and act as folks really act. That is pedantry, and the silliest thing in the world is pedantry. Look it up in the dictionary, and then cross your heart never to be guilty of it."

Yes, but what if those folks speak so badly that one can't understand them, eh?—what about that? I would like to know what good Thorvald gets out of books full of "slang." It's true that perfection of language may become pedantic if it is overdone. But if one wants to write the way people talk, one should first teach them to speak correctly. That is my opinion, and as no one else is going to pay attention to it, I tell it to you, little Diary.

May 17. On Sunday we went to Edgemere and spent the afternoon there. The weather was beautiful, but no one came to look at the bungalow. We saw Letty and her entire family and that reminded me of all that we did in Edgemere last summer. Nothing has changed except that there are more people than ever and one can see that this little beach town is going to turn into a city.

On Saturday I wrote to Marcus, who had finally answered me. And oh! little Diary, he sent me such a beautiful poem! I tried to explain to him the special value that I find in the three poems: "Tennyson," "Easter," and the last one, "Madonna Mia." I am perplexed when I realize that it isn't a boy who wrote those beautiful lines, but a poet who had a vision and knew how to express it with a golden tongue. And yet Marcus, the Marcus with whom I went to the theatre, the one with whom I *talk*, is a child—I don't understand that.

The tone of his last letter makes me realize that when I write, I am too cold. I know that I talk with warmth and enthusiasm; I don't know how many times I have seen indifferent faces light up a little because of the way I talk. I have had that happen a thousand times with Cuca. As I realize that, I wrote Marcus simply. "I like you more than any boy in the world." It is so true. I can (and I do it without meaning to) compare all the boys around me to Marcus, and he is always the one who comes closest to my ideal. Lucky that Eduardo is my cousin and I can love him tremendously and it doesn't count, and luckily I am beginning to forget Enric and think of him only when I hear a violin.

Jimmy is a person who amuses me very much. First he falls seriously in love with me for 4 or 5 days—and two or three dances. Without my knowing it, he finds me too proud and distant (he told that to Thorvald) and decides to be perfectly "indifferent." He didn't dance with me on Friday—I didn't even notice. Then his curiosity is aroused—he spends hours observing me as though I were a particularly abnormal person, and now he is suddenly in love again. Since the first time we met, I told you I was going to make a study of Mr. Jim. That is why I have wasted a perfectly good page today in an analysis of my neighbor's vicissitudes.

May 23. The other day I was wakened at 6 o'clock by a "Special Delivery" from Marcus. His school is going to have a public-speaking contest on June 4, with a little dance in the evening, the distribution of prizes on Saturday morning, and a great ball Saturday evening. He has asked me to go. My first impulse was to refuse. Just now Maman is going through one of the most difficult periods of her business life. Each day, with an anxiety that borders on desperation, I see the traces of her worries in her eyes, in the wrinkles on her brow that never were there before, in the gray hairs that I can no longer count—Oh! I haven't the heart to enjoy myself—dancing is the last thing I feel like doing these days!

I told him that Maman was sick. After sending my answer, I

had a feeling that despite that "no," I would see Marcus soon. Two days later, I received another "Special Delivery," a letter so full of arguments, prayers, commandments—for "he will not take 'no' for an answer"—that my reasons seemed very weak ones and I did not have the courage to say "no" a second time. So it is done. Furthermore, Maman took Marcus's side and, without realizing it, I let myself be persuaded to do something that deep in my heart I wanted to do, if for no other reason than that I want to see Marcus again almost as much as he wants to see me.

I never think of those two days (and I think of them all day long) without being as disturbed as I can be. I am literally in the clouds night and day; I burn the toast, put salt in the chocolate, sugar in the soup, mend black socks with yellow thread— Oh! I am so ashamed!

Maman is always sure that I am "funny," but she doesn't say that in an angry way. On the contrary, she says it with pride, and for a long time I have associated the word "funny" with one of my meager qualities. This time it is because of a "dance card" which, it seems, has been full ever since Marcus's friends saw my picture on his desk. Maman asked me if I was not delighted. The idea made no impression on me, and I shrugged my shoulders calmly.

"Yes, but it's all the same to me, you know."

"It's true, Linotte," said Maman, "You have always been 'funny'! Other girls would be tickled to death."

May 24.
Dearest little Papa:

*   *   *

I summoned enough courage to send a poem in French to "La France"— Naturally, it came back to me, and yet I am not discouraged because the Editor, Monsieur Claude Rivière, was kind enough to let me know my faults, principally "lack of experience," and ending: "But the sentiment is *charming.*" That I try, that I dare to write poetry in French seems almost ridiculous—but the ideas are always there in my head and I have to get rid of them.

However, Papa, I have changed a great deal in regard to my ambition. Perhaps you think that this comes from life in America, which in truth is the least artistic in the world; you probably believe that if I had been fortunate enough to live my life in Europe, I would have been quite different. How can I say? But I am sure, Papa, about what I think. It's all very well to push away practical and banal things, common sense, the platonic and prosaic way of looking at life, to try to rise above mediocre things and to disdain the stupid necessity of money, if one can do that. I am the first (and you know it) to admire what is known as the "madness" of poets. Sublime madness which lends golden wings to fly away from reality!

A long time ago, I think I was romantic; I dreamed of living in a garret as though it were a palace—perhaps (doubtless) hungry, no matter—but with pen and ink, paper, imagination and talent! A few years ago, I could still see that picture, perfectly clear and intact. At present, perhaps too because I am a woman, I don't believe in that in the same way. First, I have no talent, and second, I know surely and absolutely that the literary life requires sacrifices and a complete forgetfulness of self, which up to a certain point is pure egoism when one has a family and not much talent. Also the world is full of poets, full of dreamers, full of madmen and prose writers—their joys and sorrows are for themselves and for the public. Without realizing it, I have learned little by little that certain people have a duty to be practical, to undertake only those tasks that are not a risk to the family happiness. If I tried to write, I would only be an ornament to those I love. Who would bake the cakes? (poets don't know how to do such things)— who would do the marketing? the mending? I help Maman in her work—and only when I have nothing to do do I write and devour books, in the idle moments that follow hours well spent. For all that which gives pleasure only to oneself is useless, isn't that true, Papa? And I am not romantic any more—I judge boys as coldly and seriously as possible, and you should see how difficult I am to please! I have only to imitate Thorvald to learn to be just the opposite of romantic— The only thing I can't control is my imagination, even if I try only to dream at night. There's no use talking, I spend half of my life in the clouds. Divide 17 years in half. I make mistakes, naturally (almost as many as if I were 8 1/2 years old), and about people's characters. It's almost unbelievable!

See the P.S.—

Thorvald often comes into my room when he is doing his lessons, with a book in his hand, or poetry. Nothing makes him as angry as poetry; he says it is a pile of words put together from the dictionary, and he doesn't understand it at all, but not at all. I help him out of his difficulties and I always tell him that it's too bad he has so little imagination. He shrugs his shoulders—he thinks that imagination is more or less another word for "*lies*." But you should see him—he does a perfect job of repairing all the clocks in the house, fixing the doorbell or cutting down the dead branches on the trees, and he discusses with me how to make cakes, after a few science lessons of which he is very proud.

Maman makes Joaquin study. He goes to a private school in Kew Gardens. Joaquin is a boy who is too sensitive to his companions, and rather weak—that is, Thorvald and I got all the good from the superb and incomparable education (ahem! ahem!) offered by the public schools, choosing our friends very carefully and not being changed at all by the atmosphere of a public school. But Joaquin is different—he is so young! So that great sacrifices are absolutely necessary for his education, on which his life's happiness depends. His school is full of children from the best families in Kew Gardens, and Joaquin's pride keeps him on top: he works hard and his behavior is almost exemplary. In any case, he is better lately, not so devilish, but always very quarrelsome and domineering, and he doesn't love anyone deeply except his mother. He loves his brother and sister, of course, but even with us he demonstrates a kind of selfishness in his way of loving. What I don't understand is how he can be such a saint when he is good—

I am going to Massachusetts soon for two or three days of dissipation. I will tell you about it if it will amuse you. You must not have much time to read all my descriptions, but I beg you, write, write to me soon.

I love you and send you kisses,

Anaïs

P.S. Just the same, I have lost my literary ambitions, and I write only for the pure pleasure of writing. My ambition is to be a little woman of whom Maman can be proud—perhaps a business-woman, who knows? But all I know is that I will still be up in the clouds.

May 29. 8:30. If I don't go crazy these days, it won't be for lack of trying. Marcus just had me called on the telephone to be sure that I am going. And just when I thought that by talking out loud to myself half the day, talking to my mirror, to the parlor chairs, to the trees and the walls, I couldn't be intimidated by conversation anymore— Alas! Sad mirage! As soon as I heard Marcus's voice over the telephone, I thought I was going to faint. A pretty spectacle, isn't it? Fortunately he had many things to tell me and I had time to recover. And Maman was laughing heartily!

Maman's trip to Cuba was relatively a "failure." The few

pennies that she earned over there were thrown to the four winds by Mrs. Thayer. We are already planning to rent some of the rooms in our house. Face to face with these facts, these truths, with the realization that as long as I can remember we have had to struggle to make money, struggle to live, I have lost all my courage, and I spent one night weeping that I shall be ashamed of all my life. One phrase spoken by my little mother brought me to my senses: "I am fifty years old, little girl, and I am not yet weary of the struggle."

I asked Maman if she thinks it is fair that we have only one life, and that during that life we have to struggle endlessly for a thing as stupid and detestable as *money!* Maman answered that when it isn't a struggle for money, it's a struggle for health or happiness—and that anyhow, it isn't a question of justice or injustice, it's a question of not complaining too much and of taking life as one finds it.

All that storm quickly passed, and the ignoble bitterness that I felt for some hours is gone. I quickly began to think about the Future, which consists principally and uniquely of the two days that I am going to spend in Massachusetts. In my dreams, since I am a girl, I attach a great deal of importance to what I wear. My Godmother, with her magic wand, gave me a feather fan, a new hat trimmed with flowers, and some gloves (the other things were already in my closet). But when I awoke, it turned out that on Tuesday Maman will buy me the gloves and perhaps the hat, but the fan is an extravagance. Maman is fixing one of her taffeta dresses for me, she sewed a lining for my cape, and my ball dress is still fresh. It's Marcus's aunt, Mrs. Fain, who is going to chaperone me. I discovered that they are rich, alas. I don't care much for rich people, and a rich poet is so modern! I am as afraid as I can be of Marcus's aunt. I imagine her as tall, proud and disdainful. Will she say something if she learns that I am poor? Well, it doesn't matter, I won't be ashamed, oh, no!—I am proud to have a mother who is capable of supporting us—and if I am not the equal of Marcus's family in money, to make up for that I am going to Massachusetts with the whole army of my Spanish ancestors and their escutcheons, as Maman has taught me, and with the strange "thrill" in my heart that comes from being the daughter of an Artist. If only I could be as brave in front of the people I am going to meet as I am right now, as calm and as confident! But I know that I will be troubled, that I will want to run away from everyone except Marcus.

June 5. Oh! Little Diary, what an adventure—You made the 3-hour trip with me from New York to Sheffield, Massachusetts, in my suitcase with my fairy-queen dress, etc. Now it is nine o'clock in the morning and I am writing in the nicest little room imaginable, in a cottage in the style of the little house at Lake Placid. But let's tell things in order. The train stopped at Sheffield about noon. In Stamford, I met Marcus's aunt, a nice, pleasant lady.

Marcus was waiting at the station. They brought us here in an automobile, we had lunch, we talked a little together, then Marcus left and the "ladies" dressed for the Declamation. Berkshire School is a long way from here and entirely surrounded by mountains—a most delightful setting.

Little Diary, I don't know what Love is, and furthermore, I don't want to know, so I can't find a name for my happiness yesterday when Marcus was near me. All the rest meant little to me and the other boys were nice but unimportant, as usual.

I was very sorry because Marcus was nervous and had to stop a moment in the midst of his eloquent speech—and in that way probably lost 2nd prize. Afterward there was a tea, a walk and dinner—and a dance in the gymnasium. The son of Madame Homer, the famous singer, danced with me often, and many others. But when I danced with Marcus, I was "thrilled"—to the point where I forgot to talk. During the day, his aunt asked him not to give me his arm, because of propriety, and I was so embarrassed—!

We came back at 11, along dark, dark roads as at Lake Placid—a light rain whipped our faces—quickly, quickly, so quickly that I closed my eyes and again I felt that delicious "thrill" filling me so completely. At moments like that, one wonders how one can sometimes go for years and be happy without that delightful "tingling" in the blood, that sensation in the heart which seems like the last feeling before death.

At midnight I was in bed, but a real "Sandman" was needed to put me to sleep. I would have liked to begin it all over, except the trip, and I did begin it all over—in my dreams. . . .

I could write pages and pages more, but I am a little bit frozen, for the weather is nice and cold the way it is in the mountains. I hope that my heart is as cold as my hands. It would be better like that, so that it doesn't suddenly melt completely and flow away like a little stream into that great Ocean—Love.

I am not romantic but, as Maman says, I take things so dramatically, tragically. Well! I am too old to reform—let's just try to be good—that's simpler. Last night I was not a coquette—that's one battle won.

June 6. Yesterday morning, amidst mad applause, Marcus received first prize for his poem, "Tennyson," and 2nd prize for his Declamation. He seemed as (interruption—return home) I was going to say, I think, that he seemed as happy as a king (not a modern king).

June 9. At home. I have literally fallen from the clouds, and the landing hurt. Since my return, I have been unreasonably bad-tempered. I haven't wanted to write; and an unusual thing: I go to bed gladly, thinking that I will continue to dream the way I did during the three days I was away. I have written to Marcus to thank him. Sunday morning I thought I would be able to write because it was raining, but we left Sheffield at noon by automobile with the Lewis family from Greenwich, Conn. On Saturday the day was very full. I haven't forgotten a single detail, and yet I would rather think about it than write it because I absolutely cannot describe all the hours of that day, which I lived through exactly as in a dream. I know that after the distribution of the prizes, I visited the school with Marcus while his aunt was looking everywhere for us, that we rode in an automobile as far as Great Barrington, had dinner, and dressed for the big dance.

I am keeping my little program in my diary and the unforgettable memory in my heart. I say unforgettable because I was so "thrilled" and it is so delicious to be "thrilled." I wasn't happy all the time; as I wrote to Godmother, I was on pins and needles with some of the young gentlemen. Saturday I was even sad and disappointed by some things in Marcus. Perhaps I hurt his feelings, too —we are so silly, both of us, to idealize each other like this. . . .

And then I think I told him everything except what I really wanted to tell him. There were always so many people that our conversation was quite "commonplace." Last night I talked with Maman for a long time—I asked her why Marcus suddenly acted a little bit, a tiny little bit colder. His letters are so sincere, but when he talks, he has a certain vague way of seeming proud. His aunt, his teachers, his friends seem firmly convinced that he needs to be cured of egoism and lack of modesty. In awarding him the prize, one teacher said: "I would give it to you more gladly if I knew it would make you modest."

And in spite of that, half of which I attribute to the fact that they don't understand him, Marcus is still the most worthwhile boy I know.

I shall never forget the way he once told me how my eyes seem to him. Oh! Little Diary, that meant so much—especially that I would be very sorry if I learned that my features, my face, are *Me*. What do those things matter? If Marcus had never expressed anything except his enthusiasm for my eyes, he came close to the real Me—my emotions, my thoughts, my dreams, the things that don't die and which are in my eyes as in a mirror—

June 11.
To Eduardo.[1]
I have just been writing to Cuca, sending her a poem of wishes for her birthday. I have tried to convey to her in rhyme my belief that kindness and sunshine are lovelier than jewels, friends are rarer than flowers, the music flowing from the depth of the toiler's heart sweeter than any music, that the loveliest castle in the world is a heart throbbing with life and happiness. I wish her Life, Youth, Happiness and Love. What more could she have, what more could she want?

June 16. It has been a pretty long time since I have written in my diary. And I had to search a long while in the calendar to know on what day, in what month and what year I am living. I have been truly unbearable. You already know that we have fallen back into a hole, and that there are many things we are forced to do without. All that is nothing, except that I had entertained the silliest ideals about my house. Maman has now made an arrangement with one of her school friends, Rosette Riley, who is now Mrs. A. Norman. She has rented Thorvald's room, Maman's room and the study. Maman occupies Joaquin's little room, and my little brothers have moved to the attic. That way Mrs. Norman is helping us to pay for the house. She is an interesting, amiable woman, terribly sociable, and she disturbs us very little, but oh! the idea of strangers in our home once again, when the nightmare of 158 W. 75th St. seemed so far away. For a time I had the feeling that we were not going to worry any more about money, and then . . . it began again.

The very hot days have arrived. Otherwise, the days pass very peacefully. Marcus and I write each other very serious letters. I think that he is tired of telling me he loves me. It's all the same to me; I have fallen into a deep philosophical meditation, a

1 *Written in English.*

sort of intellectual lethargy. Eduardo and I write each other very amusing letters, and perhaps I shall see him the 25th or 26th of June. At that time he will leave for Havana with Billin, and I suppose that once there, Eduardo will fall in love, he won't write any more, and there it is—I don't care about that either. "Ships that pass in the night—"

The other day Maman received a telegram from Bernabecito asking her to send two dozen red roses to Ana Maria Macia,[1] who has just arrived in New York. Everyone is talking about them. Oh! How I have dreamed of those two dozen red roses. I could see them here, so beautiful and fragrant, and I thought of Burns' line: "My love is like a red, red rose"—And I asked myself a question that is too frivolous to be worthy of the Serious Miss Linotte: Will the day ever come when someone will think to send me dozens of red roses?

Maman saw Ana Maria Macia. She says that she is small and delicate, with beautiful eyes and black hair, and very nice. . . .

And I—I am so tall, so pale, so "homely," and so far from being nice! But what does it matter? I am going to Columbia University next year, I shall study, I shall wear my glasses all the time, I shall become an old maid and a businesswoman. Let romanticism be banished! No more frivolity, no more coquettishness— Come now, Miss Linotte, that's enough foolishness, those longings to have dozens of little gingham dresses, pretty lingerie, and especially books— And what do roses matter, Miss Linotte, roses and lovers, dreams and desires— We must think of stockings, of money, of economy—we must be well behaved and not lose our head, even when the moonbeams shine into my little room and I am in bed murmuring, "I would like to have roses, roses, roses—"

June 20. Oh! Sundays! Everyone looks so angelic and peaceful—I always imagine that the big castle in which the princess slept for a hundred years must have been exactly like Sundays in the 20th century. (*Is* it the 20th century?) There isn't even the exciting arrival of the postman, nor the engrossing visit of the "vegetable man," with his high-priced merchandise. . . . Nothing, nothing, except tepid weather, tepid sunshine, a pale sky, quiet trees, quiet people—in a word, an atmosphere of silence and respectable appearances. The bells ring from time to time and trouble my conscience deeply—"I should go to Mass, I should go to Mass"—

I don't want to go to Mass.

[1] *Wife of Bernabé Sánchez.*

Oh! Sundays!

Thorvald and Joaquin left Friday for Boy Scout camp, so Maman and I are enjoying ourselves together, making the smallest dinners and going to the cinema. On Friday evening I saw a film that I shall never forget: "The Stolen Kiss." Every scene left such deep feeling engraved in my memory, a mixture of delight and melancholy.

Yesterday on the way to the village, I stopped the postman on his rounds and he gave me a letter from Marcus. I spent several hours this evening studying the ceiling.

And every 5 minutes, from her bed, Maman asked me:

"What are you doing, fifille?"

"Nothing, 'Mommy' dear."

"What are you doing, fifille?"

"I'm thinking, 'Mommy' dear—"

"What are you doing, fifille?"

"Still thinking, 'Mommy' dear—"

A long silence.

"Fifille, you don't very often lie around without doing anything. What's the matter with you?"

"My disillusionments have started, Mommy—"

Then Maman gave a laugh like a rain of little silver bells—and I went back to thinking.

A long silence.

" 'Mommy,' do you think anyone else will ever fall in love with me?"

The rain of little bells started in again.

"I want an engineer this time. Poets aren't what I thought they were. Oh, 'Mommy'—!"

And Maman interrupted Act I of my Tragedy with her silver cascade. I talked with her a long time and we decided we would both remain old maids. We will have parrots, cats, canaries, dogs. . . .

Maman made a face.

I explained to her why Miss Anaïs Jeanne Nin loved Mr. Marcus Taylor Anderson—because said young lady was dying of thirst for a little bit of Romance. *But:* since Mr. Anderson didn't please Miss *Linotte* too much, said young lady was calm and cool and completely indifferent to the masculine charms that she kept discovering. And she understood (which is more than I can say because I don't understand anything) that that's how things are done (or rather, *undone*) in this world.

"Let's go to Mass, let's go to Mass!"—The bells are insistent.

I don't want to go to Mass—I am afraid that I have taken my toothbrush and moved to the moon, so I might as well stay there a few days. A few days! No, in a few days I have to be back here to entertain Marcus and to see Eduardo and Billin again. Do *you* understand, at least, why I don't want to go to Mass? My head is full of foolishness and my heart is in the icebox, with the butter and eggs. What a realist I am becoming! Alas! In a few years I shall be unrecognizable—if I am already starting!

The other day someone brought us what is called a "married" loaf of bread—two loaves that had baked into one. Joaquin wanted to know why they called it "married." I took the two loaves and opened them: "You see, something is *missing*. They don't have a crust on one side and that's why they call them 'married.' " And I turned to Maman: "It's just like people—they are lacking something when they get married, aren't they?"

Maman laughed heartily and answered: "That's true—common sense!"

Such cynicism seems unforgivable to me—but what can you expect—I am already 17, and the heart that I keep in the icebox is beginning to hurt.

But oh! Even if I must search around the world, I shall find my Shadow—tall, and strong, and noble, generous, faithful. No one as yet bears the least resemblance to the image that I have idealized since those starry nights at 158 W. 75th. He will be poor, very poor, and he will need me.

June 27. One day I received a letter from Eduardo which, as usual, I found enchanting. But in addition, he announced he was coming to visit us—on June 25th!

At the same time, Marcus telephoned to invite me to go to the theatre with him on Saturday.

Finally! the 25th arrived. Maman had bought some things for the children (because my cousin Thorvald was coming too—but that isn't very important) and she spent a miserable day waiting for their telephone call. Not a word. I felt sure that Eduardo wouldn't leave without saying anything (Thorvald might), and when evening came, I thought that something must have happened. So we telephoned the school and learned that Eduardo had been in the Infirmary with the measles. We went immediately to the hotel where Thorvald was staying; he said he didn't have our telephone number and that anyhow his suitcase was too full. Then he called Eduardo "un bobo," which made me think that he was the only stupid one, and I liked Eduardo more than ever. Contrariness—you were born a woman!

Well, Saturday arrived and Marcus came here to Richmond Hill to have lunch with us. For the first time in my life, my nerves were perfectly calm at the critical moment—and at exactly the same moment, Marcus's calm deserted him and he did several funny things: he ate his salad with a spoon, and in cutting his chop put it on the table.

After lunch, Maman sang, Joaquin gave a concert, the taxi came, and we left. The theatre was superb. It was Drinkwater's famous play: "Abraham Lincoln," which at times was almost sublime—tragic and inspired.

After the theatre we had lemonade and ice cream at the Astor. I learned why Marcus had told me once that he had never had a home—his parents are divorced. As he said this, the painful realization came to me that mine are too—in one sense. . . .

When I arrived at the Station, I took the wrong train. This wasn't exactly my fault but—almost. I went to Hammel [Boulevard], near Far Rockaway, and without a cent in my purse! I was delighted—just imagine, an adventure at last! I was almost laughing as I asked a handsome young policeman for money, offering him my bracelet and my name and address. His eyes began to dance like mine; he seemed very much amused. I was delighted, I repeat.

"Here's a dollar," he told me. "You needn't return it."

I had to ask repeatedly to get his address. I bought my ticket and as I waited for my train, Mr. Policeman came back several times to offer me more money if I were in need of it.

Finally I went to East New York, and from there to Jamaica, and from there to Kew Gardens. From 6 o'clock until 8 I enjoyed myself, arriving back home very pleased.

June 29. Today I talked to Marcus on the telephone. I am to see him tomorrow and we are going to the theatre. I really want very much to be with him, and sometimes when I realize what a child he is, I wonder how and why such a community of feeling attracts us to each other. Saturday he told me, in that "gentle" way of talking that he has, that he will be so unhappy when I go to Cuba (Maman had talked to him about my *début*), because naturally I will fall in love with a handsome Cuban and will forget about him. At that moment I smiled to myself as I remembered the line:

"Faint heart never won fair lady . . ."

And I thought that this time the "faint heart was *almost* winning fair lady"—! What I can never understand is the "thrill" that Marcus has for me—no, pardon me, I mean for Anaïs Nin, because Linotte is implacable.

I often reread my Diary to encourage myself a little, for sometimes I wonder whether the foolish things I write at certain times are good for anything. Oh! And yet, as a journalist said in his ordinary language:

"A man at forty realizes what a fool he was at twenty, and yet can't see what a fool he is now!"

Although I sometimes realize also that a thing is foolish at the time I do it. So writing in my Diary is sometimes painful, a kind of penitence—at 17. It was not when I was at the carefree age, but it is now, when I am forced to write the outrageous things that go through my head under the dangerous influence of Spring, Youth, and Romance. Well, I get even by being a little ashamed.

And oh! Little Diary, I want an Adventure so much—something grand, something sublime! And I don't think that it is love— no. Perhaps when I go to Columbia I will know. Perhaps it is "Fame." The one who best understood that great desire, in the days when it attacked me most strongly, was Eduardo because he loves that "thrill" too. I want very much to ask him, when I see him, whether he has found it—

It is raining, with thunder and lightning. The sky is black as ink. Everything harmonizes with the whims of my mood this evening. I am solemn, I am troubled, I feel like crying. I am cynical— From time to time, the lights go out because of the force of the elements—exactly like the little light that shines on the horizon of my Destiny and that I never cease to follow, except when the tempest swells.

Suddenly I am thinking of Enric. What is he doing? Who is he thinking of? Maman is right when she says I am "fickle," and yet—what can I say? I have not forgotten the former hero of my most beautiful dreams, the happy Prince for whom I let down my hair—and perhaps my philosophy. For my fatal transformation dates from that time—as does the birth of my vanity.

Ambitious people never look back—but oh! what charm there is in memory. I was going to bed tonight feeling very gloomy, but when I think of the good things, of the joy that is part of our life at present, in contrast with the old days, I can't help but be grateful and happier. Oh, yes! I will end by getting better, Miss Linotte— people who complain are good for nothing in the world. And pessimists are monsters!

Let's be gay! It's easy when one is lighthearted—but when one has no heart? . . .

Oh! I have a marvelous idea—how could I not have thought of it before—

Heavens! Listen: I admit that I have lost my head, like everyone else where love is concerned. I confess that I do not think of Browning when I look at the stars, the clouds, and when I breathe the flower-laden air on these warm evenings, but rather of a Prince. I confess (in shame and despair) that my loveliest dreams are like the dreams of all young girls, and not like those of a "Wise Man." And the worst of all is that I don't find my Prince, and I am dying of thirst for a drop of Romance, a bit of "thrill"—So—Sir Diary, I name you my Prince of Princes and my only King on earth. I am madly in love with you—do you want vows? words of tenderness?

It's up to you now to fill all the spaces remaining in my heart, my moments of "loneliness"—I entrust my heart to you. Our plan is to visit the world with care and—patience—to share our opinions and our thoughts. Then, the day that we are—tired (I was going to say "sick of it"), we will lock ourselves up in our castle, you and I, with a great many little adopted children—and Maman. It is done. Now you must act as though you are dying of passion for me, with a noble and supreme disdain for my lack of beauty and grace, and I must be faithful to you and forget Henri, Enric, John, Jack, Jimmy, Edward and Marcus.

July 1. Today I went with Maman to see Ana Maria Macia. With the delightful memory of the two dozen red roses, I expected to find a beauty, like the heroine of Dumas' "Brigand"—someone unapproachable and perfect. But no, Ana Maria has beautiful eyes, but her beauty did not blind me; she is pleasant, simple and extremely nice, but Rita Allie is still my ideal. I compare all the girls to her, and Ana Maria doesn't look very much like her.

Yesterday I went out with Marcus. We went together to see "Lightning," a comedy that is full of good humor, "cleverly acted." Afterward we walked from the theatre to the station, talking. Marcus told me in a terribly serious way:

"You are the prettiest girl in New York."

"And you are the greatest flatterer in New York!" answered Miss Linotte with her cheeks aflame. But we aren't always moonstruck. I tried to explain to him about my search for a great Adventure and to my great despair, he didn't understand. That is the first time that Marcus has not been able to follow the flight of my imagination— We talked about Greenwich Village, which I am crazy to see, and Marcus told me about his visit there and his disappointment. I was very sorry. I have so idealized Greenwich Village!

July 2. Oh! What a scatterbrain! We were packing this morning to go to Edgemere and at the last minute I put what I thought was my Diary in the suitcase that Thorvald was taking, but it was an old notebook! Then I put in the brand new one, knowing that I have only a few pages left in the old notebook. I just discovered my mistake, so while we wait for the automobile, I am writing to tell you that I am going to take you, after all. It's difficult to explain, but it is always *you* that I carry with me, isn't that so?

You seem like an old friend. And perhaps before writing your last page, a little adventure will happen to me, and you will enjoy that, I'm sure.

Maman is sick and has just enough strength to go to Edgemere, where she is sure she will feel better. I feel unbearably sad, myself—what is happening to me?

July 4. Brace yourself—I am not nice. I think that my poor family has had to put up with a sort of attack of cynicism. Superficially, these days have been very enjoyable. We have been swimming every day since we arrived. Friday evening I went to the cinema with Thorvald and Joaquin—Maman was too tired. Saturday evening Maman and I went together to see Olive Tell in "Love Without Question" at the theatre in Far Rockaway.

Our little dinners are very exciting. We lack a little bit of everything, including gas, so we are using an alcohol lamp. But the real secret of these little dinners and their success is our gigantic appetites.

Maman and I, sitting on the porch, have just remarked, "What little boys men are!" For the Fourth of July, the great American Independence holiday, those big "boys" walk around in bathing suits with whistles and firecrackers that soon will be exploding by the dozen.

I still have the memory of the beach—so much noise that one could not think. I wrote on the sand to pass the time—remembering that last year I wrote Enric's name there.

Tomorrow night we go back home.

July 9. I am writing these lines at home, several days later. Eduardo came back from school and is spending several days here.

I made him a present of one of the two new diaries and we decided we would begin them at the same time, in English, and see who would be the more interesting and sincere, and who would be the first to have a "Great Adventure." Perhaps in these remaining pages, when Eduardo has left, I will write the impressions I have had of him these last days. Thank you for your sincere patience, your kind sympathy, and all the good you do me.

Ma Librairie en 1920.

The Book of Knowledge   20 vol.

Cahiers d'une Élève de St. Denis 12 vol.

Le Tour de la France

Le Mauvais Génie - Cnce Ségur

The Peak of the Load - M. Aldrich

Books of Poetry 3 vol.   Baker.

The Song of the Cardinal - G.S. Porter

Egypt   C. E. Clement

Le Choix de Ginette - C. Trouessart

The Miseries of Paris - E. Sue

Tunisie   Brieux

Keeping Up with Lizzie - Bacheller

Chronique des Grandes Époques - de Commines

Petite Madame   A. Lichtenberger

Best Son of Battle - A. Ollivant

Abbé Constantin   Halévy

The Hand of Mercy   Alexander

Robinson Crusoe   Defoe

Guy Mannering   Scott

Alice au Pays des Merveilles   L. Carrol

Égypte   J. Bayet

Le Japon   J. Gautier

En Chine   J. Gautier

Le Juif Polonais   Eckmann Chatrian
Michel Strogoff - J. Verne

MEMORANDA

1920
Livres

The Reckoning *Jan. 10-12*	R. Chambers
Adventures of François *Jan.*	Mitchell
The Shepherd of the Hills *Jan.*	H. B. Wright
St. Ives *Jan. 1-3-*	Stevenson
The Shuttle *Jan. 18-19-*	Burnett
The Younger Set *Jan. 17-18*	R. Chambers
Jan. 18 The Times	Newspaper
" " Delineator	Butterick Pub.
Literary Digest	Magazine
Jan 23 Poetry I	Francis Thompson
Jan. 23 - Poetry II	Francis Thompson "
" " - Prose III	Francis Thompson "
" " Proverbial Philosophy	Tupper
" " Poems	P. Shelley
Jan 24 - When I Was Czar	N. Marchmont

MEMORANDA
1920

Feb. 3	Italian Romance Writers	J. S. Kennard
Feb	Works of Chaucer	Chaucer
Feb	Works of Coleridge	Coleridge
Feb	Four Socratic Dialogues	Plato (unfin
Feb. 4	Voyage de Mr Perrichon	Labiche - Marti
Feb.	David Copperfield	Charles Dicken
Feb. 17	Snow-bound	Whittier
Feb. 22	Poems	Goethe
Feb. 23	Poems from Chaucer to Kipling	
April	Short Stories	Hendrick
April	Posthumous Poems	Swinburne
April	Poems	Swinburne
April	A Childs Garden of Verses	Stevenson
April		
April	Poems	Ruskin
April	Saracinesca	F. M. Crawford
April	Cloister & the Hearth	C. Reade
April	Selections from Songs of Innocence	W. Blake
May	A Roman Singer	Crawford
"	Pietro Ghisleri 1020	Crawford
"	Don Orsino (horror')	Crawford
"	Marietta (delicious) abominable	Crawford
May	Katherine Lauderdale	Crawford

June The Worlds best Poetry I
      The World's best Poetry II

June 22 Operas Every Child   Dolores Bacon
         Should Know   Interesting but
         not well-written.

"   "   A Warning to Lovers P. L. Ford
         Absurdly Amusing —

"   23 The Brigand   A. Dumas
"   "   Blanche de Beaulieu A. Dumas
         Splendid — dramatic

Jun 27 The Fortunate Youth Wm. Locke
        Delicious and fine.

June 28 Incomparable Bellairs A.&E. Castle
         Charming but Useless

"   "   Eleanor Payton   N. Stephenson
         Too modern — I don't
         like it, though
         Eleanor is a well-
         drawn character

Page no. 1 —

Livres

Oct. 9 —
The Ingoldsby Legends   T. Ingoldsby.

Oct. 10
Literary Digest

Oct. 11 Writers Monthly

Oct. 14 Colette Baudoche   Maurice Barrès

Oct. 27 - L'ami des Mauvais Jours

" " Le Lac Noir

Nouveaux Récits Révolutionaires   Daudet

Oct. 28 - When A Man Marries

" " You Never Know Your Luck

Oct. 29 - The Girl of O. K. Valley

" " Greatheart

Oct. 30 Literary Digest

" " "

La France

Pictorial Review

Nov. 5 - Mrs Lecks and Mrs Aleshine   by Stockton

Nov. 6 - Delineator - Nov.

Book of Knowledge vol. 5

The Chimes   Dickens

Nov. 9 - The Times   Newspaper

N. Y. American

Literary Digest   Magazine

Page No. 2.

Nov. 20 - Catherine   Lavedan

Nov. 19 Madeleine, Jeune Femme   Boylesve

Nov. 20 Une Ville flottante   Verne

Nov. 27 Love Affairs of a Bibliomaniac E. Field

Cook Book   Mrs Norton

Night and Morning   Nov. 28-29-30-   Lytton

Nov. 28 - Dernier jours d'un Condamné   Hugo

Dec 1 - Delineator   Magazine

Dec 12 - Leila   E. B. Lytton

Dec   Pelham   "   "   "   "

Dec 4-5 - Le Grand Meaulnes   A. Fournier

Dec 10 - Eugene Aram   Lytton

Dec 8-9 - Choice of Books

Dec 9-10 Pensées de Pascal   Pascal

Dec. 8-9 Salome   O. Wilde

  "   "Comtesse de St Géran

Dec 23 Casa Braccio   2 Vol.   Crawford

Dec 20 Aurette   Durand

  Petite Madame   Lichtenburger

  Le Choix de Ginette   Trouessart

  Bob Son of Battle   Ollivant

  Zoroaster   M. Crawford

  Taquisara   Dec. 28   M. Crawford

℀ *Appendix* ℀

August 11, 1914. We were all dressed and on deck. It was 2 o'clock and one could vaguely see a city, but very far away. The sea was gray and heavy. How different from the beautiful sea of Spain! I was anxious to arrive, but I was sad. I felt a chill around my heart and I was seeing things all wrong.

Suddenly we were wrapped in a thick fog. A torrential rain began to fall, thunder rumbled, lightning flashes lit the heavy black sky. The people promptly took refuge in the lounge. None of the Spanish passengers had ever seen weather like that, so the frightened women wept, the men prayed in low tones. We were not afraid. Maman had seen many other storms and her calmness reassured us. We were the first to go back up on the wet deck. But the fog continued and we waited.

It was 4 o'clock when the ship began to move again, slowly, as though she approached the great city with fear. Now, leaning on the railing, I couldn't hear anything. My eyes were fixed on the lights that drew closer, I saw the tall buildings, I heard the whistling of the engine, I saw a great deal of movement. Huge buildings went by in front of me. I hated those buildings in advance because they hid what I love most—flowers, birds, fields, liberty.

Maman came up to me and took me for a walk, whispering in my ear the wonderful things that I was going to see. But although

I admire New York for its progress, I hate it, I find it superficial. I saw it as an ugly prison. Maman was still walking, but seeing that I wasn't paying the slightest attention, she didn't talk to me anymore, but her eyes looked worried. My head felt heavy, my heart seemed full enough to burst, I felt sad and unhappy. I envy those who never leave their native land. I wanted to cry my eyes out.

Maman went away again and again I leaned on the railing and filled my lungs with the pure evening air. It was growing dark, we were arriving, and I had to come out of my sad reverie. I cast a last glance around me at this last bit of Spain, which seemed to have wanted to accompany me this far, to remind me of my promise that I would return. Inside myself I answered, Oh, yes, I shall return to Spain.

Maman led me away and I set foot on land. The earth was burning hot. I woke up. People were running, shouting and waving. I found myself on a large quay. I kissed Godmother, Rafael, Carlos and Coquito, who had come to meet us. Uncle Gilbert arrived soon afterward. They decided that Thorvald and I would spend the night at Aunt Antolina's and that the next day we would rejoin Maman and Joaquinito, who were going to Aunt Edelmira's.

The night went quite well. Before going to bed, I resigned myself to not feeling sad about New York, to keep still and keep my thoughts against this country to myself. Only I am indiscreet and I have told my diary everything. You won't say anything, will you, if I tell you that I hate New York and that I find it too big, too superficial, everything goes too fast. It is just *hell*.

❧ *Glossary of Family Names* ❧

Ana: Ana María Sánchez; a cousin, daughter of Bernabé Sánchez and Anaïs Culmell

Anaïs: Anaïs Sánchez; a cousin, daughter of Bernabé Sánchez and Anaïs Culmell

Antolina, Aunt: Antolina Culmell de Cárdenas; Rosa Culmell's sister

Antolinita: Antolina de Cárdenas; a cousin, daughter of Rafael de Cárdenas and Antolina Culmell

Bernabecito: Bernabé Sánchez; a cousin, son of Bernabé Sánchez and Anaïs Culmell

Bernabé, Uncle: Bernabé Sánchez

Billin: Thorvald Sánchez; a cousin, son of Bernabé Sánchez and Anaïs Culmell

Carlos: Carlos de Cárdenas; a cousin, son of Rafael de Cárdenas and Antolina Culmell

Coco, Ti(a): Aunt Edelmira

Coquito: Gilbert Chase; a cousin, son of Gilbert Chase and Edelmira Culmell

Cuca: Caridad Sánchez; a cousin, daughter of Bernabé Sánchez and Anaïs Culmell

Edelmira, Aunt: Edelmira Culmell de Chase; Rosa Culmell's sister

Eduardo: Eduardo Sánchez; a cousin, son of Bernabé Sánchez and Anaïs Culmell

Felo: Rafael de Cárdenas; a cousin, son of Rafael de Cárdenas and Antolina Culmell

Fifille: Nickname for A.N., meaning "little girl"

Gilbert, Uncle: Gilbert P. Chase

Godmother: Juana Culmell

Grandfather: Joaquín María Nin y Tudó; paternal grandfather

Grandmother: Angela Castellanos de Nin; paternal grandmother

Graziella: Graziella Sánchez; a cousin, daughter of Bernabé Sánchez and Anaïs Culmell

Henry, Uncle: Enrique Culmell; Rosa Culmell's brother

Joaquín Nin: father

Joaquinito, Joaquín: Joaquín Nin-Culmell; the younger of A.N.'s two brothers

Juana, Aunt: Juana Culmell; A.N.'s godmother, Rosa Culmell's sister

Kiki: Joaquín Nin-Culmell

Linotte: A.N.'s nickname for herself, meaning "linnet"

Lolita, Aunt: Dolores Culmell; first wife of Thorvald Culmell

Maria Louisa: María Luisa Rodríguez; second wife of Joaquín Nin

Nuna, Nunita: Maria Teresa Chase; a cousin, daughter of Gilbert Chase and Edelmira Culmell

Rosa Culmell de Nin: mother

Thorvald: Thorvald Nin; the older of A.N.'s two brothers

Thorvald, Uncle: Thorvald Culmell; Rosa Culmell's brother

Tina: Constantina Xuclà; a cousin, daughter of Joaquín Nin's only sister, Angelina

Vaurigaud, Mr. and Mrs.: Théodore and Catherine Vaurigaud; maternal grandparents

❧ Index ❧

God (*Cont.*)
goodness of, 355
gratitude toward, 63
fear of, 54
and future, 61
and life's purpose, 133–34
and longing for father, 24, 34,
58–59, 76, 97–98
love of, 72, 73
on making souls, 107
and marriage, 85–86
and obedience, 160
poems on, 71, 108, 117, 444
prayer to, to deliver family from
illness, 133
praying to, for health of mother, 58
praying to, to protect father, 62
praying to, for parents, 72
praying to, to save France, 45, 47,
48
reawakened to, 248
receiving, 127
See also Communion
and separation of parents, 27
and sickness, 133
on the side of Germany, 129–30
and sin, 63
and understanding separation of
parents, 85
and world inside out, 325
See also Jesus
Godmother, *see* Culmell, Juana
Godoy, Armand, 217*n*
Godoy, Julia Cordovés de, 217
"God's Handiwork" (Nin), 444
Golondrina (small steamboat), 5–7
Good Gracious Annabella (film), 225
Gounod, Charles, 243, 247, 436
Governess, dislike for, 16
Granados, Enrique, 113, 178, 211*n*,
388
Granados, Mrs. E., 113
Grandmother, *see* Nin, Angela
Castellanos de
Gray, Mrs., 455
Graziella (cousin), *see* Sánchez,
Graziella
Grieg, Edvard, 87
Guerin, Mrs., 31, 32
Guillermo, 127
Gypsy, meeting a, 299–300, 302

Hamlet (Shakespeare), 461, 462
Happiness, prescription for, 320, 321,
325
Hard Times (Dickens), 210
Hart, Miss, 220
Hart, William, 225
Hawkers, 4–5
Hayakawa, Sessue, 225
Hayes, Charlie, 135
Health, *see* Nin, Anaïs, health of
Health and success, as goals, 308, 309
Healy, Miss, 381
Hearn, Marian, 112, 116, 118–20
"Heart of Gold" (Nin), 142
Heatwave, 1917, 181–82
Hedrick, Mrs., 135
Heller, 421
Henry (uncle), *see* Culmell, Enrique
"Here below, everything takes flight"
(Nin), 71
"Here Lies" (Nin), 103
Hippodrome, 22, 314, 315
Histoire de France (book), 119
Holmes, Oliver Wendell, 198
Holt, Mrs., 367
Holy Trinity School, 161–62
Homer, Madame Louise, 481
Homesickness, 272, 276
"Hope" (Nin), 75
Horace, 384
Horace (Corneille), 169
Horseback riding, 237–40, 255–57
Hostelé, Mr., 39, 61
Hostelé, Mrs., 39, 41
Housekeeping, 171–72, 178, 181,
288–89, 294, 295, 297–99, 303,
306, 324, 331, 333, 345, 376
"How can they go to an entertain-
ment?" (Nin), 133
Huff, Michael, 155
Hugo, Victor, 41, 100, 153, 220, 307
Humans
as vile, 112
See also Boys; Children; People
Hypnotizing a cat, 146

"I approach the altar" (Nin), 71
Icicle Chronicle, The (Nin), 454
"If the weather is good" (Nin), 71–72
"If She Were Alive" (Nin), 102–03
Il Trovatore (Verdi), 386

Nin, Anaïs (*Cont.*)
nicknames of, 68, 503, 504
physical characteristics of, 65–66,
105–06, 414, 440, 441
glasses, 437, 438
M. Hearn description of, 118
views of, *see specific views; for
example:* Children; Life; Love
Nin, Angela Castellanos de (paternal
grandmother)
and death of Tina, 34
drifting away from, 285
heaven for, 10
and her son, 144, 208–09, 221, 415
and Joaquinito, 165
leaving, 3, 14, 17, 61
love for, 66
marriage of, 320
missing, 12
no news from, 58, 187
poem on, 4
scarf for, 10–11
and separation of parents, 85
vision of, 9
writing to, 20, 22, 178
poems, 90
Nin, Joaquín J. ("Papa") (father)
letters to, copied in diary, 56,
136–39, 144–46, 164–68, 176–78,
186–91, 191–93, 204–07,
208–10, 221–22, 245–47,
269–72, 345–46, 357–59, 388–90,
397–99, 414–16, 449–50, 477–79
longing to be reunited with, 14,
21–22, 23–24, 25, 27, 34–38,
39–42, 45, 47, 48, 57–60, 68,
70, 76, 80–82, 84–88, 90, 94, 95,
97–98, 100–01, 138–39
presence of, in daily life, 44, 54, 57,
62, 64–66, 72–73, 74, 78, 96,
105, 107, 113, 116, 119, 127,
130, 144, 149, 151, 157, 186,
223–24, 230, 259, 265, 285, 297,
343, 352–53, 377, 392, 421,
436–38, 440, 449, 504
and life with Rosa Nin, 263–64
Rosa Nin on, 326–27, 328, 364–66,
426
sketch and musical abilities of, 9
Nin, Rosa Culmell de ("Maman")
(mother), 3, 5–7, 9–21, 22, 23,
27, 29–31, 37, 40, 43–46, 48,

49, 51–54, 56–66, 68, 72–73, 76,
79–82, 83–89, 92, 94, 96,
99–101, 105–07, 113, 114, 117,
120, 121, 122, 124, 127, 129–31,
132–35, 139, 140, 141, 142, 143,
144, 148–51, 152–54, 156–57,
160–61, 162–65, 168–70, 171–
76, 179–81, 182–86, 187, 189,
196, 197, 199–200, 207, 212,
216–26, 227, 229–32, 234, 237,
238, 239, 241, 246–50, 252–57,
261–64, 265, 269, 270, 277–86,
289, 291–315, 316, 318, 320–23,
326–36, 339, 340–46, 348–56,
360–400, 402–10, 414, 417–20,
422–24, 426, 427, 428, 430,
432–33, 435–38, 441–42, 444,
446, 449, 451–53, 454, 457–63,
464–66, 468–71, 472–80, 481–
88, 491, 492, 501–02, 504
singing career of
biographical sketch, 79
concerts, 30, 31, 33
poem on, 59
practice, 74
as singer, 9–11
as teacher, 60
views expressed on husband by,
223–24, 263–64, 325–28, 364–
66, 426
Nin, Thorvald (brother), 6, 9, 11, 13,
16, 18, 21, 30, 31, 37, 38, 40, 41,
44, 45, 49, 56, 58–60, 64–66,
73, 74, 80, 82, 83, 94, 96, 97,
100, 101, 106, 116, 117, 120,
122, 124, 125, 132, 134–36, 138,
139, 142, 144, 146, 149, 150,
153–57, 161, 170–71, 175, 180,
181, 183–85, 189, 196, 198–200,
209, 212, 216, 218, 221, 222,
227, 235, 244, 253–55, 257,
261–63, 264, 265, 270, 277, 280,
281, 283, 284, 285–87, 289, 291,
292, 294–302, 305–07, 310–14,
318, 320, 322–29, 333–39, 345–
50, 354, 357, 361–64, 366, 368,
373–82, 395, 398, 400, 402,
407, 410, 412, 415, 417, 420,
422, 423, 425, 427, 430, 435,
437, 438, 446, 449, 450, 454–56,
464, 465, 468, 471, 472–76, 478,
483, 485, 492, 502, 504